Lecture Notes in Computer Science 11983

More information about this series at http://www.springer.com/series/7410

Jaideep Vaidya · Xiao Zhang ·
Jin Li (Eds.)

Cyberspace Safety
and Security

11th International Symposium, CSS 2019
Guangzhou, China, December 1–3, 2019
Proceedings, Part II

Springer

Editors
Jaideep Vaidya
Rutgers University
Newark, NJ, USA

Xiao Zhang
Beihang University
Beijing, China

Jin Li
Guangzhou University
Guangzhou, China

ISSN 0302-9743   ISSN 1611-3349 (electronic)
Lecture Notes in Computer Science
ISBN 978-3-030-37351-1   ISBN 978-3-030-37352-8 (eBook)
https://doi.org/10.1007/978-3-030-37352-8

LNCS Sublibrary: SL4 – Security and Cryptology

This Springer imprint is published by the registered company Springer Nature Switzerland AG
The registered company address is: Gewerbestrasse 11, 6330 Cham, Switzerland

Preface

Welcome to the proceedings of the 11th International Symposium on Cyberspace Safety and Security (CSS 2019), which was organized by Guangzhou University and held in Guangzhou, China, during December 1–3, 2019.

CSS 2019 was the 11th event in a series of international symposiums devoted to research on cyberspace safety and security. Previous iterations of the symposium include CSS 2018 (Amalfi, Italy), CSS 2017 (Xi'an, China), CSS 2016 (Granada, Spain), CSS 2015 (New York, USA), CSS 2014 (Paris, France), CSS 2013 (Zhangjiajie, China), CSS 2012 (Melbourne, Australia), CSS 2011 (Milan, Italy), CSS 2009 (Chengdu, China), and CSS 2008 (Sydney, Australia).

The CSS symposium aims to provide a leading-edge forum to foster interaction between researchers and developers with the cyberspace safety and security communities, and to give attendees an opportunity to network with experts in this area. It focuses on cyberspace safety and security, such as authentication, access control, availability, integrity, privacy, confidentiality, dependability, and sustainability issues of cyberspace.

CSS 2019 attracted 235 high-quality research papers highlighting the foundational work that strives to push beyond the limits of existing technologies, including experimental efforts, innovative systems, and investigations that identify weaknesses in existing cyber technology. Each submission was reviewed by at least three experts in the relevant areas, on the basis of their significance, novelty, technical quality, presentation, and practical impact. According to this stringent peer-review process involving about 65 Program Committee members and several additional reviewers, 61 full papers were selected to be presented at the conference, giving an acceptance rate of 26%. Additionally, we also accepted 40 short papers.

CSS 2019 was made possible by the behind-the-scene effort of selfless individuals and organizations who volunteered their time and energy to ensure the success of this conference. We would like thank all authors for submitting and presenting their papers. We also greatly appreciated the support of the Program Committee members and the reviewers. We sincerely thank all the chairs–without their hard work, the success of CSS 2019 would not have been possible.

Last but not least, we would like to thank all the contributing authors and all conference attendees, as well as the great team at Springer that assisted in producing the conference proceedings, and the developers and maintainers of EasyChair.

December 2019

Jaideep Vaidya
Xiao Zhang
Jin Li

Organization

Honorary General Chair

Binxing Fang   Guangzhou University, China

General Chairs

Jin Li   Guangzhou University, China
Zhihong Tian   Guangzhou University, China

Program Chairs

Jaideep Vaidya   Rutgers University, USA
Xiao Zhang   Beihang University, China

Publication Chair

Yu Wang   Guangzhou University, China

Publicity Chairs

Xiaochun Cheng   Middlesex University, UK
Nan Jiang   East China Jiaotong University, China
Zheli Liu   Nankai University, China
Weizhi Meng   Technical University of Denmark, Denmark

Track Chairs

Xu Ma   Qufu Normal University, China
Hui Tian   National Huaqiao University, China

Steering Committee Chair

Yang Xiang   Swinburne University of Technology, Australia

Program Committee

Andrea Abate   University of Salerno, Italy
Silvio Barra   University of Cagliari, Italy
Carlo Blundo   University of Salerno, Italy
Yiqiao Cai   Huaqiao University, China
Luigi Catuogno   University of Salerno, Italy

Lorenzo Cavallario	Royal Holloway, University of London, UK
Fei Chen	Shenzhen University, China
Laizhong Cui	Shenzhen University, China
Frederic Cuppens	Enst Bretagne, France
Massimo Ficco	Second University of Naples, Italy
Dieter Gollmann	Hamburg University of Technology, Germany
Lorena Gonzalez	Carlos III University of Madrid, Spain
Zhitao Guan	North China Electric Power University, China
Jinguang Han	Nanjing University of Finance and Economics, China
Saeid Hosseini	Singapore University of Technology and Design, Singapore
Xinyi Huang	Fujian Normal University, China
Shuyuan Jin	Sun Yat-sen University, China
Lutful Karim	Seneca College of Applied Arts and Technology, Canada
Sokratis Katsikas	University of Piraeus, Greece
Xuejun Li	Anhui University, China
Kaitai Liang	Manchester Metropolitan University, UK
Jay Ligatti	University of South Florida, USA
Huiting Liu	Anhui University, China
Xiapu Luo	Hong Kong Polytechnic University, Hong Kong, China
Liangfu Lv	Tianjin University, China
Xiaobo Ma	Xi'an Jiaotong University, China
Fabio Martinelli	IIT-CNR, Italy
Mehrnoosh Monshizadeh	Nokia Bell Labs, Finland
Vincenzo Moscato	University of Naples, Italy
Francesco Moscato	Second University of Naples, Italy
Richard Overill	King's College London, UK
Umberto Ferraro Petrillo	Sapienza University of Rome, Italy
Florin Pop	University Politehnica of Bucharest, Romania
Jianzhong Qi	The University of Melbourne, Australia
Lianyong Qi	Qufu Normal University, China
Alim Al Islam Razi	Bangladesh University of Engineering and Technology, Bangladesh
Dharmendra Sharma	University of Canberra, Australia
Willy Susilo	University of Wollogon, Australia
Zhiyuan Tan	Edinburgh Napier University, UK
Donghai Tian	Beijing Institute of Technology, China
Ding Wang	Peking University, China
Hua Wang	Victoria University, Australia
Jianfeng Wang	Xidian University, China
Wei Wang	Beijing Jiaotong University, China
Lingyu Wang	Concordia University, Canada
Bing Wu	Fayetteville State University, USA
Tao Xiang	Chongqing University, China
Ping Xiong	Zhongnan University of Economics and Law, China

Jingfang Xu	Central China Normal University, China
Bin Yan	Shandong University of Science and Technology, China
Zhe Yang	Northwestern Polytechnical University, China
Shaojun Yang	Fujian Normal University, China
Xun Yi	RMIT University, Australia
Stefano Zanero	Politecnico di Milano, Italy
Xuyun Zhang	The University of Auckland, New Zealand
Yuan Zhang	Nanjing University, China
Yuexin Zhang	Swinburne University of Technology, Australia
Hongli Zhang	Harbin Institute of Technology, China
Xianfeng Zhao	Chinese Academy of Sciences, China
Zhiwei Zhao	University of Electric Science and Technology of China, China
Tianqing Zhu	University of Technology Sydney, Australia
Lei Zhu	The University of Queensland, Australia

Contents – Part II

Information Security

Machine Learning and Security

Cyberspace Safety

Contents – Part I

Information Security

Privacy Preservation

Machine Learning and Security

Cyberspace Safety

Big Data and Security

Cloud and Security

Network Security

IoT-Based DDoS Attack Detection
and Mitigation Using the Edge of SDN

Yinqi Yang[✉], Jian Wang[✉], Baoqin Zhai, and Jiqiang Liu

Beijing Jiaotong University, Beijing, China
{17120486,wangjian}@bjtu.edu.cn

Abstract. Nowadays, the Internet of Things (IoT) has developed rapidly and changed people's life into a more convenient style. However, a huge number of vulnerable IoT devices are exploited to constitute botnet by many attackers, which forms a serious problem for network security. To solve it, we propose a novel detection and mitigation mechanism. In our method, we use Software Defined Networking (SDN), a promising network architecture, for dropping malicious traffic in propagation path to avoid avalanche effect on the victim server in the traditional network. For the existing works, a lot of time and resources are wasted in using the controller of SDN to detect attacks. Unlike them, we take the features of IoT traffic into consideration and utilize the edge computing to provide local services by putting detection and mitigation method into the OpenFlow (OF) switches of IoT. This achieves a distributed anomaly detection to detect and respond IoT-based DDoS attacks in real time, and avoids the overload of the controller. Machine learning is used in the OF switches with around 99% precision. Experimental results demonstrate that our method is capable to mitigate IoT-based DDoS attacks in a short time.

Keywords: IoT-based DDoS attack · Attack detection · Attack mitigation · SDN · Edge computing · Machine learning

1 Introduction

Nowadays, the ubiquity of the Internet of Things (IoT) has contributed to the exponential rise of IoT devices. Gartner predicted that by 2020 there will be over 26 billion IoT devices, while other analysts believe that the amount of the devices will exceed 100 billion [1]. However, due to their limitations of computing ability and storage capacity, the IoT devices have become the new weak link in network security. According to the report of HP, around 60% of IoT devices will be insecure and vulnerable [2]. Because of the large amount of the vulnerable IoT devices, attackers are attracted to exploit them to launch Distributed Denial of Service (DDoS) attacks.

DDoS attacks aim to control a large number of zombies to exhaust the resources of the victim, resulting in its failure to respond to normal service. In the past, traditional desktops and laptops were the main targets for attackers to build botnets. However,

J. Vaidya et al. (Eds.): CSS 2019, LNCS 11983, pp. 3–17, 2019.
https://doi.org/10.1007/978-3-030-37352-8_1

more and more PC anti-virus schemes have emerged. As a result, DDoS attack criminals have turned their attention to the IoT devices. The notorious Mirai IoT botnet was utilized to launch a DDoS attack on October 21, 2016. The Dyn DNS service was attacked causing the Internet paralysis in almost half of the United States and inaccessibility to many major websites such as Twitter, Amazon, and Netflix. However, after the Mirai's source code has been released, not much improvement has been made. Instead, there are more and more variants of Mirai used to exploit IoT devices to launch DDoS attacks such as the attack to Deutsche Telekom [3]. It can be inferred that using IoT devices as zombies has become the mainstream of DDoS attacks, but the existing methods cannot solve this problem very well. Therefore, this issue has become one of the most concerned problems in network security.

In the traditional network infrastructure, the equipment itself is in charge of forwarding packets. Due to the constraints of computing capability and the heavy decision-making work, the packets cannot be examined in detail among the network devices. As a result, the DDoS attack detection and mitigation mechanisms in the traditional networks rely on the firewall/Anomaly Detection Systems (ADS) of the destination servers. There are two ways of the firewall/ADS to detect the attacks. One is the in-line and the other is the out-of-path. When a huge number of packets arrive, the in-line method which relies on sampling-based anomaly detection cannot analyze them in detail to provide the accurate classification, and the out-of-path method will cause a lot of delays. So, the target server cannot handle it well even with firewall/ADS.

Therefore, it is significant and urgent to find a way to drop malicious traffic before the packets accumulate in the target server. Software Defined Networking (SDN) is a promising network architecture to solve this problem. This architecture decouples the network control plane and data plane. The OpenFlow (OF) protocol is the standard communications interface defined between the controller and forwarding layers of the SDN architecture. Each OF switch has at least one flow table containing a set of flow entries including match fields, statistics and a set of rules. Based on these match fields, OF switches use the concept of flow to identify the network traffic, record its statistics by the counters and forward packets according to the rules. The flow tables can be changed dynamically enabling the network to be highly scalable and flexible. With the help of SDN, it is allowed to examine network traffic in propagation path dropping malicious flows before they accumulate to take avalanche effect on the target server. The DDoS attack detection and mitigation mechanisms using SDN have been widely studied [4–13]. Most of these works focus on the controller, which is aware of the complete topology of the network to get flow tables from each OF switch periodically and examine statistics of each flow entry to check whether the DDoS attacks occur. If the attacks are detected, the controller issues relevant security policies to the OF switches by modifying rules of forwarding malicious flows such as dropping flows.

However, the design of DDoS attack detection using SDN still needs further improvement. It works well when the network is small but in a large-scale network, there are lots of problems to be solved. The problems are summarized as follows:

- The DDoS detection mechanisms depend on controller polling time. If we need a quick response, it will aggravate the overload of the controller. If we use the sampling technologies, such as sFlow [14] and NetFlow [15], we need to consider the tradeoff between sampling rate and detection accuracy.
- Because of its huge size, collection and statistics processes of the flows from all the OF switches will overload the controller.
- The controller needs to communicate with the OF switches to get the flow's statistics, which prolongs the detection duration.
- The detection mechanism counting on the controller, is a single point vulnerability threat towards the frame. Once the controller is hacked, the system is not secure anymore.

In this paper, we use the edge computing [16] which is a more effective new scheme to solve the above problems, for the reason that IoT traffic has the different characteristic comparing with other Internet-connected devices. For example, IoT devices often communicate with a small finite set of servers and also have repetitive network traffic patterns [17]. As a result, it is easier to recognize the IoT traffic even at the edge of the network.

In many IoT deployments, IoT devices are often coordinated under a gateway which serves to connect IoT devices to the network. We use SDN-based IoT gateways (SDNIGs) which are OF switches in SDN to detect IoT-based DDoS attacks. More specifically, we regard the controller as the cloud computing layer and the SDNIGs as the edge computing layer by bringing intelligence to the SDNIGs. The SDNIGs process the detection requests to be resolved by the controller originally with no need for the controller's intervention, which has the advantages of relieving the pressure of the controller, allowing requests to be processed in real time, and improving framework security by adopting multi-point defense mechanism. The main contributions of this paper can be summarized as follows:

- Unlike the existing works, we put IoT-based DDoS attack detection and mitigation mechanism in the SDNIGs. By analyzing the flow statistics and making decisions while a DDoS attack occurs in the edge switches, it is detected and responded in real time and the overload of the controller is avoided.
- Taking advantage of the OF tables in switches, it is easy for us to figure out whether there is a DDoS attack by analyzing the flow statistics.
- By using the machine learning based method in the SDNIGs, we can distinguish the IoT-based DDoS attacks effectively and locate the malicious flows exactly. Our experimental results show that our method can detect the attacks with high accuracy and mitigate the attacks in a short time.

The organization of this paper goes as: first of all, we present related works on IoT-based DDoS attacks and then we propose our method of DDoS attack mitigation. Experimental settings and results are presented to evaluate the effectiveness of our method. Finally, we conclude our work and discuss future work.

2   Related Work

We classify the work of detecting IoT-based DDoS attacks into two categories. They are either host-based or network-based.

2.1   Host-Based

The host-based methods focus on the detection mechanisms in the IoT and try to figure out the algorithm as lightweight as possible. For example, Summerville et al. [18] put the lightweight deep packet anomaly detection in the IoT devices and Sedjelmaci et al. [19] proposed a lightweight anomaly detection method based on game theory to be applied to IoT devices. These methods are not realistic enough. They need to work with IoT device manufacturers to put the detector into the IoT devices which has low feasibility. In addition, the restriction of IoT devices' computing capability is also a big challenge to run these algorithms efficiently and guarantee devices' functionality.

2.2   Network-Based

The network-based methods are categorized according to the network features adopted to detect the attacks.

One is the features of the early steps of DDoS attacks such as propagation of the zombies. [20] is one of the examples. Ozcelik et al. combined two different scanning algorithms including Threshold Random Walk with Credit Based Rate Limiting [21] and Rate Limiting [22] in SDN. They used the controller to check whether the devices were compromised. Once the malicious devices were found, they would be added to the blacklist and drop all of the packets from the compromised devices by adding the rules to the OF switches. In our opinion, those methods focusing on the early step of DDoS attacks will be eliminated in the long run because they depend on the features of zombie propagation which may mutate to bypass detection.

The other is the network features of the DDoS attack traffic. Doshi et al. [17] collected the IoT device traffic and DDoS attack traffic in the real world and used machine learning to achieve high accuracy to classify the malicious traffic. Meidan et al. [23] proposed using deep autoencoders to detect anomalous network traffic and made a contribution to the IoT DDoS attack dataset. Both of the works focused on the algorithms to achieve high accuracy, the patterns of IoT devices traffic and the features of traffic to choose. However, they did not analyze the effect of the mechanisms on the network and how they work to mitigate the DDoS attacks. Braga et al. [8] used Self Organizing Maps (SOM) on the controller to detect which OF switch has the DDoS traffic. Bhunia et al. [4] proposed to use Support Vector Machine (SVM) to detect and mitigate DDoS attacks in SDN. Ahmed et al. [7] proposed the Dirichlet process mixture model (DPMM) to detect DNS Query-Based DDoS attacks. These three works all used the controller in the SDN to poll the flow tables periodically, which has the problems as discussed above. There are some researchers who try to bring some intelligence to the OF switches. Shin et al. [12] used OF switches to deal with DDoS attacks with two modules. The first module can only detect DDoS SYN flooding and the second one is a trigger module for responding to the network threat. Wang et al. [6] proposed an entropy-based distributed DDoS detection mechanism in the OF switches but it cannot identify and locate the malicious flows to mitigate DDoS attacks.

3 DDoS Detection and Mitigation Framework

In this section, we describe the proposed DDoS detection and mitigation mechanism in detail. First of all, we introduce the attack scenario which we are going to defend and then we propose our mechanism.

3.1 Attack Scenario

The DDoS attacks are a type of attacks which need as many as possible devices from multiple sources to produce a huge number of malicious packets to the target server. In our attack scenario, we consider attackers exploit compromised IoT devices to constitute their botnet for sending malicious traffic to make the target server unavailable to serve legitimate users.

3.2 Framework Components

Figure 1 illustrates the framework of the following five components: IoT devices, legitimate users, servers, OF switches and SDN controller.

IoT Devices. There are a number of IoT devices in the network such as various activity sensors, smart lighting systems, wearable devices. These devices are connected to the SDNIG and they are easy to be hacked.

Legitimate Users. Legitimate users refer to the users who use the network legally to acquire information in their own life. The devices used such as laptop and telephone are connected to the OF switches. These users are victims who cannot get service from the target server when the DDoS attacks occur.

Servers. Servers such as file server, database server, web server and IoT server are equipment that provide computing services and respond as well as process service requests. They are connected to the OF switches and attacked by the compromised IoT devices in the DDoS attacks.

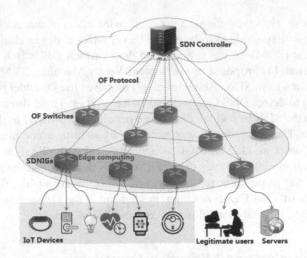

Fig. 1. Framework components

OF switches. The SDN-compatible OF switches are the end-point of the service provider's network and they are responsible for forwarding packets. Each OF switch has at least one flow table of flow statistics. The SDNIGs are a subset of OF switches and they are the platform of edge computing, to which we apply DDoS attack detection and mitigation mechanism. The flow statistics in SDNIGs are analyzed to detect the IoT-based attacks. When the attacks are detected, the policies and rules will be issued in the OF switches for security purpose.

SDN Controller. A cluster of controllers provides high reliability and availability services. They are aware of the complete topology of the network to issue forwarding rules to the OF switches.

3.3 Operation of the Mechanism

All the IoT devices are connected to the SDNIGs and the SDNIGs continuously monitor traffic and get the statistics. We put the statistics of each flow into the trained classifier to detect suspicious flows. When the statistics of the flows are classified as malicious, we add the rules in the SDNIGs to drop traffic which matches the malicious flows' head field and put the malicious hosts into the blacklist.

As illustrated in the Fig. 2 there are three main modules in the mechanism: learning module, detection module and flow management module.

Learning Module. There are three parts in the learning module: flow collection, feature extraction, and training classification. First is the flow collection. To replicate typical traffic flows, we simulate the traffic of IoT devices and legitimate users. We simulate the IoT devices traffic in four scenarios including smart home, wise

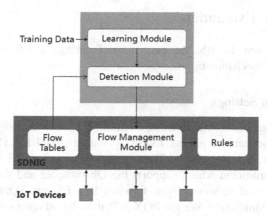

Fig. 2. Operation of the mechanism

information technology of 120 (WIT120), intelligent agriculture and automated driving. Besides, we also imitate the behavior of legitimate users browsing the website. To collect DDoS attack traffic, we launch two kinds of attacks with the use of source IP address spoofing, ICMP flooding attack and TCP SYN flooding attack, to a web server constructed by ourselves. All of the simulated traffic and DDoS attack traffic are provided to the feature extraction to get the dataset classified into two categories as benign and malicious.

It is very important to extract features from the traffic. The pattern of features is flow-level as in the flow tables. The flow-level is aggregated by source IP, source MAC, target IP, and target MAC for a period of time. Considering the characteristics of DDoS attacks, we employ five features in our method including the duration of the flow, the number of packets per flow, the packet size per flow, the type of the flow and the growth of a single flow. The first four features are easy to obtain from the flow tables and to compute the growth of a single flow, we take the total number of packets per flow and divide by the duration of the flow.

Three algorithms are used in the training classification. The training set is put into these three algorithms to train the classification module. After training, we choose one of these trained modules to be the detection module.

Detection Module. Detection module gets input from the learning module and it polls the flow tables in real time to get statistics of the flows. After the feature extraction, the data is put into the detector to analyze whether there is a DDoS attack or not. When the malicious flow is detected, the detection module will send the source's address matching the head field of the flow to the flow management module.

Flow Management Module. When the flow is classified as an anomalous flow, the flow management module will get the malicious source's address of the flow from the detection module. First, the flow management module will block the traffic from the malicious host by adding rules in the flow tables which set the flow's action to be "drop" with malicious host's address in the match field. Then, the malicious host will be put into the blacklist to be shared in all the OF switches.

4 Performance Evaluation

In this section, we first describe the experimental settings and then we evaluate the performance of our mechanism.

4.1 Experimental Settings

The hardware settings of the experimental environment for evaluating the performance of the proposed mechanism are as follows: Ubuntu 16.04.1 LTS, Intel i7 6700 3.40 GHz processor, 8 GB memory. The experiment is simulated by using Mininet [24] emulation environment which supports the OF protocol and the SDN system to create a realistic virtual network. Open vSwitch is a famous SDN software switch implemented in our simulation. We use POX, a Python-based open source controller, to perform the controller in SDN.

The topology of the experiment is shown in Fig. 3. The IoT-based DDoS attack detection and mitigation mechanism is put in S1 and S2. H18, the web server, is an http server which is used to return simple web contents. H12, H17 act like users who visit the website by using the command of curl to connect to the web server. IoT devices are simulated by H1–11 while H14–16 are simulated as IoT servers. These IoT devices, H1–4 are emulated as smoke sensor, safety center, light sensor and temperature sensor in smart home. H6–9 are emulated as electrocardiography (ECG) transducer, blood pressure sensor, pulse sensor and body temperature sensor in WIT120. H10, H11 are emulated as air temperature sensor and soil temperature sensor in intelligent agriculture. Automated driving car is emulated by H5. According to [25, 26], the traffic

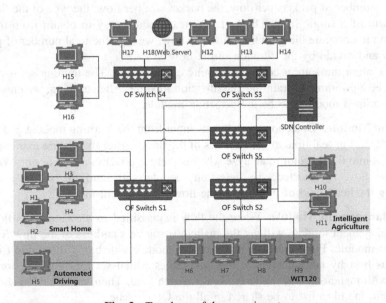

Fig. 3. Topology of the experiment

Table 1. The traffic simulation of the IoT devices

IoT scenario	IoT device	Interval	Packet's size (Bytes)
Smart home	Smoke sensor	600 s	83
	Safety center	600 s	81
	Light sensor	1800 s	119
	Temperature sensor	1800 s	99
WIT120	ECG	0.25 s	125
	Blood pressure sensor	0.4 s	125
	Pulse sensor	0.4 s	125
	Temperature sensor	5 s	27
Intelligent agriculture	Air temperature sensor	60 s	127
	Soil temperature sensor	60 s	127
Automated driving	Automated driving car	Normal distribution ($\mu = 80$, $\sigma = 8$) ms	149

simulation of the IoT devices is shown in Table 1 in detail. All the IoT devices traffic is generated by DITG (Distributed Internet Traffic Generator) [27]. When the DDoS attacks occur, H1, H2, H6, H7, H10 will become compromised IoT devices which launch mixed attacks to H18. ICMP flooding attack is conducted by H2, H6 while H1, H7, H10 launch TCP SYN flooding attack. The Scapy [28] library is used to generate DDoS attack traffic from compromised IoT devices to the victim. To evaluate the performance of the mechanism, H13 is used to execute the command of ping to test the time delay every 0.5 s.

We use the experimental network to collect realistic benign and malicious IoT devices traffic, producing a dataset of 550,109 flows, comprised of 185,449 benign flows and 364,660 malicious flows.

The dataset collected is used to train the learning module and evaluate the performance of our detection algorithms. Three machine learning algorithms have been tested to distinguish DDoS flows from legitimate flows:

- SVM with RBF kernel (SVM)
- Random Forest using Gini impurity scores (RF)
- Neural Network: 4 layers fully connected feedforward neural network (NN)

The classifiers are trained on a training set with 80% of the dataset combined with normal and DDoS traffic and are calculated performance on the remaining data.

4.2   Analysis of the Results

First of all, we obtain Precision, Ture Positive Rate (TPR) and False Positive Rate (FPR) in Eqs. 1, 2 and 3 respectively to evaluate our learning module.

$$\text{Precision} = \frac{TP}{TP + FP} \tag{1}$$

TP means attack traffic detected as attack traffic and FP is legitimate traffic detected as attack traffic. As a result, Precision reflects the number of real attacks of all detected ones.

$$\text{TPR} = \frac{TP}{TP + FN} \tag{2}$$

FN means attack traffic detected as legitimate traffic. It turns out that TPR means how many attacks are detected of all attacks.

$$\text{FPR} = \frac{FP}{FP + TN} \tag{3}$$

TN means legitimate traffic detected as legitimate traffic. FPR reflects that how much legitimate traffic is classified as attack traffic among all legitimate traffic.

The performance of our detection is shown in Table 2. As we can see, owing to the unique features of IoT traffic and DDoS attack traffic, the classifiers perform very well even at the edge of the network. SVM performs the best in Precision and FPR, but it has the poorest performance in TPR which is only 87.3% while the other algorithms are nearly 99%. It means that SVM will miss a lot of attacks, which is the last thing we want to see. The RF performs the best. NN performs surprisingly well even in the training set with only around 500 thousand flows. We believe that the NN would perform better in a larger training dataset.

Table 2. The results of detection methods

Detection module	Precision (%)	TPR (%)	FPR (%)
SVM	100	87.34	0
RF	99.99	99.98	0.0108
NN	99.98	99.93	0.0215

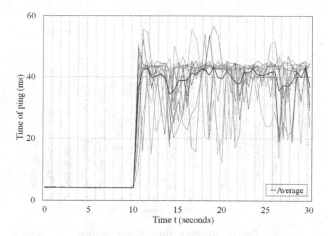

Fig. 4. The time delay results without defense of 15 simulation runs

We use trained NN as the detection module to detect malicious flows and use the results of the classifier to mitigate IoT-based DDoS attacks. To investigate the negative effect of IoT-based DDoS attacks and the effectiveness of our mechanism, we design two scenes. In each scene, the simulation runs last 30 s and is repeated 15 times. In the first scene, there are no defense methods used to mitigate IoT-based DDoS attacks while our mechanism is used in the second scene to mitigate attacks. The experiment results about the time delay of ping which is sent by the normal user in the two scenes respectively, are shown in Figs. 4 and 5.

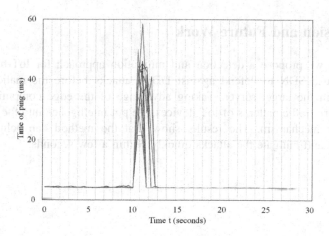

Fig. 5. The time delay results with our method of 15 simulation runs

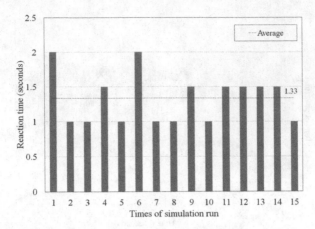

Fig. 6. Reaction time of our method

As we can see in the Fig. 4, the time delay of ping under normal circumstances is around 4 ms (ms). At the 10th second when the IoT-based DDoS attacks happen, the time delay of the normal user rises to around 40 ms without any relief for a long time in the context of no defense.

Figures 5 and 6 show the performance of our method. As we can see in Fig. 5, the time delay of the normal user is recovered with the help of our mechanism and continues its usual interaction time in a short time after the detection and response of the compromised IoT devices' attacks. Figure 6 shows how much time it takes our mechanism to detect and mitigate the DDoS attacks. The maximum detection time is 2.0 s, the shortest time is 1.0 s and the average time is 1.33 s, which means our mechanism takes steps and controls the attacks quickly when the DDoS attacks occur.

5 Conclusion and Future Work

In this work, we propose a detection and mitigation approach for IoT-based DDoS attacks. We use SDN to defend against DDoS attacks before the malicious traffic accumulates in the target server. Taking advantage of the edge computing and the unique network traffic patterns of IoT devices, we put intelligence into the SDNIGs to complete our mechanism. The results show that the method can achieve a high detection rate and mitigate the attacks quickly within a few seconds.

In the future, we are going to improve the framework in these two ways:

- Include more sophisticated DDoS attacks such as Crossfire attack [29], pulsing DDoS attack [30] and so on, to evaluate our method.
- Use the controller of SDN to sense the situation of the whole network and improve the monitoring ability of the framework.

Acknowledgements.. This work was supported in part by the Natural Science Foundation of China under Grants 61672092, in part by the Fundamental Research Funds for the Central Universities of China under Grants 2018JBZ103 and Major Scientific, and in part by the Technological Innovation Projects of Shandong Province, China (No. 2019JZZY020128).

References

1. Pettey, C.: The Internet of Things and the Enterprise. Gartner, August 2015
2. HP Enterprise: Internet of things research study -2015 report, vol. 2 (2015). http://www8.hp.com
3. Kolias, C., Kambourakis, G., Stavrou, A., Voas, J.: DDoS in the IoT: Mirai and other botnets. Computer **50**(7), 80–84 (2017)
4. Bhunia, S.S., Gurusamy, M.: Dynamic attack detection and mitigation in IoT using SDN. In: 2017 27th International Telecommunication Networks and Applications Conference (ITNAC), pp. 1–6. IEEE, November 2017
5. Yin, D., Zhang, L., Yang, K.: A DDoS attack detection and mitigation with software-defined internet of things framework. IEEE Access **6**, 24694–24705 (2018)
6. Wang, R., Jia, Z., Ju, L.: An entropy-based distributed DDoS detection mechanism in software-defined networking. In: 2015 IEEE Trustcom/BigDataSE/ISPA, vol. 1, pp. 310–317. IEEE, August 2015
7. Ahmed, M.E., Kim, H., Park, M.: Mitigating DNS query-based DDoS attacks with machine learning on software-defined networking. In: MILCOM 2017–2017 IEEE Military Communications Conference (MILCOM), pp. 11–16. IEEE, October 2017
8. Braga, R., Mota, E., Passito, A.: Lightweight DDoS flooding attack detection using NOX/OpenFlow. In: IEEE Local Computer Network Conference, pp. 408–415. IEEE, October 2010
9. Zheng, J., Li, Q., Gu, G., Cao, J., Yau, D.K., Wu, J.: Realtime DDoS defense using COTS SDN switches via adaptive correlation analysis. IEEE Trans. Inf. Forensics Secur. **13**(7), 1838–1853 (2018)
10. Yan, Q., Huang, W., Luo, X., Gong, Q., Yu, F.R.: A multi-level DDoS mitigation framework for the industrial internet of things. IEEE Commun. Mag. **56**(2), 30–36 (2018)

11. Hyun, D., Kim, J., Hong, D., Jeong, J.P.: SDN-based network security functions for effective DDoS attack mitigation. In: 2017 International Conference on Information and Communication Technology Convergence (ICTC), pp. 834–839. IEEE, October 2017
12. Shin, S., Yegneswaran, V., Porras, P., Gu, G.: Avant-guard: scalable and vigilant switch flow management in software-defined networks. In: Proceedings of the 2013 ACM SIGSAC Conference on Computer & Communications Security, pp. 413–424. ACM, November 2013
13. Ahmed, M.E., Kim, H.: DDoS attack mitigation in Internet of Things using software defined networking. In: 2017 IEEE Third International Conference on Big Data Computing Service and Applications (BigDataService), pp. 271–276. IEEE, April 2017
14. sFlow. http://www.sflow.org/
15. Cisco NetFlow. http://www.cisco.com/go/netflow
16. Dolui, K., Datta, S.K.: Comparison of edge computing implementations: fog computing, cloudlet and mobile edge computing. In: 2017 Global Internet of Things Summit (GIoTS), pp. 1–6. IEEE, June 2017
17. Doshi, R., Apthorpe, N., Feamster, N.: Machine learning DDoS detection for consumer internet of things devices. In: 2018 IEEE Security and Privacy Workshops (SPW), pp. 29–35. IEEE, May 2018
18. Summerville, D.H., Zach, K.M., Chen, Y.: Ultra-lightweight deep packet anomaly detection for internet of things devices. In: 2015 IEEE 34th International Performance Computing and Communications Conference (IPCCC), pp. 1–8. IEEE, December 2015
19. Sedjelmaci, H., Senouci, S.M., Al-Bahri, M.: A lightweight anomaly detection technique for low-resource IoT devices: a game-theoretic methodology. In: 2016 IEEE International Conference on Communications (ICC), pp. 1–6. IEEE, May 2016
20. Özçelik, M., Chalabianloo, N., Gür, G.: Software-defined edge defense against IoT-based DDoS. In: 2017 IEEE International Conference on Computer and Information Technology (CIT), pp. 308–313. IEEE, August 2017
21. Schechter, S.E., Jung, J., Berger, A.W.: Fast detection of scanning worm infections. In: Jonsson, E., Valdes, A., Almgren, M. (eds.) RAID 2004. LNCS, vol. 3224, pp. 59–81. Springer, Heidelberg (2004). https://doi.org/10.1007/978-3-540-30143-1_4
22. Williamson, M.M.: Throttling viruses: restricting propagation to defeat malicious mobile code. In: 18th Annual Computer Security Applications Conference 2002 Proceedings, pp. 61–68. IEEE (2002)
23. Meidan, Y., et al.: N-BaIoT—network-based detection of IoT Botnet attacks using deep autoencoders. IEEE Pervasive Comput. **17**(3), 12–22 (2018)
24. Mininet. http://mininet.org/
25. Zhao, J.: Analysis of the characteristics of M2 M traffic. Master's thesis, Southwest Jiaotong University (2014)
26. Hou, S., Tan, X.: Research and analysis of traffic characteristics of typical internet of things. Internet Things Technol. **7**(6), 40–42 (2017)
27. Botta, A., Dainotti, A., Pescapé, A.: A tool for the generation of realistic network workload for emerging networking scenarios. Comput. Netw. **56**(15), 3531–3547 (2012)
28. Scapy. http://www.secdev.org/projects/scapy/

29. Kang, M.S., Lee, S.B., Gligor, V.D.: The crossfire attack. In: 2013 IEEE Symposium on Security and Privacy, pp. 127–141. IEEE. May 2013
30. Rasti, R., Murthy, M., Weaver, N., Paxson, V.: Temporal lensing and its application in pulsing denial-of-service attacks. In: 2015 IEEE Symposium on Security and Privacy, pp. 187–198. IEEE, May 2015

Location Consistency-Based MITM Attack Detection in 802.11ad Networks

Xianglin Wei[1] and Chaogang Tang[2(✉)]

[1] National University of Defense Technology, Nanjing 210007, China
[2] School of Computer Science and Technology,
China University of Mining and Technology, Xuzhou 221116, China
cgtang@cumt.edu.cn

Abstract. IEEE 802.11ad-enabled millimeter-wave communication systems are becoming a key enabler for bandwidth-intensive and delay-sensitive indoor applications, due to their potentials to provision multiple-Gigabytes. However, the weak built-in security scheme renders them vulnerable to various cyber-physical attacks, such as beam-stealing and man-in-the-middle (MITM) attack. A MITM attacker aims to intercept a legitimate communication through deceiving the victims into steering their signals towards the attacker's location. Then, the attacker pretends to be a relay between the victims and eavesdrop or even manipulate the relayed packets. Hence, it is crucial to detect the existence of MITM attacks in a timely manner and thus to restore network service. In this backdrop, a location consistency-based MITM detection scheme is put forward. For each transmitter in the network, it will check for the beamforming information table and location consistency of its neighbors after the beam training process. An attack will be declared if an inconsistency is found by a legitimate node in the network. To validate the effectiveness of the algorithms, a simulator is developed and a series of simulations are conducted. Results have shown that the proposed algorithms could effectively determine the existence of MITM attacks.

Keywords: Millimeter-wave communication · Man-in-the-middle attack · Detection

1 Introduction

60 GHz millimeter-wave (mm-wave) communication is capable of providing high-directional and multiple-Gigabytes data-rates. This characteristic enables it a promising solution for bandwidth-intensive and delay-sensitive indoor applications. Furthermore, no other wiring overheads are introduced such as wireless high definition video, virtual reality, and augmented reality. To fully exploit this

This research was supported in part by the National Natural Science Foundation of China under Grant No. 61402521, Jiangsu Province Natural Science Foundation of China under Grant No. BK20140068, and BK20150201.

characteristic, beam steering-based directional transmission is widely adopted to compensate high attenuation by various standards, including IEEE 802.11ad and WirelessHD [1].

To increase the transmission gain, exploit space reusability, and reduce interference, a transmitter and a receiver should point their antennas to each other through a beam training process before data transmission. This training process is called sector sweeping in IEEE 802.11ad networks. However, this process is proved to be stealing-vulnerable since it does not provide any authentication scheme in the sweeping duration. Steinmetzer et al. have presented a man-in-the-middle (MITM) attack towards IEEE 802.11ad networks, in which the attacker will forge fake feedbacks to force victims to steer their signals to the attacker [2]. In other words, all the packets interchanged between two victims will be relayed, eavesdropped, and even manipulated by the attacker. An MITM attacker can threat the legitimate communication from three aspects. First, extra relay introduced by the attacker will increase the communication delay. Second, privacy leakage will happen if the attacker eavesdrop and investigate the transmitter packets. Third, the attacker may force legitimate nodes to act as what it wants through forged or manipulated packets. Worse, this type of MITM attack can be applied to those medium access control (MAC) protocols based on IEEE 802.11ad, as presented in references [3–5]. Therefore, how to detect the existence of a MITM attacker will be critical for the successful deployment of mm-wave communication networks.

Steinmetzer et al. have discussed four possible detection metrics that can be utilized to find MITM attacks [2], i.e. (1) the switching between sectors, (2) changes in the received signal strength, (3) beacon interval length, and (4) beacon counters to be valuable for a detection scheme. For each metric, a threshold for no-attacking scenario is determined in a learning phase, and it is adopted to raise an alarm when the running value exceeds it in the detection phase. In other words, it is a network and environment dependent method and needs a long training time. To enhance the security of the sweeping process, they have put forward a lightweight authentication scheme, named sector sweep with authentication (SSA), which ensures that devices only accept authenticated feedback [6]. With SSA, they extended the existing IEEE 802.11ad sector sweep by amending the frame format. However, protocol modification is a time-consuming process and will introduce extra computation and delay overhead.

In this paper, a location consistency-based MITM detection scheme is put forward. For each node in the network, it will check for the location consistency of its neighbors after the beam training process. An attack will be declared if an location inconsistency is found. To validate the effectiveness of the algorithms, a simulator is developed and a series of simulations are conducted. Results have shown that the proposed algorithms could effectively determine the existence of a MITM attack without modifying the protocol or a pre-training phase.

This rest of the paper is organized as follows. Section 2 introduces IEEE 802.11ad beam sweep process and presents the MITM attack. Section 3 describes the detection algorithm. Section 4 shows the evaluation results of the proposal. Finally, we conclude our main work and further research in Sect. 5.

2   Related Work

2.1   Sector Sweep Process in IEEE 802.11ad

In the Association Beamforming (BF) Training (A-BFT) period, two nodes that want to communicate with each other need to conduct the beam sweep process to determine their mutual sectors with the highest received signal strength. To be specific, the initiator of the beamforming exchange transmits training frames for each transmit antenna sector when the responder configures its antenna to have a quasi-omni directional pattern. This is followed by the responder sending a set of training frames for each antenna sector, in which the initiator configures it's antenna to have a quasi-omni directional pattern. Then, the sector sweep feedback information is exchanged between the two nodes. At this point in the process, both the initiator and the responder each possess their best transmit sector [1].

2.2   The MITM Attack

From the above introduction, we know that no authentication is performed in the sweeping period. An attacker can easily intervene in the training process through injecting forged response frames. The initiator's antenna sector will be directed to the attacker as long as its forged response arrives before the legitimate response frame from the responder. This is also true for the feedback process of the responder's sector training period. Then, the attacker can act as a relay between them and investigates all the transmitted packets, as shown in Fig. 1. In Fig. 1, the legitimate link between the initiator and the responder is replaced by the relayed links established between them and the attacker.

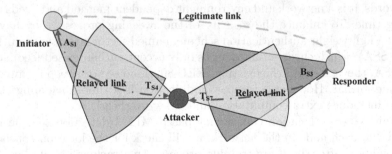

Fig. 1. The MITM attack scenario.

2.3   MITM Detection and IEEE 802.11ad Security

As mentioned above, four metrics are adopted by Steinmetzer et al. to detect the existence of MITM attacks, i.e. (1) the switching between sectors, (2) changes in the received signal strength, (3) beacon interval length, and (4) beacon counters to be valuable. Generally speaking, a threshold is learned or observed in the no-attack scenario [2]. Then, an attack is claimed if a threshold-exceeding event happens. The effectiveness of these threshold-based anomaly detection methods depends on the environments and the feasibility of the learning phase.

Mubarak et al. have proposed a new updates of Control and provisioning of wireless access points (CAPWAP) 802.11 binding for enabling the use of CAP-WAP capabilities in conjunction with IEEE 802.11ad-based wireless local area networks (WLANs) [7]. Balakrishnan et al. have discussed eavesdropper attack strategies for 802.11ad mmWave systems and provided an analytical model to characterize the success possibility of eavesdropping in both opportunistic stationary attacks and active nomadic attacks [8,9]. Aftab et al. have designed a self-organized security framework for Intrusion Detection and Prevention system (IDPS) for Wireless Gigabit alliance (WiGig) networks [10].

3 Location Consistency-Based MITM Detection

3.1 Basic Idea

Note that in many directional transmission-oriented MAC protocols, each node will remember the mutual sector information between itself and its neighbors. For each neighbor, the node will store two sector numbers in the table. The first (second) one is the number of the node's (neighbor's) sector in which the neighbor (node) can have the highest received signal strength from the node (neighbor). This table is usually called the beamforming information (BFI) table. Each node's BFI table will be filled and updated after each beam sweeping and packet receiving events. A MITM attacker can introduce errors into a victim's BFI table through injecting forged feedback frames in the sector sweep feedback and ACK period. Without loss of generality, we assume that the attacker can freely take any position in the surrounding but is unlikely to reside directly between the devices on the line-of-sight. This is also the assumption made in reference [2].

Figure 2 shows a scenario where a location inconsistency event happens when a MITM attacker exists. In the network consisting three nodes shown in Fig. 2, after the beam sweeping process with MITM attack, the possible established BFI tables of nodes A, B, and C can be shown in Fig. 3. We can see that the legitimate link between A and B is intercepted by the attacker and their BFI tables are polluted as shown in the dashed rectangles in Fig. 3. To be specific, node A's sector number to node B is set to be 2 rather than the correct number 1 (5), while node B's sector number to node A is set to 5.

If we want to find the existence of a MITM attacker, we need to exploit the inconsistency of the BFI tables. Moreover, we can also consider the mapping between the sector number and geographical location. This is due to the fact that a node's sector number also represents a particular area that can be covered by its signal if it transmits in this sector.

3.2   BFI Table Inconsistency-Based MITM Detection

In the example shown in Fig. 3, it is easy to design a detection algorithm for a IEEE 802.11ad network. To be specific, every λ seconds, node A exchanges BFI table with its neighbors and gets their BFI tables for inconsistency detection. Then, it can use Algorithm 1 to find out the existence of a MITM attacker. In Algorithm 1, a node needs to compare its BFI table with all its neighbors' BFI tables to find the inconsistency and thus to locate the potential victim nodes.

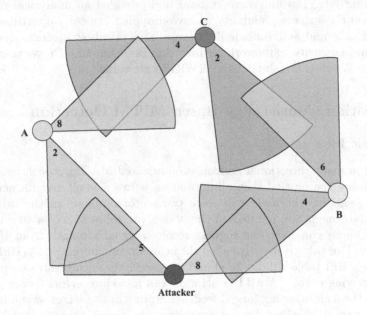

Fig. 2. Location inconsistency when a MITM exists.

Dest.	From	To
A	0	0
B	5	2
C	4	8

Dest.	From	To
A	8	4
B	0	0
C	2	6

Dest.	From	To
A	8	4
B	6	2
C	0	0

(a) A's BFI table   (b) B's BFI table   (c) C's BFI table

Fig. 3. Established BFI tables after the beam sweeping process.

The effectiveness of Algorithm 1 depends on the fact that the attacker will honestly relay nodes' BFI tables to each other. Then, node A and B can find the existence of the attack based on Algorithm 1. However, this algorithm will fail if the attacker dedicatedly modify its relayed BFI tables to remove the inconsistency from the tables. Algorithm 2 shows a possible strategy that the attacker

---

Algorithm 1. BFI Table Inconsistency Detection

Input: BFI tables of this node and all its neighbors
Output: Potential victim neighbors set $\mathbf{V}$

1 **for** *each neighbor* **do**
2 $\quad$ Choose the row vector v_1 in this node's BFI table where the
$\quad$ destination is equal to this neighbor;
3 $\quad$ Choose the row vector v_2 in the neighbor's BFI table where the
$\quad$ destination is equal to this node;
4 $\quad$ **if** $v_1(2) \neq v_2(3)$ & $v_1(3) \neq v_2(2)$ **then**
5 $\quad\quad$ An inconsistency is found ;
6 $\quad\quad$ Add this neighbor to $\mathbf{V}$;
7 $\quad$ **end**
8 **end**
9 **return** $\mathbf{V}$;

Algorithm 2. BFI Table Manipulation

Input: Transmitted BFI table from a legitimate node l, victim node set
$\quad\quad\quad$ $\mathbf{V}$, the attacker's key-value pairs
Output: Manipulated BFI table

1 **if** $l \in \mathbf{V}$ **then**
2 $\quad$ **for** *each row vector v_i in the BFI table* **do**
3 $\quad\quad$ **if** $v_i(1) \in \mathbf{V}$ & $v_i(1) \neq l$ **then**
4 $\quad\quad\quad$ **if** The key $(l, v_i(1))$ or $(v_i(1), l)$ exists in the key-value pairs
$\quad\quad\quad$ stored at the attacker **then**
5 $\quad\quad\quad\quad$ Fetch the value pair (v_1, v_2) for the key;
6 $\quad\quad\quad\quad$ **if** The key (l, v_i) is the key stored **then**
7 $\quad\quad\quad\quad\quad$ $v_i(3) = v_1$;
8 $\quad\quad\quad\quad\quad$ $v_i(2) = v_2$;
9 $\quad\quad\quad\quad$ **else**
10 $\quad\quad\quad\quad\quad$ $v_i(2) = v_1$;
11 $\quad\quad\quad\quad\quad$ $v_i(3) = v_2$;
12 $\quad\quad\quad\quad$ **end**
13 $\quad\quad\quad$ **end**
14 $\quad\quad$ **end**
15 $\quad$ **end**
16 **end**
17 **return** the manipulated BFI table;

---

can adopt when it receives a BFI table sharing frame from the victims. Note
that, for each pair of victim nodes, the attacker needs to maintain a sector number pair for them to manipulate the received BFI tables. For example, for nodes
A and B, the attacker will maintain a key-value pair. The key for the pair is

(A, B), and the value is set to be (2, 4), i.e. node A and B's respective sector number for each other with the attacker as the relay. After receiving each BFI table from a victim node, the attacker needs to modify the sector numbers in the table to remove the inconsistency between BFI tables to fail Algorithm 1.

3.3   Location Inconsistency-Based MITM Detection

In this backdrop, we try to calculate the geographical location consistency of the nodes, and determine the existence of MITM attacks.

An example of this location inconsistency detection process is shown in Fig. 4. Figure 4 shows the results inferred from nodes A, B, and C's BFI tables. In Fig. 4, A firstly estimates its distance to node C based on the channel model established in [11], and then obtains C's feasible locations based on the estimated distance and the sector number stored in A's BFI table, i.e. the arc from C1 to C2 in Fig. 4. Then, node A can calculate B's possible location based on its own

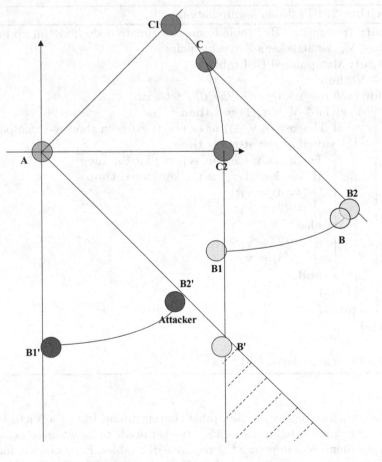

Fig. 4. Location Inconsistency detection.

observation and node C's observation. In one hand, based on its own distance estimation and sector number, several possible locations of node B from B1' to B2' can be obtained. On the other hand, based on both B and C's BFI tables and the estimated distance between them, there are a few positions that B can locate. In Fig. 4, B1 to B2 is one of the possible arcs that B can locate on. However, based on C's BFI table, we know that B' and its nearby positions are the final locations that B can locate on based on A and C's observations. This will cause an inconsistency with the arc from B1' to B2'. Therefore, a MITM attack will be declared. The detection process is illustrated in Algorithm 3. In Algorithm 3, the distance to each node is estimated based on the channel model established in [11], and the possible area of each node is determined based on both the distance and the sector numbers stored in the BFI tables. If no possible location exists in the intersection area that can fulfill both the distance and the sector number constraint, an inconsistency is claimed. In other words, a MITM attacker is detected.

Note that Algorithms 1 and 3 can be applied in conjunction with those four metrics-based detection methods presented by Steinmetzer et al. in reference [2].

Algorithm 3. Location Inconsistency Detection

Input: BFI tables of this node and all its neighbors
Output: Potential victim neighbors set $\mathbf{V}$

1 **for** *each neighbor* n_i **do**
2   **for** *each neighbor* n_j *and* $j \neq i$ **do**
3   Estimate the distance d_{ji} from n_j to n_i based on the channel model established in [11];
4   Estimate the distance d_j from this node to n_j based on the channel model established in [11];
5   Estimate n_j's position based on the sector number and d_j ;
6   Estimate n_i's possible area A_{ji} based on n_j's BFI table, d_{ji} and n_j's position;
7   **end**
8   Calculate the intersection area of all A_j, $j = 1, 2, \ldots, n, and, j \neq i$;
9   Estimate the distance d_i to n_i based on the channel model [11];
10   Derive the most feasible position of n_j;
11   Calculate the distance from the most feasible position of n_j based on n_i's observation and this node's own observation;
12   **if** The distance is larger than a threshold β **then**
13   An inconsistency is found ;
14   Add node i to $\mathbf{V}$;
15   **end**
16 **end**
17 **return** $\mathbf{V}$;

---

4   Simulation and Discussion

4.1   Simulator Design

To evaluate the effectiveness of the detection algorithms, we have extended the simulator implemented by Akhtar et al. [4]. A few events are defined according to IEEE 802.11ad MAC protocol, including sector sweeping, feedback event, feedback ACK, and so on.

We have implemented the MITM attack logic into the simulator. To be specific, it will keep listening to the channel for the sector sweeping frames and reply with forged sector numbers to force the victims to direct their signals to itself. Moreover, for BFI tables sharing, we have added the information sharing process, in which each node will exchange its BFI table with its neighbors. To simplify the simulator design, only four nodes are deployed in an indoor environment, and three of them are legitimate node and one acts as the MITM attacker. Node A locates at the $(0, 0)$. For each node, the total number of sectors are set to be 8, and each sector covers $45°$ of the total area. The transmission power, mainlobe gain, sidelobe gain, background noise, SINR threshold, and other transmission parameters are the same as those in reference [4]. Node B, the MITM attacker, and C locate at the 1_{th}, 2_{th}, and 8_{th} quadrant of node A respectively. The locations of the nodes are randomly selected and the maximum distance between any two nodes are set to be $10\,m$ to ensure the connectivity of the network. Moreover, we assume that non-AP mode communication is supported here, i.e. each two nodes can communicate with each other directly.

4.2   Simulation Results

To validate the effectiveness of our proposed algorithms, we first investigate the scenario where the attacker cannot change the content of the BFI table exchange frames. In this circumstance, nodes can find the inconsistency based on Algorithm 1. Simulation results have shown that nodes in the network can always find the inconsistency in their BFI tables since we assume that the attacker does not locate at the LoS link between victims. Moreover, based on the victim set derived in Algorithm 1, the attacker's possible locations can also be determined.

To evaluate the effectiveness of Algorithm 3 with different sector numbers and threshold settings, a series of simulations have been conducted. Figure 5 shows the results. We can see that Algorithm 3 cannot detect the attacks when the sector number is too small, i.e. 4 in the simulation. This is due to the fact that the coverage area of a single sector is too large. When the sector number is equal or larger than 16, Algorithm 3 can detect the attack with a nearly 100% probability. Therefore, we suggest to select a relatively large sector number in the real deployment of IEEE 802.11ad networks to facilitate MITM attack detection.

4.3   Discussion

The Existence of Neighbor Nodes. The effectiveness of the presented algorithms depends on the situation that there exists at least one neighbor near the victim nodes that is not attacked by the MITM attack. This assumption is based on the fact that the wireless nodes are densely deployed due to the very limited transmission range of 60 GHz communication devices.

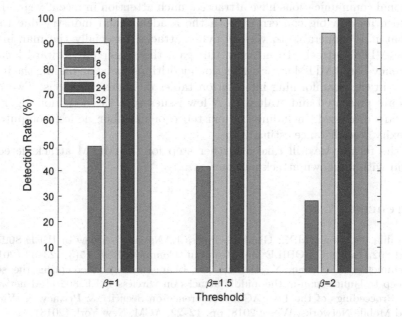

Fig. 5. Detection results with different threshold and sector numbers.

Computation Complexity. Besides, the locations of the attacker and the victims can also affect the detection capability of the presented algorithms. First of all, it is assumed that the attacker cannot locate at the line-of-sight path between two victims. Second, in the calculation process, the distance estimation is not assumed to be very accurate. In other words, each node can only infer another device's position based on its sector number and distance estimation results. An arc rather than a point is obtained as the estimation result. This introduces extra computation complexity into Algorithm 3. Therefore, we can see that there exists a trade-off between the number of sectors and the estimation accuracy in the MITM detection scenarios. Furthermore, the increase of the number of sectors will also increase the sector sweeping time if no attack happens.

Distance Estimation. Note that in this paper, the attacker is assumed to have the same capability with other devices, and the same transmitting power and gain. However, to avoid being caught by the detection algorithms, the attacker can change its transmitting power or gain over time to increase the detection difficulty. In this circumstance, the distance estimation error may be large to decrease the detection accuracy of the algorithms.

5   Conclusion

As a promising technology for supporting bandwidth-intensive applications, like wireless high definition video etc., high-bandwidth IEEE 802.11ad-based 60 GHz directional communications have attracted much attention in recent years. However, security is a big concern of both the academia and industry due to the fact that it is vulnerable to various cyber attacks, especially the man-in-the-middle (MITM) attack. To mitigate this gap, this paper put forward location consistency-based MITM attack detection algorithms based on finding the inconsistency in the beamforming information tables or nodes' locations. Two algorithms are presented and evaluated. A few issues with the detection algorithm design are discussed, including the existence of neighbor nodes, computation complexity, and distance estimation.

In the future, we will take a further step for the MITM attack detection problem with unknown attack parameters.

References

1. Perahia, E., Gong, M.X.: Gigabit wireless LANs: an overview of IEEE 802.11ac and 802.11ad. SIGMOBILE Mob. Comput. Commun. Rev. **15**(3), 23–33 (2011)
2. Steinmetzer, D., Yuan, Y., Hollick, M.: Beam-stealing: intercepting the sector sweep to launch man-in-the-middle attacks on wireless IEEE 802.11ad networks. In: Proceedings of the 11th ACM Conference on Security & Privacy in Wireless and Mobile Networks. WiSec 2018, pp. 12–22. ACM, New York (2018)
3. Jakllari, G., Broustis, I., Korakis, T., Krishnamurthy, S.V., Tassiulas, L.: Handling asymmetry in gain in directional antenna equipped ad hocnetworks. In: 2005 IEEE 16th International Symposium on Personal, Indoor and Mobile Radio Communications, vol. 2, pp. 1284–1288. IEEE (2005)
4. Akhtar, A., Ergen, S.C.: Directional MAC protocol for IEEE 802.11ad based wireless local area networks. Ad Hoc Netw. **69**, pp. 49–64 (2018)
5. De Rango, F., Inzillo, V., Quintana, A.A.: Exploiting frame aggregation and weighted round robin with beamforming smart antennas for directional MAC in MANET environments. Ad Hoc Netw. **89**, 186–203 (2019)
6. Steinmetzer, D., Ahmad, S., Anagnostopoulos, N., Hollick, M., Katzenbeisser, S.: Authenticating the sector sweep to protect against beam-stealing attacks in IEEE 802.11ad networks. In: Proceedings of the 2nd ACM Workshop on Millimeter Wave Networks and Sensing Systems. mmNets 2018, pp. 3–8. ACM, New York (2018)
7. Mubarak, A.S.A., Esmaiel, H., Mohamed, E.M.: New CAPWAP architectures for IEEE 802.11ad based Wi-Fi/WiGig WLANs. In: 2018 International Conference on Innovative Trends in Computer Engineering (ITCE), pp. 231–235, February 2018
8. Balakrishnan, S., Wang, P., Bhuyan, A., Sun, Z.: On success probability of eavesdropping attack in 802.11ad mmWave WLAN. In: 2018 IEEE International Conference on Communications (ICC), pp. 1–6, May 2018
9. Balakrishnan, S., Wang, P., Bhuyan, A., Sun, Z.: Modeling and analysis of eavesdropping attack in 802.11ad mmWave wireless networks. IEEE Access **7**, 70355–70370 (2019)

10. Aftab, F., Suntu, S.L., Zhang, Z.: Self-organized security framework for WiGig WLAN against attacks and threats. In: 2018 10th International Conference on Communication Software and Networks (ICCSN), pp. 249–253, July 2018
11. Maltsev, A., Maslennikov, R., Sevastyanov, A., Lomayev, A., Khoryaev, A.: Statistical channel model for 60 GHz WLAN systems in conference room environment. In: Proceedings of the Fourth European Conference on Antennas and Propagation, pp. 1–5. IEEE (2010)

Multi-view DDoS Network Flow Feature Extraction Method via Convolutional Neural Network

Yifu Liu[1], Jieren Cheng[1,2(✉)], Xiangyan Tang[1], Mengyang Li[1], and Luyi Xie[1]

[1] School of Computer and Cyberspace Security, Hainan University,
Haikou 570228, China
cjr22@163.com

[2] State Key Laboratory of Marine Resource Utilization in South China Sea,
Haikou 570228, China

Abstract. Distributed Denial of Service (DDoS) has caused tremendous damage to the network in large data environment. The features extracted by existing feature methods can not accurately represent the characteristics of network flow, and have the characteristics of high false alarm rate and high false alarm rate. This paper presents a multi-view distributed denial of service attack network flow feature extraction method based on convolutional neural network. According to the different characteristics of attack flow and normal flow in TCP/IP protocol, the related attributes of network flow are transformed into binary matrix, and the IP address and port number are reorganized into dual-channel matrix. Then, the multi-view perspective is composed of IP dual-channel matrix, port number dual-channel matrix, packet size grayscale matrix and TCP flag grayscale matrix. According to the characteristics of each attribute, different convolutional neural network models are used to extract the local features of each view, and the extracted local features are fused to form quaternion features to describe the characteristics of network flow. We use MVNFF to train the model, a distributed denial of service (DDoS) classifier based on multiple views is constructed. Experiments show that the features extracted by this method can more accurately represent the characteristics of network traffic and it can improve the robustness of the classifier and reduce the false alarm rate and false alarm rate.

Keywords: DDoS attack · Multi view · Feature extraction · Convolutional neural network

1 Introduction

Distributed Denial of Service (DDoS) flooding attacks are one of the biggest concerns for security professionals. DDoS flooding attacks are typically explicit attempts to disrupt legitimate users' access to services. Attackers usually gain access to a large number of computers by exploiting their vulnerabilities to set up attack armies [19]. This attack attacks maliciously from multiple systems, making it impossible for

© Springer Nature Switzerland AG 2019
J. Vaidya et al. (Eds.): CSS 2019, LNCS 11983, pp. 30–41, 2019.
https://doi.org/10.1007/978-3-030-37352-8_3

computer or network resources to provide services to their established users. It's usually expressed as a service that interrupts or suspends connections to the Internet, thereby reducing the performance of the network. In this way, it can make the network paralyze [16]. Despite the increasing popularity of cloud services, ensuring the security and availability of data, resources and services remains an ongoing research challenge [8]. Distributed denial of service (DDoS) attacks in cloud computing environments are growing due to the essential characteristics of cloud computing [17].

2 Related Work

2.1 DDoS Attack Detection Method Based on Statistics

Statistics-based DDoS attack detection by analyzing the regularity of eigenvalue statistics from large amount of data. Statistical methods are used to describe the changes in network traffic and packet structure caused by DDoS attacks [20]. Quantitative analysis of aggressive behavior is carried out, statistical features are extracted and math model is used to detect aggressive behavior. This kind of method mainly includes entropy, information theory, statistical analysis, etc.

2.2 DDoS Attack Detection Method Based on Machine Learning

Machine learning-based DDoS attack detection by extracting features sample sequences from the network traffic. This kind of method uses machine learning algorithms to learn the training samples, then building ca classifier to classify the test samples.

2.3 DDoS Attack Detection Method Based on Deep Learning

Deep learning allows computational models that are composed of multiple processing layers to learn representations of data with multiple levels of abstraction [8, 13]. These methods have dramatically improved the state-of-the-art in speech recognition, visual object recognition, object detection and many other domains such as drug discovery and genomics [4]. In recent years, with the development of deep learning methods, deep learning methods have been applied to DDoS attack detection [15].

3 Framework of This Paper

Figure 1 is the framework of this paper. A multi-view DDoS network flow feature extraction method via convolutional neural network is proposed. Firstly, we initialize the original data to get the GNM matrix, and then merge the channels to form multiple view matrices. The processed data are brought into the neural network model for feature extraction, and the sub-features of each view are obtained. We use quaternion to fuse the sub-features and get the multi-view network flow features. The features obtained by this method can be applied to the method of artificial intelligence to detect DDoS attacks.

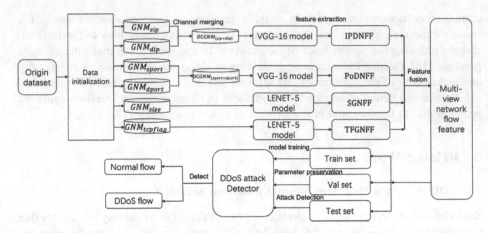

Fig. 1. Framework of the paper

4   Data Initialization

Given a network flow F with n sample IP packets, we define each IP packet as $(t_i, sip_i, dip_i, sp_i, dp_i, size_i, tf_i)$.

4.1   Binary Conversion

In order to preserve each original attribute of the network flow F, we perform number conversion on the above $s_i, d_i, sp_i, dp_i, size_i, tf_i$. For the hexadecimal conversion, the bit-weight conversion method [12] is used. Any hexadecimal data can be in the form of a sum of polynomials spread by bit weight. For example, the number N. n be expressed by the following formula:

$$N = A_{n-1} \times R^{n-1} + A_{n-2} \times R^{n-2} + \ldots + A_1 \times R^1 + A_0 \times R^0 = \sum_{i=0}^{n-1} (A_i \times R^i) \quad (1)$$

4.2   Formal Conversion

Among them, due to the problem that the number of bits in the network flow is inconsistent after being converted into binary, the digits are formally converted as following formula:

$$(data_i)_2 = \begin{cases} Precomplement\ 0, & len\left[(data_i)_2\right] < L_x \\ (data_i)_2, & len\left[(data_i)_2\right] = L_x \end{cases} \quad (2)$$

4.3 Sampling by Time

Converted by the above number system to obtain a binary form network flow
$F' = \ <(t_i, s_i, d_i, sp_i, dp_i, size_i, tf_i)> , i = 1, 2, \ldots, n$

Definition 1. Based on the binary representation, the network flow data is sampled by
unit time Δt, Packet sampling time $T \in (0, N), \Delta t = 0.01$ s, 0.05 s, 0.1 s, we extract
the packet set (PS):

$$PS = \Sigma \{t_i, s_i, d_i, sp_i, dp_i, size_i, tf_i\}_{\Delta t} \qquad (3)$$

In the definition of PS, in order to analyze the state characteristics of the PS more
efficiently, statistics on the network flow $F' = (t_i, s_i, d_i, sp_i, dp_i, size_i, tf_i)$ per unit time
are performed, we analyze the law of network traffic generation.

Definition 2. According to the above sampling method, the grayscale network flow
matrix (GNM$_i$) is obtained by extracting the PS set that has been sampled. GNM$_{sip}$ is
the grayscale network flow matrix of source IP address. GNM$_{dip}$ is the grayscale
network flow matrix of destination IP address. GNM$_{sport}$ is the grayscale network flow
matrix of source port number. GNM$_{dport}$ is the grayscale network flow matrix of
destination port number. GNM$_{size}$ is the grayscale network flow matrix of network
packet size. GNM$_{tcpflag}$ is the grayscale network flow matrix of TCP flag.

Grayscale Network Flow Matrix in Normal Flow

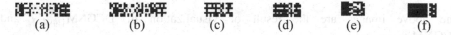

(a)   (b)   (c)   (d)   (e)   (f)

Fig. 2. Grayscale network flow matrix in normal flow

As shown in Fig. 1, under normal flow conditions, among them, (a) is GNM$_{sip}$, (b) is
GNM$_{dip}$, (c) is GNM$_{sport}$, (d) is GNM$_{dport}$, (e) is GNM$_{size}$, (f) is GNM$_{tcpflag}$.

Grayscale Network Flow Matrix in DDoS Attack Flow

(a)   (b)   (c)   (d)   (e)   (f)

Fig. 3. Grayscale network flow matrix in normal flow

As shown in Fig. 2, under DDoS flow conditions, among them, (a) is GNM$_{sip}$, (b) 为
GNM$_{dip}$, (c) is GNM$_{sport}$, (d) is GNM$_{dport}$, (e) is GNM$_{size}$, (f) is GNM$_{tcpflag}$ (Fig. 3).

4.4   Channel Merging

In order to better reflect the corresponding relationship between source IP address, destination IP address and source port number, destination port number. We combine GNM_{sip} and GNM_{dip}, GNM_{sport} and GNM_{dport} into $DCGNM_{\{sip,dip\}}$, $DCGNM_{\{sport,dport\}}$ in the form of two channels. The aim is to highlight the correspondence between the source and the destination through a dual-channel approach (Fig. 4).

Definition 4. Dual-channel Grayscale network flow matrix (DCGNM).

Fig. 4. Visualization of $DGNM_{\{sip,dip\}}$ and $DGNM_{\{sport,dport\}}$.

The above images are the result of visualization of $DCGNM_{\{sip,dip\}}$ and $DCGNM_{\{sport,dport\}}$.

5   Network Flow Feature Extraction via Multi-view

5.1   Input Data Initialization

Because of the complexity of $DCGNM_{\{sip,dip\}}$ and $DCGNM_{\{sport,dport\}}$, we need a better neural network model to extract its features, so we use VGG16 pre-training model to extract these two features. For GNM_{size} and $GNM_{tcpflag}$ are both single channel grayscale matrices, in order to save computing resources, we use LeNet-5 [5] model with fewer parameters to extract features.

We initialize the format of the input data, we reshape our DCGNM data to 128 * 128 * 3 pixels, because the VGG16 [11] pre-training model is three-channel matrix for the input tensor. We combine our DCGNM matrix with a set of empty matrices as one of them. We merge the original two-channel DCGNM matrix into a three-channel matrix to facilitate data input. Since the LeNet-5 model does not require the number of channels for the input matrix, we use the reshape of the GNM matrix as the matrix of 128 * 128 * 1.

The VGG16 pre-training model we use is the VGG16 pre-training model provided by Keras library. We fix the parameters of the convolution layer of the vgg16 model. We use our data to train the full connection layer of the model and fine-tune the parameters of the full connection layer.

We divide the data set into training set, validating set and test set. Training set is used for model fitting, validating set is used to adjust the hyper parameters of the model and preliminarily evaluate the capability of the model. Test set is used to evaluate the generalization ability of the model. We randomly scrambled the sample data. When the sampling time is 0.01 s. The number of training samples is 120540, the number of validation samples is 30457, and the number of detection samples is 32244.

5.2 Feature Extraction

Definition 5. Define the features extracted from $DCGNM_{\{sip,dip\}}$ as the IP dual-channel network flow feature ($IPDNFF_i$) [6]. Define the features extracted from $DCGNM_{\{sport,dport\}}$ as the Port dual-channel network flow feature ($PoDNFF_i$), define the features extracted from GNM_{size} as the size grayscale network flow feature ($SGNFF_i$), define the features extracted from $GNM_{tcpflag}$ as the TCPflag grayscale network flow feature ($TFGNFF_i$).

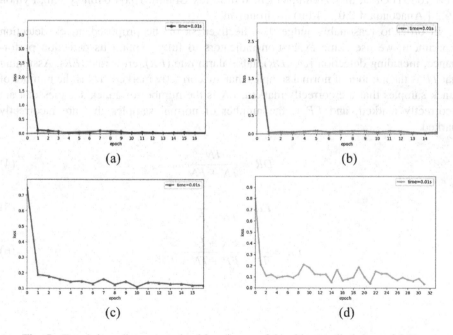

Fig. 5. Epoch-loss diagrams trained by view models with sampling time of 0.01 s

When the sampling time is 0.01 s, we can see that DCGNM$_{\{sip,dip\}}$ is retrained using VGG16 pre-training model. Convergence is achieved at the 16-th epoch. We store and use the model at the model to extract features, we get 128 -dimensional IPDNFF$_i$ feature, we can see when the epoch is 14, the loss function converges,we save the parameters of the model,and we use the model to extract PoDNFF$_i$ feature (Fig. 5).

We train the LeNet-5 model with GNM$_{size}$ and GNM$_{tcpflag}$. We extract the features of the 15-th epoch and 31-th epoch models respectively, and get the SGNFF$_i$ and TFGNFF$_i$ features.

Definition 6. We combine the features extracted by the neural network with the quadruple format. Define the four tuples [IPDNFF$_i$, PoDNFF$_i$, SGNFF$_i$, TFGNFF$_i$] as Multi-view network flow features (MVNFF$_i$)$_{\Delta t}$.

Through the above methods, we extract (MVNFF$_i$)$_{\Delta t=0.01s}$, (MVNFF$_i$)$_{\Delta t=0.05s}$, (MVNFF$_i$)$_{\Delta t=0.1s}$.

6 Experiment

6.1 Dataset and Evaluation Criteria

The experimental hardware devices in this article are 128G memory, i5 processor, and GTX 1080Ti GPU, they are implemented in Linux Ubuntu 16.04 64bit system, Python 3.6.2 | Anaconda 4.2.0 (64-bit) environment.

In order to reasonably judge the effectiveness of the proposed attack detection experiment, we use some evaluation indicators to fully explain its detection performance, including detection rate (*DR*), false alarm rate (*FR*), error rate (*ER*). Assuming that *TP* is the number of normal samples that are correctly marked, TN is the number of attack samples that are correctly marked, *FN* is the number of attack samples that are incorrectly marked, and *FP* is the number of normal samples that are incorrectly marked.

$$DR = \frac{TN}{TN + FN} \tag{4}$$

$$FR = \frac{FP}{TN + FP} \tag{5}$$

$$ER = \frac{FN + FP}{TP + FP + TN + FN} \tag{6}$$

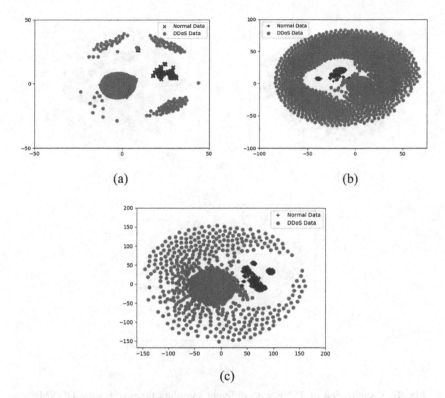

(a)

(b)

(c)

Fig. 6. Visualization of TSNE with different sampling times of feature MVNFF

6.2 Comparison of Experimental Results

Comparison of Network Flow Feature via Multi-view and Discrete Network Flow Feature

We use TSNE method [8] to reduce dimensionality based on multi-view network flow characteristics and discrete GMF features. We set the parameter of $n\_components = 2$, $learning\,rate = 300$ that is to reduce the characteristics of multi-view network flow (4 * 128) and discrete GMF positive matrix (1 * 128) to 2 - dimensional data (Figs. 6 and 7).

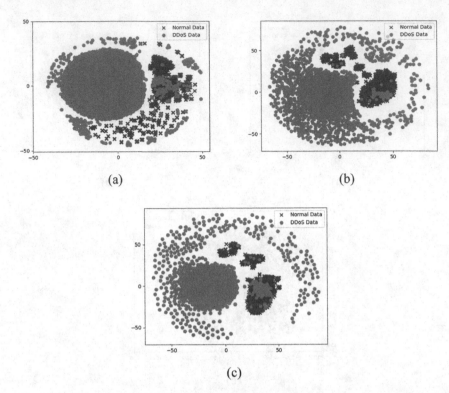

(a)   (b)

(c)

Fig. 7. Visualization of TSNE with different sampling times of feature DGNMF

Table 1. Comparison of MVNFF feature and DGNMF feature Evaluation Index in Sample Time Variation

Feature		MVNFF			DGNMF		
Sample time(s)		0.01	0.05	0.1	0.01	0.05	0.1
SVM	DR (%)	96.56	95.39	95.68	93.53	93.11	94.78
	FR (%)	3.47	3.63	3.90	4.73	7.36	6.90
	ER (%)	4.67	4.20	3.22	5.47	6.49	5.08
KNN	DR (%)	95.68	93.69	94.59	94.39	94.38	93.83
	FR (%)	4.10	5.10	5.53	6.21	4.86	7.88
	ER (%)	4.22	6.22	5.47	5.77	5.31	6.04
Bayes	DR (%)	95.63	94.18	95.92	91.77	95.73	93.73
	FR (%)	4.49	3.86	4.44	8.45	5.19	5.19
	ER (%)	4.40	4.07	4.24	8.29	4.69	6.69
RF	DR (%)	95.26	94.09	92.21	95.09	94.40	94.40
	FR (%)	5.81	4.31	7.46	3.95	5.82	5.66
	ER (%)	4.70	5.53	4.20	3.92	5.70	5.62

From the results of Table 1, we can conclude that the classification results of network traffic characteristics based on multi-view and discrete GMF network characteristics without multi-view processing proposed by us show that the network flow characteristics processed by multi-view can be better reflected by the two-channel combination of source IP, destination IP, source port and destination port. The correspondence between requester and server. We use VGG16 pre-training model to extract features from $DGNMF_{\{sip,dip\}}$ and $DGNMF_{\{sport,dport\}}$ matrices.

Comparison of Network Flow Feature via Multiple Views and FFV feature Based on Statistics

We extract features according to the methods described in [2]. According to the feature extraction rules in this paper, we use FFV feature values of one-dimensional features of quintuple features for experimental comparison.

Table 2. Comparison results of different features evaluation Indicators in the change of sample time

Feature		MVNFF			FFV [2]		
Sample time(s)		0.01	0.05	0.1	0.01	0.05	0.1
SVM	DR (%)	96.56	95.39	95.68	89.04	87.63	86.47
	FR (%)	3.47	3.63	3.90	13.33	14.28	15.26
	ER (%)	4.67	4.20	3.22	9.60	11.36	11.51
KNN	DR (%)	95.68	93.69	94.59	84.76	82.42	73.09
	FR (%)	4.10	5.10	5.53	9.63	9.13	25.00
	ER (%)	4.22	6.22	5.47	6.53	9.19	26.89
Bayes	DR (%)	95.63	94.18	95.92	84.76	82.42	73.09
	FR (%)	4.49	3.86	4.44	9.63	9.13	25.00
	ER (%)	4.40	4.07	4.24	6.53	9.19	26.89
RF	DR (%)	95.26	94.09	92.21	87.65	88.79	88.93
	FR (%)	5.81	4.31	7.46	10.53	7.54	6.91
	ER (%)	4.70	5.53	4.20	10.34	7.28	8.00

From the results of Table 2, we use support vector machine (SVM), nearest neighbor algorithm (KNN), Nave Bayes and random forest models to model and classify the network flow characteristics and FFV statistical features characteristics of multi-view.

7 Conclusion

Aiming at the problem of false alarm rate and false alarm rate of DDoS attack detection method in large data environment, a method of feature extraction for multi-view network DDoS network flow based on convolutional neural network is proposed. On the basis of GMF, multi-view method is used to extract the local features of each GNM matrix using different network models and fuse the features to improve the segmentation accuracy. This method extracts global and local features of network flow to resist over-fitting, improve computational efficiency and improve classification accuracy by using context relations of features. The classifier is trained with conventional samples and DDoS attack samples, and the MVNFF is modeled by machine learning method. The optimal classifier parameters are obtained. A distributed denial of service (DDoS) classifier based on multi-view network flow features is constructed. Experiments show that this method has higher accuracy than similar detection methods, reduces false alarm rate and false alarm rate, and can effectively detect DDoS attacks in large data.

Acknowledgement. This work was supported by the Hainan Provincial Natural Science Foundation of China [2018CXTD333, 617048]; National Natural Science Foundation of China [61762033, 61702539]; Hainan University Doctor Start Fund Project [kyqd1328]; Hainan University Youth Fund Project [qnjj1444].

References

1. Cheng, J., Yin, J., Liu, Y., Cai, Z., Li, M.: DDoS attack detection algorithm using IP address features. In: Deng, X., Hopcroft, J.E., Xue, J. (eds.) FAW 2009. LNCS, vol. 5598, pp. 207–215. Springer, Heidelberg (2009). https://doi.org/10.1007/978-3-642-02270-8_22
2. Cheng, J., Zhang, C., Tang, X., Sheng, V.S., Dong, Z., Li, J.: Adaptive DDoS attack detection method based on multiple-kernel learning. Secur. Commun. Netw. **2018**, 19 (2018)
3. Cheng, J., Xu, R., Tang, X., Sheng, V.S., Cai, C.: An abnormal network flow feature sequence prediction approach for DDoS attacks detection in big data environment. Comput. Mater. Continua **55**(1), 095 (2018)
4. LeCun, Y., Bengio, Y., Hinton, G.: Deep learning. Nature **521**(7553), 436 (2015)
5. LeCun, Y., Bottou, L., Bengio, Y., Haffner, P., et al.: Gradient-based learning applied to document recognition. Proc. IEEE **86**(11), 2278–2324 (1998)
6. Li, J., Liu, Z., Chen, X., Xhafa, F., Tan, X., Wong, D.: L-EncDB: a lightweight framework for privacy-preserving data queries in cloud computing. Knowl.-Based Syst. **79**, 18–23 (2015)
7. Li, J., Wang, Q., Wang, C., Cao, N., Ren, K., Lou, W.: Enabling efficient fuzzy keyword search over encrypted data in cloud computing. IACR Cryptology ePrint Archive **2009**, 593 (2009)
8. Ma, X., Li, J., Zhang, F.: Outsourcing computation of modular exponentiations in cloud computing. Cluster Comput. **16**(4), 787–796 (2013)
9. Maaten, L.V.D., Hinton, G.: Visualizing data using t-SNE. J. Mach. Learn. Res. **9**, 2579–2605 (2008)
10. Mirkovic, J., Reiher, P.: A taxonomy of DDoS attack and DDoS defense mechanisms. ACM SIGCOMM Comput. Commun. Rev. **34**(2), 39–53 (2004)
11. Simonyan, K., Zisserman, A.: Very deep convolutional networks for large-scale image recognition. arXiv preprint arXiv:1409.1556 (2014)
12. Stevanovic, D., Vlajic, N., An, A.: Detection of malicious and non-malicious website visitors using unsupervised neural network learning. Appl. Soft Comput. **13**(1), 698–708 (2013)
13. Tian, H., Li, J.: A short non-delegatable strong designated verifier signature. Front. Comput. Sci. **8**(3), 490–502 (2014)

14. Toklu, S., Simsek, M.: Two-layer approach for mixed high-rate and low-rate distributed denial of service (DDoS) attack detection and filtering. Arab. J. Sci. Eng. **43**(12), 7923–7931 (2018)
15. Wang, B., Zheng, Y., Lou, W., Hou, Y.T.: DDoS attack protection in the era of cloud computing and software-defined networking. Comput. Netw. **81**, 308–319 (2015)
16. Wei, Y., et al.: Cross-modal retrieval with cnn visual features: a new baseline. IEEE Trans. Cybern. **47**(2), 449–460 (2016)
17. Xu, J., Wei, L., Zhang, Y., Wang, A., Zhou, F., Gao, C.: Dynamic fully homomorphic encryption-based merkle tree for lightweight streaming authenticated data structures. J. Netw. Comput. Appl. **107**, 113–124 (2018)
18. Xu, R., Cheng, J., Wang, F., Tang, X., Xu, J.: A DRDoS detection and defense method based on deep forest in the big data environment. Symmetry **11**(1), 78 (2019)
19. Yadav, V.K., Trivedi, M.C., Mehtre, B.M.: DDA: an approach to handle DDoS (Ping Flood) attack. In: Satapathy, S.C., Joshi, A., Modi, N., Pathak, N. (eds.) Proceedings of International Conference on ICT for Sustainable Development. AISC, vol. 408, pp. 11–23. Springer, Singapore (2016). https://doi.org/10.1007/978-981-10-0129-1_2

DDoS Attack Detection Method Based on V-Support Vector Machine

Xiangyan Tang[1], Rui Cao[1(⊠)], Jieren Cheng[1,2], Dong Fan[1],
and Wenxuan Tu[1]

[1] School of Computer Science and Cyberspace Security,
Hainan University, Haikou 570228, China
410208626@qq.com
[2] State Key Laboratory of Marine Resource Utilization in South China Sea,
Hainan University, Haikou 570228, China

Abstract. The characteristics of distributed denial of service (DDoS) attack diversity, distribution and burstiness in the new network environment make it difficult to detect the current detection methods. This paper proposes a DDoS attack detection method based on V-Support Vector Machine (SVM). This method defines a nine-tuple network service association feature to extract the feature of the network flow, then normalizes the feature data and reduces the dimension by principal component analysis. Finally, select the appropriate kernel function and introduce the parameter V control support vector and the number of error vectors, establish a V-SVM-based DDoS attack classification model to detect attacks. The experimental results show that compared with similar methods, this method not only improves the accuracy, reduces the false negative rate, but also ensures the stability and timeliness of the classification model.

Keywords: DDoS attack detection · Support Vector Machine · Network flow feature extraction · Parameter optimization

1 Introduction

With the development of cloud technology, Distributed denial of service (DDoS) attacks gather a large number of botnets and send a large number of continuous attack requests to the target system to increase the attack power by taking advantage of cloud computing bandwidth network access and rapid rebound performance [1–3], and make the victims face huge amounts of economic losses.

The Arbor Networks report shows that [4] in recent years, as many as 48% of DDoS attacks in all cyber threats, it is clear that DDoS attacks have become the main cybercrime in today's society. Although we minimize the number of DDoS attacks, they have rapidly expanded the frequency and scale of target networks and computers, and are evolving to exploit flash population agents, low-rate attacks, and exploit vulnerabilities in DNS servers to scale up attacks. DDoS attacks continue to threaten today's network environments, and these threats have grown significantly in terms of the size and impact of Internet service providers and governments. DDoS attack features such as diversity, distribution, suddenness and concealment, as well as network

© Springer Nature Switzerland AG 2019
J. Vaidya et al. (Eds.): CSS 2019, LNCS 11983, pp. 42–56, 2019.
https://doi.org/10.1007/978-3-030-37352-8_4

flow scale, mass and complexity in the new network environment make current DDoS attack detection methods have such problems as high false alarm rate, high false alarm rate and poor timeliness. Accurate and efficient detection of DDoS attacks, reducing economic losses and negative social impacts is imminent. Therefore, this paper proposes a DDoS attack detection method based on V-SVM. Compared with similar methods, this method not only improves the accuracy, reduces the false negative rate, but also ensures the stability and timeliness of the classification model.

2   Related Work

In recent years, researchers have proposed a large number of DDoS attack detection methods. The existing DDoS attack detection methods are classified into two types: statistics-based attack detection and machine learning-based attack detection.

2.1   Attack Detection Method Based on Statistics

The statistically based detection methods mainly include entropy method, principal component analysis method, correlation and covariance. Christiane et al. [5] proposed an attributional selection method based on Renyi and Tsallis entropy, and evaluated the advantages and disadvantages of Renyi and Tsallis entropy by comparing with shannon entropy, so as to obtain the optimal attribute subset to distinguish normal flow or attack flow. Qi et al. [6] proposed a dynamic model based on entropy to detect DDoS attacks. This model used the conversational relationship of network flow from different perspectives to compare the change rates of dynamic and static entropy values in anomaly detection, and found that the dynamic entropy method is more sensitive and more suitable for anomaly detection. Mohiuddin et al. [7] developed the problem of detecting DDoS attacks as a collective anomaly, and proposed a framework for collective anomaly detection. The statistical analysis of the characteristics of the attack flow and the use of classification clustering techniques to achieve the detection purpose; Cheng et al. [8] ignore the redundancy filtered from the dynamic feature set according to the sparse distribution pattern of network anomalies and its low-dimensional feature attributes, and design a new detection scheme by using the sparsity of network anomaly distribution; Park et al. [9] proposed a method for detecting traffic flood attacks by using probabilistic model to analyze abnormal data detection.

2.2   Attack Detection Method Based on Machine Learning

Machine learning-based detection methods include Support Vector Machine (SVM), Naive Bayes algorithm (NB, Naive Bayes), and decision trees. Karnwal et al. [10] converted the one-dimensional time series into multi-dimensional AR model parameter timings, and used the support vector machine to learn and classify the data stream. Tama et al. [11] used the method of anomaly detection to model the network data stream according to the header attribute, and used the naive Bayesian algorithm to score each arriving data stream to evaluate the rationality of the message. Gao et al. [12] focuses on constructing a privacy-preserving NB classifier that is resistant to an easy-to-perform, but difficult-to-detect attack, which we call the substitution-then-comparison (STC) attack. Latif et al. [13] proposed an enhanced decision tree algorithm for the impact of noise on the accuracy of sensor generation data, which can effectively detect the occurrence of DDoS attacks in Wireless Body Area Network (WBAN). Ma et al. [14] present the generic secure outsourcing schemes enabling users to securely outsource the computations of exponentiations to the untrusted cloud servers. Li et al. [15] introduce Significant Permission IDentification (SigPID), a malware detection system based on permission usage analysis to cope with the rapid increase in the number of Android malware. Because the cloud servers are usually untrusted, Li et al. [16] propose a framework for privacy-preserving outsourced classification in cloud computing (POCC). Li et al. [17] propose a new secure provenance scheme based on group signature and attribute-based signature techniques.

3   DDoS Attack Characteristics

3.1   Analysis of DDoS Attack Characteristics

In the actual network environment, there are external factors such as noise, delay and congestion. To effectively detect a DDoS attack, selecting a group of features that can comprehensively reflect the attack is the core factor to ensure the classifier to speed up learning, reduce computational complexity, improve accuracy and stability [18, 19]. The DDoS attack has a strong correlation with time. Lee et al. [20] use 2 s as a time interval to count the current number of target host connections compared with the number of previous connections or the number of incorrect connections before and after the service as a percentage of the total number of connections. These metrics increase dramatically when the victim detects that the host or server has received a large number of connection requests within a certain period of time. Experiments and related research [21–23] have shown that statistics on network traffic based on fixed time intervals can effectively reflect the characteristics of DDoS attacks. Therefore, a nine-node Network service association feature (NSAF) is defined to describe the changing state of the network flow.

$$NSAF = (T, S, L, N, J, R, P, Y, C) \tag{1}$$

Where the number of hosts with the same connection and the same target is represented by T; The number of the same service with the same connection is denoted by S; L = {The number of SYN error connections during sampling time/T}; N = {The number of SYN error connections during sampling time/S}; J = {The number of REJ error connections during sampling time/T}; R = {The number of REJ error connections during sampling time/S}; P = {The number of connections with the same service as the current connection/T}; Y = {Number of connections with different services from the current connection/T}; C = {The number of connections with different target hosts from the current connection/S}.

3.2 Data Normalization

The classification accuracy of the model will be affected due to the possible interference of default values, singularities or noises in the samples. Therefore, it is necessary to normalize the data to solve the influence of the dimension between the data indicators to speed up the gradient and find the optimal solution speed. This paper analyzes the following two common data normalization methods: Z-score Standardization and Min-Max Scaling.

Z-Score standardization is a numerical unification of the mean and standard deviation of the original data. The processed data basically conforms to the standard normal distribution, i.e. "Z-distribution". The sample average is 0, the variance is 1, and the conversion function is:

$$Z = \frac{x - \mu}{\delta} \tag{2}$$

Where μ is mean of all sample data and δ is the standard deviation of all sample data.

Min-Max normalization, also known as dispersion normalization, is a linear transformation of the original data, mapping the resulting values between [0, 1] or [−1, 1]. The conversion function is as follows:

$$x^* = \frac{x - min}{max - min} \tag{3}$$

Where max and min are the maximum and minimum values of the training set or test set respectively. Since z-score method has the defect of changing the distribution of original data, sample points are distributed within the interval [0, 1] after the normalization of min-max, and all indexes are in the same order of magnitude, without changing the distribution between the data. For attributes with very small variances, the method can also enhance its stability and maintain an entry of 0 in the sparse matrix. The index values of the data sets used in this experiment are distributed in a fixed interval, and min and max are stable and do not involve cluster analysis. Therefore, this paper adopts the min-max method to normalize data, which simplifies the complexity of comparability among various indicators and is suitable for comprehensive evaluation of data.

3.3 Feature Extraction Based on Principal Component Analysis

Principal Component Analysis (PCA) is widely used in the field of network security. It recombines a group of previously correlated indexes into a new set of unrelated comprehensive indexes. The fewer the number of Principal components, the better the dimensionality reduction effect [24].

This paper proposes a feature extraction algorithm based on PCA, as shown in Table 1. Through the PCA dimension reduction, the nine characteristic indicators in the training set are converted into three comprehensive indicators. The sum of the cumulative variances of the three eigenvalues accounts for about 97% of the total variance, and the residual contribution rate is very low. Each of the principal components can reflect most of the information of the original features, and the information contained therein is not repeated.

PCA algorithm simplifies the process of data analysis, achieves the purpose of reconstructing the original high-dimensional vector, and obtains more scientific and effective data.

Table 1. PCA-based feature extraction algorithm

Algorithm 1: PCA-based feature extraction algorithm
Input: original network flow data;
Output: new data samples;
1: Data normalization;
2: Establish a standardized variable covariance matrix;
3: Calculate the NSAF feature value and its corresponding feature vector;
4: Calculate the variance contribution rate p;
5: while(The sum of the variance contribution rates of all indicator values is greater than 85%)do;
6: Calculate the number of principal components m;
7: Calculate the result matrix T;
8: determining m vectors of corresponding principal components;
9: end while.

4 Detection Method of DDoS Attack Based on V-SVM

The support vector machine method is based on the VC dimension theory of statistical learning and the principle of structural risk minimization. Based on the information of finite samples, it seeks the best compromise between the complexity and learning ability of the model to obtain the optimal promotion ability. Compared with other machine learning algorithms such as neural network, decision tree and Adaboost, SVM classifier has simpler structure design, moderate computational complexity and better generalization performance. It has many outstanding advantages in solving small sample, nonlinear and high dimensional pattern recognition.

Although the data preprocessing technology successfully solves the problems of irregular data distribution, singular values or noise points, the unstructured attributes of the network data itself often affect the accuracy of the classification model. Shortly after the advent of the SVM, Vapnik et al. [25] proposed a nonlinear soft-spaced support vector machine, C-SVM, which introduced the slack variable ζ and the penalty parameter C to obtain a more accurate classification hyperplane, thus eliminating the interference of external factors.

Since C is a weight value, it only depends on the selection of artificial experience and has no practical theoretical basis. Based on C-SVM, Schölkopf et al. [26] proposed a V-SVM to cancel parameter C, adding parameters V and variables p that can control the number of support vectors and error vectors.

In order to fully reflect the value of parameter V, improve the detection efficiency of DDoS attacks and reduce the failure rate, this paper proposes a detection method of DDoS attacks based on V-SVM.

4.1 Detection Model of DDoS Attack Based on V-SVM

After the network flow is collected, the NSAF feature vector is calculated at a time interval of 2 s to indicate the change of the state before and after the network flow.

$T = \{(x_1, y_1), \ldots, (x_l, y_l)\} \in (X \times Y)^l$, is as the training set, among them $x_n \in X = R^D$, indicates that the nth sample is a normal flow or an attack flow; $y_n \in Y = \{1, -1\}, n = 1, \ldots, l$, indicates the true label of the nth sample, and l indicates the size of the training set. The initial classification model that substitutes the training set T into the V-SVM can be expressed as:

$$\min_{w,b,\xi,\rho} \left(\frac{1}{2}\|\omega\|^2 - v\rho + \frac{1}{l}\sum_{n=1}^{l} \xi_n \right)$$

$$s.t. \quad y_n((w \cdot x_n) + b) \geq \rho - \xi_n, \xi_n \geq 0 \tag{4}$$

$$n = 1, 2, \ldots, l \quad \rho \geq 0$$

Where $\frac{1}{2}\|\omega\|^2$ is the idealized maximum classification interval, $\frac{1}{l}$ is the upper limit of the outliers, ξ_n is the classification interval error, and b is the decision function constant term.

Under the premise of satisfying the Karush-Kuhn-Tucker condition, the initial problem is equivalent to its dual problem. The dual model of Eq. (4) is:

$$\min_{\alpha} \frac{1}{2}\sum_{n=1}^{l}\sum_{m=1}^{l} y_n y_m \lambda_n \lambda_m K(x_n, x_m)$$

$$s.t. \quad \sum_{n=1}^{l} y_n \lambda_n = 0, 0 \leq \lambda_0 \leq \frac{1}{l} \tag{5}$$

$$n = 1, 2, \ldots, l \quad \sum_{n=1}^{l} \lambda_0 \geq v$$

Among them, λ_n is a lagrange multiplier. In order to ensure the validity of the classification model, the appropriate parameter V and kernel function $K(x_n, x_m)$ should be selected to obtain the optimal lagrange multiplier λ^*:

$$\lambda^* = (\lambda_1^*, \ldots, \lambda_l^*)^T \tag{6}$$

Further solve:

$$w^* = \sum_{n=1}^{l} \lambda_n^* y_n x_n$$

$$b^* = -\frac{1}{2}\sum_{n=1}^{l} \lambda_n^* y_n (K(x_n, x_m) + K(x_n, x_k)) \tag{7}$$

Bring (7) into (4) to get the optimal hyperplane in the high dimensional feature space:

$$f(z) = \text{sgn}\left(\sum_{n=1}^{l} \lambda_n^* y_n K(x_n, x_m) + b^*\right) \tag{8}$$

Among them, A is the classification result of the network flow.

4.2   Determination of the Kernel Function of the Classification Model

Most of the classification problems existing in real life are nonlinear. The support vector machine method is to choose a kernel function for nonlinear expansion. According to the actual problem and the research object, choosing the appropriate kernel function often plays a decisive role in the classification effect of the model. Under the conditions of Linear, Polynomial, Radial Basis Function and Sigmoid four different types of kernel functions, the first two dimensions of the partial training set are selected for visualization. The red and green marks represent normal sample points and attack sample points respectively. Black marks indicate support vectors. As shown in Fig. 1, the effect of the kernel function on the decision hyperplane position is visually reflected.

The experimental results based on different types of kernel functions are shown in Sect. 4, and the results are verified by accuracy, detection rate, false negative rate, and run time. As shown in the formula (9), it is a calculation method of the DDoS attack detection false negative rate.

$$MR = \frac{N_{FP}}{N_{TN} + N_{FP}} \tag{9}$$

Among them, NFP is the number of negative samples that are misjudged as positive by the classification model, NTN is the number of negative samples that are judged to be negative by the classification model, and MR is the false negative rate.

4.3   Determination of V-Values of Classification Model Parameters

Although the parameter V controls the number of support vectors and error vectors very well, the specific detection effects may not be achieved due to the differences in the specific objects of the training and the different influences of the features on the classification results. At present, there is no uniform set of best methods for the selection of V values at home and abroad. This paper analyzes the influence of artificial empirical value V on DDoS attack detection based on specific data, so as to select an appropriate V value. The experimental results are shown in Sect. 4.

4.4   Detection Process of Attack Detection Method

As shown in Fig. 2, the data set is first analyzed, the appropriate features are selected, and the training set is normalized and PCA dimensionality reduction processing; The second step is to construct various SVM classification models, and study the process of classification model parameters and kernel function parameters optimization; The third

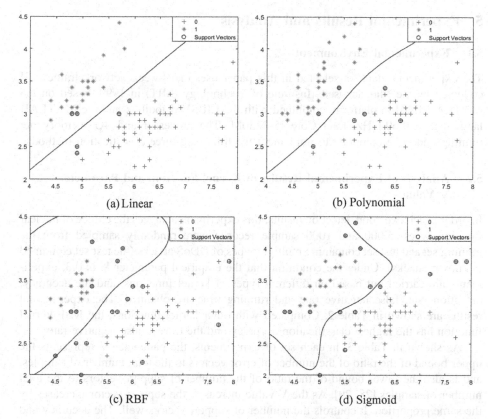

Fig. 1. Schematic diagram of V-SVM classification under different types of kernel functions (Color figure online)

step initializes the training model, introduces the training set to start the training of the model, and obtains the coefficients w and b of the decision function through the Sequential Mini Optimization; Finally, the constructed classification model is tested on a test set containing unknown tags, and the experimental results are analyzed.

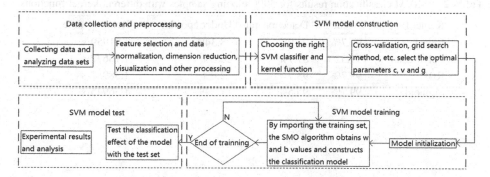

Fig. 2. DDoS attack detection process

5   Experimental Results and Analysis

5.1   Experimental Environment

The experimental data set selected in this paper uses the 9-week network traffic [27] collected by the Massachusetts Institute of Technology (MIT) in 1999, based on the MATLAB R2014a platform, combined with the LIBSVM toolbox and the MATLAB language, at 2.60 GHz, Intel Core i5-3230M. The processor and 4G memory are running under the computer to implement the following three classification methods.

5.2   Analysis of Experimental Results of Kernel Function and Parameter V Value

In order to achieve good detection results, this experiment analyzes the choice of nuclear function types. 5,000 and 1000 sample records were randomly sampled from the training set and test set containing multiple types of DDoS attacks (the test set contained unknown attacks). Under the condition that the empirical parameter V is 0.3, experiments are carried out based on different types of kernel functions, and the accuracy, detection rate, false negative rate and running time are obtained. The experimental results are shown in Table 2. Compared with other kernel functions, the RBF kernel function has the highest classification accuracy and the lowest false negative rate.

As shown in Table 3, in each set of experiments, the parameter V represents the upper bound of the ratio of the number of error vectors to the total number of samples, and is also the lower bound of the ratio of the number of support vectors to the total number of samples [28, 29]. As the V value increases, the support vector increases by the same proportion. It controls the number of support vectors well. The accuracy and detection rate remain stable, the false negative rate decreases and tends to be stable, but the running time will increase. When the V value is 0.2, the overall performance of the classifier is optimal. The experiment also shows that the selection of the V value is too small or too large will seriously affect the classification effect of the model, resulting in low classification accuracy and even classification error reporting. By analyzing the experimental results, the V value is 0.2 to study the performance of the D-S attack detection model based on V-SVM.

Table 2. V-SVM classification results for 5000 training samples with different kernel functions

Kernel function	Accuracy	Detection rate	Underreporting rate	Running time
Linear	99.7%	94.9%	8.34%	1.21959 s
Polynomial	99.52%	87.7%	20.5%	1.16672 s
RBF	99.7%	98.7%	2.0%	1.38957 s
Sigmoid	99.7%	95.5%	7.34%	1.36945 s

Table 3. V-SVM classification results for 1000 test samples with different V values

Parameter nu	Kernel function	TN (SV)	Accuracy	Detection rate	Underreporting rate	Running time
V = 0.01	RBF	102	99.81%	90.8%	16.3%	0.28190 s
V = 0.1	RBF	1003	99.81%	99.05%	2.5%	1.22487 s
V = 0.2	RBF	2002	99.81%	99.05%	1.5%	2.92453 s
V = 0.3	RBF	3003	99.81%	99.05%	1.5%	4.43277 s
V = 0.4	RBF	4003	99. 81%	99.05%	1.5%	6.59913 s
V = 0.5	RBF	5001	99. 81%	99.05%	1.5%	7.43371 s

5.3 Comparison and Analysis of Three Models

In this experiment, 5 training samples were randomly selected from the training concentration containing normal flow and attack flow in the first 7 weeks, with the sizes of 1000, 2500, 5000, 10000 and 20000 records successively. Samples with sizes of 200, 500, 1000, 2000 and 4000 were randomly selected from the mixed traffic containing normal, known and unknown attacks in the following 2 weeks as the test set.

Through five sets of experiments with different sample sizes, the classification results of C-SVM parameters before and after optimization (C, g) were compared. In the optimization process, as the sample size increases, the grid search method and cross validation will have an impact on the timeliness of the C-SVM algorithm. The detection time of the grid search based C-SVM method is much longer than that of the traditional C-SVM algorithm. However, compared with the empirical parameters, the classification accuracy of the latter is significantly improved, and the false negative rate after parameter optimization is reduced, which proves the effectiveness of the C-SVM method based on grid search. As shown in Tables 4 and 5.

Although the C-SVM classification method based on grid search is improved compared with the traditional C-SVM classification method, the number of error vectors and the number of support vectors are too large or too small, which will result in poor classification of support vector machines and poor anti-interference performance of SVM. In view of the shortcomings of the above two methods, this paper proposes a DDoS attack detection method based on V-SVM. The experimental results are shown in Table 6.

As shown in Fig. 3, it is the visualization result of the increase of the detection rate with the sample capacity in Tables 4, 5 and 6. The traditional C-SVM detection method is represented by the blue dotted line. It has the lowest classification accuracy and the highest false negative rate. As the data increases, the accuracy of the algorithm tends to be stable. The green dotted line indicates the C-SVM detection method based on grid search. The classification effect is the worst at the beginning. With the increase of traffic, the classification accuracy is improved by 2% to 10%. It solves the problem of difficult parameter selection of traditional C-SVM well, but occupies a large amount of CPU memory and increases the system overhead.

In DDoS attack detection [30], timeliness is also one of the important indicators to measure the effectiveness of attack detection algorithms. As shown in Fig. 3, the solid red line indicates the V-SVM-based DDoS attack detection method, which successfully avoids the problem of too long running time, saves a lot of computing resources and system overhead, and makes the training time acceptable. Within the scheme, the stability of the algorithm is good, which not only improves the classification accuracy and reduces the false negative rate, but also ensures the stability and timeliness of DDoS attack detection.

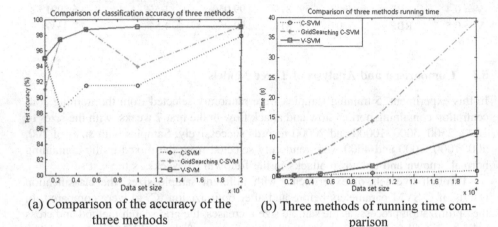

(a) Comparison of the accuracy of the three methods

(b) Three methods of running time comparison

Fig. 3. Comparison of three methods for classification test results (Color figure online)

Finally, this paper summarizes the performance of the three algorithms, as shown in Table 7.

In summary, the V-SVM-based DDoS attack detection method proposed in this paper not only improves the classification accuracy, reduces the false negative rate, but also ensures the stability and timeliness of the classification model.

Table 4. Classification results based on RBF kernel function C-SVM

Sample size	Experience parameters	Accuracy	Detection rate	False negative rate	Running time
1000	C = 1 g = 0.1	99.9%	95%	7.76%	0.14409 s
2500	C = 1 g = 0.1	99.6%	88.4%	19%	0.20170 s
5000	C = 1 g = 0.1	99.7%	91.5%	14%	0.39528 s
10000	C = 1 g = 0.1	99.86%	91.5%	14.1%	0.82539 s
20000	C = 1 g = 0.1	99.88%	97.85%	3.5%	1.35009 s

Table 5. Results of C-SVM classification based on grid search

Sample size	Optimal parameter pairs (C, g)		Accuracy	Detection rate	False negative rate	Running time
1000	C = 0.03125	g = 0.0625	99.5%	91%	13.9%	1.50818 s
2500	C = 0.5	g = 16	99.72%	97.4%	4.0%	4.00166 s
5000	C = 0.5	g = 32	99.86%	98.7%	2.0%	6.22163 s
10000	C = 0.0625	g = 4	99.9%	93.9%	10.0%	14.03318 s
20000	C = 32	g = 32	99.94%	99.1%	1.25%	39.01831 s

Table 6. Results of V-SVM classification based on RBF kernel function

Sample size	Optimal parameter	TN (SV)	Accuracy	Detection rate	False negative rate	Running time
1000	V = 0.2	203	99.9%	95.0%	7.8%	0.20467 s
2500	V = 0.2	502	99.6%	97.4%	4.0%	0.29484 s
5000	V = 0.2	1001	99.7%	98.7%	2.0%	0.69763 s
10000	V = 0.2	2001	99.81%	99.05%	1.5%	2.58873 s
20000	V = 0.2	4002	99.81%	99.05%	1.5%	0.20467 s

Table 7. Comparison of the three methods

Algorithm	Accuracy	Stability	Timeliness	Comprehensive performance
C-SVM	General	General	Fine	General
GS C-SVM	Higher	General	Poor	Better
V-SVM	Tall	Tall	Fine	Good

6 Conclusion and Future Work

6.1 Conclusion

In view of the diversity, distribution, suddenness and concealment of DDoS attacks and the large scale, mass and complexity of network flows under the new network environment, the current DDoS attack detection methods have some problems, such as high false alarm rate, high false negative rate and poor timeliness, etc., this paper proposes a detection method of DDoS attacks based on V-SVM. The method defines a nine-tuple NSAF to extract features of the network flow to describe the state characteristics of the network flow, and perform Min-Max normalization and PCA dimensionality reduction on the data. The kernel function is used to map the preprocessed samples to the high-dimensional feature space, and then the number of the parameter V control support vector and error vector is introduced, and the classification model based on V-SVM is established to detect attacks. The experimental results show that compared with similar methods, the detection method proposed in this paper not only improves the classification accuracy and reduces the missing report, but also ensures the stability and timeliness of the classification model.

6.2 Future Work

In this paper, theoretical and experimental analysis of DDoS attack detection based on V-SVM is carried out, which proves a lot of excellent performance of SVM in theory and experiment. However, SVM still has shortcomings in terms of data volume, degree of fit, and robustness. There is still room for further improvement.

(1) The mode in which the SVM processes data: With the advancement of the Internet of Things era, servers often have to deal with a large amount of data, and cloud technology can solve problems such as insufficient memory and excessive system overhead. Due to the limitations of the SVM itself, the data cannot be processed in parallel like the network flow collection method based on the cloud service model. Therefore, a hybrid model of V-SVM and distributed detection architecture remains to be studied.

(2) Regularization of the V-SVM parameter V: In the experiment, the problem of over-learning usually occurs, which results in the unsatisfactory results of the obtained model test and the weakening of the generalization ability. Due to the operability of the V value, it has a different degree of influence on different features. Therefore, it is worth thinking about how to regularize the parameter V to avoid overfitting when DDoS attacks tend to be more professional.

(3) The robustness of V-SVM: In the actual network environment, it is often accompanied by external factors such as noise points, network delays or network congestion. In the future research work, how to improve the robustness of the method needs to be continuously explored.

Acknowledgments. Thanks are due to Tang and Cheng for assistance with the experiments and to Tu and Fan for valuable discussion. Thanks to the equipment support provided by the School of Information Science and Technology of Hainan University and the State Key Laboratory of Marine Resources Utilization in South China Sea.

References

1. Behal, S., Kumar, K.: Characterization and comparison of DDoS attack tools and traffic generators -a review. Int. J. Netw. Secur. **19**(3), 383–393 (2017)
2. Cheng, J.R., Tang, X.Y., Yin, J.: A change-point DDoS attack detection method based on half interaction anomaly degree. Int. J. Auton. Adapt. Commun. Syst. **10**(1), 38 (2017)
3. Yadav, V.K., Trivedi, M.C., Mehtre, B.M.: DDA: an approach to handle DDoS (Ping Flood) attack. In: Satapathy, S.C., Joshi, A., Modi, N., Pathak, N. (eds.) Proceedings of International Conference on ICT for Sustainable Development. AISC, vol. 408, pp. 11–23. Springer, Singapore (2016). https://doi.org/10.1007/978-981-10-0129-1_2
4. Arbor Networks: Infrastructure Security Report (2012). http://tinyurl.com/ag6tht4. Accessed 22 May 2019
5. Ferreira, L.L.C., Assis, F.M., De Souza, C.P.: A comparative study of use of Shannon, Rényi and Tsallis entropy for attribute selecting in network intrusion detection. In: Proceedings of IEEE International Workshop on Measurements & Networking, vol. 7435, pp. 77–82 (2012)
6. Zhu, J.Q., Feng, F., Yin, K.X., et al.: Dynamic entropy based DoS attack detection method. Comput. Electr. Eng. **39**(7), 2243–2251 (2013)

7. Mohiuddin, A., Abdun, N.M.: Novel approach for network traffic pattern analysis using clustering-based collective anomaly detection. Inf. Sci. **2**(1), 111–130 (2015)
8. Cheng, G.Z., Chen, H.C., Cheng, D.N., et al.: Uncovering network traffic anomalies based on their sparse distributions. Sci. China Inf. Sci. **57**(9), 1–11 (2014)
9. Park, J., Choi, D.H., Jeon, Y.-B., Min, S.D., Park, D.-S.: Network anomaly detection based on probabilistic analysis. In: Park, J.J., Pan, Y., Yi, G., Loia, V. (eds.) CSA/CUTE/UCAWSN -2016. LNEE, vol. 421, pp. 699–704. Springer, Singapore (2017). https://doi.org/10.1007/978-981-10-3023-9_107
10. Karnwal, T., Sivakumar, T., Aghila, G.: A comber approach to protect cloud computing against XML DDoS and HTTP DDoS attack. In: IEEE Students' Conference on Electrical, Electronics and Computer Science, pp. 1–5. IEEE, India (2012)
11. Tama, B.A., Rhee, K.H.: Data mining techniques in DoS/DDoS attack detection: a literature review. Inf. Japan **18**(8), 3739–3747 (2015)
12. Gao, C., Cheng, Q., He, P., Susilo, W., Li, J.: Privacy-preserving Naive Bayes classifiers secure against the substitution-then-comparison attack. Inf. Sci. **444**, 72–88 (2018)
13. Abbas, H., Latif, R., Latif, S., et al.: Performance evaluation of Enhanced Very Fast Decision Tree (EVFDT) mechanism for distributed denial-of-service attack detection in health care systems. Ann. Telecommun. **71**(9), 1–11 (2016)
14. Ma, X., Li, J., Zhang, F.: Outsourcing computation of modular exponentiations in cloud computing. Cluster Comput. **16**(4), 787–796 (2013)
15. Li, J., Sun, L., Yan, Q., et al.: Significant permission identification for machine-learning-based android malware detection. IEEE Trans. Ind. Inform. **14**(7), 3216–3225 (2018)
16. Li, P., Li, J., Huang, Z., et al.: Privacy-preserving outsourced classification in cloud computing. Cluster Comput. **21**(1), 277–286 (2018)
17. Li, J., Chen, X., Huang, Q., et al.: Digital provenance: enabling secure data forensics in cloud computing. Future Gener. Comput. Syst. **37**, 259–266 (2014)
18. Iglesias, F., Zseby, T., et al.: Analysis of network traffic features for anomaly detection. Mach. Learn. **101**, 59–84 (2015)
19. Usha, M., Kavitha, P.: Anomaly based intrusion detection for 802.11 networks with optimal features using SVM classifier. Wireless Netw. **21**, 1–16 (2016). ISSN: 1022-0038
20. Lee, W., Stolfo, S.J., Mok, K.W.: Mining in a data-flow environment: experience in network intrusion detection. In: ACM SIGKDD International Conference on Knowledge Discovery and Data Mining, pp. 114–124. ACM, USA (2000)
21. Cheng, J.R., Zhou, J.H., Tang, X.Y., et al.: A DDoS detection method for socially aware networking based on forecasting fusion feature sequence. Comput. J. **61**(7), 959–970 (2018)
22. Siddiqui, M.K., Naahid, S.: Analysis of KDD CUP 99 dataset using clustering based data mining. Int. J. Database Theory Appl. **6**(5), 23–34 (2013)
23. Cheng, J.R., Xu, R.M., Tang, X.Y., et al.: An abnormal network flow feature sequence prediction approach for DDoS attacks detection in big data environment. Comput. Mater. Continua **55**(1), 95–119 (2018)
24. Niu, L., Sun, Z.L.: PCA-AKM algorithm and its application in intrusion detection system. Comput. Sci. **45**(2), 226–230 (2018)
25. Vapnik, V.N.: The Nature of Statistical Learning Theory. Springer, New York (2000). https://doi.org/10.1007/978-1-4757-3264-1
26. Schölkopf, B., Smola, A.J., Williamson, R.C., et al.: New support vector algorithms. Neural Comput. **12**(5), 1207–1245 (2000)
27. KDD Cup 1999 Dataset. http://kdd.ics.uci.edu/databases/kddcup99/kddcup99.html. Accessed 24 May 2019
28. Hao, P.Y.: New support vector algorithms with parametric insensitive/margin model. Neural Netw. Official J. Int. Neural Netw. Soc. **23**(1), 60 (2010)

29. Zhu, Y., Zhang, Y.-F., Du, A.-Y.: Study on fault classification of power-shift steering transmission based on v-support vector machine. In: Qi, E., Shen, J., Dou, R. (eds.) The 19th International Conference on Industrial Engineering and Engineering Management, pp. 647–654. Springer, Heidelberg (2013). https://doi.org/10.1007/978-3-642-38433-2_70

30. Lenders, V., Tanner, A., Blarer, A.: Gaining an edge in cyberspace with advanced situational awareness. IEEE Secur. Privacy **13**(2), 65–74 (2015)

DDOS Multivariate Information Fusion Model Based on Hierarchical Representation Learning

Xiangyan Tang[2], Yiyang Zhang[2(✉)], Jieren Cheng[1,2], Jinying Xu[2], and Hui Li[2]

[1] Key Laboratory of Internet Information Retrieval of Hainan Province,
Hainan University, Haikou 570228, China
[2] College of Computer and Cyberspace Security,
Hainan University, Haikou 570228, China
1073646111@qq.com

Abstract. The existing DDOS detection methods have the problems of single acquisition node and low detection rate. A multi-source DDOS information fusion model (HRM) based on hierarchical representation learning network and a FlowMerge algorithm based on three network flow merging modes are proposed. Firstly, the network traffic is transformed into triples, and the dimensionality reduction of Tsne algorithm is used to transform it into network IP topology structure graph. Then, the network flow is merged by FlowMerge algorithm, which is decomposed into a series of smaller and approximate coarse-grained topology structure graphs. Then, the features are embedded into more fine-grained graphs iteratively, and the HRM model is established. The experimental results show that the model can better reflect the temporal and spatial characteristics of network traffic, improve the detection accuracy, and have better robustness.

Keywords: Hierarchical representation learning · Multi-source information fusion · Feature embedding · Graph neural network

1 Introduction and Related Work

In recent years, the number, scale and type of distributed denial of service (DDoS) attacks have increased dramatically. In March 2018, GitHub, a well-known code hosting site, suffered the worst DDoS network attack ever, with peak traffic reaching 1.35 Tbps. Many scholars at home and abroad have proposed many methods for detection, early warning and confrontation. Doshi et al. proposed a low-cost DDOS detection algorithm based on machine learning for Internet of Things equipment [1]. Hodo et al. proposed a network threat analysis and anomaly classification method based on artificial neural network [2]. Cheng et al. proposed DDOS attack detection methods based on time series model, semi-interactive anomaly degree and address correlation degree [3–5]. Spaulding et al. proposed a DDOS detection method based on long-term and short-term memory (LSTM) neural network for DNS extraction and filtering [6]. Nam et al. designed two detection methods of DoS attacks based on

© Springer Nature Switzerland AG 2019
J. Vaidya et al. (Eds.): CSS 2019, LNCS 11983, pp. 57–66, 2019.
https://doi.org/10.1007/978-3-030-37352-8_5

self-organizing mapping (SOM) [7]. Li, Li and others propose the Privacy Protection Outsourcing Classification Framework (POCC) signature technology in cloud computing [8]. Li, Chen and others proposed a new secure source scheme based on group signature and attribute [9]. These algorithms often use a single node to collect data. The extracted data do not have multi-source, and are prone to local over-fitting. They can not respond to DDOS attack flow as a whole, thus affecting the accuracy of final detection, classification and recognition.

To solve the problems above, this study proposes a network information fusion model based on hierarchical representation learning and FlowMerge algorithm based on three network flow merging modes. Firstly, the information in the network flow is quantified into triples and stored in the graph structure. Then, the remaining information is quantified into 12-dimensional vectors by using SimHash, weighted and numerical conversion method, and the initial network IP topology is obtained. After that, the topology structure graph is merged into sub-graphs with smaller granularity and upper spatial and data characteristics by using FlowMerge algorithm, and the sub-graph sequence is used to embedding features layer by layer in order from coarse to fine granularity. Finally, the fusion result at decision level is obtained. This model can make full use of the multi-source information in network flow, and make pertinent decisions for different network environments.

2 Construction of Multi-source DDOS Information Fusion Model

Network information sampling can obtain information of various data types and data structures. Taking the classical WireShark network data package analysis tool as an example, the sampled single data stream can include number, time, source address, destination address, network protocol, packet size, message information, text in the package, etc. [11]. In this study, firstly, the network topology is modeled. IP source address and destination address field are coordinates, and a pair of source address and destination address form an edge, that is, a network flow containing information. Since IP addresses contain up to eight-dimensional data (ipv6), the Tsne algorithm is used to reduce the dimensions to two-dimensional or three-dimensional vectors for visualization. Then the data model of other information in the flow is built to facilitate the subsequent calculation of flow similarity.

Definition. For any flow F of network flow (NF), it contains source IP vector $S = (a_1, a_2, a_3 \ldots a_n)$, destination IP vector $D = (b_1, b_2, b_3 \ldots b_n)$ and in-stream information vector $I = (c_1, c_2, c_3 \ldots c_m)$. All vacancies in S and D are filled with 0.

TSNE interprets the total distance between data points in high-dimensional space as a symmetrical joint probability distribution P, and codes its similarity. At the same time, the joint probability distribution Q describing the similarity of low-dimensional space is calculated. The purpose is to realize embedding in low-dimensional space and let Q represent P. The algorithm realizes [12] by optimizing the location in low-dimensional space and minimizing the cost function C (cross-entropy between joint probability distribution P and q).

$$C(P,Q) = KL(P||Q) = \sum_{i=1}^{N} \sum_{i=1,j\neq 1}^{N} p_{ij} \ln(\frac{p_{ij}}{q_{ij}}) \tag{1}$$

At this time the graph $G(V,E) = \{V = (S,D), E = I\}$ is obtained, and then the information vector I is quantified according to rich text classes (such as message information), limited text classes (such as protocol name) and time classes (sampling time), which are transformed by SimHash, weighted and numerical conversion method respectively, as well as a specific similarity judgment value is obtained. Similar traffic can be judged if the difference between two traffic is less than a certain threshold. This value will be iterated in the information fusion algorithm, gradually approaching the true threshold.

3 Information Fusion Algorithms Based on Hierarchical Representation Learning

3.1 Hierarchical Representation Learning

Hierarchical representation learning is a general method of low-dimensional embedding of graphical nodes, which can maintain higher structural characteristics. The principle is to get a smaller global structure graph by information fusion, which is similar to the input. This simplified graph is used for a set of initial inputs of machine learning, which is an excellent initialization for learning the features of the original detailed graph. The idea decomposes the graph into a series of layers, and then gradually embeds the hierarchical features of the graph from the thickest level into the original hierarchical structure, effectively avoiding the complex graph embedding configuration [13]. This method can improve all the most advanced neural network algorithms for graph embedding, including DeepWalk, LINE and node2vec [13, 14].

When normal traffic dominates the network, there are traces for the generation and termination of each traffic, and there are few large-scale similar traffic. When anomalies occur, a large number of similar traffic containing false IP source address and the same destination address will appear in the network in a short time. These similar traffic flows can be merged while retaining the original space-time relationship, and merged into a simplified graph with similar features of the merged pre-graph, which can be used as input for hierarchical representation learning.

3.2 Network Flow Merging Algorithm

In the information fusion algorithm based on hierarchical representation, the quality of the coarse-grained algorithm of graph will directly affect the correlation between the final different hierarchical graphs. Based on the existing network IP topology, we discuss the methods of flow merging in different situations.

1. One-to-one network flow merging

Fig. 1. A one-to-one flow merging diagram

In Internet interaction, there are many times when a single IP repeatedly visits another fixed ip. It may be normal access to a web site, or there may be server or switch nodes in both. These flows can then be merged into one, as shown in Fig. 1. By statistic the forward-to-backward ratio of internal flow after fusion (under normal circumstances, the forward flow and the reverse flow between two nodes are roughly the same), we can preliminarily judge whether there is an anomaly.

2. Multi-to-one network flow merging

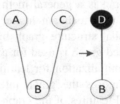

Fig. 2. Multi-to-one flow merging diagram

Many-to-one traffic is the standard network attack flow model. When DDOS attacks occur, a large number of false source IP traffic will rapidly flow to the same destination IP within the time node. Similar traffic that conforms to this model can be merged in the way of Fig. 2. It is worth noting that the traffic characteristics of large-scale network congestion are similar to DDOS attacks. When network congestion occurs, the positive-negative ratio will remain at approximately the same level for a long period of time, but will drop sharply when arriving at a specific node, i.e. network crash node. On the contrary, DDOS attack flow will maintain a stable and low proportion.

3. Unrelated network flow merging

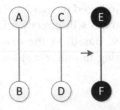

Fig. 3. Schematic diagram of unrelated traffic consolidation

After flow fusion to a certain extent, the relationship between traffic in the network becomes more sparse, and the complex traffic information graph is coarsely granularized into a variety of information clusters containing specific traffic characteristics. At this time, similar information clusters can be merged to get more streamlined information graph with decision-level fusion effect as shown in Fig. 3. At the same time, in the initial flow graph, there will be some noisy traffic free from the high-access nodes, which is not related but has certain similarity. It can merge the unrelated traffic after the similarity check is passed, and be marked as noise and then removed in the subsequent machine learning program operation.

In summary, the stream merging algorithm can be summarized as pseudo-code as follows (Tables 1 and 2):

Table 1. Multi-source information fusion model algorithms for DDOS

Algorithm 1: HierarchicalRep(G,$Detect()$)

Input:

    Graph G

    Machine learning detection algorithm Detect()

Output: matrix of vertex representation $\Phi \in R^{|V| \times d}$

    $G_0, \ G_1,...G_L \leftarrow FlowMerge(G)$

    Initialize Φ'_{G_L} by assigning zeros

    $\Phi_{G_L} \leftarrow FlowMerge(G_L, \Phi'_{G_L})$

    For i = L - 1 to 0 **do:**

        $\Phi'_{G_i} \leftarrow \Pr olongate(\Phi_{G_{i+1}}, G_{i+1}, G_i)$

        $\Phi_{G_i} \leftarrow Detect(G_i, \Phi'_{G_i})$

    end for

    return Φ_{G_0}

Table 2. Network flow merging algorithms

Algorithm 2: FlowMerge(G)

Input:

    Graph G

Output: Series of Coarsened Graphs $G_0, \ G_1,...G_L$

    $G_0, \ G_1,...G_L \leftarrow FlowMerge(G)$

    $L \leftarrow 0$

    $G_0 \leftarrow G$

    While $V_L \geq threshold$ **do:**

        $L \leftarrow L+1$

        $G_L \leftarrow InnerCollapse(MultoOneCollapse(G))$

        If similar flow exist **then:**

            $G_L \leftarrow NonConnectCollapse(G)$

    end while

    return $G_0, \ G_1,...G_L$

Among them, FlowMerge algorithm merges streams according to the three merging methods given above, until the final size of the graph is not less than a specific value, or until the merging of a specific number of rounds is completed.

3.3 Verification Model

In this model, Xavier is used to initialize network parameters, and random gradient descent back propagation algorithm is used to minimize the cost function, so as to optimize and update network parameters. After selecting the detection algorithm, the fusion algorithm is implemented to generate graph sequence, and the same detection algorithm is executed for each layer, and the results are obtained and recycled as the input of the next layer. Because the whole model uses the storage of graph structure, it can grasp the whole spatial characteristics better in the learning process.

In the training process, traffic from normal network flow is marked as 1, and traffic from abnormal network flow is marked as 0. If further classification is needed, the anomaly flow can be subdivided into more tags, corresponding to worm virus, DNS attack, reflection attack and so on. After learning, unlabeled unknown network traffic is input into the trained model for identification. DA is defined as the total number of anomalous flows identified, PA is the recognition accuracy, SF is the total number of attack flows. The detection rate formula is shown in (2):

$$P(D) = \frac{DA \times PA}{SF} \tag{2}$$

Among the existing DDOS attack detection algorithms based on machine learning, we select Doshi et al.'s device detection method based on Internet of Things (hereinafter referred to as IoT method) [16], V. Srihari et al.'s semi-supervised machine learning classification method (hereinafter referred to as SSL method) [17], Jeffrey Spaulding's DDOS attack detection method based on LSTM neural network for DNS filtering and extraction (hereinafter referred to as LD method). Contrast experiment [18]. In the experiment, we will compare the size of the same data set in HRM with that in non-HRM model, so as to verify whether HRM can improve the accuracy and robustness of DDOS attack detection algorithm based on machine learning.

4   Experiment and Analysis

The selected normal flow data sets were collected from the network traffic of two weeks under the simulated environment of ns3, and the real monitoring data of Hainan University campus network by WireShark for one week were added. A total of 15 days (total min) traffic was randomly selected as the training set, and the remaining 6 days (total min) traffic as the test set. The anomaly flow data set is selected from DARPA_Scalable_Network_Monitoring-20091103 data set under USC/ISI ANT [15] project, and the anomaly flow data set is selected from the monitoring network from November 3 to 12, 2009. There are synthetic HTTP, SMTP and DNS background data in the traffic, including large-scale network attacks, such as DNS attacks, worm viruses and DDoS attacks. Min traffic is added to the training set and test set as the final set.

The experiment is divided into three parts. Firstly, the training traffic is modeled by HRM and the traffic merging algorithm is implemented. Then, a hierarchical representation learning neural network is trained for the sequence of IP network topology structure diagrams. Finally, test the trained model with test set to verify whether it can effectively fuse the information in the model, improve the detection accuracy and reduce the false alarm rate. TensorFlow is used to model the experiment, and then DDoS attack, DNS attack, worm virus and other complex attack modes are detected.

4.1 Modeling and Merging of Training Flow

Firstly, the previous test set, which totals min and 1.37T, is modeled, and the flow merging algorithm is implemented. The merging times are set to 100. The traffic from normal flow set is marked green, and the traffic from abnormal flow set is marked red. As can be seen from Figs. 4, 5 and 6, the traffic marked as abnormal flow is gradually merged into at least a number of target nodes. This further proves that the model has the possibility of improving the prediction accuracy.

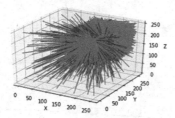

Fig. 4. Initial network IP topology (Color figure online)

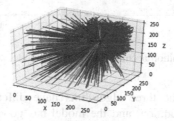

Fig. 5. Network IP topology after the 10th merge (Color figure online)

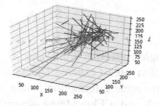

Fig. 6. Network IP topology after the 100th merge (Color figure online)

4.2 Comparisons with Various Detection Methods

Firstly, three different DDOS attack detection methods are used to train the network IP topology diagram obtained in Sect. 3.1, and tested in the test set, which is set as the control group. Then, the network IP topology diagram is replaced by the sequence of graphs obtained by the network flow merging algorithm in Sect. 3.1. The training model is iterated with the idea of hierarchical representation learning, and tested in the test set, which is set as the experimental group. The detection accuracy of the control group and the experimental group was calculated under different test set sizes.

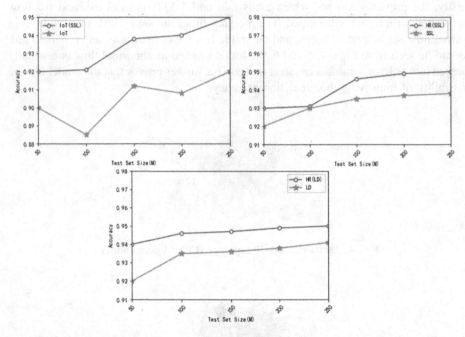

Fig. 7. Comparison of recognition accuracy using HRM model addition under three methods

As shown in Fig. 7, the three algorithms have different degrees of accuracy improvement after HRM addition, and the model has good robustness. HRM information fusion model simplifies the model in each layer of network flow merging, makes it easier to extract features, and thus enhances its recognition accuracy.

5   Conclusion

Aiming at the problems of single collection point, lack of multi-source and local over-fitting affecting the final detection rate of existing DDOS attack detection methods, this paper proposes a DDOS multi-source information fusion model based on hierarchical representation learning network and a FlowMerge algorithm based on three network flow merging modes. This method defines a new network information fusion model, which retains the spatial characteristics of network traffic as much as possible. Based on the idea of hierarchical representation learning, it learns the characteristics of the whole IP topology model step by step from coarse to fine granularity. Experiments show that this fusion method can effectively add the existing DDOS attack detection methods based on machine learning. In the future work, we will continue to study the usability of this method in network early warning, situational awareness and other fields.

Acknowledgements. This work was supported by the Hainan Provincial Natural Science Foundation of China [2018CXTD333, 617048]; National Natural Science Foundation of China [61762033, 61702539]; Hainan University Doctor Start Fund Project [kyqd1328]; Hainan University Youth Fund Project [qnjj1444]; Social Development Project of Public Welfare Technology Application of Zhejiang Province [LGF18F020019]; Ministry of Education Humanities and Social Sciences Research Planning Fund Project (19YJA710010).

References

1. Doshi, R., Apthorpe, N., Feamster, N.: Machine Learning DDoS Detection for Consumer Internet of Things Devices, pp. 29–35 (2018)
2. Hodo, E., Bellekens, X., Hamilton, A., et al.: Threat analysis of IoT networks using artificial neural network intrusion detection system. In: 2016 International Symposium on Networks, Computers and Communications (ISNCC), Yasmine Hammamet, pp. 1–6 (2016)
3. Cheng, J., Zhou, J., Liu, Q., Tang, X., Guo, Y.: A DDoS detection method for socially aware networking based on forecasting fusion feature sequence. Comput. J. **61**(7), 959–970 (2018)
4. Cheng, J., Xu, R., Tang, X., Sheng, V.S., Cai, C.: An abnormal network flow feature sequence prediction approach for DDoS attacks detection in big data environment. Comput. Mater. Continua **55**(1), 95–119 (2018)
5. Cheng, J., Tang, X., Yin, J.: A change-point DDoS attack detection method based on half interaction anomaly degree. Int. J. Auton. Adapt. Commun. Syst. **10**(1), 38–54 (2017)
6. Spaulding, J., Mohaisen, A.: Defending internet of things against malicious domain names using D-FENS. In: 2018 IEEE/ACM Symposium on Edge Computing (SEC). ACM (2018)
7. Nam, T.M., Phong, P.H., Khoa, T.D., et al.: [IEEE 2018 International Conference on Information Networking (ICOIN) - Chiang Mai, Thailand (2018.1.10–2018.1.12)] 2018 International Conference on Information Networking (ICOIN) - Self-organizing map-based approaches in DDoS flooding detection using SDN. In: International Conference on Information Networking, pp. 249–254. IEEE Computer Society (2018)
8. Li, P., Li, J., Huang, Z., et al.: Privacy-preserving outsourced classification in cloud computing. Cluster Comput. **21**(1), 277–286 (2018)
9. Li, J., Chen, X., Huang, Q., et al.: Digital provenance: enabling secure data forensics in cloud computing. Future Gener. Comput. Syst. **37**, 259–266 (2014)
10. Li, J., Chen, X., Chow, S.S.M., Huang, Q., Wong, D.S., Liu, Z.: Multi-authority fine-grained access control with accountability and its application in cloud. J. Netw. Comput. Appl. https://doi.org/10.1016/j.jnca.2018.03.006
11. Cheng, J., Yin, J., Liu, Y., Cai, Z., Li, M.: Detecting distributed denial of service attack based on address correlation value. J. Comput. Res. Dev. **46**(8), 1334–1340 (2009)
12. Pezzotti, N., Lelieveldt, B.P.F., Maaten, L.V.D., et al.: Approximated and user steerable tSNE for progressive visual analytics. IEEE Trans. Vis. Comput. Graph **23**(7), 1739–1752 (2017)

13. Chen, H., Perozzi, B., Hu, Y., et al.: HARP: Hierarchical Representation Learning for Networks (2017)
14. Wang, D., Cui, P., Zhu, W.: Structural deep network embedding. In: Proceedings of the 22nd ACM SIGKDD International Conference on Knowledge Discovery and Data Mining (2016)
15. Cao, Y., Zhou, Z., Sun, X., Gao, C.: Coverless information hiding based on the molecular structure images of material. Comput. Mater. Continua **54**(2), 197–207 (2018)
16. Agarwal, A., Dawson, S., Mckee, D., et al.: Detecting abnormalities in IoT program executions through control-flow-based features: poster abstract. In: International Conference on Internet-of-Things Design and Implementation (2017)
17. Doshi, R., Apthorpe, N., Feamster, N.: [IEEE 2018 IEEE Security and Privacy Workshops (SPW) - San Francisco, CA, USA (2018.5.24–2018.5.24)] 2018 IEEE Security and Privacy Workshops (SPW) - Machine Learning DDoS Detection for Consumer Internet of Things Devices, pp. 29–35 (2018)
18. Srihari, V., Anitha, R.: DDoS detection system using wavelet features and semi-supervised learning. In: Mauri, J.L., Thampi, S.M., Rawat, D.B., Jin, D. (eds.) SSCC 2014. CCIS, vol. 467, pp. 291–303. Springer, Heidelberg (2014). https://doi.org/10.1007/978-3-662-44966-0_28

A Method of Malicious Bot Traffic Detection

Mengying Wu[1], Zhendong Wu[1(✉)], Hao Lv[1,2], and Jingjing Wang[1]

[1] School of Cyberspace, Hangzhou Dianzi University, Hangzhou, China
wmy_lcw@163.com, wzd@hdu.edu.cn, 1205728818@qq.com,
alilliam@sina.com
[2] School of Cyberspace Security, Beijing University of Posts
and Telecommunications, Beijing, China

Abstract. The traditional malicious bot traffic detection technology is usually based on rule matching or statistical analysis, which is not flexible enough and has low detection accuracy. This article systematically analyzes the formation and characteristics of malicious bot traffic. And the WEB log traffic information is extracted, analyzed and selected as feature, finally we use support vector machine algorithm to train the malicious bot traffic detection model and the detection accuracy appears to be quite high. This is a good reference for applying machine learning to the field of cyber security.

Keywords: Malicious bot traffic · Web crawlers · Machine learning

1 Introduction

With the advancement and development of Internet technology, human beings have entered the information age, and the Internet has become the main carrier of human information. How to extract useful information quickly and effectively from the Internet has become the focus of attention [1]. In order to solve this problem, there are some companies in the Internet that provide search engine services. Search engines collect information on the web mainly relying on web crawlers, which is a computer program or script that is responsible for crawling information on the Internet. In the online world, a large number of crawlers constantly crawl the website information every day. It can be said that the bot-traffic generated by the web crawler occupies a large proportion in the network traffic, which seriously affects the performance and availability of the network.

It is undeniable that the network is also full of malicious crawlers. Some of these crawlers are used to crawl private information on the Internet, and some illegally obtain commercial profits in order to falsify false website visit traffic or advertisement click-through rate, which poses a great threat to people's information security and the healthy development of the Internet industry [2]. In addition, the crawling algorithm of malicious crawlers is often less intelligent and does not optimize the crawling algorithm, so the crawler of the professional search engine will bring more access pressure to the website. Therefore, malicious bot traffic generated by malicious crawlers seriously affects network performance. For websites with normal server performance, malicious crawlers may even cause the website fails to provide normal services. Therefore, how

J. Vaidya et al. (Eds.): CSS 2019, LNCS 11983, pp. 67–76, 2019.
https://doi.org/10.1007/978-3-030-37352-8_6

to detect and stop malicious crawlers in the network has become a hot spot for major companies and researchers.

Traditional malicious bot traffic detection methods usually identify a set of rules to identify malicious traffic by analyzing certain statistics or statistical methods for certain traffic samples [10, 12, 13]. The traditional traffic detection method is difficult to adapt to the real-time and changing network environment, and it is difficult to identify various new abnormal traffic. It is necessary to manually maintain and update the system identification rules to maintain the accuracy of system traffic identification.

With the rise of artificial intelligence technologies such as machine learning, more and more experts and scholars have applied artificial intelligence algorithms such as machine learning algorithms to malicious bot traffic detection problems. In [5], the author uses a supervised learning algorithm Bayesian classifier algorithm to analyze and detect web crawlers, and compares the experimental results with the results of using decision trees. Bomhardt et al. [8] used a neural network algorithm and used the ratio of total transmitted bytes and 4xx type status codes to train the model. Stassopoulou et al. [9] used a semi-automated method to label training sets and used Bayesian algorithms to distinguish between different sessions. In addition, some scholars have used logistic regression and decision tree algorithms to study the detection of malicious web crawlers [3].

This paper will establish a new type of malicious bot traffic detection method based on random forest algorithm, so as to make full use of the characteristics of network traffic data, and make timely and accurate response to malicious bot traffic.

The rest of this paper is structured as follows: Sect. 2 introduces the overview of malicious bot traffic. Section 3 describes our proposed method in detail. Section 4 shows experimental performances. Finally, the conclusion is presented in Sect. 5.

2   Overview of Malicious Bot Traffic

2.1   Malicious Bot Traffic Detection Problem

By analyzing relevant scientific research in the field of malicious bot traffic detection, it is concluded that the current malicious bot traffic detection methods mainly include the following.

(1)   Use Web Robot Exclusion Criteria

The method is based on the very simple fact that the most regular web crawlers access the robots.txt file in the root directory of the website before crawling the website. As mentioned above, robots.txt specifies the pages that web crawlers can crawl and not crawl. If the web crawler accesses robots.txt before crawling, then the crawler is classified as a normal crawler; if no robots.txt is accessed, the crawler is classified as a malicious crawler. Obviously this method has certain limitations, because Web robot exclusion criteria are not mandatory.

Malicious crawlers can also access robots.txt before crawling to avoid blocking the target site.

(2) Using the web page member table

When a normal user requests a simple page resource such as HTML or PHP, the browser analyzes the page and requests the page.

Other resources embedded in the page, such as cascading style sheets, image/audio files, web scripts, etc., required for the page, so that the user can see the complete page.

In general, browser requests for these embedded resources are usually completed within 0–5 s after the initial page request, and in the slowest case within 30 s.

The web crawler is different. The web crawler also needs to analyze the embedded resources required by the page. After the analysis, the request is not immediately requested, but the resource URL is added to the queue to be crawled, so the web crawler completes the embedded resource on the page. The time between the request and the initial request is usually much longer than the normal user, and even some web crawlers do not request embedded resources in the page at all.

Table 1. Web member list

Url	Number of member	Requested number
index.html	6	0
introduction.html	1	0
about.html	4	0
faq.html	0	0
contact.html	2	0
...	...	...

The method is based on the difference between normal users and web crawlers in requesting page-embedded resources. As shown in Table 1, when constructing a web page member table, you need to manually specify a time threshold as the statistical period of each entry.

A typical page member table contains the following three entries:

(1) The URL (Url) being accessed.
(2) The number of embedded resources in this page (NumberOfMember).
(3) The number of embedded resources requested in the specified time threshold (RequestedNumber).

As described above, the method mainly distinguishes between normal users and web crawlers by specifying the number of embedded resources requested within the time threshold.

(3) Web log analysis

The method mainly distinguishes normal users and web crawlers by analyzing web logs. The steps of the method are as follows:

(1) Log preprocessing: extracts IP address, date, time, status code and other information from the web log.
(2) Session differentiation: The HTTP request in the web log is divided into several groups according to the IP address and the access time.

(3) Crawler recognition: mainly relies on whether to access robots.txt, access to hidden connections Refer

(4) **Machine Learning Analysis**

Machine learning analysis mainly uses various machine learning methods to detect malicious BOT traffic. For example, Tan and Kumar [4] and others applied the C4.5 algorithm (i.e., decision tree classifier) to the 25-dimensional feature vector space to distinguish different web crawling sessions. The features they selected included: the percentage of different types of resources. (pictures, multimedia, HTML pages, etc.), time characteristics (average time interval, standard deviation of time intervals, etc.), HTTP request types (GET, POST, HEAD, etc.) and other features (IP address, User-Agent, etc.). Their research results show that by applying the C4.5 algorithm to the selected feature set, the prediction accuracy of the model is more than 90% after learning through only four web sessions. In the literature [2], a web crawler detection algorithm is designed based on Hidden Markov Model HMM, which considers the stability of the sudden crawler access request of ordinary users requesting resources, that is, ordinary users tend to be very Multiple requests are sent within a short time interval to request embedded resources of the current page, while web crawlers are computer programs whose access time tends to change more often, resulting in a 97.2% detection rate and a 0.2% error rate.

The characteristics of the data, the trained model prediction accuracy is also high, and save a lot of manual participation especially.

The unsupervised learning clustering algorithm is outstanding in anomaly detection and can make a good judgment on various emerging malicious bot traffic. Therefore, this article will be combined with related machine learning algorithms to explore the problem of malicious bot traffic detection, mainly related to the study of content:

(1) On the basis of analyzing the background of malicious bot traffic detection. This paper studies the feature preprocessing and feature selection in the design flow of malicious bot traffic detection model.
(2) Study the performance of support vector machine on malicious bot traffic detection and adjust the parameters to obtain better performance model.
(3) Implement malicious bot traffic detection software and deploy it to the actual web server.

3 Design of Malicious Bot Traffic Detection Algorithm Based on SVM

3.1 Support Vector Machine

In this paper, support vector machine algorithm is used to classify. Support vector machine mainly aims at the problem of binary classification. It tries to find the partitioned hyperplane with the largest interval as the classification boundary in the plane of the current dimension or the feature space of the higher dimension. The optimal objective function of soft margin support vector machine can be expressed as:

$$\min_{w,b} \frac{1}{2} \|w\|^2 + C \sum_{i=1}^{m} \ell_{0/1} y_i(w^T x_i + b) \tag{3.1}$$

Among them: $C > 0$ is constant, $\ell_{0/1}$ is loss function $\ell_{0/1}$ is a non-concave, non-continuous function with poor mathematical properties, which makes it difficult to calculate (3.1). Therefore, in practice, convex continuous functions are usually used to replace these functions, which are called 'surrogate loss function'. The most commonly used alternative loss function is hinge loss function. If hinge loss function is used, the optimization objective becomes:

$$\min_{w,b} \frac{1}{2} \|w\|^2 + C \sum_{i=1}^{m} \max(0, 1 - y_i(w^T x_i + b)) \tag{3.2}$$

In order to solve the problem of classification of non-linearly separable dataset, we need to use kernel function. Sample datasets are mapped from the original low-dimensional space to a higher-dimensional feature space, so that the sample datasets can be linearly separable in this feature space. The commonly used kernel function are:

(1) Linear core: $k(x_i, x_j) = x_i^T x_j$
(2) Polynomial kernel: $k(x_i, x_j) = (x_i^T x_j)^d$, $d \geq 1$ is degree of polynomial.
(3) Gaussian RBF core: $k(x_i, x_j) = e^{-\frac{\|x_i - x_j\|^2}{2\sigma^2}}$, $\sigma > 0$ is the bandwidth of Gaussian core
(4) Sigmoid core: $k(x_i, x_j) = \tan(\beta x_i^T x_j + \theta)$, $\beta > 0$, $\theta < 0$

3.2   Feature Scaling of Data

Standardization and scaling of data is an important step in the machine learning workflow. When the raw data is on the order of magnitude.

Some machine learning algorithms may not work properly when there is a big difference. For example, most machine learning classification algorithms involve the calculation of Euclidean distance. If a feature is of a large order of magnitude compared to other features, then the final Euclidean distance will be mainly affected by the feature distance. Impact, which greatly weakens the contribution of other features to the pre-dictions. Therefore, in some machine learning algorithms, we need to standardize and feature the original data.

In this experiment, the feature scale function StandardScaler() of the scikit-learn preprocessing module was used to feature the original data set. StandardScaler() will take data for each feature

Scale to a distribution with a mean of 0 and a variance of 1.

3.3 PCA Dimensionality Reduction

In order to facilitate the visual exploration and analysis of data, save computing resources and speed up the calculation, this experiment carried out PCA dimensionality reduction on the original data, and selected n_components = 3, that is, the original data was reduced to three-dimensional space. As shown in Fig. 1, PCA has a good effect after dimensionality reduction, and the distribution of the two types of data has obvious differences.

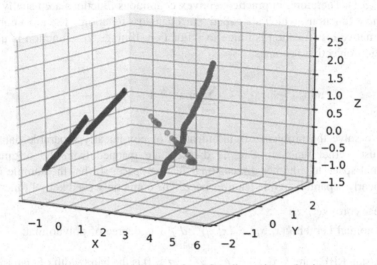

Fig. 1. Data distribution after PCA dimension reduction

3.4 Support Vector Machine Kernel Function Selection

The core part of the kernel function support vector machine(SVM) is how to choose the kernel function. This step ultimately affects the classification performance. The data set of this experiment is about 1,000, and 20% of them are selected as the test set, and then the linear kernel, polynomial kernel, Gaussian RBF kernel, and Sigmoid kernel were trained and evaluated. The algorithm for evaluating the kernel function in this test is as follows:

```
kernels = ['linear', 'poly', 'rbf', 'sigmoid']
for kernel in kernels:
    clf = SVC(kernel=kernel)
    clf.fit(X_train, y_train)
    y_pred = clf.predict(X_test)
    accuracy = accuracy_score(y_test, y_pred)
```

Table 2. Prediction accuracy of SVM for various kernel functions

Kernel function	Accuracy
Linear core	99.858%
Polynomial kernel	97.573%
Gaussian RBF core	99.813%
Sigmoid core	99.757%

It can be seen from Table 2 that the prediction accuracy of the model trained by linear kernel, Gaussian RBF kernel and Sigmoid kernel is relatively high, but because the number of data sets in this experiment is relatively small and the data distribution is relatively simple, Gaussian RBF kernel SVM and Sigmoid The nuclear SVM is too complicated and is likely to have an over-fitting phenomenon. Therefore, the linear kernel is selected as the final kernel function in this experiment.

3.5 Parameter Selection of Kernel Function Support Vector Machine

The kernel function selected in this experiment is a linear kernel. For a linear kernel support vector machine, the only parameter that can be adjusted is the multiplication factor C. The penalty factor C is used to punish the misclassification of the sample: the larger the C, the smaller the interval of dividing the hyperplane, indicating that the support vector machine has less tolerance to errors, and the model at this time has higher classification accuracy, but generalization. The ability is very weak, so choosing the right penalty factor can not be ignored for the final model.

The set of penalty factor C selected in this experiment is [0.00001, 0.0001, 0.001, 0.01, 0.1, 10, 100], and the support vector machine model under different penalty factors is evaluated by cross-validation method. This process mainly relies on the GridSearchCV function of the scikit-learn model selection module. The parameters of the function include: the classifier, the parameter list of the classifier, the number of cross-validation, and the evaluation criteria of each model. The function eventually returns an instance whose grid_scores_ attribute records the score of each incoming parameter and the corresponding machine learning model. The algorithm for selecting and evaluating model parameters using GridSearchCV in this experiment is as follows:

```
params = {'C': [0.00001, 0.0001, 0.001, 0.01, 0.1, 10, 100]}
clf = SVC(kernel='linear')
grid = GridSearchCV(clf, params, cv=10, scoring='accuracy')
grid.fit(X, Y)
print(grid.grid_scores_)
```

It is the final different penalty factor C and its corresponding prediction accuracy. When the penalty factor C = 0.1, the best prediction accuracy is 99.858% (Fig. 2).

```
mean: 0.68279, std: 0.00443, params: {'C': 1e-05},
mean: 0.68279, std: 0.00443, params: {'C': 0.0001},
mean: 0.98720, std: 0.02712, params: {'C': 0.001},
mean: 0.99573, std: 0.01268, params: {'C': 0.01},
mean: 0.99858, std: 0.00423, params: {'C': 0.1},
mean: 0.99806, std: 0.00423, params: {'C': 10},
mean: 0.99823, std: 0.00423, params: {'C': 100}
```

Fig. 2. Prediction accuracy of SVM for varies penalty factor

The experiment decided to use the linear kernel support vector machine with the penalty factor C = 0.1 as the final malicious bot traffic detection model with a prediction accuracy of 99.858%.

4 Implementation of Malicious Bot Traffic Detection Platform

The experimental environment of this experiment is shown in Table 3.

Table 3. Experimental environment of malicious bot traffic detection

Front-end language	HTML/JavaScript/jQuery/CSS
Back-end language	PHP
Web server	Apache2 + Mysql
Server operation system	Ubuntu 17
Detection module language	Python 3

After statistics, the crawler program generated 150 accesses in this test, and the simulated normal users generated 357 accesses.

Table 4 is the Confusion matrix.

Table 4. Confusion matrix over access data

	Attack (predicted)	Normal (predicted)
Attack (actual)	148	2
Normal (actual)	2	355

Table 5 is the performance of the experiment.

From the tables above, the malicious bot traffic detection model showed good performance.

Table 5. The performance of the experiment.

	Accuracy	Precision	Recall
Proposed method	99.21%	98.6%	98.6%

5 Summary

This paper discusses the working principle of web crawler, and systematically analyzes the existing malicious bot traffic detection method, and further puts forward the main research content of this paper: designing malicious bot traffic detection software using support vector machine algorithm, and the model design process The issues of feature selection and parameter optimization are discussed.

This paper implements the development of malicious bot traffic detection software based on linear kernel support vector machine, and completes the functional modules such as preprocessing of web server logs, collection and storage of data sets, and real-time prediction of website traffic.

Due to the lack of actual website log data, this paper uses its own simulated website log data. The malicious bot traffic detection algorithm designed in this paper has obtained ideal results on this data set.

Acknowledgement. This research is supported by National Natural Science Foundation of China (No. 61772162), National Key R&D Program of China (No. 2018YFB0804102), Zhejiang Key R&D Program of China (No. 2018C01088).

References

1. Tan, P.N., Kumar, V.: Discovery of web robot sessions based on their navigational patterns. In: Zhong, N., Liu, J. (eds.) Intelligent Technologies for Information Analysis, pp. 193–222. Springer, Heidelberg (2004). https://doi.org/10.1007/978-3-662-07952-2_9
2. Stassopoulou, A., Dikaiakos, M.D.: Web robot detection: a probabilistic reasoning approach. Comput. Netw. **53**(3), 265–278 (2009)
3. Bomhardt, C., Gaul, W., Schmidt-Thieme, L.: Web robot detection-preprocessing web log files for robot detection. In: Bock, H.H., et al. (eds.) New Developments in Classification and Data Analysis, pp. 113–124. Springer, Heidelberg (2005)
4. Ju, X.: Simulation of web crawler detection algorithm based on hidden Markov model. Comput. Mod. (4), 122–126 (2017)
5. Stevanovic, D., Vlajic, N., An, A.: Unsupervised clustering of Web sessions to detect malicious and non-malicious website users. Procedia Comput. Sci. **5**, 123–131 (2011)
6. Xia, Z.: Adaptive detection method for abnormal traffic based on self-similarity. Comput. Eng. **36**(5), 23 25 (2010)
7. Thatte, G., Mitra, U., Heidemann, J.: Parametric methods for anomaly detection in aggregate traffic. IEEE/ACM Trans. Netw. **19**(2), 512–525 (2011)
8. Zou, J., Li, H.: Detection of anonymous crawler based on website access behavior. Comput. Technol. Dev. **27**(12), 103–107 (2017)
9. Lei, Y.: Network anomaly traffic detection algorithm based on SVM. In: 2017 International Conference on Robots & Intelligent System (ICRIS), Huai'an, pp. 217–220 (2017)

10. He, H., Li, N.: An RBF network approach to flatness pattern recognition based on SVM learning. In: 2006 International Conference on Machine Learning and Cybernetics, Dalian, China, pp. 2959–2962 (2006)
11. Zhao, Z.-D., Lou, Y., Ni, J.-H., Zhang, J.: RBF-SVM and its application on reliability evaluation of electric power system communication network. In: 2009 International Conference on Machine Learning and Cybernetics, Hebei, pp. 1188–1193 (2009)
12. Deng, Q., Cai, A.: SVM-based loss differentiation mechanism in mobile ad hoc networks. In: 2009 Global Mobile Congress, Shanghai, pp. 1–4 (2009)
13. Qiu, G., Liao, L., Wu, Z., Du, Q.: Thunderstorm prediction study based on PCA and least square support vector machine. In: 2011 International Conference on Consumer Electronics, Communications and Networks (CECNet), XianNing, pp. 2828–2831 (2011)

Intrusion Detection Traps within Live Network Environment

Xiaochun Cheng$^{(\boxtimes)}$ and Matus Mihok

Faculty of Science and Technology, Middlesex University, London, UK
xiaochun.cheng@gmail.com, matus.mihok.uk@gmail.com

Abstract. The aim of this project is the design and implementation of the solution able to detect an intruder in the internal network. We advocate that, instead of deploying additional fake systems in the corporate network, the production systems themselves should be instrumented to provide active defense capabilities. The proposed concept of traps can be implemented in any corporate production network, with little upfront work and little maintenance.

Keywords: Active defense · Intrusion detection and prevention system · Network security · Production network · Computer network security · Honeypot · Trap

1 Introduction

As can be seen from the definition of zero-day vulnerability, the attacks that exploit these vulnerabilities are difficult to prevent [1]. Active defence aims to hinder an attacker's progress by design, rather than reactively responding to attack only after its detection. Popular active defence systems include honeypots. Honeypots are fake systems, designed to look like genuine systems, for trapping an attacker and analyzing his observed attack strategy and goals. This paper researches the situation when the attacker managed to penetrate the network, and his activity has not been detected by existing defence and detection mechanisms. Our goal is to detect the attacker in the network as soon as possible, as well as to inform the relevant administrators about such attack. Nowadays, we use honeypots to gain the information about attack techniques we have no prior knowledge about yet.

The goal of honeypots is either to divert the attacker's attention from the actual target or to obtain information about the attacker, attack patterns, such as popular targets and request-response frequency [2]. Honeypots should not be considered as an implementation of a particular problem solving solution, rather than a generic concept [3].

In August 2015, the idea of using honeypots on the internal network was presented by Thinkst during the BlackHat conference. The solution is also offered as an open source package under the name Open canary. However, this is just a service emulation, which falls into the category of low interaction honeypots [4]. Particularly service emulation can be recognised by an attacker, as is shown by several tools on the GitHub [5, 6].

© Springer Nature Switzerland AG 2019
J. Vaidya et al. (Eds.): CSS 2019, LNCS 11983, pp. 77–89, 2019.
https://doi.org/10.1007/978-3-030-37352-8_7

HonSSH is the only currently available up-to-date open-source high-interaction honeypot software. The alternative open-source honeypots such as Honeyd and Honeywall, are either restricted to low- or medium-interaction or out of date and difficult to install on modern Linux distributions [18].

The concept of traps represents real production servers that can be used for performing other tasks. For example, "read the file" trap can be installed on every server deployed within the production environment. However, most important factor will be the correct configuration of such a trap.

Configuring the honeypot, so that the attacker is not able to distinguish a honeypot from a production server, is extremely challenging [7]. Usually, the honeypots that emulate the service can behave differently from real service. Thus honeypots carry unique characteristics. A number of recent researches analyse this problem and introduce the solutions to make honeypots look more like real production systems. However, a big percentage of these solutions are only theoretical and nearly impossible to deploy them into real production environments [7]. Experienced attackers are able to detect both LIHP and HIHP [8]. Reference item [9] introduces a hybrid honeypot framework for improving IDSs to protect organizational networks. The main idea is to deploy LIHP as an emulator of services and operating systems, which directs traffics to HIHP, where attackers engage with the real services. Compared to our solutions, this method lacks the simplicity of implementation to the production environment. [9] does not explain much about alerting functions. Our solution in the form of traps skips the LIHP part of solution in [9], so traps do not need to emulate the services, as they are real services installed on real production servers.

[10] introduces the architecture for active defence. Researchers tried to implement more realistic-looking target and to improve attack analysis. The solution is easy to deploy for active defence on any corporate network, and its advantages include very simple maintenance and deployment. The solution consists of two elements: AHEAD Controller and AHEAD-pot. AHEAD controller includes an administrator interface that communicates with the honeypot via a secure channel. The solution is not able to connect with the already existing alerting system, so installation of the additional controller could lead to creating new vulnerabilities, as a result, more false positive.

None of the research papers we went through meet requirements of the simplicity and availability for our industry case. The existing solutions require installing custom applications, or heavy networking that may not be very feasible for small companies or companies with a small budget on security. The existing solutions may be similar to the concept of traps, but are very far from proposed solution in the sense of simplicity, as traps do not require much of additional maintenance once installed correctly. Every trap alert should mean real intrusion and should be connected to the existing alerting system. For companies with a small budget, it can be secure and easy to outsource the logs analysis task to a third party organization that has better expertise in IDS than IT administrator of the small company.

2   Concept of Traps

We define the trap as a system located on the internal network, which acts as an error/inattention caused by administrators, or an intentionally vulnerable system. However, the trap will not contain any confidential data. The main goal of the trap is to detect the presence of the attacker on the internal network and inform the system administrator about it. As the trap contains false/not confidential data and behaves as a "lowest hanging fruit", the attacker will try to take control over it, and the trap will distract his attention from the real/more valuable target on the network.

The aim of the trap is to identify the attacker's presence while not to arouse attacker's suspicion that it is a defensive mechanism. In this respect, it is important that honeypots are real services. Eventual detection of the honeypots could lead to an attacker's withdrawal or increased carefulness, then he could potentially try to override these security mechanisms.

Traps can be divided into the following three categories:

- Service based – honeypot emulates the service on the internal network, then access to the relevant service will trigger the alarm.
- File based – the system will have files that will be attractive for the attacker to read. Reading or any other manipulation (copy, write, read, delete) of these files will trigger an alarm.
- Data based – In the trap system, there will be false data besides the real data. In particular, this can be implemented in the database system. Operations on such data will trigger the alarm. Using data based trap where an attacker, along with legitimate data, reads false data, should not be a primary detection method. In the case of data based trap, an attacker has already been able to read a legitimate data, so detection comes late. The goal is to detect an attacker as soon as possible and respond appropriately to avoid data manipulation. The concept of data based trap can be another layer of protection, which is useful in the event that an attacker was able to bypass other forms of protection.

2.1   Concept Architecture

The overall solution consists of two main parts, single traps and a central log server that collects logs and generates alarms. The principle of each trap is to produce a detailed log of the event immediately after the trap has been launched by an attacker. This log will be immediately sent to the central log server. Here are accumulated logs from individual traps and generated alarms. These event logs from central log server are sent to Security Information and Event Management (SIEM) where they are visualized and monitored by security analysts. The Trap concept architechture is illustrated in Fig. 1.

2.2   Alerting

As mentioned in the previous section, logs from individual traps are collected at the central log server. This server can be directly on the network with actual traps installed or may be remote. Log transfer is encrypted. We are getting to the issue of alarms

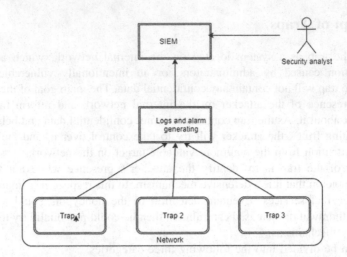

Fig. 1. Trap concept architecture

generating. If the company has its own alerting system, it is advisable to implement the traps alerting directly. Otherwise, we can create a custom tool or use already existing software solution. For this purpose, Elasticsearch Logstash Kibana (ELK) has been used [11]. It is important to note that an alarm created by a trap means a real penetration, in contrast to generic IDS alarms that can be false positive. Therefore, this alarm cannot be overlooked. If a company has its own Security Operation Centre (SOC), then these alerts must be set to high priority. If the processes are not set up, it is important to highlight this alarm via communication channels such as automatic phone calls or text messages. When an attacker launches the trap, the most important is to generate an alarm as soon as possible. When attacker manipulates a trap, additional logs are created. This raises the question whether these logs generate additional alarms or not. The solution can be the combining of multiple logs created at a short time to one alert.

2.3 Traps Description

For this research, we have created five different traps that were installed on the internal network used for functionality testing of the traps.

(1) **SSH Trap**

- Form – trap is in the form of service.
- What problem does it solve – detecting the attacker on the internal network that is trying to use the SSH service.
- How it works – a device that contains the OpenSSH service is connected to the internal network. This service deliberately contains logins with weak passwords that are easily guessed by the attacker. These logins are not normally used, but login attempts, whether successful or not, indicate an attacker in the network and trigger an alarm.

- Implementation details at a glance – we used Linux host machine. As we assume the attacker logs on the server, his rights are limited to the minimum. We will use chroot jail and whitelist commands that can be used in bash.

(2) **SAMBA Trap**

- Form – trap is in the form of service.
- What problem does it solve – detecting the attacker on the internal network that is trying to transfer data using the Samba service.
- How it works – the device that includes the real Samba service is connected to the internal network. This server contains users with weak passwords for Samba service. Any attempts to data transfer with a given user trigger an alarm. The shared files themselves do not contain any valuable information.
- Implementation details at a glance – we used Linux host machine. An attacker cannot log on to the server, the only thing he can do is to use the Samba service.

(3) **MySQL Trap**

- Form – trap is in the form of service.
- What problem does it solve – detecting the attacker on the internal network that is trying to manipulate data in the database.
- How it works – the device that contains exclusively false data is connected to the internal network. However, these data should be as close as possible to real data in order to avoid a suspicion from the attacker. This service deliberately contains logins with weak passwords that are easily guessed by an attacker, or password-free logins. Reading this data, manipulation of the database, or any manipulation of the user, indicates the presence of the attacker and triggers the alarm.
- Implementation details at a glance – the database server runs on the Linux platform. The attacker can manipulate only the database. We expect the attacker to gain root access to the database if it does not get it directly via the root user. Eventual deletion of the database is no problem as the database does not contain real data.

(4) **"Read the File" Trap**

- Form – trap is in the form of data.
- What problem does it solve – detecting an attacker on the internal network that is reading data
- How it works – on the internal network are stored files with an appealing name, for example, "backup", that do not contain actual valuable data.
- Implementation details at a glance – this type of trap is deployed on production servers. The inotify is used on Linux platform. This service tracks files or folders, and the log is created when manipulating them. If we want to get more detailed information than the user who manipulated the file, we will use auditd.

(5) **Port Scanning Detection Trap**

- Form – trap is in the form of service.
- What problem does it solve – detecting an attacker that is scanning the network

- How it works – on the internal network is deployed a server that is configured to create logs for every attempt to establish a network connection.
- Implementation details at a glance – this type of trap is deployed in a production environment as a server that does not contain any sensitive data. The purpose of this server is to be scanned by an attacker. The server has no open ports except the port for SSH. Ping is achievable, because nmap first ping a host, and then it scans hosts. If the server did not have ping enabled, it would look invisible for an attacker, and the server would not be scanned.

3 Implementation of the Proposed Traps

In this section, we present an experiment network topology and traps implementation details. In particular, we describe how our trap concept integrates other tools and services to help protect all the systems present in a typical production environment.

The testing environment was implemented in a virtual environment on the VMWare ESXi 6.5.0 platform [12]. Network topology consists of five networks segments that are located on one virtual switch. Of these five subnetworks, four correspond to the typical company network architecture. The fifth subnet - log-net, is created to collect logs from traps located in each network segment centrally. As a router, we used Ubuntu server that contains six network interfaces. The topology is illustrated in Fig. 2.

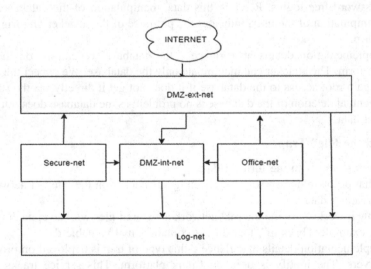

Fig. 2. Network security zones

We have deployed the traps in the test environment. Each trap in the form of service represented a custom server. The traps in the form of data are implemented directly into production servers.

We created and implemented five different traps and deployed them within the experimental production environment. Single traps were deployed as follows.

(1) "Read the File" Trap

While implementing "Read the File" trap, we used the Inotify subsystem, which offers file access monitoring [13]. This allows us to track specific files or entire directories. It is possible to modify created logs into the appropriate format. In the/tmp directory we created the backup.tar.gz file. Inotify has been set to monitor any access to this file. An alternative to this solution is to use the auditd subsystem that provides more detailed information about the event. However, it is not suitable for alerting as it requires logs pre-processing.

Logs sending to the central server is done using Filebeat, which is configured to send the log file to a centrallog server [14].

(2) Port Scanning Detection Trap

Port scanning detection is based on the firewall's ability to identify attempts to establish a connection on ports. We have set the firewall so that it also logs unsuccessful attempts to communicate. By such a configuration, we will log all events from firewall to the syslog. To evaluate these logs, we used the psad tool. It is necessary to set the psad log directory and set the port range threshold to 4 (or more) this means the minimum number of ports that must be scanned for the record to occur. Update the psad pattern database to correctly recognise the known types of scans.

Logs sending to the central server is done using Filebeat, which is configured similarly to the previous trap.

(3) SSH Trap

We installed the SSH server using apt-get install openssh-server command. We created a user with easily guessable password. Since we want to attacker log in through this account, we need to set his user rights. It is important to limit the user rights to the minimum by chroot jail [15]. Logs sending to the central server is done using Filebeat, which is configured similarly to the previous trap.

(4) SAMBA Trap

We installed the Samba service using the apt-get install samba command [16]. Then opened the /etc./samba/smb.conf configuration file and find the log level in it and set the value to 2. This determines the Samba logging level, with the lowest value being 0 and the highest being 10. We also need to modify the log file line to /var/log/samba/trap.log to determine where the logs should be stored. By default, Samba uses a security mode user, meaning clients must enter a name and password for the shared folder. We will create a user on the server, called deploy, and set a strong password. We also set a different password for the user with smbpasswd -a smbuser command. This password is deliberately weak because we want the attacker to come and log in with this password.

Logs sending to the central server is done using Filebeat, which is configured similarly to the previous trap.

(5) **MySQL Trap**

We installed the mysql server using the apt-get install mysql-server. During installation, we were prompted to enter a password for the root user. Open the /etc./mysql/ mysql.conf configuration file and find the *Logging and Replication section. We changed the default location where MySQL stores the logs by modifying general_log_file to /var/log/mysql/trap.log. After that, we set general_log to 1. To prevent the database from being empty, it is advisable to create database content or download available database samples from the internet. It is important to use a database that contains unimportant data but has an appealing name.

Logs sending to the central server is done using Filebeat, which is configured similarly to the previous trap.

Log Server, Logs Collection and Visualization

The purpose of the log server is to collect the logs from the individual traps, process the information correctly and visualize it.

The aim is to continuously collect logs from all traps using a secure communication channel and process them in a suitable form. For this purpose, we used Logstash as a server part that awaits and processes logs. As a client part, we used Filebeat, which is configured to send logs to the central log server, on which listens Logstash. The communication between the client and the server side is encrypted and runs through the SSL protocol [11]. The process of the log sending to the central log server is illustrated in Fig. 3.

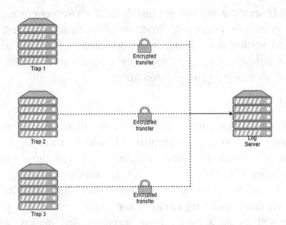

Fig. 3. Diagram representing the log sending to the central log server

Log processing takes place immediately after Logstash received a log, where this log is parsed by a filter. Processed data are stored in the Elasticsearch in JSON format, where they are easily searchable. For Logstash configuration we used the grok parser to

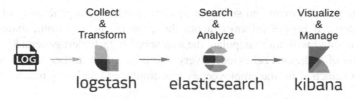

Fig. 4. ELK stack log processing [11]

identify the logs from individual traps. Alarm generating is based on the correct setting of a filter for acquired logs. This means that the logs displayed in the visualization are alarms. The process of the log is illustrated in Fig. 4.

The method of alarm generating from gathered information may vary, as companies use their own alert system. Therefore, it is advisable to create rules in an existing system that will generate alarms from trap logs.

The visualization is done using Kibana, which displays data from the Elasticsearch. Due to well-processed data is a possible quick orientation in logs as well as search by keywords [11].

We have demonstrated the implementation of the entire solution on the Ubuntu (Linux) operating system, but it is possible to perform an equivalent solution on other operating systems such as Solaris, BSD and Windows. In the case of Windows, an alternative to the Inotify subsystem is FindFirstChangeNotification [17]. Port scan detection can be performed using the Windows Firewall configuration to log all attempts to connect and subsequently generate alerts. In the case of traps in the form of service, it is possible to apply the same principles for MySQL traps, and for Samba is best to use native solutions with a high logging rate. Trap in the form of SSH service can also be implemented in the Windows environment. In older versions of Windows, SSH has not been preinstalled but could be installed, in the newer versions it is a common service.

4 False Positive and False Negative Errors

Traps in the form of service are deployed as custom servers on the production environment. The correct installation of the traps will avoid false positive generation because the trap servers will not be used as machines that will perform the same tasks as non-trap servers. The traps will be installed on these servers, and only necessary number of people will be informed about the configurations and purpose of the machines. For example, we have got a server with SAMBA trap installed, and this server will be waiting for the attacker's actions, in this case, attempt to login to Samba service and transfer the files. Employees and users of the internal network do now have a reason to scan a network and try to login to the Samba service on the server. In the case where some employee will try to do this, an alert will be generated in exactly same way as the alert of the attacker that was able to penetrate into the production network.

Trap in the form of data can be installed on any production server, even the machine that is daily used by the employees. Only manipulating the trap file will generate the alert, so to avoid the false positive detection we have to use the files that are: not stored in the Desktop directory, not in directories that are often accessed by the user.

Proper trap deployment and sufficient awareness will avoid generating of the false negative alarms. If people informed about the traps (security, admin, manager) will know the rules and will not manipulate the trap servers, each alert generated will mean real detection of malicious behaviour. Every alarm has to be further analyzed, even in case of trap launched by the employee, as this employee can be an internal threat.

5 Discussion on the Solution

Traps in the form of data are simple and do not require a lot of resources. It is, therefore, possible to deploy a number of such files on the production servers. It is not advisable to set up the trap files as monitored files, which are used and regularly accessed by legitimate system services, which could generate false positives.

Using LIHP on the internal network also makes sense, because we only need one alert to detect the attacker. This alert can be generated during first interaction with a honeypot. But the sophisticated attacker can identify and avoid the honeypot. In this research, we want to prevent this. The aim is to create a solution that would not be distinguished from a real service. We have achieved the goal because the traps represent actual services. As a result of this effort, it is possible to catch an attacker, and he will not even know that he has been caught.

When deploying a solution to the production environment, it is necessary to develop a documentation that will include details on how to deploy the solution and who will manage it. Ideally, the least people should know about a trap implementation. However, somebody has to know about it. This raises the question of the extent to which this solution is concealed in order to have an effect on potential intruders who are partly familiar with the network architecture. The case that an external company performs a security audit of the production environment where the traps are installed occurs a problem, should we share the traps description and location to such a company? This information is very sensitive, and its disclosure can potentially reduce the effectiveness of the solution. Although the attacker may have information about the existence of traps, it is very unlikely that he would be able to circumvent it and, moreover, it would be difficult for him to distinguish the trap from the real service, since the traps are designed precisely for such purpose. The solution would not fulfil its purpose if the attacker know exactly the architecture of the entire network and the exact distribution of the traps.

The ability to protect against internal attackers is based on the use of the segregation of duties principle. This principle is deployed where more than one employees are required for the work. One employee should not have all the necessary rights to perform an attack and to destroy all the tracks successfully. This principle may not be implementable if the network architecture is improperly designed.

A. Process

For the early detection of the attacker and subsequent response of the defence solution, we need more than just technical part of the solution. An important element is also the process part. It is crucial for competent administrator to monitor the alarms, who need adequate priority to respond appropriately. If IT manager checks email only during working hours, it is advisable to use 24/7 real time communication channels such as an SMS message or an automatic call because an attack can occur at any time.

B. Implementation
The solution can be implemented in autonomous way. Many companies use monitoring and alert systems. It is, therefore, appropriate to link existing alert solutions with traps to unify the alert reporting.

C. Traps' advantages
The main advantage of traps is that they are easy, fast to implement and do not require a lot of extra resources, so they are inexpensive to operate. As a result, the trap solution is feasible for small companies. The trap solution can be deployed both in the virtual environment and in the physical environment. If traps are correctly deployed to the environment, the solution can provide a high level of precision and a low false positive rate to reveal the existence of attacker. If a company that wants to use a trap solution does not have its own SOC, it is possible to use an autonomous solution, and the process can be outsourced. The trap solution can provide protection against the internal attackers.

D. Traps' disadvantages
Every deployed trap server represents management costs and potential security risks. There is still the possibility that the attacker may bypass all the traps, although it is very unlikely. In case of incorrect deployment, the trap solution can generate false positives.

6 Conclusion

The number of attacks increases with time as well as their sophistication. The existence of zero-day vulnerability challenges security experts. In this research project, we tackle the situation when the attacker manages to penetrate the network and our goal is to detect the attacker within the network, and inform timely the responsible administrator.

The aim of the project is to investigate the solution for attacker detection based on the honeypots. On the basis of the information gained from the relevant research papers and actual experiments, we have proposed a solution in the form of the trap. We have defined the trap as a system located on the internal network, which looks like an inattention caused by the administrator, or a vulnerable service for attackers. In the practical part of the project, we designed and implemented the traps. We have created an environment architecture and analyzed attack scenarios. Subsequently, we tested the concept of the traps in the test environment, and we evaluated the results. The trap concept has proven to be successful and able to detect an attacker when properly deployed. It is necessary to emphasize that for the correct functioning of the solution, the technical part is not the only factor, and the process is equally important.

One purpose of this research is to detect the attacker on the internal network. Benefits of the solution include that traps are simple, fast to implement, inexpensive to operate, and do not require a lot of resources. That is the reason why they are suitable for small companies that cannot afford complex or expensive commercial solutions.

When properly deployed, the solution provides a high level of accuracy of detection and generate only a few false positives.

Future researches include refinement of the proposed solution, in order to create a comprehensive tool for detection of intruders on the internal network environment.

With 5G communications and Internet of Things deployed for smart home, intelligent transportation, intelligent building, smart city; Internet of Things security researches [19–24] become important; we would like gear our solution for the security of emerging Internet of Things.

References

1. Bilge, L., Dumitras, T.: Before we knew it: an empirical study of zero-day attacks in the real world. In: Proceedings of the 2012 ACM Conference on Computer and Communications Security, Raleigh, North Carolina, USA, 16–18 October 2012, pp. 833–844 (2012)
2. Pomsathit, A.: Performance analysis of IDS with honey pot on new media broadcasting. In: 2017 International Conference on Circuits, Devices and Systems, 5–8 September 2017, pp. 201–204 (2017)
3. Nawrocki, M., Wahlisch, M., Schmidt, T., Keil, C., Schonfelder, J.: A Survey on Honeypot Software and Data Analysis, arXiv preprint, arXiv:1608.06249 (2016). https://arxiv.org/pdf/1608.06249.pdf. Accessed 12 June 2019
4. Opencanary.readthedocs.io: OpenCanary — OpenCanary 0.1 documentation (2019). https://opencanary.readthedocs.io/en/latest. Accessed 12 June 2019
5. Morris, A.: Kippo detect (2019). https://github.com/andrew-morris/kippo_detect. Accessed 12 June 2019
6. Wolfvan: Cowrie Detect (2019). GitHub. https://github.com/wolfvan/Cowrie_Detect. Accessed 12 June 2019
7. Campbell, R., Padayachee, K., Masombuka, T.: A survey of honeypot research: trends and opportunities. In: 2015 10th International Conference for Internet Technology and Secured Transactions (ICITST), pp. 208–212 (2015)
8. Wafi, H., Fiade, A., Hakiem, N., Bahaweres, R.: Implementation of a modern security systems honeypot: honey network on wireless networks. In: 2017 International Young Engineers Forum (YEF-ECE), pp. 91–96 (2017)
9. Artail, H., Safa, H., Sraj, M., Kuwatly, I., Al-Masri, Z.: A hybrid honeypot framework for improving intrusion detection systems in protecting organizational networks. Comput. Secur. 25(4), 274–288 (2006)
10. Gaspari, F., Jajodia, S., Mancini, L.V., Panico, A.: AHEAD: a new architecture for active defense. In: Proceedings of the 2016 ACM Workshop on Automated Decision Making for Active Cyber Defense, Vienna, Austria, 24 October 2016, pp. 11–16 (2016). ISBN 978-1-4503-4566-8
11. Elastic.co: Powering Data Search, Log Analysis, Analytics | Elastic (2019). https://ww.elastic.co/products. Accessed 12 June 2019
12. VMWare (2019). https://www.vmware.com/products/esxi-and-esx.html. Accessed 12 June 2019
13. Ibm.com: Monitor file system activity with inotify (2019). https://www.ibm.com/developerworks/library/l-ubuntu-inotify/index.html. Accessed 12 June 2019
14. Elastic.co: Filebeat: Lightweight Log Analysis & Elasticsearch | Elastic (2019). https://www.elastic.co/products/beats/filebeat. Accessed 12 June 2019

15. Kaur, N., Singh, M.: Improved file system security through restrictive access. In: 2016 International Conference on Inventive Computation Technologies (ICICT), vol. 3 (2016). https://doi.org/10.1109/inventive.2016.7830207
16. Gibbs, M.: Sharing with samba. Netw. World **20**(30), 28 (2003). https://www.networkworld.com/article/2335460/sharing-with-samba.html. Accessed 12 June 2019
17. Msdn.microsoft.com: FindFirstChangeNotification function (Windows) (2019). https://msdn.microsoft.com/enus/library/windows/desktop/aa364417(v=vs.85).aspx. Accessed 12 June 2019
18. Stockman, M., Rein, R., Heile, A.: An open-source honeynet system to study system banner message effects on hackers. In: Proceedings of the 4th Annual ACM Conference on Research in Information Technology, Chicago, Illinois, USA, 30 September–03 October 2015, pp. 19–22 (2015). https://doi.org/10.1145/2808062.2808069. ISBN 978-1-4503-3836-3
19. Gao, C., Lv, S., Wei, Y., Wang, Z., Liu, Z., Cheng, X.: An effective searchable symmetric encryption with enhanced security for mobile devices. IEEE Access **6**, 38860–38869 (2018). ISSN 2169-3536
20. Wang, C., Zhao, Z., Gong, L., Zhu, L., Liu, Z., Cheng, X.: A distributed anomaly detection system for in-vehicle network using HTM. IEEE Access **6**(1), 9091–9098 (2018)
21. Wang, C., Zhu, L., Gong, L., Zhao, Z., Yang, L., Liu, Z., Cheng, X.: Accurate sybil attack detection based on fine-grained physical channel information. Sensors **18**(3), 878 (2018). ISSN 1424-8220
22. Dinculeană, D., Cheng, X.: Vulnerabilities and limitations of MQTT protocol used between IoT devices. Appl. Sci. **9**(5), 848 (2019)
23. Shi F, Chen Z, Cheng X: Behaviour modelling and individual recognition of sonar transmitter for secure communication in UASNs. IEEE Access (2019). https://doi.org/10.1109/access.2019.2923059. Print ISSN 2169-3536, Online ISSN 2169-3536
24. Men, J., Xu, G., Han, Z., Sun, Z., Zhou, X., Lian, W., Cheng, X.: Finding sands in the eyes: vulnerabilities discovery in IoT with EUFuzzer on human machine interface. IEEE Access **7**, 103751–103759 (2019)

System Security

A Confidence-Guided Anomaly Detection Approach Jointly Using Multiple Machine Learning Algorithms

Xueshuo Xie, Zongming Jin, Qingqi Han, Shenwei Huang, and Tao Li[✉]

College of Computer Science, Nankai University, Tianjin, China
litao@nankai.edu.cn
http://ics.nankai.edu.cn

Abstract. Log data contains very rich and valuable information that records system states and behavior, which can be used to diagnose system failures. Anomaly detection from large-scale log data plays a key role in building secure and trustworthy systems. Anomaly detection model based on machine learning has achieved good results in practical applications. However, logs generated by modern large-scale distributed systems are more complex than ever before in terms of data size and variety. Therefore, the traditional single-machine learning anomaly detection model faces the model aging problem. We design an anomaly detection model that combines multiple machine learning algorithms. By using a conformal prediction, we can calculate the confidence of each algorithm for each log to be detected and use statistical analysis to tag them with a trusted label. The approach was tested on the public HDFS_100k log dataset, and the results show that our model is more accurate.

Keywords: Confidence · Anomaly detection · Statistical analysis

1 Introduction

Log data is a widely-available resource in all systems, contains very rich and valuable information, and faithfully records system state and behavior. Modern large-scale distributed systems generate a large volume of log records all the time, which can be used to discover and identify system anomalies [15,17,22], trace system behavior and malicious attacks. Anomaly detection [4] from large-scale log data plays a key role in building secure and trustworthy systems. Real-time anomaly detection helps administrators quickly locate and resolve accident issues. But traditional anomaly detection methods often use of keyword search or regular expression match, which often requires domain knowledge and low-effective manual inspection. Therefore, efficient and real-time log-based anomaly detection models are of value in academic and practical applications.

Anomaly detection model based on machine learning has achieved good results in academic research and industry practices. Researchers have designed

© Springer Nature Switzerland AG 2019
J. Vaidya et al. (Eds.): CSS 2019, LNCS 11983, pp. 93–100, 2019.
https://doi.org/10.1007/978-3-030-37352-8_8

many state-of-the-art log-based anomaly detection models using machine learning, which consists of supervised learning models and unsupervised learning models. The supervised models include: Logistic regression (LR) [1], Decision Tree [5], Support Vector Machine (SVM) [11]; and the unsupervised models include: LOF [3], One-class SVM [18], Isolation Forest [13], Principal Component Analysis (PCA) [21], Invariants Mining [14], Clustering [12], DeepLog [16], AutoEncoder [2]. To bridge the gap between the academic and industry practices, the authors give an evaluation study on some anomaly detection models in accuracy and efficiency in [8].

However, logs generated by modern large-scale distributed systems are more complex than ever before in terms of data size and variety. Log-based anomaly detection models that are built on previously logs often make poor performance when faced with new logs - a phenomenon known as concept drift (or model aging) in [9]. Anomaly detection models based on single-machine learning often use periodically retraining when facing the concept drift, but this can lead to untrusted model performance over a while.

To reduce the interference of the concept drift problem on the anomaly detection model, we design an anomaly detection model that combines multiple machine learning algorithms. By using the conformal prediction [19] method, we can calculate the confidence of each algorithm for each log to be detected and use statistical analysis to tag them with a trusted label. The approach was tested on the public HDFS_100k log dataset, and the results show that our model is more accurate.

In summary, the main contributions of this paper are the following:

- We design a confidence-guided anomaly detection model jointly using multiple machine learning algorithms, which can more effectively improve the model accuracy and reduce the interference of the concept drift problem than single-machine learning models.
- We use the conformal prediction method to calculate the new logs' confidence of each algorithm, which can give the new logs a trusted label by statistical analysis. Through tested on the public HDFS_100k log dataset, our approach is more accurate.

The remainder of this paper is organized as follows: Sect. 2 gives a problem statement on the log-based anomaly detection model's concept drift problem. Section 3 describes our confidence-guided anomaly detection model jointly using multiple machine learning algorithms. We report the experiment results in Sect. 4. Finally, Sect. 5 concludes the paper.

2   Problem-Statement

Concept drift [10] is known as the target concept in a machine-learning task that might change over time in terms of distribution, description, properties, etc. In [6,20], the authors also conclude that the data distribution changes make the old data-based model non-conformity with the new data, and regular updating of the model is necessary, so concept drift primarily refers to the relationship between the input data and the target variable changes over time.

As we all know, logs generated by modern large-scale distributed systems are more complex than ever before in terms of data size and variety. In the real world, logs are often not stable but change with time. Due to the changes in log data, log-based anomaly detection models that are built on previously logs often make poor performance when faced with new logs - a phenomenon known as concept drift (or model aging) in [10]. Anomaly detection models based on single-machine learning often use periodically retraining when facing the concept drift, but this can lead to untrusted model performance over a while.

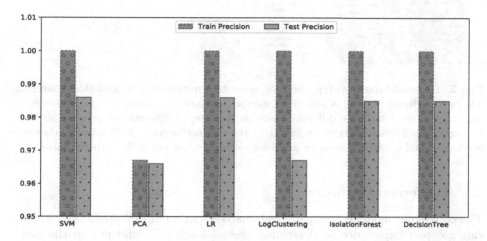

Fig. 1. The concept drift of several different anomaly detection models based on single-machine learning on the HDFS log.

Figure 1 shows the concept drift of several different anomaly detection models based on single-machine learning on the HDFS log. Due to changes between the training log and the test log, the prediction accuracy of the model is reduced and the performance of the model becomes poor. The root cause of concept drift is that traditional machine learning algorithms are often based on "yes" or "no" (either 0 or 1) when making decisions, without considering the relationship between new data and previous data. For example, SVM only checks the side of the hyperplane where the object lies while ignoring its distance from the hyperplane.

3 Methodology

In Fig. 2, we give a detailed description of the model: preprocess, non-conformity measure, statistical analysis. By using the conformal prediction method, we can calculate the confidence of each algorithm for each log to be detected and use statistical analysis to tag them with a trusted label.

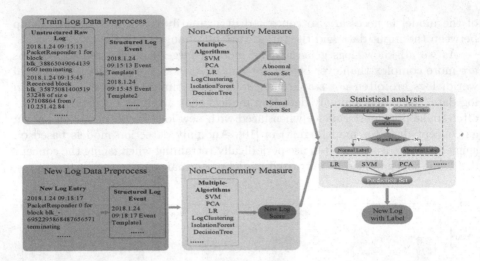

Fig. 2. The model consists of: preprocess, non-conformity measure, statistical analysis. The unstructured raw log is processed into a structured log event in the preprocessing stage; then a multiple different machine learning algorithms are selected as the non-conformity score function to calculate the non-conformity; finally, the conformal prediction and statistical analysis are used to tag the test log with a trusted label.

3.1 Conformal Prediction

The core of our model is the statistical analysis and conformal prediction, which can use past experience to determine precise levels of confidence in the new prediction, so we can use the conformal prediction [9,19] method to detect new log messages and get a confidence result.

Non-conformity Measure: In the beginning, we can choose some of multiple machine learning algorithms as non-conformity measure to calculate non-conformity scores, which can be used to measure the difference between the new log and a group training log with same labels. The real-valued scoring function is denoted as:

$$\alpha_{l^*} = A_D(L, l^*) \tag{1}$$

When give a new log message l^*, it can outputs a prediction score $A_D(L, l^*)$, where D is the training log messages and L is the group log with same label.

Conformal Prediction: Now, we can calculate the non-conformity score set by using Eq. (1). For the training log data, we can obtain the normal and abnormal non-conformity score set for each algorithm. For the detection log entry, we also can obtain one non-conformity score by each algorithm. Then, we can use the score to compute a notion of similarity through p-values. For a set of training logs K, the p-value $p_{l^*}^T$ for a new log l^* is the proportion of logs in class K that are at least as dissimilar to other logs in T as l^*. The computation of p-value for the new log is denoted as:

$$\forall i \in K, \alpha_i = A_D\left(T \backslash l_i, l_i\right) \tag{2}$$

$$p_{l^*}^T = \frac{\#\{i = 1, ..., n | \alpha_i \geq \alpha_{l^*}\}}{|K|} \tag{3}$$

When the new detection log message comes, we can calculate a p-value set (p-value with the normal label and p-value with the abnormal label) by the former Eq. (3), which can be used for anomaly detection based on statistical analysis.

Statistical Analysis: By using the p_value sets, we can obtain a label of the detection log message and calculate the algorithm's credibility (the p_value corresponding to the label) and the algorithm's confidence (1 - another p_value). The computation of credibility and confidence is denoted as:

$$
\begin{aligned}
if \quad & (p\_value\_N >= p\_value\_A): \\
& A_{Cred}(l) = p\_value\_N \\
& A_{Con}(l) = (1 - p\_value\_A) \\
else: & \\
& A_{Cred}(l) = p\_value\_A \\
& A_{Con}(l) = (1 - p\_value\_N)
\end{aligned}
\tag{4}
$$

The algorithm's confidence tells how certain or how committed the label given by the algorithm. Now, we will obtain a prediction set, which consists of multiple labels with confidence given by each algorithm for each detected log message. By setting a significance level, if the prediction set all consists of the normal label, our model will give a normal label for the detection log message; else that will give an abnormal label.

4 Evaluation

In this section, we evaluate our anomaly detection model from Precision Rate, Recall Rate, and F_measure aspects. By testing on public HDFS_100k dataset [7], the results show our model is more accurate than the single-machine learning anomaly detection model. Also, our model jointly using multiple algorithms can tag a label with confidence for the detected log messages.

4.1 Experimental Dataset

In Table 1, we give a summary of the dataset [7], which used for testing the accuracy of our model and the single-machine learning anomaly detection model. HDFS system logs record a unique block ID for each block operation, which can be utilized to slice the logs into a set of log sequences. HDFS dataset contains 104815 log messages and 7940 log sequences (separated by the block ID). In order to test the machine learning based model, we use 3969 sequences for training the model (3813 normal sequences and 156 abnormal sequences) and 3971 sequences for testing (3814 normal sequences and 157 abnormal sequences).

Table 1. Summary of dataset.

System	Total log messages	Total log sequences	Label	Train	Test
HDFS	104815	7940	Normal	3813	3814
			Abnormal	156	157

4.2   Case Study

In this case, we jointly using four machine learning algorithms (SVM, PCA, LR, and LogClustering) and set the significance level as 0.5, and then compared to the four single-machine learning anomaly detection model [7] in Precision Rate, Recall Rate, and F_measure.

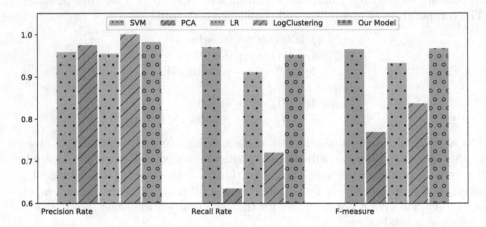

Fig. 3. The comparison of our model and the single-machine learning anomaly detection model [7] in Precision Rate, Recall Rate, and F_measure.

In Fig. 3, it clearly indicates that our model is more accurate and performance balance in Precision Rate, Recall Rate, and F_measure. Our model achieves 0.982 in Precision Rate (higher than SVM, PCA, and LR), 0.952 in Recall Rate (higher than PCA, LR, and LogClustering), and 0.967 in F_measure (the highest). In Precision Rate, although our model is slightly lower than log clustering, it only achieves 0.720 in Recall Rate and 0.837 in F_measure, which is lower than our model. In Recall Rate, our model is slightly lower than SVM, but better in Precision Rate and F_measure. Therefore, our confidence-guided anomaly detection model jointly using multiple machine learning algorithms is superior to the single-machine learning anomaly detection model in accuracy and performance.

5   Conclusion

Log-based anomaly detection models have led to extensive research and play a key role in building secure and trusted systems. Due to the complex of the log data size and variety, the single-machine learning anomaly detection model faces the concept drift (or model aging) problem. By using the conformal prediction method, we design an anomaly detection model that combines multiple machine learning algorithms, which achieves more accurate and performance balance in Precision Rate, Recall Rate, and F measure. Next, we will apply our model to the actual environment, which can better reflect the performance.

Acknowledgment. This work is partially supported by the National Key Research and Development Program of China (No. 2018YFB2100300, 2016YFC0400709), the National Natural Science Foundation (No. 61872200), the Natural Science Foundation of Tianjin (18YFYZCG00060) and Nankai University (91922299).

References

1. Bodik, P., Goldszmidt, M., Fox, A., Woodard, D.B., Andersen, H.: Fingerprinting the datacenter: automated classification of performance crises. In: Proceedings of the 5th European Conference on Computer Systems, pp. 111–124. ACM (2010)
2. Borghesi, A., Bartolini, A., Lombardi, M., Milano, M., Benini, L.: Anomaly detection using autoencoders in high performance computing systems (2018)
3. Breunig, M.M., Kriegel, H.P., Ng, R.T., Sander, J.: LOF: identifying density-based local outliers. In: ACM Sigmod Record, vol. 29, pp. 93–104. ACM (2000)
4. Chandola, V., Banerjee, A., Kumar, V.: Anomaly detection:a survey. ACM Comput. Surv. **41**(3), 1–58 (2009)
5. Chen, M., Zheng, A.X., Lloyd, J., Jordan, M.I., Brewer, E.: Failure diagnosis using decision trees. In: 2004 Proceedings of the International Conference on Autonomic Computing, pp. 36–43. IEEE (2004)
6. Gama, J., Žliobaitė, I., Bifet, A., Pechenizkiy, M., Bouchachia, A.: A survey on concept drift adaptation. ACM Comput. Surv. (CSUR) **46**(4), 44 (2014)
7. He, P., Zhu, J., He, S.: Loglizer (2016). https://github.com/logpai/loglizer
8. He, S., Zhu, J., He, P., Lyu, M.R.: Experience report: system log analysis for anomaly detection. In: 2016 IEEE 27th International Symposium on Software Reliability Engineering (ISSRE), pp. 207–218. IEEE (2016)
9. Jordaney, R., et al.: Transcend: detecting concept drift in malware classification models. In: Proceedings of the 26TH USENIX Security Symposium (USENIX Security 2017), pp. 625–642. USENIX Association (2017)
10. Li, S.Z., Jain, A. (eds.): Concept Drift, p. 190. Springer, Boston (2009). https://doi.org/10.1007/978-0-387-73003-5
11. Liang, Y., Zhang, Y., Xiong, H., Sahoo, R.: Failure prediction in IBM BlueGene/L event logs. In: Seventh IEEE International Conference on Data Mining (ICDM 2007), pp. 583–588. IEEE (2007)
12. Lin, Q., Zhang, H., Lou, J.G., Yu, Z., Chen, X.: Log clustering based problem identification for online service systems. In: IEEE/ACM International Conference on Software Engineering Companion (2016)
13. Liu, F.T., Ting, K.M., Zhou, Z.H.: Isolation forest. In: 2008 Eighth IEEE International Conference on Data Mining, pp. 413–422. IEEE (2008)
14. Lou, J.G., Fu, Q., Yang, S., Xu, Y., Li, J.: Mining invariants from console logs for system problem detection. In: Proceedings of USENIX ATC, pp. 231–244 (2010)

15. Makanju, A., Zincir-Heywood, A.N., Milios, E.E.: Fast entropy based alert detection in super computer logs. In: 2010 International Conference on Dependable Systems and Networks Workshops (DSN-W), pp. 52–58. IEEE (2010)
16. Min, D., Li, F., Zheng, G., Srikumar, V.: Deeplog: anomaly detection and diagnosis from system logs through deep learning. In: ACM SIGSAC Conference on Computer & Communications Security (2017)
17. Oprea, A., Li, Z., Yen, T.F., Chin, S.H., Alrwais, S.: Detection of early-stage enterprise infection by mining large-scale log data. In: 2015 45th Annual IEEE/IFIP International Conference on Dependable Systems and Networks (DSN), pp. 45–56. IEEE (2015)
18. Schölkopf, B., Platt, J.C., Shawe-Taylor, J., Smola, A.J., Williamson, R.C.: Estimating the support of a high-dimensional distribution. Neural Comput. **13**(7), 1443–1471 (2001)
19. Shafer, G., Vovk, V.: A tutorial on conformal prediction. J. Mach. Learn. Res. **9**(Mar), 371–421 (2008)
20. Tsymbal, A.: The problem of concept drift: definitions and related work. Comput. Sci. Dept. Trinity College Dublin **106**(2), 58 (2004)
21. Xu, W., Huang, L., Fox, A., Patterson, D., Jordan, M.: Largescale system problem detection by mining console logs. In: Proceedings of SOSP 2009 (2009)
22. Xu, W., Huang, L., Fox, A., Patterson, D., Jordan, M.I.: Detecting large-scale system problems by mining console logs. In: Proceedings of the ACM SIGOPS 22nd Symposium on Operating Systems Principles, pp. 117–132. ACM (2009)

Boosting Training for PDF Malware Classifier via Active Learning

Xinxin Wang[1]([⊠]) [ID], Yuanzhang Li[1], Quanxin Zhang[1],
and Xiaohui Kuang[2]

[1] School of Computer Science and Technology, Beijing Institute of Technology,
Beijing 100081, China
wang_xinxin2016@outlook.com,
{popular, zhangqx}@bit.edu.cn
[2] National Key Laboratory of Science and Technology
on Information System Security, Beijing 100081, China
xiaohui_kuang@163.com

Abstract. Malicious code has been a serious threat in the field of network security. PDF (Portable Document Format) is a widely used file format, and often utilized as a vehicle for malicious behavior. In this paper, machine learning algorithm will be used to detect malicious PDF document, and evaluated on experimental data. The main work of this paper is to implement a malware detection method, which utilizes static pre-processing and machine learning algorithm for classification. During the period of classifying, the differences in structure and content between malicious and benign PDF files will be taken as the classification basis. What's more, we boost training for the PDF malware classifier via active learning based on mutual agreement analysis. The detector is retrained according to the truth value of the uncertain samples, which can not only reduce the training time consumption of the detector, but also improve the detection performance.

Keywords: PDF · Malware detection · Information security · Active learning

1 Introduction

Since the birth of personal computer, malicious code has always been a problem in the field of information security. PDF file format is widely used in commercial office due to its high efficiency, stability and interactivity. With the development of non-executable file attack technology and attack methods like APT (Advanced Persistent Threat), the security of PDF has been seriously threatened, and malicious PDF files constitute the most studied infection vectors in adversarial environments [1, 2].

In recent years, researchers have developed many machine learning based systems to detect various attack types related to PDF file. Malicious PDF file detection technology can be divided into detection technology based on static analysis, detection technology based on dynamic analysis and detection technology based on both dynamic and static analysis [3].

J. Vaidya et al. (Eds.): CSS 2019, LNCS 11983, pp. 101–110, 2019.
https://doi.org/10.1007/978-3-030-37352-8_9

Our contributions are summarized as follows:

1. A PDF malware detector, which utilizes active learning based on mutual agreement analysis to augment the training set and improve the classifier constantly.
2. An experimental evaluation of the detector above, performed on nearly 15000 PDF files. In the evaluation, the detector using active learning makes using less training samples and obtaining better classifier performance possible.

The structure of this paper is as follows. We will mainly elaborate the PDF malicious code detection domestic and foreign present situation in Sect. 2. Section 3 is the background, mainly introduces the structure of PDF file format. Section 4 is the framework design, which introduces the scheme design and the key technologies used by the detector. Section 5 is the experimental evaluation. The classifier model before and after active learning is compared. Section 6 is the summary and future work, mainly summarizes the experimental process, as well as raises the prospect of future research work.

2   Related Works

The following is the research status of this field in the last decade.

In 2008, Shafiq et al. [4] used machine learning technique combined with Markov n-gram static model to detect malicious files, and adopted entropy rate to extract byte level features. It could determine the location of malicious codes and the TP rate was significantly improved compared with the previous technology. Different from Tabish et al. [5] proposed a detection method based on decision tree in 2009. Similarly, feature extraction was at byte level, and the content of each block was analyzed by using standard data mining algorithm. This method was based on non-signature, and it was possible to detect previously unknown zero-day malware, with an accuracy of over 90%. In 2010, Cova et al. [6] implemented an online malicious code detector, Wepawet, and proposed a method to detect and analyze malicious JavaScript code using a bayesian classifier. This method combined the anomaly detection with dynamic simulation to identify the abnormal JavaScript code automatically. In 2011, Laskov and Šrndic [7] presented a malicious PDF document detection technology PJScan, which was a static analysis method based on JavaScript code. This method could achieve 85% of the detection accuracy of all antivirus engines, but PJScan was more prone to appearing false positives than the most advanced dynamic methods at that time. In 2012, Maiorca et al. [8] developed Slayer, which extracted keyword features of PDF files by means of pattern recognition, and then classified them by random forest algorithm. It could be used to scan PDF file attacks of any type, not just JavaScript malicious code. At the same time, Smutz and Stavrou [9] realized the malicious PDF detector PDFRate using metadata and structure features. Even for the previously unknown malware, it could get the best results as well, with classification rate of 99% and the rate of false positives less than 0.2%. What's more, PDFRate could resist mimicry attacks effectively. In order to improve the detection accuracy and reduce the running time, Šrndić and Laskov [10] proposed a malicious PDF file detection technology SL2013 in 2013, which was based on the structured path. The learning algorithms of SL2013 included decision tree and support vector machine. Although it had strong ability to deal with the unknown security threats, its robustness was weak. In 2014, Corona et al. [11] proposed LuxOR, a new lightweight malicious JavaScript code detection method, which detected JavaScript malware through API references of JavaScript, and achieved excellent results in detection accuracy, throughput and generalization ability to malicious code. To solve the problem of evasion based on structure detection, Maiorca [12] proposed an automatic detection system Slyer NEO in 2015, which extracted information from structure and content and had an advanced parsing mechanism. It could detect various attacks, including non-javascript and parse-based attacks. The accuracy of this system was obviously higher than other static analysis technologies. However, the method was very sensitive to the training set used. In order to improve the evasion resistance of the detection system, Smutz and Stavrou [13] introduced a new method, pdfrate-new in 2016, to identify the sample files with poor performance of the ensemble classifier. During the detection process, when the inconsistent votes from individual classifiers reached sufficient numbers, it indicated that the prediction of the ensemble classifier was unreliable. The proposed mutual agreement analysis was very effective in identifying the samples to be added to the training set, which made the classifier time consumption much lower than that of random sampling. In the same year, Šrndić and Laskov [14] implemented a malware detection system Hidost, which was static, effective for multiple file formats and based on machine learning. It was an extension of SL2013, but Hidost was more robust, constantly adapting to new malware with regular retraining to update defenses.

Up to now, PDF malicious code detection technology has made great progress, however, in the face of various emerging code hiding, confusion and other technologies, there are still many shortcomings. Thus, malicious PDF detection is also a necessary research field for us.

3 Background

3.1 PDF File Structure

PDF stands for portable document format and is a document format that supports consistent rendering and printing, independent of the underlying environment. A PDF file has four components: a header, a body, a cross-reference table, and a tail [15, 16]. See Fig. 1 for particular example.

- Header: store the version number of the PDF file.
- Body: the main part of a PDF file, consists of multiple objects that define the operations to be performed by the file.
- Cross-reference table: the address index table of the indirect object, which can be queried for random access to the indirect object.
- Trailer: store the address of the cross-reference table and specify the object number of the file body root object.

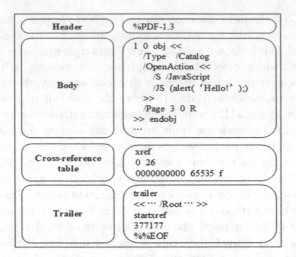

Fig. 1. Structure of PDF file

4 Scheme

When using some traditional supervised learning methods to solve classification problems, the larger the training set size, the better the classification effect. However, in many cases of the real world, the marking of large-scale samples is very difficult, requiring experts in the field to manually mark, which is time-consuming and laborious. In addition, the larger training set is, the longer the time consumption of training detection model will be. The proposal of Active learning makes it possible to use fewer training samples to acquire classifiers with better performance. Some unknown samples with the most information are selected and marked, and then the classification model is retrained with those samples to improve the accuracy of the model [17–19].

Figure 2 describes the basic design of active learning in this paper, which detects and obtains new malicious files by maintaining updates of the detector. At first, after pre-processing and feature extraction process, we transform unknown PDF files into a feature vector form. Then, we take the feature vectors as the input of classifier to classify files. If the file can be accurately classified as benign or malicious, we don't have to do additional processing of the sample. If the judgment of classifier is uncertain, we need to try to obtain real labels of samples, and deposited into the training set to retrain classifier with them in order to improve the performance of the classifier. For which, there are two things to explain. First of all, the standard of uncertainty. The uncertain files must include valuable information to improve the detector performance. How to choose the uncertain files will be detailed in the Sect. 4.2. Second, how to obtain real labels. In this paper, all the samples (including training and test sets) of experiments are all labeled in advance, so we can just query to obtain its truth value. However, the practice in the real world, need to consult security experts, and then manually label the unknown samples.

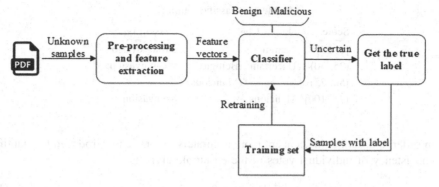

Fig. 2. Active learning model [17]

The framework is divided into two phases: the training stage and the test/update stage.

Training stage: the classifier is trained with the initial training set, which includes benign samples and malicious samples. The initial performance of the classifier is evaluated by a series of unknown files submitted for the first time.

Detection and update: for each unknown file, the detection model will provide a classification result, while the active learning method will obtain the information value contained in the file according to its uncertainty. The framework will consider obtaining some sample files based on these information values and querying the actual labels of the files, after which these information-rich files will be used to augment the training set. The updated classifier can be achieved by retraining the detection model with the augmented training set, which will be used for the next round of evaluation.

Through active learning, only the most useful samples are selected and put into the retraining of the model, which can not only effectively improve the detection performance, but also control the training time consumption to a certain extent.

4.1 Classifier

The classifier used in the experiment of this paper is improved on Hidost model, and the pre-processing adopts a structure-based static mode and the third-party tool poppler [20]. Correspondingly, the feature extraction process mainly extracts the structural features of PDF files, and the learning algorithm adopts the random forest algorithm.

4.2 Mutual Agreement Analysis

Mutual Agreement Analysis is proposed in the implementation of PDFRate-new model [13]. As shown in Table 1, in addition to benign and malicious, mutual agreement analysis adds an item to the classifier output: uncertain. Instead of splitting the vote into two parts as usual, it was split in four. In the 0% to 25% area, most votes thought that the sample was benign. Similarly, in the 75% to 100% area, most votes agreed that the sample was malicious. However, if the score is between 25% and 75%, there are differences among the classifiers, and the result output is uncertain.

Table 1. Classifier outputs

Score	Output label		Evasion type
[0, 25]	Benign		Strong evasion
(25, 50)	Uncertain	(Benign)	Weak evasion
[50, 75)		(Malicious)	
[75, 100]	Malicious		No evasion

In order to describe this concept more accurately, a metric is introduced to quantify the consistency of individual votes of the ensemble classifier:

$$A = |v - 0.5| * 2 \tag{1}$$

Where, A is the mutual agreement rate of the ensemble classifier, and v is the voting score. According to the above measurements, Fig. 3 can be obtained. When the mutual agreement rate is 50%, the result output is consistent with the above table.

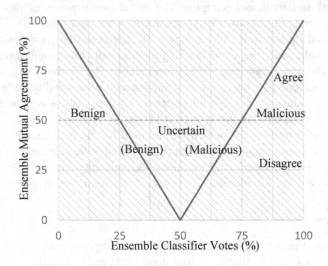

Fig. 3. Mutual agreement analysis

In active learning, the thought of how to choose the uncertain files can be obtained from the mutual agreement analysis. When we experiment, we can choose a threshold according to Fig. 3 to control the uncertain sample area. The smaller the threshold value is, the less the uncertain samples size is, but the information contained in these samples will be more valuable, because when the threshold value is close to 0, classification of uncertain samples is equivalent to blind classification of detection model. On the other hand, the larger the threshold value is, the greater the uncertain samples size is, and the more the training time consumption will be. We can imagine when the threshold is set to 100%, it's equivalent to put all of the test set into the next round of retraining, making the meaning of active learning lost.

5 Experiment

5.1 Dataset

In this paper, a small number of samples were randomly selected as the original training set. In the experiment, 354 samples, including 176 malicious samples and 178 benign samples, were evaluated for ten epochs. Each epoch, about 1400 samples were used as the test set (Table 2).

Table 2. Experimental datasets

	Size	Benign samples	Malicious samples
Original training set	354	176	178
Test set($\times 10$)	About 1400	About 700	About 700

Instead of adding all the evaluated test set samples to the next epoch as training set samples, the experiment applied active learning to the retraining process, and only a few test set samples were selected as the expansion of the original training set. In the process of selecting a small number of test set samples, mutual agreement analysis is used. When we set the threshold value to 50%, we will obtain an uncertain sample area (see Fig. 3), that is, the samples with evaluation scores between 0.25 and 0.75 are defined as uncertain samples. When the performance of the model is poor, the number of uncertain samples may be larger and even close to the number of test set samples. If they are all augmented as training sets, the significance of active learning will be lost. Therefore, the number of samples augmented to the original training set cannot exceed 20 in the experiment to limit the time of model retraining.

5.2 Evaluation

By applying active learning to Hidost model, setting the threshold value of control uncertain sample area to 50%, and setting the maximum number of uncertain sample augmented training set to 20, the Fig. 4 can be obtained. In the figure, RF all means that all the test set samples are used to augment the training set in next epoch; RF uncertain means that only part of the uncertain samples with rich information are used to augment the training set. The difference of the four measures before and after active learning is not very distinct. This explains that a small number of uncertain samples basically contain all the differential information useful for classification of the test set in this stage.

Table 3 shows the comparison the number of training set samples and training test time per epoch between the original Hidost model and Hidost model based on active learning. On the one hand, there is a big difference in the size of training sets. The number of samples of the original Hidost model in the tenth epochs reaches 13,251, while the Hidost model based on active learning only used 411, which is reduced by one third. Compared with the first epoch, Hidost model based on active learning only augmented 57 samples in the tenth epochs, less than a fifth of the original training set. On the other hand, the training test time using active learning was also significantly shorter than before.

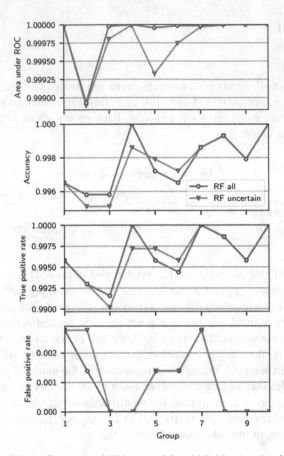

Fig. 4. The performance of Hidost models with/without active learning

Table 3. Comparison of Hidost models with/without active learning

Epoch	Test set	Original Hidost model		Hidost model based on Active learning		Training set reduction
		Training set	Time(s)	Training set	Time(s)	
1	1433	354	1.06924414635	354	1.16369819641	0
2	1433	1787	1.27057909966	362	1.22491407394	1425
3	1433	3220	1.15115809441	373	1.30330085754	2847
4	1433	4653	1.28022480011	381	1.20180821419	4272
5	1433	6086	1.39241123199	390	1.20856690407	5696
6	1433	7519	1.70291876793	395	1.33792090416	7124
7	1433	8952	1.63864588737	399	1.20936203003	8553
8	1433	10385	1.52327895164	404	1.19747900963	9981
9	1433	11818	1.53993701935	408	1.2542309761	11410
10	1421	13251	1.7291829586	411	1.19509601593	12840

Active learning greatly reduces the number of training set samples used in each epoch of the retraining period, and greatly shortens the training time. However, the performance of the detector is basically the same as the original model. This is of great significance to the malware detection model in the real world. Malicious code is always trying new ways to avoid the detector, and the detector has to retrain the model periodically in order to adapt to the new malicious code. Generally speaking, the training set is larger, the model performance will be better. However, adding all of the test samples to training set is a time-consuming effort and will cause heavy training time growth. which has little practical significance. The application of active learning makes using less training samples and obtaining better classifier performance possible. Each retraining epoch only choose some uncertain samples containing nearly all the useful information of the epoch to augment the training set. Therefore, it not only will not result in a large scale of training set to lose the practical significance, but also can improve the detector performance to keep the value of periodic retraining.

6 Conclusion

In this paper, an active learning detection model is implemented. Through periodic retraining, a small number of information-rich test set samples are selected at each epoch to augment the training set, and the detector performance is improved continuously. Compared with the traditional retraining model, the training time is greatly reduced. The main work of this paper is to implement an active learning model based on mutual agreement analysis. We apply active learning to Hidost model, and the mutual agreement analysis is used as the selection criterion of uncertain samples, which makes it possible to use fewer training samples and acquire classifiers with better performance.

PDF malicious code detection technology based on traditional machine learning has been relatively mature [21]. With the rise of deep learning, future detection models will definitely make more use of deep learning algorithms. In the future research, there is still a lot of work to be done. For instance, more deep learning models will be tried to explore deep learning algorithms that are more suitable for the detection of PDF malware, such as converting features of PDF files into image forms in a certain way, and then using convolutional neural network for binary classification.

Acknowledgment. This work is supported by National Natural Science Foundation of China (No. 61876019 & U1636213).

References

1. Blockeel, H., Kersting, K., Nijssen, S., Železný, F. (eds.): ECML PKDD 2013. LNCS (LNAI), vol. 8190. Springer, Heidelberg (2013). https://doi.org/10.1007/978-3-642-40994-3
2. Maiorca, D., Ariu, D., Corona, I., et al.: An evasion resilient approach to the detection of malicious PDF files. In: International Conference on Information Systems Security and Privacy (2015)

3. Maiorca, D., Biggio, B., Giacinto, G.: Towards adversarial malware detection: lessons learned from PDF-based attacks. ACM Comput. Surv. (CSUR) **52**(4), 78 (2018)
4. Shafiq, M.Z., Khayam, S.A., Farooq, M.: Embedded malware detection using markov n-grams. In: Zamboni, D. (ed) Detection of Intrusions and Malware, and Vulnerability Assessment. DIMVA 2008. LNCS, vol. 5137, pp. 88–107. Springer, Heidelberg (2008). https://doi.org/10.1007/978-3-540-70542-0_5
5. Tabish, S., Shafiq, M., Farooq, M.: Malware detection using statistical analysis of byte-level file content. In: ACM SIGKDD Workshop on Cybersecurity & Intelligence Informatics, pp. 23–31. ACM (2009)
6. Cova, M., Kruegel, C., Vigna, G.: Detection and analysis of drive-by-download attacks and malicious JavaScript code. In: International Conference on World Wide Web, pp. 281–290. ACM (2010)
7. Laskov, P., Šrndić, N.: Static detection of malicious JavaScript-bearing PDF documents. In: Proceedings of the 27th Annual Computer Security Applications Conference on - ACSAC 2011, pp. 373–382. ACM Press, Orlando, Florida, 05–09 December 2011
8. Maiorca, D., Giacinto, G., Corona, I.: A pattern recognition system for malicious PDF files detection. In: Perner, P. (ed.) Machine Learning and Data Mining in Pattern Recognition. MLDM 2012. LNCS, vol. 7376, pp. 510–524. Springer, Heidelberg (2012). https://doi.org/10.1007/978-3-642-31537-4_40
9. Smutz, C., Stavrou, A.: Malicious PDF detection using metadata and structural features. In: Proceedings of the 28th Annual Computer Security Applications Conference on - ACSAC 2012, pp. 239–248. ACM Press, Orlando, Florida, 03–07 December 2012
10. Šrndić, N., Laskov, P.: Detection of malicious PDF files based on hierarchical document structure. In: Proceedings of the 20th Annual Network & Distributed System Security Symposium. NDSS 2013, San Diego, California, USA, 24–27 February 2013
11. Corona, I., Maiorca, D., Ariu, D., et al.: LuxOR: detection of malicious PDF-embedded JavaScript code through discriminant analysis of API references. In: Workshop on Artificial Intelligent & Security Workshop, pp. 47–57. ACM (2014)
12. Maiorca, D., Ariu, D., Corona, I., et al.: A structural and content-based approach for a precise and robust detection of malicious PDF files. In: 1st International Conference on Information Systems Security and Privacy (ICISSP 2015), pp. 27–36. IEEE (2015)
13. Smutz, C., Stavrou, A.: When a tree falls: using diversity in ensemble classifiers to identify evasion in malware detectors. In: 23rd Annual Network and Distributed System Security Symposium, NDSS 2016, San Diego, California, USA, 21–24 February 2016
14. Šrndić, N., Laskov, P.: Hidost: a static machine-learning-based detector of malicious files. EURASIP J. Inf. Secur. **2016**(1), 22 (2016)
15. Adobe 2006: PDF Reference. Adobe Portable Document Format Version 1.7 (2006)
16. Adobe 2008: Adobe Supplement to ISO 32000 (2008)
17. Nissim, N., Cohen, A., Elovici, Y.: ALDOCX: detection of unknown malicious microsoft office documents using designated active learning methods based on new structural feature extraction methodology. IEEE Trans. Inf. Forensics Secur. **PP**(99), 1 (2017)
18. Mi, C.Z., Xua, M.W., Tong, L.: Malware detection method based on active learning. Ruan Jian Xue Bao J. Softw
19. Pimentel, T., Monteiro, M., Viana, J., et al.: A generalized active learning approach for unsupervised anomaly detection (2018)
20. FreeDesktop.org. Poppler (2018)
21. Schmidhuber, J.: Deep learning in neural networks: an overview. Neural Netw. **61**, 85–117 (2015)

Malicious Intentions: Android Internet Permission Security Risks

John Mark Andah ⓘ and Jinfu Chen⁽⊠⁾ ⓘ

Jiangsu University, Zhenjiang 212013, China
jinfuchen@ujs.edu.cn

Abstract. Many Android applications access internet networks to query, retrieve or transmit digital resources. The current version of the Android Operating System (OS) fails to provide sufficient control to the user over the amount of internet access an application has. This raises concerns for data security. Significant user data vulnerability is introduced when applications can perform unsolicited data collection in the background without user knowledge. This paper analyzes the permissions of a cross-section of android applications. We focus on the INTERNET permission, and how its classification introduces significant vulnerability onto a user's device. Subsequently, we create a proof of concept app that exploits private user data using social engineering. Our findings conclude that the INTERNET permission is a critical permission, prone to exploitation and lacks sufficient user control in the Android OS. We propose methods for the control and protection of data by the Android system.

Keywords: Android · Permissions · Internet · Vulnerability · Security

1 Introduction

Android is the most widely used mobile operating system (OS) on planet earth at the time of this writing. Its market share is 72.23% of all mobile devices according to reports from StatCounter [1] and 88% for the report from Statista in 2018 [2]. The Google Play Store, being the official application marketplace for Android applications, has seen a rise in the number of applications that are made available to users. In 2018 the Google Play Store was reported to have had about 2.6 million apps [3]. Numerous other apps are served to users by unofficial marketplaces. With such a massive number of apps in circulation, there are bound to be some bad actors and malicious apps that exploit the Android ecosystem.

Android devices have evolved to consist of a comprehensive list of functionality and sensors. These are used in various ways by applications to perform a wide range of tasks. Usage of these sensors, functions and the data generated from them, offer sensitive data on user activity, identity, location, preferences and much more. Apps installed on a device potentially have access to all this data which can be shared with advertisers [4], data mining entities and malicious actors.

An installed Android application is isolated from all others on the device because the Android OS employs the Sandbox method for its security architecture [5]. The sandbox architecture ensures that each app runs in its own virtual environment. As a

© Springer Nature Switzerland AG 2019
J. Vaidya et al. (Eds.): CSS 2019, LNCS 11983, pp. 111–120, 2019.
https://doi.org/10.1007/978-3-030-37352-8_10

result, the Android OS has in-built functionality to provide a level of fine-grained control to the critical core resources (like storage or camera) that an application has access to. There is a permission-based method of restricting access to resources until authorization is explicitly provided.

Android permissions are specified into groups depending on the sensitivity of the resources being requested. Permissions are grouped into sensitive, insensitive and system categories. Android Operating System is hereby abbreviated as Android OS. For versions of Android OS before 6.0 (API 23), the internet permission was deemed sensitive and required user authorization for use. However, in subsequent versions of the OS, the internet permission is not deemed sensitive, therefore automatic access is granted when an app requests said permission. Permissions granted in isolation can serve the purpose for which they are granted, however, coupled with the INTERNET permission, the potential for transmission of data is introduced. We seek to perform a data security risk assessment supported by experimentation.

The main contributions of this paper are,

1. We evaluate and estimate the presence and usage of the INTERNET permission in apps for Android OS (API 23) and above
2. We test the (transitive) vulnerability and importance of the INTERNET permission by creating a real-world android application that leaks user data using the INTERNET permission.
3. We propose actionable solutions for Android to make the INTERNET permission more secure.

Paper Organization. The rest of this study is organized as follows. Section 2 presents the background and previous research effort in this domain. Section 3 presents the methodology and experimentation done for this research. Section 4 details the proof of concept application using data from Sect. 3. Section 5 provides the proposed solutions. Finally, Sect. 6 concludes the study presented in this paper.

2 Preliminaries

2.1 Android Security Features

Application Sandbox. Sandboxing is a technique in which each application is securely separated and encapsulated in its own virtual environment thereby isolating it from all other applications on the device. Each application is assigned a unique UID (User ID) and caused to run on its own process i.e. a new Dalvik Virtual Machine instance is created to run it. As outlined by Armando et al. [7], sandboxing helps police app interplay such that if for example, an application tries to invoke a kill system call of another app's process, it stands in violation of the rules of the sandboxing environment hence the call is not allowed.

Runtime Permissions. These exist as a way for the android system to protect the privacy and security of a user's information [8]. Depending on the sensitivity of the functionality requested by an app, the system might grant permission automatically or prompt user approval of the request. Each Android application is required to explicitly outline the permissions it needs to operate in a file known as the Manifest file. On installation, the manifest file cannot be changed. As such, applications cannot request more permissions than outlined in the manifest file. On upload of the executable file package file (APK) to the Google Play Store (currently version 12.3.28), the manifest file of the application is scanned by Google. This is to determine and outline the permissions it requires on the app page. However, this process does not take into account the context in which these permissions are used [9]. This can lead to vulnerabilities in the system [6]. The Android developer website [8] currently categorizes its standard permissions into three designations for third-party apps, namely "normal", "dangerous", "signature". In this section, we provide a brief overview of the various permission groups.

Normal. This category of permissions cover areas where the app requires access to resources that exist outside the app's sandbox but pose a little risk to user privacy or another app's operation [8]. This category of permissions requires no authorization from the user, as such access is granted automatically.

Dangerous. As the name suggests, these permissions exist in areas that are deemed sensitive to user privacy and the integrity of the user's data. When an application requires access to permissions in this category, the user is expressly prompted to authorize access to the resource or reject it [8]. Dangerous permissions are grouped into 10 subcategories known as permission groups.

Signature. These permissions are granted at install time and are used by third-party apps but only if the requesting app is signed with the same certificate as the app that defines the permission [8].

2.2   Related Work

Prior research has been conducted into the area of Android permissions, attacks, security and privacy on the android platform. Gibler et al. [11] explored how user data is used when an application is installed by creating AndroidLeaks, a static analysis framework with the primary function of finding information leaks. They defined a privacy leak as the transfer on any personal or phone identifying information off of a user's device. They then evaluated Android leaks on a dataset of applications to determine if these applications could access private data and leak it. For their study, they focused on device-identifying data, recorded audio, WIFI state and location data. They found that at least 32% of the apps they analyzed contained leaks which were primarily due to ad libraries. A large number of leaks were also of phone identifying information.

Fang et al. [12] reviewed the coarse granularity of Android permissions. Their analysis of the INTERNET permission revealed that its use was primarily in applications within which the developer only intends to display advertising but is granted full access to the internet due to lack of fine-grained control by the OS. This allows applications to overclaim permission functionality that is not needed and could be utilized in malicious ways.

Barrera et al. [13] in 2010, after conducting an empirical analysis of a data set of android apps, concluded that one of the most widely used Android permissions is android.permission.INTERNET. It is however too coarse-grained in that it does not provide sufficient depiction of the level of internet access that an application is allowed to have. It just provides the general availability of internet access rather than restrict access to only certain URLs as specified by the developer. Majority of free apps on the Google play store are Ad-supported hence use the INTERNET permission. However, this does not sufficiently provide security from other unspecified URLs that may introduce malicious content. They proposed a much finer-grained scheme which would only provide ads internet access. Although their work bears similarities to our work, it does not do so in application, methodology or timeliness.

While Barrera et al. [13] and the other works offer substantial analyses on the state of data leaks and permissions, they contain information from dated datasets. They also fail to provide real-world implementations and explanation of privacy concerns raised by the INTERNET permission. We seek to illustrate the threats posed by the reclassification of the INTERNET permission. In doing so, we build on the research done by, Barrera et al. [13] to present a much more current view of possible exploits in the real world.

3   Methodology

The new permission model introduced in Android API 23 changes the definition of the INTERNET permission from a dangerous permission into a normal permission. In doing so, the user is not required to authorize its access. The Android system automatically grants internet access when an app requests it. This change undoubtedly arose because a lot of applications are likely to require internet access as we show in our analysis below. However, this current NORMAL status introduces leakage risks due to its automatic authorization and lack of control from the user. The internet resource cannot be turned off or restricted access to by a user for any single application, short of an entire device-wide Airplane mode. This leaves bad actors with an open channel to transmit user data without user consent or limitations.

Data Collection and Analysis. We conducted a preliminary analysis on the INTERNET permission on a much more current data set of apps on the Play Store. In this analysis, we obtained a cross-section of 130 unique free android apps and games which are among the top and trending apps in the Google Play Store. Watanabe et al. [14] found that 70% of free apps contained vulnerabilities of some kind. The apps we selected individually had 1,000,000 downloads or more and a user rating of 4.0 or higher.

Among the applications obtained were also some applications from the Editors Choice curated selection on the Google Play Store these apps are promoted as being the best in their categories as such tend to be pushed to more users and are downloaded more often. Categories selected also include Photography, Family, Music & Audio,

Entertainment, Shopping, Personalization, Social, Communication, etc. Priority was given to applications with a larger number of downloads due to the inference that these have a larger impact on users in terms of security if exploited.

Data Extraction and Preprocessing. Each Android Package (APK) file contains other files that have the actionable code, icons, XML files, and other application data [11]. An essential XML file exists in an APK known as the manifest file. It outlines all the permissions needed for the APK to accomplish tasks. It is necessary to extract the manifest file from the physical application to get the permissions it requests. We used Android Analyser for extraction, a tool provided by Android Studio IDE (Integrated Development Environment), version 3. With this, we obtained AndroidManifest.xml files for all the selected applications for preprocessing.

Preprocessing was done using the R language and RStudio. We aimed to determine the frequency with which each permission appeared across all the applications. Consequently, we would evaluate and determine the amount of control a user has over the permissions with the highest frequencies. We removed all irrelevant XML tags, various identifiers, white spaces, etc. to only leave the permission specification such as INTERNET or CAMERA or WAKE_LOCK.

Results. Using the preprocessed data, we plotted a histogram to visualize the most frequently occurring permissions. A permission frequency above 70 was used in the histogram to strip away sparse infrequently occurring permissions. The top permissions obtained were ACCESS_NETWORK_STATE, INTERNET, WAKE_LOCK, WRI-TE_EXTERNAL_STORAGE, READ_EXTERNAL_STORAGE as shown in Fig. 1. This contains 3 normal and 2 dangerous level permissions. Of the 130 apps analyzed, all of them had INTERNET and ACCESS_NETWORK_STATE permissions even for those that were offline apps.

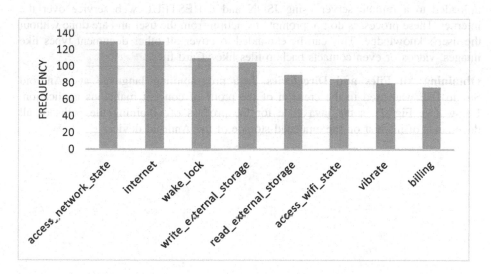

Fig. 1. Frequency distribution of permissions in the apps analyzed.

4 Proof of Concept Malicious Application

We created an Android application as a proof of concept with 4 of the most frequently occurring permissions derived from our analysis of apps. We used a social engineering exploit to trick the user to grant access so that the app can collect user data. We then transferred the data using the INTERNET permission.

We created a generic wallpaper application with which a user can obtain wallpapers. The app makes use ACCESS_NETWORK_STATE, INTERNET, WRITE_EXTERNAL_STORAGE and READ_EXTERNAL_STORAGE permissions thereby employing 2 normal permissions and 2 dangerous permissions from the analysis above. The app was created using the Android Studio IDE. The user can browse through wallpapers available, download and set wallpaper to the device home screen. For this malicious app to operate correctly, it requests authorization for WRITE_EXTERNAL_STORAGE and READ_EXTERNAL_STORAGE permissions when the action for download of a wallpaper or setting to the home screen is attempted. It is essential to note that only one system prompt for storage access is presented to the user for authorization. On authorization, access to the entire permission group is granted and the user is no longer prompted for further authorization.

Covert Data Collection. Going a step further, we created an asynchronous task to run in the background of the malicious app that uses multithreading to traverse all documents to select text documents in all directories on the external storage of the Android device. The files are of the extension .txt, .doc, .epub, .pdf, etc. This background task initially checks if it has permission to access the emulated storage on the Android device. If access has been granted, it then proceeds to read all the file paths of items on the emulated (external) storage into an array list and select the files that meet its upload criteria. Upload of the selected files begins immediately. The list of all files found is uploaded to a remote server using JSON and a RESTFUL web service over the internet. These processes do not prompt any action from the user and are done without the user's knowledge. This can be expanded to cover all other document types like images, videos or even contacts backup files like vCard files.

Obtaining All Files and Directories. Java programming language and Android Studio IDE was used in the creation of the proof of concept malicious application. Below (see Fig. 2) is the java code for the process of obtaining file paths of all documents of interest on the emulated storage of the Android device.

```
1     public ArrayList<String> getFilePaths(){
2            ArrayList<String> resultFS = new Ar-
      rayList<String>();
3            File myDirectory = new File(sdPath);
4            File[] directories = myDirectory.listFiles(new
      FileFilter() {  @Override
5               public boolean accept(File pathname) {
6                   return pathname.isDirectory();      }});
7            final int noOfDirectories = directories.length;
8            for(int i=0;i<directories.length;i++)
9            { File[] itemsList = directories[i].listFiles();
10             for (File file : itemsList) {
11                 try { if(file.isDirectory())
12                     { itemsList = file.listFiles();}
13                     if ( file.getName().contains(".txt")||
14                         file.getName().contains(".doc")  ||
      file.getName().contains(".pdf")  ||
15                         file.getName().contains(".epub"))
16                     { String path= file.getAbsolutePath();
17                       resultFS.add(path); detectedFiles++;   }
18                 } catch (Exception e) {
      e.printStackTrace();}}}
             return resultFS ;
19    }
```

Fig. 2. Java code for gathering data in our proof of concept malicious app.

Upload of Selected Device Files. Upload of the device files is performed using a background asynchronous task that continues until all files are uploaded. These background data collection processes are undetectable to the user and the Android operating system does not also provide any log of the activity of the app to the user. As such user data is being uploaded without user consent. Outlined below is the java code we used. Figure 3 shows the flow chart of this social engineering exploit of the proof of concept application.

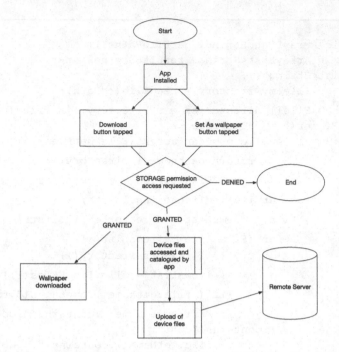

Fig. 3. Attack flow chart of covert acquisition of data without user knowledge in proof of concept app.

5 Discussion and Proposed Solutions

The INTERNET permission independently poses little threat but when coupled with other permissions, its exploitability exponentially increases. As discussed earlier, Android performs checking of permissions individually without analysis of the threat level of combined permissions. The above experiment operates as a Blackbox system where the user is unaware of the processes it undertakes. These processes of exploitation are largely made possible by the presence of the INTERNET permission. We propose the following solutions to mitigate the problems in our analysis.

Ability to Revoke Internet Access for an Application. It is of significant importance that any user should be able to turn off internet access to any application. A complete turn off of internet capabilities of an application raises issues with advertising, which is the primary source of monetization for most applications without directly asking for users to pay for the services that apps provide. We propose an expansion of the ADVERTISING permission as proposed by Barrera et al. [13] to include all other known trusted advertising providers' URLs. Google currently allows other advertisers to mediate ads through Admob [20]. This permission would work similar to the role ad mediation plays in managing ads from different advertising providers. This will enable the developers to show ads from any trusted provider while ensuring that no other URLs are allowed to communicate with the app when activated.

Temporary Permission Access for All Permissions. This concept is used in iOS to an extent for certain permissions like location access. With this concept, an app that is authorized by the user is granted one-time permission access to a device resource unless permanent access is explicitly granted by the user. Another variant of this is also access to resources only when the application is running in the foreground unless authorized by the user. This means that access to a permission is only turned on when a user is within the application. When the user switches applications or the current application is in the background, access is temporarily paused. This preemptively restricts background monitoring by applications that gather data on usage patterns of users.

App Internet Connection History Like Browsers. Routine legitimate permissions can be used to collect sensitive user data using the INTERNET permission. The Android OS also provides no way for users to view internet traffic of applications. We propose an internet history of applications much similar to how internet browsers show a log of all visited websites, detailing uploads and downloads. Possibility of internet connection history alerts for applications operating in the background is also proposed. A log of the data traffic per application will be essential in providing the user with more detailed information about an app's background activities. Such an audit is needed for finding applications that are performing suspicious activities over the network and as such compromising user data.

6 Conclusion

The Android Operating System has made several improvements in security since its first release to consumers. However, as a result of changes in permission specifications for Android 6.0 (API 23) and later, the INTERNET permission has been reclassified. Its current designation allows malicious applications to violate user privacy while adhering to the Android permission rules. We analyzed a cross-section of Android applications that have a minimum of 1,000,000 downloads and 4.0-star ratings on the Google Play Store. We determined that the INTERNET permission is one of the most requested permissions, even by "offline" apps. We created a sample malicious wallpaper app that transmits user data in the background. It can copy documents, images and other sensitive user files in the external storage of an Android device and send using the INTERNET permission. We propose 3 solutions to significantly mitigate the exploitation of user data by bad actors which are temporary permissions, connection history and a modified off-switch for the internet permission.

Acknowledgement. This study was funded by the National Natural Science Foundation of China (NSFC grant number: U1836116).

References

1. Mobile operating system market share worldwide. http://gs.statcounter.com/os-market-share/mobile/worldwide. Accessed 06 Aug 2019

2. Global mobile OS market share in sales to end users from 1st quarter 2009 to 2nd quarter 2018. https://www.statista.com/statistics/266136/global-market-share-held-by-smartphone-operating-systems/. Accessed 06 Aug 2019
3. Number of available applications in the Google Play Store from December 2009 to December 2018. https://www.statista.com/statistics/266210/number-of-available-applications-in-the-google-play-store/. Accessed 06 Aug 2019
4. Demetriou, S., Merrill, W., Yang, W., Zhang, A., Gunter, C.A.: Free for all! Assessing user data exposure to advertising libraries on Android. In: NDSS (2016)
5. Yadav, S., Apurva, A., Ranakoti, P., Tomer, S., Roy, N.R.: Android vulnerabilities and security. In: 2017 International Conference on Computing and Communication Technologies for Smart Nation (IC3TSN), pp. 204–208. IEEE (2017)
6. Rangwala, M., Zhang, P., Zou, X., Li, F.: A taxonomy of privilege escalation attacks in Android applications. Int. J. Secur. Netw. **9**(1), 40–55 (2014)
7. Armando, A., Merlo, A., Verderame, L.: An empirical evaluation of the android security framework. In: Janczewski, L.J., Wolfe, H.B., Shenoi, S. (eds.) SEC 2013. IAICT, vol. 405, pp. 176–189. Springer, Heidelberg (2013). https://doi.org/10.1007/978-3-642-39218-4_14
8. Permissions overview. https://developer.android.com/guide/topics/permissions/overview. Accessed 06 Aug 2019
9. Schlegel, R., Zhang, K., Zhou, X.-Y., Intwala, M., Kapadia, A., Wang, X.: Soundcomber: a stealthy and context-aware sound trojan for smartphones. In: NDSS, vol. 11, pp. 17–33 (2011)
10. Runtime permissions. https://source.android.com/devices/tech/config/runtime_perms. Accessed 06 Aug 2019
11. Gibler, C., Crussell, J., Erickson, J., Chen, H.: AndroidLeaks: automatically detecting potential privacy leaks in Android applications on a large scale. In: Katzenbeisser, S., Weippl, E., Camp, L.J., Volkamer, M., Reiter, M., Zhang, X. (eds.) Trust 2012. LNCS, vol. 7344, pp. 291–307. Springer, Heidelberg (2012). https://doi.org/10.1007/978-3-642-30921-2_17
12. Fang, Z., Han, W., Li, Y.: Permission based Android security: issues and countermeasures. Comput. Secur. **43**, 205–218 (2014)
13. Barrera, D., Kayacik, H.G., van Oorschot, P.C., Somayaji, A.: A methodology for empirical analysis of permission-based security models and its application to Android. In: Proceedings of the 17th ACM Conference on Computer and Communications Security, pp. 73–84. ACM (2010)
14. Watanabe, T., et al.: Understanding the origins of mobile app vulnerabilities: a large-scale measurement study of free and paid apps. In: Proceedings of the 14th International Conference on Mining Software Repositories, pp. 14–24. IEEE Press (2017)
15. App manifest overview. https://developer.android.com/guide/topics/manifest/manifest-intro. Accessed 06 Aug 2019
16. Alshehri, A., Hewins, A., McCulley, M., Alshahrani, H., Fu, H., Zhu, Y.: Risks behind device information permissions in Android OS. Commun. Netw. **9**, 219–234 (2017)
17. AdMob. https://en.wikipedia.org/wiki/AdMob. Accessed 06 Aug 2019

DeepWAF: Detecting Web Attacks Based on CNN and LSTM Models

Xiaohui Kuang[1], Ming Zhang[1(✉)], Hu Li[1], Gang Zhao[1],
Huayang Cao[1], Zhendong Wu[1], and Xianmin Wang[2]

[1] National Key Laboratory of Science and Technology on Information System
Security, Beijing, China
zm_stiss@163.com
[2] School of Computer Science, Guangzhou University, Guangzhou, China

Abstract. The increasing popularity of web applications makes the web a main
venue for attackers engaging in a myriad of cybercrimes. With large quantities
of information processing and sharing by web applications, the situation for web
attack detection or prevention becomes increasingly severe. We present a prototype implementation called DeepWAF to detect web attacks based on deep
learning techniques. We systematically discuss the approach for effective use of
the currently popular CNN and LSTM models, and their combinational models
CNN-LSTM and LSTM-CNN. The experimental results on the dataset of
HTTP DATASET CSIC 2010 demonstrate that our proposed four types of
detection models all achieve satisfactory results, with the detection rate of
approximately 95% and the false alarm rate of approximately 2%. We also
carried out case studies to analyze the causes of false negatives and false positives, which can be used for further improvements. Our work further illustrates
that machine learning has a promising application prospect in the field of web
attack detection.

Keywords: Web attacks · CNN · LSTM · Detection models

1 Introduction

The web is the abbreviation for the World Wide Web, which plays a central role in the
development of the Information Age and has become the primary tool for billions of
people to interact on the Internet. Currently, the majority of services on the Internet are
provided by web applications with a myriad of information, entertainment, education,
commercial and governmental utilities. However, the web security situation is not
optimistic. For cyber-criminals, the web has become a main venue for spreading
malware and launching cyber-attacks, thus engaging in a wide range of cybercrimes,
including information theft, fraud, espionage and blackmail. As early as 2008,
Symantec [1] observed that attackers tended to adopt stealthier and more focused
techniques targeting computers through the web instead of trying to penetrate networks
with high-volume broadcast attacks, and the web-based vulnerabilities had outnum-
bered traditional computer security concerns with the majority of effective malicious

© Springer Nature Switzerland AG 2019
J. Vaidya et al. (Eds.): CSS 2019, LNCS 11983, pp. 121–136, 2019.
https://doi.org/10.1007/978-3-030-37352-8_11

activities targeting the web. According to Trustwave [2], hackers are increasingly focusing on and succeeding with application layer attacks.

Among the numerous web security protection solutions, the web application firewall (WAF) is a type of application firewall that applies specifically to web applications. By inspecting HTTP traffic, it can prevent attacks stemming from web application security flaws, such as SQL injection [3], cross-site scripting (XSS) [4], and path traversal [5]. However, the current WAFs typically work in a rule-based mode and rely highly on signatures to detect and prevent attacks. They must have enough characterization and generalization ability to cover normal or malicious behaviors, whereas in practice it is a time-consuming and labor-intensive task to update rules against new emerging attacks. Notably, the renaissance of machine learning, especially the rise of deep learning provides us with new ideas for solving problems. We can build a mathematical model based on sample data to make predictions or decisions without using explicit instructions. Inspired by this, we explore and study how to use deep learning techniques to design a novel and effective WAF—DeepWAF. In this paper, we systematically discuss the approach for using two currently popular deep learning models, namely, convolutional neural network (CNN) and long short-term memory (LSTM), to build web attack detection models.

The rest of the paper is organized as follows. The related work is introduced in Sect. 2. The details of DeepWAF are described in Sect. 3. Experimental results and discussions are presented in Sect. 4. Finally, Sect. 5 concludes the paper.

2 Related Work

Considerable web attacks detection or prevention research [6, 7] has been proposed. Such research ranges from narrow solutions used to prevent only some specific attacks, to generic methods aiming to provide comprehensive protection for web applications.

SQL injections are one of the most common web attacks; thus, a large number of protection methods are proposed specifically to circumvent SQL injection attacks [8–12]. Kar et al. [13] presented an approach for detecting SQL injection attacks by modeling SQL queries as a graph of tokens and using the centrality measure of nodes to train a support vector machine (SVM).

XSS attacks are a type of injection attack in which malicious scripts are injected into the targeted website. Gupta et al. discussed a detailed comprehensive analysis of the exploitation, detection and prevention mechanisms of XSS attacks in [14]. XSS attacks are generally categorized into two categories: stored and reflected. The stored attacks usually rely on client protections to monitor the outgoing HTTP responses [15]. The reflected attacks are generally circumvented by user input sanitizing [16, 17].

HTTP parameter pollution is a special type of attack that supplies multiple HTTP parameters with the same name and may cause a web application to interpret values in unanticipated ways, thus allowing it to be exploited to bypass input validation, trigger application errors or modify internal variable values. Balduzzi et al. [18] presented an automated approach for the discovery of HTTP parameter pollution vulnerabilities in web applications to prevent attackers from compromising application logic to perform attacks.

Protection techniques against other types of web attacks have also been explored. For example, Su and Wassermann [19] proposed a method for preventing command injection based on context-free grammar and compiler parsing techniques. Tajbakhsh and Bagherzadeh [20] presented a framework for preventing local file inclusion attacks. Han [21] introduced a system to detect directory traversal attacks by analyzing web server logs. Saxe and Berlin [22] used a character-level CNN to detect malicious URLs, file paths and registry keys.

Unlike the above work, some research has concentrated on uniform solutions to detect or prevent many types of attacks. Kruegel et al. [23, 24] presented a multi-model approach to detect web-based attacks. They built many statistical detection models on different features, including attribute length, attribute character distribution, attribute order, and access frequency. Corona et al. proposed a formulation of query analysis through hidden Markov models (HMM) to detect attacks on web applications in [25], and presented SuStorID in [26, 27], which is a multiple classifier system that can model legitimate inputs towards web services. Zolotukhin et al. [28] considered analyzing HTTP logs to detect web attacks and employed support vector data description (SVDD), K-means and density-based spatial clustering of Applications with Noise (DBSCAN) to model normal user behaviors.

Choras and Kozik [29] proposed a model consisting of patterns obtained using graph-based segmentation techniques and dynamic programming based on information from HTTP requests to detect cyberattacks on web applications. Bronte et al. [30] proposed an anomaly detection approach that utilizes three measures: cross-entropy for parameters, value and data type, which are intended to compare the deviation between learned request profiles and a new web request. Zhang et al. [31] designed a CNN model to detect web attacks, and the experimental results showed that the model achieves satisfactory results with a high detection rate and a low false alarm rate.

The above work has made great achievements, but only a few have tried to develop protection solutions by using machine learning techniques. Defending web applications is very difficult because there are so many and different attacks. It is necessary to use machine learning, especially deep learning techniques to develop effective protection solutions that are easily implementable and capable of learning. In this paper, we systematically present how to apply two currently popular deep learning models, i.e., CNN and LSTM, and their combinational models to the detection of web attacks.

3 DeepWAF

In this section, we describe the details of DeepWAF. First, the architecture of Deep-WAF is introduced. Second, the HTTP request preprocessing algorithm is described. Finally, the four types of detection models, i.e., CNN, LSTM, CNN-LSTM and LSTM-CNN, are presented.

3.1 Architecture of DeepWAF

Figure 1 shows the architecture of DeepWAF with the main focus on the detection phase. Because DeepWAF is a machine learning-based detection system, it must be trained with real web requests before deployment in a real environment to provide protection for web applications. In practical use, DeepWAF can be deployed inline as a reverse proxy.

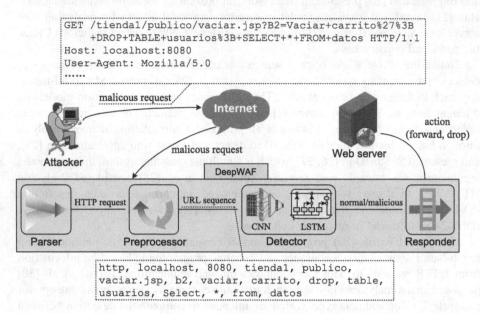

```
GET /tienda1/publico/vaciar.jsp?B2=Vaciar+carrito%27%3B
    +DROP+TABLE+usuarios%3B+SELECT+*+FROM+datos HTTP/1.1
Host: localhost:8080
User-Agent: Mozilla/5.0
......
```

```
http, localhost, 8080, tienda1, publico,
vaciar.jsp, b2, vaciar, carrito, drop, table,
usuarios, Select, *, from, datos
```

Fig. 1. Architecture of DeepWAF.

DeepWAF is composed of four modules: parser, preprocessor, detector and responder. The typical process for DeepWAF to detect a malicious web request is as follows. First, the request to the web server is parsed and analyzed by the parser into HTTP headers and body. Next, the preprocessor preprocesses the HTTP request and generates a URL sequence that can be fed to the detector. Then the detector detects whether the request is normal or malicious based on the built-in deep learning models. Finally, the responder performs suitable actions according to the detection results. For example, it can forward the request to the web server if the detection result is normal but may drop it if malicious. Since the parser and the responder are similar to those in ordinary WAFs, the following will focus on the implementation of the preprocessor and the detector.

3.2 Preprocessing the HTTP Request

Web attacks exclusively leverage the HTTP protocol to perform malicious activities. If a web server is attacked, that means it receives one or more malicious HTTP requests. Based on this, DeepWAF is designed by inspecting HTTP requests to detect the server-side web attacks. Like other WAFs, DeepWAF can also support the HTTPS protocol by copying the private key used by the server.

The following snippet shows a GET HTTP request from the dataset HTTP DATASET CSIC 2010 [32]. An HTTP request consists of a request line, several request headers and an optional message body (for the POST request). The request line is composed of three components: the HTTP-method, the HTTP-URL and the HTTP-version. Because the vast majority of web attacks are implemented by manipulating the HTTP-URL, and the dataset used in our experiments only contain attacks in HTTP-URL, we focus the detection object on the HTTP-URL. However, without loss of generality, our detection method can be applied to other fields of the HTTP request. A special case is that the POST request contains a message body that can be exploited by injection attacks. So for the POST request, the detection object is defined as the combination of the HTTP-URL and the HTTP-body. For convenience, the detection object is simply called URL in later sections.

```
1: GET http://localhost:8080/tienda1/publico/vaciar.jsp?B2=Vaciar
        +carrito%27%3B+DROP+TABLE+usuarios%3B+SELECT+*+FROM+datos HTTP/1.1
2: User-Agent: Mozilla/5.0
3: Pragma: no-cache
4: Cache-control: no-cache
5: Accept: text/xml,application/xml;q=0.9,text/plain
6: Accept-Encoding: x-gzip, x-deflate, gzip, deflate
7: Accept-Charset: utf-8, utf-8;q=0.5, *;q=0.5
8: Accept-Language: en
9: Host: localhost:8080
10:Cookie: JSESSIONID=11F98280E08EE19274786F4EDDDC821F
11:Connection: close
```

Algorithm 1 Preprocess the HTTP request

Input: HTTP request *Request*

Output: URL sequence *url_seq*

1: **function** PREPROCESSREQUEST(*Request*)
2:    **if** *Request.method* == "POST" **then**
3:        *url* ← *Request.url* + *Request.body*
4:    **else**
5:        *url* ← *Requst.url*
6:    **end if**
7:    *url* ← DECODE(*url*)
8:    *url* ← LOWERCASE(*url*)
9:    *url_seq* ← SPLIT(*url*, "/, ?, &, =, +")
10:    **return** *url_seq*
11: **end function**

The procedure of the HTTP request preprocessing, which is used to process the HTTP request into a URL sequence that can be fed to the detector, is shown in Algorithm 1. The main steps are Decode, Lowercase and Split. Since the HTTP URL allows users to encode special characters, attackers often leverage the encodings to hide attack payloads. To effectively detect web attacks, the URL should be decoded first. Because the URL is not case-insensitive, we lowercase all the characters in URL, which can reduce the size of the training vocabulary. The URL is finally split into a sequence by special characters "/", "?", "&", "=", "+", etc. In practice, the preprocessing may be continuously optimized according to the detection results.

For the above HTTP request, one result of the preprocessing is as follows.

```
http, localhost, 8080, tienda1, publico, vaciar.jsp, b2, vaciar, carrito,
drop, table, usuarios, select, *, from, datos
```

3.3   CNN- and LSTM-Based Detection Models

CNN Model. CNN was initially designed for image recognition but has become a versatile model used for a wide array of tasks. CNN can recognize local or high-order structural features of the input. For example, in our detection model, CNN might be able to distinguish that a request containing the words "*table*", "*select*", "*from*", etc. is malicious. The architecture of the CNN-based detection model is shown in Fig. 2. The one-hot encodings X of the URL sequence are input to the embedding layer. The embedding vectors E are convolved on the Convolutional layer with different types of filters, i.e., if the size of E is $l \times k$, the filter sizes are set to $s \times k$ ($s = 3, 4, 5...$), with k equaling the embedding dimension and s taking different values. The max-pooling (over time) takes the largest element from each feature map output by the convolutional layer, and then concatenates them to pass to the Softmax layer. The Softmax layer outputs a label "0" or "1", which indicates whether the request is normal (by label "0") or malicious (by label "1").

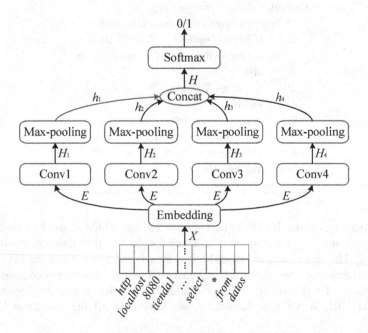

Fig. 2. CNN-based detection model.

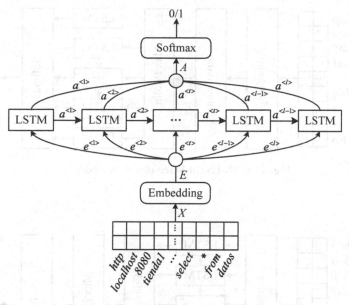

Fig. 3. LSTM-based detection model.

LSTM Model. LSTM is a variant of the recurrent neural network (RNN), which has been proven to perform extremely well on sequential data. In our detection model, LSTM might be able to remember that the word *"from"* appearing in a malicious URL sequence usually follows the word *"select"*. The architecture of the LSTM-based detection model is shown in Fig. 3. The length of the time steps is the same as the length of the URL sequence. The embedding vectors of the one-hot encodings are sequentially distributed to different LSTM units. Then, the outputs of all the LSTM units are gathered together to be input to the Softmax layer.

CNN-LSTM Model. The CNN-LSTM model is a combination of CNN and LSTM. As Fig. 4 shows, the convolutional layer receives the embedding vectors as input. Its output is pooled and then fed to the LSTM layer. The output of the LSTM layer is input to the Softmax layer. The intuition behind the CNN-LSTM model is that the CNN will extract structure features, from which the LSTM will learn the sequential features to classify the input.

LSTM-CNN Model. The LSTM-CNN model is a combination of LSTM and CNN. As Fig. 5 shows, the LSTM layer receives the embedding vectors as input. Its output is directly input to the convolutional layer. The output of the convolutional layer is pooled and then input to the Softmax layer. The intuition behind the LSTM-CNN model is that the LSTM generates new sequential encodings of the input, from which the CNN extracts structural features to classify the input.

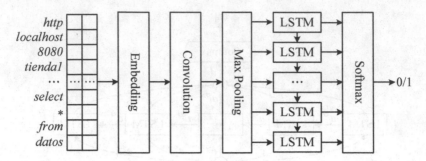

Fig. 4. CNN-LSTM-based detection model.

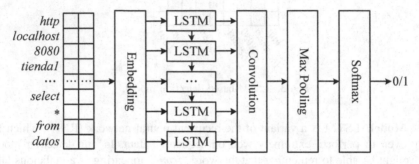

Fig. 5. LSTM-CNN-based detection model.

4   Experiments

To evaluate the performance of models on detecting web attacks, we experimented on the dataset of HTTP DATASET CSIC [32].

4.1   Data Preparation

The HTTP DATASET CSIC 2010 dataset contains thousands of web requests automatically generated by the Information Security Institute of CSIC (Spanish Research National Council), and has been widely used for testing web attack detection systems. The dataset contains 36,000 normal requests and 24,668 malicious requests. The malicious requests include web attacks such as SQL injection, XSS, buffer overflow, information gathering, and file disclosure.

As shown in Table 1, we randomly select approximately 70% of the dataset as training data, approximately 5% as the validation data, and the remaining approximately 25% as the testing data. We train the detection models using the "training data", tune the parameters using the "validation data" and then test the performance of the detection models on the unseen "testing data".

Table 1. Experimental data distribution.

	Training	Validation	Testing
Normal	25,200	1,800	9,000
Malicious	17,268	1,233	6,167
Total	42,468	3,033	15,167

4.2 Parameter Settings and Evaluating Criteria

Based on empirical experiences, we set the necessary hyperparameters as Table 2 shows. The embedding dimension is set to 128. The CNN utilizes 4 types of filters with sizes of $3 \times 128, 4 \times 128, 5 \times 128$ and 6×128. The number of each type of filter is 128. For the LSTM model, the dimensionality of the output space, i.e., the number of hidden units, is set to 64. We train the models by the batch training approach. The learning rate is set to 1e-3, and the batch size is 128.

Table 2. Hyperparameter settings.

	Hyperparameter	Value
Embedding	Dimension	128
CNN	Filter sizes	$3 \times 128, 4 \times 128$ $5 \times 128, 6 \times 128$
	# of filters	128
LSTM	# of hidden units	64
Training	Learning rate	1e−3
	Batch size	128

To evaluate the detection models, we adopted criteria usually used in intrusion detection systems, i.e., *detection rate* and *false alarm rate*, as well as criteria used in machine learning, i.e., *precision, recall, F_1-measure* and *accuracy*. We use *TP* (*true positive*) to represent the number of malicious requests that are correctly detected as malicious. *FP* (*false positive*) represents the number of normal requests that are incorrectly detected as malicious. *TN* (*true negative*) represents the number of normal requests that are correctly detected as normal. *FN* (*false negative*) represents the number of malicious requests that are incorrectly detected as normal. The evaluation criteria are defined as follows. Note that the *recall* has the same definition as the *detection rate*.

$$Detection\ rate/Recall = \frac{TP}{TP+FN} \tag{1}$$

$$False\ alarm\ rate = \frac{FP}{FP+TN} \tag{2}$$

$$Precision = \frac{TP}{TP+FP} \tag{3}$$

$$F_1 - measure = \frac{2 * Precision * Recall}{Precision + Recall} \qquad (4)$$

$$Accuracy = \frac{TP + TN}{TP + FP + TN + FN} \qquad (5)$$

4.3   Experimental Results

The detection model must first be adequately trained on the training data to perform well on the testing data, i.e., effectively detect web attacks. In practice, the testing data (i.e., the requests to be detected) are unknown to us, so we can only improve the performance of the detection models with training and validation data.

In the experiment, we first observe the model performance on training and validation data, and then adjust the training strategies based on validation accuracy. Finally, we evaluate the detection models on the testing data.

Training Results

There are two commonly used methods to enhance the generalization of the detection model during the training phase, i.e., selecting adequate training epochs and applying dropout. We first simply trained each model for 10 epochs and added dropout after the max-pooling layer with the keeping probability being 0.5, and then performed adjustment depending on the results. The training accuracy and loss were recorded every one step and the validation accuracy and loss were recorded every 100 steps. The results are shown in Fig. 6, where blue curves denote the training metrics and orange curves denote the validation metrics. The CNN, LSTM and LSTM-CNN models exhibit good performance, with accuracy rapidly achieving above 95% and loss decreasing towards 0 on both the training and validation data. The CNN-LSTM model may not seem ideal. It fits the training data well but has a large generation error on the validation data. It also demonstrates that 10 epochs of training are sufficient for these models to achieve stable performance.

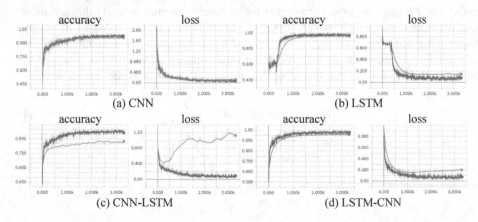

Fig. 6. Training results of the four types of detection models.

Effects of Dropout

In this part, we test the effects of dropout. Dropout has a tunable hyperparameter p (the probability of retaining a neuron in the network, or called the keeping probability). A small p indicates that very few neurons work during training, and "$p = 1$" means no adoption of dropout. We added dropout after the max-pooling layers and trained the models with different keeping probabilities. The results are shown in Table 3. Since the LSTM model does not contain a max-pooling layer and no dropout is applied, its validation accuracy is always 96.11%. For the CNN and LSTM-CNN models, the dropout provides a very limited contribution to improving the model performance. The validation accuracy varies little with p. However, for the CNN-LSTM model, the dropout has a significant negative impact on the validation accuracy. It increases the generalization error. As long as the dropout exists, whatever value the keeping probability takes (i.e., $p = 0.2$, 0.5 or 0.8), the validation accuracy is significantly smaller than that without dropout (i.e., $p = 1$), Which also explains why the CNN-LSTM model does not behave as expected as other models in Fig. 6, where all the models were trained with dropout of the keeping probability being 0.5.

Table 3. Effects of dropout.

Dropout (p)	Validation accuracy			
	CNN	LSTM	CNN-LSTM	LSTM-CNN
0.2	0.9608	0.9611	**0.5897**	0.9548
0.5	0.9618	0.9611	**0.8912**	0.9574
0.8	0.9710	0.9611	**0.8945**	0.9568
1.0	0.9651	0.9611	**0.9601**	0.9588

We retrained the CNN-LSTM model without dropout, and the training results are shown in Fig. 7. Obviously, the CNN-LSTM model regains its outstanding performance on both training and validation data.

We think that the aforementioned dropout is improper for the CNN-LSTM model. The dropout is added after the max-pooling layer and before the LSTM layer. It randomly drops some neurons at training time, which is disastrous for the LSTM. The LSTM is learned by sequential information, some of which is unfortunately removed by the dropout. We can conclude that if the CNN and LSTM are sequentially combined to form a CNN-LSTM model, it is not appropriate to apply the dropout before the LSTM, which will undermine LSTM's learning process.

Given the above results, the four types of detection models (i.e., CNN, LSTM, CNN-LSTM and LSTM-CNN) are all trained for 10 epochs without dropout.

Detection Results

After completing the training, we ran the trained models on testing data to evaluate their performance on detecting web attacks. The detection results are as shown in Table 4. In terms of intrusion detection evaluation criteria, each detection model achieves both a high *detection rate* (average approximately 95%) and a low *false alarm*

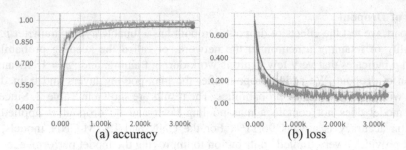

(a) accuracy   (b) loss

Fig. 7. Training results of CNN-LSTM without dropout.

rate (average approximately 2%). In terms of machine learning evaluation criteria, every model achieves satisfactory performance with high *precision* (average 96.92%), *recall* (average 94.27%), F_1-*measure* (average 95.57%) and *accuracy* (average 96.44%). Because the numerical difference in each criterion is very small (approximately 1–2%), it is hard to determine which model is the best.

Table 4. Detection results.

	CNN	LSTM	CNN-LSTM	LSTM-CNN	Average
Detection rate (recall)	0.9549	0.9372	0.9428	0.9359	0.9427
False alarm rate	0.0153	0.0077	0.0367	0.0231	0.0207
Precision	0.9771	0.9882	0.9463	0.9652	0.9692
F_1-measure	0.9659	0.9621	0.9445	0.9504	0.9557
Accuracy	0.9726	0.9699	0.9550	0.9602	0.9644

All the models achieved satisfactory detection results, which were obtained just by using the basic CNN and LSTM models with little hyperparameter tuning. Theoretically, the detection results will be better if we adopt more optimal hyperparameter values. Obviously, the results demonstrate that machine learning has great potential to be applied in the field of web attack detection.

Discussions and Case Studies

In this subsection, we provide an intuitive grasp of the number of false negatives (*FN*) and the number of false positives (*FP*), and carry out case studies to explain why some requests are incorrectly detected.

As stated above, the testing dataset contains 9,000 normal requests and 6,167 malicious requests. The *FN* and *FP* of different detection models are shown in Table 5, where "COM" represents the number of requests that are incorrectly detected by all four types of models. Specifically, the same 233 malicious requests are incorrectly reported as normal, and 21 normal requests are incorrectly reported as malicious, which demonstrates that these detection models are more likely to produce the same false negatives but different false positives. Theoretically, if we construct an ensemble model with these four types of models, the *detection rate* can be increased to 96.22% (i.e.,

233/6,167), and the *false alarm rate* can be decreased to 0.23% (i.e., 21/9,000), but that will be time consuming.

Table 5. *FN* and *FP* of different models.

	CNN	LSTM	CNN-LSTM	LSTM-CNN	COM
FN	278	387	353	395	233
FP	138	69	330	208	21

We choose a false negative and a false positive for case studies. The following snippets show two requests. The upper is a malicious testing request that is incorrectly detected as normal and the below is a normal request in the training data. We can see that the following two requests are very similar except that the upper request contains a "%2F", which is the encoding of "/". In our preprocessing algorithm, "/" is regarded as a special character used to split the URL and will not appear in the URL sequence. In other words, the following two requests have the same type of URL sequence after the preprocessing, which explains the reason why the upper request is incorrectly detected as normal.

```
A "malicious" testing request incorrectly detected as "normal":
1: GET http://localhost:8080/tienda1/publico/anadir.jsp?id=3&nombre=Vino
   +Rioja&precio=100%2F&cantidad=55&B1=A%F1adir+al+carrito HTTP/1.1
2: User-Agent: Mozilla/5.0
3: Pragma: no-cache
......
```

```
A "normal" training request:
1: GET http://localhost:8080/tienda1/publico/anadir.jsp?id=3&nombre=Vino
   +Rioja&precio=100&cantidad=55&B1=A%F1adir+al+carrito HTTP/1.1
2: User-Agent: Mozilla/5.0
3: Pragma: no-cache
......
```

The following snippet shows a normal testing request that is detected as malicious. Through analysis, we find that the following request contains some strings such as "pasar", "por" and "caja", which never appear in the training vocabulary. Such types of requests are very likely to be detected as malicious by the detection models.

```
A "normal" testing request incorrectly detected as "malicious":
1: GET http://localhost:8080/tienda1/publico/pagar.jsp?modo=insertar
   &Precio=6505&B1=Pasar+por+caja HTTP/1.1
2: User-Agent: Mozilla/5.0
3: Pragma: no-cache
......
```

The above case studies can be used for further improvements, which we leave as future work.

5 Conclusion

We present a novel web application firewall called DeepWAF by using deep learning techniques to detect web attacks. We first described the architecture of DeepWAF. Then we provided detailed explanations of the HTTP request preprocessing and the principles of the proposed four types of detection models based on CNN, LSTM, CNN-LSTM and LSTM-CNN. Finally, we evaluated the detection models on the dataset of HTTP DATASET CSIC 2010 and verified their good performance in detecting web attacks.

We simply tried the basic CNN and LSTM models with little hyperparameter tuning. Future work can be concentrated on adopting more sophisticated deep learning models, tuning model hyperparameters and inspecting all the fields of the HTTP request, thus resulting in much more powerful web attack detection models.

References

1. Symantec Corporation: Symantec internet security threat report, Trends for July–December 07 (2008)
2. Trustwave: Cenzic application vulnerability trends 2014 (2014)
3. Halfond, W.G.J., Viegas, J., Orso, A.: A classification of SQL injection attacks and countermeasures. In: Proceedings of the IEEE International Symposium on Secure Software Engineering, pp. 13–15. IEEE (2006)
4. Kieyzun, A., Guo, P.J., Jayaraman, K., Ernst, M.D.: Automatic creation of SQL injection and cross-site scripting attacks. In: Proceedings of the 31st International Conference on Software Engineering, pp. 199–209. IEEE Computer Society (2009)
5. Li, H.-F., Lee, S.-Y., Shan, M.-K.: DSM-PLW: single-pass mining of path traversal patterns over streaming Web click-sequences. Comput. Netw. **50**, 1474–1487 (2006)
6. Jensen, M., Gruschka, N., Herkenhoner, R.: A survey of attacks on web services. Comput. Sci. Res. Dev. **24**, 185 (2009)
7. Prokhorenko, V., Choo, K.-K.R., Ashman, H.: Web application protection techniques: a taxonomy. J. Netw. Comput. Appl. **60**, 95–112 (2016)
8. Valeur, F., Mutz, D., Vigna, G.: A learning-based approach to the detection of SQL attacks. In: Julisch, K., Kruegel, C. (eds.) DIMVA 2005. LNCS, vol. 3548, pp. 123–140. Springer, Heidelberg (2005). https://doi.org/10.1007/11506881_8
9. Halfond, W.G.J., Orso, A.: Preventing SQL injection attacks using AMNESIA. In: Proceedings of the 28th International Conference on Software Engineering, pp. 795–798. ACM (2006)
10. Kemalis, K., Tzouramanis, T.: SQL-IDS: a specification-based approach for SQL-injection detection. In: Proceedings of the 2008 ACM Symposium on Applied Computing, pp. 2153–2158. ACM (2008)
11. Liu, A., Yuan, Y., Wijesekera, D., Stavrou, A.: SQLProb: a proxy-based architecture towards preventing SQL injection attacks. In: Proceedings of the 2009 ACM Symposium on Applied Computing, pp. 2054–2061. ACM (2009)
12. Bisht, P., Madhusudan, P., Venkatakrishnan, V.N.: CANDID: dynamic candidate evaluations for automatic prevention of SQL injection attacks. ACM Trans. Inf. Syst. Secur. **13**, 1–39 (2010)

13. Kar, D., Panigrahi, S., Sundararajan, S.: SQLiGoT: detecting SQL injection attacks using graph of tokens and SVM. Comput. Secur. **60**, 206–225 (2016)
14. Gupta, S., Gupta, B.B.: Cross-site scripting (XSS) attacks and defense mechanisms: classification and state-of-the-art. Int. J. Syst. Assur. Eng. Manag. **8**, 512–530 (2017)
15. Nadji, Y., Saxena, P., Song, D.: Document structure integrity: a robust basis for cross-site scripting defense. In: Network & Distributed System Security Symposium (2009)
16. Wassermann, G., Su, Z.: Static detection of cross-site scripting vulnerabilities. In: Proceedings of the 30th International Conference on Software Engineering, pp. 171–180. ACM (2008)
17. Weinberger, J., Saxena, P., Akhawe, D., Finifter, M., Shin, R., Song, D.: A systematic analysis of XSS sanitization in web application frameworks. In: Atluri, V., Diaz, C. (eds.) ESORICS 2011. LNCS, vol. 6879, pp. 150–171. Springer, Heidelberg (2011). https://doi. org/10.1007/978-3-642-23822-2_9
18. Balduzzi, M., Gimenez, C.T., Balzarotti, D., Kirda, E.: Automated discovery of parameter pollution vulnerabilities in web applications. In: Proceedings of the 18th Annual Network and Distributed System Security Symposium, pp. 1–16 (2011)
19. Su, Z., Wassermann, G.: The essence of command injection attacks in web applications. In: Conference Record of the 33rd ACM SIGPLAN-SIGACT Symposium on Principles of Programming Languages, pp. 372–382. ACM, Charleston (2006)
20. Tajbakhsh, M.S., Bagherzadeh, J.: A sound framework for dynamic prevention of Local File Inclusion. In: 2015 7th Conference on Information and Knowledge Technology (IKT), pp. 1–6 (2015)
21. Han, E.E.: Detection of web application attacks with request length module and regex pattern analysis. In: Zin, T.T., Lin, J.C.-W., Pan, J.-S., Tin, P., Yokota, M. (eds.) GEC 2015. AISC, vol. 388, pp. 157–165. Springer, Cham (2016). https://doi.org/10.1007/978-3-319-23207-2_16
22. Saxe, J., Berlin, K.: eXpose: a character-level convolutional neural network with embeddings for detecting malicious URLs, file paths and registry keys. arXiv:1702.08568 [cs] (2017)
23. Kruegel, C., Vigna, G.: Anomaly detection of web-based attacks. Presented at the Proceedings of the 10th ACM Conference on Computer and Communications Security (2003)
24. Kruegel, C., Vigna, G., Robertson, W.: A multi-model approach to the detection of web-based attacks. Comput. Netw. **48**, 717–738 (2005)
25. Corona, I., Ariu, D., Giacinto, G.: HMM-Web: a framework for the detection of attacks against web applications. In: 2009 IEEE International Conference on Communications, pp. 1–6. IEEE (2009)
26. Corona, I., Giacinto, G.: Detection of server-side web attacks. In: Proceedings of the First Workshop on Applications of Pattern Analysis, pp. 160–166 (2010)
27. Corona, I., Tronci, R., Giacinto, G.: SuStorID: a multiple classifier system for the protection of web services. In: Proceedings of the 21st International Conference on Pattern Recognition (ICPR 2012), pp. 2375–2378. IEEE (2012)
28. Zolotukhin, M., Hamalainen, T., Kokkonen, T., Siltanen, J.: Analysis of HTTP requests for anomaly detection of web attacks. In: 2014 IEEE 12th International Conference on Dependable, Autonomic and Secure Computing, pp. 406–411. IEEE, Dalian (2014)
29. Choras, M., Kozik, R.: Machine learning techniques applied to detect cyber attacks on web applications. Log. J. IGPL **23**, 45–56 (2015)

30. Bronte, R., Shahriar, H., Haddad, H.: Information theoretic anomaly detection framework for web application. In: 2016 IEEE 40th Annual Computer Software and Applications Conference (COMPSAC), pp. 394–399. IEEE (2016)
31. Zhang, M., Xu, B., Bai, S., Lu, S., Lin, Z.: A deep learning method to detect web attacks using a specially designed CNN. In: Liu, D., Xie, S., Li, Y., Zhao, D., El-Alfy, E.S. (eds.) ICONIP 2017. LNCS, vol. 10638, pp. 828–836. Springer, Cham (2017). https://doi.org/10.1007/978-3-319-70139-4_84
32. Gimenez, C.T., Villegas, A.P., Maranon, G.A.: HTTP dataset CSIC 2010 (2012). http://www.isi.csic.es/dataset/

Research on Intrusion Detection Based on Semantic Re-encoding and Multi-space Projection

Jingjing Wang[1], Zhendong Wu[1(✉)], and Zhang Zhang[1,2]

[1] School of Cyberspace, Hangzhou Dianzi University, Hangzhou, China
alilliam@sina.com, wzd@hdu.edu.cn, 3ricccz@gmail.com
[2] School of Systems Science, Beijing Normal University, Beijing, China

Abstract. In recent years, with the continuous popularization of the cyber-attacking technology, the network intrusion events tend to be frequent and concealed. The accuracy of the traditional rule-based intrusion detection system is affected. And the false alarm rate of machine learning-based intrusion detection system is high due to the lack of causal link analysis among sampled data and attack events. Aiming at the problem, this paper proposes an intelligent intrusion detection algorithm, named SRMPC, which based on semantic re-encoding and multi-space projection. The key idea of the SRMPC algorithm is that the semantics of the network traffic is differentiated, and the normal network traffic and the attack network traffic often have obvious differences in the narrative semantics. The SRMPC algorithm re-encodes the semantics of the network traffic, and uses the multi-space projection technology to make the re-encoded semantic space boundaries clearing, thus, effectively improving the detection accuracy and robustness of the algorithm. The SRMPC algorithm can get > 99% accuracy of general Web attack detection, and when identifying NSL-KDD data sets with CNN, an average performance improvement of 8% is achieved.

Keywords: Intrusion detection · Semantic recoding · Multi-space projection · CNN

1 Introduction

In recent years, we have witnessed incredible progress in cyberspace attack which can cause enormous damage if undetected. The Intrusion detection system (IDS) needs further developing because of the rate of missed detection and false alarm are still high.

In general, Intrusion detection can be divided into two types, misuse detection and anomaly detection. Misuse-based detection detects network traffic and system logs according to detection rules. While the rules with attack character is already known, easily bypassed. Anomaly-based detection models the normal state of the system and treats network behavior deviations from normal as exceptions [1, 2].

Anomaly detection methods based on machine learning (ML) have received extensive attentions [3]. It can continuously adjust the detection model according to the changes of network traffic through training. A number of researchers use ML

© Springer Nature Switzerland AG 2019
J. Vaidya et al. (Eds.): CSS 2019, LNCS 11983, pp. 137–150, 2019.
https://doi.org/10.1007/978-3-030-37352-8_12

techniques like C4.5, random forest, k-NN, SVM for anomaly detection, which improves the accuracy and automation of anomaly detection [4, 5].

However, restrict to a single ML method, the accuracy of identifying attacks is limited regardless of how much data is given for training. So a hybrid method combined with various data ML methods to form a hybrid classifier to further improve the accuracy of recognition [6–9].

Recently, Deep Learning (DL) is widely used for various pattern recognition and network applications, due to their capability of learning a computational process in depth. Additionally, some DL algorithms have been used for intrusion detection [10–16]. Yin et al. [15] proposed a deep learning approach for intrusion-detection using recurrent neural networks (RNN-IDS). The model can effectively improve both the accuracy of intrusion detection and the ability to recognize the intrusion type. Wu et al. [14] used CNN to select traffic features from raw data set automatically, and he set the cost function weight coefficient of each class based on its numbers to solve the imbalanced data set problem. The model not only reduces the false alarm rate (FAR) but also improves the accuracy of the class with small numbers. Blanco et al. [10] used CNN as a multiclass network attack classifier. A Genetic Algorithm (GA) was used to find a high-quality solution by rearranging the layout of the input features, reducing the amount of different features if required.

And there are also researchers combined the ML method and DL method. Al-Qatf et al. [17] proposed an approach combing sparse autoencoder with SVM ((STL)-IDS). The autoencoder is for feature extraction, and SVM is the classifier. The proposed approach improved SVM classification accuracy and accelerated training and testing times.

Although the DL-based IDS has achieved high recognition accuracy in the laboratory, the accuracy in actual use is still questionable. The main reason is that the existing DL algorithms are insufficient in both the interpretability and certainty. In addition, the existing intelligent detection algorithms can be easily adapted by attackers to bypass detection. In this paper, an intelligent intrusion detection algorithm based on semantic re-encoding and multi-space projection is proposed. Semantic re-encoding is used to highlight the difference between positive and negative traffic, raise the interpretability; while using multi-space projection techniques can reduce the possibility of an attacker adapting to the detection algorithm.

The rest of this paper is organized as follows: Sect. 2 introduces the residual network. Section 3 describes our proposed method in detail. Section 4 shows experimental performances. Finally, the conclusion is presented in Sect. 5.

2 Residual Network (ResNet)

Convolutional Neural Networks are very similar to ordinary neural networks, and they all consist of neurons with learnable weights and biases. ResNet is based on CNN. As the parameters of ResNet are easier to optimize than the other CNN structures and with good performance, the detection rate of intrusion detection will be increased using ResNet. As shown in Fig. 1. The ResNet [19] is composed of the image input, convolution layer, subsampling layer, full connection layer. The main purpose of convolution layer is to extract features from the input image. The subsampling layer reduces the dimensions of each feature map and preserves the most important information. The role of pooling is to gradually reduce the size of the input space. Put an image into the network, then output the class that the image belong to.

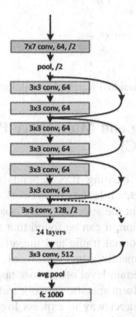

Fig. 1. The architecture of ResNet.

Unlike other CNN, ResNet reformulate the layers as learning residual functions with reference to the layer inputs, instead of learning unreferenced functions. The residual networks proved to be easier to optimize, and gain greater accuracy than other CNN models before.

Resnet provides 2 types of mapping, one is identity mapping and the other is residual mapping, those two maps are to solving the problem of the accuracy decreases as the network deepens. The Resnet is stacked by the building blocks. As shown in Fig. 2, the building block is made up of identity mapping and residual mapping. The identity mapping is the "curved curve" part. Formally, denoting the desired underlying mapping as $H(x)$, we let the stacked nonlinear layers fit another mapping of $F(x) := H(x) - x$. The original mapping is recast into $F(x) + x$.

We hypothesize that it is easier to optimize the residual mapping than to optimize the original, unreferenced mapping. To the extreme, if an identity mapping were optimal, it would be easier to push the residual to zero than to fit an identity mapping by a stack of nonlinear layers. The formulation of $F(x) + x$ can be realized by feed-forward neural networks with "shortcut connections". Shortcut connections are those skipping one or more layers. Identity shortcut connections add neither extra parameter nor computational complexity.

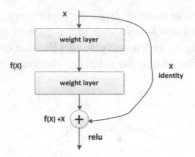

Fig. 2. Residual learning: a building block.

3 Semantic Re-encoding and Multi-space Projection Based Classification (SRMPC)

The detection accuracy of the existing IDS depends greatly on the accuracy and specificity of the training data set, while the raw network traffic data has a large amount of noise. It's difficult to highlight the specificity. By observing the attack and defense features of the network application, it can be found that for the network attack applied on a specific application, the normal traffic and the attack traffic often have obvious differences in the narrative semantics. In other words, the attacker will inevitably change the original logic of a certain level of network application. As long as the logic can be clearly expressed, it can form specific network traffic characteristic. While inter-symbol semantics is the most direct way to express logic, so we raised an algorithm based on semantic re-encoding and multi-space projection (SRMP).

3.1 Network Traffic Semantic Re-encoding

For the network traffic dataset, we re-sequence the network traffic characteristics to a new feature space by re-encoding.

The dataset of network traffic can be divided into raw data and features that are extracted from raw data. So in our method, we first judge whether the dataset is made up of raw data or not. And then do semantic re-encoding using separately.

Raw Data

The existing network traffic raw data can easily be converted into a form of character stream. For example, the network application on the Internet, which uses the HTTP protocol to express its semantics in the form of a character stream. And the network traffic of the non-http protocol can be analyzed through the protocol and then we can extract its key parameter fields and transform them to a character stream.

We first create a word table extracted from the dataset. We use delimiters such as breakpoint punctuation and special characters to split character stream. After that, we split the character stream into word string named word segmentation. Put words in the word string into a word table separately, then we get a word table. In the HTTP protocol, for example, '&', '|', ', ', '\', '?', '||' are delimiters. As delimiters will vary with the HTTP protocol, we need to update them continuously.

According to the origin word table, we can transform all the records in the character stream to a word array. We rearrange the HTTP access string into a record composed of words in the word table, and access one record at a time.

Extract all positive and the negative sample from the HTTP access traffic, and perform the operations of the former steps. Then we get a sample record set.

Then we want to get a new word table to map the origin word table. The new word table is ordered by the difference between the positive and the negative sample. So we need to first calculate the difference between positive and the negative sample, we define it as comprehensive word frequency (CWF). We calculate the positive and negative word frequency (WF) in the original word table separately and sort word array according to the word frequency. If a word appears in one line multiple times then count just once. Set threshold T1, T2, we can easily see from the Fig. 3 that T1 > 0 and T2 < 0. If CWF > T1 or CWF < T2, means that the WF between positive and negative is huge, do One-to-one re-encoding. While if CWF < T1 and CWF > T2, do Many-to-one re-encoding. As shown in Fig. 3, the multiple words that CWF < T1 and CWF > T2 are combined into word WordM. In addition, unknown words are also encoded as WordM. Sort the original word table by CWF, and we get the word-table-after.

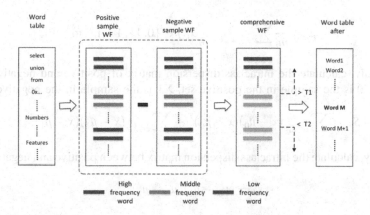

Fig. 3. The procedure of reordering the word table.

The next step is re-mapping the positive and negative samples to a word bag according to the new code table. As shown in Fig. 4, when n words in the sample are mapped to the same word, the value at the corresponding position of the word is added by n. The mapping procedure makes any unequal-length word sequence to the same word sequence. After all the positive and negative samples are remapped, we get a set of training samples of equal length. The transformation function is as follows:

$$S = \{(x_i, y_i)\}, 1 \le i \le m, y \in \{0, 1\}, \tag{1}$$

m is the number of training samples, Xi means the record (word sequence) in the training set. The length of word bag is n.$y \in \{0, 1\}$ is the label of sample.

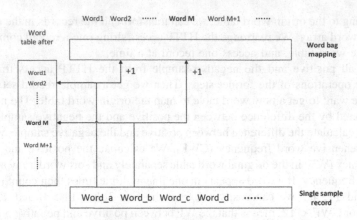

Fig. 4. Re-mapping a sample into a word bag.

Finally, we do dimension reduction. Here are the steps:

Firstly, calculate the mean of positive and negative samples μ_j respectively, j means the class type, positive and negative.

$$\mu_j = \frac{1}{m_j}\sum\nolimits_{(x_i,y_i \in s \& y_i = j)} x_i, j \in \{0,1\}, 1 \le i \le m, \tag{2}$$

Secondly, calculate the intraclass dispersion matrix of positive and negative samples Sw. X0 is the sample in the positive set, X1 is the sample in the negative one.

$$S_w = \sum\nolimits_{x \in X_0} (x - \mu_0)(x - \mu_0)^T + \sum\nolimits_{x \in X_1} (x - \mu_1)(x - \mu_1)^T, \tag{3}$$

Thirdly, calculate the intraclass dispersion matrix between positive and negative one.

$$s_d = (\mu_0 - \mu_1)(\mu_0 - \mu_1)^T, \tag{4}$$

Finally, calculate positive and negative sample space separation projection vectors W. W is the corresponding eigenvector of largest eigenvalue of the matrix $S_w^{-1}S_d$. Then we do the a dimensionality reduction operation, the new feature space is $w^T x_i$.

$$S1 = \{(x_{i1}, y_{i1})\}, 1 \le i1 \le m, y \in \{0,1\}, \tag{5}$$

x_{i1} is the record in the training set, the dimension is n1, n1 $<$n.

The purpose of dimension reduction is to further open the spatial distance between positive and negative samples.

Features Extract from Raw Data

For the data made up of features extract from raw data such as the benchmark dataset NSL-KDD. We change the feature to a matrix made up of four parts in order to do the semantic re-encoding. The four parts are the original part, the difference of the original feature between the mean of positive sample and the negative sample separately, and the square of the original part.

We first do some preprocess. And then we calculated the mean feature map of positive data and the negative data. We then let the original features subtract the two feature maps separately, resulting two parts of feature maps. The last part of feature map is the square of the original part.

We link the four parts of features and transform it from 1D vector to a 2D matrix. The result of the steps may seem like Fig. 5.

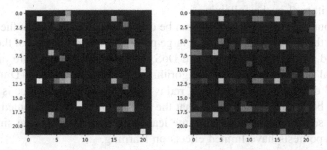

Fig. 5. The mean feature map of normal connections (left) and abnormal connections (right).

From the figure above, we can obviously see that the feature map between the positive samples and the negative samples are different. Through the semantic re-encoding, we amplify the gap between the two types.

We formalize this algorithm in Algorithm 1.

Alg. 1 Network character stream semantic re-encoding algorithm

    if the dataset is made up of raw data:

        1. Transform data to character stream.

        2. Word segmentation.

        3. Build a word table. Put the word string split by (1) into a word table separately.

        4. Rearrange the HTTP access string into a record composed of words, and access one record at a time.

        5. Extract the abnormal and the normal sample from the HTTP access traffic, and perform the operations of steps (1) (2) (3) to form a sample record set.

        6. Sort the word table.

        7. Re-encode the word list.

        8. Re-mapping the positive and negative samples to a word bag according to the new code table.

        9. Dimension reduction.

    else:

        10. Preprocess data, get original vector v1.

        11. Calculate the positive and negative mean vector separately. And subtract from original vector separately. Then we get v2, v3.

        12. Calculate the square of the original vector v4.

        13. Combine the v1, v2, v3, v4.

        14. Transpose 1D vector to 2D matrix.

3.2 Multi-space Projection

Algorithm 1 semantically re-encodes the network dataset to form a new network traffic feature space. So that he network traffic detection model can be trained on the feature space using classical machine learning methods such as SVM and CNN. In order to further separate the feature space formed by positive and negative samples, we proposed an algorithm called Algorithm 2 using multi-space projection. We describe the steps of Algorithm 2 in the following.

The distribution of the same attack can be different. For example, in the NSL-KDD attack dataset, the DoS attack type has a large proportion, and the data of the same type is not balanced. As shown in Fig. 6, the DoS and Normal data sets are processed by PCA (principal component analysis) algorithm for easy observation. Dimensionality reduction (2–3 dimensions) observation, red is the DoS dataset, and blue is the Normal dataset. It can be seen from the figure that the DoS datasets are distributed in different three regions, so that the various machine learning methods under the single normal distribution hypothesis have limited effects on learning.

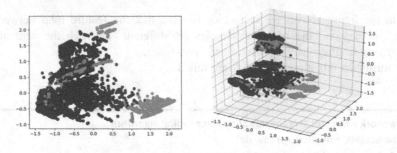

Fig. 6. Dos & normal hybrid distribution in 2D and 3D values. (Color figure online)

The first step in Algorithm 2 is that we use K-means to get more negative set. In other words, we separate the negative sets into more groups. While the positive sample set is still in a group. For example, we changed the attack type of DoS into DoS1, DoS2, and DoS3. The purpose of this step is to make the classification of the sample set closer to the multi-dimensional normal distribution.

The second step is that we can use multiple types of binary classifier (BC) to divide the positive and negative samples.

One of BCs we used is ResNet. Assuming that the network flow feature space obtained by Algorithm 1 has a better specific feature distribution, we may think the new distribution as a multidimensional normal distribution, and it can be effectively distinguished by BCs. Although ResNet can be stacked to very deep layers, we think that even network are not so deep is enough to handle the problem. The structure of ResNet is shown in Fig. 7.

The architecture of classifier is shown in Fig. 8. There are several BCs and each of them classify one types of sample. For an incoming connection x, BCs make their decision, and if the BCi considers that it belongs to normal, we define $BCi(x) = 1$, and when it belongs to abnormal, we define $BCi(x) = 0$.

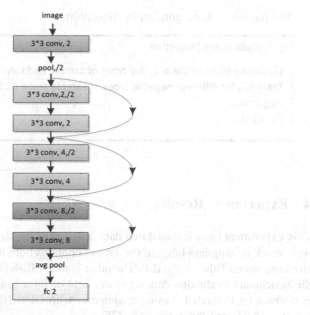

Fig. 7. The structure of ResNet in the proposed method.

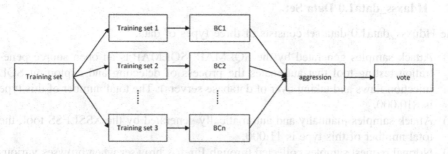

Fig. 8. The architecture of classifier.

The third step collects the outcomes of the BCs, and then calculates the sum of the outcomes.

The final step judges if the result is more than 1, then the x is a normal sample, or else the x is an attack sample. That is, if any of the 4 outcomes vote the connection to be an attack type, then we make the decision that the connection is an attack. The transformation function is as follows:

$$\sum_{i=0}^{3} BC_i > = 1,\qquad(6)$$

We formalize this algorithm in Algorithm 2.

Alg. 2. Multi-space Projection

1. Clustering some of the negative types of sample and form new negative groups.
2. Train BCs for different negative types of sample and a BC for positive type.
3. Aggression.
4. Final judge.

---

4   Experiment Results

This experiment has examined two data sets, one is the dataset collected especially for web attack in hangdian lab, and the dataset contains both the normal and abnormal http streams, named Hduxss_data1.0. The other is the NSL-KDD, which is considered to be the benchmark evaluation data set in the field of intrusion detection; the experiment is performed on Pytorch 1.0 using a computer with GPU 1050ti, the operating system is Ubuntu 18.04, and the memory is 32G.

4.1   Hduxss_data1.0 Data Set

The Hduxss_data1.0 data set consists of three types of data:

(1) Attack samples generated by the SQLMAP (SQLMAP is an open source pene-tration testing tool that automates the process of detecting and exploiting SQL injection flaws and taking over of database servers); The total number of this type is 810,000.
(2) Attack samples manually and automatically generated by the XSSLESS tool; the total number of this type is 11,000.
(3) Normal request samples collected through Firefox browser when browses various web pages. We extracted parameters from them, and obtains 130,000 normal samples.

We separate the dataset of Hduxss_data1.0 dataset evenly into training set and testing set. The results are shown in Table 1. In the test process, all data is processed by SRMPC Algorithm 1, and the processing result is processed by support vector machine, naive Bayes, and SRMPC Algorithm 2. It can be seen from Table 1, the SRMPC algorithm achieves the best recognition performance comparing with the classical machine learning algorithm. At the same time, all the machine learning methods involved in the test obtained more than 99% accuracy and F1 value. This performance was mainly achieved by SRMPC Algorithm 1 performing a round of semantic re-encoding processing on the HTTP data stream, highlighting the network data. The specificity of the flow has achieved good test results.

Table 1. The result of Hduxss_data1.0 dataset

	Accuracy	Precision	Recall	F1
Naive Bayes	99.02%	99.10%	99.12%	0.9911
SRMPC	99.56%	99.99%	99.53%	0.9976

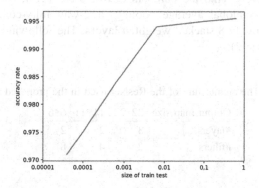

Fig. 9. The data demand of SRMPC algorithm.

The experiment tests the data demand of SRMPC algorithm. The result is shown in Fig. 9. It can be seen from the figure that the algorithm requires less data, even in the case of only five-tenths of the data is trained. High classification accuracy (>99%), with the increase of the training set, the accuracy rate is gradually close to 1. Tests show that the SRMPC algorithm has good stability.

4.2 NSL-KDD Data Set

Each record of NSL-KDD dataset is a vector that contains 41 features and a label which means the attack types. The attack types include four categories: DoS, probe, U2R, R2L.

The NSL-KDD data set has 41 attribute and one class attribute. In the preprocessing step, we used 1-to-n encoding to convert the non-numeric features into numeric features. Then we get 122-dimensional features. Observation of NSL-KDD dataset shows that the 7th feature has almost all zero values in dataset [18]. So we removed the features to get 121-dimensional features.

We apply the min-max normalization to address the data in this paper. The transformation function is as follows:

$$X_{std} = \frac{X - X.min}{X.max - X.min},$$ (7)

Here we describe the details of the experiment. And then analyze the performance on the NSL-KDD data set.

As ResNet showing a great performance on image, and the residual networks is easier to optimize, we did our experiment on ResNet.

The semantic difference between positive and negative sample will be highlighted in intrusion detection, the complexity of classifier is low. So we use ResNet without much deep in our experiment.

We use the architecture of ResNet in [19]. We changed the feature maps of sizes to {22, 11, 6} respectively. And the numbers of filters are {2, 4, 8} respectively. The network ends with a global average pooling, a 2-way fully-connected layer, and softmax. There are totally 8 stacked weighted layers. The following table summarizes the architecture (Table 2):

Table 2. The architecture of the ResNet used in the proposed method.

Output map size	22*22	11*11	6*6
#layers	3	2	2
#filters	2	4	8

We train the BCs over the KDDTrain+ . The following table shows the contrast experiment on NSL-KDD, In order to see the effect of semantic re-encoding and the multi-space projection.

Table 3. Performance of the proposed method for KDDTest+.

	Precision	Recall	F1
(STL)-IDS [17]	–	–	–
ANN [18]	96.59%	69.35%	0.8073
RNN-IDS [15]	96.92%	72.95%	0.8324
SRMPC	93.46%	93.75%	0.9360

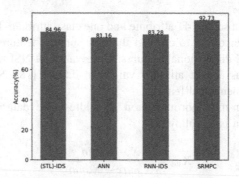

Fig. 10. Accuracy of the proposed method for KDDTest+.

As shown in Table 3 the SRMPC have both high precision and high recall. And from the Fig. 10, the experimental results show that the SRMPC exceed than the other two classifiers, almost an average performance improvement of 8%. We can infer the Fig. 10 that the semantic re-encoding with ResNet improved the gap between the attack and the normal sample. In addition, as the ResNet has the strength of CNN, it runs less time than RNN-IDS.

5 Summary

This paper proposes a SRMPC intrusion detection algorithm based on semantic space re-encoding and multi-space projection. The semantic re-encoding technique proposed by the algorithm characterizes different semantic spaces using different methods, such as frequency of use of words, DNN, and can effectively separate different types of semantic expressions in the field where semantic differences are obvious. The SRMPC intrusion detection algorithm uses this technology and further multi-space projection operation to make different types of semantic network data streams further highlight differences in space, form a new feature space, and achieve better recognition accuracy. The algorithm has good dynamics and is not easy to be analyzed by attackers, thus avoiding the situation that the intrusion detection algorithm often encounters the "adaptation" of the attacker. Semantic re-encoding technology in network security can have multiple encoding methods. This paper only proposes one of them. Ideally, semantic re-encoding technology can distinguish between normal and attack data streams in an environment where the offensive and defensive semantic differences are obvious. We will carry out further research work in this follow-up.

Acknowledgement. This research is supported by National Natural Science Foundation of China (No. 61772162), National Key R&D Program of China (No. 2018YFB0804102), Zhejiang Key R&D Program of China (No. 2018C01088).

References

1. Folino, G., Sabatino, P.: Ensemble based collaborative and distributed intrusion detection systems: a survey. J. Netw. Comput. Appl. **66**, 1–16 (2016)
2. Moustafa, N., Hu, J., Slay, J.: A holistic review of network anomaly detection systems: a comprehensive survey. J. Netw. Comput. Appl. **128**, 33–55 (2019)
3. Bhuyan, M.H., Bhattacharyya, D.K., Kalita, J.K.: Network anomaly detection: methods, systems and tools. IEEE Commun. Surv. Tutor. **16**, 303–336 (2013)
4. Prabhu Kavin, B.: Data mining techniques for providing network security through intrusion detection systems: a survey. Int. J. Adv. Comput. Electron. Eng. **2**(10), 1–6 (2017)
5. Aburomman, A.A., Reaz, M.B.I.: A survey of intrusion detection systems based on ensemble and hybrid classifiers. Comput. Secur. **65**, 135–152 (2017)
6. Colom, J.F., Gil, D., Mora, H., Volckaert, B., Jimeno, A.M.: Scheduling framework for distributed intrusion detection systems over heterogeneous network architectures. J. Netw. Comput. Appl. **108**, 76–86 (2018)

7. Ji, S.-Y., Jeong, B.-K., Choi, S., Jeong, D.H.: A multi-level intrusion detection method for abnormal network behaviors. J. Netw. Comput. Appl. **62**, 9–17 (2016)
8. Li, L., Yu, Y., Bai, S., Hou, Y., Chen, X.: An effective two-step intrusion detection approach based on binary classification and k-NN. IEEE Access **6**, 12060–12073 (2018)
9. Kabir, E., Hu, J., Wang, H., Zhuo, G.: A novel statistical technique for intrusion detection systems. Futur. Gener. Comput. Syst. **79, Part 1**, 303–318 (2018)
10. Blanco, R., Malagon, P., Cilla, J.J., Moya, J.M.: Multiclass network attack classifier using CNN tuned with genetic algorithms. In: 2018 28th International Symposium on Power and Timing Modeling, Optimization and Simulation (PATMOS), pp. 177–182. IEEE, Platja d'Aro (2018)
11. Hsu, C.-M., Hsieh, H.-Y., Prakosa, S.W., Azhari, M.Z., Leu, J.-S.: Using long-short-term memory based convolutional neural networks for network intrusion detection. In: Chen, J.-L., Pang, A.-C., Deng, D.-J., Lin, C.-C. (eds.) WICON 2018. LNICST, vol. 264, pp. 86–94. Springer, Cham (2019). https://doi.org/10.1007/978-3-030-06158-6_9
12. Diro, A.A., Chilamkurti, N.: Distributed attack detection scheme using deep learning approach for Internet of Things. Futur. Gener. Comput. Syst. **82**, 761–768 (2018)
13. Naseer, S., et al.: Enhanced network anomaly detection based on deep neural networks. IEEE Access **6**, 48231–48246 (2018)
14. Wu, K., Chen, Z., Li, W.: A novel intrusion detection model for a massive network using convolutional neural networks. IEEE Access **6**, 50850–50859 (2018)
15. Yin, C., Zhu, Y., Fei, J., He, X.: A deep learning approach for intrusion detection using recurrent neural networks. IEEE Access **5**, 21954–21961 (2017)
16. Mohammadpour, L., Ling, T.C., Liew, C.S., Chong, C.Y.A.: Convolutional neural network for network intrusion detection system. Proc. Asia-Pacific Adv. Netw. **46**, 50–55 (2018)
17. Al-Qatf, M., Lasheng, Y., Al-Habib, M., Al-Sabahi, K.: Deep learning approach combining sparse auto encoder with SVM for network intrusion detection. IEEE Access **6**, 52843–52856 (2018)
18. Ingre, B., Yadav, A.: Performance analysis of NSL-KDD dataset using ANN. In: 2015 International Conference on Signal Processing and Communication Engineering Systems (SPACES), pp. 92–96. IEEE, Guntur (2015)
19. He, K., Zhang, X., Ren, S., Sun, J.: Deep residual learning for image recognition. In: 2016 IEEE Conference on Computer Vision and Pattern Recognition (CVPR), pp. 770–778. IEEE, Las Vegas (2016)

Software Defect Prediction Model Based on GA-BP Algorithm

Mengtian Cui, Yameng Huang$^{(\boxtimes)}$, and Jing Luo$^{(\boxtimes)}$

Key Laboratory of Computer System, State Ethnic Affairs Commission,
Southwest Minzu University, Chengdu 610041, China
dbsd_dbsd@163.com, hangkongzy@163.com

Abstract. The novel software defect prediction model based on GA-BP algorithm was proposed in the paper considering the disadvantage of traditional BP (abbreviated for Back Propagation) neural network, which has the problem of easy to fall into local optimization when constructing software defect prediction model, and finally affects the prediction accuracy. Firstly, the optimization ability of GA (abbreviated for Genetic Algorithms) is introduced to optimize the weights and thresholds of Back Propagation neural network. Then the prediction model was constructed based on the GA-BP. Meanwhile the public dataset MDP from NASA was selected and the tool WEKA was used to clean the data and format conversion and as the result, four datasets is available. In the end, experimental results show that the proposed method in the paper is effective for software defect prediction.

Keywords: Software defect prediction · Machine learning · Genetic Algorithms · BP neural network

1 Introduction

With the development of the Internet, software products can be seen everywhere in people's lives. In the development of software technology, people pay more and more attention to the prediction of software defects [1, 2]. Recently related class imbalance problem [3], model algorithm research and semi-supervised and unsupervised research are becoming the main research of software defect prediction [4, 5]. Machine learning plays a huge role in the field of software defect prediction. Regarding to model algorithms, many researchers have done many works on WSDP (Within-Project Software Defect Prediction) [1], CSDP (Cross-Project Software Defect Prediction) and the HDP (Heterogeneous Defect Prediction) [6, 7]. Artificial neural network algorithm has a strong fault tolerance and has a strong ability to deal with nonlinear relations, can build very complex functions and nonlinear relations, so the use of neural networks to build software defect prediction model has great advantages [8]. However, because the convergence speed of BP neural network is slow and it is difficult to find its optimal weights and thresholds in the prediction of software defects, it is becoming a new research focus to resolve it.

The main task of this research is to study the existing software defect prediction model, combine the BP neural network algorithm in machine learning, optimized the

© Springer Nature Switzerland AG 2019
J. Vaidya et al. (Eds.): CSS 2019, LNCS 11983, pp. 151–161, 2019.
https://doi.org/10.1007/978-3-030-37352-8_13

weights and thresholds of neural network by using the optimization ability of GA. Experiments were carried out on the basis of research, and the conclusions were drawn from statistical analysis and comparative experimental data.

2 Constructing a Software Defect Prediction Model Based on GA-BP Algorithm

2.1 Construction of GA-BP Defect Prediction Model

Although the BP network has been widely used, there are still many shortcomings including the slow convergence speed and easy to local optimal solution. So genetic algorithm is used to find the global optimal solution of BP network in the paper [9]. The GA-BP prediction model combines BP neural network and genetic algorithm, calculates the predicted value and the loss function value by BP neural network algorithm, and then uses the genetic algorithm to iterate continuously to find the optimal weight of the neural network. The GA-BP algorithm model is divided into two stages, the first stage is the training stage, and the second stage is the prediction stage. The software defect Prediction Model based on GA-BP algorithm is shown in Fig. 1, which include the following steps.

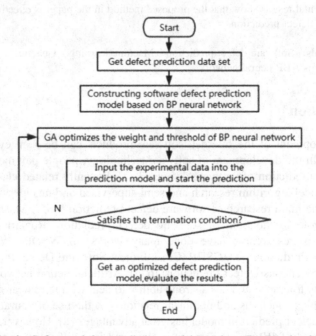

Fig. 1. Software defect prediction model based on GA-BP algorithm

Step1. Acquisition of software defect prediction data sets for training and predicting.

Step2. Construction of software defect prediction model of BP neural network based on training samples.

Step3. Using GA to optimize the weights and thresholds of BP neural networks.

Step4. Input the experimental dataset into the prediction model and start the prediction.

Step5. Determine whether the prediction results satisfy the termination condition, if so, stop the optimization, get the optimized software prediction model and evaluated the prediction results. Otherwise return **Step3**. The core part is the use of GA to optimize the weight and threshold of BP neural network, with three-layer BP network. The algorithm flow of genetic algorithm to optimize BP neural network, which is shown in Fig. 2, which include the following steps.

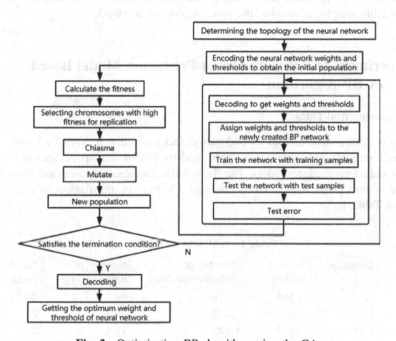

Fig. 2. Optimization BP algorithm using the GAs

Step1. Initialization of population P, including population size, crossover scale, crossover probability P_c and mutation probability P_m.

Step2. Calculating each individual evaluation function and sorting it. The probability values for selecting individuals are as follows [10].

$$P_s = \frac{f_i}{\sum_{i=1}^{N} f_i}$$

(1)

Where, f_i is for the suitability values of individual i, which is measured by the sum of squared errors E, which is as follows.

$$f(i) = \frac{1}{E(i)}, E(i) = \sum_p \sum_k (V_k - T_k)^2 \tag{2}$$

Where, $i = 1, \ldots, N$ is for the number of chromosomes; k is for the number of nodes in the output layer; p is for the number of learning samples.

Step3. The new individuals G'_i and G'_{i+1} are generated by the crossover operation of the individuals G_i and G_{i+1} with the probability P_c, and the individuals who do not perform the crossover directly start the copying.

Step4. Using the probability P_m mutation to generate a new individual G'_j of G_j.

Step5. The new individual G'_j is inserted into the population P, and the evaluation function of G'_j is calculated.

Step6. If an optimal individual that satisfies the condition is found, the process ends, and the optimized individual is decoded to obtain the optimized network connection weight, otherwise, the process proceed to **step3**.

3   Experiment of Software Defect Prediction Model Based on GA-BP Algorithm

3.1   Experimental Data

A common open source dataset for software defect prediction is NASA's Metrics Data Program, a publicly available dataset published by NASA that specializes in building software defect prediction models. The data of the database are collected from actual software system projects [8], which contains 13 datasets, the dataset information is shown in Table 1.

Table 1. NASA MDP dataset

Dataset name	Language	Total of modules	Number of defective modules	Number of defects (%)	Number of features
CM1	C	505	48	9.5	40
JM1	C	10878	2102	19.3	21
KC1	C++	2107	325	15.4	21
KC3	JAVA	458	43	9.4	40
KC4	Perl	125	75	60.0	40
MC1	C++	9466	68	0.7	39
MC2	C	161	52	32.3	40
MW1	C	403	31	7.7	40
PC1	C	1107	76	6.9	40
PC2	C	5589	23	0.41	40
PC3	C	1563	160	10.2	40
PC4	C	1458	178	12.2	40
PC5	C++	17186	516	3.0	39

The defect rate of the dataset in Table 1 is calculated as follows.

$$DefectRate(\%) = \frac{Number\ of\ defective\ modules}{Number\ of\ all\ modules} * 100 \tag{3}$$

The number of features is the number of nodes in the dataset. That is to say, the number of columns remaining after removing the last column of label column values, such as part of the dataset KC4, are shown in Fig. 3 below. Where, the number of columns remaining after removing the last column of label values is 40, so the number of features in the dataset KC4 is 40. In neural network training, the number of features needs to be modified according to the different datasets.

```
0,7,5,0,0,0,4,1,0,0,4,1,93,1,0,0,0,0,0,0,0,0,0,0,0,0.25,0,0,91,0.04,0,0,0,0,100,1,0,100,N
0,125,11,0,0,0,63,1,0,0,56,0.89,462,1,0,0,0,0,0,0,0,0,0,0,0,0,0.02,0,0,401,0.13,0,0,0,0,489,
0,23,2,0,0,0,12,1,0,0,2,0.17,64,1,0,0,0,0,0,0,0,0,0,0,0,0.08,0,0,54,0.19,0,0,0,0,62,1,0,62
0,3,8,0,0,0,2,1,0,0,2,1,37,1,0,0,0,0,0,0,0,0,0,0,0,0,0.5,0,0,37,0.03,0,0,0,0,58,1,0,58,Y
0,1,1,0,0,0,1,1,0,0,1,1,6,1,0,0,0,0,0,0,0,0,0,0,0,0,1,0,0,7,0,0,0,0,0,613,1,0,613,N
0,9,2,0,0,0,5,1,0,0,2,0.4,29,1,0,0,0,0,0,0,0,0,0,0,0,0,0.2,0,0,26,0.12,0,0,0,0,41,1,0,41,Y
0,1,3,0,0,0,1,1,0,0,1,1,24,1,0,0,0,0,0,0,0,0,0,0,0,0,1,0,0,25,0.03,0,0,0,0,36,1,0,36,Y
0,1,1,0,0,0,1,1,0,0,1,1,5,1,0,0,0,0,0,0,0,0,0,0,0,0,1,0,0,6,0.01,0,0,0,0,81,1,0,81,N
0,29,9,0,0,0,15,1,0,0,14,0.93,133,1,0,0,0,0,0,0,0,0,0,0,0,0,0.07,0,0,120,0.1,0,0,0,0,145,1,0
0,3,8,0,0,0,2,1,0,0,2,1,38,1,0,0,0,0,0,0,0,0,0,0,0,0,0.5,0,0,38,0.03,0,0,0,0,58,1,0,58,Y
0,1,1,0,0,0,1,1,0,0,0,1,1,6,1,0,0,0,0,0,0,0,0,0,0,0,1,0,0,7,0,0,0,0,0,269,1,0,269,N
```

Fig. 3. The number of dataset KC4 features

Reference [8] indicates that because of the many redundant properties of the original dataset provided by NASA, this property reduces predictive accuracy and requires data preprocessing to be suitable for use in experiments. Before the experiment, the open source machine learning tool WEKA was first used to preprocess the data. In addition, the format of the dataset running in Python code needs to be converted, and after converting the arff formatted file to csv format, only four datasets JM1, KC4, MC2, PC5 can be used for experiment. The four datasets information used for the experiment is simplified from Table 1 as follows in Table 2.

Table 2. Dataset information for experiments

Dataset	Defection rate (%)	Number of features
JM1	19.3	21
KC4	60.0	40
MC2	32.3	40
PC5	3.0	39

Among them, the defect rate of dataset KC4 and dataset MC2 is relatively high, the defect rate of dataset JM1 is general, the defect rate of dataset PC5 is only 3 percent, and the lower the defect rate, the worse the prediction effect may be.

3.2   Experimental Process

The comparative experiment was done in the paper. On the one hand, the original BP network is used for training, and the dataset is put into the defect prediction, and the results are output to the file BP-log.txt. On the other hand, the BP neural network optimized by GAs is used for training and prediction, and the results are output to the file log.txt. First, it is necessary to first create BP neural network model, then GAs is used to optimize BP network before making prediction. GAs is set iteratively 5 times based on experience, which is easy to reflect the role of GAs optimization. The more iterations there are, the slower the network converges. Also based on experience, each time the neural network is set to 20.

4   Experimental Results and Analysis

4.1   Model Evaluation Criteria

In order to evaluate the performance of the predictive model, the evaluation indexes of software defect prediction model mainly include accuracy (Accuracy), accuracy (Precision), recall rate (Recall), F1 value (F1_Score) and loss rate (Loss) is used based on the hybrid matrix [11, 12], which is shown in Table 3. The experiment randomly selects 80 percent of the dataset as the training dataset, and the remaining 20 percent is used as the prediction dataset. For the traditional BP neural network model, because the convergence speed is slow, the optimal value of the first 5 experimental measures is taken as the experimental running result, and for the BP network model with GA optimization, the optimal value of the experimental measure in 8 iterations is taken as the experimental running result.

Table 3. Hybrid matrix

	Error-prone module of predictive values	Not easy to error module of predictive values
Error-prone module of actual values	True positive	False negative
Not easy to error module of actual values	False positive	True negative

As shown in the table above, the final prediction results of the model can be divided into four categories in the table: TP (correct positive example), FP (positive example of error), TN (correct negative example), FN (negative example of error). The evaluation criteria indicators are defined as follow.

Accuracy is as follows [11].

$$Accuracy = \frac{TP + TN}{TP + FP + TN + FN} \tag{4}$$

Precision is as follows [11].

$$Precision = \frac{TP}{TP + FP} \tag{5}$$

The recall rate is as follows [11].

$$Recall = \frac{TP}{TP + FN} \tag{6}$$

The value of $F1$ is as follows [12].

$$F1\_Score = 2 \times \frac{Precision \times Recall}{Precision + Recall} \tag{7}$$

The loss rate is calculated by the logarithmic loss (Log Loss) function, which is used to measure the degree of inconsistency between the predicted value $F(x)$ of the model and the true value Y, which is a non-negative real value function and is usually represented by $L(Y, f(x))$. The less the loss function value is the smaller the loss rate, the better the robustness of the model.

4.2 Experimental Data Analysis

The best prediction results obtained by the dataset KC4 in both models are shown in Figs. 4 and 5 below, and it can still be seen that the optimized model predicts better.

```
2019-04-28 13:15:52,607 - INFO - {'nb_neurons': 256, 'nb_layers': 1,
'activation': 'relu', 'optimizer': 'adamax'}
2019-04-28 13:15:52,607 - INFO - Network loss: 0.44
2019-04-28 13:15:52,607 - INFO - Network accuracy: 88.00%
2019-04-28 13:15:52,607 - INFO - Network f1_score: 90.32%
2019-04-28 13:15:52,608 - INFO - Network precision: 82.35%
2019-04-28 13:15:52,608 - INFO - Network recall: 100.00%
```

Fig. 4. The best prediction results for datasets KC4 using GA-BP algorithm

```
2019-04-28 12:41:57,388 - INFO - {'nb_neurons': 64, 'nb_layers': 1,
'activation': 'relu', 'optimizer': 'adam'}
2019-04-28 12:41:57,388 - INFO - Network loss: 0.56
2019-04-28 12:41:57,389 - INFO - Network accuracy: 80.00%
2019-04-28 12:41:57,389 - INFO - Network f1_score: 80.00%
2019-04-28 12:41:57,389 - INFO - Network precision: 100.00%
2019-04-28 12:41:57,390 - INFO - Network recall: 66.67%
```

Fig. 5. The best prediction results algorithm for predicting datasets KC4 using the traditional BP algorithm

Among them, the parameters randomly selected 256 neurons, one layer of hidden layer, activation function relu, and adamax optimizer. The lower the loss rate, the better the robustness of the model, the higher the accuracy, $F1$ value, accuracy and recall rate, the better. The predicted loss rate, accuracy, $F1$ value and recall rate are 44%, 88%, 90.32%, 82.35%, 100%, which respectively shown in Fig. 4, which indicates that the model has good robustness. Compared with the results predicted by the optimized BP neural network model, the results predicted by the traditional BP neural network model are not better except for the accuracy of 100%.

The best prediction results obtained by the dataset JM1 in both models are shown in Figs. 6 and 7 below, and it can still be seen that the optimized model predicts better, and all evaluation index values are superior to the traditional predicted values.

```
2019-04-28 14:51:34,949 - INFO - {'nb_neurons': 64, 'nb_layers': 1,
 'activation': 'relu', 'optimizer': 'adadelta'}
2019-04-28 14:51:34,951 - INFO - Network loss: 0.28
2019-04-28 14:51:34,956 - INFO - Network accuracy: 92.00%
2019-04-28 14:51:34,960 - INFO - Network f1_score: 95.91%
2019-04-28 14:51:34,960 - INFO - Network precision: 92.31%
2019-04-28 14:51:34,961 - INFO - Network recall: 100.00%
```

Fig. 6. The best prediction results for datasets JM1 using GA-BP algorithm

```
2019-04-28 11:43:15,630 - INFO - {'nb_neurons': 64, 'nb_layers': 1,
 'activation': 'relu', 'optimizer': 'adam'}
2019-04-28 11:43:15,631 - INFO - Network loss: 0.51
2019-04-28 11:43:15,631 - INFO - Network accuracy: 78.79%
2019-04-28 11:43:15,631 - INFO - Network f1_score: 25.00%
2019-04-28 11:43:15,631 - INFO - Network precision: 50.00%
2019-04-28 11:43:15,631 - INFO - Network recall: 16.67%
```

Fig. 7. The best prediction results algorithm for predicting datasets JM1 using the traditional BP algorithm

The best predictive results of the dataset MC2 predicted in both models are shown in Figs. 8 and 9 below, and the optimized model is more robust and better predictive, but the overall predictive effect of the dataset is not very good, the $F1$ value, recall rate are very low, the accuracy is only 50%, This may be due to a low defect rate in the dataset.

```
2019-04-28 10:09:32,905 - INFO - {'nb_neurons': 256, 'nb_layers': 2,
 'activation': 'tanh', 'optimizer': 'adadelta'}
2019-04-28 10:09:32,905 - INFO - Network loss: 0.44
2019-04-28 10:09:32,905 - INFO - Network accuracy: 84.85%
2019-04-28 10:09:32,905 - INFO - Network f1_score: 28.22%
2019-04-28 10:09:32,905 - INFO - Network precision: 50.00%
2019-04-28 10:09:32,906 - INFO - Network recall: 34.29%
```

Fig. 8. The best results of the traditional BP algorithm for predicting datasets MC2

```
2019-04-28 11:43:15,630 - INFO - {'nb_neurons': 64, 'nb_layers': 1,
 'activation': 'relu', 'optimizer': 'adam'}
2019-04-28 11:43:15,631 - INFO - Network loss: 0.51
2019-04-28 11:43:15,631 - INFO - Network accuracy: 78.79%
2019-04-28 11:43:15,631 - INFO - Network f1_score: 25.00%
2019-04-28 11:43:15,631 - INFO - Network precision: 50.00%
2019-04-28 11:43:15,631 - INFO - Network recall: 16.67%
```

Fig. 9. The best results of the traditional BP algorithm for predicting datasets MC2 using the traditional BP algorithm

The best prediction results of a dataset PC5 predicted in both models are shown in Figs. 10 and 11 below. It can be seen that although the predicted $F1$ value, accuracy and recall rate are very low, the optimized effect is not as good as the prediction effect of the traditional BP neural network model. This is because the defect rate of dataset PC5 is only 3%, the defect module is too few, and the probability of using GA optimization to find the global optimal solution of BP neural network in a short time is also very low.

```
2019-04-28 17:54:04,248 - INFO - {'nb_neurons': 256, 'nb_layers': 3,
 'activation': 'tanh', 'optimizer': 'adam'}
2019-04-28 17:54:04,248 - INFO - Network loss: 0.04
2019-04-28 17:54:04,248 - INFO - Network accuracy: 98.75%
2019-04-28 17:54:04,248 - INFO - Network f1_score: 12.82%
2019-04-28 17:54:04,248 - INFO - Network precision: 15.38%
2019-04-28 17:54:04,248 - INFO - Network recall: 11.54%
```

Fig. 10. The best prediction results for datasets PC5 using GA-BP algorithm

```
2019-04-28 17:26:26,474 - INFO - {'nb_neurons': 64, 'nb_layers': 1,
 'activation': 'relu', 'optimizer': 'adam'}
2019-04-28 17:26:26,474 - INFO - Network loss: 0.03
2019-04-28 17:26:26,474 - INFO - Network accuracy: 99.50%
2019-04-28 17:26:26,474 - INFO - Network f1_score: 23.08%
2019-04-28 17:26:26,475 - INFO - Network precision: 23.08%
2019-04-28 17:26:26,475 - INFO - Network recall: 23.08%
```

Fig. 11. The best prediction results algorithm for predicting datasets PC5 using the traditional BP algorithm

BP Neural network model and GA-BP neural network model are predicted for defects on the four datasets KC4, JM1, MC2 and PC5, and the results obtained are statistically shown in Fig. 12 below.

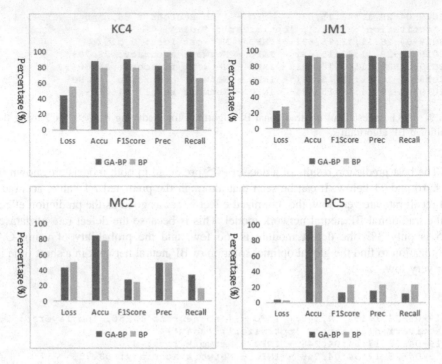

Fig. 12. Statistical histogram of forecast results of BP model and GA-BP model

It's shown from Fig. 12 that the datasets are different and the predicted results may be very different because of the factor of different datasets and different neural network parameters. However, it can be seen that the prediction results of the two datasets KC4 and JM1 are very good. The dataset MC2 is second, the dataset PC5 has the worst prediction effect, and even the traditional BP neural network model predicts better results than the GA optimized results. The reason for this is that the defect rate of both KC4 and JM1 is high, and the defect rate of PC5 is very low, so it is difficult to get a good prediction. In general, the overall prediction effect after using BP to optimize BP neural network is better than that of traditional BP neural network prediction.

5   Conclusions

The novel software defect prediction model based on GA-BP algorithm was proposed in the paper considering the disadvantage of traditional BP. Then the prediction model was constructed based on the GA-BP. In addition, the public dataset MDP from NASA was selected and the tools WEKA was used to clean the data and format conversion and as the result, 4 datasets is available. In the end, experimental results show that the proposed method in the paper is effective for software defect prediction.

Acknowledgements. This work was supported by Sichuan Science and Technology Programs (Grant No. 2019YJ0252), the Fundamental Research Funds for the Central Universities, SWUN (Grant No. 2019YYXS04) and Key laboratory of Computer System, State Ethnic Affairs Commission, Southwest Minzu University.

References

1. Okutan, A., Olcay, T.Y.: Software defect prediction using Bayesian networks. Empir. Softw. Eng. **19**(1), 154–181 (2014). https://doi.org/10.1007/s10664-012-9218-8
2. Gong, L.N., Jing, S.J., Jiang, L.: Research progress of software defect prediction. J. Softw. **30**(10), 3090–3114 (2019). https://doi.org/10.13328/j.cnki.jos.005790
3. Yu, Q., Jiang, S.J., Zhang, Y.M., et al.: The impact study of class imbalance on the performance of software defect prediction models. Chin. J. Comput. **41**(4), 809–824. https://dx.doi.org/10.11897/SP.J.1016.2018.00809
4. Xiang, Z.Y., Tang, Z.T.: Research of software defect prediction model based on gray theory. In: International Conference on Management & Service Science. IEEE (2009). https://dx.doi.org/10.1109/ICMSS.2009.5301677
5. Li, M., Zhang, H.Y., Wu, R.X., et al.: Sample-based software defect prediction with active and semi-supervised learning. Autom. Softw. Eng. **19**(2), 201–230 (2012). https://doi.org/10.1007/s10515-011-0092-1
6. Ni, C., Liu, W.S., Chen, X., et al.: A cluster based feature selection method for cross-project software defect prediction. J. Comput. Sci. Technol. **32**(6), 1090–1107 (2017). https://doi.org/10.1007/s11390-017-1785-0
7. Nam, J., Kim, S.: Heterogeneous defect prediction. IEEE Trans. Softw. Eng. **PP**(99), 1 (2015). https://doi.org/10.1109/TSE.2017.2720603
8. Wang, H.L., Yu, Q., Li, T., et al.: Research of software defect prediction model based on CS-ANN. Appl. Res. Comput. **34**(2), 467–472, 476 (2017). http://dx.doi.org/10.3969/j.issn.1001-3695.2017.02.033
9. Cui, M.T., Zhong, Y., Zhao, H.J.: Realization to multimedia network QoS routing based on ACOGA. J. Univ. Electron. Sci. Technol. China **38**(02), 266–269 (2009). https://doi.org/10.3969/j.issn.1001-0548,2009.02.26
10. Wang, Z., Fan, X.Y., Zhou, Y.G., et al.: Genetic algorithm based multiple faults localization technique. J. Softw. **27**(04), 879–900 (2016). https://doi.org/10.13328/j.cnki.jos.004970
11. He, J.Y., Meng, Z.P., Chen, X., et al.: Semi-supervised ensemble learning approach for cross-project defect prediction. J. Softw. **28**(06), 1455–1473 (2017). https://doi.org/10.13328/j.cnki.jos.005228
12. Menzies, T., Dekhtyar, A., Distefano, J., et al.: Problems with precision: a response to "comments on 'data mining static code attributes to learn defect predictors'". IEEE Trans. Softw. Eng. **33**(9), 637–640 (2007). https://doi.org/10.1109/TSE.2007.70706

Security Solution Based on Raspberry PI and IoT

Bahast Ali⑩ and Xiaochun Cheng(✉)⑩

Middlesex University, London NW4 4BT, England, UK
BA644@live.mdx.ac.uk, x.cheng@mdx.ac.uk

Abstract. This project focuses on building and developing a secure smart home IoT system that can give near real-time information about the status of the home, with the aid of cloud and wireless sensor communication technologies. In this paper, the capabilities and limitations of smart home systems were researched. The project built a smart Internet of Things (IoT) system for the security of the home. This project uses inexpensive and commercially available hardware, and the software solutions were developed based on open source packages. The performance and the security of the home IoT system were tested. Further security analysis was conducted to analyse the vulnerabilities of the connected IoT devices. The solutions presented in this paper are applicable to the real world and not limited to a controlled environment.

Keywords: Smart home · Raspberry PI · Sensors · Internet of Things · Cloud · Security · Vulnerability

1 Introduction

Internet of Things (IoT) solutions are developing rapidly. With 5G communication, IoT solutions are deployed for more applications. Security, privacy and performance are the key research areas. This section is to highlight some of the contemporary issues that are being faced and to outline the stages that must be taken for the research.

Governments and companies [1] are investing into developing and building intelligent cities. Recently, the UK government has funded over a billion pounds (GBP) into transforming modern cities. Berkshire Hathaway stated that the market share of smart infrastructures will increase drastically by 2023 to over $2,000 billion [2].

Knowing all this, it is worth noting that smart and intelligent cities cannot exist without smart homes. Therefore, it is only logical to develop a cost-effective, less intrusive and simple system. This project will aim to investigate and examine the challenges and limitations of building smart homes today. There are many smart home systems currently developed. However, not many have met the smart home requirements framework by Beckel et al. [3]. For example, there have been many cases of Amazon Echo privacy breaches [4]. Other reports show that Nest devices are becoming victims of botnets. Data is increasingly being moved to the cloud and devices are being connected, therefore, it is important to investigate security vulnerabilities and to find proper solutions. Some of the largest companies [5] were hacked despite their efforts on security.

© Springer Nature Switzerland AG 2019
J. Vaidya et al. (Eds.): CSS 2019, LNCS 11983, pp. 162–171, 2019.
https://doi.org/10.1007/978-3-030-37352-8_14

This illustrates that there is strong demand of security solutions. Furthermore, systems like the Philips Hue smart lights are not scalable.

The structure of this paper is as follows. In Sect. 2, current developed projects and systems are reviewed and critically analysed; so that their limitations are manifested. Section 3 is about the methodology of the research. It includes the approaches and the methods of experiments. The design of the system will be elaborated in Sect. 4. This section includes how the system was designed and developed. This section also includes some testing and results of the project. Finally, Sect. 5 concludes the project to manifest major findings, as well as the limitations. In addition, there is a discussion about the technical applicability and final evaluation.

2 Literature Review

In this section, prevalent works are critically analysed and studied, not only to gain more understanding, but also to identify gaps in the knowledge. Many IoT research papers have been published but very few have addressed the security and user privacy concerns, others have merely dealt with matter superficially. It is incumbent for smart homes to implement security mechanisms to ensure the integrity of data and protect against the outside world [6]. Tabassum et al. report [7] is a good illustration of using technology to secure modern homes. However, the authors have given no explanation about how the network will be secured. Logic would dictate that since the network is not secured; the home is not secured.

In Nath et al. [8] research paper, they improved their project by using voice commands to control the system. An advantage of the project was that they used OpenShift which is a cloud platform. This means that the actual code and program is not on the Raspberry PI hardware. The study in this paper is similar to Dey et al. [9] research, both papers use cloud services to minimise hardware failures. The advantage of this is that the system can be scaled up or down, without consideration of performance, data space size, hardware resources of local devices. The authors also acknowledge that smart homes must have economics advantages for it become widespread and adopted.

Sahani et al. [10], argues that one of the features of their proposed system is portability, and they never explain why a smart home security system would need to be portable. Their project sends a SMS message every time a user enters the door. However, they will need to counter and mitigate the false positives. Dey et al. [9] had undertaken identical approaches for human interaction. However, the system used face recognition. Nevertheless, their system did not escape from drawbacks, they purposely decreased the image resolution to increase processing time. It is clear the authors have preferred performance over security. A fatal flaw in the design was that the data is transported with UDP, this means the connection is unreliable and prone to failure.

Smart homes are not protected by a fortress, a similar statement is made by Apthorpe et al. [11]. They studied regular smart home devices for privacy vulnerabilities. They found out that although the data passing through the network was encrypted, they were still able to see the DNS traffic and frequency of requests and responses. DNS uses clear text for queries and responses. Even though the data was encrypted and passive observers were unable to read or change the data. Attackers may still can learn more about the user from deep learning.

The evaluation criteria aided this project to stay focused on the goals and objectives set. This is necessary because it allowed all the project's outcomes to be analysed using a scientific approach. The previous works and the final product of this project is compared using the evaluation criteria as follows:

The system must have near real-time notification to alert the user of changes in the home environment. For example, if the home temperature rises to a defined abnormal degree in Celsius then the user should be notified of this change. Another example, if the window or door opens are a defined abnormal time.

The final system product must be accessible anytime and anywhere with internet connectivity. Even if the user does not have Internet connectivity they should be able to make changes to their home and the changes update when they have internet access. In addition, the user should be able to view the last known state if the server goes down.

Security is one of the biggest problems as it relates to networks and user data. The system must have been tested to ensure user data integrity, data confidentiality, and system availability. These three principles may be breached by someone with malicious intent. Hence, the final product system must have been tested to some degree to ensure that the system is reliable. The results must indicate that it is safe for users. Performance will be a key driver for the development of smart homes. It is compulsory for the system to provide at a minimum decent performance. The keyword performance is used to indicate the fulfilment of speed relating to the latency and bandwidth in regard to the network and the smart home controllers. Scalability is another problem that many of the reviewed works suffered from. If a system is scalable the system architecture and program codes should not add major complexity to the design of the system. In addition, the changes needed to be made to scale up or scale down should not require redesign and reconfiguration of settings.

3 Methodology

The methodology explained and elaborated below will help to conceptualise the building blocks and the actual framework for the planning of this project. No project plan is without weaknesses, thus the more ideas that were generated and produced the more the weaknesses were able to be minimised and mitigated.

A Chaotic approach was taken based on the Chaos Model [12]. This was beneficial because it allowed all the problems to be considered, and no single issue was considered less important than others. This approach also helped to think about every small and minuscule problem and how it related to the rest of the project overall. In a software development sense, it is how a single line of code relates to a function or a method, and how a class relates to the overall functionality of the program.

The proposed methodology took a loop approach, whereby the end of the loop new problems were realised. Thus, by the end of the next loop phase the problem was defined, understood and then a solution was proposed. The solution was then implemented to see the results and to check whether the proposed solution solved the issue. The strength of the method is that it was not dependent on a specific organisational structure. New changes were able to be adapted easily as the project progression was unpredictable. Moreover, this approach helped to address the issues with smart homes as some of the ideas were not tried and tested.

The weakness of this methodology is that it was not direct, and the flexibility of the project might have hindered the focus of the aims and objectives. There was not be a single way to solve a problem, to design a solution or to implement the solution. So, there were many different routes that could have been taken for the researches.

4 Design

4.1 Notification System

Firebase is a Google mobile application development platform that enables developers to do an array of tasks. For example, authorising and authenticating users, cloud storage, real-time database, application hosting etc. This project used the Firebase Cloud Messaging (FCM) system and the real-time database. FCM is free and the real-time database can be simultaneously connected to 100 devices, and 1 GB can be stored at a time, and up to 10 GB data transfer per month.

The FCM service provides near real-time notification to the user. The sensors collect data about its environment and sends it to the Raspberry Pi. The coded programs analyse the sensor data. If the data is something which requires the user's attention then it will be pushed upstream to the FCM service. The FCM then sends a notification to the client mobile application alerting the user.

Sending notification to users is faster than sending an email which may take some time for the user to receive. This type of notification is also more effective than sending an SMS because it is free. Some SMS API service providers charge low rates but it can accumulate over time. Additionally, this would mean the security of the home would be dependent on a third-party service provider. Table 1 below shows that there are many SMS services, and all have per message or monthly charge. Many projects reviewed above use SMS for their notification system. It is difficult to determine how much a user will spend per month knowing that every individual users' activities are different.

Table 1. SMS service providers

Service provider	Pricing	Frequency
Pricing frequency PLivo (2019)	£0.04	Per message
Fast SMS (2019)	£0.04	Per message
Twilio (2019)	£10.00	Per month
SMS API (LINK Mobility, 2019)	£0.033	Per message
Clockwork SMS (2019)	£0.04	Per message

The Fig. 1 illustrates the architecture of the implemented system. The sensors send their data to the Raspberry Pi controller. If the Raspberry Pi detects that the user should

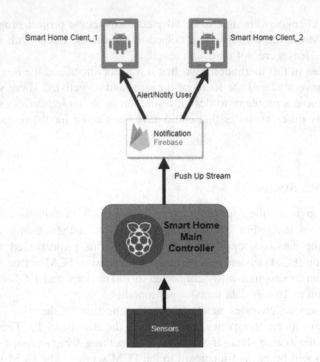

Fig. 1. Notification alert system

be notified, it sends a message to the Firebase Messaging Service, which forwards the request to the user to be alerted (Fig. 1).

4.2 Object Positioning System

The original idea was to put a collection of ultrasonic sensors in an array. This was not successful and did not go as anticipated. The problem was that there were many gaps between each sensor. Therefore, estimating a near accurate result was unlikely. When an object was between the sensors sound wave burst path, the previously known location of the object had to be used. This led to numerous other problems. Moreover, when the size of the room increased the number of sensors required also increased. This further increases the complexity of the data management, measuring and calculation.

The second plan was to put two ultrasonic sensors each at a corner of the room, and when the sound wave hits the walls it creates a ripple and echo effect. This also failed, as the expected behaviour of the sound was not produced. When the sound wave bounced off the walls, it bounced back in the same angle it was hit the wall. It was expected to increase the size (height and width) of the wave. However, the height and width of the wave remained the same from when the sound wave was produced to when it was received back at the sonar sensor.

The last plan for being able to find the coordinates of an object in 2D space is as explained. Although the second plan had failed, it allowed for further idea exploration. Firstly, having two sensors (A and B) and triangulating an object (C) was a correct concept. Secondly, the distance between the two sensors (AB) is known and it is a fixed length. The distance between the sensors and the object (AC and BC) will also be calculated with the ultrasonic program. The coordinates of sensor A and sensor B are known. What is left is to find the coordinates of the object C. The initial problem was that a single formula was needed to be used to programmatically calculate the coordination of object C. The problem became more severe when it was discovered that the triangle could be a right angle, isosceles or an irregular. The coordination of all three points was needed so that the shape can be drawn on the user application. This was done to visually reproduce the object in the room remotely to the user.

The first step was to work out the area of the triangle with the Heron theorem, as illustrated in Eqs. 1 and 2 below.

$$S = (dist(AB) + dist(BC) + dist(AC))/2 \tag{1}$$

The equation above is used to find the semi-perimeter of the triangle. Where S is half of the perimeter. To calculate the perimeter of the triangle; the sum of the distances between point A and B; B and C, A and C.

$$Area = \sqrt{(S(S - A)(S - A)(S - C))} \tag{2}$$

Equation 2 above is used to work out the area of the triangle using S.

$$Height = 2(Area/Base) \tag{3}$$

The next step was to find the height of the triangle, this can be calculated using the equation above. When the height of the triangle is calculated then the Y-axis of the object has been determined. Working out the height creates a line in the triangle, starting at point C and finishing between points A and B. The line creates a right-angle (Fig. 2).

The next step was to work out the X coordinate of the object. This can be described as the width of the new triangle or the distance between point A and the line (the right-angle). Pythagoras can be used to calculate the width, as shown in Eq. 4 below.

$$a^2 = c^2 - b^2 \tag{4}$$

The equation above is used for the X coordinates.

4.3   Security

The user interface of the application was password protected to keep intruders out. This also meant that the credentials being transferred over the network had to be encrypted as well with TLS. The first module that was used is the Unix IRCD backdoor, where it creates a Unix bind shell to penetrate through the network infrastructure. The first step was to generate a payload to send over the network and then trigger the exploit, and then finally connect to the bind shell remotely via NC [13]. After a few attempts, the tests failed repeatedly and so this testing was successful because it meant the correct

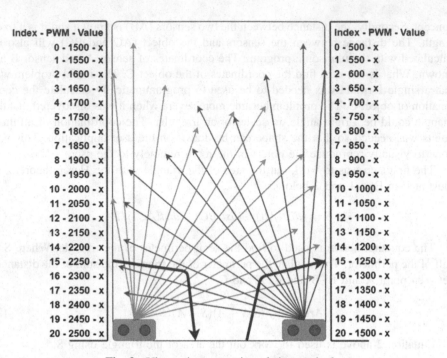

Index - PWM - Value
0 - 1500 - x
1 - 1550 - x
2 - 1600 - x
3 - 1650 - x
4 - 1700 - x
5 - 1750 - x
6 - 1800 - x
7 - 1850 - x
8 - 1900 - x
9 - 1950 - x
10 - 2000 - x
11 - 2050 - x
12 - 2100 - x
13 - 2150 - x
14 - 2200 - x
15 - 2250 - x
16 - 2300 - x
17 - 2350 - x
18 - 2400 - x
19 - 2450 - x
20 - 2500 - x

Index - PWM - Value
0 - 500 - x
1 - 550 - x
2 - 600 - x
3 - 650 - x
4 - 700 - x
5 - 750 - x
6 - 800 - x
7 - 850 - x
8 - 900 - x
9 - 950 - x
10 - 1000 - x
11 - 1050 - x
12 - 1100 - x
13 - 1150 - x
14 - 1200 - x
15 - 1250 - x
16 - 1300 - x
17 - 1350 - x
18 - 1400 - x
19 - 1450 - x
20 - 1500 - x

Fig. 2. Ultrasonic sensor triangulation method

procedures were implemented to protect against attacks. NMap software was used to check for open and vulnerable ports on the network. No port vulnerability was detected. The final test involved using a Wi-Fi microchip that is highly durable, compact and energy efficient [14]. The hardware is formally called the ESP8266. It has a wide range of applications and can be used for sensor networks. However, the hardware was used for disruption and interference with the smart home network. The device can be used with the Arduino IDE to write and develop programs. A custom software was used, often called Deauther that allows the Wi-Fi microchip to scan nearby wireless devices and block their connections [15]. The program can also be used to create Wi-Fi access point with a similar name to the router causing turmoil for the users.

The first attack involved de-authorisation the devices connected to the wireless router. It was required to connect to the ESP8266 hardware device Wi-Fi network and access the webpage with a browser. When the webpage is loaded, the device will scan for nearby Wi-Fi networks and connected devices. The option is given to choose the access points and devices that should be attacked. When they are added to the saved list, on the attack page several options are given to start the attack.

4.4   Performance

The Raspberry Pi based system was tested when it was stressed and overloaded with mathematical computation, and when no processes were running (stress-free).

The CPU utilisation reached 99% to 100% when stressed. Popular websites in the UK were tested to sever. Web application was limited to a payload of 1024 bytes because of the MTU. The Raspberry Pi performed well when transferring small payloads. However, there was a noticeable difference when transferring packets of large size payloads. Overall the system displayed decent data throughput.

5 Conclusion

Among increasing researches on smart IoT systems, cloud services, multimedia communication and security [16–24], this project was completed using consumer available hardware and software packages. The software was programmed and the system is suitable for low budget applications. The hardware which were used were all inexpensive. The system overall provided decent performance and was reliable. Object positioning system was completed and can triangulate the position of an object. Two ultrasonic sensors were used to pinpoint the exact location of the object. When movement was detected by the sensors, the program to triangulate the object was executed. Once the object was been found, the software collected the sensor readings and uploaded the data to the cloud DB. Users are notified of the changes in the smart home environment. Users may open the Android application and see the location and movement of the object. This system and its design methodology are not restricted to the security of the smart home and can have other applications. For example, the object tracking system can be used as a baby monitor so that the parents can be aware of their child's activity remotely. The benefit of this solution is that the data being transferred over the network is small when compared to video footage. Another benefit is, in the event of a hacker getting into the smart home system, the hacker would not be able to see inside the house. However, the adopted sensors have few limitations. One flaw is that the sensor cannot give accurate enough readings for it to be completely reliable. The selected sensor is limited to 4 m of distance and a room could be bigger. For the sensor rotation, servo motors were used to provide the flexibility for rotating the sensor to a specific angle. The servo motor allows the speed and orientation as well as the direction to be amended and changed dynamically. At first, the standard GPIO libraries were used to control the motor. Later it was realised the pigpio libraries were better optimised for the purpose. The main reason for the change was because the standard GPIO library made the servo randomly twitch and jitter, which caused abnormal responses.

The reed sensors wiring and circuitry implementation was successful. Using the Android application, users can see the status of doors and windows of their home. When the state changes, the user receives a notification, for the user to be aware of the changes. Similar status monitoring solutions may be used for letterboxes, wardrobes, etc. A door in the home can be opened or closed through the Android IoT application. As suggested by the latency analysis results, there was reasonable delay, so the likelihood of someone being locked out of their home would not happen. This methodology can be expanded into garage shutters, controlling windows with motors. These 'on' and 'off' states were also used for controlling the home lights, which proves to be useful and over time it can reduce energy consumption.

The system enables users to have control and awareness over their home, such as for security monitoring. The implemented system not only provides network resilience against intruders, but the security of the actual home is also conceptualised. For example, real-time notification would be sent to the user if the temperature reached a pre-determined threshold, this would indicate a fire.

The security of the system was tested to prove that the smart home system has adequate methods to protect user data. The level of security also entailed that the system is in fact reliable. Numerous implementation measures and procedures were undertaken to provide a dependable system. There was only a single security chasm that was realised after the testing. This showed that the system needs to develop to become more secure. Because it may seem distrusting to know that a relatively cheap microchip device can bring the whole smart home network down. However, the major of the results gives assurance that the user data was protected and that the system maintains data integrity without being affected by this flaw.

References

1. Shields, N.: Urban development: why investors are growing more interested in smart cities (2018).   http://uk.businessinsider.com/siemens-head-urban-development-martin-powell-investors-interested-smart-cities-2018-3
2. Gov.UK: The UK's leadership in smart cities (2018). https://www.gov.uk/government/speeches/the-uks-leadership-in-smart-cities
3. Beckel, C., Serfas H., Moritz G.: Requirements for smart home applications and realization with WS4D-pipesBox. De Bosch (2011)
4. Montag, A.: Former NSA privacy expert: here's how likely it is that your Amazon Echo will be hacked (2018). https://www.cnbc.com/2018/09/04/ex-nsa-privacy-expert-how-likely-your-amazon-echo-is-to-be-hacked.html. Accessed Jun 2019
5. Taylor, A.: The 17 biggest data breaches of the 21st century (2018). https://www.csoonline.com/article/2130877/data-breach/the-biggest-data-breaches-of-the-21st-century.html. Accessed Jun 2019
6. Dinculeana, D., Cheng, X.: Vulnerabilities and limitations of MQTT protocol. Appl. Sci. J. 9(5), 848 (2019). https://doi.org/10.3390/app9050848
7. Tabassum, A., Ahmed, F., Ahmed, Z.: Smart home security using Raspberry PI. Int. J. Sci. Res. Eng. Technol. 4(7), 164–169 (2018)
8. Nath, R.K., Bajpai, R., Thapliyal, H.: IoT based indoor location detection system for smart home environment. In: 2018 IEEE International Conference on Consumer Electronics (ICCE), Las Vegas, NV, pp. 1–3 (2018). https://doi.org/10.1109/icce.2018.8326225
9. Dey, P., Syed, S., Mitul, J., Ahmed, N.: Embedded system for automatic door access using face recognition. Int. Res. J. Eng. Technol. 06(06), 67–70 (2018). e-ISSN: 2395-0056
10. Sahani, M., Nanda, C., Sahu, A.K., Pattnaik, B.: Web-based embedded door access control and home security system. In: International Conference on Circuit, Power and Computing Technologies (ICCPCT), pp. 1–6 (2015). https://doi.org/10.1109/iccpct.2015.7159473
11. Apthorpe, N., Reisman, D., Feamster, N.: A smart home is no castle: privacy vulnerabilities of encrypted IoT traffic. Princeton University, Princeton, New Jersey (2017)
12. Raccoon, L.B.S.: The chaos model and the chaos cycle. SIGSOFT Softw. Eng. Notes 20(1), 55–66 (1995). https://doi.org/10.1145/225907.225914. ACM Digital Library, New York

13. MetalKey: UnrealIRCD 3.2.8.1 Backdoor Command Execution (2017). https://metalkey. github.io/unrealircd-3281-backdoor-command-execution.html
14. Espressif: ESP8266 - Low-power, highly-integrated Wi-Fi solution (2019). https://www. espressif.com/en/products/hardware/esp8266ex/overview
15. Kremser, S.: esp8266_deauther (2018). https://github.com/spacehuhn/esp8266_deauther. Accessed Jun 2019
16. Xie, W., Cheng, X.: Imbalanced big data classification based on virtual reality in cloud computing. Multimedia Tools Appl., 1–18 (2019). http://dx.doi.org/10.1007/s11042-019-7317-x
17. Yu, G., Xu, J., Cheng, X.: Platform of quality evaluation system for multimedia video communication based NS2. J. Ambient Intell. Humanized Comput., 1–12 (2018). https://doi.org/10.1007/s12652-018-1164-x. Print ISSN: 1868-5137, Online ISSN: 1868-5145
18. Xie, X., Yuan, T., Zhou, X., Cheng, X.: Research on trust model in container-based cloud service. Comput. Mater. Continua 56(2), 273–283 (2018). https://doi.org/10.3970/cmc.2018.03587. ISSN: 1546-2218 (printed), ISSN: 1546-2226
19. Gao, C., Lv, S., Wei, Y., Wang, Z., Liu, Z., Cheng, X.: an effective searchable symmetric encryption with enhanced security for mobile devices. IEEE Access 6, 38860–38869 (2018). ISSN 2169-3536
20. Wang, C., Zhao, Z., Gong, L., Zhu, L., Liu, Z., Cheng, X.: A distributed anomaly detection system for in-vehicle network using HTM. IEEE Access 6(1), 9091–9098 (2018)
21. Wang, C., et al.: Accurate Sybil attack detection based on fine-grained physical channel information. Sensors 18(3), 878 (2018). ISSN 1424-8220
22. Dinculeană, D., Cheng, X.: Vulnerabilities and limitations of MQTT protocol used between IoT devices. Appl. Sci. J. 9(5), 848 (2019). https://doi.org/10.3390/app9050848. Special issue "Access Control Schemes for Internet of Things"
23. Shi, F., Chen, Z., Cheng, X.: Behaviour modelling and individual recognition of sonar transmitter for secure communication in UASNs. IEEE Access (2019). https://doi.org/10.1109/access.2019.2923059. Print ISSN: 2169-3536, Online ISSN: 2169-3536
24. Men, J., et al.: Finding sands in the eyes: vulnerabilities discovery in IoT with EUFuzzer on human machine interface. IEEE Access 7, 103751–103759 (2019)

Information Security

Design of Anonymous Communication Protocol Based on Group Signature

Haojia Zhu[1], Can Cui[1], Fengyin Li[1(✉)], Zhongxing Liu[1], and Quanxin Zhang[2]

[1] School of Information Science and Engineering, QuFu Normal University,
Rizhao 276826, Shandong, China
lfyin318@126.com
[2] School of Computer Science and Technology, Beijing Institute of Technology,
Beijing 100081, China

Abstract. The onion routing protocol enables low-latency anonymous communication over the public network. Currently, many onion routing protocols have been proposed to enable anonymous connections between users, such as Tor. Even though existing onion routing protocols appear to have a secure structure, there are still some disadvantages in terms of efficiency and security. This paper proposes a new onion routing protocol based on certificateless group signature, which uses the new designed certificateless group signature scheme to achieve anonymous authentication of messages. In the protocol, this paper modifies the data encapsulation format of the transmission, and uses only the key shared with the receiver to encrypt the data payload in a single layer. The proposed protocol not only reduces the encryption and decryption operations of the data packets in the transmission process, but also improves the forwarding efficiency of the message, and further realizes the anonymous authentication and integrity of the message forwarding.

Keywords: Privacy protection · Certificateless group signature · Onion routing · Anonymous communication · Group signature

1 Introduction

With the rapid development of the Internet and its related emerging industries, the network has been integrated with the whole society. The network have been deeply connected with the real world. The boundaries between online and offline have disappeared. Any security issue in cyberspace will directly map to the security of the real world, which will profoundly affect the normal operation and stability of society. While the network brings convenience to the world, it also brings many new security threats and challenges to the country, enterprises and individuals [15]. In May 2017, the global outbreak of the WannaCry ransomware incident was a good example [8].

How to protect the privacy of users in the public network and enable users to realize fast and secure communication in an open communication environment is one of the urgent problems to be solved [1]. Because the network device

© Springer Nature Switzerland AG 2019
J. Vaidya et al. (Eds.): CSS 2019, LNCS 11983, pp. 175–181, 2019.
https://doi.org/10.1007/978-3-030-37352-8_15

needs to know some information about the user to complete the routing and data forwarding functions, its identity cannot be completely hidden [17]. Therefore, anonymous communication hides important information from untrusted parties and discloses appropriate information to trusted parties [11]. The means of anonymous communication can hide the user's personal information in the communication process, such as user identity, network location, and uses the encryption technology to separate the sender's identity and location information from its network activity, so that it can transmit data with the receiver without reveal of the privacy of the user [12].

It is also the most commonly method in current anonymous communication networks to achieve user identity anonymity with onion routing [9]. In 2004, Dingledine et al. introduced the second generation onion routing (Tor (the second-generation onion routing)), which adds forward secrecy, directory servers, and user location hiding services through node sets. In [3], Florian et al. proposed an architecture for various desktops and mobile devices in an anonymous networks and this architecture based on P2P (Peer-to-Peer) technology locates the established anonymous layer, but the server in the scheme is more vulnerable to attacks. The certificateless onion routing protocol proposed by Catalano et al. [5] in 2016 greatly improved the computing load of the relay router and obtained a higher data transmission rate. However, the packet structure used by it cannot counter the data tampering attack of the relay node.

2   A New Group Signature Scheme

2.1   Mathematical Foundation

Definition 1 (Discrete Logarithm Problem) Known a prime order q, if given y and generator g, computing integer x of $y = g^z \bmod q$ is difficult.

Definition 2 (Computational Diffie-Hellman Problem) (CDH Problem) A finite-loop group of known prime orders is a generator. If given a sum, the solution is difficult [6].

Certificateless Group Signature Scheme. The certificateless group signature scheme consists of the following algorithms [4,13,16].

Setup: KGC inputs the security parameter l, generates a prime number q (length is 2l), and selects g as a generator of the cyclic multiplication group G. Three hash functions are $H_1 : \{0,1\}^* \to Z_q$, $H_2 : \{0,1\}^* \times G \to Z_q$, $H_3 : G \to \{0,1\}^*$. Uniform random select $sk_{sys} \xleftarrow{\$} Z_q$ as a system secret key, obtain $pk_{sys} = g^{sk_{sys}} \bmod q$ as the system public key, then the public parameters are $(q, g, G, H_1, H_2, H_3, pk_{sys})$. $m \epsilon \{0,1\}^*$ as message space, $c \epsilon \mathbb{C}$ as ciphertext space.

Partial Private Key Extraction: The KGC generates a partial private key for the user after it verifies that the user with the identifier A is legal. First randomly choose $k_A \xleftarrow{\$} Z_q$, calculate $s_{D_A} = g^{k_A}$. Let $r_{D_A} = k_A + sk_{sys} H_2(\text{ID}, s_{D_A}) \bmod q$ get a partial private key (s_{D_A}, r_{D_A}) and KGC sends it.

SetPublic-PrivateKey: The user receives the (s_{D_A}, r_{D_A}) sent by the KGC and runs this algorithm to generate his own public-private key pair. It picks a random number $t_A \xleftarrow{\$} Z_q$ and sets it $u_A = g^{t_A}$. Then, the user's public key is $pk_A = (s_{D_A}, u_A)$, private key is $k_{ID} = (r_{D_{ID}}, t_{ID})$. The user transmits its public key to the KGC over a secure channel, and the KGC publishes it in a public list. The private key is reserved by the user.

If the user is the group manager GM, the public key $pk_G = (s_{D_G}, u_G)$ and the private key $sk_G = (r_{D_G}, t_G)$ of the GM are as the public and private key of the group.

Join: User A sends a request to the GM. After verifying that the user's identity is legal, the GM allows the user to join the group, and generates the credential $cert_A$ for the users identity.

Sign: The user A signs the message m using the signing private key h_A and the credential $cert_A$. Calculate $h_1 = H_1(m \parallel ID_G \parallel U_A \parallel pk_G)$ and set $\sigma = h_A h_1 + cert_A$. A outputs group signature (U_A, σ).

Verify: The receiver acts as a verifier and first checks if the user's signing public key is in the revocation list. If the U_A is not in the revocation list, the receiver calculates whether $g^\sigma = U_A^{h_1} \cdot u_{G}s_{D_G}(pk_{sys}^{H_2(ID, s_{D_G})})^{H_1(ID_G \parallel U_A \parallel pk_G)}$ is established according to the public parameters.

If equal, the verifier outputs "Accept"; if not equal, it outputs "Reject". If U_A is in the revocation list, it indicates that the user is not a member of the group, the signature is invalid, and the verifier should output "reject" [2].

2.2 Security Analysis

The proposed certificateless group signature technology meets the security requirements of group signatures [14]:

(1) Identity anonymity
    For a legitimate group signature, even if the attacker owns the signature key, it is impossible to open the group signature to determine the identity of the signing user, that is, it is impossible to track the true identity of the signer through limited calculations. In the signature algorithm of this paper, the group signature is in the form of (U_A, σ), where U_A and σ are both random numbers, and the randomness of the group signature (U_A, σ) makes it impossible for anyone other than the one to know the identity of the signer, and the users anonymity can be guaranteed.
(2) Unforgeability of signature
    We say that only legitimate group members can generate the corresponding legal signature key h and the valid group signature σ. No other attacker can fake a legitimate signature. Since the signature key h_{ID} is randomly selected, and the group administrator uses its own private key to sign the member certificate U_{ID} on its signature public key $cert_{ID}$, in the limited polynomial time algorithm, as long as the attacker cannot obtain the user signature secret The key, and can not solve the CDH problem, then there is no case where the attacker can forge a valid signature.

3   Anonymous Communication Protocol Based on Group Signature

3.1   Packet Structure During Forwarding

In order to improve the transmission efficiency, this paper strips the anonymous message from the onion packet and uses only the session key K_D shared between the user A and the target receiver D to encrypt the message m, and designs a new packet format (as shown in Fig. 1 below), greatly reducing the number of encryption and decryption operations of anonymous messages, improving the efficiency of anonymous message forwarding.

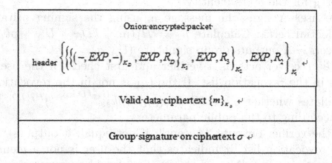

Fig. 1. Anonymous message packet format

User A and the three onion routers sequentially encrypt the next hop routing information R and the session expiration time EXP on the anonymous link using the session keys K_D and $K_i(i = 1, 2, 3)$, respectively, to form an onion routing packet for anonymous message forwarding [7,10]. Instead, we use K_D to encrypt a valid anonymous message m, and then perform subsequent group signature operations, attaching the group signature to the onion routing packet.

The packet structure in the anonymous message forwarding process is as follows:

$$\left\{ \left\{ \left\{ \begin{matrix} \{(-, EXP, -)_{K_D}, EXP, R_D\}_{k_3}, \\ EXP, R_3 \\ EXP, R_2 \end{matrix} \right\}_{k_2} \right\}_{k_1} \| \{m\}_{k_D} \| \{\{m\}_{k_D}\}_{Sign} \right\}$$

Conversely, if destination D wants to communicate anonymously with user A, D records the anonymous message as m, forwards m by the onion routers in the reverse direction of the anonymous communication link. Destination D first encrypts the anonymous message m' and the expiration time EXP with K_D, and returns it to the previous router on the anonymous link. The previous router continues to encrypt the data packet with the session key shared by itself and the source user, to return along the anonymous link. Until the anonymous message is returned to the source user A, A uses the session keys $K_i(i = 1, 2, 3)$ and K_D

shared by the three routers $R_i(i = 1, 2, 3)$ and the destination D to decrypt the onion packet in turn to obtain the anonymous message m' sent to it by D. The corresponding packet format is as follows:

$$\left\{ \left\{ \{(m', EXP)_{K_D}, EXP\}_{k_3}, EXP \right\}_{k_2}, EXP \right\}_{k_1}$$

The anonymous message forwarding process between User A and Destination D ends.

3.2 Anonymous Communication Protocol Security

We say that if the group signature scheme is anonymous, the new anonymous communication protocol is anonymous [10].

Proof If A can break the anonymity of the group signature scheme, then a simulation algorithm can be constructed. Challenger C breaks the anonymity of the group signature scheme. Challenger C generates the group administrators public key pk_G, the users signature key Sk_0 and Sk_1 and generates all signature-related parameter values. Then C will give $(pk_G, Sk_0, Sk_1, params, sk_{sys})$ to the A. In the challenge phase, C gets the ID^* from A, generates the group signature σ^* as the output of the Sign algorithm, and runs other query algorithms accordingly. A outputs b as a guess bit for the Sk_b pair. Then C can attack the anonymity of the group signature with the same advantage of A. This contradicts the anonymity of the previously proven group signature scheme.

3.3 Anonymous Communication Protocol Efficiency Analysis

In order to achieve the analysis of the anonymous communication protocol in this paper, the efficiency of the protocol is discussed in this section, and the efficiency achieved by the specific parameters is compared with other protocols. The cost of establishing a link of length n is analyzed from the perspective of the source user and the onion routing node. In the protocol, the process of establishing a link involves the following operations.

The comparison of the protocol in this paper with other protocols [5,10] is shown in the following table.

Time	Room					
	IBE		CL-OR		This protocol	
	User	Routing node	User	Routing node	User	Routing node
Encryption	1	0	1	0	1	0
Decrypt	0	1	0	1	0	1
Modular exponentiation	1	0	3	2	3	3
Algorithms in groups	3	1	0	0	0	0
Pair	2	0	0	0	0	0

As can be seen in the table, the protocol of this paper is basically the same as the other two protocols except for the modulus exponentiation, because in the protocol of this paper, the value of each onion routing node with ID can be pre-calculated, SAS. Is part of its public key. In addition, since the KGCs key does not change, the pre-calculated value does not need to be changed repeatedly.

The point is that the anonymous communication protocol of this article does not require KGC to change the system key frequently. The user only needs to obtain the KGC key once, and the same is true when the onion routing node re- quests part of the private key. From KGC, it does not require repeated operations during the key generation phase and has a lower computational load. Secondly, the protocol in this paper also has a signature mechanism. Compared with other protocols, it not only implements security in the encryption process, but also detects whether the data has been modified. The protocol can still achieve better efficiency.

4   Conclusions

In order to ensure the anonymity of user communication and to protect users privacy in the next generation network, this paper implements the forwarding process of anonymous messages in the anonymous communication link based on the new proposed certificateless group signature scheme, thus realizing confidentiality and integrity protection for anonymous messages. In the forwarding process of anonymous message, this paper applies a new onion routing data packet format, which effectively reduces the number of encryption and decryption operations of the relay node, and is beneficial for the node to forward the message efficiently and improves the efficiency of anonymous communication.

References

1. Asoni, D.E., Chen, C., Barrera, D., Perrig, A.: On building onion routing into future internet architectures. In: Camenisch, J., Kesdoğan, D. (eds.) iNetSec 2015. LNCS, vol. 9591, pp. 71–81. Springer, Cham (2016). https://doi.org/10.1007/978-3-319-39028-4_6
2. Backes, M., Goldberg, I., Kate, A., Mohammadi, E.: Provably secure and practical onion routing. In: Computer Security Foundations Symposium, vol. 6. IEEE (2012)
3. Burgstaller, F., Derler, A., Kern, S., Schanner, G., Reiter, A.: Anonymous communication in the browser via onion-routing. In: International Conference on P2P, Parallel, Grid, Cloud and Internet Computing, vol. 4 (2016)
4. Catalano, D., Fiore, D., Gennaro, R.: Certificateless onion routing, vol. 3, no. 51, pp. 151–160 (2009)
5. Catalano, D., Fiore, D., Gennaro, R.: A certificateless approach to onion routing. Int. J. Inf. Secur. 16(3), 327–343 (2017)
6. Chen, H., Zhu, C., Song, R.: Efficient certificateless signature and group signature schemes. J. Comput. Res. Dev. 2, 231–237 (2010)
7. Chen, C., Asoni, D.E., Barrera, D.: HORNET: high-speed onion routing at the network layer, vol. 4, no. 5, p. 51 (2015)

8. Chen, Q., Bridges, R.A.: Automated behavioral analysis of malware a case study of wannacry ransomware, vol. 2, pp. 454–460. arXiv preprint (2017)
9. Dhankani, M., Dhameja, A., Darda, S., Bohra, D.: Anonymous communication system based on onion routing. Int. J. Comput. Appl. **23**, 12–15 (2015)
10. Emura, K., Kanaoka, A., Ohta, S., Takahashi, T.: Building secure and anonymous communication channel: formal model and its prototype implementation. In: Proceedings of the 29th Annual ACM Symposium on Applied Computing, vol. 4, no. 1, pp. 1641–1648 (2014)
11. Jiang, L., Li, T., Li, X.: Anonymous communication via anonymous identity-based encryption and its application in IoT. In: Wireless Communications and Mobile Computing, vol. 4, p. 2018. IEEE (2018)
12. Mahmood, K., Li, X., Chaudhry, S.A., Naqvi, H., Kumari, S., Sangaiah, A.K., Rodrigues, J.J.: Pairing based anonymous and secure key agreement protocol for smart grid edge computing infrastructure. Future Gener. Comput. Syst. **88**, 491–500 (2018)
13. Tsai, J.L.: A new efficient certificateless short signature scheme using bilinear pairings. IEEE Syst. J. **11**(4), 2395–2402 (2015)
14. Liang, Y., Zhang, X., Zheng, Z.: Electronic cash system based on certificateless group signature. J. Commun. **37**(5), 184–190 (2016)
15. Shirazi, F., Simeonovski, M., Asghar, M.R., Backes, M., Diaz, C.: A survey on routing in anonymous communication protocols, vol. 3, no. 51, pp. 70–74 (2016)
16. Yameng, C., Xiangguo, C.: Certificateless group signature scheme from bilinear pairings, vol. 3, no. 51, pp. 262–267 (2017)
17. Yang, X., Yi, X., Khalil, I.: A new privacy-preserving authentication protocol for anonymous web browsing. Concurr. Comput. Pract. Exp. **3**(11), 4706 (2018)

Research on K-Means Clustering Algorithm Over Encrypted Data

Chen Wang, Andi Wang, Xinyu Liu, and Jian Xu[(✉)]

Software College, Northeastern University, Shenyang 110169, China
xuj@mail.neu.edu.cn

Abstract. Aiming at the privacy-preserving problem in data mining process, this paper proposes an improved K-Means algorithm over encrypted data, called HK-means++ that uses the idea of homomorphic encryption to solve the encrypted data multiplication problems, distance calculation problems and the comparison problems. Then apply these security protocols to the improved clustering algorithm framework. To prevent the leakage of privacy while calculating the distance between the sample points and the center points, it prevents the attacker from inferring the cluster grouping of the user by hiding the cluster center. To some extent, it would reduce the risk of leakage of private data in the cluster mining process. It is well known that the traditional K-Means algorithm is too dependent on the initial value. In this paper, we focus on solving the problem to reduce the number of iterations, and improve the clustering efficiency. The experimental results demonstrate that our proposed, HK-Means algorithm has good clustering performance and the running time is also reduced.

Keywords: K-means algorithm · Privacy-preserving clustering · Homomorphic encryption · Security protocol

1 Introduction

With the rapid development of science and technology, people are facing more and more data information. In order to analyze and extract valuable information, data mining technology is born, which can predict future trends and behaviors by analyzing data. However, there are large amount of user sensitive data, the process of processing data has a certain degree of leakage of user's private information, which brings serious threat to the user sensitive data. If the data is used by a thief for a malicious attack, the user or business will be forced to suffer huge losses. In the past, many people hold view that the data privacy protection brought by data mining through analyzing data is often considered to be contradictory. In fact, Data mining can satisfy privacy protection. The data mining of privacy protection can mine and protect the privacy of user data, and extract valuable information, thus effectively solving the relationship between data leakage and privacy protection. In today's rapidly expanding data, it is increasingly important to protect the privacy of data from leaks. Data mining methods are mainly divided into three types: association rule methods, classification methods and clustering methods [1]. Clustering is a very important part of data mining, there are many clustering methods such as partitioning and density. The purpose of clustering is to divide

© Springer Nature Switzerland AG 2019
J. Vaidya et al. (Eds.): CSS 2019, LNCS 11983, pp. 182–191, 2019.
https://doi.org/10.1007/978-3-030-37352-8_16

the data points into several classes. The data items in the same class have great similarities, and the data items in the different class have great dissimilarity. Privacy is revealed while calculating the distance between the sample point and the center point, so it is possible to prevent the attacker from inferring the cluster group which the user belongs by hiding the cluster center. Privacy-preserving means that in the process of clustering information, private information cannot be obtained by non-authorized participants, and the accuracy of mining results is also ensured [2]. The K-Means algorithm is a fundamental clustering algorithm based on distance division that has the characteristics of simplicity and high efficiency, also has been widely used in many fields. However, it is sensitive to the initial cluster center and needs to input the cluster number in advance.

In this paper, we proposed an algorithm called HK-Means++ which combines the K-Means++ idea, as well as automatically obtains the best cluster number to solve the problems existing in the current K-Means clustering. Meanwhile, it uses the homomorphic encryption idea to solve the encrypted data multiplication, distance calculation and comparison problem, then these security protocols are applied to the HK-Means++ algorithm framework to implement clustering algorithm.

2 Related Work

Currently, privacy-preserving data mining methods include data perturbation and cryptography. Data perturbation based on data mining mainly uses differential privacy method, but the traditional differential privacy protection K-Means algorithm is sensitive to the selection of its initial center point, which reduces the availability and stability of clustering results [3]. Yu et al. [4] proposed the differential privacy k-means method, which first eliminated the anomaly points in the dataset, then selected the initial cluster center point according to the density distribution, lastly added noisy to the original data. The disadvantage of this method has not been proved to be applicable by privacy-preserving clustering for large-scale dataset. Ren et al. [5] proposed an improved the traditional clustering named DPK-Means which satisfies the differential privacy protection. He used the method of randomly dividing the dataset into multiple subsets to obtain the initial center point. However, the number of dataset divided is difficult to determine, which affects the stability of the clustering results. Cryptography research based on data mining is to use homomorphic encryption, which is the most popular encryption technology at present. Due to it supports arithmetic operations directly on encrypted data, it is used to implement data security through encryption. By using homomorphic encryption, some data mining methods have developed corresponding encryption versions, such as gradient descent, linear regression, support vector machine, naive Bayes, decision tree, K-NN and other algorithms [6]. These technologies are part of supervised learning and focus on classification issues in data mining tasks. Due to the highly computational complexity of homomorphic encryption, these schemes cannot handle multidimensional data efficiently. K-Means clustering as an unsupervised learning range is a basic key data mining algorithm, which has been widely used in practical applications.

Encrypted data calculation is a major difficulty. Homomorphic Encryption (HE) scheme can support a series of arithmetic operations applied to cryptographic data [7]. In 2009, Gentry [8] proposed Fully Homomorphic Encryption (FHE), an encryption algorithm that finds its corresponding homomorphic operations for both addition and multiplication. At present, distributed privacy protection data mining based on homomorphic encryption has achieved rich research results. Vaidya [7] realized privacy-preserving K-Means clustering under vertical partitioning, which based on the algorithm of homomorphic encryption and secure permutation. Gentry [8] proposed a distributed clustering algorithm based on fully homomorphic encryption. However, due to insufficient computing power of the client, the encryption and decryption calculations take a long time. Fang et al. [9] designed a secure comparison protocol based on the fully homomorphic public key encryption protocol and data perturbation method, which is feasible through experimental verification. Erkin et al. [10, 11] used the Paillier encryption mechanism and the ElGamal encryption mechanism, they also has the same homomorphic nature.

Secure Muti-Party Computation (SMC), an important branch of cryptography, aimed to solve the problem of collaborative privacy protection computing between a group of untrusted participants, and provided data with no disclosure of raw data [12]. Recently, researchers have built several privacy-preserving K-Means clustering schemes using SMC protocols [13–15]. SMC is only available for the required clustering of data belonging to two or more data owners. The basic idea is that most of the processing is done internally by the data owner, and only the centroid on each K-Means iteration is shared [15]. Aggarwal et al. [13] think that, data owners generated local clusters using their respective datasets in each K-Means iteration. Then each party computed the cluster center of its local cluster class, encrypted it, and shared the encrypted cluster center with other owners. A similar mechanism is proposed by Gheid et al. [14], except that one of the users calculated the global centroid and then shared it. Due to the data is stored locally and not shared with other parties, data confidentiality is preserved. However, as K-Means clustering progresses, data owners performed similarity calculations that usually required a large number of such calculations.

In this paper, the Paillier homomorphic encryption method is applied to the encrypted data multiplication protocol, distance calculation protocol and comparison protocol, and iterative calculation is performed in K-Means algorithm.

3 Security Protocol

K-Means clustering algorithm consists of three steps: selecting the center point, clustering and recalculating the center point. In the process of clustering, we first calculate the Euclidean distance between data points and each central point, and then compare the nearest central points to cluster. These data points may come from different participants, so privacy leakage may occur in the process of computing. There are two main problems: how to calculate the distance between the data point and the center point safely, and how to compare the distance between the data points. This experiment adopts homomorphic encryption method, which is oriented to encrypted operation. To solve the problem of how to calculate the distance between data points and center points safely, we propose a distance calculation protocol based on the secure multiplication protocol, and encrypted data comparison protocols for how to compare the distance between data points and multiple centroid points.

3.1 Secure Multiplication Protocol

The secure multiplication protocol mainly realizes the multiplication homomorphism through attributes of homomorphic encryption, so that their results can be obtained from two encrypted data. Specifically, A has two encrypted data such as $E_{pk}(x)$ and $E_{pk}(y)$. The goal is to get $E_{pk}(xy)$ through interaction with B and ensure the privacy of x and y. B has the private key encrypted by Paillier and the public key is public. The basic idea of secure multiplication protocol is based on this formula:

$$x * y = (x + r_x) * (y + r_y) - x * r_x - y * r_y, \; r_x, r_y \in Z_n \tag{1}$$

Specific security protocols are shown in Protocol 1.

Protocol 1. Secure multiplication protocol

Input A: $E_{pk}(x)$ and $E_{pk}(y)$, public keys pk_p

Input B: Secret keys sk_p

Output: $E_{pk}(xy)$

1. A: randomly select two numbers $r_x, r_y \in Z_n$

2. A: compute $x' \leftarrow E_{pk}(x) E_{pk}(r_x)$

3. A: compute $y' \leftarrow E_{pk}(y) E_{pk}(r_y)$

4. A: send x' and y' to B

5. B: decrypt x' and y', compute $h_x \leftarrow D_{pk}(x')$, $h_y \leftarrow D_{pk}(y')$, $h \leftarrow h_x h_y \bmod N$ and $h' \leftarrow E_{pk}(h)$

6. B: send h' to A

7. A: compute $s \leftarrow h' E_{pk}(x)^{N-r}$, $s' \leftarrow s E_{pk}(x)^{N-r}$ and $E_{pk}(xy) \leftarrow s' E_{pk}(r_x r_y)^{N-1}$

8. A: output $E_{pk}(xy)$

3.2 Secure Distance Computing Protocol

The secure distance protocol implements the Euclidean distance calculation between two encrypted vectors. The basic idea is based on the following equation:

$$\left(|x - y|^2\right) = \sum_{i=1}^{l} (x_i - y_i)^2 \qquad (2)$$

Firstly, for all $1 \le i \le l$, A calculates $E_{pk}(x_i - y_i) = E_{pk}(x_i)E_{pk}(y_i)^{N-1}$ by the properties of Paillier homomorphic encryption, and then $E_{pk}\left((x_i - y_i)^2\right)$ is calculated by multiplying security protocol M and B. Finally, A uses the properties of homomorphic encryption to sum $E_{pk}\left((x_i - y_i)^2\right)$ and get the final calculation result $E_{pk}\left(|x - y|^2\right)$.

$$E_{pk}\left(|x - y|^2\right) = \prod_{i=1}^{l} E_{pk}\left((x_i - y_i)^2\right) \qquad (3)$$

Specific security protocols are shown in Protocol 2.

Protocol 2. Safety distance calculation protocol

Input A: $E_{pk}(x)$ and $E_{pk}(y)$, the bit length l of x and y, public keys pk_p

Input B: Secret keys sk_p, the bit length l

Output: $E_{pk}\left(|x - y|^2\right)$

1. A: for i=1 to l do

2.   compute $E_{pk}(x_i - y_i) \leftarrow E_{pk}(x_i)E_{pk}(y_i)^{N-1}$

3. A and B: for i=1 to l do

4.   compute $E_{pk}\left((x_i - y_i)^2\right) \leftarrow M\left(E_{pk}(x_i - y_i), E_{pk}(x_i - y_i)\right)$

5. A: compute $E_{pk}\left(|x - y|^2\right) \leftarrow \prod_{i=1}^{l} E_{pk}\left((x_i - y_i)^2\right)$

6. A: output $E_{pk}\left(|x - y|^2\right)$

3.3   Security Comparison Protocol

The main idea of the comparison protocol is to compute encrypted data $2^l + y - x$, and then refer to bit $l + 1$ which corresponds to bit 2^l. If the result is 1, then $y \ge x$; otherwise $y < x$. This paper assumes that the encryption scheme is additive homomorphism, N denotes encrypted modulus.

Protocol 3. Safety Comparison protocol

Input A: $E_{pk}(x), E_{pk}(y)$, the bit length l of x and y, public keys pk_p

Input B: Secret keys sk_p, the bit length l

Output A: 1 or 0

1. A: compute $x' \leftarrow E_{pk}(y) * 2^l * E_{pk}(x)^{-1} \bmod N^2$

2. A: randomly select a number r from $\left(0, 2^{l+1}\right) \cap \mathbb{Z}$

3. A: adding noisy r to the encrypted data x' makes it impossible for the B party to know the

real data x' : $z \leftarrow x' E_{pk}(r) \bmod N^2$

4. A: send z to B

5. B: compute decrypted data z' : $z' \leftarrow D_{pk}(z)$

6. A: compute $c \leftarrow r \bmod 2^l$

7. B: compute $d \leftarrow r \bmod 2^l$

8. transfer DGK comparison protocol, A, B as input, c, d as input data, B gets comparison result

$E_{pk}(t')$, where t=(d<c)

9. A: sent $E_{pk}(r_{l+1})$ to B, where r_{l+1} is the $l+1$ th bit of r

10. B: encrypt the $l+1$ th bit of z to get $E_{pk}(z_{l+1})$

11. B: compute $t' \leftarrow E_{pk}(t')E_{pk}(r_{l+1})E_{pk}(z_{l+1})$

12. B: send t' to A

13. A: compute decrypted data t, $t \leftarrow D_{pk}(t')$

14. output t

---

4   HK-Means + + Algorithm Over Encrypted Data

In this section, we proposed an improved K-Means algorithm over encrypted data, named HK-Means++ algorithm, that is designed based on the above security protocol and the idea of K-Means++.

4.1   Improved K-Means Algorithm

Based on the previous research, experiments combined with the idea of k-means++, a clustering algorithm which can automatically obtain the best clustering cluster number is adopted. The dataset is divided into K clusters by iteration process, so that each data point belongs to the cluster corresponding to its nearest vector, which makes the similarity within classes larger and the similarity between the classes lower. The detailed process description is as follows.

$$\frac{D(x)^2}{\sum_{x \in X} D(x)^2} \tag{4}$$

Step 1: Random Selection of Cluster Center C1 from Training Data Set X;

Step 2: Calculate the probability from other data points to cluster center C1 according to formula 4, and the biggest probability value becomes the next cluster center C2, where D (x) represents the Euclidean distance from the data point to the nearest center;

Step 3: Allocate the remaining data points to the nearest clustering center;

Step 4: Find out the data points farthest from the center and check whether they can become a new clustering center. If conditions are met, repeat steps 3 and 4; Otherwise, the algorithm ends.

In order to determine whether a point can become a new clustering center, this experiment takes 0.5 times of the average distance of all clustering centers as the lower limit and 1 as the upper limit. If the distance Di from point Xi to its clustering center falls within this range, it can become a new clustering center, which ensures that the new cluster center is far away from other centers.

4.2   HK-Means+ + Algorithm Over Encrypted Data

The algorithm using homomorphic encryption, encrypt the sensitive data appearing in k-means++ algorithm, and the above two protocols are invoked by encrypted operation.

Step 1: Encryption of data by public key;

Step 2: Randomly select the initial clustering center C1 and transfer protocol 1 to calculate the Euclidean distance from the remaining encrypted data points to the clustering center C1;

Step 3: Transfer protocol 2 according to distance to compare encrypted data, and assign the remaining data points to the nearest clustering center. At this time, the clustering center is protected, which is unknown to others;

Step 4: Find out the data points farthest from the center and check whether they can become a new clustering center. If the condition is satisfied, repeat steps 3 and 4 and assign encrypted data points again for the next iteration. Until no new clustering centers are generated;

Step 5: Use private key to decrypt data, and obtain clustering analysis results.

The above process is carried out in a encrypted environment to prevent privacy disclosure while calculating the distance between the sample point and the center point. Hiding the cluster center can prevent the attacker from inferring the cluster group which the user belongs.

5   Evaluation

The evaluation of the proposed method is presented in this section using Last_fm data set, which describes information about users, singers and types of singers. For each user in the data set, include a list of their most popular artists and the number of playback times, as well as the type of singer that the user tagged. Include the number of times each user listens to each singer's music. Among them, there are 1892 users, 17632 singers and 11946 types of singers. The metric used is Silhouette Coefficient and run time.

Clustering Performance. Silhouette Coefficient is a popular method to measure the performance of clustering. The goal of clustering algorithm is to make the similarity between clusters smaller and within clusters larger, and the larger the Silhouette Coefficient, the better the clustering performance. Compare to the traditional K-Means algorithm, the improved K-Means++ algorithm, the privacy-preserved K-Means algorithm named HK-Means and we proposed in this paper named HK-Means++ and observe the effect of K value on clustering results. The experimental results are shown in Fig. 1.

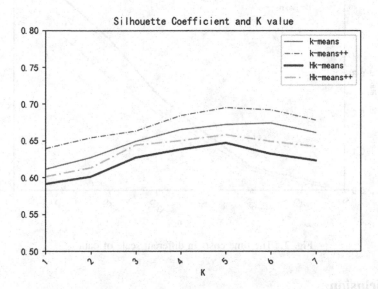

Fig. 1. The relationship between the silhouette coefficients and the k value of four algorithms

As shown in Fig. 1, with the increase of K value, the Silhouette Coefficient of the four algorithms generally shows an upward trend. When k = 5, the Silhouette Coefficient are larger, and the clustering effect is better. The clustering effect of HK-Means++ algorithm we proposed is better than that of HK-Means on the whole, and the clustering performance of the HK-Means++ algorithm is close to K-Means++ with non-privacy protection. For example, when k = 3, S(K-Means++) = 0.663, S(HK-Means) = 0.627, S(HK-Means+) = 0.644, for K-Means++, the performance of HK-Means++ is only reduced by 0.7%; compared with HK-Means, the performance of HK-Means++ is increased by about 2.7%.

Runtime. Figure 2 shows the time cost of four algorithms, the runtime is the time to complete the clustering excluding encryption. The results show that the time overhead increases with the scale of the data sets increasing. Since the user needs to generate a key and perform SMC encrypted calculation, the time overhead of HK-Means algorithm and HK-Means++ algorithm we proposed is higher than that of non-privacy-protected K-Means algorithm and K-Means++ algorithm. It can be seen from the figure that the time cost of the K-Means++ algorithm and the HK-Means++ algorithm which automatically obtained cluster numbers are smaller than the traditional K-Means algorithm and HK-Means algorithm. This shows that the algorithm proposed in this paper can improve the clustering efficiency as well as reduce runtime.

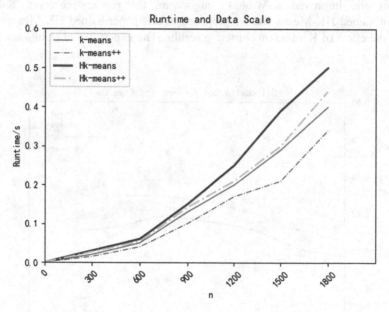

Fig. 2. The time costs in different scale of data

6   Conclusion

The traditional K-Means clustering algorithm is sensitive to the initial value and has some blindness in the selection of the clustered number of K value. At the same time, while calculating the distance between the sample point and the center point, privacy will be revealed. Hide the cluster center to prevent an attacker from inferring the cluster of classes to which the user belongs. This paper proposes an algorithm named HK-Means++ over encrypted data based on K-Means++, which aims the problem that the traditional K-Means algorithm is too dependent on the initial value. The algorithm is based on homomorphic encryption, which supports encrypted multiplication, distance calculation and comparison in the operation process. Meanwhile, it not only guarantees the security of data but also obtains correct results of K-Means mining tasks. Due to insufficient computing power of the client itself, encryption and decryption calculations take a long time. As a future work we intend to solve it.

Acknowledgments. This work is supported, in part, by the National Natural Science Foundation of China under grant No. 61872069, in part, by the Fundamental Research Funds for the Central Universities (N171704005), in part, by the Shenyang Science and Technology Plan Projects (18-013-0-01).

References

1. Bonawitz, K., Ivanov, V., Kreuter, B., et al.: Practical secure aggregation for privacy-preserving machine learning. In: Proceedings of the 2017 ACM SIGSAC Conference on Computer and Communications Security, pp. 1175–1191. ACM, New York (2017)
2. Neha, B., Gordhan, B.: Privacy-preserving using distributed k-means clustering for arbitrarily partitioned data. Int. J. Eng. Res. Dev. **2**(2), 2291–2295 (2014)
3. Su, D., Cao, J., Li, N.: Differentially private k-means clustering and a hybrid approach to private optimization. ACM Trans. Priv. Secur. **20**(4), 1–33 (2017)
4. Yu, Q., Luo, Y., Chen, C., et al.: Outlier-eliminated k-means clustering algorithm based on differential privacy preservation. Appl. Intell. **45**(4), 1179–1191 (2016)
5. Ren, J., Xiong, J., Yao, Z., et al.: DPLK-means: a novel differential privacy k-means mechanism. In: 2017 IEEE Second International Conference on Data Science in Cyberspace, Shenzhen, pp. 133–139. IEEE (2017)
6. Raphael, B., Raluca, P., Stephen, T., et al.: Machine learning classification over encrypted data. In: Network and Distributed System Security Symposium. NDSS Symposium, San Diego (2015)
7. Vaidya, J., Clifton, C.: Privacy-preserving k-means clustering over vertically partitioned data. In: Proceedings of the Ninth ACM SIFKDD International Conference on Knowledge Discovery & Data mining, pp. 206–215. ACM, New York (2003)
8. Gentry, G.: Computing arbitrary function of encrypted data. Commun. ACM **53**(3), 97 (2010)
9. Fang, W., Yang, R., Xia, K.: SMC-based privacy protection clustering model. Syst. Eng. Electron. **54**(7), 1505–1510 (2012)
10. Erkin, Z., Veugen, T., Toft, T., et al.: Privacy-Preserving Distributed Clustering. EURASIP J. Inf. Seur. **1**, 1–15 (2013)
11. Yi, X., Zhang, Y.: Equally contributory privacy-preserving k-means clustering over vertically partitioned data. Inf. Syst. **38**(1), 97–107 (2013)
12. Almutairi, N., Coenen, F., Dures, K.: K-means clustering using homomorphic encryption and an updatable distance matrix: secure third party data clustering with limited data owner interaction. In: Bellatreche, L., Chakravarthy, S. (eds.) DaWaK 2017. LNCS, vol. 10440, pp. 274–285. Springer, Cham (2017). https://doi.org/10.1007/978-3-319-64283-3_20
13. Aggarwal, A., Kaur, D., Mittal, D., et al.: Secure data mining in cloud using homomorphic encryption. In: 2014 IEEE International Conference on Cloud Computing in Emerging Markets, Bangalore. IEEE (2014)
14. Gheid, Z., Challal, Y.: Efficient and privacy-preserving k-means clustering for big data mining. In: Proceedings of the IEEE Trustcom/BigdataSE/ISPA, Tianjin, pp. 791–798. IEEE (2016)
15. Angela, J., Frederik, A.: Unsupervised machine learning on encrypted data. In: Cid, C., Jacobson, M. (eds.) SAC 2018. LNCS, vol. 11349, pp. 453–478. Springer, Cham (2017). https://doi.org/10.1007/978-3-030-10970-7_21

Requester-Centric CP-ABE Combining Removing Escrow and Outsourcing Decryption

Wang Yao[1,2,3], Faguo Wu[1,2,3], and Xiao Zhang[1,2,3]([✉])

[1] Key Laboratory of Mathematics, Informatics and Behavioral Semantics,
Ministry of Education, and School of Mathematics and Systems Science,
Beihang University, Beijing 100191, China
xiao.zh@buaa.edu.cn
[2] Peng Cheng Laboratory, Shenzhen 518055, Guangdong, China
[3] Beijing Advanced Innovation Center for Big Data and Brain Computing,
Beihang University, Beijing 100191, China

Abstract. Key escrow and low efficiency are two practical bottlenecks of attribute-based encryption. In this paper, a Requester-Centric CP-ABE (RC-CP-ABE) combining removing escrow and outsourcing decryption is proposed. By the bilinear map of composite order, we optimized the computational complexity of key transformation in the case of a large number of attributes. Without adding roles in the system, data requesters can undertake the key transformation which make them the center in the interactive process and the bridge linking removing escrow with outsourcing decryption. Security analysis has been made to prove our algorithm secure.

Keywords: Ciphertext-policy attribute-based encryption ·
Requester-centric · Outsourcing decryption · Removing Escrow

1 Introduction

Attribute-based encryption is first proposed by Sahai and Waters [23] in 2005. Then, the idea was further extended and key-policy attribute-based encryption (KP-ABE) was formally proposed by Goyal et al. [5]. In 2007, ciphertext-policy attribute-based encryption was first proposed by Bethencourt et al. [1]. ABE scheme is used to share information securely [15] and support fine-grained access control [2,18]. ABE has many applications in different fields [4,9,12,13,19,21, 28]. Attribute-based encryption is considered as a good way to share information securely in cloud [27]. As encrypted information can be decrypted by specific access control policy and attribute set instead of identity, scope of information

Supported by Program of National Natural Science Foundation of China Grant No. 11871004, Fundamental Research of Civil Aircraft Grant No. MJ-F-2012-04.

dissemination is well extended. But practical bottlenecks exist. Key escrow and low efficiency are two prominent problems.

Key escrow is caused by the too high authority of attribute authority. The attribute authority is able to compute the attribute secret keys corresponding to any attribute, and is free to decrypt and read data meant for any data owner. This could be a potential threat to data confidentiality [7]. There are two typical ways to solve key escrow problem. One is multi-authority attribute-based encryption (MA-ABE) [8,19]. MA-ABE is a nature way to solve key escrow problem, as there exists multiple attribute authorities who can generate different partial private keys. Another way to solve key escrow problem is in situation only single authority exists [7,24]. By this kind of methods, attribute authority cooperates with cloud service provider to generate private keys. Two-party computation protocols or other protocols are needed to make sure neither authority nor cloud service provider can get the other's master key.

In terms of efficiency, generally, the number of exponential power operations is proportional to the number of attributes used, which occupy a large amount of computing resources in ABE. The lightweight design of encryption and decryption operations is thus particularly important. ABE has many directions of optimization measures, such as offline/online encryption and outsourced decryption. Here, we focus on outsourced decryption [14,16,17,22]. Outsourced decryption is firstly proposed by Green et al. in 2011 [6]. Its main idea is transforming the decryption keys in a secure way, and by using the transformed key, making an outsourced decryption server undertake most decryption operations. Mao et al. [20] establish verifiable attribute-based encryption algorithm with outsourcing decryption based on CPA security and RCCA security. Wang et al. [25] propose a CP-ABE with outsourced decryption and directionally hidden policy. Zuo et al. [29] extended the verifiable outsourcing decryption algorithm to the CCA security model, and provided the corresponding security proof.

Due to the key transformation phase, removing escrow and outsourcing decryption can hardly coexist. Chen et al. [3] construct a key issuing protocol where AA and MAA not noly cooperate with but also restrain each other skillfully to generate users' secret keys to realize an outsourced attribute-based encryption without key escrow. We also focus on this problem, but propose an algorithm in a completely different way.

The contributions of this paper are as follows:

(1) We presents a requester-centric CP-ABE to remove key escrow with outsourced, where data requesters become the center in the interactive process and undertake the key transformation. In this way, we do not need to add roles in the system, and traditional defenses against those two problems work well together.
(2) We prove the security of the algorithm from four aspects, namely Basic Structure Security, Escrow-Free Guarantee, Outsourced Security Guarantee and Outsourced Decryption Security.

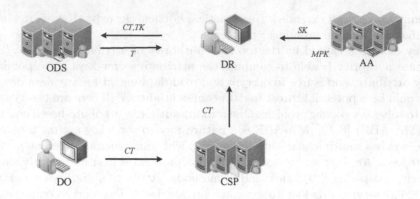

Fig. 1. System model.

2   Preliminaries

2.1   Bilinear Maps

Let G and T two multiplicative cyclic groups of prime order p with generator g and h respectively. We define $e : G \times T \to G_T$ to be a bilinear map if it has the following properties: (1) Bilinear: for all $g \in G$, $h \in T$ and $a, b \in Z_p^*$, we have $e(g^a, h^b) = e(g, h)^{ab}$; (2) Non-degeneracy: $e(g, h) \neq 1$; (3) Computability: For all $g \in G$, $h \in T$, there is an efficient algorithm to compute $e(g, h)$ [1].

But if G is a multiplicative cyclic group of composite order $N = pq$, p and q distinct primes. G_p and G_q are two subgroups of G with prime orders p and q respectively. $e : G \times G \to G_T$ is a bilinear map. For all $g \in G_p$, $h \in G_q$, we have $e(g, h) = 1_{G_T}$ [25].

2.2   Linear Secret-Sharing Schemes

A LSSS is a share-generating matrix $A_{l \times n}$whose rows are labeled by attributes. When we consider the column vector $v = (s, r_2, ..., r_n)$, where $s \in Z_p$ is the secret to be shared and $r_2, ..., r_n \in Z_p$ are randomly chosen, then Av is the vector of l shares of the secret s. A user's set of attributes S satisfies the LSSS access matrix if the rows labeled by the attributes in S have the linear reconstruction property, which means there exist constants $\{\omega_i\}$ such that, for any valid shares $\{\lambda_i\}$ of a secret s according to the LSSS matrix, we have: $\sum_i \omega_i \lambda_i = s$. Essentially, a user will be able to decrypt a ciphertext with access matrix A if and only if the rows of A labeled by the user's attributes include the vector $(1, 0, ..., 0)$ in their span [10].

3   System Model

System consists of 5 parts: Data Owner (DO), Data Requester (DR), Attribute Authority (AA), Cloud Service Provider (CSP) and Outsourced Decryption

Server (ODS), shown as Fig. 1. We suppose AA, CSP and ODS are semi-trusted, which means they will follow the protocols in an honest way but are curious in the stored information.

AA is responsible for the management of users' attributes and CSP stores ciphertexts. ODS is a serve used for outsourcing the complicated decryption computation to reduce the computing overhead of requesters.

4 Basic Structure

The basic structure of RC-CP-APE without outsourced decryption and removing escrow consists of 4 phases: Setup, Key Generation, Encryption, and Decryption.

4.1 Setup

AA inputs a security parameters λ and a monotone universal attribute space $\sum$. And it generates $N = p_1 p_2$, G, G_T and e, where p_1 and p_2 are distinct primes, G and G_T are two multiplicative cyclic groups of composite order N, and $e : G \times G \rightarrow G_T$ a bilinear map. Then it selects random generators $g_1 \in G_{p_1}$, $g_2 \in G_{p_2}$. G_{p_1} and G_{p_2} are subgroups of G with prime orders p_1, and p_2 respectively. There is also a hash function $F : \sum \rightarrow: G_{p_1}$. a is selected randomly from Z_{p_1}.It also picks $\alpha \in Z_{p_1}$, and computes $e(g_1, g_1)^\alpha$. AA's master public key is set as

$$MPK_{AA} = <N, G, Gp_1, Gp_2, G_T, e, g_1, g_2, F, g_1^a, e(g_1, g_1)^\alpha>$$

and AA's master secret key is set as

$$MSK_{AA} = <a, \alpha>$$

4.2 Key Generation

AA inputs DR's attribute set S and picks random number $t \in Z_{p_1}$. And the secret key of DR is computed as

$$SK = <K_1 = g_1^t, K_2 = g_1^\alpha g_1^{at}, [K_x = F(x)^t]_{x \in S}>$$

4.3 Encryption

DO inputs a LSSS $\prod = <A, \rho>$ and a message M to encrypt. A is a $l \times n$ matrix, and function ρ maps rows of A to attributes. DO chooses secret value $s \in Z_N$ and random number $v_1, ... v_n \in Z_N$ to construct vector $\vec{v} = (s, v_1, ..., v_n)$. For $i - 1$ to n, it computes $\lambda_i = \vec{v} \cdot A_i$, where A_i is ith row of A. DO picks randomly $r_1, ..., r_l, \tau_1, \tau_2 \in Z_N$ and computes ciphertext CT as

$$CT = <C = M \cdot e(g_1, g_1)^{\alpha s}, C_{TK1} = e(g_2, g_2)^{\tau_1}, C_{TK2} = e(g_2, g_2)^{\tau_2}, C_v$$

$$= g_1^s g_2^{\tau_1}, [C_{i1} = g_1^{a\lambda_i} F(\rho(i))^{-r_i} g_2^{\tau_2}, C_{i2} = g_1^{r_i} g_2^{\tau_2}]_{i \in [l]}, \prod >$$

And DO must keep τ_1 and τ_2 secret, and $\tau_1 - 2\tau_2 \sum_{i \in [l]} \omega_i \neq 0$.

4.4 Decryption

If DR's attribute set S is an authorized set, then let $I \subset [l]$ be defined as $I = \{i : \rho(i) \in S\}$. Then it can compute a set $\{\omega_i \in Z_N\}_{i \in I}$ such that $\sum_{i \in I} \omega_i \lambda_i = s$, if $\{\lambda_i\}_{i \in I}$ are valid shares according to A.

Then, Y^s can be computed by DR as follow

$$Y^s = \frac{e(C_v, K_2)}{\prod_{i \in [l]}[e(C_{i1}, K_1)e(C_{i2}, K_{\rho(i)})]^{\omega_i}}$$

Thus, DR can compute M by $M = C/Y^s$.

4.5 Correctness

$$
\begin{aligned}
Y^s &= \frac{e(C_v, K_2)}{\prod_{i \in [l]}[e(C_{i1}, K_1)e(C_{i2}, K_{\rho(i)})]^{\omega_i}} \\
&= \frac{e(g_1^s g_2^{\tau_1}, g_1^\alpha g_1^{at})}{\prod_{i \in [l]}[e(g_1^{a\lambda_i}F(\rho(i))^{-r_i}g_2^{\tau_2}, g_1^t)e(g_1^{r_i}g_2^{\tau_2}, F(\rho(i))^t)]^{\omega_i}} \\
&= \frac{e(g_1, g_1)^{\alpha s}e(g_1, g_1)^{ats}e(g_2, g_1)^{\alpha \tau_1}e(g_2, g_1)^{at\tau_1}}{\prod_{i \in [l]}[e(g_1, g_1)^{at\lambda_i}e(F(\rho(i)), g_1)^{-r_i t}e(g_2, g_1)^{t\tau_2}e(g_1, F(\rho(i)))^{r_i t}e(g_2, , F(\rho(i)))^{t\tau_2}]^{\omega_i}} \\
&= \frac{e(g_1, g_1)^{\alpha s}e(g_1, g_1)^{ats}}{\prod_{i \in [l]}e(g_1, g_1)^{at\lambda_i \omega_i}} \\
&= \frac{e(g_1, g_1)^{\alpha s}e(g_1, g_1)^{ats}}{e(g_1, g_1)^{ats}} \\
&= e(g_1, g_1)^{\alpha s}
\end{aligned}
$$

5 Escrow-Free Structure

For solving the key escrow problem, the basic structure can easily be modified to [8,19]where muliti-authorities exists or to [7,24] where escrow is removing by the secure two-party computation between the AA and the CSP. What we need to do is to modify the ciphertexts like the basic structure and to adjust the local decryption equation according to the decryption.

6 Proposed Algorithm

Due to the centric role of DR, the key transformation phase will be token by DR and the escrow-free structure has little influence on the outsourced decryption of our proposed algorithm. Thus, we will introduce our algorithm by improving the basic structure.

The proposed RC-CP-ABE consists of 6 phases: Setup, Key Generation, Encryption, Key Transformation, Outsourced Decryption and Local Decryption. The first two phases are same with those of basic structure. We will introduce the last four here.

6.1   Encryption

We adds two hash functions $H_1 : \{0,1\}^* \rightarrow Z_{p_1}$ and $H_2 : \{0,1\}^* \rightarrow \{0,1\}^*$ in the public keys.

DO picks a random $R \in G_T$ and computes $s = H_1(R, M)$ and $r = H_2(R)$. The ciphertexts will be

$$CT = <C = R \cdot e(g_1, g_1)^{\alpha s}, C' = M \oplus r, C_{TK1} = e(g_2, g_2)^{\tau_1}, C_{TK2} =$$

$$e(g_2, g_2)^{\tau_2}, C_v = g_1^s g_2^{\tau_1}, [C_{i1} = g_1^{a\lambda_i} F(\rho(i))^{-r_i} g_2^{\tau_2}, C_{i2} = g_1^{r_i} g_2^{\tau_2}]_{i \in [l]}, \prod >$$

6.2   Key Transformation

DR picks the transformation private key as $TSK = \{\psi, \phi\} \in Z_{p_2}$ and computes the transformation keys as

$$TK = \{TK_1 = g_1^t g_2^{\psi}, TK_2 = g_1^{\alpha} g_1^{at} g_2^{\phi}, [TK_x = F(x)^t g_2^{\psi}]_{x \in S}\}.$$

6.3   Outsourced Decryption

By obtaining CT and TK, the ODS can calculate the semi-decrypted information T as

$$T = \frac{e(C_v, TK_2)}{\prod_{i \in [l]} [e(C_{i1}, TK_1) e(C_{i2}, TK_{\rho(i)})]^{\omega_i}}$$

6.4   Local Decryption

DR can get Y^s from the result of outsourced decryption T by computing $Y^s = T \cdot C_{TK1}^{-\phi} \cdot C_{TK2}^{2\psi \sum_{i \in [l]} \omega_i}$. Then DR can compute $R = C/Y^s$, $M = H_2(R) \oplus C'$ and $s = H_1(R, M)$. If $C = R \cdot e(g_1, g_1)^{\alpha s}$ and $T = e(g_1, g_1)^{\alpha s} C_{TK1}^{\phi} C_{TK2}^{-2\psi \sum_{i \in [l]} \omega_i}$, it outputs M; otherwise, it outputs the error symbol.

6.5 Correctness

$$T = \frac{e(C_v, TK_2)}{\prod_{i \in [l]}[e(C_{i1}, TK_1)e(C_{i2}, TK_{\rho(i)})]^{\omega_i}}$$

$$= \frac{e(g_1^s g_2^{\tau_1}, g_1^{\alpha} g_1^{at} g_2^{\phi})}{\prod_{i \in [l]}[e(g_1^{a\lambda_i} F(\rho(i))^{-r_i} g_2^{\tau_2}, g_1^t g_2^{\psi})e(g_1^{r_i} g_2^{\tau_2}, F(\rho(i))^t g_2^{\psi})]^{\omega_i}}$$

$$= \frac{e(g_1, g_1)^{\alpha s} e(g_1, g_1)^{ats} e(g_2, g_2)^{\tau_1 \phi}}{\prod_{i \in [l]}[e(g_1, g_1)^{at\lambda_i} e(F(\rho(i)), g_1)^{-r_i t} e(g_2, g_2)^{\tau_2 \psi} e(g_1, F(\rho(i)))^{r_i t} e(g_2, , g_2)^{\psi \tau_2}]^{\omega_i}}$$

$$= \frac{e(g_1, g_1)^{\alpha s} e(g_1, g_1)^{ats} e(g_2, g_2)^{\tau_1 \phi}}{(\prod_{i \in [l]} e(g_1, g_1)^{at\lambda_i \omega_i})(\prod_{i \in [l]} e(g_2, g_2)^{2\psi \tau_2 \omega_i})}$$

$$= \frac{e(g_1, g_1)^{\alpha s} e(g_1, g_1)^{ats} e(g_2, g_2)^{\tau_1 \phi}}{e(g_1, g_1)^{ats} e(g_2, g_2)^{2\psi \tau_2 \sum_{i \in [l]} \omega_i}}$$

$$= e(g_1, g_1)^{\alpha s} e(g_2, g_2)^{\tau_1 \phi - 2\tau_2 \sum_{i \in [l]} \omega_i \psi}$$

$$= Y^s C_{TK1}^{\phi} C_{TK2}^{-2\psi \sum_{i \in [l]} \omega_i}$$

7 Security Analysis

7.1 Basic Structure Security

Basic structure security means the security of the basic CP-ABE scheme without removing escrow and outsourced decryption.

Theorem 1. *When the decisional q-parallel BDHE assumption [26] holds, no polynomial time adversary can break the basic structure under selective CPA model [26].*

Proof. Suppose we have an adversary $\mathscr{A}$ with non-negligible advantage $Adv_{\mathscr{A}} = \epsilon$ in the selective CPA game against the basic structure. We now build a simulator $\mathscr{B}$ that plays the decisional q-parallel BDHE.

Init. The simulator $\mathscr{B}$ takes in a decisional q-BDHE challenge $input, T$. The adversary $\mathscr{A}$ declares the challenge access structure $\prod^* = <A^*, \rho^*>$, where A^* is a $l^* \times n^*$ matrix, $l^*, n^* \leq q$.

Setup. The simulator $\mathscr{B}$ chooses random $\alpha' \in Z_{p_1}$ and sets $\alpha = \alpha' + a^{q+1}$. X is a set of index i with $\rho^*(i) = x$. $U = \{\rho^*(i)\}_{i=1,\ldots,l^*}$ is the set of attributes needed by A^*. $\mathscr{B}$ chooses random $z_x \in Z_{p_1}$ for each attribute x. Under random oracle model, the simulator $\mathscr{B}$ can program $F(x) = g_1^{z_x} \prod_{i \in X} g_1^{aA_{i,1}^*/b_i} \cdot g_1^{a^2 A_{i,2}^*/b_i} \cdots g_1^{a^{n^*} A_{i,n^*}^*/b_i}$. If $X = \emptyset$, $F(x) = g_1^{z_x}$.

Phase I. In this phase the simulator $\mathscr{B}$ answers private key queries. Suppose the simulator is given a private key query for a set S where S does not satisfy

$A*$.By the definition of a LSSS, there must exist a vector $\vec{\omega} = (\omega_1, ..., \omega_{n^*})$ that $\omega_1 = -1$ and for all i where $\rho^*(i) \in S$, we have $\vec{\omega} * A_i^* = 0$.

The simulator then chooses a random $r \in Z_{p_1}$ and sets $t = r + a^q \omega_1 + a^{q-1}\omega_2 + \cdots + a^{q-n^*+1}\omega_{n^*}$. Thus, we have $K_1 = g_1^t = g_1^r \prod_{i=1,...,n^*} g_1^{a^{q-n^*+1}\omega_{n^*}}$ and $K_2 = g_1^\alpha g_1^{at} = g_1^{\alpha'} g_1^{ar} \prod_{i=2,...,n^*} g_1^{a^{q+2-i}\omega_i}$. Also, we have

$$
\begin{aligned}
K_x &= \left(g_1^{z_x} \prod_{i \in X} g_1^{aA_{i,1}^*/b_i} \cdot g_1^{a^2 A_{i,2}^*/b_i} \cdots g_1^{a^{n^*} A_{i,n^*}^*/b_i}\right)^t \\
&= K_1^{z_x} \cdot \prod_{i \in X} \prod_{j=1,...,n^*} \left[g_1^{(a^j/b_i)r} \prod_{\substack{k=1,...,n^* \\ k \neq j}} (g_1^{a^{q+1+j-k}/b_i})^{\omega_k}\right]^{A_{i,j}^*} \quad x \in S \cap U
\end{aligned}
$$

If $x \in S \setminus (S \cap U)$, $K_x = g_1^{z_x \cdot t} = K_1^{z_x}$.

Challenge. The adversary $\mathcal{A}$ gives two messages of equal length M_0 and M_1. The simulator flips a coin and selects a random $b \in \{0, 1\}$. The simulator encrypt the message M_b by $\prod^*$. Then, $\mathcal{B}$ selects randomly $\tau_1, \tau_2 \in Z_{p_2}$, and sets $C = M_b \cdot T \cdot e(g_1^s, g_1^{\alpha'})$, $C_{TK1} = e(g_2, g_2)^{\tau_1}$, $C_{TK2} = e(g_2, g_2)^{\tau_2}$, $C_v = g_1^s g_2^{\tau_1}$. $\mathcal{B}$ selects randomly $u_2', ..., u_{n^*}' \in Z_{p_1}$ and defines the secret sharing vector as $\vec{v} = (s, sa + u_2', ..., sa^{n^*-1} + u_{n^*}') \in Z_{p_1}^{n^*}$. $\mathcal{B}$ also selects randomly $r_1', ..., r_{l^*}'$. For $i = 1, ..., n^*$, we defines R_i as the set of i where $\rho^*(i) = \rho^*(k)$ when $k \neq i$. Thus we can set the last ciphertexts as

$$
\begin{aligned}
C_{i1} &= g_2^{\tau_2} F(\rho^*(i))^{r_i'} \left(\prod_{j=2,...,n^*} (g_1^a)^{A_{*i,j} u_j'}\right) (g_1^{b_i \cdot s})^{-z_{\rho^*(i)}} \\
&\quad \cdot \left(\prod_{k \in R_i} \prod_{j=1,...,n^*} (g_1^{a^j \cdot s \cdot b_i/b_k})^{A_{k,j}^*}\right) \\
C_{i2} &= g_2^{\tau_2} g_1^{-r_i'} g_1^{-sb_i}
\end{aligned}
$$

Phase II. Same as Phase I.

Guess. The adversary $\mathcal{A}$ will give a guess b' of b. if $b' = b$, $T = e(g_1, g_1)^{a^{q+1}}$ and $\mathcal{B}$ outputs 0. Otherwise, T is a random element in G_T and $\mathcal{B}$ outputs 1.

When $T = e(g_1, g_1)^{a^{q+1}}$, the the simulator $\mathcal{B}$ gives a perfect simulation.

$$
Pr\left[\mathcal{B}(Input, T = e(g_1, g_1)^{a^{q+1}}) = 0\right] = \frac{1}{2} + Adv_{\mathcal{A}}
$$

When T is a random element in G_T, the adversary $\mathcal{A}$ knows nothing about M_b.

$$
Pr\left[\mathcal{B}(Input, T = R) = 0\right] = \frac{1}{2}
$$

Thus, $\mathcal{B}$ can play the decisional q-parallel BDHE game with non-negligible advantage.

7.2 Escrow-Free Guarantee

Based on the former proof, we can find that the difference between the basic structure and the algorithm of [26] has little influence on security. Thus, the escrow-free modification can easily be migrated from ones based on [26] to ones based on the basic structure. Meanwhile, security is not affected.

7.3 Outsourced Security Guarantee

Outsourced security guarantee means the modification for outsourced decryption will not leak the message.

Firstly, we introduce Theorem 2 [11].

Theorem 2. *Let $N = \sum_{i=1}^{m} p_i$ be a product of distinct primes, each greater than 2^λ. Let $\{A_i\}$ be random variables over G, and let $\{B_i\}$, T_0, T_1 be random variables over G_T, where all random variables have degree at most t. Consider the following experiment in the generic group model:*

An algorithm is given N, $\{A_i\}$ and $\{B_i\}$. A random bit b is chosen, and the adversary is given T_b. the algorithm outputs a bit b', and succeeds if $b' = b$. The algorithm's advantage is the absolute value of the difference between its success probability and $\frac{1}{2}$.

Say each of T_0 and T_1 is independent of $\{B_i\} \cup \{e(A_i, A_j)\}$. Then given any algorithm $\mathscr{A}$ issuing at most q instructions and having advantage δ in the above experiment, $\mathscr{A}$ can be used to find a nontrivial factor of N (in time polynomial in λ and the running time of $\mathscr{A}$) with probability at least $\delta - \mathscr{O}(q^2 t/2^\lambda)$.

Then we prove Theorem 3.

Theorem 3. *When Theorem 2 holds, it is hard to find a nontrivial factor of N in the outsourced decryption structure.*

Proof. Similarly with the proof of Assumption 3 in [11], we define two operations.

$$(a, b) = g_1^a g_2^b$$

$$[a, b] = e(g_1, g_1)^a e(g_2, g_2)^b$$

where $a \in Z_{p_1}$, $b \in Z_{p_2}$, $g_1 \in G_{p_1}$, $g_2 \in G_{p_2}$. G_{p_1} and G_{p_2} are subgroups of G with prime orders p_1, and p_2 respectively.

Now, we can transform the ciphertexts and transformation keys into new forms.

$$C_{TK1} = [0, \tau_1], C_{TK2} = [0, \tau_2], C_v = (s, \tau_1)$$

$$C_{i1} = (\theta_{i1}, \tau_2), \theta_{i1} = a\lambda_i - r_i(z_{\rho(i)} \sum_{j \in X} aA_{j,1}^*/b_j)$$

$$C_{i2} = (r_i, \tau_2), TK_1 = (t, \psi), TK_2 = (\alpha + at, \phi)$$

$$TK_x = (-r_i t \sum_{j \in X} aA_{j,1}^*/b_j, \psi)$$

We define $B_1 = C_{TK1}$, $B_2 = C_{TK2}$ and the others as A_i, $i = 1, \ldots$.

And we also have $T_0 = [\alpha s, 0]$, $T_1 = [Z_1, Z_2]$. T_1 is independent of $\{B_i\} \cup \{e(A_i, A_j)\}$. T_0 is independent of B_1 and B_2. Due to the random numbers, we can't get $(0, \tau_1)$, $(0, \tau_2)$, $(0, \phi)$ and $(0, \psi)$. The only way to get the αs in the first coordinate is to take $\frac{e(C_v, TK_2)}{\prod_{i \in [l]} [e(C_{i1}, TK_1) e(C_{i2}, TK_{\rho(i)})]^{\omega_i}}$, but we are left a $\tau_1 \phi - 2\tau_2 \sum_{i \in [l]} \omega_i \psi$ in the second coordinate which can't be canceled. Thus, it is hard to find a nontrivial factor of N.

7.4   Outsourced Decryption Security

Outsourced decryption security means the security of the proposed algorithm.

Theorem 4. *When the basic structure is secure under selective CPA model, no polynomial time adversary can break the proposed algorithm under RCCA model [6].*

Proof. We have proven that the basic structure is secure under selective CPA model earlier. Suppose we have an adversary $\mathscr{A}$ with non-negligible advantage $Adv_{\mathscr{A}} = \epsilon$ in RCCA model against the proposed algorithm. We now build a simulator $\mathscr{B}$ with non-negligible advantage in the selective CPA game against the basic structure.

Init. The simulator $\mathscr{B}$ runs $\mathscr{A}$. The adversary $\mathscr{A}$ declares the challenge access structure $\prod^* = <A^*, \rho^*>$, where A^* is a $l^* \times n^*$ matrix, $l^*, n^* \leq q$.

Setup. The simulator $\mathscr{B}$ obtain the public parameters of the basic structure and sends these to $\mathscr{A}$.

Phase I. The simulator $\mathscr{B}$ initializes three empty tables T, T_1 and T_2, an empty set D and a counter $j = 0$. It answers the adversary $\mathscr{A}$'s queries as follows:

* Random Oracle Hash $H_1(R, M)$: If there is an entry (R, M, s) in T_1, return s. Otherwise, choose a random $s \in Z_{p_1}$, record (R, M, s) in T_1 and return s.
* Random Oracle Hash $H_2(R)$: If there is an entry (R, r) in T_2, return r. Otherwise, choose a random $r \in \{0.1\}^k$, record (R, r) in T_2 and return r.
* Create((S)): $\mathscr{B}$ sets $j = j + 1$. It proceeds one of two ways.
    – If S satisfies $\prod^*$, then it chooses a fake transformation key as follows: choose a random $\delta \in Z_{p_2}$ and run Key Generation and Key Transformation to obtain SK and TK'. TK' is properly distributed if ϕ was replaced by the unknown value $\delta = \phi\tau_1 - 2\psi\tau_2 \sum_{i \in [l]} \omega_i$.
    – Otherwise, it obtains the key SK' and chooses a random value $\delta \in Z_{p_2}$, and runs Key Transformation to obtain TK'.
    Finally, store (j, S, SK, TK) in table T and return TK to $\mathscr{A}$.
* Corrupt(i): $\mathscr{A}$ can't ask to corrupt any key corresponding to the $\prod^*$. If there exists an ith entry in table T, then $\mathscr{B}$ obtains the entry (j, S, SK, TK) and sets $D = D \cup \{S\}$. It then returns SK to $\mathscr{A}$, or $\perp$ if no such entry exists.

* Decrypti(i): Let $CT = (C, C_v, T)$ be associated with structure $\prod$. Obtain the record (i, S, SK, TK) from table T. If it is not there or $S \notin \prod$, return $\bot$ to $\mathscr{A}$. If key i does not satisfy $\prod^*$, proceed as follows:

1. Compute $R = C/(T \cdot C_{TK1}^{-\phi} \cdot C_{TK2}^{2\psi \sum_{i \in [l]} \omega_i})$
2. Obtain the records (R, M_i, s_i) from table T_1. If none exist, return $\bot$ to $\mathscr{A}$.
3. If in this set, there exists indices $y \neq x$ such that (R, M_x, s_x) and (R, M_y, s_y) are in table T_1, $M_y \neq M_x$ and $s_y = s_x$, then $\mathscr{B}$ aborts the simulation.
4. Otherwise, obtain the record (R, r) from table T_2. If it does not exist, $\mathscr{B}$ outputs $\bot$.
5. For each i, test if $C = R \cdot e(g_1, g_1)^{\alpha s_i}$, $C' = M_i \oplus r$ and $T = e(g_1, g_1)^{\alpha s_i} \cdot C_{TK1}^{\phi} \cdot C_{TK2}^{-2\psi \sum_{i \in [l]} \omega_i}$.
6. If there is an i that passes the above test, output the message M_i; otherwise, output $\bot$.

If key i does satisfy $\prod^*$, proceed as follows:
1. Compute $\beta = Te(g_2, g_2)^\delta$.
2. For each record (R_i, M_i, S_i) in table T_1, test if $\beta = e(g_1, g_1)^{\alpha s_i}$.
3. If zero matches are found, output $\bot$.
4. If more than one matches are found, aborts the simulation.
5. Otherwise, let (R, M, s) be the sole match. Obtain the record (R, r) from table T_2. If it does not exist, output $\bot$.
6. Test if $C = R \cdot e(g_1, g_1)^{\alpha s}$, $C' = M_i \oplus r$ and $\beta = Te(g_2, g_2)^\delta$.
7. If all tests pass, output M; else, output $\bot$.

Challenge. $\mathscr{B}$ acts as follows:

* $\mathscr{B}$ chooses random messages $R_0, R_1 \in G_T$ and passes them on to the basic structure challenger to obtain a ciphertext $CT = (C, C_v, T)$ under $\prod^*$.
* $\mathscr{B}$ chooses a random value $C' \in \{0,1\}^k$.
* $\mathscr{B}$ sends to $\mathscr{A}$ the challenge ciphertext.

Phase II. Same as Phase I, except that if the response to a Decrypt query would be either M_0 or M_1, then $\mathscr{B}$ responds with the message test instead.

Guess. $\mathscr{A}$ must either output a bit or abort, either way $\mathscr{B}$ ignores it. Next, $\mathscr{B}$ searches through tables T_1 and T_2 to see if the values R_0 or R_1 appear as the first element of any entry. If neither or both values appear, $\mathscr{B}$ outputs a random bit as its guess. If only value R_b appears, then $\mathscr{B}$ outputs b as its guess.

8   Conclusion

In this paper, we propose a Requester-Centric CP-ABE combining removing escrow and outsourcing decryption. Proposed algorithm uses outsourced decryption based on composite order bilinear map to be more practical in cloud. In this way, data requesters can undertake the key transformation and become the center in the system. Traditional defenses against key-escrow and low-efficiency work well together in the case of a large number of attributes. With security analysis, we can figure out that proposed algorithm can realize removing escrow and outsourced decryption at the same time without adding roles in system. Therefore, proposed algorithm is secure and efficient.

References

1. Bethencourt, J., Sahai, A., Waters, B.: Ciphertext-policy attribute-based encryption. In: IEEE Symposium on Security and Privacy, pp. 321–334 (2007)
2. Castiglione, A., et al.: Hierarchical and shared access control. IEEE Trans. Inf. Forensics Secur. **11**(4), 850–865 (2016)
3. Chen, Y., Wen, Q., Li, W., Zhang, H., Jin, Z.: Generic construction of outsourced attribute-based encryption without key escrow. IEEE Access **6**, 58955–58966 (2018). https://doi.org/10.1109/ACCESS.2018.2875070
4. Fan, L., Zhao, R., Gong, F.K., Yang, N., Karagiannidis, G.: Secure multiple amplify-and-forward relaying over correlated fading channels. IEEE Trans. Commun. **65**(7), 2811–2820 (2017)
5. Goyal, V., Pandey, O., Sahai, A., Waters, B.: Attribute-based encryption for fine-grained access control of encrypted data. In: ACM Conference on Computer and Communications Security, pp. 89–98 (2006)
6. Green, M., Hohenberger, S., Waters, B.: Outsourcing the decryption of abe ciphertexts. In: Proceedings of the 20th USENIX Conference on Security, SEC 2011, p. 34. USENIX Association, Berkeley (2011). http://dl.acm.org/citation.cfm?id=2028067.2028101
7. Huang, Q., Zhaofeng, M.A., Yang, Y., Jingyi, F.U., Niu, X.: Eabds:attribute-based secure data sharing with efficient revocation in cloud computing. Chin. J. Electron. **24**(4), 862–868 (2015)
8. Jiang, R., Wu, X., Bhargava, B.: SDSS-MAC: secure data sharing scheme in multi-authority cloud storage systems. Comput. Secur. **62**, 193–212 (2016). https://doi.org/10.1016/j.cose.2016.07.007
9. Jiang, W., Wang, G., Bhuiyan, M.Z.A., Wu, J.: Understanding graph-based trust evaluation in online social networks: methodologies and challenges. ACM Comput. Surv. **49**(1), 1–35 (2016)
10. Lewko, A., Okamoto, T., Sahai, A., Takashima, K., Waters, B.: Fully secure functional encryption: attribute-based encryption and (hierarchical) inner product encryption. In: Gilbert, H. (ed.) EUROCRYPT 2010. LNCS, vol. 6110, pp. 62–91. Springer, Heidelberg (2010). https://doi.org/10.1007/978-3-642-13190-5_4
11. Lewko, A., Waters, B.: New techniques for dual system encryption and fully secure HIBE with short ciphertexts. In: Micciancio, D. (ed.) TCC 2010. LNCS, vol. 5978, pp. 455–479. Springer, Heidelberg (2010). https://doi.org/10.1007/978-3-642-11799-2_27
12. Li, H., Liu, D., Dai, Y., Luan, T., Yu, S.: Personalized search over encrypted data with efficient and secure updates in mobile clouds. IEEE Trans. Emerg. Top. Comput. **6**(1), 97–109 (2015)
13. Li, H., Liu, D., Dai, Y., Luan, T.H., Shen, X.S.: Enabling efficient multi-keyword ranked search over encrypted mobile cloud data through blind storage. IEEE Trans. Emerg. Top. Comput. **3**(1), 127–138 (2015)

14. Li, J., Huang, X., Li, J., Chen, X., Xiang, Y.: Securely outsourcing attribute-based encryption with checkability. IEEE Trans. Parallel Distrib. Syst. **25**(8), 2201–2210 (2014). https://doi.org/doi.ieeecomputersociety.org/10.1109/TPDS.2013.271

15. Li, J., et al.: Secure attribute-based data sharing for resource-limited users in cloud computing. Comput. Secur. **72**, 1–12 (2017)

16. Li, J., Jia, C., Li, J., Chen, X.: Outsourcing encryption of attribute-based encryption with MapReduce. In: Chim, T.W., Yuen, T.H. (eds.) ICICS 2012. LNCS, vol. 7618, pp. 191–201. Springer, Heidelberg (2012). https://doi.org/10.1007/978-3-642-34129-8_17

17. Lin, S., Zhang, R., Ma, H., Wang, M.: Revisiting attribute-based encryption with verifiable outsourced decryption. IEEE Trans. Inf. Forensics Secur. **10**(10), 2119–2130 (2015). https://doi.org/10.1109/TIFS.2015.2449264

18. Liu, J.K., Man, H.A., Huang, X., Lu, R., Li, J.: Fine-grained two-factor access control for web-based cloud computing services. IEEE Trans. Inf. Forensics Secur. **11**(3), 484–497 (2015)

19. Luo, E., Liu, Q., Wang, G.: Hierarchical multi-authority and attribute-based encryption friend discovery scheme in mobile social networks. IEEE Commun. Lett. **20**(9), 1772–1775 (2016)

20. Mao, X., Lai, J., Mei, Q., Chen, K., Weng, J.: Generic and efficient constructions of attribute-based encryption with verifiable outsourced decryption. IEEE Trans. Dependable Secure Comput. **13**(5), 533–546 (2016). https://doi.org/10.1109/TDSC.2015.2423669

21. Pan, G., Lei, H., Deng, Y., Fan, L., Yang, J., Chen, Y., Ding, Z.: On secrecy performance of MISO SWIPT systems with TAS and imperfect CSI. IEEE Trans. Commun. **64**(9), 3831–3843 (2016)

22. Qin, B., Deng, R.H., Liu, S., Ma, S.: Attribute-based encryption with efficient verifiable outsourced decryption. IEEE Trans. Inf. Forensics Secur. **10**(7), 1384–1393 (2015). https://doi.org/10.1109/TIFS.2015.2410137

23. Sahai, A., Waters, B.: Fuzzy identity-based encryption. In: Cramer, R. (ed.) EUROCRYPT 2005. LNCS, vol. 3494, pp. 457–473. Springer, Heidelberg (2005). https://doi.org/10.1007/11426639_27

24. Wang, S., Liang, K., Liu, J.K., Chen, J.: Attribute-based data sharing scheme revisited in cloud computing. IEEE Trans. Inf. Forensics Secur. **11**(8), 1–1 (2016)

25. Wang, Z., Liu, W.: CP-ABE with outsourced decryption and directionally hidden policy. Secur. Commun. Netw. **9**(14), 2387–2396 (2016)

26. Waters, B.: Ciphertext-policy attribute-based encryption: an expressive, efficient, and provably secure realization. In: Catalano, D., Fazio, N., Gennaro, R., Nicolosi, A. (eds.) PKC 2011. LNCS, vol. 6571, pp. 53–70. Springer, Heidelberg (2011). https://doi.org/10.1007/978-3-642-19379-8_4

27. Xhafa, F., Feng, J., Zhang, Y., Chen, X., Li, J.: Privacy-aware attribute-based PHR sharing with user accountability in cloud computing. J. Supercomput. **71**(5), 1607–1619 (2015)

28. Zhao, R., Yuan, Y., Fan, L., He, Y.C.: Secrecy performance analysis of cognitive decode-and-forward relay networks in nakagami-m fading channels. IEEE Trans. Commun. **65**(2), 549–563 (2017)

29. Zuo, C., Shao, J., Wei, G., Xie, M., Ji, M.: CCA-secure ABE with outsourced decryption for fog computing. Future Gener. Comput. Syst. https://doi.org/10.1016/j.future.2016.10.028. http://www.sciencedirect.com/science/article/pii/S0167739X16304745

An Efficient Dynamic Group Signatures Scheme with CCA-Anonymity in Standard Model

Xiaohan Yue[✉][iD], Mingju Sun, Xibo Wang, Hong Shao, and Yuan He

School of Information Science and Engineering,
Shenyang University of Technology, Shenyang 110870, China
xhyue@sut.edu.cn

Abstract. Group signatures is a cryptographic primitive, simultaneously supporting anonymity and traceability. Though many group signatures schemes have been presented, some drawbacks still exist in these schemes at the aspects of security, performance and functionality. In order to overcome these issues, this paper proposes a new dynamic group signatures scheme with CCA-anonymity, allowing the members enroll the group dynamically. By making use of the Groth-Sahai proof system and verifiable encryption technologies, this paper constructs the scheme in detailed under the decisional linear assumption and q-strong diffie-hellman assumption. And in standard model, we prove our scheme meet CCA-anonymity, traceability and non-frameability. Finally, compared with other existing group signatures schemes, the proposed scheme is more secure and efficient on both the computation cost and communication cost.

Keywords: CCA-anonymity · Dynamic group signatures · Groth-Sahai proof system · Verifiable encryption · Standard model

1 Introduction

In 1991, Chaum and Heyst first proposed the concept of Group Signatures [1]. The group signatures scheme allows members of the group to sign messages on behalf of the group and keeps the anonymity of members. Namely, the verifier can only verify the signature generated by members of the group, but he can't reveal the identity of the signer. In special cases, for example legal disputes, the specified group manager can reveal the identity of the signer by opening the group signature, ensuring the traceability of the group signature. Meanwhile, the group signatures has the features of unforgeability, even the group manager cannot be able to forge the signature of the members of the group. Because group signatures has the above features, it is used as a prototype of digital signature in various privacy preserving scenarios on the Internet. For example, direct anonymous attestation [2] in trusted computing environment, network identity hosting [3], online anonymous electronic voting [4] and anonymous certificate system [5] etc. Furthermore, it is also used in wireless MESH network [36] and VANET network [37].

© Springer Nature Switzerland AG 2019
J. Vaidya et al. (Eds.): CSS 2019, LNCS 11983, pp. 205–219, 2019.
https://doi.org/10.1007/978-3-030-37352-8_18

1.1   Related Work

The group signatures has attracted the attention from many scholars and research institutions since it was proposed. And they have performed researches on the construction of group signatures scheme from the aspects of function and security. The first highly effective anti-collusion attack group signatures scheme was proposed by Ateniese et al. [6] Namely the famous ACJT group signatures scheme. Focusing on the security attributes of group signature, Bellare et al. proposed the definition and security model of static group signatures, namely BMW model [7]. This model assumes that all group members and their identities are fixed during the group initialization phase, and the corresponding group signatures keys are also given in a correct way. Obviously, this assumption isn't applicable to the actual situation. Later, Bellare et al. strengthened this security model, and they proposed the definition and security model of dynamic group signature [8], namely the BSZ model. This model made up for the functional lack of the BMW model, which allowed members to dynamically join the group and divided the roles of the group manager into two parts: the issuer and the opener. Many group signatures schemes are proposed based on the above two models. At the aspect of security proof, there are two proof models can be used, the one is random oracle model (ROM), and the other is standard model (SM).

Under the random oracle model, the cryptography scheme has high efficiency [9], therefore many efficient group signature schemes are proposed. The ACJT group signature scheme is one of them. In addition, Boneh et al. [10] proposed a more efficient short group signature scheme, which has short signature length and low computational cost. In the same year, Camenish et al. [11] constructed an efficient group signature scheme based on the LRSW assumption. Delerablee et al. [12] proposed a dynamic short group signature scheme based on the BSZ model; Moreover, more group signature schemes under ROM were proposed [13–15]. However, Canetti et al. [16] pointed out that any specific object in the random oracle model, for example a hash function, is treated as a completely random object. However, completely random objects don't exist in practice. Therefore, the cryptographic schemes under ROM aren't secure in practical applications. And more scholars [17, 18] pointed out that security drawbacks exist in random oracle model.

Due to the drawbacks of ROM, many scholars focused on the standard model, and proposed many constructions of the group signature scheme under the standard model. According to the group signatures model, the proposed schemes in standard model also can be divided into two types: the first type is based on the BMW model. Boyen and Waters proposed a group signature scheme using two-level signature technology [19], but there are some problems in this scheme, such as the problem of logarithmic relation between the size of group signature and the number of group members. Boyen and Waters proposed a more efficient group signature scheme [20]. Libert et al. used this scheme [20] to propose revocable group signature scheme [21]. Zhou et al. [22] proposed a group signature scheme based on the hybrid order group assumption, but the anonymity of these four group signature schemes is only secure under Chosen Plaintext Attack (CPA).It is also worth mentioning that the anonymity of the scheme [19, 20, 22] is based on the hybrid order group deterministic assumption. Due to this type of assumption is based on the large integer factorization problem, thus this hybrid order group is very large and difficult to be used in practice. Libert et al. [31] proposed a short group signature scheme, which used weak hypotheses and maintained structural signature algorithms, but it was only constructed under the BMW model; The second scheme was based on the BSZ model. Ateniese et al. [23] proposed a practical group signature scheme, but the anonymity of the scheme can only be guaranteed under the non-adaptive Chosen Ciphertext Attack. Namely, once the group members' signature private key is revealed, the adversary can identify all the group signatures generated by the group members. In addition, The computational cost of the scheme's opening algorithm is non-constant. In order to avoid these problems, Groth proposed two specific group signature schemes [24, 25], which were based on an efficient non-interactive zero-knowledge proof. However, the length of these two group signature schemes are too large and computationally inefficient, therefore Masayuki and Groth proposed a group signature scheme with smaller signature length and CCA anonymity [38]. However, in the process of group signature generation, the group membership certificate issued by the issuer is randomized, and this randomization will lead to the difficulty in certificate management. Moreover, in order to guarantee the anonymity of the signature algorithm, it uses a one-time signature technology. Therefore, each time a signature operation is performed, a new signature key pair needs to be generated for signing the message. It doesn't only increase the complexity of the algorithm, but also increases the computational cost of the signer. Other group signature schemes based on the BSZ model were also proposed a few years ago [26–28, 35]. And Libert [28] proposed a group signature scheme with further security, which avoided the problems in the scheme [24], but the signature length and calculation cost were still large. Slamanig et al. [35] proposed a group signature prototype with controllable relevance, but he didn't give a specific scheme.

1.2   Our Contributions

Aim at the above security and performance issues, this paper puts forward a new type of CCA anonymity dynamic group signature scheme. The works of this paper are as followings:

(1) Define the entities and algorithms of dynamic group signature, and formalizes the security model of dynamic group signature scheme.
(2) Use the Groth-Sahai proof system and verifiable encryption technology to construct our dynamic group signature scheme with CCA anonymity.
(3) Prove our scheme meet CCA anonymity, traceability and non-frameability based on DLIN assumption and q-SDH assumption in standard model.
(4) Compared with existing group signature schemes in terms of security and performance, the results show that our scheme is better than other schemes in the above two aspects.

The roadmap of this paper is as followings. The second section introduces the relevant cryptographic assumptions and cryptographic tools used by our scheme construction; The third section gives the definition of the CCA anonymity dynamic group signature scheme and its formal description of the security model; The fourth section constructs the CCA anonymity; The fifth section proves the security properties of the scheme, and compares the security and performance with the existing group signature scheme.

2 Cryptographic Assumptions and Tools

2.1 Bilinear Pairings and Cryptography Assumptions

Bilinear Pairing. Let G be an n-order cyclic group, where n is a prime number, g is the generator of group G, and the bilinear mapping on the group is defined as: $e : G \times G \rightarrow G_T$, and satisfies the following properties:

- bilinear: $e(g^a, g^b) = e(g, g)^{ab}$, all of $a, b \in \mathbb{Z}_n^*$ are established;
- non-degenerate: $e(g, g) \neq 1_{G_T}$, among them 1_{G_T} is the unit element of G_T;
- computability: there is an effective algorithm to calculate $t = e(g, g)$.

The description of the specific bilinear pairing algorithm mentioned above can be found in paper [40].

Cryptographic Assumptions

Definition 1. q-Strong Diffie-Hellman (q-SDH) assumption that the q-SDH assumption in order to prime number n group $G = g$ defined as follows, with $(q + 1)$ tuple $\left(g, g^x, g^{x^2}, \cdots, g^{x^q}\right) \in G^{q+1}$ as input, there is no probability of a polynomial time algorithm is able to not ignore the probability output of a binary group (A, c), makes $A^{(x+c)} = g$, including $c \in \mathbb{Z}_n^*$.

This assumption was proposed and proved by Boneh et al. [34], and is valid in bilinear group.

Definition 2. Decision Linear (DLIN) assumption: the DLIN assumptions in order for the prime number n group $G = g$ is defined in the following, the given five yuan group $(g^\alpha, g^\beta, g^{\alpha-r}, g^{\beta-s}, g^t)$ does not exist a probability polynomial time algorithm to probability judgments that cannot be ignored is $t = r + s$ or $t \in_R \mathbb{Z}_n^*$.

This assumption was proposed and proved by Boyen et al. [10], and is valid in bilinear group.

2.2 Cryptography Tools

Groth-Sahai Non-interactive Proof System. Groth and Sahai [29] proposed an efficient non-interactive proof system for bilinear group under the standard model, and proposed the non-interactive witness-indistinguishable NIWI proof system and non-interactive zero-knowledge NIZK proof system based on DLIN assumption. The system using $\vec{g}_1 = (g_1, 1, g)$, $\vec{g}_2 = (1, g_2, g)$ and $\vec{g}_3 = \vec{g}_1^{-\xi_1} \circ \vec{g}_2^{-\xi_2}$ as a Common Reference String (CRS), where $(g_1, g_2, g) \in G^3$ and the operator $\circ$ is Hadamard product. Commitment to elements in the group of X can be expressed as $\vec{C} = \iota(X) \circ \vec{g}_1^r \circ \vec{g}_2^s \circ \vec{g}_3^t$, where $\iota(X) = (1, 1, X)$, $r, s, t \leftarrow \mathbb{Z}_n^*$, the commitment of key for $\alpha_1 = log_g^{g_1}$, $\alpha_2 = log_g^{g_2}$.

For scalar $x \in \mathbb{Z}_n^*$, the commit algorithm is $\vec{D} = \vec{\varphi}^x \circ \vec{g}_1^r \circ \vec{g}_2^s$. In order to ensure the soundness, we let $\vec{\varphi} = \iota(g) \circ \vec{g}_3$ that means the $\vec{\varphi}, \vec{g}_1, \vec{g}_2$ are linearly independent.

In order to prove that secret values satisfy some pairing or multi-exponential product equation, Groth-Sahai proof system replaces these values with corresponding commitment values in the equation, and outputs the proof values. For each pairing product equation, the proof contains nine group elements and for each multi-exponential product equation, the proof contains two group elements.

In the definition [28] of Groth-Sahai(GS) proof system, F represents symmetric bilinear mapping function $F : G^3 \times G^3 \rightarrow G_T^9$; $\iota_T(u)$ is a 3×3 matrix, where the position $(3, 3)$ is $u \in G_T$ and the rest parts is the identity element 1; $\widehat{\iota}_T(v) = F(\vec{\varphi}, \iota(v))$.

Verifiable Encryption. Verifiable encryption [30] is one of the common cryptography tools used to build cryptography algorithms or protocols, allowing any entity to verify the consistency of encrypted message and committed message without disclosing any information about the message. Generally, a verifiable encryption algorithm consists of an encryption algorithm and a zero-knowledge proof system, therefore the security of verifiable encryption meets three secure properties: completeness, soundness and zero-knowledge.

In order to ensure the CCA-anonymity of our scheme, this paper use the verifiable encryption to construct the group signature algorithm. The CCA-encryption algorithm we used is the CCA-PKE encryption scheme based on chameleon hash function proposed by zhang [31], and the zero-knowledge proof system we used is the Groth-Sahai non-interactive zero-knowledge proof system [28].

Groth Sub-protocol. Groth proposed a five-step zero-knowledge proof protocol based on Discrete Logarithm assumption, which is called Groth sub-protocol [25]. The protocol is performed by two entities (group member M and issuer) and outputs the member's private key value $sk := x$ with public key value $pk := g^x$. The protocol is constructed as follows:

(1) Group members select random numbers $a, r \in_R \mathbb{Z}_n$, $\eta \in_R \mathbb{Z}_n^*$ and send $A = g^a$, $R = g^r$ and $h = g^\eta$ to the issuer;
(2) Issuer randomly select $b, s \in_R \mathbb{Z}_n$ and send commitment $B = g^b \cdot h^s$ to group member M;
(3) Group member M randomly select $c \in_R \mathbb{Z}_n$ and send C to the issuer;
(4) The issuer sends the promised object B (challenge value) and the open key s to the group member M;
(5) Member M verify the validity of commitment $B = g^b \cdot h^s$, and send response values $z = (b + c) \cdot a + r \, mod \, n$ and η to the issuer, and output $sk := x = a + b + c \, mod \, n$;
(6) Issuer verify whether $h = g^\eta$ and $A^{b+c} R = g^z$ hold, if positive, output $pk := A \cdot g^{b+c} = g^x$.

Theorem 1. The Sub-protocol has perfect correctness and if the discrete logarithm problem is difficult, then there exists a black box simulator to simulate the view of group members and issuers.

Groth proves the theorem in paper [25]. In his proof, for the group member M, the simulator can extract their private key x by rewind, and for issuer, the simulator can simulate member's views without knowing the private key value x.

3   Dynamic Group Signature Scheme Definition

As shown in Fig. 1, the dynamic group signature scheme consists of four entities and six algorithms (protocols). The four entities include:

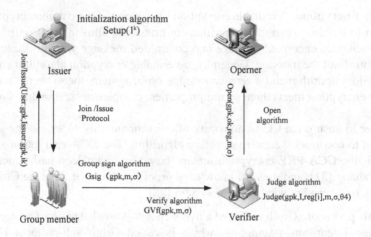

Fig. 1. Diagram of dynamic group signature scheme

(1) Issuer: It interacts with members of the group and issues group membership certificates for members with its issuer key (ik), and maintains the group membership registry $reg[i]$, where i is the group membership identifier;

(2) Opener: It can use its open key (ok) to open a group signature and obtain the identifier i of the corresponding member;

(3) Group Member: A user can dynamically join the group as the group member/signer, and use the group certificate issued by issuer with its public-private key pairs (pk, sk) to sign messages;

(4) Verifier: The verifier can use group public key (gpk) to verify group signatures. If the verification passes, the group signatures are accepted; otherwise, rejected.

The six algorithms or protocols for dynamic group signature, as shown in Fig. 1, including:

(1) Setup Algorithm: Input security parameter 1^K generation (gpk, ik, ok), where gpk is a group public key, with the group public key can verify the group signature, ik

and *ok* are the key of the issuer and the opener, respectively provided to the issuer and the opener. The formal description is: $Setup(1^k) \to (gpk, ik, ok)$.

(2) Join/Issue Protocol: This is an interactive protocol between member M_i and issuer. When the protocol performs successfully, the issuer creates a registration information for the member M_i into the group member registration table $reg[i]$. The content of the registration information is the final state of the output of the Issue algorithm, including the membership certificate and the member public key. On the other hand, if the group member M_i accepts the group membership certificate issued by the issuer, the final state of the output of the Join algorithm is its group signatures private key $gsk[i]$. Thus, the above description can be denoted as: Join/Issue $(M_i : gpk, I : gpk, ik) \to (M_i : gsk[i], I : reg[i])$.

(3) Group Sign (*GSig*) Algorithm: The group member M_i uses its signature key $gsk[i]$ to perform the group signature algorithm *GSig* to obtain the signature σ of the message m. The formal description is: $GSig(gpk, gsk[i], m) \to \sigma$.

(4) Group Signature Verify (*GVf*) Algorithm: When the verifier obtains the message-signature pair (m, σ), it can perform this algorithm *GVf* to check the validity of the signature, if the output is 1 then accept; otherwise reject. The formal expression of this algorithm is: $GVf(gpk, m, \sigma) \to 1/0$.

(5) Open Algorithm: The opener has the permission to access the group member registry reg, and runs the Open algorithm with the open key ok to open the group signature σ, then obtains the group member identifier i and the unencrypted signature part θ of the group signature. Notes that, if $i = \perp$ indicates that the member of the group is not in the member registration table reg. The algorithm can be denoted as: Open $(gpk, ok, m, reg, \sigma) \to (i, \theta)$.

(6) Judge Algorithm: This algorithm is used to judge the correctness of the open algorithm, that is, the validity of θ. If valid, the output is 1; otherwise, the output is 0. The algorithm is formally described as: Judge $(gpk, i, reg[i], m, \sigma, \theta) \to 1/0$.

4 CCA Anonymous Dynamic Group Signature Scheme

4.1 Initialization Algorithm

Setup(1^K): Input the security parameter 1^K. The parameter initialization algorithm is as follows:

(1) Select a bilinear group (n, g, G, G_T, e) where $G = g$, the order is prime number $n > 2^k$ and the bilinear map is $e \sim G \times G \to G_T$;

(2) Randomly select the generator h from the group G and randomly select $\gamma, \alpha_1, \alpha_2$, from $\mathbb{Z}_n^*$, calculate $\Omega = g^\gamma$, $g_1 = g^{\alpha_1}$, $g_2 = g^{\alpha_2}$;

(3) Generate a general reference string CRS $(\vec{g}_1, \vec{g}_2, \vec{g}_3)$ based on the non-interactive proof system under the DLIN assumption, where $\vec{g}_1 = (g_1, 1, g) \in G^3$, $\vec{g}_2 = (1, g_2, g) \in G^3$ and $\vec{g}_3 = (g_{3,1}, g_{3,2}, g_{3,3}) = \vec{g}_1^{\xi_1} \circ \vec{g}_2^{\xi_2} \in G^3$ where $\xi_1, \xi_2 \in_R \mathbb{Z}_n^*$;

(4) Select $(u_1, u_2, w) \in G^3$, a hash function $H : \{0, 1\}^* \rightarrow \{0, 1\}^n$ and g, g_1, g_2 as the public of the CCA encryption scheme key parameters, the corresponding decryption key/open key is α_1, α_2;

(5) The group public key, the issuer private key and the opening key of the group signatures are as follows:

$$\{gpk, ik, ok\} := \{(n, G, G_T, e, h, g, g_1, g_2, \vec{g}_1, \vec{g}_2, \vec{g}_3, \Omega, u_1, u_2, w, H), \gamma, (\alpha_1, \alpha_2)\}.$$

4.2 Join/Issue Protocol

Join/Issue(User: gpk, Issuer: gpk, ik): The interactive protocol runs as follows:

(1) The group member M and issuer run the Groth sub-protocol, then the group member M gets $sk := x \in \mathbb{Z}_n^*$ and $pk := g^x \in G$, and the issuer only knows pk;

(2) The issuer chooses $S_{id} \in \mathbb{Z}_n^*$ to generate the group membership certificate $K_1 = (h \cdot pk)^{1/(\gamma + S_{id})}$ and $K_2 = g^{S_{id}}$, forwards (K_1, K_2) to member M, then restores $(S_{id}, K_1, pk) \rightarrow reg[i]$ where i is the identifier;

(3) On receiving (K_1, K_2), the group member checks whether the equation $e(K_1, \Omega \cdot K_2) = e(g, h)e(g, pk)$ is hold. If positive, the private key is $gsk := (sk, pk, K_1, K_2)$.

4.3 Sign Algorithm

$GSig(gpk, gsk, m)$: The group signature for a message m is calculated as follows:

(1) Let $\theta_1 = K_1$, $\theta_2 = K_2$, $\theta_3 = pk$, the signature value for the message m is $\theta_4 = g^{1/(x + H(m))}$ where x is its private key sk;

(2) To calculate the commitments of $\theta_1, \cdots, \theta_4$, group member M randomly selects $r_i, s_i, t_i \in \mathbb{Z}_n^*$ where $i = 1, \cdots, 4$, and calculates the commitment values $\vec{c}_i = \iota(\theta_i) \circ \vec{g}_1^{r_i} \circ \vec{g}_2^{s_i} \circ \vec{g}_3^{t_i}$;

(3) Calculate the NIWI proof that $\vec{\pi}_1$, $\vec{\pi}_2$ satisfy the below equations:

$$e(\theta_1, \Omega \cdot \theta_2) = e(g, h)e(g, \theta_3) \tag{1}$$

$$e\left(\theta_4, g^{H(m)} \cdot \theta_3\right) = e(g, g) \tag{2}$$

The NIWI proof can be formalized as:

$$\text{NIWI}\left\{(\theta_1, \theta_2, \theta_3, \theta_4) : e(\theta_1, \Omega \cdot \theta_2) = e(g, h)e(g, \theta_3) \wedge e\left(\theta_4, g^{H(m)} \cdot \theta_3\right) = e(g, g)\right\}$$

Because Eqs. (1) and (2) are quadratic pairing product equations for $\theta_1, \cdots, \theta_4$, the proof π of each equation should contain 9 group elements. For Eq. (1), $\vec{\pi}_1$ is calculated as follows:

$$\vec{\pi}_1 = \begin{pmatrix} \vec{\pi}_{1,1} \\ \vec{\pi}_{1,2} \\ \vec{\pi}_{1,3} \end{pmatrix} = \begin{pmatrix} \iota(\theta_1)^{r_2} \circ (\iota(\Omega) \circ \vec{c}_2)^{r_1} \circ \iota(g)^{-r_3} \\ \iota(\theta_1)^{s_2} \circ (\iota(\Omega) \circ \vec{c}_2)^{s_1} \circ \iota(g)^{-s_3} \\ \iota(\theta_1)^{t_2} \circ (\iota(\Omega) \circ \vec{c}_2)^{t_1} \circ \iota(g)^{-t_3} \end{pmatrix}.$$

For Eq. (2), $\vec{\pi}_2$ is calculated as follows:

$$\vec{\pi}_2 = \begin{pmatrix} \vec{\pi}_{2,1} \\ \vec{\pi}_{2,2} \\ \vec{\pi}_{2,3} \end{pmatrix} = \begin{pmatrix} \iota(\theta_4)^{r_3} \circ \left(\iota\left(g^{H(m)}\right) \circ \vec{c}_3\right)^{r_4} \\ \iota(\theta_4)^{s_3} \circ \left(\iota\left(g^{H(m)}\right) \circ \vec{c}_3\right)^{s_4} \\ \iota(\theta_4)^{t_3} \circ \left(\iota\left(g^{H(m)}\right) \circ \vec{c}_3\right)^{t_4} \end{pmatrix}$$

(4) Select $z_1, z_2 \in_R \mathbb{Z}_n^*$, and encrypt θ_1 with CCA-PKE encryption algorithm: $(e_1, e_2, e_3) = (g_1^{z_1}, g_2^{z_2}, \theta_1 \cdot g^{z_1 + z_2})$;

(5) Because (e_1, e_2, e_3) and $\vec{c}_1 = (c_{1,1}, c_{1,2}, c_{1,3}) = \left(g_1^{r_1} \cdot g_{3,1}^{t_1}, g_2^{s_1} \cdot g_{3,2}^{t_1}, \theta_1 \cdot g^{r_1 + s_1} \cdot g_{3,3}^{t_1}\right)$ are encryption and commitment to the same value θ_1, so the following three equations are hold:

$$e_1^{-1} \cdot c_{1,1} = g_1^{\bar{r}} \cdot g_{3,1}^{\bar{t}} \tag{3}$$

$$e_2^{-1} \cdot c_{1,2} = g_2^{\bar{s}} \cdot g_{3,2}^{\bar{t}} \tag{4}$$

$$e_3^{-1} \cdot c_{1,3} = g^{\bar{s}+\bar{r}} \cdot g_{3,3}^{\bar{t}} \tag{5}$$

Where $\bar{r} = r_1 - z_1, \bar{s} = s_1 - z_2, \bar{t} = t_1$. Then we can use NIZK to prove that $(\bar{r}, \bar{s}, \bar{t})$ meets the relationship Eqs. (3)–(5), that is:

$$\text{NIZK}\left\{ (\bar{r}, \bar{s}, \bar{t}) : e_1^{-1} \cdot c_{1,1} = g_1^{\bar{r}} \cdot g_{3,1}^{\bar{t}} \wedge e_2^{-1} \cdot c_{1,2} = g_2^{\bar{s}} \cdot g_{3,2}^{\bar{t}} \wedge e_3^{-1} \cdot c_{1,3} = g^{\bar{s}+\bar{r}} \cdot g_{3,3}^{\bar{t}} \right\}$$

The commitment values of $(\bar{r}, \bar{s}, \bar{t})$ are calculated as follows:

$$\vec{d}_1 = \vec{\varphi}^{\bar{r}} \circ \vec{g}_1^{\tau_1} \circ \vec{g}_2^{v_1}$$

$$\vec{d}_2 = \vec{\varphi}^{\bar{s}} \circ \vec{g}_1^{\tau_2} \circ \vec{g}_2^{v_2}$$

$$\vec{d}_3 = \vec{\varphi}^{\bar{t}} \circ \vec{g}_1^{\tau_3} \circ \vec{g}_2^{v_3}$$

where τ_1, τ_2, τ_3 ensure that the commitment values are soundness, namely $\vec{g}_1, \vec{g}_2, \vec{\varphi}$ are linearly independent.

Since the above three equations belong to the linear multi-exponential equation, the NIZK ϕ for each equation should contain two group elements.

For Eq. (3):

$$\vec{\phi}_1 = (\phi_{1,1}, \phi_{1,2}) = \left(g_1^{\tau_1} \cdot g_{3,1}^{\tau_3}, g_1^{v_1} \cdot g_{3,1}^{v_3}\right);$$

For Eq. (4):

$$\vec{\phi}_2 = (\phi_{2,1}, \phi_{2,2}) = \left(g_2^{\tau_2} \cdot g_{3,2}^{\tau_3}, g_2^{\upsilon_1} \cdot g_{3,2}^{\upsilon_3} \right);$$

For Eq. (5):

$$\vec{\phi}_3 = (\phi_{3,1}, \phi_{3,2}) = \left(g_1^{\tau_1 + \tau_2} \cdot g_{3,3}^{\tau_3}, g_1^{\upsilon_1 + \upsilon_2} \cdot g_{3,3}^{\upsilon_3} \right);$$

(6) Calculate the hash $H = H(m \| \vec{c}_1 \| \vec{c}_2 \| \vec{c}_3 \| \vec{c}_4 \| \vec{d}_1 \| \vec{d}_2 \| \vec{d}_3 \| e_1 \| e_2 \| e_3 \| \vec{\pi}_1 \| \vec{\pi}_2 \| \vec{\phi}_1 \| \vec{\phi}_2 \|$
$\vec{\phi}_3)$, select the random number $\beta \in \mathbb{Z}_n^*$, calculate the hash value $\widetilde{H} = H(g^H \cdot w^\beta)$, and generate the encryption value $v_1 = g^{\widetilde{H} \cdot z_1} \cdot u_1^{z_1}$, $v_2 = g^{\widetilde{H} \cdot z_2} \cdot u_2^{z_2}$;

(7) The group member M sends the following group signature values to the verifier:

$$\sigma = \left(\vec{c}_1, \vec{c}_2, \vec{c}_3, \vec{c}_4, \vec{d}_1, \vec{d}_2, \vec{d}_3, e_1, e_2, e_3, \vec{\pi}_1, \vec{\pi}_2, \vec{\phi}_1, \vec{\phi}_2, \vec{\phi}_3, \beta, v_1, v_2 \right).$$

4.4   Verify Algorithm

$GVf(gpk, m, \sigma)$: After the verifier receives the group signature, it performs the following steps to check the validity of group signature.

(1) Calculate the hash $H = H(m \| \vec{c}_1 \| \vec{c}_2 \| \vec{c}_3 \| \vec{c}_4 \| \vec{d}_1 \| \vec{d}_2 \| \vec{d}_3 \| e_1 \| e_2 \| e_3 \| \vec{\pi}_1 \| \vec{\pi}_2 \| \vec{\phi}_1 \| \vec{\phi}_2 \|$
$\vec{\phi}_3)$ and $\widetilde{H} = H(g^H \cdot w^\beta)$, verify that whether $e\left(g^{\widetilde{H}} \cdot u_1, e_1 \right) = e(v_1, g_1)$ and $e\left(g^{\widetilde{H}} \cdot u_2, e_2 \right) = e(v_2, g_2)$ is hold;

(2) Verify that the NIWI proves that the following relationship is satisfied:

$$F(\vec{c}_1, \iota(\Omega) \circ \vec{c}_2) = \iota_T(e(g, h)) \circ F(\iota(g), \vec{c}_3) \circ F(\vec{g}_1, \vec{\pi}_{1,1}) \circ F(\vec{g}_2, \vec{\pi}_{1,2}) \circ F(\vec{g}_3, \vec{\pi}_{1,3}),$$
$$F\left(\vec{c}_4, \iota\left(g^{H(m)} \right) \circ \vec{c}_3 \right) = \iota_T(e(g, g)) \circ F(\vec{g}_1, \vec{\pi}_{2,1}) \circ F(\vec{g}_2, \vec{\pi}_{2,2}) \circ F(\vec{g}_3, \vec{\pi}_{2,3});$$

(3) Verify that the NIZK certificate satisfies the following relationship:

$$F\left(\vec{d}_1, \iota(g_1) \right) \circ F\left(\vec{d}_3, \iota(g_{3,1}) \right) = \hat{\iota}_T(c_{1,1} \cdot e_1^{-1}) \circ F(\vec{g}_1, \iota(\phi_{1,1})) \circ F(\vec{g}_2, \iota(\phi_{1,2})),$$
$$F\left(\vec{d}_2, \iota(g_2) \right) \circ F\left(\vec{d}_3, \iota(g_{3,2}) \right) = \hat{\iota}_T(c_{1,2} \cdot e_2^{-1}) \circ F(\vec{g}_1, \iota(\phi_{2,1})) \circ F(\vec{g}_2, \iota(\phi_{2,2})),$$
$$F\left(\vec{d}_1, \iota(g) \right) \circ F\left(\vec{d}_2, \iota(g) \right) \circ F\left(\vec{d}_3, \iota(g_{3,3}) \right) = \hat{\iota}_T(c_{1,3} \cdot e_3^{-1}) \circ F(\vec{g}_1, \iota(\phi_{3,1})) \circ F(\vec{g}_2, \iota(\phi_{3,2}));$$

(4) If the above steps are true, then the verifier returns 1 (accept); otherwise returns 0 (reject).

4.5   Open Algorithm

$Open(gpk, ok, reg, m, \sigma)$: When the group signature needs to be enabled, the opener performs the following operations:

(1) Using the open key (α_1, α_2) to calculate $\theta_1 = e_3 / \left(e_1^{1/\alpha_1} \cdot e_2^{1/\alpha_2} \right)$ and the message signature value $\theta_4 = c_{4,3} / \left(c_{4,1}^{1/\alpha_1} \cdot c_{4,2}^{1/\alpha_2} \right)$;

(2) Find whether there is an entry $K_1^{(i)} = \theta_1$ in the registration list $reg[]$, and return the corresponding identifier i if it exists, otherwise return $i = \perp$.

4.6 Judge Algorithm

$Judge(gpk, i, reg[i], m, \sigma, \theta_4)$: To verify the correctness of the algorithm, the Judge algorithm performs the following calculations:

For the signature θ_4 of the message m, verify that $i \neq \perp$ and whether the equation $e(\theta_4, g^{H(m)} \cdot pk_i) = e(g, g)$ is hold, if positive, return 1 (correct), otherwise return 0 (incorrect).

5   Security and Performance Analysis

5.1   Security Analysis

Here, we discuss the security of our scheme. That is, we explain that our scheme satisfies CCA-anonymity, traceability and non-frameability defined. For traceability, the adversary is essentially concerned with faking a valid group membership certificate. This case can be reduced to the q-SDH assumption. For non-frameability, in our join protocol, a user chooses its secret signing key $sk := x$ and it is unknown to the issuer. Therefore, from a forged signature output by the adversary of framing attacks, we can construct an algorithm that extracts such an unknown secret key and uses it to solve the q-SDH problem. Moreover, due to the CCA security of the CCA-PKE encryption scheme [31], our scheme is anonymous. Due to space constraints, we give the security proofs of following theorems in the full version of this paper.

Theorem 2. The proposed group signatures scheme is CCA-anonymity in the standard model if the DLIN assumption holds in (G, G_T).

Theorem 3. The proposed group signatures scheme has non-frameability in the standard model under the q-SDH assumption.

Theorem 4. The proposed group signatures scheme has traceability in the standard model under the q-SDH assumption.

5.2   Security and Performance Analysis

In security analysis, the proposed dynamic group signature scheme is compared with the current group signature schemes [10, 12, 20–22, 24, 27] in terms of security properties, group signature model and proof model, as shown in Table 1.

Table 1. Comparison of the security

Scheme	Anonymity	Traceability	Non-frameability	Group signature model	Proof model
BBS [10]	CPA	√	×	BMW	ROM
BW [20]	CPA	√	×	BMW	SM
Gro [25]	CCA	√	√	BSZ	SM
LV [21]	CPA	√	×	BMW	SM
Zhou [22]	CPA	√	×	BMW	SM
DP [12]	CCA	√	√	BSZ	ROM
LV [28]	CCA	√	√	BSZ	SM
LPY [31]	CCA	√	√	BMW	SM
AFG [38]	CCA	√	√	BSZ	SM
Ours	CCA	√	√	BSZ	SM

It can be seen from Table 1 that the security of schemes [25, 28, 38] are the same with the proposed dynamic group signatures scheme, so the performance comparison of the above three schemes is shown in Table 2:

Table 2. Comparison of the performance

Scheme	Communication cost (signature length)		Computational cost (signature algorithm)	
	Element in G	Element in $\mathbb{Z}$	Exponentiation operation	"∘" operation
Gro [25]	50	1	92	33
LV [28]	62	1	143	57
AFG [38]	42	1	78	27
Ours	37	1	59	36

It can be seen from Table 2 that the proposed dynamic group signature scheme is better than schemes [25, 28, 38], in terms of communication cost and computational cost. Although the Hadamard product "∘" is more than the scheme [38], the computational cost of the Hadamard product operation is much lower than that of the power operation calculation, so the proposed scheme performance is better than the scheme [38].

6   Conclusion

Firstly, this paper analyzes the existing problems of the current group signature scheme in terms of security, performance and functionality. In order to solve these problems, a new group signature scheme is presented by using Groth-Sahai non-interactive proof system and verifiable encryption technology. This scheme has dynamic membership in terms of functionality, and it also has CCA anonymity in terms of security and provable security under the standard model. Furthermore, in terms of performance, compared with the existing group signature schemes, it has the advantages of less signature length and lower computational cost.

References

1. Chaum, D., van Heyst, E.: Group signatures. In: Davies, D.W. (ed.) EUROCRYPT 1991. LNCS, vol. 547, pp. 257–265. Springer, Heidelberg (1991). https://doi.org/10.1007/3-540-46416-6_22
2. Brickell, E., Camenisch, J., Chen, L.: Direct anonymous attestation. In: CCS 2004, pp. 132–145. ACM, New York (2004)
3. Kilian, J., Petrank, E.: Identity escrow. In: Krawczyk, H. (ed.) CRYPTO 1998. LNCS, vol. 1462, pp. 169–185. Springer, Heidelberg (1998). https://doi.org/10.1007/BFb0055727
4. Nakanishi, T., Fujiwara, T., Watanabe, H.: A linkable group signature and its application to secret voting. IPSJ J. 40(7), 3085–3096 (1999)
5. Camenisch, J., Lysyanskaya, A.: Dynamic accumulators and application to efficient revocation of anonymous credentials. In: Yung, M. (ed.) CRYPTO 2002. LNCS, vol. 2442, pp. 61–76. Springer, Heidelberg (2002). https://doi.org/10.1007/3-540-45708-9_5
6. Ateniese, G., Camenisch, J., Joye, M., Tsudik, G.: A practical and provably secure coalition-resistant group signature scheme. In: Bellare, M. (ed.) CRYPTO 2000. LNCS, vol. 1880, pp. 255–270. Springer, Heidelberg (2000). https://doi.org/10.1007/3-540-44598-6_16
7. Bellare, M., Micciancio, D., Warinschi, B.: Foundations of group signatures: formal definitions, simplified requirements, and a construction based on general assumptions. In: Biham, E. (ed.) EUROCRYPT 2003. LNCS, vol. 2656, pp. 614–629. Springer, Heidelberg (2003). https://doi.org/10.1007/3-540-39200-9_38
8. Bellare, M., Shi, H., Zhang, C.: Foundations of group signatures: the case of dynamic groups. In: Menezes, A. (ed.) CT-RSA 2005. LNCS, vol. 3376, pp. 136–153. Springer, Heidelberg (2005). https://doi.org/10.1007/978-3-540-30574-3_11
9. Bellare M., Rogaway P.: Random oracles are practical: a paradigm for designing efficient protocols. In: CCS 1993, pp. 62–73. ACM, New York (1993)
10. Boneh, D., Boyen, X., Shacham, H.: Short group signatures. In: Franklin, M. (ed.) CRYPTO 2004. LNCS, vol. 3152, pp. 41–55. Springer, Heidelberg (2004). https://doi.org/10.1007/978-3-540-28628-8_3
11. Camenisch, J., Lysyanskaya, A.: Signature schemes and anonymous credentials from bilinear maps. In: Franklin, M. (ed.) CRYPTO 2004. LNCS, vol. 3152, pp. 56–72. Springer, Heidelberg (2004). https://doi.org/10.1007/978-3-540-28628-8_4
12. Delerablée, C., Pointcheval, D.: Dynamic fully anonymous short group signatures. In: Nguyen, P.Q. (ed.) VIETCRYPT 2006. LNCS, vol. 4341, pp. 193–210. Springer, Heidelberg (2006). https://doi.org/10.1007/11958239_13
13. Fan, C.-I., Hsu, R.-H., Manulis, M.: Group signature with constant revocation costs for signers and verifiers. In: Lin, D., Tsudik, G., Wang, X. (eds.) CANS 2011. LNCS, vol. 7092, pp. 214–233. Springer, Heidelberg (2011). https://doi.org/10.1007/978-3-642-25513-7_16
14. Bichsel, P., Camenisch, J., Neven, G., Smart, N.P., Warinschi, B.: Get shorty via group signatures without encryption. In: Garay, Juan A., De Prisco, R. (eds.) SCN 2010. LNCS, vol. 6280, pp. 381–398. Springer, Heidelberg (2010). https://doi.org/10.1007/978-3-642-15317-4_24
15. Kiayias, A., Yung, M.: Group signatures with efficient concurrent join. In: Cramer, R, (ed.) EUROCRYPT 2005. LNCS, vol. 3494, pp. 198–214. Springer, Heidelberg (2005). https://doi.org/10.1007/11426639_12
16. Canetti, R., Goldreich, O., Halevi, S.: The random oracle methodology. STOC J. 51(4), 557–594 (2004)

17. Canetti, R., Goldreich, O., Halevi, S.: On the random-oracle methodology as applied to length-restricted signature schemes. In: Naor, M. (ed.) TCC 2004. LNCS, vol. 2951, pp. 40–57. Springer, Heidelberg (2004). https://doi.org/10.1007/978-3-540-24638-1_3

18. Bellare, M., Boldyreva, A., Palacio, A.: An uninstantiable random-oracle-model scheme for a hybrid-encryption problem. In: Cachin, C., Camenisch, Jan L. (eds.) EUROCRYPT 2004. LNCS, vol. 3027, pp. 171–188. Springer, Heidelberg (2004). https://doi.org/10.1007/978-3-540-24676-3_11

19. Boyen, X., Waters, B.: Compact group signatures without random oracles. In: Vaudenay, S. (ed.) EUROCRYPT 2006. LNCS, vol. 4004, pp. 427–444. Springer, Heidelberg (2006). https://doi.org/10.1007/11761679_26

20. Boyen, X., Waters, B.: Full-domain subgroup hiding and constant-size group signatures. In: Okamoto, T., Wang, X. (eds.) PKC 2007. LNCS, vol. 4450, pp. 1–15. Springer, Heidelberg (2007). https://doi.org/10.1007/978-3-540-71677-8_1

21. Libert, B., Vergnaud, D.: Group signatures with verifier-local revocation and backward unlinkability in the standard model. In: Garay, J.A., Miyaji, A., Otsuka, A. (eds.) CANS 2009. LNCS, vol. 5888, pp. 498–517. Springer, Heidelberg (2009). https://doi.org/10.1007/978-3-642-10433-6_34

22. Zhou, F., Xu, J., Wang, L., Chen, C.: A group signature in the composite order bilinear groups. Chin. J. Comput. 35(4), 581–592 (2012)

23. Ateniese, G., Camenisch, J., Hohenberger, S., Medeiros, B.: Practical group signatures without random oracles. LNCS Homepage. http://eprint.iacr.org/2005/385. Accessed 06 Jun 2019

24. Groth, J.: Simulation-sound NIZK proofs for a practical language and constant size group signatures. In: Lai, X., Chen, K. (eds.) ASIACRYPT 2006. LNCS, vol. 4284, pp. 444–459. Springer, Heidelberg (2006). https://doi.org/10.1007/11935230_29

25. Groth, J.: Fully anonymous group signatures without random oracles. In: Kurosawa, K. (ed.) ASIACRYPT 2007. LNCS, vol. 4833, pp. 164–180. Springer, Heidelberg (2007). https://doi.org/10.1007/978-3-540-76900-2_10

26. Yue, X., Xi, M., Chen, B., Gao, M., He, Y., Xu, J.: A revocable group signatures scheme to provide privacy-preserving authentications. Mob. Netw. Appl. 1–30, online first

27. Libert, B., Peters, T., Yung, M.: Scalable group signatures with revocation. In: Pointcheval, D., Johansson, T. (eds.) EUROCRYPT 2012. LNCS, vol. 7237, pp. 609–627. Springer, Heidelberg (2012). https://doi.org/10.1007/978-3-642-29011-4_36

28. Libert, B., Yung, M.: Fully forward-secure group signatures. In: Naccache, D. (ed.) Cryptography and Security: From Theory to Applications. LNCS, vol. 6805, pp. 156–184. Springer, Heidelberg (2012). https://doi.org/10.1007/978-3-642-28368-0_13

29. Groth, J., Sahai, A.: Efficient non-interactive proof systems for bilinear groups. In: Smart, N. (ed.) EUROCRYPT 2008. LNCS, vol. 4965, pp. 415–432. Springer, Heidelberg (2008). https://doi.org/10.1007/978-3-540-78967-3_24

30. Ghadafi, E.: Formalizing group blind signatures and practical constructions without random oracles. In: Boyd, C., Simpson, L. (eds.) ACISP 2013. LNCS, vol. 7959, pp. 330–346. Springer, Heidelberg (2013). https://doi.org/10.1007/978-3-642-39059-3_23

31. Libert, B., Peters, T., Yung, M.: Short group signatures via structure-preserving signatures: standard model security from simple assumptions. In: Gennaro, R., Robshaw, M. (eds.) CRYPTO 2015. LNCS, vol. 9216, pp. 296–316. Springer, Heidelberg (2015). https://doi.org/10.1007/978-3-662-48000-7_15

32. Camenisch, J., Shoup, V.: Practical verifiable encryption and decryption of discrete logarithms. In: Boneh, D. (ed.) CRYPTO 2003. LNCS, vol. 2729, pp. 126–144. Springer, Heidelberg (2003). https://doi.org/10.1007/978-3-540-45146-4_8

33. Zhang, R.: Tweaking TBE/IBE to PKE transforms with chameleon hash functions. In: Katz, J., Yung, M. (eds.) ACNS 2007. LNCS, vol. 4521, pp. 323–339. Springer, Heidelberg (2007). https://doi.org/10.1007/978-3-540-72738-5_21

34. Boneh, D., Boyen, X.: Short signatures without random oracles. In: Cachin, C., Camenisch, J.L. (eds.) EUROCRYPT 2004. LNCS, vol. 3027, pp. 56–73. Springer, Heidelberg (2004). https://doi.org/10.1007/978-3-540-24676-3_4

35. Slamanig, D., Spreitzer, R., Unterluggauer, T.: Adding controllable linkability to pairing-based group signatures for free. In: Chow, S.S.M., Camenisch, J., Hui, L.C.K., Yiu, S.M. (eds.) ISC 2014. LNCS, vol. 8783, pp. 388–400. Springer, Cham (2014). https://doi.org/10.1007/978-3-319-13257-0_23

36. Yue, X., Chen, B., Wang, X., Duan, Y., Gao, M., He, Y.: An efficient and secure anonymous authentication scheme for VANETs based on the framework of group signatures. IEEE Access **2018**(6), 62584–62600 (2018)

37. Shao, J., Lin, X., Lu, R.: A threshold anonymous authentication protocol for VANETs. IEEE Trans. Veh. Technol. **65**(3), 1711–1720 (2016)

38. Masayuki, A., Georg, F., Groth, J.: Structure- preserving signatures and commitments to group elements. J. Cryptology **29**(2), 363–421 (2016)

39. Hwang, J., Chen, L., Cho, H.: Short dynamic group signature scheme supporting controllable linkability. IEEE Trans. Inf. Forensics Secur. **10**(6), 1109–1124 (2015)

40. Galbraith, S.D., Paterson, K.G., Smart, N.P.: Pairings for cryptographers. Discrete Appl. Math. **156**(16), 3113–3121 (2008)

41. Barreto, Paulo S.L.M., Naehrig, M.: Pairing-friendly elliptic curves of prime order. In: Preneel, B., Tavares, S. (eds.) SAC 2005. LNCS, vol. 3897, pp. 319–331. Springer, Heidelberg (2006). https://doi.org/10.1007/11693383_22

42. Hess, F., Smart, N.P., Vercauteren, F.: The Eta pairing revisited. IEEE Trans. Inf. Theory **52** (10), 4595–4602 (2006)

43. Blazy, O., Fuchsbauer, G., Izabachène, M., Jambert, A., Sibert, H., Vergnaud, D.: Batch Groth–Sahai. In: Zhou, J., Yung, M. (eds.) ACNS 2010. LNCS, vol. 6123, pp. 218–235. Springer, Heidelberg (2010). https://doi.org/10.1007/978-3-642-13708-2_14

An Efficient Property-Based Authentication Scheme in the Standard Model

Xiaohan Yue[(⊠)] [iD], Xin Wang, Xibo Wang, Wencheng Cui,
and Yuan He

School of Information Science and Engineering,
Shenyang University of Technology, Shenyang 110870, China
xhyue@sut.edu.cn

Abstract. In order to solve the problem of platform configuration information leakage that are caused by the traditional platform authentication in the trusted computing environment, this paper proposes a novel property-based authentication (PBA) scheme. In this paper, we design the framework and define the security model of our scheme. Then we give the detail construction of our scheme. Comparing with existing PBA schemes, our PBA scheme is more effective than other schemes. At the aspect of security, this paper proves that our scheme meets correctness, unforgeability and configuration privacy in the standard model.

Keywords: Property-based attestation · Trusted computing · Bilinear pairing · Standard model

1 Introduction

In today's open distribute network environment, the spread of malicious code has caused huge losses to users and service providers. Therefore, it is necessary to establish a distributed trusted computing environment to ensure the predictable behavior of all parties. To achieve this goal, the computer industry has established a trusted computing organization TCG [1] and developed a trusted platform module TPM to ensure the integrity, confidentiality and authentication of the platform. In terms of platform authentication, TCG provides a solution for platform authentication, called binary authentication [2], that is, TPM as the verifier sends the measurement results (usually binary hash value) of software and hardware on the platform, also called integrity report, to the verifier, who checks the integrity report and evaluates its security. However, this method will destroy the privacy of the platform. As the authenticator reports the identification of the software and hardware in his own system, the adversary obtains the characteristics of the platform through the identification, which will lead to the following situations: first, differentiated services, remote service providers may refuse to provide services due to the business model adopted by the other party, for example, denial of service for Linux, or denial of service for certain platform configuration information by some chat software, etc.; Second, attacks on configuration. If the adversary knows that some hardware or software configurations exist on a large number of platforms by collecting platform configuration information, the adversary

© Springer Nature Switzerland AG 2019
J. Vaidya et al. (Eds.): CSS 2019, LNCS 11983, pp. 220–233, 2019.
https://doi.org/10.1007/978-3-030-37352-8_19

can implement targeted attacks according to these configurations. Third, anonymity is destroyed, and adversaries can uniquely determine a platform based on platform configuration information.

Aim at the above problems, in 2004, Sadeghi et al. [3] proposed the definition of property-based attestation (PBA), but there is no construction of PBA in this paper. The advantage of PBA is that different platforms may have different configuration specification (cs), but they have the same property specification (ps) to meet the same secure requirements. Compared with the binary attestation, the property-based attestation converts the original binary attestation into the attestation of the platform property, and the attestor can give the attestation of satisfying the property according to the target property that the verifier needs to verify. In terms of PBA scheme research, Chen et al. [4] first proposed an property-based attestation scheme, and then proposed another property attestation scheme without a trusted third party [5]; Due to the efficiency bottleneck of the above schemes, Feng Dengguo et al. [6] proposed a more efficient PBA scheme based on bilinear pairings. In recent years, Abir et al. [19] presented a secure cloud monitoring system by using PBA scheme; Nazanin et al. [20] proposed platform property certificate, based on the current certificates of the system as the model's property, and designed a practical PBA protocol.

However, these schemes are proved to be security in the random oracle model. But this model is an ideal model, which was proposed by Bellare and Rogaway in 1993 [7]. In this model, any object, such as hash function, can be regarded as a completely random object. However, in the actual scheme, because the hash function we used usually is specified, the output of hash function for each time is not really random, which may lead to the insecurity of the scheme. In fact, the defects of the random oracle model have been pointed out in several papers [8, 9]. The proof under the standard model can clearly show that a provable secure cryptographic scheme cannot be corrupted unless the underlying mathematic problem is solved. Therefore, designing a PBA scheme which security can be proved in the standard model is the main research work of this paper.

Based on bilinear pairing, this paper uses group signature [10–14] technology and Groth-Sahai proof system [15, 16] to propose a novel property-based attestation scheme that is provable secure and efficient in the standard model. The scheme has security properties such as unforgeability of attestation and configuration privacy. In terms of performance cost, compared with the existing schemes [4–6], our scheme has higher efficiency and shorter attestation value length.

2 Preliminaries

2.1 Bilinear Pairing

Let g and G_T be two cyclic groups of order n, where n is a prime number and g is the generator of G. Bilinear mapping on two groups is defined as $e : G \times G \to G_T$, and satisfies the following properties:

Bilinear: $e(g^a, g^b) = e(g, g)^{ab}$, holds for all $a, b \in \mathbb{Z}_n^*$;

Non-degeneracy: $e(g, g) \neq 1_{G_T}$, where 1_{G_T} is a unit of G_T;

Computability: there is an effective algorithm to calculate $t = e(g, h)$.

2.2   Assumptions

Assumption 1. Subgroup Decision Assumption (SDA): Given that $n = pq$, $h \in G_n$, and $h \in G_p$, it is indistinguishable in polynomial time to determine which group h belongs to. The formal expression is as follows:

$$Pr[(p, q, G, G_T, e, g) \leftarrow \text{BilinearSetup}(1^k); n = pq; h \in G_n : A(n, G, G_T, e, g, h) = 1] \approx$$
$$Pr[(p, q, G, G_T, e, g) \leftarrow \text{BilinearSetup}(1^k); n = pq; h \in G_p : A(n, G, G_T, e, g, h) = 1]$$

Assumption 2. q-Hidden Diffie-Hellman(q-HSDH) Assumption: Given that g, g^x, $u \in G_1$, $h, h^x \in G_2$ and $\{g^{\frac{1}{x+c_l}}, h^{c_l}, u^{c_l}\}_{l=1\ldots q}$, it is difficult to calculate $\left(g^{\frac{1}{x+c}}, h^c, u^c\right)$ in polynomial time, so there is a negligible function v that:

$$Pr[(p, G_1, G_2, G_T, e, g, h) \leftarrow BilinearSetup(1^k); u \in G_1; x, \{c_l\}_{l=1\ldots q} \leftarrow$$
$$Z_p; (A, B, C) \leftarrow A(p, G_1, G_2, G_T, e, g, g^x, h, h^x, u, \{g^{\frac{1}{x+c_l}}, h^{c_l}, u^{c_l}\}_{l=1\ldots q}) :$$
$$(A, B, C) = \left(g^{\frac{1}{x+c}}, h^c, u^c\right) \wedge c \notin \{c_l\}_{l=1\ldots q}] < v(k)$$

2.3   Property-Based Attestation

Property-based attestation (PBA) scheme involves three entities, namely: attestor P (including host H and trusted platform module PTM), verifier $\mathcal{V}$ and trusted third party issuer $\mathcal{I}$. In the whole PBA scheme, Attestor P asks issuer I for an property certificate of the current platform configuration information, and then proves to verifier γ that the current platform configuration information is consistent with the property certificate and has corresponding property. The issuer main work consists of two parts: issuing property certificates for platform configuration information and checking whether the property certificates are revoked; Verifier $\mathcal{V}$ verify the certificate given by attestor $\mathcal{P}$. In general, PBA scheme is mainly composed of five algorithms:

(1) **Setup:** Input the security parameter 1^k, issuer $\mathcal{I}$ use random algorithm to generate a pair of keys (ppk, tsk), where tsk is the private key of issuer and ppk is the public key.

(2) **Join:** TPM collects platform configuration information cs and sends cs to issuer $\mathcal{I}$, who evaluates the cs as ps, then signs (cs, ps) with its own private key γ to generate property certificate cre and sends the certificate and (cs, ps) to attestor P.

(3) **Attest:** This process is to prove to verifier $\mathcal{V}$ that attestor P has a certificate on the property ps and that the current relevant platform configuration information is consistent with that in the certificate. Firstly, TPM carries out commitment

calculation on the current platform configuration information cs to obtain a commitment value C_{cs} and signs it to obtain a signature value σ_M; Then host H blinds the certificate cre and calculates relevant witness values; Finally, attestor P obtains the property-based attestation σ_{PBA} according to the calculation results of TPM and host, and sends σ_{PBA} to verifier $\mathcal{V}$.

(4) **Verify:** Verifier $\mathcal{V}$ obtains the property-based attestation σ_{PBA} from attestor P. First verifier $\mathcal{V}$ verifies TPM's signature σ_M to ensure that the attestation information comes from a real TPM; Then verifier $\mathcal{V}$ checks correctness of the other parameters of σ_{PBA}. If positive, it indicates that attestor P has a valid property certificate cre and that **attestor** P's current platform configuration information cs is consistent with the certificate cre. Finally verifier $\mathcal{V}$ sends C_{cs} and ps to issuer $\mathcal{I}$ to verify whether the property certificate for (cs,ps) has been revoked. If all the above checks pass, verifier $\mathcal{V}$ outputs accept, otherwise reject.

(5) **Check:** On receiving the query from verifier $\mathcal{V}$, issuer uses its private key tsk to obtain the corresponding (cs, ps) pair, then checks the configuration-property database whether the (cs, ps) pair is existed in the revocation list RL, and forwards the result to verifier $\mathcal{V}$.

2.4   PBA Security Model

If a PBA scheme is secure, it will satisfy the following security properties:

(1) **Correctness.** If both the attestor and verifier are honest, (cs, ps) is not in the revocation list RL, then the attestation generated by the attestor will be regarded as valid by the verifier with overwhelming probability. This means that the PBA scheme must meet the following consistency requirements.

$$((ppk, tsk) \leftarrow \text{Setup}(1^k), \quad (cs, cre) \leftarrow \text{Join}(ppk, tsk),$$
$$\sigma_{PBA} \leftarrow \text{Attest}(cs, ps, cre, ppk)) \Rightarrow 1 \leftarrow \text{Verify}(ps, \sigma_{PBA}, ppk, RL)$$

(2) **Configuration Privacy.** This PBA scheme has configuration privacy, that is, no adversary can win the following games in polynomial time.

– **Initialization:** Challenger $\mathcal{C}$ runs $\text{Setup}(1^k)$ and sends public key ppk and private key tsk to adversary $\mathcal{A}$.

– **Queries:** Adversary $\mathcal{A}$ adaptively queried challenger $\mathcal{C}$ in the following method:

Join: $\mathcal{A}$ sends the i-th Join request to challenger $\mathcal{C}$, challenger $\mathcal{C}$ selects $cs_i \in CS = \{cs_1, cs_2, \ldots, cs_n\}$, where CS is the same property set, and runs join algorithm to obtain certificate cre_i about property ps, then sends cre_i and ps to adversary $\mathcal{A}$.

Attest: Adversary $\mathcal{A}$ sends the i-th Attest request to challenger $\mathcal{C}$, and challenger $\mathcal{C}$ runs attest algorithm to generate certificate $\sigma_{PBA}^{(i)}$ and takes it as a response to Adversary $\mathcal{A}$. Corrupt: Taking the index i as input, challenger $\mathcal{C}$ outputs cs_i.

- **Challenging response:** At this stage, challenger $\mathcal{C}$ randomly selects a cs from CS set and generates the corresponding attestation σ_{PBA} as the query on adversary $\mathcal{A}$. At this time, adversary $\mathcal{A}$ needs to output the index j as the response. If $cs_j = cs$, then the query is successful, otherwise fails.

Definition 1 (Configuration Privacy). Let $Adv\left[\mathcal{A}_{PBA}^{anon}\right] = |\Pr[\mathcal{A} \, wins] - 1/n|$ denotes that the advantage of the adversary $\mathcal{A}$ wins the above game. If $Adv\left[\mathcal{A}_{PBA}^{anon}\right]$ is negligible for any probabilistic polynomial time adversary $\mathcal{A}$, then the PBA scheme meets configuration privacy.

(3) **Unforgeability.** This PBA scheme is unforgeable, that is, no adversary can win the following games in polynomial time.

- **Initialization:** Challenger $\mathcal{C}$ runs $Setup(1^k)$ and the adversary $\mathcal{A}$ only knows the public key ppk.
- **Queries:** Adversary $\mathcal{A}$ adaptively query challenger $\mathcal{C}$ in the following manner:

Join: Adversary $\mathcal{A}$ sends the i-th Join request to challenger $\mathcal{C}$, challenger $\mathcal{C}$ selects a attestor's platform configuration information $cs_i(i \in \{1, \ldots, q-1\})$ to run the join algorithm to create a certificate cre_i bout the property ps_i for the attestor, and sends cre_i to adversary $\mathcal{A}$;

Attest Query: This query is divided into two cases. The first is that adversary $\mathcal{A}$ issues the i-th Attest query, challenger C runs Attest algorithm to generate the unblinded attestation S_i and returns it to $\mathcal{A}$; The second is that when $i = i^*$, challenger $\mathcal{C}$ will run the Attest algorithm to generate an attestation S^*, and use it as a response to the $\mathcal{A}$.

Corrupt Query: adversary $\mathcal{A}$ sends the i-th Corrupt request to challenger $\mathcal{C}$. $i \neq i^*$. challenger $\mathcal{C}$ will respond to $\mathcal{A}$ with cs_i corresponding to the index i. challenger C will not respond when $i = i^*$.

- **Forgery:** Adversary $\mathcal{A}$ outputs attestor's property-based attestation S and a challenge value N_v. If Verify$(N_v, S, ppk, RL) = 1(ACCEPT)$ and adversary $\mathcal{A}$ has not made a Corrupt query to cs corresponding to attestation S, the attack is successful, otherwise failed.

Definition 2 (Unforgeability). Adversary $\mathcal{A}$ as the adversary in the above-mentioned attack game, and use $Adv\left[\mathcal{A}_{PBA}^{unforgery}\right] = Pr[\mathcal{A} \, wins]$ to represent the advantage of $\mathcal{A}$ against the above-mentioned unforgeable game. If adv $Adv\left[\mathcal{A}_{PBA}^{unforgery}\right]$ is negligible for any probabilistic polynomial time adversary $\mathcal{A}$, then the PBA scheme is said to have proved unforgeability.

3 Our Scheme

3.1 Setup Algorithm

(1). Input the secure parameter 1^k to generate a bilinear cyclic group G of order n, where $n = p \cdot q$, p and q are prime numbers, G_p and G_q are subgroups of group G, and bilinear map is $e : G \times G \rightarrow G_T$. Select generator g and h from G and G_p respectively;

(2). Randomly select a number γ from $\mathbb{Z}_n$ and calculate $\omega := g^\gamma$ and $T := e(g, g)$;

(3). Selecting l generators $\tau_1, \ldots, \tau_l$ and u, τ' from group G;

(4). Output PBA public key ppk and TTP private key tsk:

$$(ppk, tsk) := ((G, G_T, n, e, g, h, u, \tau', \tau_1, \ldots \tau_l, \omega, T), \gamma)$$

3.2 Join Algorithm

(1). TPM collects the platform configuration information cs, then sends cs to issuer I through a secure channel and asks for an property certificate. When issuer I receive TPM's platform configuration information verifier $\mathcal{V}$, issuer I evaluate the property of cs. if the evaluated property are ps, then issuer I issues an property certificate $cre := (g^{cs}, (g^{ps})^{\frac{1}{\gamma+cs}}, u^{cs})$ and sends the property certificate and (cs, ps) to TPM, then issuer I restore cre and (cs, ps) into the configuration-property certificate database, which is convenient for later verification and query.

(2). TPM receives the property certificate cre and (cs, ps) and checks them as follows: let $U_1 := g^{cs}$, $U_2 := (g^{ps})^{\frac{1}{\gamma+cs}}$, $U_3 := u^{cs}$, and check whether $e(U_1 \cdot \omega, U_2) = T^{ps}$ and $e(U_1, u) = e(U_3, g)$ are valid. If it passes the check, TPM saves the property certificate cre.

3.3 Attest Algorithm

(1). Verifier $\mathcal{V}$ query TPM with a challenge value $N_v = (m_1 \cdots m_l) \in \{0, 1\}^l$;

(2). After TPM obtains the challenge value N_v, it randomly selects $r \leftarrow \mathbb{Z}_n$, calculates the commitment value $C_{cs} = g^{cs} \cdot h^r$ to cs, and generates an anonymous authentication signature (The signature algorithm uses AIK signature method in TCG standard, the corresponding private key is sk_M) $\sigma_M := \text{Sign}(sk_M, C_{cs} \| N_v)$;

(3). TPM sends $(\sigma_M, C_{cs}, U_2, U_3, r, N_v)$ to host;

(4). Host randomly selects $t \leftarrow \mathbb{Z}_n$ and computes:

$$S := (S_1, S_2, S_3, S_4) = \left(C_{cs}, U_2, U_3 \cdot \left(\tau' \cdot \prod_{i=1}^{l} \tau_i^{m_i}\right)^t, g^{-t}\right)$$

(5). To ensure privacy, host $\mathcal{H}$ needs to re-randomize attestation $\mathcal{S}$

Select $r_1, r_2, r_3 \leftarrow \mathbb{Z}_n$, and compute:

$$\Omega := (\Omega_1, \Omega_2, \Omega_3, \Omega_4) = (S_1, S_2 \cdot h^{r_1}, S_3 \cdot h^{r_2}, S_4 \cdot h^{r_3})$$

(6). Host computes the corresponding proof as follows:

$$\pi_1 := h^{r \cdot r_1} \cdot (\Omega_1 \cdot \omega)^{r_1} \cdot (\Omega_2)^r$$

$$\pi_2 := u^r \cdot g^{-r_2} \cdot \left(\tau' \cdot \prod_{i=1}^{l} \tau_i^{m_i}\right)^{-r_3}$$

(7). Host $\mathcal{H}$ sends $\sigma_{PBA} := (\sigma_M, \Omega_1, \Omega_2, \Omega_3, \Omega_4, \pi_1, \pi_2)$ to verifier.

3.4   Verify Algorithm

(1). After receiving σ_{PBA}, the verifier checks whether $\Omega_1, \Omega_2, \Omega_3, \Omega_4, \pi_1, \pi_2$ is belong to G and verifies the validity of σ_M;
(2). Verifier $\mathcal{V}$ computes and checks:

$$e(\Omega_1 \cdot \omega, \Omega_2) \cdot T^{-ps} = e(h, \pi_1)$$

$$e(\Omega_1, u) \cdot e(\Omega_3, g)^{-1} \cdot e(\Omega_4, \tau' \cdot \prod_{i=1}^{l} \tau_i^{m_i})^{-1} = e(h, \pi_2)$$

(3). If the above equations are hold, Verifier $\mathcal{V}$ sends (Ω_1, ps) to issuer $\mathcal{I}$ to judge whether the platform configuration-property pair (cs, ps) is in the revocation list;
(4). If all the checks pass, then Verifier $\mathcal{V}$ outputs accept.

3.5   Check Algorithm

On receiving a request (Ω_1, ps) from verifier, issuer should check whether the platform configuration information cs about (Ω_1, ps) is in the revocation list. The issuer computes $\rho := (\Omega_1)^p = g^{cs \cdot p}$, then research the certificate database with ρ and ps to check whether $\rho^{\frac{1}{p}}$ is equal to a certain g^{cs^*} value, where $cs* \in CS$ (CS is the set of platform configuration specification). If the corresponding certificates exists, issuer inform Verifier $\mathcal{V}$ that the property certificate for platform configuration information cs is valid; Otherwise, the platform configuration information cs was revoked.

4 Security and Performance Analysis

4.1 Security Proof

In this section, under the standard model we prove the security of our scheme. An PBA protocol must satisfy the following security properties: correctness, unforgeability and configuration privacy. According to the security model in the Sect. 2, the following theorems is proved.

Theorem 1 (Correctness). The PBA scheme proposed in Sect. 3 is correct.

Proof: To prove the correctness of the proposed PBA scheme, it is necessary to prove that the signature generated by the valid signer can be successfully verified by any verifier.

$$e(\Omega_1 \cdot \omega, \Omega_2) \cdot T^{-ps} = e\left(g^{cs} \cdot h^r \cdot g^\gamma, (g^{ps})^{\frac{1}{(cs+\gamma)}} \cdot h^{r_1}\right) \cdot e(g,g)^{-ps}$$

$$= e\left(g^{cs+\gamma}, (g^{ps})^{\frac{1}{(cs+\gamma)}}\right) \cdot e(g^{cs+\gamma}, h^{r_1}) \cdot e\left(h^r, (g^{ps})^{\frac{1}{(cs+\gamma)}}\right) \cdot e(h^r, h^{\gamma_1})$$

$$= e(g,g)^{ps} \cdot e(h, (g^{cs+\gamma})^{r_1}) \cdot e\left(\left((g^{ps})^{\frac{1}{(cs+\gamma)}}\right)^\gamma\right) e(h, h^{\gamma \cdot r_1}) \cdot e(g,g)^{-ps}$$

$$= e(h, h^{\gamma \cdot r_1} \cdot (\Omega_1 \cdot \omega)^{r_1} \cdot (\Omega_2)^\gamma)$$

$$= e(h, \pi_1)$$

$$e(\Omega_1, u) \cdot e(\Omega_3, g)^{-1} \cdot e\left(\Omega_4, \tau' \cdot \pi_{i=1}^\tau \tau_i^{m_i}\right)^{-1}$$

$$= e(g^{cs} \cdot h^r, u) \cdot e\left(u^{cs} \cdot h^{r_2} \cdot (\tau' \cdot \pi_{i=1}^\tau \tau_i^{m_i})^t, g\right)^{-1} \cdot e(g^{-t} \cdot h^{r_3}, \tau' \cdot \pi_{i=1}^\tau \tau_i^{m_i})^{-1}$$

$$= e\left(h, u^r \cdot g^{-r_2} \cdot (\tau' \cdot \pi_{i=1}^\tau \tau_i^{m_i})^{-r_3}\right)$$

$$= e(h, \pi_2)$$

Theorem 2 (Unforgeability). Based on q-HSDH assumption, PBA protocol has the attestation unforgeability. Under adaptive chosen message attack, if an adversary $\mathcal{A}$ can forge a valid attestation with non-negligible probability in probability polynomial time, then there is an algorithm attestation $\mathcal{S}$ that can solve q-HSDH assumption with non-negligible probability in probability polynomial time.

Proof: The idea of proof here is based on papers [12–14]. In addition, since TPM is physically secure, adversary $\mathcal{A}$ can only control the behavior of host $\mathcal{H}$ for attestor $\mathcal{P}$. Assuming that an Adversary $\mathcal{A}$ can forge an unblinded PBA with non-negligible probability, then a polynomial time simulator attestation $\mathcal{S}$ can be constructed to solve the q-HSDH problem through interaction with adversary $\mathcal{A}$. It is worth noting that if an adversary can forge an unblinded PBA, it can also forge σ_{PBA}. First, an example of attestation $\mathcal{S}$ is given: $g, u \in G$, $h \in G_p$, $w = g^\gamma$ and $q - 1$ $(A_i = g^{\frac{1}{\gamma+cs_i}}, B_i = g^{cs_i}, C_i = u^{cs_i})_{i=1,\dots,q-1}$ q-HSDH example, where γ value is unknown. The interaction process between adversary $\mathcal{A}$ and attestation $\mathcal{S}$ is as follows:

Setup. Attestation S executes the Setup(1^k) algorithm as follows: first, attestation S selects random numbers $\mu \in \mathbb{Z}_l$, $t \in \mathbb{Z}_n$ and a series of random numbers $(x', x_1, \ldots, x_l) \in \mathbb{Z}_{2q-1}^{l+1}$; Then, S randomly selects $(z', z_1, \ldots, z_l) \in \mathbb{Z}_n^{l+1}$, so that $(v' = g^{z'}, v_1 = g^{z_1}, \ldots, v_l = g^{z_l}) \in G$ for ease of analysis, the following three parameters are defined: $X = -2\mu q + x' + \Sigma_{i=1}^l x_i m_i$, $Y = z' + \Sigma_{i=1}^l z_i m_i$, $Z = \tau' \prod_{j=1}^l \tau_j^{m_j}$.

Attestation S constructs PBA system parameters as follows: $f = \omega^{-1} g^t$, $\tau' = f^{x'-2kl} v'$, $\tau_1 = f^{x_1} v_1, \ldots, \tau_l = f^{x_l} v_l$ and $(g, \omega = g^y, h, u, \tau', \tau_1, \ldots \tau_l, T)$ as PBA system parameters; Finally, attestation S maintains a list that records the results of the queries and maps the query results regarding platform configuration information cs_i with *indexes* $i \in \{1, \ldots, q-1\}$.

Join Queries. When adversary $\mathcal{A}$ applies for the property certificate to S for the first time, there are two situations to consider:

When $i \neq i^*$, s selects $cre_i = (A_i^{ps}, B_i, C_i)$ as a response from the q-HSDH instance, saves the certificates cre_i and ps in the i item in the list, and uses this as a return value; if the i times query has occurred before, then S will take the content corresponding to the i item in the list as a response to adversary $\mathcal{A}$.

When $i = i^*$, attestation S will not respond and terminate because s does not know the value of $cs^* = |t - \gamma|$.

Attest Queries. When adversary $\mathcal{A}$ asks S for a query, there are two cases:

When $i \neq i^*$, in order to answer adversary $\mathcal{A}$'s query i, attestation S will do the following. If this i times queries has been conducted before, then attestation S selects the contents of the i table item from the list and uses cre_i as the return value; If the i times query has not occurred before, then attestation S selects the number i from q-HSDH instances, takes $cre_i = (A_i^{ps}, B_i, C_i)$ and ps_i as responses, and records them in the list;

When $i = i^*$, Attestation S randomly selects a $r \leftarrow \mathbb{Z}_n$ and calculates $S = (S_1, S_2, S_3, S_4) = \left(g^{\frac{ps}{T}}, \omega^{-1} g^t, u^{-\frac{Y}{X}} \cdot Z^r, u^{\frac{1}{X}} g^{-r} \right)$ if $X \equiv 0 \pmod{n}$, S terminates and exits.

Because $cs^* = t - \gamma$, Therefore, $r' = r - \log_g^u X$, $S_3 = u^{-\frac{Y}{X}} \cdot Z^r = u^{-\frac{Y}{X}} \cdot (f^X g^Y)^r = u^{-\frac{Y}{X}} \cdot (f^X g^Y)^{r'} \cdot f^{\log_g^u} \cdot u^{\frac{Y}{X}} = u^{cs^*} \cdot Z^{r'}$ is constructed for the above formula, which is similar to $S_4 = g^{-r'}$, This certificate is:
$S = \left(g^{\frac{ps}{\gamma+cs^*}}, g^{cs^*}, u^{cs^*} \cdot Z^{r'}, g^{-r'} \right)$. It and the corresponding ps^* are taken as the response value to the adversary $\mathcal{A}$ query.

Corrupt Queries. Adversary $\mathcal{A}$ conducts the first time query, where $i \neq i^*$, attestation S will look up the i-th item from the list and will take cs_i as the return value.

Forgery. Adversary $\mathcal{A}$ passed q-1 inquiries and finally output attestation $S^* = (S_1^*, S_2^*, S_3^*, S_4^*)$. If $S_1^* \neq f$, then attestation S will terminate, otherwise calculate $X^* = -2\mu q + x' + \Sigma_{i=1}^l x_i m_i^*$ and $Y^* = z' + \Sigma_{i=1}^l z_i m_i^*$, where $N_v^* = (m_1^* \cdots m_l^*) \in \{0, 1\}^l$. If $X^* \neq 0 \pmod{n}$ then attestation S will terminate, because what is obtained is an invalid forgery. If all the conditions are met, the final simulator attestation S output $\left(S_1^{\frac{1}{ps}}, S_2, S_3 \cdot S_4^{Y^*}\right)$) is taken as the output to the q-HSDH problem.

The above proof process describes the simulation process of attestation S, and the success probability of attestation S is analyzed below. Because the entire simulation algorithm needs to be run completely to solve the q-HSDH problem, simulator attestation S cannot be terminated during the query. According to the above algorithm, three conditions must be met for attestation S not to terminate: $\Omega_1^* = f$, this probability is $\frac{1}{q-1}$; Secondly, the probability of $X \neq 0(mod\, n)$ is at least $1-1/2q$ for each attest query of $i = i^*$. if there are at least $q-1$ query, then the total probability should be greater than 1/2; Finally, in the forgery stage, the probability of $X^* \equiv 0(mod\, n)$ should be at least $1/2lq$. If adversary $\mathcal{A}$ successfully forges the proof in polynomial time with the probability of ε, then the probability of success of attestation S is $Adv\left[\mathcal{A}_{PBA}^{unforgery}\right] \geq \frac{\varepsilon}{4lq(q-1)} \geq \frac{\varepsilon}{4lq^2}$, that is, the problem of q-HSDH is solved with the advantage of $Adv\left[\mathcal{A}_{PBA}^{unforgery}\right]$ in polynomial time, which contradicts the assumption of q-HSDH. Therefore, this PBA scheme has the unforgeability of attestation.

Theorem 3 (Configuration Privacy). Based on SDA assumption, PBA protocol has the property of configuration privacy. Assuming that no polynomial time algorithm can solve the SDA assumption with a probability ε, then for each polynomial time adversary $\mathcal{A}$ there is adv $Adv\left[\mathcal{A}_{PBA}^{anon}\right] < 2\varepsilon$.

Proof: In order to prove adv $Adv\left[\mathcal{A}_{PBA}^{anon}\right] < 2\varepsilon$, then according to SDA assumption, we first need to prove that the two games when host $\mathcal{H}$ belongs to group G_p or group G, represented Υ_0 and Υ_1 respectively, are indistinguishable from adversary $\mathcal{A}$, namely adv $Adv\left[\mathcal{A}_{PBA}^{anon}\right]_{\Upsilon_0} - Adv\left[\mathcal{A}_{PBA}^{anon}\right]_{\Upsilon_1} < \varepsilon'$ is a negligible value.

In the initialization phase of the game, Attestation S will receive a subgroup decision assumption instance (n, G, G_T, e, h). As mentioned above, there are two cases for h: case 1. Host $\mathcal{H}$ belongs to group G_p, and then the game is a normal configuration privacy game, marked as Υ_0; case 2. Host $\mathcal{H}$ belongs to group G, then the game is recorded as Υ_1. The remaining parameters of the two games are the same. Then, adversary A and simulator attestation S play the configuration privacy game described in Sect. 3.4.

In the query phase, adversary $\mathcal{A}$ responds to the query of attestation S, i.e. answers an index j. if the answer is correct, i.e. $cs_j = cs$ then S outputs 1, indicating $h \in G_P$; Otherwise, attestation S outputs 0, indicating $h \in G$. $Adv\left[S_{PBA}^{anon}\right]$ is used to represent the advantage of simulator attestation S in subgroup decision game, and $Pr[h \in G_p] = Pr[h \in G] =$ is known, then there is:

$$Adv\left[\mathcal{A}_{PBA}^{anon}\right]_0 - Adv\left[\mathcal{A}_{PBA}^{anon}\right]_1$$
$$= 2Adv\left[S_{PBA}^{anon}\right] < 2e$$

Next, it needs to be further proved that adv $Adv[\mathcal{A}_{PBA}^{anon}]_{\Upsilon_1} = 0$, that is to say, when $h \in G$, the query values σ_{PBA} and cs are statistically independent of each other. The proof process is as follows:

In the query phase, given a query value $\sigma_{PBA} = (\sigma_M, \Omega_1, \Omega_2, \Omega_3, \Omega_4, \pi_1, \pi_2)$ (where σ_M is TPM authentication signature, and its security is beyond the scope of this article), it needs to be proved that σ_{PBA} can match any assumed value $\tilde{cs}$ that the adversary may adopt, that is, σ_{PBA} will not disclose any information about cs.

Under the condition of statistical independence, it is necessary to define an adversary $\tilde{A}$ with infinite computing power and obtain the following discrete logarithm:

First of all, for the four commitment values $(\Omega_1, \Omega_2, \Omega_3, \Omega_4)$, they do not disclose any information about cs because they are perfectly blinded by four uniformly distributed and independent random values $h^r, h^{r_1}, h^{r_2}, h^{r_3}$. Where Ω_1 and Ω_2 are directly related to cs, so no matter the adversary judges cs as any assumed value $\tilde{cs}$, for $\tilde{cs}$, there is $\tilde{r}, \tilde{r}_1$ makes $\Omega_1 = g^{\tilde{cs}} h^{\tilde{r}}$, ω $\Omega_2 = g^{1/(\gamma+\tilde{cs})} h^{\tilde{r}_1}$, so blindness does not reveal any information about cs.

Secondly, for evidence π_1, which involves Ω_1 and Ω_2, it needs to be proved that the given evidence π_1 value is consistent with the evidence value constructed by the adversary based on the assumed value. Let $\tilde{cs}, \tilde{r}, \tilde{r}_1$ be the values assumed by adversary $\tilde{A}$, then there are:
$$\begin{cases} \omega\Omega_1 = g^{\gamma+cs} h^r = g^{\gamma+cs+\beta \cdot r} \\ \omega\Omega_1 = g^{\gamma+\tilde{cs}} h^{\tilde{r}} = g^{\gamma+\tilde{cs}+\beta \cdot \tilde{r}} \end{cases},$$ the two equations are combined to obtain $\tilde{r} = r + (1-\xi) \cdot (\gamma+cs)/\xi \cdot \beta (mod\, n)$.

$$\begin{cases} \Omega_2 = g^{ps/(\gamma+cs)} h^{r_1} = g^{ps/(\gamma+cs)+\beta r_1} \\ \Omega_2 = g^{ps/(\gamma+\tilde{cs})} h^{\tilde{r}_1} = g^{(ps/(\gamma+cs))*((\gamma+cs)/(\gamma+\tilde{cs}))+\beta\tilde{r}_1} \end{cases}$$

The two equations are combined to obtain $\tilde{r}_1 = r_1 + ps(1-\xi)/\beta(\gamma+cs)$ For the evidence $\tilde{\pi}_1 = h^{\tilde{r} \cdot \tilde{r}_1} (g^{\tilde{cs}+\gamma})^{\tilde{r}_1} (g^{ps/(\tilde{cs}+\gamma)})^{\tilde{r}}$ constructed by adversary $\tilde{A}$, the above $\tilde{r}, \tilde{r}_1$ and ξ can be substituted into the formula to derive $\tilde{\pi}_1 = \pi_1$, which indicates that the equation holds no matter what the assumed value of adversary $\tilde{A}$ is, it is not helpful to exclude the value of $\tilde{cs}$, and further proves that π_1 does not disclose any information about cs.

The same proof method and conclusion apply to evidence π_2.

Through the analysis of $\sigma_{PBA} = (\sigma_M, \Omega_1, \Omega_2, \Omega_3, \Omega_4, \pi_1, \pi_2)$, it is proved that the query attestation values σ_{PBA} and cs are statistically independent of each other, so adversary $\tilde{A}$ has an advantage of 0 in the Υ_1 game, namely $Adv[\mathcal{A}_{PBA}^{anon}]_{\Upsilon_1} = 0$

In summary, according to SDA assumption, $Adv\left[\mathcal{A}_{PBA}^{anon}\right]_{\Upsilon_0} - Adv\left[\mathcal{A}_{PBA}^{anon}\right]_{\Upsilon_1} < 2\varepsilon$ holds, and $Adv[\mathcal{A}_{PBA}^{anon}]_{\Upsilon_1} = 0$ is obtained according to analysis of various parameters of σ_{PBA} in game Υ_1, thus $Adv[\mathcal{A}_{PBA}^{anon}]_{\Upsilon_0} < 2\varepsilon$ holds, which is proved.

4.2 Performance Analysis

In this section, the scheme proposed in this paper is compared with the existing PBA scheme based on bilinear pairings [6] called PBA-BM scheme. It is worth noting that this paper does not compare with other existing schemes [4, 5], because these schemes are not as efficient as PBA-BM schemes based on bilinear pairing.

First, we compare the size of certificate and attestation value. The following parameters are defined:$\mathbb{Z}_n$ denotes the size of the element in $\mathbb{Z}_n$, $\hbar$ denotes the size of the HASH value, G denotes the size of the element in group G, G_T denotes the size of the element in group G_T, and σ_M denotes the size of $|\sigma_M|$. For bilinear mapping satisfying 128-bit security, G_T needs to be about 3072 bit [17]. The comparison results are shown in Table 1.

Table 1. Comparison on communication cost

PBA scheme	Certificate (cre) size	Attestation (σ_{PBA}) size
PBA-BM	$2h + 5G$	$\sigma_M + \hbar + 6G + 5Z_n$
This scheme	$2h + 3G$	$\sigma_M + 6G$

1. The size of certificates and certificates of this scheme are smaller than that of PBA-BM scheme, i.e. the communication cost of this scheme is smaller than that of PBA-BM scheme.

Secondly, we compare the efficiency of the two schemes in proving algorithm, checking algorithm and revocation algorithm. Define the following parameters: p represents a pairing operation, G represents an exponential operation in group G, G^k represents a k times exponential operation, and G_T represents an exponential operation in group G_T. It is worth noting that a multiple exponential operation is slightly more efficient than an exponential operation [18], and the exponential operation in group g is much more efficient than the exponential operation in group G_T. The comparison results are shown in Table 2.

Table 2. Comparison on computation cost

PBA algorithm	PBA-BM scheme[]	our scheme
Attest (TPM)	$G + G^2$	G^2
Attest (Host)	$8G + G^2 + G^3 + 4G_T$	$3G^2 + G^3 + 2G^4$
Verify	$2G^2 + G^3 + G_T^4 + 4P$	$G_T + G$
Check	G^2	G^2

Because TPM is much less efficient than host, the Attest algorithm is divided into two parts for comparison. Compared with PBA-BM scheme, the Attest algorithm of our scheme is more efficient on both TPM and host. Compared with Verify algorithm, the efficiency of our scheme is better than PBA-BM scheme, while the execution efficiency of Check algorithm is the same. Therefore, our scheme is better than PBA-BM scheme.

5 Summary

The proposed property-based attestation scheme solves the problem of privacy leakage caused by the original binary attestation scheme and enhances the configuration privacy of the platform. Compared with the existing schemes on performance, our scheme is better than PBA-BM scheme and other PBA schemes. On the other hand, in terms of security, since the security of the existing property-based attestation schemes is proved under the random oracle model, our scheme can be proved under the standard model based on SDH assumption and SDA assumption, the security is better than other existing schemes. In the future work, the scheme will continue to be further improved to make it more efficient and practical.

References

1. Trusted Computing Group. TPM Main Part 1, Design Principles Specification, Version 1.2 Revision 62[EB/OL], 02 November 2003. https://www.trustedcomputinggroup.org/home
2. Jaeger, T., Sailer, R., Shankar, U.: PRIMA: policy-reduced integrity measurement architecture. In: Proceedings of the 11th ACM Symposium on Access Control Models and Technologies, New York, pp. 19–28 (2006)
3. Sadeghi, A., Stuble, C.: Property-based attestation for computing platforms: caring about properties, not mechanisms. In: Proceedings of the 2004 Workshop on New Security Paradigms. ACM, Nova Scotia, pp. 67–77 (2004)
4. Chen, L., Landfermann, R., Lohr, H., et al.: A protocol for property-based attestation. In: Proceedings of the First ACM Workshop on Scalable Trusted Computing. ACM, New York, pp. 7–16 (2006)
5. Chen, L., Löhr, H., Manulis, M., Sadeghi, A.-R.: Property-based attestation without a trusted third party. In: Wu, T.-C., Lei, C.-L., Rijmen, V., Lee, D.-T. (eds.) ISC 2008. LNCS, vol. 5222, pp. 31–46. Springer, Heidelberg (2008). https://doi.org/10.1007/978-3-540-85886-7_3
6. Dengguo, F., Qin, Y.: A property-based attestation protocol for TCM. Sci. Chin. Inf. Sci. 53(3), 454–464 (2010)
7. Bellare, M., Rogoway, P.: Random oracles are practical: a paradigm for designing efficient protocols. In: Proceedings of the First Conference on Computer and Communications Security. ACM, New York, pp. 62–73 (1993)
8. Bellare, M., Boldyreva, A., Palacio, A.: An uninstantiable random-oracle-model scheme for a hybrid-encryption problem. In: Cachin, C., Camenisch, J.L. (eds.) EUROCRYPT 2004. LNCS, vol. 3027, pp. 171–188. Springer, Heidelberg (2004). https://doi.org/10.1007/978-3-540-24676-3_11
9. Canetti, R., Goldreich, O., Halevi, S.: The random oracle methodology, revisited (preliminary version). In: Proceedings of the 30th Annual ACM Symposium on the Theory of Computing. STOC 1998, pp. 209–218. ACM. New York (1998)
10. Chaum, D., van Heyst, E.: Group signatures. In: Davies, D.W. (ed.) EUROCRYPT 1991. LNCS, vol. 547, pp. 257–265. Springer, Heidelberg (1991). https://doi.org/10.1007/3-540-46416-6_22
11. Bellare, M., Micciancio, D., Warinschi, B.: Foundations of group signatures: formal definitions, simplified requirements, and a construction based on general assumptions. In: Biham, E. (ed.) EUROCRYPT 2003. LNCS, vol. 2656, pp. 614–629. Springer, Heidelberg (2003). https://doi.org/10.1007/3-540-39200-9_38

12. Boneh, D., Boyen, X., Shacham, H.: Short group signatures. In: Franklin, M. (ed.) CRYPTO 2004. LNCS, vol. 3152, pp. 41–55. Springer, Heidelberg (2004). https://doi.org/10.1007/978-3-540-28628-8_3

13. Boyen, X., Waters, B.: Compact group signatures without random oracles. In: Vaudenay, S. (ed.) EUROCRYPT 2006. LNCS, vol. 4004, pp. 427–444. Springer, Heidelberg (2006). https://doi.org/10.1007/11761679_26

14. Boyen, X., Waters, B.: Full-domain subgroup hiding and constant-size group signatures. In: Okamoto, T., Wang, X. (eds.) PKC 2007. LNCS, vol. 4450, pp. 1–15. Springer, Heidelberg (2007). https://doi.org/10.1007/978-3-540-71677-8_1

15. Groth, J., Sahai, A.: Efficient non-interactive proof systems for bilinear groups. In: Smart, N. (ed.) EUROCRYPT 2008. LNCS, vol. 4965, pp. 415–432. Springer, Heidelberg (2008). https://doi.org/10.1007/978-3-540-78967-3_24

16. Jens, G.: Simulation-sound NIZK proofs for a practical language and constant size group signatures. In: Proceedings of ASIACRYPT 2006, Shanghai, pp. 444–459 (2006)

17. Koblitz, N., Menezes, A.: Pairing-based cryptography at high security levels. In: Smart, Nigel P. (ed.) Cryptography and Coding 2005. LNCS, vol. 3796, pp. 13–36. Springer, Heidelberg (2005). https://doi.org/10.1007/11586821_2

18. Wenbo, M.: Modern Cryptography: Theory and Practice. Prentice Hall Press, New Jersey (2003)

19. Awad, A., Kadry, S., Lee, B., et al.: IEEE 2014 IEEE/ACM 7th International Conference on Utility and Cloud Computing (UCC) - London, United Kingdom (8.12.2014–11.12.2014). 2014 IEEE/ACM 7th International Conference on Utility and Cloud Computing - Property Based Attestation for a Secure Cloud Monitoring System, pp. 934–940 (2014)

20. Qin, Y., Feng, D.G.: Component property based remote attestation. J. Softw. 20(6), 1625–1641 (2009)

Group Identification via Non-threshold Leakage-Resilient Secret Sharing Scheme

Ping Li[1], Jin Li[2(✉)], and Alzubair Hassan[2]

[1] School of Computer Science, South China Normal University,
Guangzhou 510631, China
liping26@mail2.sysu.edu.cn
[2] School of Computer Science and Cyber Engineering, Guangzhou University,
Guangzhou, China
jinli71@gmail.com

Abstract. In this work, we construct a non-threshold secret sharing scheme that realizes a non-threshold access structure by using linear codes, in which any element of the non-threshold access structure can reconstruct the secret key. We prove that our scheme is a multiprover zero-knowledge proof system in the random oracle model, which shows that a passive adversary gains no information about the secret key. Our scheme is also a leakage-resilient secret sharing scheme (LRSS) in the bounded-leakage model, and it is (ε, l)-secure as long as the overall amount of information about the secret key learned by a malicious adversary is bounded by l bits. As an application, we propose a new group identification protocol (GID-scheme) from our LRSS, and we prove that it is a leakage-resilient GID-scheme. In our leakage-resilient GID-scheme, the verifier believes the validity of qualified group members and tolerates l bits of adversarial leakage in the distribution protocol, whereas for unqualified group members, the verifier cannot believe their valid identifications in the proof protocol.

Keywords: Privacy-preserving · Outsourcing computation · Machine learning · Dynamic secret sharing

1 Introduction

The secret sharing scheme originally and independently introduced by Shamir [14] and Blakley [2], is a method in which a dealer selects a secret and distributes it as shares among a set of participants in the distribution stage. Only the predefined subsets of participants can reconstruct the secret from their shares, while others learn nothing about the secret in the reconstruction stage. These subsets are called qualified, and the monotonic collection of qualified subsets is called an access structure of the secret sharing scheme. As a basic primitive in cryptography, the secret sharing scheme has been used widely in security

This work was supported by National Natural Science Foundation of China (No. 61702126).

© Springer Nature Switzerland AG 2019
J. Vaidya et al. (Eds.): CSS 2019, LNCS 11983, pp. 234–241, 2019.
https://doi.org/10.1007/978-3-030-37352-8_20

applications and protocols, such as threshold cryptography, secure multiparty computation, oblivious transfer and access control.

In general, in the secret sharing scheme (n participants and access structures are known in advance), there are two types of access structures: *threshold* and *non-threshold*. In the *threshold* access structure, at least $t = t(n)$ qualified participants can reconstruct the secret key. In [12], the authors constructed an evolving secret sharing scheme for a dynamic threshold access structure. In their scheme, the size of the qualified sets increases if the number of participants increases. However, in the *non-threshold* access structure, the size of the qualified set is not limited, i.e., any collection of the qualified subsets can reconstruct the secret key. If a non-threshold access structure (a small monotonic span program) can be described, then an efficient secret-sharing scheme is realized [10].

Leakage-Resilient Secret Sharing Scheme. In previous work, most researchers generally used *leakage-resilient primitives* [8,9,11] and *leakage-resilient devices* [1] to protect the security of the secret key even if an adversary can learn some partial information about it. A cryptographic primitive and device is said to be *leakage-resilient*, if it remains secure in the presence of *bounded-leakage* of an internal state. In work presented in [7], the authors defined the assumption that only the computation leaks information. In other words, there is no leakage without computation. However, this assumption does not guarantee security in the model, because cold-boot attacks may work. Therefore, motivated by the work of Dziembowski and Pietrzak [3], we describe the leakage assumptions considered in this work as follows:

- Independent leakage: the computation can be organized into rounds, the leaks in each round are independent.
- Bounded leakage: in each round, the number of leakages is bound to some parameter l bits, whereas the total can be arbitrarily large.
- Bounded domain: in fact, the leakage function takes as input *only* the secret state during the invocation.

1.1 Our Contributions

In this work, we construct a secret sharing scheme for a given non-threshold access structure arising from linear correcting codes. The basic construction of our scheme relies on the following considerations: (1) Assume that a private channel exists in the distribution protocol of our protocol between every participant and the dealer and that all the participants have an individual broadcast channel. (2) Given the public key pk and l bits of secret key sk leakage, our protocol is performed between any probabilistic polynomial -time adversarial verifier V^* and an honest prover P, maintaining information-theoretic entropy and achieving security in the bounded-leakage model. (3) For any adversarial prover, the corresponding secret key of the emulated identity's public key should be known. (4) For one public key, the probability of an algorithm to find two distinct secret keys is negligible.

2 Preliminaries

Definition 1 *(Linear Codes).* *An* $[n, k]$ *code* C *is a* k-*dimensional linear subspace of* $\mathbb{F}_q^n$, *which means that the sum of the two codewords of* C *is a codeword and that the product of any codeword by a field element is a codeword.*

Definition 2 *(Generator Matrix).* *If* $\boldsymbol{g}_0, \boldsymbol{g}_0, \cdots, \boldsymbol{g}_{k-1}$ *is a basis for* $[n, k]$ *code* C, *where* $\boldsymbol{g}_i = (g_{i0}, g_{i1}, \cdots, g_{i,n-1})$, *for* $i = 0, 1, \cdots, k-1$, *then the matrix*

$$
G = \begin{pmatrix} \boldsymbol{g}_0 \\ \vdots \\ \boldsymbol{g}_{k-1} \end{pmatrix} = \begin{pmatrix} g_{00} & \cdots & g_{1,n-1} \\ \vdots & \ddots & \vdots \\ g_{k-1,1} & \cdots & g_{k-1,n-1} \end{pmatrix}
$$

is called a generator matrix of an $[n, k]$ *code* C.

Let $\mathscr{P}_n = \{P_1, \cdots, P_n\}$ be a set of n participants. The definition of (monotone) access structure is given as follows.

Definition 3 *(Access Structure, [13]).* *A set* $AS = \{A \subseteq 2^{\mathscr{P}_n} \mid A \text{ can reconstruct the secret}\}$ *is called an* access structure, *if it satisfies the* monotone *property, i.e.,*

$$
\text{for any } A' \in AS \text{ and } A' \subseteq A \subseteq 2^{\mathscr{P}_n}, \text{ it holds } A \in AS.
$$

Any subsets in AS are called *qualified* (or *authorized*), and the subsets that do not belong to AS are called *unqualified* (or *unauthorized*).

Definition 4 *(Leakage-resilient Secret Sharing, LRSS).* *We say scheme* $LRSS_{n,\rho} = (\mathsf{Share}_{n,\rho}, \mathsf{Recon}_{n,\rho})$ *is a leakage-resilient secret sharing scheme between dealer* D *and participant set* $\mathscr{P}_n = \{P_1, \cdots, P_n\}$, *if it satisfies*

- $(s_1, \cdots, s_n) \leftarrow \mathsf{Share}_{n,\rho}(m)$: *This probabilistic algorithm is performed by* D. *It takes as input a message* $m \in \{0, 1\}^N$ *and returns a sequence of shares* $s_1, \cdots, s_n$. *Each share* s_i $(1 \in [1, n])$ *with length* a, *where* $a, N \in \mathbb{N}$, $\rho \in \mathbb{N}$ *is the number of 'loops' that required to reconstruct the secret* s *for participants, one loop is a sequence of* n *(short) messages. Then,* D *issues share* s_i *to* P_i *for each* $i \in [1, n]$.
- $m \leftarrow \mathsf{Recon}_{n,\rho}(\mathsf{Share}_{n,\rho}(m))$: *This deterministic algorithm is executed among* $P_1, \cdots, P_n$ *in* $n\rho$ *rounds. It takes as input a sequence of shares* $s_1, \cdots, s_n$ *and outputs the correct message* m *in* $n\rho$ *rounds.*

Definition 5 *(Corruption Path Length).* *Let* $\mathscr{P}^b = \{P_{p_1}, \cdots, P_{p_b}\} \in \mathscr{P}_n$ *be a corruption set with* $b \in \mathbb{N}$ *participants. We write* $cpl(\mathscr{P}^b)$ *by the corruption path length of* $\mathscr{P}^b$, *which is described as the length of the maximal prefix of* $\mathscr{P}_n^*$ *and is the subset of* $\mathscr{P}^b$. *We say that* $\mathscr{P}^b$ *makes* ρ *loops, if there is* $cpl(\mathscr{P}^b)/n > \rho$.

Definition 6 *(l-Bounded Adversary).* *We say an adversary* $\mathscr{A}$ *is* l-*bounded, if the corruption set* $\mathscr{P}^b = \{P_{p_1}, \cdots, P_{p_b}\} \in \mathscr{P}_n$ *picked by* $\mathscr{A}$ *satisfies the following property: for per* $P_j \in \mathscr{P}^b$, *it holds* $\sum_i l_i \leqslant l$, *where* i *is a index such that* $P_{p_i} = P_j$, *and* l_i *denotes the length of the output an arbitrary (leakage) function* $f_i : \{0, 1\}^a \rightarrow \{0, 1\}^{l_i}$.

Definition 7 (Security of LRSS). *We say scheme $LRSS_{n,\rho}$ is (ε, l)-secure if every ρ-admissible l-bounded adversary $\mathscr{A}$ breaks $LRSS_{n,\rho}$ with an advantage at most ε, where ε is a small positive constant.*

Definition 8 (Multi-Prover Computational Zero-knowledge, [5]). *Let $(P_1, \ldots, P_n, V)$ be multi-prover interactive proof system with some language L. We say that $(P_1, \ldots, P_n, V)$ is computational zero-knowledge, if for every interactive PPT turning machine V^*, there exists a PPT machine $\mathscr{M}$ such that for all $x \in L$, two ensembles $View\{(P_1, \ldots, P_n, V^*)(x)\}_{x \in L}$ and $\{\mathscr{M}(x)\}_{x \in L}$ are computationally indistinguishable.*

Definition 9 (Leakage Oracle, [9]). *Let $\mathcal{O}_w^{\lambda, l}(\cdot)$ be a leakage oracle, which is parameterized by a prover's witness w and a leakage parameter l and a security parameter λ. A query to the leakage oracle is constitute by a leakage function $f_i : \{0,1\}^* \to \{0,1\}^{l_i}$, and the oracle answers with $f_i(w)$. The oracle $\mathcal{O}_w^{\lambda, l}(\cdot)$ is restricted in the total number of l bits. For all queries received, $\mathcal{O}_w^{\lambda, l}(\cdot)$ only responds to the jth leakage query and computes the function $f_i(w)$ for at most $poly(\cdot)$ steps if $\sum_{i=1}^{j} l_i \leqslant l$. Otherwise, the oracle ignores the queries.*

Definition 10 (Leakage-Resilient ID-Scheme). *Let $\{KeyGen, P, V\}$ be an ID-scheme, which is parametreized by security parameter λ and holds the property of completeness. We say $\{KeyGen, P, V\}$ is secure against the pre-emulation leakage l if the advantage of any PPT adversary $\mathscr{A}$ in the attack game $ID_{pre_l}^{\lambda}(\mathscr{A})$ is negligible in λ. Also, it is secure against the arbitrary time leakage l if the above adversary $\mathscr{A}$ for the attack game $ID_{arb_l}^{\lambda}(\mathscr{A})$ is negligible in λ.*

3 Our Protocol

3.1 PROTOCOL : Non-threshold Secret Sharing Scheme via Linear Codes

Initialization: Let λ be a security parameter and q be a large prime number, and p is a prime factor of $q-1$. Let $\mathbb{F}_q$ be a finite filed. We write $\langle g \rangle$ to indicate a cyclic group generated by an element $g \in \mathbb{F}_q^*$ with order $|\langle g \rangle| = p$, and $\langle g \rangle \subset \mathbb{F}_q^*$. Let C be a linear code over $\mathbb{F}_q$ with length $n+1$ and G be the generator matrix.

Distribution Protocol: This protocol is divided into two steps:

(1) Distribution of shares: D defines $s_0 = s$, calculates and publishes $B_0 = Enc(s_0)$ by a broadcast channel. To distribute the master secret key s_0 among n participants $P_1, \cdots, P_n$, D executes the following program of SECRET DISTRIBUTION:

$\qquad$ D's SECRET DISTRIBUTION ON INPUT (s_0, pk, B_0, G) :

$\qquad\qquad$ CHOOSE random $\mathbf{u} = (u_0, u_1, \cdots, u_{k-1}) \in \mathbb{F}_p^k$ such that $u_{k-1} = (s_0 - \sum_{j=0}^{k-2} u_j g_{j0})/g_{k-1,0} \pmod{p}$

$\qquad\qquad$ COMPUTE $B_j = g^{u_j} \bmod q$, where $j \in [1, k-1]$

CONSTRUCT a polynomial $s(x) = \sum_{j=0}^{k-1} u_j g_{jx} \pmod{p}$, where $x \in [0, n]$

COMPUTE $s(i) = \sum_{j=0}^{k-1} u_j g_{ji} \pmod{p}$ and set $sk_i = s_i = s(i)$, where $j \in [0, k-1]$.

PUBLISH B_j, where $j \in [1, k-1]$.

SEND s_i to P_i, where $i \in [1, n]$

(2) Verification of the shares: After receiving the share $sk_i = s_i$, every participant P_i performs $pk_i = g^{s_i} = B_0 \prod_{j=1}^{k-1} B_j^{g_{ji}} \pmod{q}$. If it is satisfied, then accepts the valid shares.

Proof Protocol: According to the above subprotocols, B_0, p, q, g, G are common inputs of $\mathscr{P}_n$ and V. Every participant $P_i \in \mathscr{P}_n$ has a secret input s_i for $i \in [1, n]$.

Let $\{P_{i_1}, P_{i_2}, \cdots, P_{i_m}\}$ be a size-m subset of $\mathscr{P}_n$, and every participant P_{i_j} has a secret input s_{i_j}, $j \in [1, m]$. If all of them have corresponding correct shares, then there is a polynomial function $F(\cdot)$, such that $F(s_{i_1}, s_{i_2}, \cdots, s_{i_m}) = \sum_{j=1}^{m} s_{i_j} c_j = s$, where i_j is an integer number and c_j can be computed publicly by $c_j = \prod_{1 \leqslant j, k \leqslant m, k \neq j} \frac{i_k}{i_k - i_j}$, according to the Lagrange interpolation function.

(1) Proof of the secret s: This step can be described as follows:

Step $P1$: Every participant P_{i_j} chooses random $r_j \in \mathbb{F}_p$, computes that $x_j = g^{r_j} \pmod{q}$, and sends x_j to V, where $j \in [1, m]$.

Step $V1$: V chooses a random number $t \in \{1, 2\}$, then sends t to all participants P_{i_j}, where $j \in [1, m]$.

Step $P2$: Every participant P_{i_j} computes $y_j = r_j - t c_j s_{i_j} \pmod{p}$, then sends y_j to V, where $j \in [1, m]$.

(2) Verification of the secret s:

Step $V2$: If it holds $g^{y_1 + y_2 + \cdots + y_m} B_0^t = \prod_{j=1}^{m} x_j \pmod{q}$, then V believes that $P_{i_1}, P_{i_2}, \cdots, P_{i_m}$ share the secret s satisfying $B_0 = g^s \pmod{q}$; otherwise V rejects it.

4 Security Analysis of PROTOCOL

4.1 Properties from PROTOCOL

The property of completeness and soundness are obviously satisfied. We only proof the property of zero-knowledge.

A passive verifier V does not choose randomly t_η in the η-th time when running the protocol. Thus, he can use some $\{0, 1\}$-valued function f to compute t_η in deterministic, polynomial time [6]. So, we define $f(p, q, g, B_0, G, h, V_{\eta-1}, x_{1,\eta}, \cdots, x_{n,\eta}) = t_\eta$, where h is a secret input; $V_{\eta-1}$ denotes all data of viewed when V executes the protocol in the $\eta - 1$-th time; $x_{1,\eta}, \cdots, x_{n,\eta}$ denote a message sent to V in Step $P1$ when running the PROTOCOL in the η-th time. Suppose a simulator $\mathscr{M}$ has constructed with the input p, q, g, h, B_0, G and successfully simulated the PROTOCOL for $\eta - 1$ times, then $\mathscr{M}$ will simulate the η-th time according to the following program.

DO FOREVER
  $t'_\eta :=$ a random umber of $\{1,2\}$
  $y_{i,\eta} :=$ a random number of $\mathbb{F}_p$ for $i \in [1,n]$
  $c_{i,\eta} :=$ a random number of $\mathbb{F}_p$ for $i \in [1, n-1]$
  $s_{i,\eta} :=$ a random number of $\mathbb{F}_p$ for $i \in [1, n-1]$
  COMPUTE $r_{i,\eta} := y_{i,\eta} + t'_\eta c_{i,\eta} s_{i,\eta} \pmod{p}$, $x_{i,\eta} := g^{r_{i,\eta}} \pmod{q}$
  for $i \in [1, n-1]$, and $x_{n,\eta} = \dfrac{g^{y_{1,\eta} + y_{2,\eta} + \cdots + y_{n,\eta}} B_0^{t'_\eta}}{\prod_{i=1}^{n-1} x_{i,\eta}} \pmod{q}$
  IF $t'_\eta = f(p, q, g, h, B_0, V_{\eta-1}, x_{1,\eta}, \cdots, x_{n,\eta})$ THEN
    OUTPUT $(x_{1,\eta}, x_{2,\eta}, \cdots, x_{n,\eta}, t'_\eta, y_{1,\eta}, y_{2,\eta}, \cdots, y_{n,\eta})$ and HALT
  ELSE
    GO back to the first step and repeat again
END DO

According to the Definition 8, we can get the fact that if two ensembles $\mathcal{M}(p, q, g, h, B_0, G)$ and $\mathrm{View}\{(P_1(c_1 s_1), \cdots, P_n(c_n s_n)), V(h)\}(p, q, g, B_0, G)$ are *computational indistinguishability*, then the protocol which we constructed is zero-knowledge. Hence, to prove $\mathcal{M}(p, q, g, h, B_0, G)$ and $\mathrm{View}\{(P_1(c_1 s_1), \cdots, P_n(c_n s_n)), V(h)\}(p, q, g, B_0, G)$ are *computational indistinguishability*, we use mathematical induction method to perform the following steps:

1. Assume that the probability of Out_{V_η} is denoted by $P_{\mathcal{M}V,\eta}$ if $\mathrm{Out}_{V_\eta} \subseteq \mathcal{M}(p, q, g, h, B_0, G)$; the probability of Out_{V_η} is denoted by $P_{P_1,P_2,\cdots,P_n,V,\eta}$ if $\mathrm{Out}_{V_\eta} \subseteq \mathrm{View}\{(P_1(c_1 s_1), \cdots, P_n(c_n s_n)), V(h)\}(p, q, g, B_0, G)$

2. When $\eta = 0$, it is the initial state of interactive proof system $(P_1, \cdots, P_n, V)$ and turning machine $\mathcal{M}$. Hence, Out_{V_0} and $\mathcal{M}$ are the empty set. There is $Pr_{\mathcal{M}V,0} = Pr_{P_1,P_2,\cdots,P_n,V,0}$ and $|Pr_{\mathcal{M}V,0} - Pr_{P_1,P_2,\cdots,P_n,V,0}| < \varepsilon$, where $\varepsilon > 0$ is an arbitrarily small constant.

3. In the $\eta-1$-th operation, we assume that $|Pr_{\mathcal{M}V,\eta-1} - Pr_{P_1,P_2,\cdots,P_n,V,\eta-1}| < \varepsilon$ is satisfied for each $\eta \geqslant 1$.

4. In the η-th operation, we consider two models:
In fact, t_η and t'_η, $y_{1,\eta}, \cdots, y_{n,\eta}$ are selected randomly and independently, the case $t = 1$ yields that $Pr_{P_1,P_2,\cdots,Pr_n,V,\eta} = P_{P_1,P_2,\cdots,P_n,V,\eta-1} \cdot \frac{\vartheta}{p^n}$, and $t = 2$ results in $Pr_{P_1,P_2,\cdots,Pr_n,V,\eta} = Pr_{P_1,P_2,\cdots,P_n,V,\eta-1} \cdot \frac{1-\vartheta}{p^n}$.
Suppose in the $(\eta-1)$-th time $|Pr_{\mathcal{M}V,\eta-1} - Pr_{P_1,P_2,\cdots,P_n,V,\eta-1}| < \varepsilon$, then in the η-th time, we have

$$|Pr_{\mathcal{M}V,\eta} - Pr_{P_1,P_2,\cdots,P_n,V,\eta}|$$

$$= \left| Pr_{P_1,P_2,\cdots,P_n,V,\eta-1} \cdot \frac{\vartheta}{p^n} - Pr_{P_1,P_2,\cdots,P_n,V,\eta-1} \cdot \frac{1-\vartheta}{p^n} \right|$$

$$= |Pr_{\mathcal{M}V,\eta-1} - Pr_{P_1,P_2,\cdots,P_n,V,\eta-1}| \cdot \frac{\max\{\vartheta, 1-\vartheta\}}{p^n}$$

$$= \varepsilon \cdot \frac{\max\{\vartheta, 1-\vartheta\}}{p^n},$$

this is a negligible amount, so we know $\mathcal{M}(p, q, g, h, B_0, G)$ and $\mathrm{View}\{(P_1(c_1 s_1), \cdots, P_1(c_n s_n)), V(h)\}(p, q, g, B_0, G)$ are computational indistinguishability.

4.2   Theorems from PROTOCOL 2

Theorem 1. _PROTOCOL 2 is n-prover computational zero-knowledge proof system._

Proof. According to the context of Sect. 4.1, PROTOCOL satisfies completeness, soundness, zero-knowledge, and also satisfies the Definition 8. Consequently, PROTOCOL is n-prover computational zero-knowledge proof system.

Theorem 2. _Under the Discrete Logarithm assumption, PROTOCOL is LRSS$_{n,\rho}$ scheme, which is (ε, l)-secure._

5   Group Identification via PROTOCOL

We can construct a group identification protocol GID-scheme with the following properties: only for the qualified group members, their valid identities can be believed by the verifier, but not for the unqualified members; the verifier gains nothing except believing that the qualified members have valid identities.

According to the work presented in [4], our GID-scheme is secure against (classical) passive attacks.

Theorem 3. _Let_ (ParGen, KeyGen _ba a GID-scheme and_ $\mathscr{R} = \{(\bar{pk}, \bar{sk}) | \bar{sk} = \{s_0\} \cup \{s_i\}_{i=1}^n, \bar{pk} = \{pk_0\} \cup \{pk_i = g^{sk_i} \bmod q\}_{i=1}^n\}$ _be a hard relation with key generator_ KeyGen. _We write_ $(\mathscr{P}_n, V)$ _to denote the prover set and the verifier in a sigma-protocol for_ $\mathscr{R}$ _with 2-bit challenges. Suppose the_ $\sum$-_protocol is complete, 2-special sound, and honest verifier zero-knowledge. Then our GID-scheme is secure against emulation under (classical) passive attacks._

In the bounded-leakage model, we have the following theorem.

Theorem 4. _Under the Discrete Logarithm assumption, our GID-scheme is secure for pre-emulation leakage of up to_ $l = (n-1)log(q) - \lambda \geqslant (1 - \frac{2}{n})|sk|$ _bits. It is secure against arbitrary time leakage attack with_ $l^* = \frac{1}{2}l$ _bits._

6   Conclusions and Future Work

We proposed a non-threshold secret sharing scheme realizing a non-threshold access structure based on linear codes. According to the definitions of zero-knowledge proof system and security model, we proved that our protocol is a multi-prover zero-knowledge proof system and (ε, l)-secure LRSS scheme. In our LRSS scheme, the secret key can be repeatedly shared as many times as desired, and the security is guaranteed even though the adversary learns an amount of information bound by l bits.

Meanwhile, we presented a GID-scheme from our LRSS scheme, and it is leakage-resilient under the leakage attacks $\mathrm{ID}_{\mathrm{pre}_l}^{\lambda}(\mathscr{A})$ and $\mathrm{ID}_{\mathrm{arb}_l}^{\lambda}(\mathscr{A})$. In our leakage-resilient GID scheme, any authorized participant sets can prove to a verifier that they share the secret key without leaking any information about their individual shares to a passive adversary, and can guarantee security even though l bits are retrieved by the malicious adversary; any authorized participants can prove themselves to keep the corresponding valid secret share.

References

1. Ajtai, M.: Secure computation with information leaking to an adversary. In: Proceedings of the Forty-Third Annual ACM Symposium on Theory of Computing, pp. 715–724. ACM (2011)
2. Blakley, G.R., et al.: Safeguarding cryptographic keys. In: Proceedings of the National Computer Conference, vol. 48, pp. 313–317 (1979)
3. Dziembowski, S., Pietrzak, K.: Leakage-resilient cryptography. In: 2008 IEEE 49th Annual IEEE Symposium on Foundations of Computer Science, FOCS 2008, pp. 293–302. IEEE (2008)
4. Galbraith, S.D., Petit, C., Silva, J.: Identification protocols and signature schemes based on supersingular isogeny problems. In: Takagi, T., Peyrin, T. (eds.) ASIACRYPT 2017. LNCS, vol. 10624, pp. 3–33. Springer, Cham (2017). https://doi.org/10.1007/978-3-319-70694-8_1
5. Goldreich, O.: Foundations of cryptography (fragments of a book) (1995)
6. Goldwasser, S., Micali, S., Rackoff, C.: The knowledge complexity of interactive proof systems. SIAM J. Comput. **18**(1), 186–208 (1989)
7. Goldwasser, S., Rothblum, G.N.: Securing computation against continuous leakage. In: Rabin, T. (ed.) CRYPTO 2010. LNCS, vol. 6223, pp. 59–79. Springer, Heidelberg (2010). https://doi.org/10.1007/978-3-642-14623-7_4
8. Goyal, V., Kumar, A.: Non-malleable secret sharing for general access structures. In: Shacham, H., Boldyreva, A. (eds.) CRYPTO 2018. LNCS, vol. 10991, pp. 501–530. Springer, Cham (2018). https://doi.org/10.1007/978-3-319-96884-1_17
9. Hazay, C., López-Alt, A., Wee, H., Wichs, D.: Leakage-resilient cryptography from minimal assumptions. J. Cryptol. **29**(3), 514–551 (2016)
10. Karchmer, M., Wigderson, A.: On span programs. In: Proceeding of the 8th IEEE Structure in Complexity Theory, pp. 102–111 (1993)
11. Kiltz, E., Pietrzak, K.: Leakage resilient elgamal encryption. In: Abe, M. (ed.) ASIACRYPT 2010. LNCS, vol. 6477, pp. 595–612. Springer, Heidelberg (2010). https://doi.org/10.1007/978-3-642-17373-8_34
12. Komargodski, I., Paskin-Cherniavsky, A.: Evolving secret sharing: dynamic thresholds and robustness. In: Kalai, Y., Reyzin, L. (eds.) TCC 2017. LNCS, vol. 10678, pp. 379–393. Springer, Cham (2017). https://doi.org/10.1007/978-3-319-70503-3_12
13. Okada, K., Kurosawa, K.: MDS secret-sharing scheme secure against cheaters. IEEE Trans. Inf. Theory **46**(3), 1078–1081 (2000)
14. Shamir, A.: How to share a secret. Commun. ACM **22**(11), 612–613 (1979)

A Standard Model Secure Verifiably Encrypted Signature Scheme Based on Dual System

Pengtao Liu[✉]

College of Cyberspace Security, Shandong University of Political Science
and Law, Jinan, China
ptwave@163.com

Abstract. In this paper, we propose a new standard-model verifiably encrypted signature scheme (VES) based on dual system. The VES scheme is provably secure under the decisional Bilinear Diffie-Hellman and decisional Linear assumptions. Our security proof is based on a newly-introduced strategy called dual system by Waters. In our proof, we divide the signature space into two types and prove that neither type of the signature could be forged or extracted by defining a game sequences in which we can change the query signatures from one type to another one by one without the notice of the adversary.

Keywords: Verifiably encrypted signature · Standard model · Dual system · Opacity · Unforgeability

1 Introduction

Verifiably encrypted signature was first introduced in 1998 by Asokan [1], its first and major usage is in optimistic fair exchange. Following Asokan's pioneering optimistic fair exchange protocol which involve highly intricate interactive ZK proof, lots of VES schemes in the random oracle model have been proposed with only NIZK proof. In 2003, Boneh et al. [2] proposed a non-interactive VES scheme via signature aggregation based on pairings and Zhang et al. [3] proposed a VES scheme derived from their own pairing-based signature [4]. Subsequently, many works have been proposed to construct a VES without random oracle. A standard model secure VES derived from Waters' signature [5] was proposed by Lu et al. [6] in 2006, and in 2007, Zhang et al. [7] proposed another VES scheme which is also derived from Waters' signature [5]. Both VES schemes above have large public parameters. Yet Zhang et al. [7] have not provided a sound security proof. In 2009, Ruckert and Schroder [8] proposed a VES from multilinear maps which has not yet been proved to be constructable. In 2015, Hanser et al. [9] proposed a standard model secure VES scheme from structure-preserving signatures on equivalence classes. Some works also add new attributes to the VES scheme, such as [10] and [11].

Recently, Waters [12] introduced a novel strategy to construct security proof in the standard model. Nishimaki and Xagawa [13] proposed a standard model VES scheme with short keys based on Waters' scheme. In this paper, we also explore Waters' new

© Springer Nature Switzerland AG 2019
J. Vaidya et al. (Eds.): CSS 2019, LNCS 11983, pp. 242–252, 2019.
https://doi.org/10.1007/978-3-030-37352-8_21

strategy and construct a new VES which is fully secure under the decisional Bilinear Diffie-Hellman and decisional Linear assumptions. Our VES scheme is a standard model VES scheme with short system parameters whose signature consists of a constant number of group elements. Specifically, our scheme has shorter verification key compared with that in [13]. In our proof, we have two types of signatures and prove that neither type of the signature could be forged or extracted by defining a sequence of games where we can change the query signatures from one type to another one by one without the notice of the adversary.

The rest of this paper is organized as follows. First, some preliminaries are given in Sect. 2. Then in Sect. 3, we present our VES scheme with its security proof. Section 4 concludes our work.

2 Preliminaries

In this Section, we present some relevant complexity assumptions. In order to save spaces, we omit here the description of bilinear groups [12] and the model of Verifiably Encrypted Signature [13].

2.1 Decisional Bilinear Diffie-Hellman Assumption [12]

Let g be a generator of group G of prime order p. Let $e : G \times G \to G_T$ be a bilinear map. Select three random elements $c_1, c_2, c_3 \in Z_p$. Given $\vec{T} = (g, g^{c_1}, g^{c_2}, g^{c_3})$, it is hard to distinguish $e(g, g)^{c_1 c_2 c_3}$ from a random element R in G_T.

Let D be an algorithm to distinguish $e(g, g)^{c_1 c_2 c_3}$ from R with advantage ϵ, i.e.,

$$\epsilon = \left| Pr[D(\vec{T}, e(g, g)^{c_1 c_1 c_3}) = 0] - Pr[D(\vec{T}, R) = 0] \right|$$

Definition 1. We say that the decisional BDH assumption holds if for all polynomial-time algorithms D, ϵ is negligible.

2.2 Decisional Linear Assumption [12]

Let g, f, μ be generators of group G of prime order p. Select two random elements $c_1, c_2 \in Z_p$. Given $\vec{T} = (g, f, \mu, g^{c_1}, f^{c_2})$, it is hard to distinguish $\mu^{c_1 + c_2}$ from a random element R in G.

Let D be an algorithm to distinguish $\mu^{c_1 + c_2}$ from R with advantage ϵ, i.e.,

$$\epsilon = \left| Pr[D(\vec{T}, \mu^{c_1 + c_2}) = 0] - Pr[D(\vec{T}, R) = 0] \right|$$

Definition 2. We say that the decisional Linear assumption holds if for all polynomial-time algorithms D, ϵ is negligible.

3 Our Scheme

We now present our verifiably encrypted signature scheme along with our proof of its security.

3.1 The Concrete Scheme

VES.Setup. The setup algorithm first chooses groups G, G_T of prime order p, for which there exists an admissible bilinear pairing $e : G \times G \to G_T$. And choose randomly a generator $g \in G$.

VES.SignKGen. The signer's key generation algorithm chooses randomly generators $v, v_1, v_2, \omega, u, h \in G$ and exponents $a_1, a_2, b, \alpha \in Z_p$. Let $\tau_1 = v v_1^{a_1}$, $\tau_2 = v v_2^{a_2}$. The public key is

$$PK = \left\{ g, g^b, g^{a_1}, g^{a_2}, g^{ba_1}, g^{ba_2}, \tau_1, \tau_2, \tau_1^b, \tau_2^b, \omega, u, h, e(g,g)^{\alpha a_1 b} \right\},$$

and the private key is $SK = \{ g^\alpha, g^{\alpha a_1}, v, v_1, v_2 \}$. The message space is Z_p.

VES.Sign(SK, M). The signature algorithm chooses random $r_1, r_2, z_1, z_2, tag_k \in Z_p$. Let $r = r_1 + r_2$. Then calculate $\sigma_1 = g^{\alpha a_1} v^r$, $\sigma_2 = g^{-\alpha} v_1^r g^{z_1}$, $\sigma_3 = \left(g^b \right)^{-z_1}$, $\sigma_4 = v_2^r g^{z_2}$, $\sigma_5 = \left(g^b \right)^{-z_2}$, $\sigma_6 = g^{r_2 b}$, $\sigma_7 = g^{r_1}$, $\sigma_k = \left(u^M \omega^{tag_k} h \right)^{r_1}$. The signature is

$$\sigma = (\sigma_1, \sigma_2, \sigma_3, \sigma_4, \sigma_5, \sigma_6, \sigma_7, \sigma_k, tag_k).$$

VES.Verify(PK, σ, M). The verification algorithm first chooses random s_1, s_2, t, and $tag_c \in Z_p$ where $tag_c \neq tag_k$. Let $s = s_1 + s_2$. It creates $C_1 = \left(g^b \right)^{s_1 + s_2}$, $C_2 = \left(g^{ba_1} \right)^{s_1}$, $C_3 = \left(g^{a_1} \right)^{s_1}$, $C_4 = \left(g^{ba_2} \right)^{s_2}$, $C_5 = \left(g^{a_2} \right)^{s_2}$, $C_6 = \tau_1^{s_1} \tau_2^{s_2}$, $C_7 = \left(\tau_1^b \right)^{s_1} \left(\tau_2^b \right)^{s_2} \omega^{-t}$, $E_1 = \left(u^M \omega^{tag_c} h \right)^t$, $E_2 = g^t$. Then it computes:

$$A_1 = e(C_1, \sigma_1) e(C_2, \sigma_2) e(C_3, \sigma_3) e(C_4, \sigma_4) e(C_5, \sigma_5), \quad A_2 = e(C_6, \sigma_6) e(C_7, \sigma_7)$$

Let $A_3 = A_1 / A_2$. Then the verification algorithm computes

$$A_4 = \left(e(E_1, \sigma_7) / e(E_2, \sigma_k) \right)^{1/(tag_c - tag_k)}.$$

Finally, it tests the following equation $\left(e(g,g)^{\alpha a_1 b} \right)^{s_2} = A_3 / A_4$ and outputs "1" if the equation holds meaning that the VES signature is valid. Otherwise, it outputs "0".

VES.AdjKGen. The adjudicator-key generate algorithm chooses randomly $S_a \in Z_p$, and set public key $APK = g^{S_a}$, private key $ASK = S_a$.

VES.ESign(APK, SK, M). The verifiably encrypted signature algorithm randomly chooses $r_1, r_2, z_1, z_2, tag_k \in Z_p$. Let $r = r_1 + r_2$. Then calculate $\sigma_1 = g^{\alpha a_1} v^r$,

$\sigma_2 = g^{-\alpha}v_1^r g^{z_1}$, $\sigma_3 = (g^b)^{-z_1}$, $\sigma_4 = v_2^r g^{z_2}$, $\sigma_5 = (g^b)^{-z_2}$, $\sigma_6 = g^{r_2 b}$, $\sigma_7 = g^{r_1}$,

$\sigma_k = (u^M \omega^{tag_k} h \cdot APK)^{r_1}$. The signature is $\sigma = (\sigma_1, \sigma_2, \sigma_3, \sigma_4, \sigma_5, \sigma_6, \sigma_7, \sigma_k, tag_k)$.

VES.Everify(PK, APK, σ, M). The verification algorithm first chooses random s_1, s_2, t, and $tag_c \in Z_p$ where $tag_c \neq tag_k$. Let $s = s_1 + s_2$. It creates $C_1 = (g^b)^{s_1 + s_2}$, $C_2 = (g^{ba_1})^{s_1}$, $C_3 = (g^{a_1})^{s_1}$, $C_4 = (g^{ba_2})^{s_2}$, $C_5 = (g^{a_2})^{s_2}$, $C_6 = \tau_1^{s_1} \tau_2^{s_2}$, $C_7 = (\tau_1^b)^{s_1}$ $(\tau_2^b)^{s_2} \omega^{-t}$, $E_1 = (u^M \omega^{tag_c} h)^t$, $E_2 = g^t$. Then it computes:

$$A_1 = e(C_1, \sigma_1)e(C_2, \sigma_2)e(C_3, \sigma_3)e(C_4, \sigma_4)e(C_5, \sigma_5), \quad A_2 = e(C_6, \sigma_6)e(C_7, \sigma_7)$$

Let $A_3 = A_1/A_2$. Then the verification algorithm computes $A_4 = (e(E_1, \sigma_7)$ $e(APK, \sigma_7^t)/e(E_2, \sigma_k))^{1/(tag_c - tag_k)}$. Finally, it tests the following equation $\left(e(g, g)^{\alpha a_1 b}\right)^{s_2} = A_3/A_4$ and outputs "1" if the equation holds meaning that the VES signature is valid. Otherwise, it outputs "0".

VES.Adjudicate(ASK, PK, σ, M). The adjudicate algorithm first verify the validity of σ, if rejected, the algorithm output $\perp$. Else, it calculates $\sigma_k' = \sigma_k/(\sigma_7^{ASK})$ and keeps other elements unchanged. The algorithm outputs a new signature $\sigma' = (\sigma_1, \sigma_2, \sigma_3, \sigma_4, \sigma_5, \sigma_6, \sigma_7, \sigma_k', tag_k)$.

3.2 Proof of Security

Correctness. The correctness of the VES.Verify algorithm is obviously trivial. The correctness of the VES.Adjudicate algorithm follows from the fact that all the temporary values calculated out in both the VES.Verify and the VES.EVerify algorithms are equal. Given a valid verifiably encrypted signature σ, it satisfies that

$$A_4 = \left(e(E_1, \sigma_7)e(APK, \sigma_7^t)/e(E_2, \sigma_k)\right)^{1/(tag_c - tag_k)}$$
$$= \left(e(E_1, \sigma_7)/e\left(E_2, \sigma_k'\right)\right)^{1/(tag_c - tag_k)}$$

So, if a signature σ is accepted by VES.EVerify algorithm, then its adjudicated version σ' would definitely be accepted by VES.Verify algorithm.

Unforgeability. The Unforgeability of this VES scheme comes handily from the unforgeability of Waters' dual system signature scheme.

Theorem 1. *If Waters' dual system signature scheme is unforgeable, then our verifiably encrypted signature scheme is unforgeable.*

Proof. Assume that A is an adversary who can $(t, q_{es}, q_{adj}, \epsilon)$-break the unforgeability of our scheme, then we can construct an algorithm B which can (t', q_s, ϵ)-break the unforgeability of Waters' dual system signature scheme, where $t' = t + O(q_{es} + q_{adj})$ and $q_s = q_{es}$.

When playing the unforgeability game of waters' original dual system signature scheme, algorithm B is given all the public parameters, then B takes these public parameters as the public parameters in our scheme and runs the VES.AdjKGen to get adjudicator's key (ASK, APK). B give all the public parameters and adjudicator's public key APK to the adversary A.

- VES.ESign query. When the adversary A makes VES.ESign queries, B forwards the query parameters to the signing oracle in waters' game, and get a signature $\sigma = (\sigma_1, \sigma_2, \sigma_3, \sigma_4, \sigma_5, \sigma_6, \sigma_7, \sigma_k, tag_k)$, then B set $\sigma'_k = \sigma_k \sigma_7^{ASK}$, and output a verifiably encrypted signature $\sigma' = (\sigma_1, \sigma_2, \sigma_3, \sigma_4, \sigma_5, \sigma_6, \sigma_7, \sigma'_k, tag_k)$.
- VES.Adjudicate query. When the adversary A makes VES.Adjudicate queries, B runs the VES.Adjudicate algorithm and output its result.

Output: Finally, the adversary A forges a VES signature σ^* on a message M^*, then the algorithm B could run the VES.Adjudicate algorithm on σ^* and M^*, and get a forged normal signature on M^* which has not been submitted to the signing oracle in Waters' game. Hence the algorithm B could break the unforgeability of the Waters' dual system signature scheme.

Opacity. To prove the opacity security, we partition the whole normal signature space into two different types and argue that an adversary could not extract a normal signature of either type. First, we define a new verification algorithm and divide the normal signature space into two part using the new verification algorithm.

VES.SemiVerify(PK, σ, M). The semi-verification algorithm first chooses randomly x, s_1, s_2, t, and $tag_c \in Z_p$ where $tag_c \neq tag_k$. Let $s = s_1 + s_2$. It creates $C_1 = (g^b)^{s_1 + s_2}$, $C_2 = (g^{ba_1})^{s_1}$, $C_3 = (g^{a_1})^{s_1}$, $C_4 = (g^{ba_2})^{s_2} g^{ba_2x}$, $C_5 = (g^{a_2})^{s_2} g^{a_2x}$, $C_6 = \tau_1^{s_1} \tau_2^{s_2} v_2^{a_2x}$, $C_7 = (\tau_1^b)^{s_1} (\tau_2^b)^{s_2} \omega^{-t} v_2^{a_2bx}$, $E_1 = (u^M \omega^{tag_c} h)^t$, $E_2 = g^t$. Then it computes

$$A_1 = e(C_1, \sigma_1) e(C_2, \sigma_2) e(C_3, \sigma_3) e(C_4, \sigma_4) e(C_5, \sigma_5), A_2 = e(C_6, \sigma_6) e(C_7, \sigma_7)$$

Let $A_3 = A_1/A_2$. Then the verification algorithm computes $A_4 = (e(E_1, \sigma_7)/e(E_2, \sigma_k))^{1/(tag_c - tag_k)}$. Finally, it tests the following equation

$$\left(e(g, g)^{\alpha a_1 b} \right)^{s_2} = A_3/A_4$$

and outputs "1" if the equation holds meaning that the VES signature is valid. Otherwise, it outputs "0". Notice that to run VES.SemiVerify, a secret $v_2^{a_2b}$ is needed. Together with VES.Verify, we can divide normal signatures into two types.

1. **Type A* normal signatures.** The signature that could be accepted by both VES. Verify and VES.SemiVerify with significant probability.
2. **Type B* normal signatures.** The signature that could be accepted by VES.Verify with significant probability and be accepted by VES.SemiVerify with negligible probability.

And we define two concrete types of signatures which could be used in our proof.

1. **Type A normal signature** and **type A verifiably encrypted signature**
   As defined in the VES.Sign and VES.ESign algorithm. It could be easily verified that a type A normal signature is also a type A* normal signature and has 100% probability of being accepted by verify algorithms.
2. **Type B normal signature** and **type B verifiably encrypted signature**
   Taken a type A normal signature or a type A verifiably encrypted signature σ, choose randomly a value $\gamma \in Z_p$ and compute $\sigma'_1 = \sigma_1 g^{-a_1 a_2 \gamma}$, $\sigma'_2 = \sigma_2 g^{a_2 \gamma}$, $\sigma'_4 = \sigma_4 g^{a_1 \gamma}$. The type B signature is $\sigma' = (\sigma'_1, \sigma'_2, \sigma_3, \sigma'_4, \sigma_5, \sigma_6, \sigma_7, \sigma_k, tag_k)$. It could be easily verified that a type B normal signature is also a type B* normal signature and has 100% probability of being accepted by VES.Verify.

And we define a new game here

Game(i,j): Similar to the opacity game defined in Sect. 2, except that

1. The first i VES.ESign queries always yield type B verifiably encrypted signature and the other VES.ESign queries always yield type A verifiably encrypted signature.
2. The first j VES.Adjudicate queries always yield type B normal signature and the other VES.Adjudicate queries always yield type A normal signature.

Notice that Game($0,0$) is the real opacity game.

Lemma 1. No adversary could produce type B* normal signature in game($0,0$), where the VES.ESign gives out only type A verifiably encrypted signature and VES.Adjudicate gives out only type A normal signature.

Proof. Assume that there exists an algorithm A that makes at most q_s VES.ESign queries and q_{adj} VES.Adjudicate queries and has non-negligible chance of ϵ to forge a type B* normal signature which would be accepted by verify algorithms with non-negligible probability ε in game($0,0$), then we can build an algorithm B that has advantage $\epsilon \cdot \varepsilon$ in the decision linear game. Given $(g, f, \mu, g^{c_1}, f^{c_2}, T)$, the algorithm B wants to decide whether T is equal to $\mu^{c_1 + c_2}$ or T is just a random element in G.

Setup. The algorithm B chooses randomly $b, \alpha, y_v, y_{v1}, y_{v2} \in Z_p$ and $u, \omega, h, Q \in G$. It then sets $g^{a_1} = f, g^{a_2} = \mu$, $g^{ba_1} = f^b, g^{ba_2} = \mu^b, v = g^{y_v}, v_1 = g^{y_{v1}}, v_2 = g^{y_{v2}}$. And calculate $\tau_1, \tau_2, \tau_1^b, \tau_2^b$ and $e(g,g)^{aa_1 b} = e(g,f)^{ab}$ in order to publish the public key PK, and the adjudicator's public key $APK = Q$.

VES.ESign. Since the algorithm B has the secret key SK, it can run the VES.ESign and output the signature.

VES.Adjudicate. Since the algorithm B has the secret key SK, it can run the VES. Sign and output the signature.

Output. The algorithm A outputs a type B* normal signature $M, \sigma = (\sigma_1, \sigma_2, \sigma_3, \sigma_4, \sigma_5, \sigma_6, \sigma_7, \sigma_k, tag_k)$, then B random choose $s_1, s_2, t, tag_c \in Z_p$, where $\text{tag}_c \neq \text{tag}_k$ set $s = s_1 + s_2$ and calculate $C_1 = (g^b)^{s_1+s_2}(g^{c_1})^b$, $C_2 = (g^{ba_1})^{s_1}(f^{c_2})^{-b}$, $C_3 = (g^{a_1})^{s_1}f^{-c_2}$, $C_4 = (g^{ba_2})^{s_2}T^b$, $C_5 = (g^{a_2})^{s_2}T$, $C_6 = \tau_1^{s_1}\tau_2^{s_2}(g^{c_1})^{y_v}$ $(f^{c_2})^{-y_{v1}}T^{y_{v2}}$, $C_7 = (\tau_1^b)^{s_1}(\tau_2^b)^{s_2}\omega^{-t}((g^{c_1})^{y_v}(f^{c_2})^{-y_{v1}}T^{y_{v2}})^b$, $E_1 = (u^M\omega^{tag_c}h)^t$, $E_2 = g^t$; $A_1 = e(C_1,\sigma_1)e(C_2,\sigma_2)e(C_3,\sigma_3)e(C_4,\sigma_4)e(C_5,\sigma_5)$, $A_2 = e(C_6,\sigma_6)e(C_7,\sigma_7)$, $A_3 = A_1/A_2$, $A_4 = (e(E_1,\sigma_7)/e(E_2,\sigma_k))^{1/(tag_c-tag_k)}$. If the equation $\left(e(g,g)^{\alpha a_1 b}\right)^{s_2}$ $(e(g^{c_1},f)e(g,f^{c_2}))^{ba} = A_3/A_4$ holds, then T is equal to $\mu^{c_1+c_2}$ and the construction above is the same as in VES.Verify algorithm, else T is random and the construction above is the same as in VES.SemiVerify algorithm, and algorithm B solve the decision linear problem. Notice that the construction above is either a VES.Verify or a VES. SemiVerify with the implicit value $s_1' = s_1 - c_2$ and $s_2' = s_2 + c_1 + c_2$.

Lemma 2. No adversary could distinguish game$(k,0)$ from game$(k+1,0)$.

Proof. Assume that there exists an algorithm A that makes at most q_{es} VES.ESign queries and q_{adj} VES.Adjudicate queries and has non-negligible chance of ϵ to distinguish game$(k,0)$ from game$(k+1,0)$, then we can build an algorithm B that has advantage ϵ in the decision linear game. Given $(g,f,\mu,g^{c_1},f^{c_2},T)$, the algorithm B wants to decide whether T is equal to $\mu^{c_1+c_2}$ or T is just a random element in G.

Setup. Algorithm B first chooses randomly $\alpha, a_1, a_2, y_{v1}, y_{v2}, y_\omega, y_u, y_h$. And it sets $g^b = f$, $g^{ba_1} = f^{a_1}$, $g^{ba_2} = f^{a_2}$, $v = \mu^{-a_1a_2}$, $v_1 = \mu^{a_2}g^{y_{v1}}$, $v_2 = \mu^{a_1}g^{y_{v2}}$, $e(g,g)^{\alpha a_1 b} = e(f,g)^{\alpha a_1}$. Then algorithm B can create $\tau_1 = vv_1^{a_1} = g^{y_{v1}a_1}$, $\tau_2 = vv_2^{a_2} = g^{y_{v2}a_2}$, $\tau_1^b = f^{y_{v1}a_1}$, $\tau_2^b = f^{y_{v2}a_2}$. Finally, B chooses randomly $s, A, B \in Z_p$ and sets $\omega = fg^{y_\omega}$, $u = f^{-A}g^{y_u}$, $h = f^{-B}g^{y_h}$, $Q = g^s$ in order to publish all the public parameters of the system PK and the adjudicator's public key $APK = Q$. Note that although B knows the secret key of the adjudicator here, the importance here is not to break the opacity but to distinguish the two games.

VES.ESign. We break the VES.ESign queries into three cases. Consider the i-th query made by A.

Case 1: $i > k+1$. Since B has the secret key SK, it could run the VES.ESign to produce a type A verifiably encrypted signature.

Case 2: $i < k+1$. Since B has the secret key SK and $g^{a_1a_2}$, it could produce a type B verifiably encrypted signature.

Case 3: $i = k+1$. B first runs the VES.ESign to generate a type A verifiably encrypted signature $M, \sigma = (\sigma_1, \sigma_2, \sigma_3, \sigma_4, \sigma_5, \sigma_6, \sigma_7, \sigma_k, tag_k)$ where $tag_k = A*M+B$, let r_1, r_2, z_1, z_2 be the random exponents used in VES.ESign algorithm. It then sets $\sigma_1' = \sigma_1 T^{-a_1a_2}$, $\sigma_2' = \sigma_2 T^{a_2}(g^{c_1})^{y_{v1}}$, $\sigma_3' = \sigma_3(f^{c_2})^{y_{v1}}$, $\sigma_4' = \sigma_4 T^{a_1}(g^{c_1})^{y_{v2}}$, $\sigma_5' = \sigma_5(f^{c_2})^{y_{v2}}$, $\sigma_6' = \sigma_6 f^{c_2}$, $\sigma_7' = \sigma_7(g^{c_1})$, $\sigma_k' = \sigma_k(g^{c_1})^{M*y_u+y_h+tag_k*y_\omega+s}$, and return the new signature $M, \sigma' = (\sigma_1', \sigma_2', \sigma_3', \sigma_4', \sigma_5', \sigma_6', \sigma_7', \sigma_k', tag_k)$. If T is equal to $\mu^{c_1+c_2}$, then this new signature is a type A verifiably encrypted signature under randomness $r_1' = r_1 + c_1$ and $r_2' = r_2 + c_2$. Otherwise, if T is random, then we can write $T = \mu^{c_1+c_2}g^r$ for random $r \in Z_p$. This is a type B verifiably encrypted signature where r is the added randomness.

VES.Adjudicate. Since B has the secret key SK, it could run the VES.Sign algorithm to produce a type A normal signature.

Output. If algorithm A decides that the game constructed above is game$(k, 0)$, then B could claim that T is equal to $\mu^{c_1 + c_2}$, otherwise B could claim that T is a random group element.

Lemma 3. If an adversary could produce a type A* normal signature in game$(k, 0)$, then it could also produce a type A* normal signature in game$(k+1, 0)$.

Proof. If there is an adversary who can produce a type A* normal signature in game $(k, 0)$ but could not produce any normal signature in game$(k+1, 0)$, we can easily construct a algorithm to distinguish game$(k, 0)$ from game$(k+1, 0)$ and break Lemma 2 above. So we only need to prove that under this condition the adversary could not produce a type B* normal signature in game$(k+1, 0)$.

Assume that the adversary A has non-negligible chance of ϵ to produce a type A* normal signature which would be accepted by verifying algorithms with non-negligible probability ε in game$(k, 0)$ and had non-negligible chance of ϵ' to produce a type B* normal signature which would be accepted by veirfing algorithms with non-negligible probability ε' in game$(k+1, 0)$, then we can build an algorithm B that has advantage $\epsilon \cdot \varepsilon \cdot \epsilon' \cdot \varepsilon'$ in the decision linear game. Given $(g, f, \mu, g^{c_1}, f^{c_2}, T)$, the algorithm B wants to decide whether T is equal to $\mu^{c_1 + c_2}$ or T is just a random element in G.

The constructions of Setup, VES.ESign and VES.Adjudicate are the same as that in the proof of Lemma 2.

Output. The algorithm A output a type B* normal signature $M, \sigma = (\sigma_1, \sigma_2, \sigma_3, \sigma_4, \sigma_5, \sigma_6, \sigma_7, \sigma_k, tag_k)$. Since algorithm A has no knowledge of the value of A and B, we claim that it has negligible chance to produce a signature with $tag_k = A * M + B$. Assuming $tag_k \neq A * M + B$, B randomly chooses $x, s_1, s_2, t \in Z_p$. Set $s = s_1 + s_2$, $tag_c = A * M + B$ and calculate $C_1 = (g^h)^{s_1 + s_2}$, $C_2 = (g^{ba_1})^{s_1}$, $C_3 = (g^{a_1})^{s_1}$, $C_4 = (g^{ba_2})^{s_2} f^{a_2 x}$, $C_5 = (g^{a_2})^{s_2} g^{a_2 x}$, $C_6 = \tau_1^{s_1} \tau_2^{s_2} v_2^{a_2 x}$, $C_7 = (\tau_1^b)^{s_1} (\tau_2^b)^{s_2} \omega^{-t} f y_{v2} \cdot x \cdot a_2 \mu^{-a_1 \cdot x \cdot y_\omega \cdot a_2}$, $E_1 = (u^M \omega^{tag_c} h)^t (\mu^{My_u + y_h + tag_c y_\omega})^{a_1 a_2 x}$, $E_2 = g^t \mu^{a_1 a_2 x}$. Then B computes:
$A_1 = e(C_1, \sigma_1) e(C_2, \sigma_2) e(C_3, \sigma_3) e(C_4, \sigma_4) e(C_5, \sigma_5)$, $A_2 = e(C_6, \sigma_6) e(C_7, \sigma_7)$, $A_3 = A_1/A_2$ and $A_4 = (e(E_1, \sigma_7)/e(E_2, \sigma_k))^{1/(tag_c - tag_k)}$. If the following equation $\left(e(g, g)^{\alpha a_1 b}\right)^{s_2} = A_3/A_4$ holds, the algorithm B could decide that the signature produced by A is a type A* normal signature, otherwise the signature is a type B* normal signature. In either case, B could distinguish game$(k, 0)$ from game$(k+1, 0)$ and break the decision linear problem. Notice that the construction above is essentially the same as in VES.SemiVerify algorithm which could distinguish a type A* normal signature from a type B* normal signature with significant probability.

Lemma 4. No adversary could distinguish game(q_{es}, k) from game$(q_{es}, k+1)$

Proof. Assume that there exists an algorithm A that makes at most q_{es} VES.ESign queries and q_{adj} VES.Adjudicate queries and has non-negligible chance of ϵ to distinguish game(q_{es}, k) from game$(q_{es}, k+1)$, then we can build an algorithm B that has advantage ϵ in the decision linear game. Given $(g, f, \mu, g^{c_1}, f^{c_2}, T)$, the algorithm B wants to decide whether T is equal to $\mu^{c_1 + c_2}$ or T is random in G.

Setup. Algorithm B first chooses randomly $\alpha, a_1, a_2, y_{v1}, y_{v2}, y_\omega, y_u, y_h$. And it sets $g^b = f, g^{ba_1} = f^{a_1}, g^{ba_2} = f^{a_2}, v = \mu^{-a_1 a_2}, v_1 = \mu^{a_2} g^{y_{v1}}, v_2 = \mu^{a_1} g^{y_{v2}}, e(g, g)^{\alpha a_1 b} = e(f, g)^{\alpha a_1}$. Then algorithm B can create $\tau_1 = v v_1^{a_1} = g^{y_{v1} a_1}, \tau_2 = v v_2^{a_2} = g^{y_{v2} a_2}$, $\tau_1^b = f^{y_{v1} a_1}, \tau_2^b = f^{y_{v2} a_2}$. At last, B chooses randomly $s, A, B \in Z_p$ and sets $\omega = f g^{y_\omega}, u = f^{-A} g^{y_u}, h = f^{-B} g^{y_h}, Q = g^s$ to publish all the public parameters of the system PK and the adjudicator's public key $APK = Q$. Note that although B knows the secret key of the adjudicator here, the importance here is not to break the opacity but to distinguish the two games.

VES.ESign Query. Since B has the secret key SK and $g^{a_1 a_2}$, it could run the VES. ESign algorithm to generate a type A VES signature and apply the algorithm in the definition of type B VES signature to generate a type B VES signature.

VES.Adjudicate Query. We break the VES.Adjudicate queries into three cases. Consider the i-th query made by A.

> Case 1: $i > k + 1$. Since B has the secret key SK, it could run the VES.Sign to produce a type A normal signature.
>
> Case 2: $i < k + 1$. Since B has the secret key SK and $g^{a_1 a_2}$, it could produce a type B normal signature.
>
> Case 3: $i = k + 1$. B first runs the VES.Sign to generate a type A normal signature $M, \sigma = (\sigma_1, \sigma_2, \sigma_3, \sigma_4, \sigma_5, \sigma_6, \sigma_7, \sigma_k, tag_k)$ where $tag_k = A * M + B$, let r_1, r_2, z_1, z_2 be the random exponents used in VES.Sign algorithm. It then sets $\sigma_1' = \sigma_1 T^{-a_1 a_2}$, $\sigma_2' = \sigma_2 T^{a_2} (g^{c_1})^{y_{v1}}$, $\sigma_3' = \sigma_3 (f^{c_2})^{y_{v1}}$, $\sigma_4' = \sigma_4 T^{a_1} (g^{c_1})^{y_{v2}}$, $\sigma_5' = \sigma_5 (f^{c_2})^{y_{v2}}$, $\sigma_6' = \sigma_6 f^{c_2}$, $\sigma_7' = \sigma_7 (g^{c_1})$, $\sigma_k' = \sigma_k (g^{c_1})^{M * y_u + y_h + tag_k * y_\omega}$, and return the new signature $M, \sigma' = (\sigma_1', \sigma_2', \sigma_3', \sigma_4', \sigma_5', \sigma_6', \sigma_7', \sigma_k', tag_k)$. If T is equal to $\mu^{c_1 + c_2}$, then this new signature is a type A normal signature under randomnesses $r_1' = r_1 + c_1$ and $r_2' = r_2 + c_2$. Otherwise, if T is random, then it can be written as $T = \mu^{c_1 + c_2} g^r$ for random $r \in Z_p$. This is a type B normal signature where r is the added randomness.

Output. If algorithm A decides that the game above is game(q_{es}, k), then B could claim that T is equal to $\mu^{c_1 + c_2}$, otherwise B could claim that T is a random element.

Lemma 5. If an adversary could produce a type A* normal signature in game(q_{es}, k), then it could also produce a type A* normal signature in game$(q_{es}, k + 1)$.

Proof. Similar proof sketch as in Lemma 3.

Lemma 6. No adversary could produce a type A* normal signature in game(q_{es}, q_{adj}), where the oracles give out only type B normal signatures and verifiably encrypted signatures.

Proof. Assume that there exists an algorithm A that makes at most q_{es} VES.ESign queries and q_{adj} VES.Adjudicate queries and has non-negligible chance of ϵ to forge a new type A* normal signature which would be accepted by veirfy algorithms with non-negligible probability ε, then we can build an algorithm B that has advantage $\varepsilon \cdot \epsilon$ in the BDH game. Given a BDH instance $(g, g^{c1}, g^{c2}, g^{c3}, T)$, algorithm B wants to decide whether T is equal to $e(g, g)^{c_1 c_2 c_3}$.

Setup. The algorithm B first chooses randomly $a_1, b, y_v, y_{v1}, y_{v2}, y_\omega, y_h, y_u \in Z_p$, $Q \in G_1$. It then sets $g^b, g^{a_1}, g^{a_2} = g^{c_2}, g^{ba_1}, g^{ba_2} = (g^{c_2})^b$, $v = g^{y_v}, v_1 = g^{y_{v1}}, v_2 = g^{y_{v2}}, \omega = g^{y_\omega}, u = g^{y_u}, h = g^{y_h}, e(g, g)^{a_1 \alpha b} = e(g^{c_1}, g^{c_2})^{a_1 b}$ and calculates $\tau_1 = vv_1^{a_1}$, $\tau_1^b, \tau_2 = v(g^{c_2})^{y_{v2}}, \tau_2^b$ in order to public the public key PK and $APK = Q$. Notice that B dose not know the secret key SK.

VES.ESign. Given a message M, B randomly chooses $r_1, r_2, z_1, z_2, \gamma, tag_k \in Z_p$ and defines $r = r_1 + r_2$. It creates a signature as: $\sigma_1 = (g^{c_2})^{-\gamma a_1} v^r$, $\sigma_2 = (g^{c_2})^\gamma v_1^r g^{z_1}$, $\sigma_3 = (g^b)^{-z_1}$, $\sigma_4 = (g^{c_1})^{a_1} g^{a_1 \gamma} v_2^r g^{z_2}$, $\sigma_5 = (g^b)^{-z_2}$, $\sigma_6 = g^{r_2 b}$, $\sigma_7 = g^{r_1}$, $\sigma_k = (u^M \omega^{tag_k} hQ)^{r_1}$ and outputs the signature as $M, \sigma = (\sigma_1, \sigma_2, \sigma_3, \sigma_4, \sigma_5, \sigma_6, \sigma_7, \sigma_k, tag_k)$.

VES.Adjudicate. Given a message M, the algorithm B randomly chooses $r_1, r_2, z_1, z_2, \gamma, tag_k \in Z_p$ and defines $r = r_1 + r_2$. It creates a signature as: $\sigma_1 = (g^{c_2})^{-\gamma a_1} v^r$, $\sigma_2 = (g^{c_2})^\gamma v_1^r g^{z_1}$, $\sigma_3 = (g^b)^{-z_1}$, $\sigma_4 = (g^{c_1})^{a_1} g^{a_1 \gamma} v_2^r g^{z_2}$, $\sigma_5 = (g^b)^{-z_2}$, $\sigma_6 = g^{r_2 b}$, $\sigma_7 = g^{r_1}$, $\sigma_k = (u^M \omega^{tag_k} h)^{r_1}$ and outputs the signature as $M, \sigma = (\sigma_1, \sigma_2, \sigma_3, \sigma_4, \sigma_5, \sigma_6, \sigma_7, \sigma_k, tag_k)$.

Output. Algorithm A output a type A* normal signature $M, \sigma = (\sigma_1, \sigma_2, \sigma_3, \sigma_4, \sigma_5, \sigma_6, \sigma_7, \sigma_k, tag_k)$, algorithm B could use this signature to solve the BDH problem. B randomly chooses $s_1, t, tag_c, x \in Z_p$ and calculates $C_1 = g^{s_1 b} (g^{c_3})^b$, $C_2 = g^{ba_1 s_1}$, $C_3 = g^{a_1 s_1}$, $C_4 = (g^{c_2})^{xb}$, $C_5 = (g^{c_2})^x$, $C_6 = \tau_1^{s_1} (g^{c_3})^{y_v} (g^{c_2})^{y_{v2} x}$, $C_7 = (\tau_1^b)^{s_1} (g^{c_3})^{y_v b} (g^{c_2})^{y_{v2} xb} \omega^{-t}$, $E_1 = (u^M \omega^{tag_c} h)^t$, $E_2 = g^t$; $A_1 = e(C_1, \sigma_1) \; e(C_2, \sigma_2) e(C_3, \sigma_3) e(C_4, \sigma_4) e(C_5, \sigma_5)$, $A_2 = e(C_6, \sigma_6) e(C_7, \sigma_7)$, $A_3 = A_1 / A_2$, $A_4 = (e(E_1, \sigma_7) / e(E_2, \sigma_k))^{1/(tag_c - tag_k)}$. If the equation $T^{a_1 b} = A_3 / A_4$ holds, then T is equal to $e(g, g)^{c_1 c_2 c_3}$ or else T is just random.

Lemma 7. No adversary could produce a type A* normal signature in game(0,0), where the oracles give out only type A normal signatures and verifiably encrypted signatures.

Proof. Directly from Lemmas 3, 5 and 6.

Theorem 2. No adversary should break the opacity game.

Proof. Directly from Lemmas 1 and 7.

4 Conclusion

In this paper, we construct another verifiably encrypted signature scheme in standard model based on Waters' newly introduced Dual System and give its security analysis. Compared with other standard model verifiably encrypted signature schemes, our construction has const number of public parameters and uses simple assumptions for security analysis. The drawback is that the signature size is somewhat larger than in other system.

References

1. Asokan, N., Shoup, V., Waidner, M.: Optimistic fair exchange of digital signatures. In: Nyberg, K. (ed.) EUROCRYPT 1998. LNCS, vol. 1403, pp. 591–606. Springer, Heidelberg (1998). https://doi.org/10.1007/BFb0054156
2. Boneh, D., Gentry, C., Lynn, B., Shacham, H.: Aggregate and verifiably encrypted signatures from bilinear maps. In: Biham, E. (ed.) EUROCRYPT 2003. LNCS, vol. 2656, pp. 416–432. Springer, Heidelberg (2003). https://doi.org/10.1007/3-540-39200-9_26
3. Zhang, F., Safavi-Naini, R., Susilo, W.: Efficient verifiably encrypted signature and partially blind signature from bilinear pairings. In: Johansson, T., Maitra, S. (eds.) INDOCRYPT 2003. LNCS, vol. 2904, pp. 191–204. Springer, Heidelberg (2003). https://doi.org/10.1007/978-3-540-24582-7_14
4. Zhang, F., Safavi-Naini, R., Susilo, W.: An efficient signature scheme from bilinear pairings and its applications. In: Bao, F., Deng, R., Zhou, J. (eds.) PKC 2004. LNCS, vol. 2947, pp. 277–290. Springer, Heidelberg (2004). https://doi.org/10.1007/978-3-540-24632-9_20
5. Waters, B.: Efficient identity-based encryption without random Oracles. In: Cramer, R. (ed.) EUROCRYPT 2005. LNCS, vol. 3494, pp. 114–127. Springer, Heidelberg (2005). https://doi.org/10.1007/11426639_7
6. Lu, S., Ostrovsky, R., Sahai, A., Shacham, H., Waters, B.: Sequential aggregate signatures and multisignatures without random Oracles. In: Vaudenay, S. (ed.) EUROCRYPT 2006. LNCS, vol. 4004, pp. 465–485. Springer, Heidelberg (2006). https://doi.org/10.1007/11761679_28
7. Zhang, J., Mao, J.: A novel verifiably encrypted signature scheme without random Oracle. In: Dawson, E., Wong, D.S. (eds.) ISPEC 2007. LNCS, vol. 4464, pp. 65–78. Springer, Heidelberg (2007). https://doi.org/10.1007/978-3-540-72163-5_7
8. Rückert, M., Schröder, D.: Aggregate and verifiably encrypted signatures from multilinear maps without random Oracles. In: Park, J.H., Chen, H.-H., Atiquzzaman, M., Lee, C., Kim, T.-h., Yeo, S.-S. (eds.) ISA 2009. LNCS, vol. 5576, pp. 750–759. Springer, Heidelberg (2009). https://doi.org/10.1007/978-3-642-02617-1_76
9. Hanser, C., Rabkin, M., Schröder, D.: Verifiably encrypted signatures: security revisited and a new construction. In: Pernul, G., Ryan, P.Y.A., Weippl, E. (eds.) ESORICS 2015. LNCS, vol. 9326, pp. 146–164. Springer, Cham (2015). https://doi.org/10.1007/978-3-319-24174-6_8
10. Wang, Y., Pang, H., Deng, R.H.: Verifiably encrypted cascade-instantiable blank signatures to secure progressive decision management. Int. J. Inf. Secur. **17**, 347–363 (2018)
11. Wang, Z., Luo, X., Wu, Q.: Verifiably encrypted group signatures. In: Okamoto, T., Yu, Y., Au, M.H., Li, Y. (eds.) ProvSec 2017. LNCS, vol. 10592, pp. 107–126. Springer, Cham (2017). https://doi.org/10.1007/978-3-319-68637-0_7
12. Waters, B.: Dual system encryption: realizing fully secure IBE and HIBE under simple assumptions. In: Halevi, S. (ed.) CRYPTO 2009. LNCS, vol. 5677, pp. 619–636. Springer, Heidelberg (2009). https://doi.org/10.1007/978-3-642-03356-8_36
13. Nishimaki, R., Xagawa, K.: Verifiably encrypted signatures with short keys based on the decisional linear problem and obfuscation for encrypted VES. Des. Codes Crypt. **77**, 61–98 (2015)

Lightweight Encryption Algorithm Containing SPN Structure for IoT

Yiming Qin[1], Xinchun Cui[1(✉)], Yuefan Wang[1], Hong Qiao[2], and Shancang Li[3]

[1] School of Information Science and Engineering,
Qufu Normal University, Rizhao, China
cxcsd@126.com
[2] Business School, Shandong Normal University, Jinan, China
[3] Department of Computer Science,
University of the West of England (UWE), Bristol, UK

Abstract. With the development of information technology, the Internet of Things has increasingly entered all aspects of people's work and life. In the IoT environment, in order to provide better and faster services, while ensuring data integrity, confidentiality and privacy, people put forward higher requirements for the efficiency of encryption algorithms. However, although the traditional encryption algorithm can guarantee the security, it is not suitable for the security of the Internet of Things in terms of encryption efficiency and energy consumption. In this paper, we propose a lightweight packet encryption algorithm based on the Substitution Permutation Network (SPN) structure. The algorithm consists of several P-boxes and S-boxes. It avoids the problems of high energy consumption and low efficiency caused by the large number of rounds of AES algorithm. Based on the SPN-based block cipher, it introduces the S-box and P-box and the multiple-pass authentication encryption scheme. As well, by proving its block cipher variance and linear analysis, the proposed solution is effective and provides sufficient security through authentication and encryption. This algorithm can be used for low-energy and IoT information transmission processes that require only moderate security.

Keywords: SPN · Lightweight encryption · Block cipher · IoT

1 Introduction

With the rapid development of information technology, the application of IoT has increased dramatically, and it has become ubiquitous in industry, commerce, everyday life, and administration. Along with that, there is a need for rapid encryption algorithms over the user's credentials so that no unauthorized user can access the confidential data in the IoT [1–3].

The lightweight encryption algorithm is applied in a restricted environment, such as RFID, sensors, smart cards and medical devices [3]. As well, the Internet of Things must have the characteristics of small occupied area, low energy consumption and high speed when transmitting data. Although AES and SHA work well together in computer

© Springer Nature Switzerland AG 2019
J. Vaidya et al. (Eds.): CSS 2019, LNCS 11983, pp. 253–262, 2019.
https://doi.org/10.1007/978-3-030-37352-8_22

systems, since the processing capability, their use in the Internet of Things is not widespread, physical space, and excessive battery power consumption. Li et al. [4] identified the breadth and diversity of existing IoT research in the industrial sector and highlighted the challenges and opportunities that researchers face in the future [5]. It has been proposed to use a large number of lightweight encryption algorithms on devices with limited resources. National (NIST) and international (ISO/IEC) organizations have outlined a number of methods that can be used for lightweight encryption for IoT and RFID devices [6].

Recently introduced CLEFIA is a famous lightweight encryption algorithm [7]. The CLEFIA-128 algorithm uses a four-branch Feistel structure and 18 iterations. In each round, two branches are used to update the other two branches. However, tests show that the diffusion effect of the algorithm is not significant. It takes 5 rounds to basically achieve the avalanche effect, and using two round functions in each round reduces the software and hardware implementation efficiency. Besides, Zhang have proposed a block encryption algorithm for nested SPN structure, but the algorithm has obvious lightweight defects [8].

In that paper, the CLEFIA-128 algorithm requires 5 rounds to basically achieve the avalanche effect, the diffusion effect is not obvious, and the design of the two round functions in each round lead to the problem of soft and hardware implementation efficiency reduction. The algorithm has been improved on the structure and round function. And based on the idea of SPN, we developed a lightweight encryption algorithm based on SPN. The algorithm consists of several P-boxes and S-boxes. It avoids the problems of high energy consumption and low efficiency caused by the large number of rounds of AES algorithm. Based on the SPN-based block cipher, it introduces the S-box and P-box and the multiple-pass authentication encryption scheme. As well, the algorithm can be applied to Internet of Things.

The past of paper is organized as follows: in Sect. 2 - review the most prominent research. In Sect. 3 - algorithmic cryptography is proposed. In Sect. 4 - discuss the encryption process, decryption process and the security analysis of this algorithm. Finally, we concluded this paper by linear probability, and discussed its application.

2   SPN-Based Block Cipher

Block ciphers have many advantages in terms of information confidentiality and are therefore widely used. However, the security of the block cipher algorithm is generally difficult to prove. There is a great risk in using the block cipher algorithm without security proof. In this paper, the provable security of nested substitution-permutation network (SPN) structure block cipher algorithm against differential analysis and linear analysis is analyzed. The purpose is to analyze the security of SPN structure under differential analysis and linear analysis, which is beneficial to the design of block cipher. The main structure of the block cipher algorithm of nested SPN structure is SPN structure, and the round function is one round or two rounds of SPN structure. This combination can effectively utilize the advantages of SPN structure and avoid the shortcomings of this structure. The security standard NESSIE, one of the two grouping algorithms, Camellia algorithm is a Feistel-type block cipher algorithm with a nested

SPN structure [9]. The E2 algorithm in the AES candidate algorithm is a Feistel-type block cipher algorithm with two loops of SPN structure [10].

E2 cryptographic algorithm is one of 15 AES candidate algorithms submitted by Japanese cryptographers to the National Institute of Standards and Technology. The E2 cipher algorithm has a packet length of 128 bits, a key length of 128/192/256 bits, and a round of 12 rounds. The overall structure is a Feistel structure, and the wheel function is a two-turn SPN structure. The SPN structure uses eight identical S-boxes. Both the linear transformation and the key addition operation in the SPN structure use an exclusive OR operation. In the literature, Choy mainly analyzes the algebraic properties of the S-box of the E2 cryptographic algorithm, and gives the upper bound of the differential probability of the three-round E2 cryptographic algorithm $2^{(-55.39)}$ [11]. This paper focuses on AES encryption algorithm, and designs and implements the AES encryption algorithm based on SPN structure. This paper introduces the method of block security of nested SPN structure against the provable security of differential analysis and linear analysis. This method mainly considers the independent variable of linear transformation of E2 cryptographic algorithm. The nature of this paper is used to analyze the provable security of the cryptographic algorithm that reduces the number of rounds against differential analysis and linear analysis.

SPN structure is designed according to Shannon's confusion and diffusion guidelines. Each round of its structure consists of a replacement layer, a diffusion layer, and a key plus three parts. The permutation layer is composed of a plurality of S-box (non-linear replacement), and the linear transformation of the diffusion layer is used to spread the cryptographic characteristics of the permutation layer pairs into more packets. The role of key addition is to apply the round key of the password to each round.

2.1 The Encryption Process

The basic elements of the "dissipative" cipher design in the statistic of diffusion statistics in the explicit statistics include: block size, key size, rounds, subkey generation algorithm, round function, fast software encryption. Block ciphers are considered duplicate ciphers because they change the plaintext sized plaintext block to the same size ciphertext by repeatedly applying reversible transformations. This conversion is called round function [4] (Fig. 1).

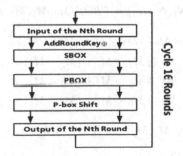

Fig. 1. Flowchart of algorithm steps.

In this section, we give the encryption algorithm in detail as follows.

i. AddRoundKey: The input of the Nth round and the key of the Nth round are XORed by each bit.

ii. S-box Shift: The result obtained in 'i' is sequentially entered into 16 identical 8*8 S-box, and the input 16-byte data is sequentially replaced with another 16-byte data, and the algorithm adopts the same structure of AES.

iii. P-box Mix: The result obtained in 'ii' is sequentially entered into P-box (input and output are all four 32-bit data). The P-box uses exclusively XOR, modular addition operation and cyclic shift, and mix them in the encryption algorithm, which makes P-box differential branching number and linear branching number is 16, so the algorithm is very resistant to differential cryptanalysis and linear analysis.

iv. P-box shift: The P-box shift is a Quick Trickle Permutation, and the result obtained in 'iii' is subjected to a P-box replacement (the input and output of the P-box shift are both 16-bit numbers). After the transposition operation, the position between the data is sufficiently disturbed. This makes all the possibilities of distance between data elements appear. The output of the P-box shift is used as the input to the next round functions (Table 1).

Table 1. Symbol description table.

Symbol	Description
$\oplus$	XOR operation
$+$	Modulus 2's 32th power
$\&$	AND operation
$\vert$	OR operation
$\ll$	Loop left shift
$-$	Modulus 2's 32th reduction

2.2 P-Box Mix

The diffusion layer PBOX (P-box) (the inverse of PBOX is $PBOX_{INV}$) is defined as follows.

$$(N_0, N_1, N_2, N_3) = PBOX(M_0, M_1, M_2, M_3)$$

$$\{ \begin{aligned} M_0 &= M_0 \oplus M_2 \oplus M_3 + (M_2 + M_3) \ll 8 \\ M_1 &= M_1 \oplus M_2 \oplus M_3 + (M_2 + M_3) \ll 16 \\ M_2 &= M_2 \oplus M_0 \oplus M_1 + (M_0 + M_1) \ll 8 \\ M_3 &= M_3 \oplus M_0 \oplus M_1 + (M_0 + M_1) \ll 16 \} \end{aligned} \tag{1}$$

$$(M_0, M_1, M_2, M_3) = PBOX_{INV}(N_0, N_1, N_2, N_3)$$

$$\{M_3 = (M_3 - (M_0 + M_1) \lll 16) \oplus M_0 \oplus M_1$$
$$M_2 = (M_2 - (M_0 + M_1) \lll 8) \oplus M_0 \oplus M_1$$
$$M_1 = (M_1 - (M_2 + M_3) \lll 16) \oplus M_2 \oplus M_3$$
$$M_0 = (M_0 - (M_2 + M_3) \lll 8) \oplus M_2 \oplus M_3\} \tag{2}$$

Where $N_0 = M_0, N_1 = M_1, N_2 = M_2, N_3 = M_3$ (where M, N is 32 bits), where PBOX is the diffusion of the P-box and where PBOX is the diffusion of the P-box and $PBOX_{INV}$. is the inverse if the P-Box.

2.3 P-Box Shift

Quick trickle permutation P (P_INV is the inverse of P-box) is defined as follows. Hypothesis,

$$P = (1, 2, 3, 4, 5, 6, 7, 8, 9, 10, 11, 12, 13, 14, 15, 16) \tag{3}$$

$$P_{INV} = (2, 4, 1, 8, 14, 6, 7, 13, 9, 12, 10, 15, 3, 11, 5, 16) \tag{4}$$

The result of the shift is as follows (where Z is 8 bits).

$$(Z_1, Z_2, Z_3, Z_4, Z_5, Z_6, Z_7, Z_8, Z_9, Z_{10}, Z_{11}, Z_{12}, Z_{13}, Z_{14}, Z_{15},$$
$$Z_{16}) = P(Z_5, Z_{14}, Z_{15}, Z_{11}, Z_2, Z_6, Z_{16}, Z_{10}, Z_9, Z_{13}, Z_8, Z_3, Z_{12}, Z_4, Z_1, Z_7) \tag{5}$$

$$(Z_5, Z_{14}, Z_{15}, Z_{11}, Z_2, Z_6, Z_{16}, Z_{10}, Z_9, Z_{13}, Z_8, Z_3, Z_{12}, Z_4, Z_1,$$
$$Z_7) = P_{INV}(Z_1, Z_2, Z_3, Z_4, Z_5, Z_6, Z_7, Z_8, Z_9, Z_{10}, Z_{11}, Z_{12}, Z_{13}, Z_{14}, Z_{15}, Z_{16}) \tag{6}$$

2.4 Encryption and Decryption Algorithm

Assume plaintext block: X_0, X_1, X_2, X_3(X is 32 bits);ciphertext: Y_0, Y_1, Y_2, Y_3 (Y is 32 bits); Seed key: K_0, K_1, K_2, K_3; AddRoundKey: RK_0, RK_1, RK_2, RK_3 (RK is 32 bits). The plaintext is processed as follows.

$$Y_0, Y_1, Y_2, Y_3 = F(X_0, X_1, X_2, X_3, RK_0, RK_1, RK_2, RK_3) = P(PBOX(SBOX(X_0 \oplus RK_0, X_1 \oplus RK_1, X_2 \oplus RK_2, X_3 \oplus RK_3) \tag{7}$$

Decryption algorithm:

$$X_0, X_1, X_2, X_3 - F(Y_0, Y_1, Y_2, Y_3, RK_0, RK_1, RK_2, RK_3) =$$
$$SBOX_{INV}(P_{INV}(Y_0, Y_1, Y_2, Y_3)) \oplus (RK_0, RK_1, RK_2, RK_3) \tag{8}$$

$$PBOX\left[SBOX\begin{bmatrix}X_0\\X_1\\X_2\\X_3\end{bmatrix}\oplus\begin{bmatrix}RK_0\\RK_1\\RK_2\\RK_3\end{bmatrix}\right]SBOX_{INV}\left[P_{INV}\begin{bmatrix}Y_0\\Y_1\\Y_2\\Y_3\end{bmatrix}\oplus\begin{bmatrix}RK_0\\RK_1\\RK_2\\RK_3\end{bmatrix}\right]$$

(9)

2.5 Key Expansion Algorithm

The key expansion algorithm uses four system keys ($WK_0 = 0x3E93DC59$, $WK_1 = 0x8B40E6E8$, $WK_2 = 0xD9C580BF$, $WK_3 = 0x723A13A6$) for sixteen rounds of key addition. The encryption algorithm is as follows.

i. $RK_0 = SBOX(K_0 \ll N) \oplus SBOX((K_0 + WK_0) \ll (N+8) \bmod 32 \oplus$
    $SBOX(K_1 \& WK_1) \ll (N+12) mod 32 \oplus SBOX((K_2|WK_2) \ll (N+16)$ (10)
    $mod32 \oplus SBOX((K_3 \oplus WK_3) \ll (N+20) mod 32$

ii. $RK_1 = SBOX(K_1 \ll N) \oplus SBOX((K_1 + WK_0) \ll (N+8) \bmod 32 \oplus$
    $SBOX(K_2 \& WK_1) \ll (N+12) mod 32 \oplus SBOX((K_3|WK_2) \ll (N+16)$ (11)
    $mod32 \oplus SBOX((K_0 \oplus WK_3) \ll (N+20) mod 32$

iii. $RK_2 = SBOX(K_2 \ll N) \oplus SBOX((K_2 + WK_0) \ll (N+8) \bmod 32 \oplus$
    $SBOX(K_3 \& WK_1) \ll (N+12) mod 32 \oplus SBOX((K_0|WK_2) \ll (N+16)$ (12)
    $mod32 \oplus SBOX((K_1 \oplus WK_3) \ll (N+20) mod 32$

iv. $RK_3 = SBOX(K_3 \ll N) \oplus SBOX((K_3 + WK_0) \ll (N+8) \bmod 32 \oplus$
    $SBOX(K_0 \& WK_1) \ll (N+12) mod 32 \oplus SBOX((K_1|WK_2) \ll (N+16)$ (13)
    $mod32 \oplus SBOX((K_2 \oplus WK_3) \ll (N+20) mod 32$

3 Security Analysis

The SPN structure for two rounds includes key addition, S-displacement layer, p-diffusion, and P-displacement, The S-displacement is made up of 16 identical 8*8 S-box, and the input 16-byte data is sequentially replaced with another 16-bite data. All S-boxes are mapped one by one. That is, the input difference of the S-box is 0. Here in, the S-box with input differential not 0 is the active S-box, and the S-box with input differential of 0 is the inactive S-box. Similarly, for linear analysis, when the output mask is not zero, the S-box is called a linear active S-box.

3.1   S-Box Maximum Differential and Linear Probability

The maximum value of the differential probability of the S-box in the defined packet cipher round function is p, and the maximum value of the linear probability is q, Γ_a, Γ_b are the input mask and the output mask, respectively. then:

$$p = \max_{1 \le i \le n} \max_{a \ne 0,b} DP^{S_i}(a,b) \tag{14}$$

$$q = \max_{1 \le i \le n} \max_{a \ne 0,b} LP^{S_i}(\Gamma_a, \Gamma_b) \tag{15}$$

By calculating the maximum differential propagation probability of the S-box of the algorithm is $(1/2)^6$ and the maximum linear correlation probability is $(1/2)^4$. In the SPN structure, when p and q are small enough, the replacement layer is more secure, but although it is highly secure, it cannot guarantee that the SPN structure can resist differential analysis and linear analysis. Therefore, the linear transformation layer plays an important role in the SPN structure, which is directly related to the security of block ciphers. Therefore, the main analysis is as follows for the diffusivity of block cipher linear transformation.

3.2   P-Displacement Diffusivity

Linear branch number of differential analysis:

$$\beta_d = \min_{p \ne 0} \{Hw(p) + Hw(L(p))\} \tag{16}$$

Linear branch number of linear analysis:

$$\beta_l = \min_{\Gamma_y \ne 0} \{Hw(\Gamma_y) + Hw(L^t\Gamma_y)\} \tag{17}$$

Where $\mathbf{p} = (Z_1, Z_2, \ldots, Z_n)$, L^t represents the matrix transpose after linear transformation, and HW(x) is the Hamming weight function.

The definition is as follows:

$$HW(p) = \#\{i | 1 \le i \le n, Z_i \ne 0\} \tag{18}$$

It can be seen from the above formula that the larger the number of linear branches, the faster the differential diffusion, and the safer the SPN structure. When β_d, β_l take the maximum value, the linear transformation becomes the maximum linear transformation.

3.3   Upper Bound of Two Rounds Cipher

The 2-round SPN structure is an iterative structure. Assuming that the two-wheel key is independently and randomly distributed, the differential probability of the two-round

SPN structure can be represented by the differential probability of the less-represented SPN structure. Assuming that the input difference XOR of the N rounds of SPNs is $a = (a_1, a_2, \ldots, a_n)$, the output differential exclusive XOR is $b = (b_1, b_2, \ldots, b_n)$. Then the difference probability of the N-round SPN structure is recorded as $DP_r(a, b)$. Then the difference probability of a round of SPN structure is $DP_1(a, b) = \prod_{i=1}^{n} DP^{S_i}(a_i, b_i)$.

For the N-round SPN structure, if the differential mode δ is input and the differential mode ρ is output, the upper bound of the difference probability of the N-round SPN structure is denoted by $dp_r(\delta, \rho)$.

$$dp_r(\delta, \rho) = \max_{\gamma_a = \delta, \, \gamma_b = \rho} DP_r(a, b) \tag{19}$$

First, we calculate the maximum value of the differential probability (the difference probability of the two-wheel SPN structure)

$$DP_z(a, b) = \sum_x \left(\prod_{i=1}^{n} DP^{S_i}(a_i, x_i) \right) \left(\prod_{j=1}^{n} DP^{S_j}(y_j, b_j) \right) \tag{20}$$

The diffusion characteristics and the number of branches of the P-box are almost optimal (the number of differential branches and the number of linear branches are 16), which makes the maximum difference probability of 2-round of the algorithm is $(1/2)^{96}$, the maximum of 2-round linear approximation probability is $(1/2)^{64}$, which indicates that algorithm is well resistant to differential cryptanalysis and linear cryptanalysis (Table 2).

$$Q = \max \left\{ \max_{1 \le i \le 8} \max_{1 \le i \le 2^8 - 1} \sum_{j=1}^{255} \left\{ DP^{S_i}(u, j) \right\}^5 \max_{1 \le i \le 8} \max_{1 \le i \le 2^8 - 1} \sum_{j=1}^{255} \left\{ DP^{S_i}(j, u) \right\}^5 = \frac{175936}{(2^8)^5} \approx 2^{-22.575} \right. \tag{21}$$

Table 2. Symbol description table.

Rounds	Linear probability streets
1	$2^{-21.875}$
2	$2^{-21.875}$
3	$2^{-43.714}$
4	$2^{-44.714}$

The diffusion characteristics and the number of branches of the P-box are almost optimal (the number of differential branches and the number of linear branches are 16), which makes the maximum difference probability of 2-round of the algorithm is $(1/2)^{-22.575}$, the maximum of 2-round linear approximation probability is $(1/2)^{-44.714}$, which indicates this is well resistant to differential cryptanalysis and linear cryptanalysis.

3.4   Analysis of Algorithms

The nonlinearity, differential uniformity, algebraic number and term distribution, completeness and avalanche effect, diffusion characteristics, and algebraic immunity order of the S-box of the algorithm are optimal or near optimal.

The maximum differential propagation probability of the S-box of the algorithm is $(1/2)^6$ and the maximum linear correlation probability is $(1/2)^4$. The diffusion characteristics and the number of branches of the P-box are almost optimal (the number of differential branches and the number of linear branches are 16), which makes the maximum difference probability of the 2-round of the algorithm is $(1/2)^{-22.575}$, the maximum of 2-round linear approximation probability is $(1/2)^{-44.714}$, which indicates that the algorithm is well resistant to differential cryptanalysis and linear cryptanalysis.

P- replacement of the algorithm is quick trickle permutation, which not only can disturb the initial position of the plaintext, but also has all the possibilities of the distance between the plaintext elements. For diffusion and permutation, quick trickle permutation has good cryptographic characteristics. And it can resist cryptanalysis methods such as differential cryptanalysis, linear cryptanalysis, impossible differential cryptanalysis, integral attack, and related key attack. And the 16 round algorithm has sufficient security redundancy.

4   Conclusion

This paper proposed a lightweight encryption algorithm which based on AES. The algorithm consists of several P-boxes and S-boxes. It avoids the problems of high energy consumption and low efficiency caused by the large number of rounds of AES algorithm. Based on the SPN-based block cipher, it introduces the S-box and P-box and the multiple-pass authentication encryption scheme. As well, the algorithm can be applied to Internet of Things. In order to solve the extreme environment of the Internet of Things, such as energy consumption, space is insufficient. The algorithm only uses primary operations such as XOR and cyclic shift, which makes the encryption and decryption efficiency of the encryption algorithm significantly improved. The energy consumption is greatly reduced, too. In order to ensure the security of the algorithm, the design of the S-box and the P-box provides chaotic layer and diffusion layer for the encryption algorithm. After a series of tests, the algorithm has better encryption and decryption effect in the same environment.

Acknowledgment. This work is partially supported by Ministry of Education Humanities and Social Sciences Project (11YJCZH021, 15YJCZH111). Shandong Social Science Planning Research Project (17CHLJ41, 16CTQJ02, 18CHLJ34).

References

1. Li, S., Xu, L.D., Zhao, S.: The Internet of Things: a survey. Inf. Syst. Frontiers **17**(2), 243–259 (2015)
2. Buchanan, W.J., Li, S., Asif, R.: Lightweight cryptography methods. J. Cyber Secur. Technol. **1**(3–4), 187–201 (2017)
3. Wang, Y., et al.: Social rational secure multi-party computation. Concurrency Comput.: Pract. Experience **26**(5), 1067–1083 (2014)
4. Li, S., Zhao, Y.Y., Sun, Q., Zhang, K.: Dynamic security risk evaluation via hybrid bayesian risk graph in cyber-physical social systems. IEEE Trans. Comput. Soc. Syst. **5**(4), 1133–1141 (2018)
5. Kim, J., Hong, S., Preneel, B.: Related-key rectangle attacks on reduced AES-192 and AES-256. In: Biryukov, A. (ed.) FSE 2007. LNCS, vol. 4593, pp. 225–241. Springer, Heidelberg (2007). https://doi.org/10.1007/978-3-540-74619-5_15
6. Li, T., Gupta, B.B., Metere, R.: Socially-conforming cooperative computation in cloud networks. J. Parallel Distrib. Comput. **117**, 274–280 (2018)
7. Chen, B., Ch., Huang, Y.H., Shi, Y.Y.: Research and improvement of CLEFIA. Comput. Technol. Dev. **24**(12), 124–127 + 132 (2014). https://doi.org/10.3969/j.issn.1673-629x.2014.12.029
8. Zhang, W.T., Qing, S.H., Wu, W.L.: Provable security for SPN block ciphers containing feistel structure. J. Comput. Res. Dev. **41**(8), 1389–1397 (2004)
9. Chun, K., Kim, S., Sung, S.H., Yoon, S.: Differential and linear cryptanalysis for 2-round SPNs. Inf. Process. Lett. **87**, 227–282 (2003)
10. Al-Rahman, S.A., Sagheer, A., Dawood, O.: NVLC: new variant lightweight cryptography algorithm for Internet of Things, 20–21 November 2018
11. Choy, J., Khoo, K.: New applications of differential bounds of the SDS structure. In: Wu, T.-C., Lei, C.-L., Rijmen, V., Lee, D.-T. (eds.) ISC 2008. LNCS, vol. 5222, pp. 367–384. Springer, Heidelberg (2008). https://doi.org/10.1007/978-3-540-85886-7_26
12. National Institute of Standards and Technology. FIPS PUB 197: Advanced Encryption Standard (AES), November 2001
13. Wang, Y., et al.: Fair secure computation with reputation assumptions in the mobile social networks. Mobile Inf. Syst. (2015)
14. Lu, J.: Cryptanalysis of block ciphers. Doctoral dissertation, Royal Holloway University of London, pp. 15–104, 30 July 2008
15. Schneier, B., Kelsey, J.: Unbalanced Feistel networks and block cipher design. In: Gollmann, D. (ed.) FSE 1996. LNCS, vol. 1039, pp. 121–144. Springer, Heidelberg (1996). https://doi.org/10.1007/3-540-60865-6_49
16. Aoki, K., et al.: *Camellia*: A 128-bit block cipher suitable for multiple platforms — design and analysis. In: Stinson, D.R., Tavares, S. (eds.) SAC 2000. LNCS, vol. 2012, pp. 39–56. Springer, Heidelberg (2001). https://doi.org/10.1007/3-540-44983-3_4
17. Handschuh, H., Naccache, D.: SHACAL. NESSIE (2001). https://www.cosic.esat.kuleuven.be/nessie
18. Biham, E., Shamir, A.: Differential cryptanalysis of DES-like cryptosystems. J. Cryptol. **4**(1), 3–72 (1991)
19. Junod, P., Vaudenay, S.: FOX: a new family of block ciphers. In: Handschuh, H., Hasan, M.A. (eds.) SAC 2004. LNCS, vol. 3357, pp. 114–129. Springer, Heidelberg (2004). https://doi.org/10.1007/978-3-540-30564-4_8
20. Biryukov, A., Khovratovich, D., Nikolić, I.: Distinguisher and related-key attack on the full AES-256. In: Halevi, S. (ed.) CRYPTO 2009. LNCS, vol. 5677, pp. 231–249. Springer, Heidelberg (2009). https://doi.org/10.1007/978-3-642-03356-8_14

A Blind Watermarking Scheme Using Adaptive Neuro-Fuzzy Inference System Optimized by BP Network and LS Learning Model

Jilin Yang[1], Chunjie Cao[1], Jun Zhang[1], Jixin Ma[2], and Xiaoyi Zhou[1(✉)]

[1] College of Computer and Cyberspace Security, Hainan University, Haikou, China
xy.zhou.xy@gmail.com
[2] Computing and Mathematical School, University of Greenwich, London, China

Abstract. To maintain a trade-off between robustness and imperceptibility, as well as secure transmission of digital images over communication channels, a digital image blind watermarking scheme on the basis of adaptive neuro-fuzzy inference system (ANFIS) is proposed in this study. To achieve better results, an optimized ANFIS (OANFIS) combines a back propagation neural network and a least-square (LS) hybrid learning model. Each 3×3 non-overlap block of the original host image is selected to form a sample dataset, which is trained to establish a model of nonlinear mapping between the input and the output. As a sequence, the host image is decomposed by wavelet transform to obtain a low frequency subband. Finally, each watermark signal is adaptively embedded into the low frequency subband by OANFIS. Results show that our scheme is robust to various attacks while effectively maintaining satisfying transparency.

Keywords: Watermarking · Neuro-Fuzzy inference system · Hybrid · Back propagation

1 Introduction

Internet technology has made the sharing and transmission of digital images easier and more convenient. However, while image transmission brings benefits to people, it leaves an opportunity for some malicious attackers. These attackers can intercept the original transmitted images and change the contents, thus affecting the receiver to obtain the real information. Therefore, it is necessary to use technical methods to ensure the copyright of the images. At the same time, the image transmission on the network is also interfered by different types of attacks, such as noise and geometric attacks. Moreover, limited by the transmission bandwidth or storage capacity, the original image will suffer a certain degree of lossy compression processing. As a result, to effectively maintain the authenticity and integrity of image content has become a hot topic in today's research. Watermarking is one of the most common and reliable methods to solve such problems.

© Springer Nature Switzerland AG 2019
J. Vaidya et al. (Eds.): CSS 2019, LNCS 11983, pp. 263–274, 2019.
https://doi.org/10.1007/978-3-030-37352-8_23

Owing to artificial intelligence technology, researchers have been applying machine learning algorithms to improve watermarking systems. To this end, a variety of techniques have emerged, for example, artificial neural networks (ANNs) [1–10], fuzzy inference systems (FIS) [11–19], genetic algorithms (GA) [20–22] and reinforcement learning (RL) [23]. However, quite a few machine learning algorithms have difficulties in dealing with large-dimensional data and nonlinear constraints, furthermore, they have slow convergence speed. Through investigation, we found that artificial neural networks have good nonlinear mapping ability, and fuzzy systems can well reduce large-scale data. Therefore, an approach of applying the adaptive network-based fuzzy inference system to watermarking is proposed.

Artificial neural network (ANN) refers to the abstract simulation of the structure and function of the human brain's central nervous system, so as to establish a model to predict and acquire relevant data knowledge by learning and training the existing data information. Yan et al. [2] propose a probabilistic neural network (PNN) based scheme to select the best watermark embedding position for the wavelet coefficients. The algorithm achieves the goal of extracting the watermark without the host image while having good robustness and transparency. However, the experiment cannot be performed when the data volume is insufficient. PNN takes the reasoning procedure into numerical calculation, resulting in certain information loss. Xu [3] propose a novel blind digital watermarking algorithm based on back propagation (BP) neural network in wavelet domain. The experimental results show that the proposed algorithm is robust against various attacks. However, BP neural network is easy to fall into local optimum, and the computational complexity is high. In addition to the above-mentioned literature, other types of neural networks have also incorporated to watermarking techniques in recent years [5–8] or applied watermarking techniques to neural networks [9, 10].

Based on the fuzziness characteristics of human brain thinking, a fuzzy system not only makes good use of expert knowledge, but also uses it to establish fuzzy logic, which reasonably solves many complex fuzzy information problems. Aiming at designing a digital watermarking method against various attacks, a fuzzy adaptive resonance theory based image watermarking scheme is introduced by Li et al. [11]. The proposed method combines fuzzy logic and human visual system (HVS). After the watermark is Arnold scrambled and error correction encoded, the HVS based entropy values and standard deviation values of image block matrix are taken as the input parameters for the fuzzy system. According to the texture masking characteristics, the corresponding fuzzy rules are formulated, and the obtained embedding strength is used as the system output. In this way, the problem of vision tomography caused by the different embedding strength of various adjacent image blocks is solved, thus enhancing the transparency of the watermark without affecting the robustness. Motwani et al. [12] propose a novel watermarking algorithm based on wavelet domain and fuzzy logic, which adapts the local geometry of the mesh to determine the optimal value of watermark amplitude in the inserted 3D model. Nevertheless, this algorithm does not implement blind detection and blind extraction.

In summary, an artificial neural network has defects such as lack of transparency, too difficult to understand, taking long time of learning and training and easy to fall into local optimum. On the other hand, a fuzzy system is not perfect as well. The fuzzy rule base is the core of a fuzzy system, but there is no way to accurately establish the fuzzy rules and membership functions, it can only be determined by expert experience. As a result, combining artificial neural networks with fuzzy systems will make them complete each other, and its advantages will be far superior to applying them respectively [16–19].

A digital image blind watermark scheme based on ANFIS is proposed in this study. By combining the artificial neural network and the fuzzy system, the robustness and transparency of the watermark is improved.

The remaining of the paper is organized as follows. Relevant theories are introduced in Sect. 2. Section 3 describes the design of the ANFIS based watermarking model. Experimental results and discussions are given in Sect. 4. Section 5 outlines conclusion and future work.

2 Background

A brief overview of the concepts used in the proposed scheme is given in this section.

2.1 A Subsection Sample

In 1991, Jyh-Shing [24] proposed a fuzzy inference system based on neural network structure. In 1993, he designed a related network structure model, and named it ANFIS [25].

ANFIS is based on Takagi-Sugeno model. Compared with the traditional models, it no longer relies entirely on expert experience to formulate fuzzy rules. Instead, it uses neural network learning algorithms to extract rules from sample data, and through training and learning it achieves self-adjustment of fuzzy rules. Therefore, ANFIS has stronger self-learning and self-adaptive capabilities. According to different ways of judging the rules, ANFIS is divided into grid-based and cluster-based. The main research object in this study is grid-based ANFIS.

Figure 1 shows the structure of the simplest double-inputs-single-output ANFIS based on the T-S model. Suppose the system has two inputs x and y and one output z. The square node in the figure represents that the parameters of the node are adjustable, while the circular node represents that the parameters are not adjustable or have no parameters.

The two equivalent if-then fuzzy rules are:

$$if \ x \ is \ A_1 \ and \ y \ is \ B_1, \ then \ z = p_1x + q_1y + r_1 \tag{1}$$

$$if \ x \ is \ A_2 \ and \ y \ is \ B_2, \ then \ z = p_2x + q_2y + r_2 \tag{2}$$

The ANFIS network consists of five layers, namely the fuzzy layer, the rule inference layer, the normalization layer, the defuzzification layer and the output layer. The first three are antecedent layers, while the latter two are consequent layers.

The structure of the simple ANFIS is not unique. One can choose to merge the third and the fourth layers, or perform the normalization process in the last layer to obtain a four-layer structure. However, it should be noted that the output of ANFIS must be single whereas the input can be multiple.

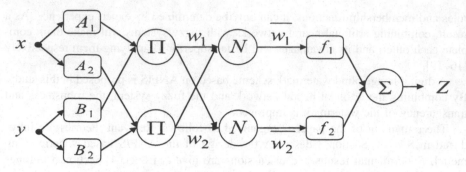

Fig. 1. Simple ANFIS Structure

2.2 A Subsection Sample

A hybrid scheme combining the BP algorithm and the least square method is proposed for improving ANFIS. For simple description, we name it optimized ANFIS (OANFIS).

(1) The forward transmission first fixes the antecedent parameters. For a double-input-single-output ANFIS structure, the total output can be denoted as a linear combination of consequent parameters, as formula (3):

$$
\begin{aligned}
f &= \sum_{i=1}^{2} \overline{\omega_i} f_i = \sum_{i=1}^{2} \overline{\omega_i}(p_l x_1 + q_l x_2 + r_l) \\
&= (\overline{\omega_1} x_1) p_1 + (\overline{\omega_1} x_2) q_1 + (\overline{\omega_1}) r_1 + (\overline{\omega_2} x_1) p_2 + (\overline{\omega_2} x_2) q_2 + (\overline{\omega_2}) r_2 \\
&= A \bullet \theta
\end{aligned} \tag{3}
$$

Where A represents the input parameter set and θ forms consequent parameter set. By extension, for an ANFIS with m inputs, single output and n fuzzy rules, if the total number of input sample sets is P, the actual output is, then A constitutes a set of input vectors of dimensions, and θ constitutes a set of consequent parameters of dimensions.

(2) Back propagation fixes consequent parameters, calculates the system error according to the actual output and the target output, applies the gradient descent method to pass the error from output to the input, and then updates the antecedent parameters in the fuzzy rules and the connection weights of the 4th and the 5th layer.

3 Proposed Algorithm

This section presents the proposed blind digital image watermarking technique, which includes the process of watermark embedding and extracting.

OANFIS integrates the learning mechanism of neural network with the language inference ability of fuzzy systems, effectively improves the black box characteristic of neural networks and increases the adaptive learning ability of fuzzy systems. As a sequence, OANFIS has favourable nonlinear mapping and fitting ability. If a mathematical model is established for calculating the relationship of the pixels in the host image, the pixels can be determined according to this model when extracting the watermark, thereby detecting and extracting the watermark without the host image.

Based on the above idea, this study uses the adaptive neural fuzzy inference system to establish the mathematical model, so as to determine the embedding position of the watermark.

3.1   A Subsection Sample

Given I is the host image with the size $M \times N$, W is a binary gray watermark image with the size $m \times n$, the watermark is $W = \{b(i,j), 1 \le i \le m, 1 \le j \le n\}$, where $b(i,j) \in \{0, 1\}$.

The detailed embedding process of the watermark is as follows:

Step 1: Preprocess the watermark image. Use the Arnold transform to encrypt the watermark, for providing security protection for the watermark. Then record the scrambling times Key1 as the secret key;

Step 2: Generate a binary array of length k by using Key1, and reducing the dimension of the watermark image by employing a row (or a column) stacking method to generate a one-dimensional array of length k. Combine the two arrays to generate a binary watermark array, denoted as formula (4):

$$W_1 = w_1(1)w_1(2)w_1(3) \cdots w_1(k) = \{w_1(i), 1 \le i \le mn\} \tag{4}$$

Where $w_1(i) \in \{0, 1\}$, the value of k can be assigned by the sender. The binary array offers the dataset to train the optimized ANFIS, so as to effectively record the original watermark information;

Step 3: Use ergodic matrix [26] to generate Key2 as a key, thus generate a random position coordinate array Z, as formula (5):

$$Z = \{(p_x, p_y) | x, y = 1, 2, 3, \cdots, n \times l\} \tag{5}$$

Where $p_x \in \{1, 2, \cdots M\}, p_y \in \{1, 2, \cdots N\}, l$ is the repeated times of each bit of watermark signal embedded in the selected region. Arbitrarily choose a pixel (p_x, p_y) and its neighboring eight pixels as a learning sample dataset. That is, the pixel-centered 3×3 sample dataset is used as an input signal for the OANFIS.

OANFIS is trained by using the sample space to establish a nonlinear mapping mathematical model of the central pixel and the domain pixel, and it can be used to achieve blind extraction;

Step 4: Perform a layer of wavelet decomposition on the original host image to obtain a low-frequency sub-band coefficient LLl of the host image;

Step 5: For a random position coordinate array Z, obtain the value of the low-frequency sub-band coefficient in 7 by the following formula (6):

$$K(p_x, p_y) = \sum\nolimits_{x_1=-1}^{1} \sum\nolimits_{y_1=-1}^{1} (LLl(p_{x+x_1}, p_{y+y_1}) - LLl(p_x, p_y)) \tag{6}$$

Step 6: Embed each bit of the watermark in the low-frequency sub-band of the original host image wavelet decomposition for times. Given the watermark is, the embedding procedure can be realized by adjusting the wavelet coefficient at the sub-band of the low-frequency by the following formula (7):

$$LLl(p_x, p_y) = K(p_x, p_y) + 2(W_s - 1) \times d \tag{7}$$

Where $x, y = sl + 1, \ sl + 2, \ \cdots, \ (s + l)l$, d is the embedding strength, which is adjusted according to the experiment results:

Step 7: Repeat step 6 until all the watermark elements are embedded into the wavelet coefficients of the low-frequency sub-band, and then carry out the inverse wavelet transform to obtain the watermarked image I'.

3.2   A Subsection Sample

The extracting process established a mathematical model, which is based on OANFIS to calculate the relationship of the pixels in the host image, thus to determine the mapping relationship between the input and the output signal, and to extract the watermark without the host image.

The detailed extracting process is as follows:

Step 1: Perform one-layer wavelet decomposition on the watermarked image to obtain a low-frequency sub-band coefficient LLl;

Step 2: Use Key2 to generate a random position coordinate array Z, as in the third step of the watermark embedding process;

Step 3: Calculate the value of the low-frequency sub-band coefficient in the coordinate array Z by formula (8):

$$K'(p_x, p_y) = \sum_{x_1 = -1}^{1} \sum_{y_1 = -1}^{1} \left(LLl(p_{x + x_1}, p_{y + y_1}) - LLl(p_x, p_y) \right) \tag{8}$$

Step 4: calculate times to extract the watermark by formula (9):

$$E(p_x, p_y) = LLl(p_x, p_y) - K'(p_x, p_y) \tag{9}$$

The extracted sample set is denoted as formula (10) and (11):

$$O = \left\{ E_{sl+1}(p_x, p_y), \ E_{sl+q}(p_x, p_y), \ E_{sl+3}(p_x, p_y), \ , E_{(s+1)l}(p_x, p_y), \ O^s \right\} \tag{10}$$

$$O^s = \begin{cases} 0, & W^s = 0 \\ 1, & W^s = 1 \end{cases} \tag{11}$$

Where O^s is the output of the neural network of the s-th sample;
Step 5: Select i samples as the training set F for OANFIS;

Step 6: Take the sample set as an input sample, using the input sample set and the trained OANFIS to obtain the output, and then extracting the watermark sequence of length k according to formula (12):

$$S = \begin{cases} 1 & O^s \geq 0.5 \\ 0, & else \end{cases} \tag{12}$$

The array is converted into a two-dimensional signal, and the final binary digital watermark image W' is recovered based on Key1.

4 Results and Discussion

In this section, we will discuss the imperceptibility of the watermarked image and the robustness of watermarks under various attacks, and compare the results of our scheme with other existing ones.

4.1 Simulation Results

In order to verify the validity and feasibility of the proposed scheme, six gray images of 256×256 pixels were selected as the host images which are shown in Table 1, and a binary image of 64×64 was selected as the watermark image. It can be seen from the second and the third rows in Table 1 that there is no significant difference between the host image and the watermarked image, which indicates that the proposed algorithm has good imperceptibility. Although only one of the NC value of the extracted watermark reaches 1, the NC value of the others are quite close to 1. Therefore, it does not affect the purpose of copyright protection.

Table 1. Experimental results on different host images.

Name of host image	Lena	Goldhill	Couple	Airplane	Barbara	Cameraman
Host image						
Watermarked image						
Extracted watermark	通信学院	通信学院	通信学院	通信学院	通信学院	通信学院
PSNR	60.2404	60.5162	60.7315	60.2104	60.7692	60.7313
NC	0.97893	0.97983	0.97873	1	0.97885	0.98647

4.2   A Subsection Sample

Watermarked Lena image was used for further simulation analysis. In the experiment, we applied various attacks to test the robustness. The extracted watermark image and NC value after the attack are shown in Table 2.

Table 2. The extracted watermark images under various attacks.

JPEG (QF=30) PSNR=0.87994	JPEG (QF=50) PSNR=0.95288	JPEG (QF=70) PSNR=0.97152	JPEG (QF=90) PSNR=0.98102	Average Filtering(3×3) PSNR=0.98374	Image Brighten PSNR=1.00
Contrast Decreasing PSNR=1.00	Salt-pepper Noise (0.01) PSNR=0.97866	Salt-pepper Noise (0.05) PSNR=0.94975	Salt-pepper Noise (0.2) PSNR=0.90858	Product Noise (0.003) PSNR=0.88932	Gaussian low-pass filtering(3,0.5) PSNR=0.94122
Median Filtering PSNR=0.82959	Motion Filtering(9,0) PSNR=0.93858	Cropping PSNR=0.97906	JPEG (QF=10) PSNR=0.70478	Rotate (0.25) PSNR=0.73319	Histogram Equalization PSNR=0.66506

As can be seen from Table 2, the proposed scheme has satisfying robustness against Gaussian low-pass filtering (3, 0.5), histogram equalization, salt and pepper noise, average filtering, cropping and resize.

Last but not least, in order to further discuss the robustness of the proposed scheme, the experiment was compared with the existing watermarking technique using the quality evaluation methods mentioned in the paper [27–31]. The comparison results are shown in Fig. 2. Conclusions can be drawn from the figure that:

(1) the transparency of proposed scheme is better than the existing ones;
(2) the robustness of the proposed scheme is superior to the compared schemes under various attacks, whatever common attacks or the geometric attacks.

From the above comparisons with different techniques, we have proved the efficiency and feasibility of the proposed scheme. In general, OANFIS-based blind watermarking scheme uses adaptive factors to maintain the trade-off between robustness and transparency.

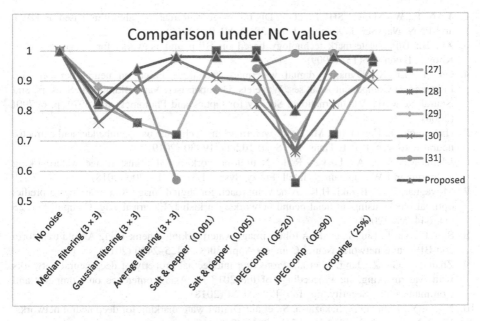

Fig. 2. NC performance comparison with paper [27–31].

5 Conclusions

Under the consideration of robustness and transparency, combined with some existing network security ideas [32–45], we propose an efficient blind digital image watermarking technique using wavelet domain-based adaptive neuro-fuzzy inference system. Back propagation algorithm and least square method is combined to optimized the system, It is a novel application of ANFIS in the security field of robust digital image watermarking. Simulation results show that, compared with existing schemes, the proposed one is robust to most attacks under the same watermarking capacity. And the transparency of the proposed scheme reaches 60.02 dB in terms of PSNR. In addition, the proposed algorithm is completely reversible, which is very important for some sensitive confidential information.

Acknowledgement. The research was supported by Hainan Provincial Natural Science Foundation (Grant No. 117063), Hainan Provincial Technology Project (Key Research and Development Project, Grant No. ZDYF2017171), Funding Scheme to Outstanding Scientific and Technological Programs by Chinese Students Abroad (Grant No. Human Society Notice [2015] 192 and [2016]176-2).

References

1. Zhang, M., Zhang, L., Huang, X.: Neural network-based digital image watermarking algorithm. J. Jiangxi Normal Univ. (Natural Sciences Edition) **31**(5), 445–449 (2007)

2. YAN, F., WANG, U., SHI, L., et al.: Digital image watermarking algorithm based on DWT and PNN. Nat. Sci. J. Xiangtan Univ. **38**(3), 89–93 (2016)

3. Xu, B.: Blind watermark technology based on BP-neural networks for image. Comput. Knowl. Technol. **5**(13) (2009)

4. Gu, T., Li, X.: Dynamic digital watermark technique based on neural network. In: Independent Component Analyses, Wavelets, Unsupervised Nano-Biomimetic Sensors, and Neural Networks VI. International Society for Optics and Photonics, vol. 6979, p. 69790I (2008)

5. Hamamoto, I., Kawamura, M.: Image watermarking technique using embedder and extractor neural networks. IEICE Trans. Inf. Syst. **102**(1), 19–30 (2019)

6. Islam, M., Roy, A., Laskar, R.H.: Neural network based robust image watermarking technique in LWT domain. J. Intell. Fuzzy Syst. **34**(3), 1691–1700 (2018)

7. Movaghar, R.K., Bizaki, H.K.: A new approach for digital image watermarking to predict optimal blocks using artificial neural networks. Turkish J. Electrical Eng. Comput. Sci. **25**(1), 644–654 (2017)

8. Sun, L., Xu, J., Liu, S., et al.: A robust image watermarking scheme using Arnold transform and BP neural network. Neural Comput. Appl. **30**(8), 2425–2440 (2018)

9. Zhang, J., Gu, Z., Jang, J., et al.: Protecting intellectual property of deep neural networks with watermarking. In: Proceedings of the 2018 on Asia Conference on Computer and Communications Security, pp. 159–172. ACM (2018)

10. Nagai, Y., Uchida, Y., Sakazawa, S., et al.: Digital watermarking for deep neural networks. Int. J. Multimedia Inf. Retrieval **7**(1), 3–16 (2018)

11. Li, L.Z., Gao, T.G., Gu, Q.L., et al.: A zero-watermarking algorithm based on fuzzy adaptive resonance theory. In: 2009 Sixth International Conference on Fuzzy Systems and Knowledge Discovery, vol. 3, pp. 378–382. IEEE (2009)

12. Motwani, M., Beke, N., Bhoite, A., et al.: Adaptive fuzzy watermarking for 3D models. In: International Conference on Computational Intelligence and Multimedia Applications (ICCIMA 2007), vol. 4, pp. 49–53. IEEE (2007)

13. Duong, D.M., Duong, D.A.: A hybrid watermarking scheme using contourlet transform and fuzzy logic. In: 2012 9th International Conference on Fuzzy Systems and Knowledge Discovery, pp. 386–390. IEEE (2012)

14. Jamali, M., Rafiei, S., Soroushmehr, S.M., et al.: Adaptive image watermarking using human perception based fuzzy inference system. J. Intell. Fuzzy Syst. 1–20 (2018, Preprint)

15. Papakostas, G.A., Tsougenis, E.D., Koulouriotis, D.E.: Fuzzy knowledge-based adaptive image watermarking by the method of moments. Complex Intell. Syst. **2**(3), 205–220 (2016)

16. Agarwal, C., Mishra, A., Sharma, A.: A novel gray-scale image watermarking using hybrid Fuzzy-BPN architecture. Egyptian Inform. J. **16**(1), 83–102 (2015)

17. Loganathan, A., Kaliyaperumal, G.: An adaptive HVS based video watermarking scheme for multiple watermarks using BAM neural networks and fuzzy inference system. Expert Syst. Appl. **63**, 412–434 (2016)

18. Mishra, A., Sehra, K., Chetty, G.: Neuro fuzzy architecture for gray scale image watermarking using fractal dimensions. In: 2018 International Joint Conference on Neural Networks (IJCNN), pp. 1–8. IEEE (2018)

19. Nobuhara, H., Pedrycz, W., Hirota, K.: A digital watermarking algorithm using image compression method based on fuzzy relational equation. In: 2002 IEEE World Congress on Computational Intelligence. 2002 IEEE International Conference on Fuzzy Systems. FUZZ-IEEE'02. Proceedings (Cat. No. 02CH37291), vol. 2, pp. 1568–1573. IEEE (2002)

20. Moosazadeh, M., Andalib, A.: A new robust color digital image watermarking algorithm in DCT domain using genetic algorithm and coefficients exchange approach. In: 2016 Second International Conference on Web Research (ICWR), pp. 19–24. IEEE (2016)

21. Takore, T.T., Kumar, P.R., Devi, G.L.: Efficient gray image watermarking algorithm based on DWT-SVD using genetic algorithm. In: 2016 International Conference on Information Communication and Embedded Systems (ICICES), pp. 1–6. IEEE (2016)
22. Lai, C.C., Yeh, C.H., Ko, C.H., et al.: Image watermarking scheme using genetic algorithm. In: 2012 Sixth International Conference on Genetic and Evolutionary Computing, pp. 476–479. IEEE (2012)
23. Latif, A., Naghsh-Nilchi, A.R., Derhami, V.: A reinforcement learning method for decision making process of watermark strength in still images. Sci. Res. Essays 6(10), 2119–2128 (2011)
24. Jang, J.S.R.: Fuzzy modeling using generalized neural networks and kalman filter algorithm. In: AAAI, vol. 91, pp. 762–767 (1991)
25. Jang, J.S.R.: ANFIS: adaptive-network-based fuzzy inference system. IEEE Trans. Syst. Man Cybernet. 23(3), 665–685 (1993)
26. Zhao, X.Y., Gang, C.: Ergodic matrix in image encryption. In: Second International Conference on Image and Graphics. International Society for Optics and Photonics, vol. 4875, pp. 394–402 (2002)
27. Kandi, H., Mishra, D., Gorthi, S.R.K.S.: Exploring the learning capabilities of convolutional neural networks for robust image watermarking. Comput. Secur. 65, 247–268 (2017)
28. Liu, J.X., Wen, X., Yuan, L.M., et al.: A robust approach of watermarking in contourlet domain based on probabilistic neural network. Multimedia Tools Appl. 76(22), 24009–24026 (2017)
29. Makbol, N.M., Khoo, B.E.: Robust blind image watermarking scheme based on redundant discrete wavelet transform and singular value decomposition. AEU-Int. J. Electron. Commun. 67(2), 102–112 (2013)
30. Rani, A., Raman, B., Kumar, S.: A robust watermarking scheme exploiting balanced neural tree for rightful ownership protection. Multimedia Tools Appl. 72(3), 2225–2248 (2014)
31. Singh, A.K., Kumar, B., Singh, S.K., et al.: Multiple watermarking technique for securing online social network contents using back propagation neural network. Future Gener. Comput. Syst. 86, 926–939 (2018)
32. Cheng, R., Xu, R., Tang, X., et al.: An abnormal network flow feature sequence prediction approach for DDoS attacks detection in big data environment. Comput. Mater. Continua 55(1), 095 (2018)
33. Cheng, J., Zhou, J., Liu, Q., et al.: A DDoS detection method for socially aware networking based on forecasting fusion feature sequence. Comput. J. 61(7), 959–970 (2018)
34. Cheng, J., Zhang, C., Tang, X., et al.: Adaptive DDoS attack detection method based on multiple-kernel learning. Secur. Commun. Networks 2018 (2018)
35. Cheng, J., Li, M., Tang, X., et al.: Flow correlation degree optimization driven random forest for detecting DDoS attacks in cloud computing. Secur. Commun. Networks 2018 (2018)
36. Wang, H., Wang, W., Cui, Z., Zhou, X., Zhao, J., Li, Y.: A new dynamic firefly algorithm for demand estimation of water resources. Inf. Sci. https://doi.org/10.1016/j.ins.2018.01.041
37. Li, J., Liu, Z., Chen, X., Tan, X., Wong, D.S.: L-EncDB: a lightweight framework for privacy-preserving data queries in cloud computing. Knowl.-Based Syst. 79, 18–26 (2015)
38. Lin, Q., Yan, H., Huang, Z., Chen, W., Shen, J., Tang, Y.: An ID-based linearly homomorphic signature scheme and its application in blockchain. IEEE Access. https://doi.org/10.1109/access.2018.2809426
39. Xu, J., Wei, L., Zhang, Y., Wang, A., Zhou, F., Gao, C.-z.: Dynamic fully homomorphic encryption-based Merkle tree for lightweight streaming authenticated data structures. J. Network Comput. Appl. (2018). https://doi.org/10.1016/j.jnca.2018.01.014

40. Li, Ya., Wang, G., Nie, L., Wang, Q.: Distance metric optimization driven convolutional neural network for age invariant face recognition. Pattern Recogn. **75**, 51–62 (2018). https://doi.org/10.1016/j.patcog.2017.10.015
41. Shen, J., Gui, Z., Ji, S., Shen, J., Tan, H., Tang, Y.: Cloud-aided lightweight certificateless authentication protocol with anonymity for wireless body area networks. J. Network Comput. Appl. (2018). https://doi.org/10.1016/j.jnca.2018.01.003
42. Ma, X., Li, J., Zhang, F.: Outsourcing computation of modular exponentiations in cloud computing. Cluster Comput. **16**(4), 787–796 (2013)
43. Tian, H., Chen, X., Li, J.: A short non-delegatable strong designated verifier signature. In: Susilo, W., Mu, Y., Seberry, J. (eds.) ACISP 2012. LNCS, vol. 7372, pp. 261–279. Springer, Heidelberg (2012). https://doi.org/10.1007/978-3-642-31448-3_20
44. Chen, W., Lei, H., Qi, K.: Lattice-based linearly homomorphic signatures in the standard model. Theor. Comput. Sci. **634**, 47–54 (2016)
45. Chen, W., et al.: Inapproximability results for the minimum integral solution problem with preprocessing over infinity norm. Theoret. Comput. Sci. **478**, 127–131 (2013)

Towards Secure Computation of Similar Patient Query on Genomic Data Under Multiple Keys

Chuan Zhao[1,2], Shengnan Zhao[3], Bo Zhang[1,2], Shan Jing[1,2(✉)],
Zhenxiang Chen[1,2], and Minghao Zhao[4]

[1] Shandong Provincial Key Laboratory of Network Based Intelligent Computing,
University of Jinan, Jinan 250022, China
jingshan@ujn.edu.cn
[2] School of Information Science and Engineering,
University of Jinan, Jinan 250022, China
[3] School of Software, Shandong University, Jinan 250101, China
[4] School of Software, Tsinghua University, Beijing, China

Abstract. Genomics plays an especial role in our daily lives. Genomic data, however, are highly-sensitive and thus normally stored in repositories with strict access control insurance. This severely restricts the associated processing on genomic data, in which multiple institutes holding their own data hope to conduct specific computation on the entire dataset. Accordingly, researchers attempt to propose methods to enable secure computation on genomic data among multiple parties. Nevertheless, most of the existing solutions fall short in efficiency, security or scalability.

In this paper, we focus on providing a secure and practical solution to perform similar patient query on distributed Electronic Health Records (EHR) databases with genomic data. To achieve this, we propose a privacy-preserving framework to execute similar patient query on genomic data owned by distributed owners in a server-aided setting. Specifically, we apply multi-key homomorphic encryption to the proposed framework, where each data owner performs queries on its local EHR database, encrypts query results with its unique public key, and sends them to the servers for further secure edit-distance computation on genomic data encrypted under multiple keys. Security and performance analysis show that our system achieves satisfactory efficiency, scalability, and flexibility while protecting the privacy of each data contributor.

Supported by National Natural Science Foundation of China (No. 61702218, 61672262), Shandong Provincial Key Research and Development Project (No. 2019GGX101028, 2018CXGC0706, 2016GGX101001), Shandong Province Higher Educational Science and Technology Program (No. J18KA349), Natural Science Foundation of Shandong Province (No. ZR2014JL042, ZR2014FL011, ZR2015FL023), Project of Independent Cultivated Innovation Team of Jinan City (No. 2018GXRC002), Doctoral Program of University of Jinan (No.160100224), and Science and Technology Program of University of Jinan (No. XKY1709).

J. Vaidya et al. (Eds.): CSS 2019, LNCS 11983, pp. 275–284, 2019.
https://doi.org/10.1007/978-3-030-37352-8_24

Keywords: Secure computation · Genomic data privacy · Homomorphic encryption · Electronic health records

1   Introduction

With the rapid development of genome sequencing technology [6,10], we are now able to obtain detailed genomic data at a very low cost. Analysis of these data provides useful information to our daily lives, especially in health care, biomedical research, direct-to-consumer genetic detection (e.g. 23 and Me) and other fields . Among the applications of genomic data, the most popular one is Similar Patient Query (SPQ) on genomic data, which is widely used to identify similar patients from Electronic Health Records (EHR) databases with genomic data, through a health information exchange system such as PatientsLikeMe [13]. To be specific, suppose a doctor or a hospital holding the genome of a patient may want to find other individuals with similar genomic data and use the EHR data of these individuals to find better treatment for that patient.

Similar patient query benefits from querying on a large amount of EHR data, but a single organization may not have sufficient data, and databases of different hospitals and medical institutions could be geographically distributed. An effective way to make the most of genomic data in similar patient query is to conduct collaborative query among distributed data owners. However, unlike ordinary data, human genomic data is personally identifiable information. It contains a large amount of sensitive information about individuals, such as personal traits, disease susceptibility, and identity information. Leakage of this information may result in discrimination or further social problems, which will lead to severe consequences. Even if genomic data are anonymized, the identifiable information contained in them cannot be completely removed, and the identity may be re-identified. Therefore, there is a common belief among researchers that genomic data-related operations, including genome-based similar patient query, should be handled carefully in a privacy-preserving manner. An applicable way to keep individuals' information private is to apply cryptographic protocols to the objective collaborative query tasks.

Researchers have proposed many techniques and frameworks to provide secure solutions to similar patient query on genomic data. Instead of proposing an efficient distributed framework for similar patient query, most of the work in the literature mainly focus on improving the efficiency of computing (an approximated version of) edit distance [1,3,12]. The most relevant research work is the scheme proposed by Aziz *et al.* [4], which is a framework designed for the count and ranked queries on genomic data distributed and owned by different owners. In their system, data owners execute count queries independently and send the encrypted outputs to a central server. In order to enable the central server to perform computation on ciphertexts, the authors adopted a typical homomorphic encryption scheme – Paillier cryptosystem [8]. However, in this framework, all participants need to rely on a crypto service provider, who is responsible for distributing a single public-secret key pair in the system. This assumption makes employment in practice very limited. Besides, this work only secures the computations in the cloud but not the final output of the query, which may leak information about genomic data of data contributors.

1.1 Our Contributions

In this paper, in order to enable a querier to efficiently perform similar patient query on distributed Electronic Health Records (EHR) databases with genomic data, we design and evaluate a new framework with multiple advantages. The main contributions of this work are summarized as follows:

– **Multi-key setting.** We propose a privacy-preserving framework to execute similar patient query on genomic data owned by distributed owners in a multi-key setting. Specifically, instead of using a single public key to encrypt different data owners' data, we consider the multi-key scenario where each party possesses its own public-secret key pair. We implement this by applying multi-key homomorphic encryption [9] to our framework, and make use of two servers to perform secure edit distance computation on genomic data encrypted under multiple public keys. In the multi-key scenario, each data owner can also be a querier and obtain query results encrypted under its own secret key.
– **Optimal interaction costs for the querier and data owners.** In the proposed framework, each data owner performs queries on its local EHR database, encrypts query results with its unique public key, and sends them to two servers for further edit-distance computation. The two servers help with avoiding interaction between the querier and data owners during the query process. Besides, the querier can be off-line after submitting the query to the server, which is preferable in server-aided settings.
– **Strong flexibility and scalability.** Each user in the platform has its own public-secret key pair. Therefore, there is no need for the system to generate new public-secret key pairs and share the secret key among all users when a new user joins in the system. From this point of view, the proposed framework is flexible and scalable.
– **Performance evaluation.** We perform security and performance analysis and show that our system achieves satisfactory efficiency, scalability, and flexibility while protecting the privacy of each data contributor.

The rest of this paper is organized as follows. Section 2 presents related preliminaries, including building blocks and the threat model. Section 3 describes the proposed framework in detail, and gives security and efficiency analysis. The last section concludes this paper and describes possible future work.

2 Preliminaries

2.1 Building Blocks

Additively Homomorphic Encryption. The main building block of our system is homomorphic encryption, a form of encryption that allows computation tasks to be carried out on ciphertext, thus generating an encrypted result which, when decrypted, matches the result of operations performed on the plaintext.

In this paper, we consider additively homomorphic encryption. Intuitively, a public-key encryption scheme $\varepsilon = (\mathsf{KeyGen}, \mathsf{Enc}, \mathsf{Dec})$ is additively homomorphic, if given two ciphertexts $c_1 = \mathsf{Enc}_{pk}(m_1)$ and $c_2 = \mathsf{Enc}_{pk}(m_2)$, it is possible to efficiently compute $c_1 \cdot c_2$ such that

$$c_1 \cdot c_2 = \mathsf{Enc}_{pk}(m_1 + m_2)$$

without any knowledge of the secret key or plaintexts, where the symbol "$\cdot$" denotes the operation in ciphertext space, and the symbol "$+$" denotes the addition operation in plaintext space. Here we require that the result of $c_1 \cdot c_2$ is a random encryption to $m_1 + m_2$.

BCP Cryptosystem. To conduct homomorphic encryption in a multi-key setting, we consider a special additively homomorphic encryption scheme—BCP cryptosystem proposed by Bresson, Catalano, and Pointcheval [5], which provides two independent decryption mechanisms. In addition to key generation algorithm KeyGen, encryption algorithm Enc and decryption algorithm Dec, BCP cryptosystem also consists of a setup algorithm Setup and a master decryption algorithm mDec. The former algorithm is responsible for generating public parameters and a master secret key, and the latter algorithm allows successful decryption of any ciphertexts generated in this cryptosystem. Specifically, the algorithms in BCP cryptosystem are presented as follows:

- $(pp, msk) \leftarrow \mathsf{Setup}(1^n)$: Given a security parameter n, outputs public parameters pp and a master secret key msk.
- $(pk, sk) \leftarrow \mathsf{KeyGen}(pp)$: Given public parameters pp, outputs a public-secret key pair (pk, sk).
- $c \leftarrow \mathsf{Enc}_{pp,pk}(m)$: Given public parameters pp, a public key pk and a message m, outputs a ciphertext c.
- $m := \mathsf{Dec}_{pp,sk}(c)$: Given public parameters pp, a secret key sk and a ciphertext c, outputs a message m.
- $m := \mathsf{mDec}_{pp,pk,msk}(c)$: Given public parameters pp, a user's public key pk, a master secret key msk and a ciphertext c, outputs a message m.

In the following sections, we omit pp in the above algorithms for a more succinct description.

Similar Patient Query on Genomic Data. Genomic data refers to the genome and DNA data of an organism. It is a pair of sequences of three billion bases taking value in $\{A, T, G, C\}$. This pair of sequences carries the genetic signature of its holder. Similar patient query on genomic data is a medical method used to identify similar patients from EHR databases with genomic data. In this setting, a doctor or a hospital holding the genome of a patient may want to find other individuals with similar genomic data, and use the EHR data of these individuals to find better treatment for that patient. In this paper, we consider the following scenario. A querier with a genomic sequence and a Structured Query Language (SQL) query, would like to obtain the identities and the corresponding EHR data of the t-closest genomic sequences in distributed EHR databases satisfying the specific SQL query.

The similarity between two genomic sequences is measured by edit distance, which represents the minimum number of insertions, deletions, and substitutions needed to convert a sequence a to a sequence b [7]. The Wagner-Fisher algorithm [2,11] is wildly used to compute edit distance.

2.2 Threat Model

In this paper, we aim at protecting the privacy of genomic data against internal adversaries in the semi-honest model, where the adversary is honest-but-curious, in the sense that it will follow protocol specifications strictly, but might try to derive private information about the honest participants' datasets. The adversary can corrupt any kinds of participants in the proposed system, including proxy server, auxiliary server, data owner, and querier. However, we assume that the adversary cannot corrupt both the cloud and server at the same time. This is a relatively reasonable assumption because it can be easily realized in the real world. For example, the proxy server belongs to a medical institution or organization, and the auxiliary server is provided by a commercial company. In this case, it is proper to assume these two servers will not collude due to reputation concerns.

During the process of similar patient query, privacy should be preserved for both the genomic data in the EHR databases as well as the query genomic sequence. Specifically, the query genomic sequence should be protected against data owners and servers in the system, while the privacy of genomic data in the EHR databases should be preserved against the querier and servers.

3 Proposed Framework

In this paper, we propose an effective similar patient query framework that enables a querier to securely have access to similar patients' DHR data in an outsourcing setting. In this section, we describe our proposed framework in detail and illustrate its efficiency and security.

3.1 Framework Participants

The proposed framework involves four kinds of participants: Querier, Data Owner, Proxy Server and Auxiliary Server. Each kind of the participant is responsible for different specific tasks, presented as follows:

- Querier: A querier, denoted as Q, may be any doctor, researcher or institution who wants to perform similar patient queries for better disease diagnosis or other purposes. In the proposed system, the querier Q possesses a key pair (pk, sk) generated from the BCP scheme for encryption/decryption of genomic data and EHR data.

- Data Owner: Suppose there are m data owners $D_1, D_2, \cdots, D_m$ in the system. These data owners can be any hospitals or biomedical research centers who locally store patients' DHR data and genomic data. These data are stored securely by data owners with strict access control insurance. After receiving the query forwarded by the proxy server, data owners will perform query operations locally on DHR databases and find the corresponding genomic data as the query result. Like the querier, each data owner D_i $(i \in [m])$ also holds a public-secret key pair (pk_i, sk_i) for further encryption/decryption of private data. Importantly, each data owner can also be a querier.
- Proxy Server: The proxy server in our system, denoted as S_1, is responsible for interacting with all other participants to accomplish secure computation of similar patient query. Specifically, it receives the query and encrypted genome data from Q, performs a query on distributed EHR databases possessed by data owners D_i, computes the edit distance between encrypted genomic data under multiple public keys with the auxiliary server securely, and sends back the final query result to the querier.
- Auxiliary Server: The auxiliary server, denoted as S_2, is responsible for running the Setup algorithm of BCP cryptosystem, and also the secure edit distance computation protocol on genomic data with the proxy server S_1.

Please refer to Fig. 1 for an intuitive description.

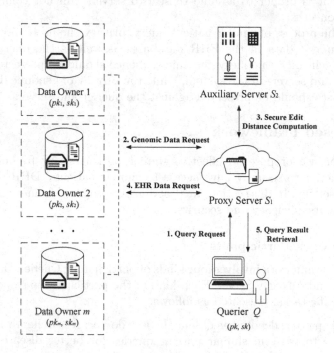

Fig. 1. Proposed framework

3.2   Execution Description

– Setup Phase

- S_2 runs the system setup algorithm Setup of BCP cryptosystem $(pp, msk) \leftarrow$ Setup(1^n), keeps the master secret key msk private and sends the public parameters pp to the querier and all data owners in the system.
- The querier Q invokes the key generation algorithm KeyGen to generate its public-secret key pairs $(pk, sk) \leftarrow$ KeyGen(pp).
- Each data owner $D_i (i \in [m])$ invokes KeyGen to generate its public-secret key pair $(pk_i, sk_i) \leftarrow$ KeyGen(pp).

– Query Phase

- **Query Request.** The querier Q invokes the encryption algorithm Enc and encrypts its genomic data g under its public key pk, and obtains the ciphertext $c \leftarrow$ Enc$_{pk}(g)$. Then Q submits a similar patient query $q = (\text{SQL}, c, t)$ to the proxy server S_1, where SQL is a SQL query to be performed on data owners' distributed EHR databases, c is the encrypted form of Q's genomic data g, and t indicates the upper bound of the edit distance between g and other genomic sequences. In other words, q determines which kind of patients' EHR data Q would like to get from this query.
- **Genomic Data Request.** After receiving $q = (\text{SQL}, c, t)$, the proxy server S_1 forward SQL to all data owners. For $i \in [m]$, D_i performs the following operations.
    * First, it performs database query SQL on its local EHR database. For example, suppose SQL = **SELECT** index **FROM** EHR **WHERE** disease type = breast cancer, D_i finds all the patient records satisfying disease type = breast cancer, and the corresponding genomic data $g_{i,j} (j \in N_i)$, where N_i is the set of the indices of the query results.
    * Second, it encrypts these genomic data $g_{i,j}$ with pk_i by invoking BCP encryption algorithm Enc, and obtains $c_{i,j} \leftarrow$ Enc$_{pk_i}(g_{i,j})$ $(j \in N_i)$.
    * Then, D_i uploads $(c_{i,j}, N_i)$ to the proxy server S_1.
- **Secure Edit Distance Computation.** With $(t, c, c_{i,j}, N_i)(i \in [m], j \in N_i)$, S_1 runs the secure edit distance computation protocol Protocol 1 (see below) with the auxiliary server S_2. As a result, S_1 obtains new indices sets $N_i'(i \in I)$, satisfying that the edit distance between g and each genomic data $g_{i,j}(i \in I, j \in N_i')$ is at most t, where I is the indices set of relevant data owners. Note that during the process of secure edit distance computation protocol, no participants will learn any information about the genomic data.
- **EHR Data Request.** S_1 sends the querier's public key pk, and the index set N_i' to the relevant data owners $D_i(i \in I)$, and requests these data owners to send back encrypted EHR data records. Each relevant data owner D_i runs Enc algorithm, encrypts corresponding EHR data records

$d_{i,j}(i \in I, j \in N_i')$, and sends the ciphertexts $c_{i,j}' \leftarrow \mathsf{Enc}_{pk_i}(d_{i,j})(i \in I, j \in N_i')$ back to S_1.

- **Query Result Retrieval.** After the querier Q receives the encrypted DHR data $c_{i,j}'(i \in I, j \in N_i')$ from S_1, it decrypts the ciphertexts with sk and obtains the query result $d_{i,j}(i \in I, j \in N_i')$.

We now describe in detail about the edit distance secure computation protocol run between S_1 and S_2 (Fig. 2).

3.3 Security and Efficiency Analysis

In this section, we elaborate on the security and efficiency of our framework.

Security Analysis. First, we state that the information about the querier's genomic data g and data owners' genomic data $g_i (i \in [m], j \in N_i)$ will not be leaked to other participants. This benefits from the fact that g and g_i are encrypted under the BCP cryptosystem, and remain encrypted or blinded during the query process. Particularly, the secure edit distance protocol ensures that neither S_1 nor S_2 will obtain any information about related genomic data g and g_i.

Second, as for the information about distributed EHR databases, we note that all EHR data are stored locally by data owners with strict access control insurance. No one will learn anything about these data except for the query result learned by the querier.

Efficiency Analysis. We now analyze the efficiency of the proposed framework.

Computation cost. The querier only needs to invoke the Enc algorithm once and the Dec algorithm $|I| * |N_i'|$ times ($i \in I$). Each data owner $D_i(i \in [m])$ performs SQL query locally without encryption operations, and only needs to invoke the Enc algorithm $|N_i|$ times to encrypt the genomic data that satisfy the SQL query. As for the proxy server and auxiliary server, they are responsible for running the secure edit distance protocol. Because the servers are rich in both computation and communication resources, the complexity of secure computation protocol would not be a bottleneck in the runtime of this framework.

Scalability. We note that there is no restriction on the number of data owners and queriers in this system. Most importantly, the runtime efficiency of the system is not related to the number of participants but the number of genomic data.

Flexibility. Because of the multi-key setting adopted in our framework, new participants can join in the system flexibly. Specifically, a new querier or a new data owner with its own public-secret key pair can join in the system any time, without requiring the auxiliary server to update system public parameters all the time.

4 Conclusions

In this paper, we proposed a new framework to enable a querier to securely and practically query distributed EHR databases with genomic data. During the query process, all the genomic data are kept private with the help of the BCP cryptosystem, a dual-trapdoor encryption scheme with additive homomorphism.

Protocol for Secure Edit Distance Computation

Inputs:

- S_1 inputs $(t, c, c_{i,j}, N_i)(i \in [m], j \in N_i)$;
- S_2 inputs msk;

Outputs:

- S_1 outputs $N_i'(i \in I)$, where I is the set of relevant data owners' indices;
- S_2 outputs nothing;

Protocol Execution:

- Blinding. Upon receiving the encrypted form c of Q's genomic data g, the proxy server S_1 blinds it with a random value r and obtains c'. Besides, it blinds the ciphertext $c_{i,j}$ of each genomic data $g_{i,j}(i \in [m], j \in N_i)$ with a random value $r_{i,j}$, and gets $c_{i,j}'$.
- Re-Encryption. With msk, the auxiliary server S_2 is able to decrypts all $c_{i,j}'$ by invoking mDec algorithm, and re-encrypts them with the querier's public key pk, denoted as $c_{i,j}''$. In this way, all ciphertexts are encrypted under the same public key pk, being ready for further computation.
- Edit Distance Computation. To compute the edit distance between g and each $g_{i,j}$ securely, the two servers collaborate together by running BCP cryptosystem. We need to perform two operations in edit distance computation, Addition and Multiplication. As BCP cryptosystem is additively homomorphic, Addition operations in edit distance computation can be performed by the proxy server S_1 alone, without any interaction with the auxiliary server S_2. However, Multiplication operations should be computed interactively between two servers. Specifically, for each multiplication operation in the edit distance computation between g and $g_{i,j}$, the proxy server S_1 sends the blinded data to the auxiliary server S_2, the latter then decrypts the data and multiplies the underlying plaintexts, re-encrypts intermediate results under pk, and returns the result to the proxy server S_1. Then S_1 removes the blinding factor with the method as described in [9].
- Computation Result. For $i \in [m], j \in N_i$, S_1 obtains the edit distance between g and $g_{i,j}$, denoted as $e_{i,j}$. Then it gets the indices of the data records satisfying $e_{i,j} \leqslant t$, and denotes the indices set as $N_i'(i \in [I])$, where I is the set of indices of relevant data owners.

Fig. 2. Protocol for secure edit distance computation

By adopting a novel method proposed by Peter *et al.*, we succeeded in accomplishing secure edit distance computation tasks on genomic data in the multi-key setting, which increased the scalability and flexibility of the system. Besides, our framework enables the data owners to perform queries on EHR databases locally and find corresponding genomic data without any interaction with the querier. This, therefore, avoided the transfer of a large amount of highly-sensitive data, and also decreased the communication costs greatly. Security and performance analysis showed that our system achieved satisfactory efficiency while protecting the privacy of each data owner.

Acknowledgments. Supported by National Natural Science Foundation of China (No. 61702218, 61672262), Shandong Provincial Key Research and Development Project (No. 2019GGX101028, 2018CXGC0706), Shandong Province Higher Educational Science and Technology Program (No. J18KA349), Project of Independent Cultivated Innovation Team of Jinan City (No. 2018GXRC002).

References

1. Aziz, M.M.A., Alhadidi, D., Mohammed, N.: Secure approximation of edit distance on genomic data. BMC Med. Genomics **10**(2), 41 (2017)
2. Andoni, A., Onak, K.: Approximating edit distance in near-linear time. SIAM J. Comput. **41**(6), 1635–1648 (2012)
3. Asharov, G., Halevi, S., Lindell, Y., Rabin, T.: Privacy-preserving search of similar patients in genomic data. Proc. Priv. Enhancing Technol. **2018**(4), 104–124 (2018)
4. Aziz, A., Momin, Md., Hasan, M.Z., Mohammed, N., Alhadidi, D.: Secure and efficient multiparty computation on genomic data. In: Proceedings of the 20th International Database Engineering & Applications Symposium, pp. 278–283. ACM (2016)
5. Bresson, E., Catalano, D., Pointcheval, D.: A simple public-key cryptosystem with a double trapdoor decryption mechanism and its applications. In: Laih, C.-S. (ed.) ASIACRYPT 2003. LNCS, vol. 2894, pp. 37–54. Springer, Heidelberg (2003). https://doi.org/10.1007/978-3-540-40061-5_3
6. Heather, J.M., Chain, B.: The sequence of sequencers: the history of sequencing DNA. Genomics **107**(1), 1–8 (2016)
7. Jurafsky, D.: Speech & Language Processing. Pearson Education (2000)
8. Paillier, P.: Public-key cryptosystems based on composite degree residuosity classes. In: Stern, J. (ed.) EUROCRYPT 1999. LNCS, vol. 1592, pp. 223–238. Springer, Heidelberg (1999). https://doi.org/10.1007/3-540-48910-X_16
9. Peter, A., Tews, E., Katzenbeisser, S.: Efficiently outsourcing multiparty computation under multiple keys. IEEE Trans. Inf. Forensics Secur. **8**(12), 2046–2058 (2013)
10. Venter, J.C., et al.: The sequence of the human genome. Science **291**(5507), 1304–1351 (2001)
11. Wagner, R.A., Fischer, M.J.: The string-to-string correction problem. J. ACM (JACM) **21**(1), 168–173 (1974)
12. Wang, X.S., Huang, Y., Zhao, Y., Tang, H., Wang, X., Bu, D.: Efficient genome-wide, privacy-preserving similar patient query based on private edit distance. In: Proceedings of the 22nd ACM SIGSAC Conference on Computer and Communications Security, pp. 492–503. ACM (2015)
13. Wicks, P., et al.: Sharing health data for better outcomes on patientslikeme. J. Med. Internet Res. **12**(2), e19 (2010)

Secure and Dynamic Outsourcing Computation of Machine Learning in Cloud Computing

Ping Li[1] and Jin Li[2(✉)]

[1] School of Computer Science, South China Normal University, Guangzhou 510631, China
liping26@mail2.sysu.edu.cn
[2] Peng Cheng Laboratory, Shenzhen, China
jinli71@gmail.com

Abstract. This paper presents a novel, secure and dynamic mechanism to train machine learning models that achieve membership privacy. Our protocol falls in the two-server-aided model and allows one server to perform most of computations and allows another server to provide auxiliary computation. In addition, users distribute their private data among two non-colluding but untrusted servers who train neural network on the adaptively select data using secure multi-party computation (MPC). In our protocol, only the selected members can reconstruct a predefined secret and jointly decrypt the computation result. This protocol is proven to be secure in the semi-honest model and passive adversary settings, and show that security is maintained even if the unselected users' drop out at any time.

Keywords: Privacy-preserving · Outsourcing computation · Machine learning · Dynamic secret sharing

1 Introduction

In recent year, machine learning has become an important tool to discover new knowledge about the data in cloud computing. Many services, applications and algorithms can be designed using much less engineering effort by relying on advanced machine learning. Due to the powerful computing and storage resources, cloud computing platforms provide many services for machine learning. a wide range of data stored and computed in cloud computing platfrom. However, cloud servers are not fully trusted, large-scale collection of sensitive data entails risks. Consequently, it is necessary and important to protect the data privacy and data confidentiality when processing machine learning related outsourcing computations [1,8,10,11]. To preserve the privacy and confidentiality of data, the cryptographic methods are used to design a secure protocol against various attacks [6,7,9].

Many previous works focused on the static data or data encrypted under a unified public key in the secure outsourcing computation of machine learning. In this work, we consider the scenario: users upload their ciphertexts (under their own public keys)

This work was supported by National Natural Science Foundation of China (No. 61702126).

to two servers for secure data storing and secure data processing; severs run an MPC protocol in order to transform these uploaded data into encryption under the same key, adaptively select which users' data can be used to compute and return the encrypted result to the users; only the selected users can jointly decrypt the result.

1.1 Our Contributions

We design a protocol for dynamic collaborative machine learning that offers privacy and secure. Our protocol is divided into two phases: setup phase and training phase. In the setup phase, multiple users share and encrypt their private data by their own private keys among two non-colluding but untrusted servers $\mathscr{S}_0$ and $\mathscr{S}_1$. In the training phase, $\mathscr{S}_0$ and $\mathscr{S}_1$ jointly train a neural network model over the adaptively selected outsourced data and get nothing except the trained model. The main contributions of this paper are summarized as follows:

- Our protocol is designed to conduct the data encrypted under different public keys and preserve the privacy and confidentiality of data. Users only perform the encryption operation and decryption operation.
- After collecting the outsourced data, $\mathscr{S}_1$ runs an MPC protocol with $\mathscr{S}_0$ in order to get the integrated encryptions under the product of selected public keys without changing the underlying plaintexts.
- $\mathscr{S}_0$ and $\mathscr{S}_1$ only perform several MPC protocols over the transformed ciphertexts (under the same key) in training phase.
- Once the training result is given, only the users corresponding to the selected public keys can reconstruct the predefined secret and jointly decrypt the training result.

2 Preliminaries

2.1 Definitions and Notations

Let $\mathbb{N}$ be natural number set. For $n \in \mathbb{N}$, we denote by $[1,n]$ as the set of $\{1,2,\cdots,n\}$. If S is a finite set, we write $s \xleftarrow{\$} S$ to denote the operation of taking element of S uniformly at random and issuing the output to variable s and $\#S$ denotes the number of elements in S. Let A be a randomized algorithm, we use $y \leftarrow A(x_1,x_2,\cdots,x_n)$ to describe the performing the algorithm A with inputs $x_1,x_2,\cdots,x_n$ and distributing the output to variable y.

Pseudorandom Generator. A secure pseudorandom generator (PRG) [2]: PRG : $\{0,1\}^n \rightarrow \{0,1\}^l$ can be described by a deterministic algorithm that expands short random seeds s into much longer bit sequences $\mathrm{PRG}(s)$ that appear to be "random".

Neural Networks (NN). Loosely speaking, in a multi-layer network, each neuron takes a vector of real-valued inputs, calculates a linear combination of these inputs, then applies a threshold to the result. That is to say, the output of neurons in layer k is defined by $\mathbf{x}_k = f(W_k\mathbf{x}_{i-1})$, where f is an activation function and W_k is the weight matrix that determines the contribution of each input signal. Given a training sample set, the task of learning a neural network is to determine the weight variables to minimize a pre-fined cost function.

3   Problem Formulation

3.1   System Model

In our work the ultimate goal is to design a privacy-preserving machine learning scheme that provides the privacy protection on the dynamic users' data, while supporting the outsourcing computation and keeping the efficiency. Therefore, there are three entities in our system: users, cloud servers and an authority party (Key Generation Center KGC) (illustrated in Fig. 1).

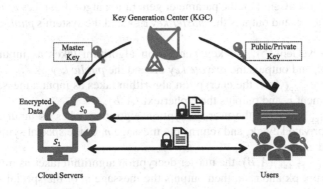

Fig. 1. Our system model under consideration

- Cloud Servers. $\mathcal{S}_0$ and $\mathcal{S}_1$ are two non-colluding but untrusted servers. There are several cryptographic protocols are performed between $\mathcal{S}_0$ and $\mathcal{S}_1$. In our system, $\mathcal{S}_0$ is distributed a master private key, which can be used to decrypt any valid ciphertext and $\mathcal{S}_1$ is distributed a public tuple from the KGC.
- Users. Let $U = \{u_1, \cdots, u_n\}$ be the user set. User $u_i \in U$ ($i \in [1,n]$) keeps private data, holds the corresponding public key and private key, and aims to outsource the computation task of machine learning to servers. User u_i divides the private data into two parts, encrypts each part of private data under its public key and uploads two ciphertexts to cloud $\mathcal{S}_0$ and cloud $\mathcal{S}_1$, respectively.
- Key Generation Center (KGC). In this system, KGC is an authority party trusted by all the entities. KGC setups the BCP cryptographic system [4] and distributes the system parameters and keys to the other entities.

3.2   Attack Model

In the semi-honest model, we stress that there is no collusion between $\mathcal{S}_0$ and $\mathcal{S}_1$, between any two of users or between any user and at most one of cloud servers. Adversary $\mathcal{A}$ has three types of abilities: (i) $\mathcal{A}$ may corrupt any subset of U to obtain all plaintexts belonging to the others; (ii) $\mathcal{A}$ may corrupt only one server to achieve plaintext of all outsourced data from the users; (iii) $\mathcal{A}$ corrupts a server and users.

4 Cryptographic Protocols

4.1 Secure Computation of the BCP Cryptosystem

BCP cryptosystem [4] is an additive homomorphic encryption scheme and has two independent decryption algorithms. One decryption algorithm is called *user decryption* (i.e., the user entity has a private key) and the other is *master decryption* algorithm (i.e., the master entity has a special key). Consider the scenario in our scheme, we describe the BCP encryption scheme, denoted by $\Pi = \{\mathsf{ParaGen}, \mathsf{KeyGen}, \mathsf{Enc}, \mathsf{uDec}, \mathsf{mDec}\}$ as follows:

- $(\mathsf{msk}, \mathsf{pp}) \leftarrow \mathsf{ParaGen}(1^\kappa)$: the parameter generation algorithm takes as input a security parameter κ, and outputs the *master key* msk and the system's *public parameters* pp.
- $(\mathsf{sk}, \mathsf{pk}) \leftarrow \mathsf{KeGen}(1^\kappa)$: the key generation algorithm takes as input a security parameter κ, and outputs the *private key* sk and the *public key* pk.
- $(A, B) \leftarrow \mathsf{Enc}_{(\mathsf{pp},\mathsf{pk})}(m)$: the encryption algorithm takes as input a message m and a random element r, and outputs the ciphertext (A, B).
- $m \leftarrow \mathsf{uDec}_{(\mathsf{pp},\mathsf{sk})}(A, B)$: the user decryption algorithm takes as input a ciphertext (A, B) and private key sk, and returns the message m or the special symbol '$\perp$' if it is an invalid ciphertext.
- $m \leftarrow \mathsf{mDec}_{(\mathsf{pp},\mathsf{pk},\mathsf{msk})}(A, B)$: the master decryption algorithm takes as input a ciphertext (A, B), pp, pk and msk, then outputs the message m or the special symbol '$\perp$' if it is an invalid ciphertext.

Let $[x]_i$ be the ciphertext of x encrypted under the public key pk_i of BCP cryptosystem. Denote by **Add** as the secure addition of BCP cryptosystem. Multiplication operation can be securely evaluated by the protocol of [5], which is based on "blinding-the-plaintext" techniques. This step is denoted by **SeMul**.

4.2 Secure Computation of Dynamic Secret Sharing Scheme

Let $\mathsf{U} = \{u_1, \cdots, u_n\}$ be a set of n parties and let $\mathscr{AS} \subseteq 2^{\mathsf{U}}$ be the access structure on U which we desire to recover the secret. We require the access structure $\mathscr{AS}$ with the property of *monotone*, that is if $B \in \mathscr{AS}$ and $B \subseteq C \subseteq \mathsf{U}$, then $C \in \mathscr{AS}$. We write by $\{p_s(x)\}_{x \in S}$ the probability distribution on the secret domain S. A dynamic secret sharing scheme with broadcast message for the access structure [3] consists of three phases:

Preprocessing Phase: The dealer D gets as input $\{p_s(x)\}_{x \in S}$, a set of parties $\mathsf{U} = \{u_1, \cdots, u_n\}$ and $\mathscr{AS} = \{\mathscr{AS}_1, \cdots, \mathscr{AS}_m\}$, generates and distributes the shares $s_1, \cdots, s_n$ to the parties $u_1, \cdots, u_n$, respectively.

Message Generation Phase: The dealer D takes as input the secret $s \xleftarrow{U} S$, the shares $\{s_1, \cdots, s_n\}$ and an index $\sigma \in [1, m]$, generates and broadcasts the broadcast message $b_\sigma \in B_\sigma$ to all participants in U. Only the subsets of participants in $\mathscr{AS}_\sigma$ are able to recover the secret s. Denote by B_σ the set of broadcast messages enabling $\mathscr{AS}_\sigma$.

Secret Reconstruction Phase: For any set $A \in \mathscr{AS}_\sigma$, there is a reconstruction function: $\mathsf{Re}^\sigma : (s_1, \cdots, s_n)|_A \times B_\sigma \to S$. The participants in A, get as input $\{s_i\}_{P_i \in A}$ and b_σ, jointly compute the reconstruction function Re^σ and recover s.

4.3 Secure Restoration Protocol

In this subsection, we give the description of secure restoration protocol **SeRes** which is performed by $\mathscr{S}_0$ and $\mathscr{S}_1$.

– $\mathscr{S}_0$ holds the users' public key h_i, msk and ciphertexts $[a_{i0}]_i$ and $[b_{i0}]_i$. $\mathscr{S}_0$ computes $h = \prod_{i \in U'} h_i$ mod N^2, decrypts $[a_{i0}]_i$ and $[b_{i0}]_i$ by using algorithm mDec.
– $\mathscr{S}_1$ holds the users' public key h_i, and ciphertexts $[a_{i1}]_i$ and $[b_{i1}]_i$. $\mathscr{S}_1$ computes $h = \prod_{i \in U'} h_i$ mod N^2. Calculate the blinded ciphertext $[c_a]_i$ and $[c_b]_i$ of $[a_{i1}]_i$ and $[b_{i1}]_i$, respectively. Send $[c_a]_i$ and $[c_b]_i$ to $\mathscr{S}_0$.
– $\mathscr{S}_0$ decrypts $[c_a]_i$ and $[c_b]_i$ by using mDec, and computes $a'_i = a_{i0} + c_a$ and $b'_i = b_{i0} + c_b$, re-encrypts $[a'_i]_h$ and $[b'_i]_h$ and sends it to $\mathscr{S}_1$;
– $\mathscr{S}_1$ removes the blinded factor and gets the ciphertexts $[a_i]_h$ and $[b_i]_h$ encrypted under the public key h.

Here, U' is a subset of U. We write $i \in U'$ to describe user u_i belonging to U.

4.4 Secure Computation of Active Function (SeAcf)

In this work, we take sigmoid $g(z) := \frac{1}{1+e^{-x}}$ as the active function. To support secure computation of the sigmoid function, the exponentiation operation and the division operation should be removed such that the equation only contains additive operation and multiplicative operation. Hence, we take Taylor theorem to approximate it

$$g(z) = \frac{1}{1+e^{-z}} = \frac{1}{2} + \frac{z}{4} - \frac{z^3}{480} + o(x^4) \approx 0.5 + 0.25z - 0.02z^3 \tag{1}$$

According to Eq. (1), the activation function can be calculated securely as follows:

– $\mathscr{S}_1$ holds $[z]_h, [0.5]_h, [0.25]_h$ and $[-0.02]_h$
– Calculate $[z_1]_h = $ **SeMul**$([0.25]_h, [z]_h)$ by using secure multiplication operation **SeMul**;
– Calculate $[z_2]_h = $ **SeMul**$([-0.02]_h, [z]_h, [z]_h, [z]_h)$ by using secure multiplication operation **SeMul**;
– Calculate $[y]_h = $ **Add**$([0.5]_h, [z_1]_h, [z_2]_h)$.

5 Privacy-Preserving Neural Networks

In our work, we consider arbitrarily partitioned data among multiple users. Denote by U the set of parties $u_1, \cdots, u_n$. Let $\mathscr{AS} = \{\mathscr{AS}_{(v_1, U_1)}, \cdots, \mathscr{AS}_{(v_t, U_t)}\}$ be the access structure on U, $\mathscr{AS}_{(v_i, U_i)}$, where $1 \leq v_i \leq |U_i| \leq n$, $U_l \subseteq U$, and $i \in [1, t]$.

Assuming the learning data of the NN with Z training samples, denoted by $\{m_k^1, \cdots, m_k^d\}_{k=1}^Z$ and is arbitrary divided into n ($n \geqslant 2$) mutually disjoint subsets, where $m_k^l = m_k^{l1} + m_k^{l2} + \cdots + m_k^{ln}$ for every $l \in [1, d]$ and d is the input number of NN. Each attribute in sample $\{m_k^1, \cdots, m_k^d\}_{k=1}^Z$ is possessed by only one user. Here, the private data set of user u_i ($i \in [1, n]$) is denoted by $m_i = \{m_k^{1i}, \cdots, m_k^{di}\}_{k=1}^Z$. Loosely speaking, our scheme can be divided into two phases **Set up Phase** and **Training Phase**.

5.1   Set up Phase

Initialization. Initially, KGC sets up BCP cryptosystem Π and generates $(\mathrm{msk}, \mathrm{pp})$ and $(\mathrm{sk}, \mathrm{pk})$ by using ParaGen and KeyGen, respectively. We suppose the $S = \mathbb{Z}_{N^2}$, where $N^2 \geq \max\{2n, m\} + 1$. Choose a $s \xleftarrow{U} S$, set $\mathrm{sk} = s$ and compute $\mathrm{pk} = h = g^{\mathrm{sk}} \bmod N^2$. KGC runs the dynamic secret sharing scheme for the access structure $\mathscr{A}\mathscr{S} = \{\mathscr{A}\mathscr{S}_{(v_1, \mathsf{U}_1)}, \cdots, \mathscr{A}\mathscr{S}_{(v_t, \mathsf{U}_t)}\}$ as follows:

Preprocessing Phase: For each $u_i \in \mathsf{U}$, KGC randomly selects $r_1, \cdots, r_n \in \mathbb{Z}_{N^2}$, such that $s = r_{I_1} + r_{I_2} + \cdots + r_{I_v}$, where $r_{I_1}, \cdots, r_{I_v}$ are arbitrary subsequence of $r_1, \cdots, r_n$ with v values. Set $s_i = r_i$ to be the share of $u_i \in \mathsf{U}$ for $i \in [1, n]$. Then, KGC sends the shares $s_1, \cdots, s_n$ to parties $u_1, \cdots, u_n$, respectively.

Message Generation Phase: Let U' be an arbitrary subset of U and $1 \leq v \leq |\mathsf{U}'| \leq n$. Especially, $\mathsf{U}' \in \{\mathsf{U}_1, \cdots, \mathsf{U}_t\}$ and $v \in \{v_1, \cdots, v_t\}$. KGC takes as input $(s, s_1, \cdots, s_n, v, \mathsf{U}')$, generates and distributes the broadcast message

$$b_{(v, \mathsf{U}')} = (\bigcup_{1 \leq i \leq |\mathsf{U}'| - v + 1} \{y_{n+i}\}) \cup (\bigcup_{\mathsf{U}_i \notin \mathsf{U}'} \{s_i\})$$

to all participants in U. Only the participants in $\mathscr{A}\mathscr{S}_{(v, \mathsf{U}')}$ can recover the secret s, where $y_1, \cdots, y_{2n}$ is the secret shares of s generated by using the threshold secret sharing scheme $(n + 1, 2n)$ in such a way that $y_i = s_i$ for $i \in [1, n]$. Finally, KGC sends $(\mathrm{msk}, \mathrm{pp}, v)$ and (pp, v) to cloud $\mathscr{S}_0$ and $\mathscr{S}_1$ by a secure channel, respectively.

Data Upload. After receiving the system's public parameters pp and private share s_i, each user u_i $(i \in [1, n])$ computes $h_i = g^{s_i} \bmod N^2$. Let $(\mathrm{sk}_i = s_i, \mathrm{pk}_i = h_i)$ be the private-public key pair of user u_i. Then u_i uses PRG to generate a pseudorandom number R_i and divides the private message $m_i \in \mathbb{Z}_N$ into two parts $m_{i0} = R_i$ and $m_{i1} = m_1 - m_{i0}$. Denote by $[m_{ij}]_i$ $(j = 0, 1)$ the ciphertext encrypted under the private key s_i according to the BCP cryptosystem Π. Later, each user u_i $(i \in [1, n])$ uploads the ciphertexts $([m_{i0}]_i, [m_{i1}]_i)$ and the public key h_i to the cloud $\mathscr{S}_0$ and $\mathscr{S}_1$, respectively.

5.2   Training Phase

After the set up phase, $\mathscr{S}_0$ and $\mathscr{S}_1$ have respectively collected a part of outsourced data from different users. Initialize the coefficients $\mathbf{w}$ to small random numbers and make them secure shared between two servers. Right now, $\mathscr{S}_0$ and $\mathscr{S}_1$ can perform the **SeNN** protocol over the adaptively selected data encrypted under different public keys, i.e., the upload data of users in U'.

Secure Neural Networks Protocol (SeNN). $\mathscr{S}_0$ keeps msk, pp, $\{\mathrm{pk}_i,\}_{i \in \mathsf{U}'}$, $\{[m_{i0}]\}_{i \in \mathsf{U}'}$ and $\{[w_{i0}]\}_{i \in \mathsf{U}'}$. $\mathscr{S}_1$ keeps $\mathrm{pp} = (N, k, g)$, $\{\mathrm{pk}_i,\}_{i \in \mathsf{U}'}$, $\{[m_{i1}]\}_{i \in \mathsf{U}'}$ and $\{[w_{i1}]\}_{i \in \mathsf{U}'}$, where $i \in [1, n]$.

- $\mathscr{S}_1$ sends two lists $\{[m_{i1}]_i\}_{i \in \mathsf{U}'}$ and $\{[w_{i1}]_i\}_{i \in \mathsf{U}'}$ to $\mathscr{S}_0$.
- Receive the two lists $\{[m_{i1}]_i\}_{i \in \mathsf{U}'}$ and $\{[w_{i1}]_i\}_{i \in \mathsf{U}'}$ sent by $\mathscr{S}_1$, $\mathscr{S}_0$ performs the **SeRes** protocol with $\mathscr{S}_1$.

- After the **SeRes** protocol, $\mathscr{S}_1$ holds two lists of encrypted data: $\{[m_i]_h\}_{i\in U'}$ and $\{[w_i]_h\}_{i\in U'}$, where $[m_i]_h$ and $[w_i]_h$ is encrypted under the product key h.
- Based on the two lists $\{[m_i]_h\}_{i\in U'}$ and $\{[w_i]_h\}_{i\in U'}$, $\mathscr{S}_1$ performs the **SeMul** protocol with $\mathscr{S}_0$. Then $\mathscr{S}_1$ holds the a list of multiplication $\{[m_iw_i]_h\}_{i\in U'}$, and calculates $[mw]_h = \mathbf{Add}([m_1w_2]_h, \cdots, [m_nw_n]_h)$, that is $[mw]_h = \prod_{i\in U'}[m_iw_i]_h \bmod N^2$.
- $\mathscr{S}_1$ securely computes the activation function f at the input $[mw]_h$ according to the **SeAcf** protocol, and sends the results $[y_i]_h$ to the user u_i.
- Each user u_i in U' holds a broadcast message $b_{(v,U')}$, only the users in the access structure $\mathscr{AS}_{(v,U')}$ can recover the secret s, which described in the secret reconstruction phase of the dynamic secret sharing scheme. Therefore, for any set $A \in \mathscr{AS}_{(v,U')}$, all the uses in A, take as input $\{s_i\}_{U_i\in A}$ and $b_{v,U'}$, jointly compute the secret $s \leftarrow \mathrm{Re}^v(\{s_i\}_{U_i\in A}, b_{(v,U')})$. Finally, $u_i \in A$ decrypts $[y_i]_h$ by using uDec under the private key s.

5.3 Semi-honest Security

In our multiparty outsourcing computation setting, the security argument is considered in the *semi-honest* model.

Theorem 1. *([4]) BCP cryptosystem is semantically secure assuming the group $\mathbb{Z}^*_{N^2}$ satisfies the decisional Diffie-Hellman assumption.*

Due to the Theorem 1, we obtain the following lemma:

Lemma 1. *Protocol **SeMult**, protocol **SeRes** and protocol **SeAcf** is secure if BCP cryptosystem is semantically secure.*

As we claimed in the Sect. 3.2, our proposed scheme is resistant to the three types attacks. We stress that the two servers $\mathscr{S}_0$ and $\mathscr{S}_1$ are non-colluding and independent. We require the adversary $\mathscr{A}$ has the polynomial bounded of computing power.

Security against users. $\mathscr{A}$ may corrupt any subset of users to obtain their ciphertext, however, $\mathscr{A}$ will not be able to decrypt the ciphertext without knowing the corrupted users' private key due to the semantic security of the BCP cryptosystem. Security against only one server. $\mathscr{A}$ may compromise $\mathscr{S}_0$ (or $\mathscr{S}_1$) to achieve the ciphertext and private data of users. However, $\mathscr{A}$ is unable to recover the users' private key to decrypt the ciphertext. Because in our protocol, the private data is splitted into two pieces, where one piece is a pesudorandom number and another price is the message reduce a pesudorandom number. If $\mathscr{S}_0$ is corrupted, it only obtains a pesudorandom number by using algorithm mDec. If $\mathscr{S}_1$ is corrupted, it only gets the blinded message. For this setting, the information of original private data is not leaked. Security against a sever and users. In this setting, a server ($\mathscr{S}_0$ or $\mathscr{S}_1$) allowed to collaborate with several users in getting the others message. Similar to the above analysis, $\mathscr{S}_0$ (or $\mathscr{S}_1$) and several users, they only obtain a pesudorandom number.

6   Conclusion and Future Work

In this work, we have proposed a protocol for securely training machine learning model while supporting that computation on the data encrypted under different public keys of the dynamic users. We show that only the users selected by the servers can reconstruct the predefined secret and jointly decrypt the training result. In this paper, we have considered the collaborative learning of neural network for the dynamic users, and we expect to deploy a full application in the near future.

References

1. Abadi, M., et al.: Deep learning with differential privacy. In: ACM SIGSAC Conference on Computer and Communications Security, pp. 308–318 (2016)
2. Blum, M., Micali, S.: How to generate cryptographically strong sequences of pseudo-random bits. In: Symposium on Foundations of Computer Science, 1982. SFCS 2008, pp. 112–117 (2008)
3. Blundo, C., Cresti, A., De Santis, A., Vaccaro, U.: Fully dynamic secret sharing schemes. In: Stinson, D.R. (ed.) CRYPTO 1993. LNCS, vol. 773, pp. 110–125. Springer, Heidelberg (1994). https://doi.org/10.1007/3-540-48329-2_10
4. Bresson, E., Catalano, D., Pointcheval, D.: A simple public-key cryptosystem with a double trapdoor decryption mechanism and its applications. In: Laih, C.-S. (ed.) ASIACRYPT 2003. LNCS, vol. 2894, pp. 37–54. Springer, Heidelberg (2003). https://doi.org/10.1007/978-3-540-40061-5_3
5. Cramer, R., Damgård, I., Nielsen, J.B.: Multiparty computation from threshold homomorphic encryption. In: Pfitzmann, B. (ed.) EUROCRYPT 2001. LNCS, vol. 2045, pp. 280–300. Springer, Heidelberg (2001). https://doi.org/10.1007/3-540-44987-6_18
6. Gilad-Bachrach, R., Dowlin, N., Laine, K., Lauter, K., Naehrig, M., Wernsing, J.: CryptoNets: applying neural networks to encrypted data with high throughput and accuracy. In: International Conference on Machine Learning, pp. 201–210 (2016)
7. Graepel, T., Lauter, K., Naehrig, M.: ML confidential: machine learning on encrypted data. In: Kwon, T., Lee, M.-K., Kwon, D. (eds.) ICISC 2012. LNCS, vol. 7839, pp. 1–21. Springer, Heidelberg (2013). https://doi.org/10.1007/978-3-642-37682-5_1
8. Li, P., Li, J., Huang, Z., Gao, C.Z., Chen, W.B., Chen, K.: Privacy-preserving outsourced classification in cloud computing. Cluster Comput. **21**(1), 1–10 (2017)
9. Li, P., et al.: Multi-key privacy-preserving deep learning in cloud computing. Future Gener. Comput. Syst. **74**, 76–85 (2017)
10. Li, T., Huang, Z., Li, P., Liu, Z., Jia, C.: Outsourced privacy-preserving classification service over encrypted data. J. Netw. Comput. Appl. **106**, 100–110 (2018)
11. Li, T., Li, J., Liu, Z., Li, P., Jia, C.: Differentially private Naive Bayes learning over multiple data sources. Inf. Sci. **444**, 89–104 (2018)

A Biometric Key Generation Method for Fingerprint and Finger Vein Fusion

Hua Yang and Zhendong Wu[✉]

School of Cyberspace, Hangzhou Dianzi University, Hangzhou, China
yh1264117935@163.com, wzd@hdu.edu.cn

Abstract. This paper proposed a biometric key generation method for fingerprint and finger vein fusion. A matrix extraction algorithm is proposed, which can fuse the aligned fingerprint and finger vein images to extract the biological key. Furthermore, blind alignment of fingerprint and finger vein biometric images are used to improve the accuracy and stability of subsequent biometric key extraction. Compared with the original direct eigenvector extraction method, the proposed bio-key extraction method is more stable and accurate.

Keywords: Key generation · Biological feature · Finger vein recognition · Fingerprint identification

1 Introduction

With the development of information technology in society, data information is not only in computers, but also in many aspects, such as mobile phones, tablets, micro-computers and other electronic products that often appear in our lives. Therefore, people are increasingly demanding the level of security and confidentiality of personal privacy, and the risk of user secret information leakage is getting higher and higher. For example, in early June 2016, a hacker code-named "Peace" got the account and password information of hundreds of millions of users on the world's second-largest social networking site, and then sold the data on the deep Internet. And such acts of stealing user passwords and selling them are not the only case. It can be found that if we simply use the traditional password and do not take other authentication measures, once the user password is stolen, it will be a huge loss. Because of the risk of the password being stolen, the use of the uniqueness of the characteristics of the organism for verification and identification has become the focus [1].

Biometrics is a technique for personal identification based on the inherent physiological characteristics of the human body. This way of using human body and behavioral characteristics to automatically recognize human identity is widely used in today's society [2]. At present, the biometric technology that has made great progress in both theory and practical application should be fingerprint recognition [3–11]. Many products in the domestic market use fingerprint recognition technology, but the response speed and stability of the fingerprint recognition system and the algorithm Accuracy still need to be improved. On the other hand, if the technical research is carried out only from the single feature of the finger vein, it is costly and cannot be solved. So if you want to solve this bottleneck, perhaps we can use multi-modal

J. Vaidya et al. (Eds.): CSS 2019, LNCS 11983, pp. 293–300, 2019.
https://doi.org/10.1007/978-3-030-37352-8_26

bio-fusion recognition technology to combine two or more kinds of biological features that complement each other [14].

In this paper, fingerprint and finger vein fusion certification research is selected. The advantage of this research is that on the one hand, fingerprint is very convenient as an identification method. Secondly, finger vein is a biological feature inside the body, which is better than fingerprint recognition. The invariance is not easy to forge. Therefore, in this paper, the fusion technology is experimentally studied, and the advantages of fingerprint and finger vein fusion technology are summarized. In general, the two features of fingerprint and finger vein have many advantages such as high security and high recognition. In civil, police, corporate and other social life scenarios, multimodal fusion recognition technology has broad application prospects and commercial value in the future [15].

The rest of this paper is organized as follows: Sect. 2 introduces the overview of fingerprint recognition and finger vein recognition technology. Section 3 describes our proposed method in detail. Section 4 shows experimental performances. Finally, the conclusion is presented in Sect. 5.

2 Overview of Fingerprint Recognition and Finger Vein Recognition Technology

2.1 The Basic Principle of Fingerprint Recognition

Fingerprint refers to the texture produced by the unevenness on the skin on the front side of the fingertip. Studies have shown that each person's fingerprint texture is different at the bifurcation point and endpoint and other physiological characteristics, and does not change with age or physical health. In fact, fingerprints have a long history of recognition. Modern fingerprint recognition technology refers to the uniqueness and stability of fingerprints, integrating modern electronic technologies such as sensor devices, image processing and image matching. The advantages of fingerprint recognition compared to other recognition methods are:

(1) The fingerprint is relatively fixed, and it is difficult to change with age in a certain period of time, and the fingerprints of different human fingers are also different.
(2) It is convenient to collect fingerprint samples. There are already standard fingerprint sample libraries in the world [4].
(3) The small amount of image storage reduces the burden of network transmission, and the matching speed and recognition speed are also improved.

2.2 The Basic Principle of Finger Vein Recognition

Finger vein recognition technology is the focus of biometrics research in recent years. The process can be roughly divided into three parts.

(1) Image acquisition.
(2) Image preprocessing and feature point extraction.
(3) Image recognition matching.

At the same time, single finger vein recognition technology has many advantages:

(1) The technique is acquired by using the characteristics of the living organism, which prevents camouflage verification using fake images or model hand tools.
(2) The finger vein is located in the skin, and the recognition result is not easily affected by the external environment.
(3) High accuracy, medically indicated that under normal circumstances, each person's finger veins are unique and non-replicable, and the vascular characteristics are relatively easy to identify, so the method has high accuracy.

3 Design of Our Method

The fingerprint and finger vein biometric image blind alignment technology are proposed to support the blind alignment of single fingerprint and finger vein images without reference images, which improved the accuracy and stability of subsequent biometric key extraction.

3.1 Fingerprint and Finger Vein Blind Alignment Technology

Step 1. Refer to the vein fusion blind alignment training.

The specific steps are as follows:

The user collects multiple samples on the same fingerprint and finger vein, and obtains more than three fingerprint grayscale images and finger vein grayscale images, and uniformly scales the fingerprint grayscale image to 354×354 pixels. The finger vein grayscale image is scaled to 256×64 or 256×256 pixel size, and the fingerprint image obtained at this stage is labeled as the first fingerprint image, the first finger vein image, as shown in Fig. 1.

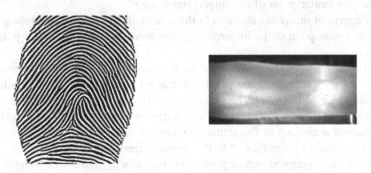

Fig. 1. Fingerprint grayscale image and finger vein grayscale image

Step 2. Equalize, converge, smooth, enhance, binarize, and refine Fig. 1, form the refined-feature-map, as shown in Fig. 2.

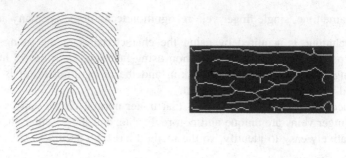

Fig. 2. Refined image after fingerprint and finger vein image preprocessing

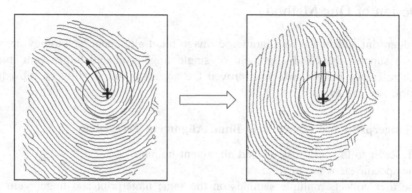

Fig. 3. Fingerprint image blind alignment process

Step 3.1. Fingerprint image blind alignment.

The alignment operation is to perform operations such as offset, rotation (Fig. 3). The specific process of blind alignment of fingerprint images is:

(1) Locate the center point of the fingerprint image;
(2) The fingerprint image is translated in the screen along the x-axis and the y-axis, so that the center point of the fingerprint image coincides with the center point of the screen.
(3) The center point of the image, that is, the center point of the fingerprint is the center of the circle, and the pixels of the ml are rounded for the radius. The specific value of the ml can be perpendicularly cut by the edge of the circle. The cutting point is marked as z, and the general ml is taken as 15–30 pixels, can be determined according to the actual situation; if there is no vertical cutting point, select the cutting point closest to the vertical, recorded as z;
(4) Connect the fingerprint center point and the point z, make a ray, and rotate the fingerprint image with the center point of the fingerprint as the center of the circle, and the rotation result is that the ray of the fingerprint center point and the point z coincides with the y-axis, as shown in Fig. 1.

Step 3.2. Finger vein image blind alignment.

In the process of collecting the finger vein, the collecting device generally presets the bayonet, and the finger will be against the top of the bayonet, so that the position of

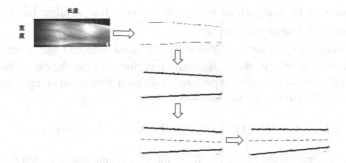

Fig. 4. Schematic diagram of blind alignment of finger vein images

the finger vein in the longitudinal direction is substantially fixed, and no alignment is required; in the width direction, since the finger may move left or right during the collecting process, so that the captured image may still have misalignment; accordingly, the blind alignment process of the finger vein image mainly considers the alignment in the width direction. As shown in Fig. 4, the specific process is:

1. Perform edge detection on the finger vein image to extract the image of the finger vein edge;
2. The image of the finger vein edge is a binarized image, with two upper and lower sides (may be left and right sides, depending on the placement of the image), and linear regression operation is performed on the point sets of the two sides to obtain two straight lines.
3. The finger vein image is placed in a Cartesian coordinate system, a certain vertex of the image rectangle is placed at the origin of the coordinate system, the length direction is parallel to the x-axis, the width direction is parallel to the y-axis, and the entire image is in the first quadrant;
4. Calculate the center line of the two lines.
5. Pan and rotate the finger vein image.

    Step. 4. Form a feature vector.

    Step. 5. Manifold learning. The fingerprint and finger vein fusion feature learning matrix, the biological key extraction matrix, is obtained W_l.

3.2   Extraction Fingerprint and Finger Vein Fusion Bio-Key Features

Step. 1 the user collects fingerprints and finger vein images.
Step. 2 the fingerprint training and the finger vein fusion feature learning matrix W_l are trained as the first part.
Step. 3 implement the PCA algorithm on the thinned fingerprint after blind alignment, taking the first 4–5 feature components $x_j^{(i)}$.

$$x_j^{(i)} \leftarrow x_j^{(i)} - \frac{1}{m} \sum_{i=1}^{m} x_j^{(i)}$$

Step. 4 implement PCA algorithm on the finger vein images after blind alignment, taking the first 4–5 feature components $x_j^{(i)}$.

Step. 5 the voiceprint vector x_t obtained by the third step and the fourth step after transposition $W_l^T \cdot x_j$, that is, the d_z dimension vector after the fusion is obtained x_{tz}.

Step. 6, a checkerboard operation is performed on each dimension component x_{tz} of the pair to further stabilize the feature vector $\bar{x}_{tz}$.

$$\Lambda(x) = k, \quad (D+1) \cdot k < x_{tzi} \leq (D+1) \cdot k + D, (k = 0, 1, \cdots)$$

Step. 7. First n components of the result vector $\bar{x}_{tz}$ are calculated in step 6. n can take values of 16, 32, 64, etc., generally a power value of 2, depending on the number of effective feature components $\bar{x}_{tz}$ and the bio-key strength requirement. The n components are spliced back and forth to form a fingerprint and a finger vein fusion biokey. If n is 64, and each component takes a value of 0 to 64, a 4-bit key calculation can be formed, and the first n components of the result vector $\bar{x}_{tz}$ can form a 64-bit bio-key.

At this point, a fingerprint and a finger vein fusion bio-key are obtained.

Alg. 1 The fingerprint and finger vein fusion bio-key generation algorithm

    if the vein fusion bio-key is not trained:

        1. Collect multiple samples on the same finger print and finger vein.

        2. Equalize, converge, smooth, enhance, binarize, and refine Fig.1, form the two-finger vein image.

        3. Fingerprint image blind alignment.

        4. Finger vein image blind alignment.

        5. Form a feature vector.

        6. Manifold learning. Obtain the fingerprint and finger vein fusion feature learning matrix, the biological key extraction matrix W_l.

    else:

        7. Collect fingerprints and finger vein images.

        8. Obtain the fingerprint and finger vein fusion feature learning matrix, the biological key extraction matrix W_l as the first part.

        9. Implement the PCA algorithm on the thinned fingerprint after blind alignment, taking the first 4-5 feature components $x_j^{(i)}$

        10. implement PCA algorithm on the finger vein images after blind alignment, taking the first 4-5 feature components $x_j^{(i)}$

        11. Obtain the vector x_{tz} and the dimension vector d_z

        12. Calculate and form a fingerprint and a finger vein fusion bio-key.

We formalize this algorithm in Algorithm 1.

4 Experiment Result

The environment of our experiment is matlab 2015b. This experiment used two data sets of fingerprint and finger vein. The fingerprint data set consists of 25 fingerprint images per person from 42 people. The finger vein data set use a library of 64 human finger veins acquired over the Internet with a high image quality.

4.1 Performance

In the experiment, we selected a total of 64 finger veins images and two fingerprint images for the experimental sample library. First, we test the recognition accuracy of bi-biometric features. During operation, one finger vein image and one fingerprint image are selected as templates to be compared to other possible combinations. 64 comparison operations were performed, and the final manual statistics are shown in Table 1. Table 2 shows the success rate of key generation, where D represents the quantization interval in pixels.

Table 1. 1:1 match result

Match number	Accept number	Reject number	Accept rate	Reject rate
64	63	1	98.4%	1.6%

Table 2. Accuracy of Key Generation in Different D Values

Decision Threshold (D)	GAR (%)
120	90.18
180	92.05

From this we can get, although the total time of the bimodal fusion recognition is longer than single fingerprint recognition and finger vein recognition. However, the overall performance of the system after fingerprint and finger vein fusion is better than single fingerprint recognition and fingerprint recognition, and the rejection rate is only about 2%. And in the case of high quality and high stability images generated by bio-key, the accuracy can reach more than 90% by adjusting the value of D appropriately. This result is satisfactory at present.

5 Summary

The method combines the fingerprint feature with the finger vein feature bit level to extract the bio-key. The two types of bio-feature fusion can expand the effective bio-feature space, extract more stable bio-features, and increase the key length. And the bit-level fusion is more favorable for extraction. Compared with the separate fingerprint and finger vein bio-key extraction methods, the method can obtain a more stable and stronger biological key. The key extraction accuracy rate can be better than 96% and the key length can be up to 64 bits.

Acknowledgement. This research is supported by National Natural Science Foundation of China (No. 61772162), National Key R&D Program of China (No. 2018YFB0804102).

References

1. Lu, S.: A review of the development and application of biometrics. Comput. Secur. (1), 63–67 (2013)
2. Hashimoto, J.: Finger vein authentication technology and its future. In: 2006 Symposium on VLSI Circuits, Digest of Technical Papers, Honolulu, HI, pp. 5–8 (2006)
3. Hitachi, Ltd. Finger vein authentication: white paper [EB/OL] (2006). [2011-11]
4. Yanagawa, T., Aoki, S., Ohyama, T.: Human finger vein images are diverse and its patterns are useful for personal identification. MHF Preprint Series **12**, 1–7 (2007)
5. Zhang, Z., Ma, S.: Multiscale feature extraction of finger-vein patterns based on curveles and local interconnection struction neural network, ICPR 2006, pp. 145–148 (2006)
6. Maio, D., Maltoni, D.: Direct gray-scale minutiae detection in fingerprints. IEEE Trans. Pattern Anal. Mach. Intell. **19**(1), 27–40 (1997)
7. Jiang, X., Yau, W.Y., Ser, W.: Detecting the fingerprint minutiae by adaptive tracing the gray-level ridge. Pattern Recogn. **34**(5), 999–1013 (2001)
8. Ratha, N.K., Bolle, R.: Automatic Fingerprint Recognition Systems. Springer, New York (2003). https://doi.org/10.1007/b97425
9. Schulingkamp, R.J., Pagano, T.C., Hung, D., et al.: Insulin receptors and insulin action in the brain: review and clinical implications. Neurosci. Biobehav. Rev. **24**(8), 855–872 (2000)
10. Liu, Y., Ma, Y., Feng, X., et al.: Fingerprint identification preprocessing algorithms based on Gabor filter. Comput. Meas. Control (2007)
11. Girgis, M.R., Sewisy, A.A., Mansour, R.F.: A robust method for partial deformed fingerprints verification using genetic algorithm. Expert Syst. Appl. **36**(2), 2008–2016 (2009)
12. Zhao, Q., Zhang, D., Zhang, L., et al.: High resolution partial fingerprint alignment using pore–valley descriptors. Pattern Recogn. **43**(3), 1050–1061 (2010)
13. Wang, Y.A., Hu, J.: Global ridge orientation modeling for partial fingerprint identification. IEEE Trans. Pattern Anal. Mach. Intell. **33**(1), 72–87 (2010)
14. Selvarani, S., Jebapriya, S., Mary, R.S.: Automatic identification and detection of altered fingerprints. In: 2014 International Conference on Intelligent Computing Applications (ICICA), pp. 239–243. IEEE (2014)
15. Nakashika, T., Garcia, C., Takiguchi, T.: Local-feature-map integration using convolutional neural networks for music genre classification (2012)

A Fingerprint and Voiceprint Fusion Identity Authentication Method

Yaoping Wu, Zhendong Wu$^{(\boxtimes)}$, and Hua Yang

School of Cyberspace, Hangzhou Dianzi University, Hangzhou, China
wuypiy@163.com, wzd@hdu.edu.cn, yh1264117935@163.com

Abstract. In the traditional biometric identification scheme, the single fingerprint feature points are used for identification, or the single voiceprint is used as the authentication standard, and it is difficult to obtain a good accuracy in a complicated environment. Different biometrics have different advantages, disadvantages and applicable scenarios. A single mode cannot have a wider coverage scene. For this reason, we propose a fusion algorithm for fingerprint recognition and voiceprint recognition, combining the recognition characteristics of fingerprint and voiceprint, an identification scheme based on fingerprint and voiceprint fusion is proposed. The eigenvalues of fingerprint and voiceprint are divided into a group. The depth neural network is used to extract the fingerprint and voiceprint features respectively, and the probability combination is used to verify the fusion. The experimental results show that the combination of the two certifications reduces the error acceptance rate (FAR) by 4.04% and the error rejection rate (FRR) by 1.54% compared to a single fingerprint or voiceprint recognition scheme.

Keywords: Multi-biometric · Deep-learning · Voiceprint identification · Fingerprint identification · Fusion

1 Introduction

With the booming Internet industry, the need for ubiquitous identity authentication is growing. At present, password authentication is still the main means of user identity authentication in the Internet-based service industry, but at the same time, identity authentication methods based on human biometrics are rapidly spreading [1, 2]. Although the password authentication is convenient to deploy, there is a problem that the user's memory ability is limited, resulting in insufficient password strength. The biometric authentication can save the burden of the human memory key, and the convenience of deployment can be improved with the software framework and the biometrics collection device. However, the safety of biometric authentication has become more prominent. The strength, stability and privacy retention of single biometric authentication are insufficient [3, 4]. In comparison, multimodal biometric authentication can enhance authentication strength, stability and provide richer. The means of privacy preservation is the trend of biometric authentication technology development. The existing multi-modal biometric authentication technology is mainly based on two categories:

© Springer Nature Switzerland AG 2019
J. Vaidya et al. (Eds.): CSS 2019, LNCS 11983, pp. 301–310, 2019.
https://doi.org/10.1007/978-3-030-37352-8_27

(1) Performing single biometric feature recognition firstly, and then calculating the multi-feature fusion score by a fixed ratio for authentication decision [5–9]. Some work has tried to use deep neural network to recognize the biological features of speech, and achieved some results, but the model of fingerprint and voiceprint recognition at the same time is rare [10–12].

(2) Integrating multiple biometric features in the feature layer, a unified feature recognition algorithm makes the decision. The two types of methods have their own advantages. At present, the second type of method is difficult to reliably guarantee due to the feature specificity of multi-feature fusion, which makes the stability of the second type of method low. The first type of method limits the accuracy limit of multimodal biometric authentication due to the fixed ratio feature fusion.

We proposed a new method, the method aims at the shortcoming of the prior art, and proposes a method for dynamic fusion calculation of fingerprint and voiceprint two kinds of biological features using depth neural network, and in the judgment stage, dynamic Bayesian analysis are used, which can improve the authentication accuracy rate by more than 4% compared with the existing methods.

The rest of this paper is organized as follows: Sect. 2 introduces the overview of voiceprint recognition. Section 3 describes our proposed method in detail. Section 4 shows experimental performances. Finally, the conclusion is presented in Sect. 5.

2   Overview of Fingerprint and Voiceprint Recognition

Fingerprint and voiceprint recognition is a kind of biometric technology. It is a technology that automatically recognizes the identity of a people based on the finger or speech parameters that reflect the physiological and behavioral characteristics of the people [13–16]. Unlike speech recognition, voiceprint recognition utilizes speaker information in a speech signal, regardless of the meaning of the words in the speech, which emphasizes the personality of the speaker. The purpose of speech recognition is to identify the verbal content in the speech signal, regardless of who the speaker is, and it emphasizes commonality.

The biometric recognition system mainly includes two parts, namely feature detection and pattern matching. The task of feature detection is to select an effective and stable feature that uniquely expresses the identity of the people. The task of pattern matching is to match the feature patterns during training and recognition.

2.1   Feature Detection

The feature detection in the fingerprint recognition system consists of fingerprint image acquisition, fingerprint image preprocessing, feature extraction, and fingerprint classification. Preprocessing usually includes image segmentation, enhancement, binarization, refinement, etc., shown as Fig. 1.

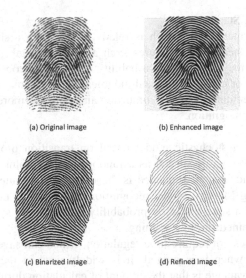

(a) Original image   (b) Enhanced image

(c) Binarized image   (d) Refined image

Fig. 1. Fingerprint preprocessing schematic

The feature detection in the voiceprint recognition system extracts the basic features of the person in the speech signal, which should effectively distinguish different speakers and maintain relatively stable changes to the same speaker. Figure 2 shows the spectrogram of different speakers in the same speech segment. We can identify different speakers by delicately dividing the details of the spectrogram. Considering the quantify ability of speech features, the number of training samples, and the evaluation of system performance, the current voiceprint recognition system mainly relies on lower-level acoustic features for recognition.

Fig. 2. Voiceprint spectrum for different speakers

In addition, people also improve the performance of the actual system by combining different characteristic parameters. When the correlation between the parameters is small, there will be better results, because they reflect different characteristics of the biometrics signal.

2.2 Pattern Matching

At present, the research on pattern matching methods proposed for various features is getting deeper and deeper. These methods can be roughly classified into the following categories: 1. Probability and Statistics. 2. Markov Model. 3. Artificial neural network.

1. Probability and Statistics

The speaker information in speech is relatively stable in a short time. Through statistical analysis of steady-state features such as pitch, glottal gain, and low-order reflection coefficient, the statistic and probability density functions such as mean and variance can be used for classification and judgment. The advantage is that the feature parameters are not regularized in the time domain, and are more suitable for text-independent speaker recognition.

2. Markov Model

Markov Model is a stochastic model based on transition probability and transmission probability. It regards speech as a random process composed of observable symbol sequences, and symbol sequence is the output of the utterance system state sequence. When using Markov Model recognition, an utterance model is established for each speaker, and a state transition probability matrix and a symbol output probability matrix are obtained through training.

Markov Model does not require time regulation, which can save computation time and storage capacity when it is judged. It is widely used in the industrial field at present, and the disadvantage is that the amount of calculation during training is large.

3. Artificial Neural Network

Artificial neural network simulates the perceptual characteristics of biological to some extent. It is a network model of distributed parallel processing structure, with self-organization and self-learning ability, strong complex classification boundary distinguishing ability and incomplete information. Robustness, its performance is approximately ideal for classifiers. The disadvantage is that the training time is long, the dynamic time warping ability is weak, and the network size may be too large to be trained as the number of speakers increases.

In general, a successful speaker recognition system should: firstly be able to effectively distinguish between different speakers, and be able to maintain relative stability when the same speaker's voice changes, such as a cold. Secondly, it is not easy to be imitated by others or can better solve the problem of being imitated by others. Finally, it is possible to maintain a certain stability when the acoustic environment changes, that is, the anti-noise performance is better.

3   Design of Our Method

Fingerprint recognition technology has been widely used in various fields, but the traditional Fourier domain filtering is less sensitive to the resolution of fingerprint singularity changes. However, with the development of deep neural networks, deep learning has shown excellent results in image processing, especially in biometrics. Through neural network training, biometrics can be extracted accurately and effectively.

Whether for fingerprints or voiceprints, each person's image has its own characteristics. Through deep learning, the model can capture fingerprints and voiceprints collected in various environments. Deep neural networks can overcome various environmental influence factors. Ability to extract accurate features.

In this paper, we use deep neural network to train learning extraction features. We chose Resnet18 as the network model of this experiment. This model can effectively solve the problem of network degradation, so as to build a deeper network and extract more detailed biometrics. Fingerprints and voiceprints require very detailed feature recognition, so Resnet18 is our choice.

Table 1. Architecture for ImageNet

Layer name	18-layer
conv1	7×7, 64, stride 2
conv2_x	3×3, max pool, stride 2
	$\begin{bmatrix} 3 \times 3, & 64 \\ 3 \times 3, & 64 \end{bmatrix} \times 3$
conv3_x	$\begin{bmatrix} 3 \times 3, & 128 \\ 3 \times 3, & 128 \end{bmatrix} \times 2$
conv4_x	$\begin{bmatrix} 3 \times 3, & 256 \\ 3 \times 3, & 256 \end{bmatrix} \times 2$
conv5_x	$\begin{bmatrix} 3 \times 3, & 512 \\ 3 \times 3, & 512 \end{bmatrix} \times 2$
fc	average pool, 128-d, softmax

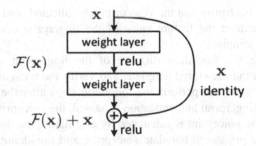

Fig. 3. Residual learning: a building block

As shown in the network architecture shown in Table 1, as the network deepens, the accuracy will reach saturation and then drop sharply, but the accuracy is not due to overfitting. To this end, Microsoft Research proposed a residual network through identity mapping. As shown in Fig. 3, for the network structure, when learning the input of x, the feature is recorded as H(x). Now we want it to learn the residual F (x) = H(x) − x, so the original learning characteristic is F(x) + x. Yes, residual learning is easier than learning original features directly.

In this paper, the fusion authentication method of fingerprint and voiceprint is used. When the fingerprint and voiceprint are within the threshold, they can pass the authentication. Through the experimental test, the threshold corresponding to the EER is selected as the threshold value (T) of the fingerprint and the voiceprint, distance is D, as shown in the experimental flow shown in Fig. 4.

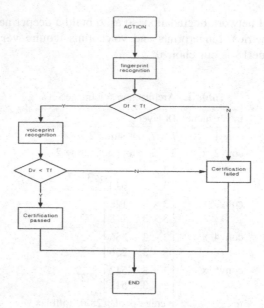

Fig. 4. Fusion recognition flow chart

Step 1: The user fingerprint and the voiceprint are collected, and the pre-processing is performed to extract the feature value of the fingerprint and the voiceprint to match the stored template.

Step 2: Calculate the Euclidean distance of the fingerprint and the voiceprint respectively from the pre-stored template, and verify the recognition when the fingerprint does not pass, and perform the following steps after the fingerprint passes

Step 3: After the fingerprint authentication is passed, the voiceprint authentication is performed, and the voiceprint is calculated by calculating the distance between the voiceprint and the pre-stored template voiceprint, and the identity authentication is passed, otherwise the authentication fails and re-authentication is required.

3.1 Fingerprint and Voiceprint Fusion Authentication Template Generation

Fingerprint and voiceprint recognition template generation:

1. Collect multiple fingerprint images of a large number of users
2. Fingerprint image preprocessing, including fingerprint image normalization, image enhancement, image binarization, fingerprint line refinement, alignment of fingerprints, rotation of the image, interception of the central area of the image as the feature area of the fingerprint
3. Using the Resnet18 deep neural network, 128-dimensional feature values are extracted from the fingerprint images, and the triple loss function (Tripletloss) is used for training learning, so that the network model parameters can correctly extract the biometric features of the fingerprint.

4. Through the deep learning network learning, after the model has correctly extracted the feature values, the 128-dimensional biometrics are extracted using the network to identify the fingerprint image, and recorded as X1.
5. Collect a large number of users' voiceprint images
6. Preprocessing of speech signals, including speech signal pre-emphasis, framing, windowing, Fourier transform, Mel frequency filter bank filtering, discrete cosine transform (DCT), generating user's voiceprint image
7. Training the voiceprint image using the same deep neural network and training method with the same fingerprint
8. Extract the 128-dimensional eigenvalues from the voiceprint image using the well-learned neural network and record it as X2.
9. Use [X1, X2] as the authentication template for fingerprint voiceprint fusion

The feature value extraction and fusion authentication template generation of the above fingerprint and voiceprint are generated.

3.2   Fingerprint and Voiceprint Dual Biometric Fusion Certification

1. Collect user fingerprints and voiceprint images, and extract feature values from the images for dynamic dual biometric fusion authentication.
2. Establish a fusion authentication template for user biometric values [XS1, XS2].
3. The fusion authentication template is matched with the already stored [X1, X2] template to obtain the Euclidean distance Df of the fingerprint and voiceprint feature values, Dv.
4. Through a large number of fingerprint and voiceprint data statistics, select the threshold corresponding to the EER as the authentication limit, set Tf as the fingerprint threshold, and set Tv as the threshold of the voiceprint.

$$D_f < T_f, D_v < T_v$$

5. According to the calculated European distance of the fingerprint and the voiceprint, the fingerprint and the voiceprint are combined and authenticated. The authentication method is as follows: when the user inputs the fingerprint and the voiceprint to meet the above conditions, it is determined that the user authentication matches the storage template, and the authentication passes; if the fingerprint or the voiceprint fails to match, the authentication is considered to be different, and the user needs to re-enter.

4   Experiment Result

This experiment used two data sets of fingerprint and voiceprint. The fingerprint data set consists of 25 fingerprint images per person from 42 people. The voiceprint data set consists of 40 people, each with 8 segments of text recording, and each text recording has 10 voiceprint images. This experiment is on the Ubuntu16.04 platform, with 32G memory, using PyTorch 1.1.0 version, accelerated by using NVIDIA 1060 6G GPU.

4.1   Performance

This experiment extracts feature values from fingerprint and voiceprint pictures using a deep neural network. For the preprocessing of the data, the image of the fingerprint is rotated at random angles, left and right, flipped up and down, and the voiceprint is turned left and right and flipped up and down. The preprocessing can make the original data cover a wider feature value. The Resnet18 network is used for feature value extraction, and the final connection layer outputs 128-dimensional feature values to calculate the Euclidean distance of the 128-dimensional feature values of the two pictures.

$$d = \sqrt{\sum_i^n (x_i - y_i)^2}$$

When the distance is less than a certain threshold, it is considered to be the same person, otherwise it is not considered to be the same person. The experimental results are shown in Tables 2 and 3.

Table 2. FAR and FRR values for different fingerprint thresholds.

thr	3.3	3.4	3.5	3.6	3.7
FRR	0.0556	0.0397	0.0317	0.0238	0.0238
FAR	0.0238	0.0317	0.0317	0.0317	0.0397

As can be seen from Table 2, FAR = FRR = 0.0317, the threshold is 3.5, and the threshold is selected as the threshold of the fingerprint.

Table 3. FAR and FRR values for different thresholds of voiceprint

thr	5.2	5.3	5.4	5.5	5.6	5.7
FRR	0.0622	0.0556	0.0489	0.0456	0.0367	0.0289
FAR	0.0378	0.0456	0.0522	0.0556	0.0589	0.0689

There are no equal FAR and FRR values in Table 3, which can be passed through the median, FAR = FRR = 0.049, and the threshold is 5.45, which is selected as the threshold for the voiceprint.

After determining the threshold, 40 fingerprints and voiceprints were selected as the 40 group of anchors, and 40 other fingerprints and voiceprints were selected as the positive group, and the other 40 fingerprints and voiceprints were selected as the negative group. When both the fingerprint and the voiceprint match, the match is considered to pass, and it is considered to be the same person. If any fingerprint or voiceprint does not pass, it is considered to be mismatched and does not pass. The experimental data is shown in Table 4.

Table 4. Positive and negative pass number

	Total	Match	Non-match
positive	40	39	1
negative	40	0	40

By comparing the accuracy of individual items and the accuracy of fingerprint and voiceprint fusion, as shown in Table 5, it can be seen that the fusion has better misunderstanding rate and false rejection rate.

Table 5. 3 ways of FRR and FAR

Type	FRR	FAR
fingerprint	0.0317	0.0317
voiceprint	0.049	0.049
fusion	0.025	0

Through the above experiments, it can be concluded that although the fusion authentication method requires more computing power and time than a single fingerprint or voiceprint authentication, the computing power of the device can almost complete the authentication process without any difference. Moreover, the performance of the fingerprint and voiceprint fusion authentication system is only about 2.5% compared with fingerprint or voiceprint recognition, and the false positive rate is almost zero. This is a very satisfactory result of the experiment.

5 Summary

The paper provides a dynamic Bayesian-based fingerprint and voiceprint dual biometric fusion authentication method, which can dynamically adjust the proportion of fingerprint and voiceprint in the fusion authentication according to the posterior probability in each authentication process, and optimize the final fusion certification effect.

Acknowledgement. This research is supported by National Natural Science Foundation of China (No. 61772162), National Key R&D Program of China (No. 2018YFB0804102).

References

1. Lu, S.: A review of the development and application of biometrics. Comput. Secur. (1), 63–67 (2013)
2. Huang, Z., Liu, S., Mao, X., Chen, K., Li, J.: Insight of the protection for data security under selective opening attacks. Inf. Sci. **412**, 223–241 (2017)
3. Li, J., Li, J., Chen, X., Jia, C., Lou, W.: Identity-based encryption with outsourced revocation in cloud computing. IEEE Trans. Comput. **64**(2), 425–437 (2015)

4. Wu, Z., Tian, L., Li, P., Wu, T., Jiang, M., Wu, C.: Generating stable biometric keys for flexible cloud computing authentication using finger vein. Inf. Sci. **433–434**, 431–447 (2018)
5. Yanagawa, T., Aoki, S., Ohyama, T.: Human finger vein images are diverse and its patterns are useful for personal identification. MHF Preprint Series **12**, 1–7 (2007)
6. Zhang, Z., Ma, S.: Multiscale feature extraction of finger-vein patterns based on curvelets and local interconnection structure neural network. In: 18th International Conference on Pattern Recognition (ICPR 2006), 20–24 August 2006, Hong Kong, China. IEEE Computer Society, pp. 145–148 (2006)
7. Liu, Y., Ma, Y., Feng, X., et al.: Fingerprint identification preprocessing algorithms based on Gabor filter. Comput. Meas. Control (2007)
8. Jiang, X., Yau, W.Y., Ser, W.: Detecting the fingerprint minutiae by adaptive tracing the gray-level ridge. Pattern Recogn. **34**(5), 999–1013 (2001)
9. Ratha, N.K., Bolle, R.: Automatic Fingerprint Recognition Systems. Springer, New York (2003). https://doi.org/10.1007/b97425
10. Hinton, G.E., Osindero, S., The, Y.-W.: A fast learning algorithm for deep belief nets. Neural Comput. **18**(7), 1527–1554 (2006)
11. Richardson, F., Reynolds, D., Dehak, N.: Deep neural network approaches to speaker and language recognition. IEEE Signal Process. Lett. **22**(10), 1671–1675 (2015)
12. Liu, Z., Wu, Z., Li, T., et al.: GMM and CNN hybrid method for short utterance speaker recognition. IEEE Trans. Ind. Inform. **14**(7), 3244–3252 (2018)
13. Girgis, M.R., Sewisy, A.A., Mansour, R.F.: A robust method for partial deformed fingerprints verification using genetic algorithm. Expert Syst. Appl. **36**(2), 2008–2016 (2009)
14. Zhao, Q., Zhang, D., Zhang, L., et al.: High resolution partial fingerprint alignment using pore-valley descriptors. Pattern Recogn. **43**(3), 1050–1061 (2010)
15. Wang, Y.A., Hu, J.: Global ridge orientation modeling for partial fingerprint identification. IEEE Trans. Pattern Anal. Mach. Intell. **33**(1), 72–87 (2010)
16. Selvarani, S., Jebapriya, S., Mary, R.S.: Automatic identification and detection of altered fingerprints. In: International Conference on Intelligent Computing Applications, pp. 239–243. IEEE Computer Society (2014)
17. He, K., Zhang, X., Ren, S., et al.: Deep Residual Learning for Image Recognition (2015)

Trust and Privacy

Research and Application of Trusted Service Evaluation Model in Social Network

Rui Ge[1], Ying Zheng[1], Fengyin Li[1(✉)], Dongfeng Wang[1], and Yuanzhang Li[2]

[1] School of Information Science and Engineering, QuFu Normal University,
Shandong Rizhao 276826, China
lfyin318@126.com
[2] School of Computer Science and Technology, Beijing Institute of Technology,
Beijing 100081, China

Abstract. In this paper, we propose a new Trusted Service Evaluation (TSE) model based on the service-oriented social network, which can realize user feedback and collect comments safely and efficiently. Each service provider independently maintains a TSE for itself, which collects and stores users' comments about its services without requiring any third trusted authority. The service comments can then be made available to interested users in making wise service selection decisions. Specifically, this new service evaluation model enables users to collaboratively submit comments by using a new digital signature scheme. It restricts the service providers to reject, modify, or delete the comments. Thus, the integrity and authenticity of comments are improved. Through security analysis and performance evaluation, it is proved that this new trustworthy service evaluation model achieves better performance in terms of current service review system submission rate, and can effectively resist mainstream service comment attacks.

Keywords: Service evaluation model · Private keys · Security model · Social network

1 Introduction

Service-oriented social networks [3,4,8] are emerging social networking platforms over which one or more individuals can communicate with local service providers using handheld wireless communication devices such as smartphones and tablets. In the service-oriented social network, service providers (restaurants and grocery stores) offer location-based services to local users and aim to attract the users by employing various advertising approaches, for example, sending e-flyers to the nearby passengers via wireless connections. Because most users choose services based on the comparison of the service quality, the user selects a service provider based on the suppliers reputation or other users comments on the supplier. Therefore, in the service-oriented social network, to establish a trustworthy

© Springer Nature Switzerland AG 2019
J. Vaidya et al. (Eds.): CSS 2019, LNCS 11983, pp. 313–317, 2019.
https://doi.org/10.1007/978-3-030-37352-8_28

service evaluation model is particularly important. However, the service-oriented social networks are autonomous and distributed networks, where no third trusted authority exists on bootstrapping to trust relations. Therefore, for the users in the service-oriented social networks, how to enable the trust evaluation of the service providers is a challenging problem.

The trustworthy service model [1,2] enables service providers or any third trusted authority to receive user feedback, known as service reviews, such as compliments and complaints about their services or products. By using the TSE model, the service providers learn the service experiences of the users and can improve their service strategy in time. Besides, the collected reviews can be made available to the public, which enhances service advertising and assists users in making wise service selections. The TSE model is often maintained by a third trusted authority that is trusted to host authentic reviews. The popular TSE model can be found in web-based social networks such as online stores like eBay and mobile app stores.

Without in-network third trusted authorities on the service-oriented social network, vendors are required to manage reviews of themselves. This requirement brings unique security problems to the review submission process. In this paper, we move the TSE model to a service-oriented social network. We require service providers to maintain a TSE model [6]. At the same time, we believe that users cooperatively participate in the TSE model, and improve the efficiency of comment submission while ensuring security. For the sake of demonstration, we will refer to the service provider as a supplier below [7].

2   System Model

In this article, we only consider the use of a single provider of service-oriented social networks. It is not general, assuming that each supplier provides a single service. By assigning unique identifiers to different vendors and services, the TSE model can be easily extended to multi-vendor and multi-business scenarios.

In the service-oriented social network of a particular single vendor, there is a Key Generator Center (KGC) that every user trusts. Each user u_j has a private unique identity id_j. KGC verifies the unique id_j of each user u_j. Generate a series of pseudonyms for each user after verification. For example, KGC can generate a series of pseudonyms $pid_{j;1}$, $pid_{j;2}$, $pid_{j;3}$ for user u_j. Each pseudonym of u_j corresponds to one Private key $pid_{j;*}$.

3   Trusted Service Evaluation Model

3.1   A New Digital Signature Scheme

In this section, a digital signature scheme for high security is proposed, which is described as follows [5] (Fig. 1):

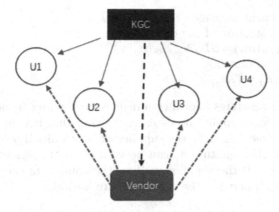

Fig. 1. Trusted service evaluation model network structure model

(1) Setup

KGC (Key Generation Center) chooses the primitive root alpha of prime q and q, and chooses an encryption hash function $H_1:\{0,1\}^* \to Z/q^z$ to get the system parameters of the digital signature scheme: params $= \{$q, alpha, $H_1\}$.

(2) Key generation

Users u_i generate random integers X_i such that $1 < X_i < q-1$.

Calculate $Y_i = \alpha^{X_i} \bmod$ q.

u_i's private key X_i is kept secret and the public key Y_i is public.

(3) Signature

Users u_i perform the following steps to sign comment content m_i, $\forall k_i \in Z_q^*$.

Calculate $K_i = \alpha^{k_i} \bmod$ q, $S_i = k_i + X_i + H_1(m_i) \bmod$ q.

Get signed $\sigma_i = (K_i, S_i)$.

(4) Verify

Verify the signature $\sigma_i = (K_i, S_i)$ of the comments received by the user u_i, verify the validity of the signature by the following equation.

$\alpha^{S_i} = K_i + Y_i + \alpha^{H_1(m_i)} \bmod$ q.

If the equation holds, the signature α_i is valid; otherwise, the signature α_i is invalid and discarded.

(5) Security Proof of Signature Scheme

This signature scheme is based on the difficulty of the discrete logarithm problem. Under the premise of secret signature private key X_i, attackers can not generate users private keys based on public-key computation simulation, so they can not forget the signature of the signer.

3.2   Generation and Submission of Comments

Assuming that the user u_i uses a pseudonym $pid_{j;*}$, the current time T_j, based on the comments on vendor v, the process of generating local comments rev_j is as follows:

(1) Generate comment messages: $m_j = (\alpha_j \| \text{v} \| T_j)$.
(2) Compute the signature of the comment message:
$\alpha_j = SIGN_{pskj;*}(m_j) = SIGN_{pskj;*}(\alpha_j \| \text{v} \| T_j)$.
(3) Generate local comments:
$rev_j = \langle pid_{j;*}, \alpha_j, \text{v}, T_j, \sigma_j \rangle$.

After a user u_j generates a local comment rev_j, the user u_j needs to submit it to the supplier. The supplier needs to verify rev_j that it is indeed generated by the user u_j in time T_j not by the supplier or by an illegal user.

The validity of the signature α_j can be verified by the signature scheme for the previous section. If the supplier verifies, the comments rev_j submitted by the user u_j revalid; otherwise, the comments are invalid.

4   Analysis of Simulated Experiments

The trusted service evaluation model designed in this paper resists the current four mainstream comment attacks through a new digital signature scheme. Comment Connectivity Attacks and Comment Modification Attacks have no effect on the process of submitting comments. Therefore, in this simulation experiment, we only study the impact of Comment Denial Attacks on system performance.

This paper defines the following performance indicators to reflect system performance: comment submission success rate (SR). SR is defined as the ratio of the number of comments submitted successfully to the total number of comments generated in the network (Fig. 2).

In the simulation experiment, 100 authenticated legitimate users were selected to submit comments to the same service provider. The 100 users were randomly divided into 10 groups, and each group was numbered. Each group was submitted 50 comments respectively. A total of 500 simulations were carried out. Each group was calculated according to the two cases of comment rejection attack (R) and no comment rejection attack. The average value of the lower SR is used for performance analysis.

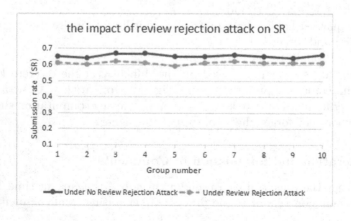

Fig. 2. The impact of review rejection attack on SR

Through the analysis of 10 groups of experimental results, the following conclusions can be drawn: in the case of comment rejection attack, the success rate of comment submission SR is only about 5% lower than that without comment rejection attack, which indicates that using this new trusted service evaluation model of digital signature scheme can effectively resist service rejection comment attack. Security analysis shows that the trusted efficient service evaluation model can effectively resist the current mainstream service comment attacks without relying on any trusted third party.

5   Conclusions

This paper proposes a new digital signature scheme, and then designs a trusted service evaluation model. In the trusted service evaluation model, the success rate of comment submission is improved, while ensuring the integrity of the comment, the vendors modification ability is reduced, and the security of the users comment is guaranteed. Security analysis shows that a trusted service evaluation model can effectively resist the current mainstream service review attacks without relying on trusted third parties. The experimental results show that trusted service evaluation model can still maintain a high success rate of comment submission under the condition of comment rejection attack.

References

1. Douceur, J.R.: The sybil attack. In: Druschel, P., Kaashoek, F., Rowstron, A. (eds.) IPTPS 2002. LNCS, vol. 2429, pp. 251–260. Springer, Heidelberg (2002). https://doi.org/10.1007/3-540-45748-8_24
2. Liang, X., Li, X., Luan, T.H., Lu, R., Lin, X., Shen, X.: Morality-driven data forwarding with privacy preservation in mobile social networks. IEEE Trans. Veh. Technol. 61(7), 3209–3222 (2012)
3. Liang, X., Lin, X., Shen, X.S.: Enabling trustworthy service evaluation in service-oriented mobile social networks. IEEE Trans. Parallel Distrib. Syst. 25(2), 310–320 (2013)
4. Liang, X., Xu, L., Lu, R., Lin, X., Shen, X.: SEER: a secure and efficient service review system for service-oriented mobile social networks. In: IEEE International Conference on Distributed Computing Systems (2012)
5. Pointcheval, D., Stern, J.: Security proofs for signature schemes. In: Maurer, U. (ed.) EUROCRYPT 1996. LNCS, vol. 1070. Springer, Heidelberg (1996). https://doi.org/10.1007/3-540-68339-9_33
6. Pointcheval, D., Stern, J.: Security proofs for signature schemes. In: International Conference on the Theory & Applications of Cryptographic Techniques (2012)
7. Rajan, H., Hosamani, M.: Tisa: toward trustworthy services in a service-oriented architecture (2008)
8. Wei, D., Dave, V., Qiu, L., Yin, Z.: Secure friend discovery in mobile social networks (2011)

Effective L-Diversity Anonymization Algorithm Based on Improved Clustering

Wantong Zheng[1], Yong Ma[2], Zhongyue Wang[1], Chunfu Jia[1(✉)], and Peng Li[3]

[1] College of Cyberspace Security, Nankai University, Tianjin 300350, China
cfjia@nankai.edu.cn
[2] Civil Aviation University of China, Tianjin, China
[3] TravelSky Technology Limited, Beijing, China

Abstract. Mass data has been collected and released everyday, at the same time, the published data contains a lot of sensitive information related to individuals. K-anonymity privacy preserving mechanisms can prevent the disclosure of individual privacy information in the scenarios of data publication. L-diversity further considers the distribution of sensitive attributes in equivalence classes to avoid homogeneity attacks. In this paper, we propose an improved L-diversity algorithm based on clustering, and we consider the L-diversity demand of sensitive attributes while clustering to achieve K-anonymity. We minimize the total information loss of each equivalence class by choosing records which has minimal loss of information, regardless of whether they have different sensitive attributes, until the number of distinct values of sensitive attribute in the equivalence class reaches L. This algorithm we conduct experiments on UCI Adult data set and compared with traditional (K,L)-member algorithm. Theoretical analysis and the experimental results demonstrate that the improved L-diversity algorithm can not only improve the privacy protection degree of sensitive data, but also effectively reduce the information loss.

Keywords: Data anonymization · L-diversity · K-anonymity · Clustering

1 Introduction

Recent years, with the rapid development of the Internet, both convenience and effectiveness let us strongly feel the power of science and technology. But at the same time, sensitive data, personally identifiable information, medical diagnoses and even non-personal sensitive data is exposed to abuse or negligence. Once the personal privacy data is excessively applied in data mining or data sharing, the privacy security of users cannot be guaranteed, their work and life will be affected and this will even endanger their lives. A large number of facts prove that more attention should be paid to data security.

Figure 1 shows a typical scenario of data collection and publishing. As we can see, data publisher is the one who collect data from record owners a data miner

© Springer Nature Switzerland AG 2019
J. Vaidya et al. (Eds.): CSS 2019, LNCS 11983, pp. 318–329, 2019.
https://doi.org/10.1007/978-3-030-37352-8_29

and the public is called data recipient. If data recipient conduct their mining on the raw data or directly disclose them to the public, all the individual privacy will be disclosed. And the anonymization technique is one of the most efficient methods to solve this important problem. In terms of data publishing technology for privacy protection, the most important task is to design or develop a data publishing tool which guarantee that personal privacy can be protected even under more adverse environmental conditions, and the utility of data can be guaranteed. This task is known as Privacy Preserving Data Publishing (PPDP).

A large amount of metrics was proposed to quantify privacy guarantees in publishing publishing anonymized data sets. Perfect privacy [4,10] was proposed to ensure that published data does not disclose any information about the sensitive data with an obvious problem that checks whether a conjunctive query discloses any information about the answer to another conjunctive query is shown to be very hard. They following implement a subsequent work to handle this problem [7]. However, perfect privacy places very strong restrictions on the types of queries that can be answered [10]. After that, less restrictive privacy definitions have been proposed [3,16].

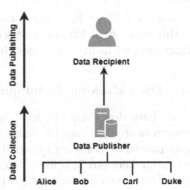

Fig. 1. Data collection and data publishing

Statistical databases allow answering aggregates over sensitive values without disclosing the exact value [1].

Except these PPDP theories, de-identification becomes one of the most creative and effective techniques in this filed. The most representative one is K-anonymity algorithm [14,15,17]. Under the influence of this theory, more and more algorithms have been proposed for better security of personal privacy, e.g., L-diversity [8] and T-closeness [6].

Some literatures realize that L-diversity has carried out prior analysis on data sets, however, in the actual application environment, there is no time to do prior analysis for large data sets that are constantly being generated.

In order to conform L-diversity standard, some algorithms force two records with very low relevance to be added to the equivalence class, resulting in that most of the generalized quasi-identifiers become suppressed. These kinds of algorithms separate K-anonymity from L-diversity, and cut off their relevance. It cause a serious information loss.

In this paper, we propose a novel clustering-based L-diversity algorithm. Our algorithm considers both K-anonymity and L-diversity, and realizes the relatively close coupling between K-anonymity and L-diversity algorithm. We relax the constraint of K-anonymity on the equivalence classes generation, and add more highly similar records to a cluster in the process of looking for L different sensitive attributes. Moreover, in the process of clustering, each generated cluster is used as a reference for selecting the new cluster centroid. This satisfies the principle of diversity between clusters to the greatest extent. Our scheme makes the records in equivalence class more compact, and greatly reduce the information loss caused by achieving L-diversity. Furthermore, we do not impose absolute limits on the size of cluster, so all the released data can be involved in the equivalence classes with no data abandoned. After this design and implementation, we demonstrate its superiority by practical experiment and theoretical reasoning.

2   Related Work

In this section, we first introduce data masking technique systematically and on this basis we briefly outline some related work in the area of K-anonymity algorithm and L-diversity algorithm which are the target of our improvement.

2.1   Data Masking Technique

As we have described in Sect. 1, privacy becomes a more and more important concern in applications. In recent years, relevant laws and regulations have been promulgated at home and abroad to protect data security. On the other hand, the researchers put in a lot of effort finding a effective solution at the technical level. Data masking as a general technique to ensure that real data sets are safely used in development, testing, and other non-production and outsourcing environments was first proposed by Adam et al. [1].

Following the idea of data masking, a large amount of researches were proposed, while some existing techniques were applied in this area. In general, data masking techniques in the literature can be categorized into two types: bottom-facing data masking and holistic data masking.

There are a number of effective and famous proposals in the first category, such as data swapping, data shuffling, data perturbation, data encryption, and so on. Data swapping method was proposed by Moore [11] where we randomly choose a value in initial data set and replace the raw data with it. Muralidhar et al. proposed data shuffling method in 2006 [12] which means swapping the locations of initial data randomly without new data generated. Data perturbation is a frequently used protection method to counter data mining [2,5] which alters individual data in a way such that the summary statistics remain approximately the same. Data encryption method encrypt initial data and utilize the ciphertext as the masking result. Each of these has different advantages and disadvantages and applicable scenarios.

In the second category, anonymous technology is one of the privacy protection technology which is main applied before data releasing and data sharing, through the method of the generalization and suppression of data attributes to achieve the effect of the privacy protection where K-anonymity is the most common algorithm which was proposed by Sweeney et al. [14,15,17]. As our improvement is based on this algorithm, we will elaborate it in Sect. 2.2. Other than this strategy, Murphy applied 3 kinds of classical ciphers in data masking [13]. On the other hand, Natalie come up with a risk assessment model to evaluate holistic data masking.

In summary, data masking technologies will always follow a simple, yet strict rule: masked data should be realistic and quasi-real. It is obvious that K-anonymity satisfies this requirement greatly. Our improvement on it is reasonable and valuable.

2.2   K-Anonymity Algorithm

As mentioned in Sect. 2.1, K-anonymity algorithm is one of the most common data masking strategies. We will describe its principle and outline some of its improvement.

We all know, the first step to implement data masking is to remove or mask Identifier (an attribute or a set of attributes that can identify a unique individual). However, a large number of facts prove that even we have done this work, attackers also have the ability to identify individuals by the help of Quasi-Identifier. K-Anonymity was proposed to counter this kind of attacks.

The high-level principle of K-anonymity is to ensure adversaries can identify at least K records by the help of Quasi-Identifier. This requires that the value of each Quasi-Identifier sequence in the published anonymous data set appear at least K $(K > 1)$ times, that is, at least K records have to use the same quasi-identifier attribute value. However, the problem is that this algorithm was demonstrated to be an NP-problem by Meyercon two years after its proposal [9].

K-anonymity can be seen as an indicator to measure the risk of privacy data disclosure, the algorithm guarantees there is only a $1/K$ probability that the attacker can relate the record to specific individual theoretically.

In practical, there are some drawbacks when utilizing K-anonymity algorithm. In this case, lots of improved algorithms appeared. For example, Zheng et al. proposed a new algorithm to achieve K-anonymity in a better way through improved clustering, and they optimized the clustering process by considering the overall distribution of Quasi-Identifier groups in a multidimensional space. Our mechanism is based on this theory.

2.3   L-Diversity Algorithm

There is no doubt that K-anonymity algorithm can be used to protect the risk of personal identity disclosure, but what needs to be concerned more is that the risk of property disclosure cannot be protected by it. For K-anonymity data sets, attackers may attack the user's attribute information in two ways, namely, homogeneity attack and background knowledge attack. In this situation, Machanavajjhala et al. introduced L-diversity to measure the risk of attribute disclosure on the basis of K-anonymity model [8].

The definition of L-diversity is that an equal set is said to be L-diversity satisfied that if it contains L "appropriate" values for a set of sensitive data corresponding to all records in any equal set and a data set is called L-diversity if all equal sets in the data set are L-diversity.

Machanavajjhala et al. defined three typical L-diversity strategies:

- **Distinct L-Diversity:** The values of sensitive attributes in each equivalence class in the anonymized data set have at least L different values. This model can defense homogeneity attack while there is no limit to the probability proportion of a single sensitive attribute.
- **Entropy L-Diversity:** The definition of entropy L-diversity of a equivalence class e_i is:

$$Encropy(e_i) = -\sum_{sa \in S} p(e_i, sa) log p(e_i, sa),$$

where S is the domain of the sensitive attribute, and $p(e_i, sa)$ is the fraction of records in e_i that have sensitive value sa. A table is said to have entropy L-diversity if for every equivalence class e_i,

$$Encropy(e_i) \geq log L.$$

- **Recurive(C,L)-Diversity:** In this case, we set m as the number of values in an equivalence class, and r_i as the number of times that the ith most frequent sensitive value appears in an equivalence class e_i. For a given constant C, if

$$r_1 < C(r_L + r_{L+1} + ... + r_m),$$

we judge e_i satisfies the recurive(C,L)-diversity and if all equivalence class in a data set is recurive(C,L)-diversity equivalence class, this dataset is a recurive(C,L)-diversity accordingly.

Comparing with standard K-anonymity, a data set in line with L-diversity standard is significantly reduced the risk of attribute data disclosure since, in theory, the probability of the attacker has at most $1/L$ can attribute disclosure attack and build relationship between specific users and their sensitive information. In general, to conform the data set to L-diversity standard is to construct a data set by inserting data perturbation. But just like data generalization, the insertion of data perturbation would cause the loss of table-level information, and the L-diversity standard also had some shortcomings in practical.

Our approach overcome some difficulty of traditional L-diversity algorithm by enhancing it with improved clustering.

3   Improved Algorithm

In this section, we will elaborate our improved algorithm.

3.1   Motivation and Design Idea

At present, most K-anonymous algorithms fail to consider that the distribution of sensitive attributes should meet the requirement of L-diversity. Many of the authors try other ways to achieve L-diversity because of the poor performance when they construct L-diversity on the basis of their K-anonymity algorithms. But our scheme makes some difference.

Our contribution can be concisely summed up in two points. First, We optimize the selection method of the new cluster centroid. We change the initial m centroids of clusters to gradual greedy selection, and the position of each generated cluster is used as a reference point to select new cluster centroids. This make objects highly dissimilar between clusters.

Second, We construct an outstanding method for L-diversity to participate in the process of K anonymous clustering. In the K-anonymity scheme, sometimes a few elements that should belong to a cluster are forced into other inappropriate clusters due to the limitation of K, this creates unnecessary information loss. So we relaxe the K-anonymity limit on the size of equivalence classes, and do not perform any active intervention while the cluster is looking for the nearest record, until the kinds of SAs come to L. Because we get rid of the K constraint, each cluster will become more compact. Improper classification will decrease appropriately, and there will be fewer residual records to be allocated in the last step. Thanks to this idea, we greatly decrease the information loss while meeting the requirement of L- diversity, and our L-diversity scheme even performs better than our K-anonymity scheme in information loss. Because of the compact clusters, there is no need to remove any complete record from the released data, the integrity of the data set is also guaranteed.

The idea of L-diversity is based on K-anonymity. So, we decide to meet the condition of L-diversity while achieving K-anonymity. First of all, we should set the parameters K and L. The parameter K means the size of the equivalence class should be at least K, While the parameter L sets limits to the kinds of Sensitive Attributes. As we mentioned above, all the implements are based on our improved K-anonymity clustering algorithm. That is, we start our clustering from a random initial centroid, and then we will find K records nearest to the centroid and append them to the cluster. We still consider the existence of all the generated cluster. Whereas, In order to achieve the requirements of L-diversity, we make some changes while generating a cluster. When the size of a new cluster come to K, the equivalence class will contain K records, but the kinds of Sensitive Attributes may not reach the limit 'L'. So we continue with our clustering process to collect L kinds of Sensitive attributes. For the equivalence classes that satisfy both K-anonymity and L-diversity, we store them and proceed to the next round of clustering. For those that do not meet the requirements, we still find the nearest record to the centroid each time and append the record to the current cluster even though the Sensitive Attribute of the record might already exist in the cluster. We repeat the steps above until we get L different kinds of Sensitive Attributes in the cluster. And then the next round of clustering starts.

3.2 Algorithm Description

Our algorithm is roughly divided into three parts.

First, we initialize the cluster set and set the parameters K and L. And then, we choose a random record as the initial centroid.

Next, we generate the equivalence classes by our improved clustering algorithm. We put the K records closest to the centroid into the cluster, and then check the number of SAs' kinds. If the number reaches L, we go into the next round of clustering. But if the number does not reach L, we continue to append records to the cluster until the diversity reach the level L. We reach both K-anonymity and L-diversity at the same time.

Finally, we deal with the residual data in the data set, and complete the clustering process.

The pseudo-code is as follows:

Input:

   The initial data set *data*;

   The anonymized parameters K and L;

Output:

   The final clusters achieved K-anonymity and L-diversity;

1: Initialize clusters=[]
2: Random select a record r_i
3: **while** len($data$) $\geq K$ **do**
4:   **if** clusters is empty **then**
5:     choose the furthest record r_j from r_i as the first centoid of the first cluster
6:     pop record r_j from *data*
7:     initialize the first cluster = Cluster(r_j)
8:   **else**
9:     choose the record r_i that has max_sum_distance from all existed cluster as the next centroid
10:     initialize the next cluster = Cluster(r_i)
11:   **end if**
12:   **while** len(cluster) $< K$ **do**
13:     choose residual $K - 1$ nearest records to add into cluster to achieve K-anonymity
14:   **end while**
15:   select all SAs of cluster into list *sa_list*
16:   transform list *sa_list* into set *sa_set*
17:   initialize *num*=len($data$) and *sa_num*=len(sa_set)
18:   **while** *sa_num* $< L$ and *num* > 0 **do**
19:     find record r_j with lowest information loss between r_j and the cluster
20:     *num* minus 1
21:     **if** r_j(sa) in *sa_set* **then**
22:       add record(r_j) into cluster
23:       pop record r_j from *data*
24:     **else**
25:       add r_j(sa) into *sa_set*
26:       *sa_num* plus 1
27:       add record(r_j) into cluster
28:     **end if**
29:   **end while**
30: **end while**

We explain the superiority of our algorithm by an example; As shown in Fig. 2, we assume the anonymization parameters K is 5 and L is 3. When given the initial data set, we first random choose a record as the centroid of `cluster 1`. Then we find 4 other closest records to add into `cluster 1`. When we choose the second centroid, our algorithm is the same as the traditional ones. We all select the record that is farthest from the cluster. But then our algorithm is different. Starting with the third cluster, we consider the positional distribution of the clusters that have been generated before. For example, point A will be selected as the third centroid in traditional algorithms because it's the furthest one from `cluster 2`. But in our algorithm, the third centroid will fall within the scope of the `cluster 3` and point A will merge into `cluster 1` during processing outliers finally. This is the first innovation of the clustering algorithm proposed in this paper.

Second, at the same time, our algorithm also takes into account the diversity of sensitive attributes. That is, green, blue and red represent the different values of sensitive attribute. Let's look at `cluster 2`, while `cluster 2` has covered two blue and two red points, we need to find another record while the third color. In traditional algorithms, the blue below will be ignored and continue to merge the green, but in this paper, we still add the blue point into `cluster 2`. This is because the process clustering will continue until the cluster satisfies the L-diversity. The blue point does not add extra information loss but makes the cluster more compact. Thus, our algorithm can greatly reduce the overall information loss of the data set.

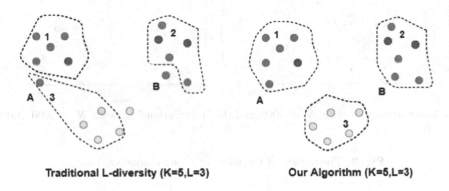

Traditional L-diversity (K=5,L=3)   **Our Algorithm (K=5,L=3)**

Fig. 2. An example for comparison

4   Evaluation

In this section, we evaluate our improved algorithm in two ways. In Sect. 4.1, we practically evaluate the effectiveness through 3 experiments. After that, we demonstrate the superiority of our method theoretically in Sect. 4.2.

4.1   Experiment

Our experiments choose the Adult data set from the UCI machine learning database to test the performance of the proposed algorithm and the traditional algorithm. The data set includes part of the US population census data. It has been widely used in the study of anonymized privacy protection and has become the de facto standard in this field. In our data preprocessing, we remove records with missing values and get 32561 records. We choose 7 attributes as `Quasi-Identifiers` which includes age, workclass, education time, marital status, race, sex, and native country, and occupation is chosen as the sensitive attribute.

To compare our approach with (K,L)-member diversity, we calculate information loss in different setting of L in these two model; see Fig. 3. First, we fix the data size N and the parameter of K-anonymity K and change the value of anonymous algorithm L to conduct experiments. As we can see in Fig. 3(a), when L increases, more records are contained into the equivalent class, causing higher information loss. When we change the setting of data quality, the same conclusion comes to us. We show this result in Fig. 3(b). We claim that our algorithm has higher data quality and outperforms (K,L)-member diversity.

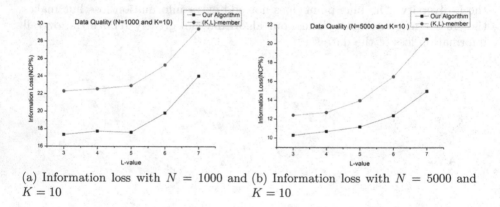

(a) Information loss with $N = 1000$ and   (b) Information loss with $N = 5000$ and
$K = 10$ $K = 10$

Fig. 3. The impact of the value of L on anonymity data

Then we change the size of data set to see its impact on the anonymity data. We set the initialization parameter K is 50 and L is 5. As shown in Fig. 4, with the increase of data size, the information loss of both algorithms all gradually reduce. Our algorithm performs better than (K,L)-member in preserving data quality.

Another interesting finding is when the N is 30000, the NCP of our algorithm is only 12.19%, while (K,L)-member is 18.33%. So we note that the more compact the records in the equivalence class, the more similar the quasi-identifiers of the records are.

4.2   Algorithm Analysis

Before the theoretically reasoning on our approach. We have the following parameters to calculate the time complexity:

- n as the total number of records contained in the raw data set S, $|S| = n$;
- m as the dimension of Quasi-Identifier;
- K as the minimum size of the groups in K-anonymity;
- L as the number of different values for sensitive attributes in each equivalence class.

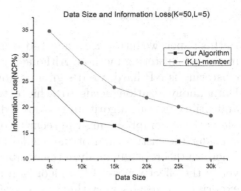

Data Size and Information Loss(K=50,L=5)

Fig. 4. The impact of data size on anonymity data

Time Complexity. As the implementation of our L-diversity benefits from our proposed clustering based K-anonymity, so locating the latest centroid holds a definite proportion. Because every new centroid is chosen according to the existed clusters. As the clustering goes on, the count of existing clusters increases at the same time. But it is a little different from the situation where we only implement K-anonymity, In the situation of K-anonymity, we end a round of clustering when the size of equivalence class comes to K. However in the L-diversity scheme, the clustering process may not stop at K, clusters usually have larger size. Hence, the number of clusters m is usually less than $\lfloor n/K \rfloor$. Due to the decrease of the total number of clusters, the calculation times of distance when we locate a new cluster based on the location information of the generated cluster will be reduced. In the worst situation m equals to $\lfloor n/K \rfloor$, the times of compare will go up from $1 \cdot (n - K)$ to $(n - mK)\lfloor n/k \rfloor$. So the time complexity of this part is $(n - K) \cdot 1 + (n - 2K) \cdot 2 + ... + (n - mK)\lfloor n/k \rfloor$, but in most cases the equivalence has less than m items. It seems clear that time complexity of this part is $O(n^2)$. Another part of time complexity comes from the selection of record, this is the inevitable cost of looking for the nearest record to a centroid. The time complexity of this part is a sum of arithmetic series from $(n-1)$ to 1, so this part is also $O(n^2)$.

Security. Since L-diversity participates in the process of K-anonymous clustering, so the security evaluation benefits from both K-anonymity and L-diversity, K-anonymity requires that each cluster contain at least K records, and all the quasi-attributes in each cluster are generalized to the same value. This forces the attacker to guess the individual's privacy information with probability $1/K$. This gives the algorithm the ability to resist SQL-connected attacks. And L-diversity makes each cluster have at least L different sensitive values, so the algorithm also has the characteristics of resisting background knowledge attack and homogeneity attack.

5   Conclusions

In this paper, we introduce a new L-diversity implementation algorithm based on improved clustering method. Although achieve optimal (K, L)-diversity through clustering is NP hard, we design an algorithm that minimizes information loss. Data anonymization needs to achieve the balance of data privacy protection and utility. So our algorithm tries to reduce information loss as much as possible without compromising the security of anonymization. In our algorithm, we consider the distribution of the whole data set and whether there are outliers. Then we theoretically analyze the complexity and security of the algorithm, and verify the effectiveness of the algorithm through comparative experiments. The experimental results show that our algorithm is better than the other traditional algorithms in data publishing.

Acknowledgement. This work was supported by the National Natural Science Foundation of China (No. 61772291), and National Science Foundation of Tianjin (No. 17JCZDJC30500). We also thank Civil Aviation University of China and TravelSky Technology Limited for supporting this paper.

References

1. Adam, N.R., Worthmann, J.C.: Security-control methods for statistical databases: a comparative study. ACM Comput. Surv. (CSUR) **21**(4), 515–556 (1989)
2. Agrawal, R., Srikant, R.: Privacy-preserving data mining, vol. 29. ACM (2000)
3. Dalvi, N., Miklau, G., Suciu, D.: Asymptotic conditional probabilities for conjunctive queries. In: Eiter, T., Libkin, L. (eds.) ICDT 2005. LNCS, vol. 3363, pp. 289–305. Springer, Heidelberg (2004). https://doi.org/10.1007/978-3-540-30570-5_20
4. Deutsch, A., Papakonstantinou, Y.: Privacy in database publishing. In: Eiter, T., Libkin, L. (eds.) ICDT 2005. LNCS, vol. 3363, pp. 230–245. Springer, Heidelberg (2004). https://doi.org/10.1007/978-3-540-30570-5_16
5. Kantarcioglu, M., Clifton, C.: Privacy-preserving distributed mining of association rules on horizontally partitioned data. IEEE Trans. Knowl. Data Eng. **16**(9), 1026–1037 (2004)
6. Li, N., Li, T., Venkatasubramanian, S.: t-closeness: privacy beyond k-anonymity and l-diversity. In: IEEE 23rd International Conference on Data Engineering, ICDE 2007, pp. 106–115. IEEE (2007)
7. Machanavajjhala, A., Gehrke, J.: On the efficiency of checking perfect privacy. In: Proceedings of the Twenty-Fifth ACM SIGMOD-SIGACT-SIGART Symposium on Principles of Database Systems, pp. 163–172. ACM (2006)
8. Machanavajjhala, A., Gehrke, J., Kifer, D.: L-diversity: privacy beyound kanonymity. ACM Trans. Knowl. Discov. Data (TKDD) **1**(1), 24–35 (2007)
9. Meyerson, A., Williams, R.: On the complexity of optimal k-anonymity. In: Proceedings of the Twenty-Third ACM SIGMOD-SIGACT-SIGART Symposium on Principles of Database Systems, pp. 223–228. ACM (2004)
10. Miklau, G., Suciu, D.: A formal analysis of information disclosure in data exchange. J. Comput. Syst. Sci. **73**(3), 507–534 (2007)
11. Moore Jr., R.A.: Controlled data-swapping techniques for masking public use microdata sets. In: Statistical Research Division Report Series RR 96–04 (1996)

12. Muralidhar, K., Sarathy, R.: Data shuffling–a new masking approach for numerical data. Manage. Sci. **52**(5), 658–670 (2006)
13. Murphy, C.: Data masking with classical ciphers. In: SAS Global Forum (2010)
14. Samarati, P., Sweeney, L.: Generalizing data to provide anonymity when disclosing information. In: PODS, vol. 98, p. 188. Citeseer (1998)
15. Samarati, P., Sweeney, L.: Protecting privacy when disclosing information: k-anonymity and its enforcement through generalization and suppression. Tech. rep., SRI International (1998)
16. Stoffel, K., Studer, T.: Provable data privacy. In: Andersen, K.V., Debenham, J., Wagner, R. (eds.) DEXA 2005. LNCS, vol. 3588, pp. 324–332. Springer, Heidelberg (2005). https://doi.org/10.1007/11546924_32
17. Sweeney, L.: k-anonymity: a model for protecting privacy. Int. J. Uncertainty Fuzziness Knowl. Based Syst. **10**(05), 557–570 (2002)

Semantic Location Privacy Protection Based on Privacy Preference for Road Network

Yonglu Wang[1,2], Kaizhong Zuo[1,2(✉)], Rui Liu[1,2], and Liangmin Guo[1,2]

[1] School of Computer and Information, Anhui Normal University, Wuhu 241002, Anhui, China
zuokz@ahnu.edu.cn
[2] Anhui Provincial Key Laboratory of Network and Information Security, Anhui Normal University, Wuhu 241002, Anhui, China

Abstract. In recent years, with the popularization of mobile intelligent terminals, location-based services (LBS) have been widely used. When users enjoy the convenience of LBS, they also face with the risk of leakage of location privacy. Therefore, it is very important to provide effective privacy protection service during the use of LBS. Previous methods of location privacy protection cannot meet the requirements of users for location privacy protection and service qualities. For this reason, an adjustable semantic location privacy protection scheme is presented in this paper. According to the road network, this scheme introduces the privacy tolerance and the deficient number to select adjacent road segment to satisfy users' requirements. Experimental results show that the proposed scheme supports users' privacy preference for location privacy protection and the required quality of service, and fully considers the user's personalized privacy requirements.

Keywords: Location-based service · Privacy preference · Privacy preservation · Road network · Semantic location

1 Introduction

With the rapid development of wireless communication technology and positioning technology, it has promoted the wide application of location-based services (LBS) [1–3]. In order to get services in LBS, the user has to share its current location information, such as querying the nearest hospital. However, the location information can be stolen by the attackers, then more private information maybe leaked by the mining methods [4]. Therefore, the personal privacy information in LBS should be protected.

The location privacy protection method for road network is mainly based on K-anonymity and L-diversity [5–9], which is an anonymous region contains both K users and L road segments. However, this method doesn't consider the influence of semantic information of the location. Based on this, Li et al. [10] divided the city map based on the Voronoi diagram, and the anonymous region is constructed according to the semantic location popularity of the Voronoi cell. Xu et al. [11] proposed an incremental query optimization method based on local optimization and global

© Springer Nature Switzerland AG 2019
J. Vaidya et al. (Eds.): CSS 2019, LNCS 11983, pp. 330–342, 2019.
https://doi.org/10.1007/978-3-030-37352-8_30

optimization, using the deficient popularity to build an anonymous region. Li et al. [12] converted the road network into road segment clustering map, balancing quality of service and privacy requirements by constructing the anonymous region with different semantic location types. Chen et al. [13] introduces the regional popularity and combines with the user-defined sensitivity to calculate the privacy of adjacent road segments, a privacy protection algorithm based on location semantic is designed. Lv et al. [14] obtained the adjacent candidate road segments efficiently until the privacy requirements are satisfied. Chen et al. [15] considered the semantic information of the dummy location and enhanced the privacy protection by constructing a location semantic tree. Xu et al. [16] proposed a sensitivity-fade algorithm, which uses the semantic location influence vector to select the road segment to construct the anonymous region and improve privacy protection.

However, none of these methods consider most the user's privacy preference for location privacy protection and quality of service. Therefore, an adjustable semantic location privacy protection scheme for road network is proposed in this paper.

2 Preliminaries

2.1 Related Definition

In this paper, the road network is denoted as an undirected connectivity diagram $G = (V, E)$, $E = \{e_1, e_2, \ldots, e_m\}$ denotes the road segments in the road network, each road segment $e_i = \{eid, v_s, v_e\}$ is an edge in the road network, with eid is the road segment number, v_s and v_e respectively denote the starting and the end point of the road segment. $V = \{v_1, v_2, \ldots, v_n\}$ denotes the intersection of road segment. Anonymous region CR is comprised of multiple adjacent road segments $Edges = \{e_1, e_2, \ldots, e_i\}$, multiple users $Users = \{u_1, u_2, \ldots, u_j\}$ and multiple semantic locations $Locs = \{loc_1, loc_2, \ldots, loc_k\}$ on the road segments, in which the number of road segments $Edges$ and users $Users$ should satisfy the personalized privacy requirement of users.

Definition 1 (*Semantic location*). $loc = \{lid, eid, (x, y), tp\}$ denotes the semantic location in the road network, with lid is the number of the semantic location, eid is the number of the road where the semantic location is located, (x, y) is the coordinate of the semantic location, and tp is the type of the semantic location. The type of semantic location is divided into n types in total, and $Type = \{tp_1, tp_2, \ldots, tp_n\}$ is the set of n semantic location types.

Definition 2 (*Semantic location popularity*). It is used to describe the popularity of a semantic location type in the road network. For each semantic location type $tp_i \in Type$ set a popularity p_{tp_i}. The set $Pop = \{p_{tp_1}, p_{tp_2}, \ldots, p_{tp_n}\}$ indicates the popularity of all semantic location.

Definition 3 (*Semantic location sensitivity*). It is used to describe the sensitivity of a semantic location type in the road network. Each user sets a sensitivity s_{tp_i} for each semantic location type $tp_i \in Type$ according to their own circumstances. The set

$S_u = \{s_{tp_1}, s_{tp_2}, \ldots, s_{tp_n}\}$ is the set of sensitivity of all semantic location types relative to user u.

Based on definition 2 and definition 3, the popularity and the sensitivity of the CR can be defined as follow:

Definition 4 (*Regional popularity*). The popularity $Popular_{CR}$ of the CR,

$$Popular_{CR} = \sum_{i=1}^{|Type|} \frac{|CR.Locs.tp = tp_i|}{|CR.Locs|} P_{tp_i} \tag{1}$$

Definition 5 (*Regional sensitivity*). The sensitivity $Sens_{CR}$ of the CR,

$$Sens_{CR} = \sum_{i=1}^{|Type|} \frac{|CR.Locs.tp = tp_i|}{|CR.Locs|} S_{tp_i} \tag{2}$$

$|Type|$ in formulas (1) and (2) is the total number of semantic location types contained in the CR; and $|CR.Locs|$ is the number of semantic locations contained in the CR.

Definition 6 (*Regional privacy*). The regional privacy RP_{CR} of the CR,

$$RP_{CR} = \frac{Popular_{CR}}{Sens_{CR}} \tag{3}$$

Definition 7 (*Privacy tolerance*). It is used to describe the importance of the user's privacy information. Assuming that all adjacent road segments of the CR are the set $NearEdges = \{e_1, e_2, \ldots, e_n\}$, and the regional privacy is formed by adding road segments in $NearEdges$ to the CR one by one, which is recorded as the set RP_{set}.

$$\forall rp_i \in RP_{set}, \delta_i = \frac{rp_{\max} - rp_i}{rp_{\max} - rp_{\min}}, \delta_i \in [0, 1] \tag{4}$$

$rp_{\max}$ is the maximum of RP_{set}, $rp_{\min}$ is the minimum of RP_{set}. Privacy tolerance reflects the user's choice of location privacy protection and the quality of service based on subjective intent, which is in a range of values [0,1]. The more attention is paid to the location privacy protection, the privacy tolerance is lower; otherwise, the quality of service is more important.

Definition 8 (*Privacy requirement*). For a user u that makes a query, his privacy requirements are expressed in $PR(K,L,\delta,S)$. In this case, K denotes the user-defined lowest number of anonymous users; L denotes the user-defined lowest number of road segments; δ denotes the user-defined highest value of privacy tolerance; and S is user-defined sensitivity of a group of different semantic location types.

Definition 9 (*Deficient number*). For a user u, it is used to describing how many anonymous users are still missing from the CR to satisfy $u.PR.K$,

$$dn = u.PR.K - |CR.Users| \tag{5}$$

$|CR.Users|$ is the number of anonymous users in the CR.

2.2 System Model

This paper is based on the central server architecture (Fig. 1), a trusted third anonymous server that exists in the client and the location server. Users send their locations, inquiry contents, and privacy requirements to anonymous servers. The anonymous server sends the users' locations after the privacy preference selection module and the anonymous module to the LBS server. The location server queries the candidate results and returns it to the anonymous server, the anonymous server analyzes the query candidate set, and returns the screening valid results to the requester. Besides, the anonymous server needs to store the city map information and the semantic location information.

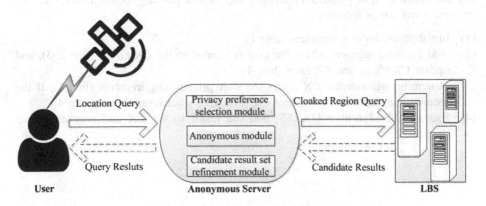

Fig. 1. Central Server Architecture

3 Adjustable Semantic Location Privacy Protection Scheme

This paper assumes that third-party servers(anonymous servers) are trustworthy to users. In order to achieve user's privacy preference for location privacy protection and the quality of service in the road network, this paper designs an adjustable semantic location privacy protection scheme. The algorithm flow as shown in Fig. 2.

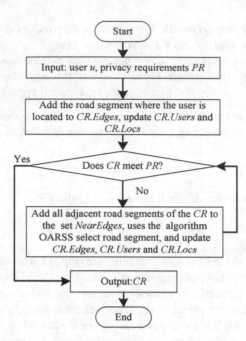

Fig. 2. Algorithm Flow

Algorithm 1 is an adjustable semantic location privacy protection scheme(ASLPP). The algorithm's input parameters include user *u* and privacy requirements *PR*. The concrete steps are as follows:

(1) Initialize the input parameters (line 1);
(2) Add the road segment where the user is located to the *CR.Edges* (line 2–3), and update *CR.Users* and *CR.Locs* (line 4);
(3) Determine whether the *CR* meets the user privacy requirements (line 5), If the requirements are satisfied, return *CR* (line 13); otherwise, execute step 4;
(4) Execute the algorithm OARSS, add the result to the *CR* and execute step 3 (line 5–12).

The pseudo-code of the algorithm is as follows:

Algorithm 1 Adjustable Semantic Location Privacy Protection Scheme

---

Input: user u, privacy requirements PR

Output: CR

1) $CR = \varnothing$;
2)   find the road segment e where u is located;
3) $CR.Edges = CR.Edges \cup e$;
4)   update $CR.Users$ and $CR.Locs$;
5)   while $|CR.Users| < u.PR.K$ or $|CR.Edges| < u.PR.L$
6) $dn(CR) = u.PR.K - |CR.Users|$;
7) $NearEdge_{set} = Findedges(CR)$; //find all adjacent road segments of the CR
8) $BestEdge = OARSS(CR, NearEdge_{set}, dn(CR), u.PR.\delta, u.PR.S)$;
9) $CR.edges = CR.edges \cup BestEdge$;
10)   update $CR.Users$ and $CR.Locs$;
11) $NearEdge_{set} = \varnothing$;
12) end while
13) return CR;

Algorithm 2 is the optimal road segment selection algorithm(OARSS). The input parameters of the algorithm are the anonymous region CRS, the deficient number dn, the privacy tolerance δ, the set of road segments $NearEdges$ and the set of sensitivity SS. The concrete steps are as follows:

(1) Initialize the input parameters (line 1–4);
(2) Calculate RP after adding the set of road segments and add it to the set RP_{set} (line 5–8), find the maximum and minimum of RP_{set} (line 9–10).
(3) Calculate the privacy tolerance of each road segment in the set $NearEdge$, and take the road segment of less than or equal to δ as the set $Cadedges_{set}$ (line 11–17).
(4) Add a road segment greater than or equal to dn in the $Cadedges_{set}$ to the set $DPEdge1_{set}$, and add a road segment smaller than dn to the set $DPEdge2_{set}$ (line 18–24).
(5) If $DPEdge1_{set}$ is not empty, return to the road segment of the minimum of anonymous users. Otherwise, return to the road segment of $DPEdge2_{set}$ with the maximum of anonymous users (line 25–30).

The pseudo-code of the algorithm is as follows:

Algorithm 2 Optimal Adjacent Road Segment Selection Algorithm

---

Input: anonymous region *CRS*, adjacent road segments set *NearEdges*, deficient
number *dn*, privacy tolerance δ, the sensitivity set *SS*

Output: *AEdge*

1) $AEdge = \varnothing$;

2) $Cadedges_{set} = \varnothing, DPEdge1_{set} = \varnothing, DPEdge2_{set} = \varnothing$;

3) $MAX=0, MIN=0$;

4) $RP_{set} = \varnothing$;

5) for each *edge* in *NearEdges* do

6) $RP_{set} = RP_{set} \cup (RP = Popular_{(CRS \cup edge)} / Sens_{(CRS \cup edge)})$;

7)   *CRS*.remove(*edge*);

8) end for

9) $MAX = \{RP \mid \max\{RP \in RP_{set}\}\}$;

10) $MIN = \{RP \mid \min\{RP \in RP_{set}\}\}$;

11) for each *edge* in *NearEdges* do

12) $RP = Popular_{(CRS \cup edge)} / Sens_{(CRS \cup edge)}$;

13)   *CRS*.remove(*edge*);

14)   if $\dfrac{MAX - RP}{MAX - MIN} \le \delta$ then

15) $Cadedges_{set} = Cadedges_{set} \cup edge$;

16)   end if

17) end for

18) for each *edge* in *Cadedges*$_{set}$ do

19)   if $(NumUser(edge) - dn) \ge 0$ then

20) $DPEdge1_{set} = DPEdge1_{set} \cup edge$;

21)   else

22) $DPEdge2_{set} = DPEdge2_{set} \cup edge$;

23)   end if

24) end for

25) if $DPEdge1_{set}.size() > 0$ then

26) $AEdge = \{edge \mid \min_{edge \in DPEdge1_{set}} \{NumUser(edge)\}\}$;

27) else

28) $AEdge = \{edge \mid \max_{edge \in DPEdge2_{set}} \{NumUser(edge)\}\}$;

29) end if

30) return *AEdge*;

---

4 Experiment and Analysis

4.1 Experiment Data Sets and Parameter Settings

The environment of the experiment is Intel Core(TM) 2 CPU @ 2.83 GHz; 2 GB RAM; the operating system is Microsoft Windows 7 Professional, and the algorithm is written in Java based on MyEclipse environment.

The experimental data is based on the Oldenburg map of Germany, which includes 6105 vertices and 7035 edges. There are 1 0000 uniform distribution users obtained from Brinkhoff based network mobile object generator [17] by introducing the highway network of Germany Oldenburg city into Brinkhoff generator. The users are distributed on the road segments, and a specific semantic information definition is labeled on the attribute of location type in location data generated by Brinkhoff generator, including 4 types of semantic location (hospital, bar, shopping mall, and school). All experimental parameters in the experiment set are shown in Table 1.

Table 1. Parameter settings

Parameter	Defaults	Evaluation rang
The number of users	10000	
K	25	[15,35]
L	6	[3, 15]
L_{max}	20	
The number of semantic locations	10000	
The number of users that request services	1000	
δ	0.7	[0.1,1]

The experiment randomly selects 1000 users who request service to simulate experiments. For the convenience of calculation, the hypothetical popularity for the type of semantic locations is as following: {hospital:0.3, bar:0, shopping mall:0.4, school:0.3}. Considering the time complexity and the quality of service, the maximum number of road segments L_{max} is set in the experiment.

4.2 Analysis of Experimental Results

The experiment compares and evaluates ASLPP with LSBASC proposed in literature [13] and Enhance-LSBASC proposed in literature [14] from the aspects of anonymous success rate, average anonymous execution time, average number of semantic locations and regional privacy.

(1) Influence of δ

Figure 3 depicts the influence of δ on the algorithm ASLPP. Since the algorithm LSBASC and Enhance-LSBASC don't consider privacy tolerance δ, only the algorithm ASLPP is experimentally verified when $K = 25$, $L = 6$, $L_{max}= 20$ and δ changes from 0.1 to 1. It can be seen from Fig. 3 that the anonymous success rate of the algorithm

ASLPP is increasing, but the number of semantic locations, average anonymous execution time, and regional privacy are decreasing, especially after δ is greater than 0.7, the trend of change is more obvious. This is because when the δ increases, more road segments meet the privacy tolerance δ. The algorithm ASLPP selects the road segment according to the deficient number, reduces the number of road segments that need to be added. Therefore, the average anonymous execution time and the number of semantic locations are reduced, the anonymous success rate is improved. However, the larger of δ, the road segment selected by the algorithm ASLPP contains more sensitive semantic locations of the user, which makes the regional privacy decrease. It can be seen that the algorithm ASLPP can effectively implement the privacy preference selection of the user's location privacy protection and the quality of service by adjusting δ.

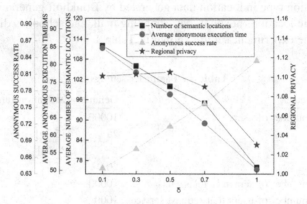

Fig. 3. Anonymous success rate, average number of semantic locations, average anonymous execution time, regional privacy and δ

(2) Influence of K

Figure 4 depicts the influence of K on the algorithm ASLPP, LSBASC, and Enhance-LSBASC when $L = 6$, $\delta = 0.7$, $L_{max} = 20$ and K changes from 15 to 35. In Fig. 4(a), the anonymous success rate of the three algorithms is decreasing and the algorithm ASLPP is higher than that of the algorithm LSBASC and Enhance-LSBASC. This is because the algorithm LSBASC chooses the best one to join the anonymous set each time, while the algorithm Enhance-LSBASC selects the optimal road segment set to join the current anonymous set each time. When the number of added road segments reaches the upper limit of the road segment tolerance L_{max}, the number of anonymous users can't meet the privacy requirements, resulting in anonymous failure. The algorithm ASLPP selects the optimal road segment by the deficient number. In Fig. 4(b), the average anonymous execution time of the three algorithms is increasing, but the algorithm ASLPP is lower than that of the algorithm LSBASC and higher than that of Enhance-LSBASC. This is because when the K increases, more road segments need to be added to meet the user's privacy requirements.

In Fig. 4(c), the number of semantic locations of the three algorithms increases, but algorithm ASLPP is lower than that of the algorithm LSBASC and Enhance-LSBASC. This is because algorithm ASLPP selects adjacent road segment based on the deficient

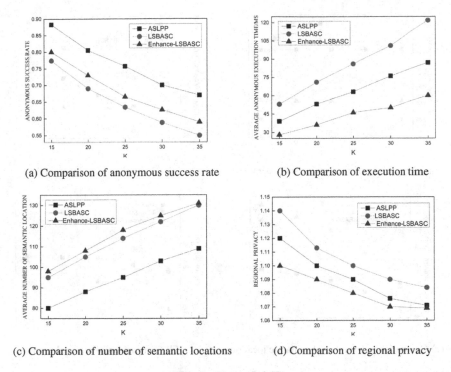

(a) Comparison of anonymous success rate

(b) Comparison of execution time

(c) Comparison of number of semantic locations

(d) Comparison of regional privacy

Fig. 4. Change of K

number, and reduces the number of road segments that need to be added. In Fig. 4(d), the regional privacy of the three algorithms is decreasing. This is because the anonymous region contains more relatively sensitive semantic locations of the user, which makes the regional privacy decrease. The algorithm ASLPP is lower than that of the algorithm LSBASC and higher than the algorithm Enhance-LSBASC. However, the algorithm ASLPP only reduces regional privacy by about 1% compared to the algorithm LSBASC.

(3) Influence of L

Figure 5 depicts the influence of L on the algorithm ASLPP, LSBASC, and Enhance-LSBASC when $K = 25$, $\delta = 0.7$, $L_{max} = 20$, and L changes from 3 to 15. In Fig. 5(a), the anonymous success rate of the three algorithms is not affected by L, and the algorithm ASLPP is higher than that of the algorithm LSBASC and Enhance-LSBASC. In Fig. 5(b), the average anonymous execution time of the three algorithms is increasing, but the algorithm ASLPP is lower than that of the algorithm LSBASC and higher than that of the algorithm Enhance-LSBASC. This is because when the L increases, the number of road segments in the anonymous region must reach a certain number. The algorithm ASLPP and LSBASC choose the best one each time, while the algorithm Enhance-LSBASC selects the optimal road segments set each time.

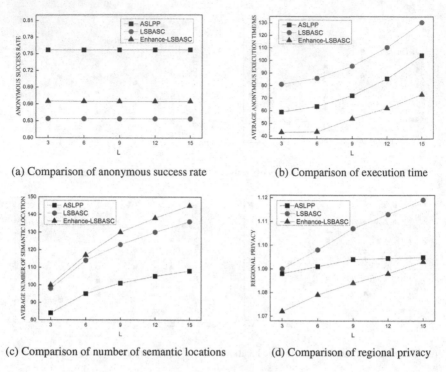

(a) Comparison of anonymous success rate   (b) Comparison of execution time

(c) Comparison of number of semantic locations   (d) Comparison of regional privacy

Fig. 5. Change of L

In Fig. 5(c), the number of semantic locations of the three algorithms is increasing, but the algorithm ASLPP is lower than that of the algorithm LSBASC and Enhance-LSBASC. This is because the algorithm ASLPP selects the road segment by the deficient number, reducing the number of road segments so that the number of semantic locations is decreasing. In Fig. 5(d), the regional privacy of the three algorithms is increasing, but the algorithm ASLPP is lower than that of the algorithm LSBASC and higher than that of the algorithm Enhance-LSBASC. This is because when the L increases, the number of road segments in the anonymous region is increasing, making the number of semantic locations are less sensitive to the increasing number of users.

5 Conclusion

In this paper, based on the existing semantic location privacy protection methods without the consideration of the user's privacy preference, we propose an adjustable semantic location privacy protection scheme for road network. The scheme selects the adjacent road segment through privacy tolerance and deficient number. Under the premise of fully satisfying personalized privacy requirements, the privacy preference of location privacy protection and service quality is realized. Finally, simulation experiments show that the proposed scheme supports the user's privacy preference.

Acknowledgement. This paper is supported by the *Natural Science Foundation of China* through projects 61672039 and 61370050, by the *Anhui Natural Science Foundation* through project 1508085QF133.

References

1. Wang, B., Yang, X., Wang, G., et al.: Energy efficient approximate self adaptive data collection in wireless sensor networks. Front. Comput. Sci. **10**(5), 936–950 (2016)
2. Sun, Y., Chen, M., Hu, L., et al.: ASA: against statistical attacks for privacy-aware users in location based service. Future Gen. Comput. Syst. **70**(4), 48–58 (2017)
3. Zhang, X.J., Gui, X.L., Wu, Z.D.: Privacy preservation for location-based services: a survey. J. Softw. **26**(9), 2373–2395 (2015)
4. Mingjie, M.A., Yuejin, D.U., Fenghua, L.I., Jiawen, L.: Review of semantic-based privacy-preserving approaches in LBS. Chin. J. Netw. Inf. Secur. **2**(12), 1–11 (2016)
5. Wang, Y., Xia, Y., Hou, J., et al.: A fast privacy-preserving framework for continuous location-based queries in road networks. J. Netw. Comput. Appl. **53**(1), 57–73 (2015)
6. Xinghua, L., Ermeng, W., Weidong, Y., et al.: DALP: a demand-aware location privacy protection scheme in continuous location-based services. Concurr. Comput. Pract. Exp. **28**(4), 1219–1236 (2016)
7. Cui, N., Yang, X., Wang, B.: A novel spatial cloaking scheme using hierarchical hilbert curve for location-based services. In: Cui, B., Zhang, N., Xu, J., Lian, X., Liu, D. (eds.) WAIM 2016, Part II. LNCS, vol. 9659, pp. 15–27. Springer, Cham (2016). https://doi.org/10.1007/978-3-319-39958-4_2
8. Niu, B., Li, Q., Zhu, X., et al.: Achieving k-anonymity in privacy-aware location-based services. J. Graph Algorithms Appl. **20**(2), 363–410 (2016)
9. Xiao, P., Weizhang, C., Yige, S., Lei, W.: Continuous queries privacy protection algorithm based on spatial-temporal similarity over road networks. J. Comput. Res. Dev. **54**(9), 2092–2101 (2017)
10. Li, M., Qin, Z., Wang, C.: Sensitive semantics-aware personality cloaking on road-network environment. Int. J. Secur. Appl. **8**(1), 133–146 (2014)
11. Xu, M., Xu, H., Xu, C.: Personalized semantic location privacy preservation algorithm based on query processing cost optimization. In: Wang, G., Atiquzzaman, M., Yan, Z., Choo, K.-K.R. (eds.) SpaCCS 2017. LNCS, vol. 10656, pp. 153–168. Springer, Cham (2017). https://doi.org/10.1007/978-3-319-72389-1_14
12. Li, Y., Yuan, Y., Wang, G., Chen, L., Li, J.: Semantic-aware location privacy preservation on road networks. In: Navathe, S.B., Wu, W., Shekhar, S., Du, X., Wang, X.S., Xiong, H. (eds.) DASFAA 2016, Part II. LNCS, vol. 9643, pp. 314–331. Springer, Cham (2016). https://doi.org/10.1007/978-3-319-32049-6_20
13. Chen, H., Qin, X.: Location-semantic-based location privacy protection for road network. J. Commun. **37**(8), 67–76 (2016)
14. Lv, X., Shi, H., Wang, A., et al.: Semantic-based customizable location privacy protection scheme. In: International Symposium on Distributed Computing and Applications for Business Engineering and Science, pp. 148–154. IEEE Computer Society (2018)
15. Chen, S., Shen, H.: Semantic-aware dummy selection for location privacy preservation. In: Trustcom/bigdatase/ispa, pp. 752–759. IEEE (2017)

16. Xu, H., Zheng, Y., Zeng, J., Xu, C.: Location-semantic aware privacy protection algorithms for location-based services. In: IEEE SmartWorld, Ubiquitous Intelligence & Computing, Advanced & Trusted Computing, Scalable Computing & Communications, Cloud & Big Data Computing, Internet of People and Smart City Innovation, pp. 1219–1224 (2018)

17. Brinkhoff, T.: A framework for generating network-based moving objects. Geoinformatica **6** (2), 153–180 (2002)

Efficient Privacy Preserving Cross-Datasets Collaborative Outlier Detection

Zhaohui Wei[1], Qingqi Pei[1(✉)], Xuefeng Liu[2], and Lichuan Ma[2]

[1] School of Telecommunications Engineering,
Xidian University, Xian 710071, Shaanxi, China
wei0612hui@163.com, qqpei@mail.xidian.edu.cn
[2] School of Cyber Engineering, Xidian University, Xian, Shaanxi, China

Abstract. Outlier detection is one of the most important data analytics tasks and is used in numerous applications and domains. It is the identification of rare items, events or observations which raise suspicions by differing significantly from the majority of the data. The accuracy of the outlier detection depends on sufficient data. However, the underlying data is distributed across different organizations. If outlier detection is done locally, the results obtained are not as accurate as when outlier detection is done collaboratively over the combined data. Unfortunately, competitive advantage, privacy concerns and regulations, and issues surrounding data sovereignty and jurisdiction prevent many organizations from openly sharing their data. In this paper, we address precisely this issue. We present new and efficient protocols for privacy preserving outlier detection to find outliers from arbitrarily partitioned categorical data. Our protocols fall in the two-server model where data owners distribute their private data among two non-colluding servers who detects on the joint data using secure two-party computation (2PC). Our method is based on Local Distance-based Outlier Factor (LDOF) using the relative location of an object to its neighbours to determine the degree to which the object deviates from its neighbourhood. We provide the privacy guarantee by using secure multiparty computation techniques. We implement our system in C++ on real data. Our experiments validate that our protocols are both effective and efficient.

Keywords: Privacy-preserving · Outlier detection · Distributed data

1 Introduction

With the rapid development of network technology and database technology, we are in an era of information explosion. Data regarding a single entity may be

Supported by the National Key Research and Development Program of China under Grant 2016YFB0800601, and the Key Program of NSFC-Tongyong Union Foundation under Grant U1636209.

J. Vaidya et al. (Eds.): CSS 2019, LNCS 11983, pp. 343–356, 2019.
https://doi.org/10.1007/978-3-030-37352-8_31

collected by many different organizations. For example, in the financial domain, users'credit records are collected by different banks and institutions. Such as the credit records of the same user in different sites, as well as the credit records of different users in the same site. As above, different banks and institutions will typically collect the same kind of data, but only of the users visiting them. In either case, the data is clearly distributed across multiple different sites. While this data can be locally analyzed, the results of local analysis may not provide complete insight. Indeed, the potential of big data can only be realized with appropriate analytics, carried out over global data. Dataset distributed among multiple parties is a tough challenge for data mining as the dataset owners are generally unwilling to disclose their sensitive information due to legal and moral considerations. It is therefore important to devise privacy-preserving data mining algorithms which can obtain meaningful result on those distributed datasets without disclosing any private information. Much privacy-preserving data mining work has been done on association rule mining [1–3], clustering [4–6] and classification [7–10]. But one of the most fundamental tasks, outlier analysis, [11] has not as yet received much attention.

Outlier detection is a key data analytics task and has numerous applications such as credit card fraud discovery, electronic commerce and search for terrorism [12]. While this data can be locally analyzed, the results of local analysis may not provide complete insight. Many different outlier detection techniques have been developed in the literature [11]. All of these techniques assume that all of the data is centrally available and do not worry about data privacy. Therefore, they automatically assume that the underlying data being analyzed is the complete global dataset. Indeed, the precision of outlier detection depends crucially on the number of data involved in the test, i.e., the more data participate in detection, the higher accuracy we get. However, privacy information in these areas is typically sensitive [13,14], so approaches for privacy-preserving outlier detection are especially expected.

While there has been some work that looks at privacy-preserving outlier detection. Literature [15] proposed a privacy-preserving scheme for distanced-based outlier detection algorithm. Unfortunately, a certain shortcoming of [15] is requiring the user to specify a distance parameter which could be difficult to determine and not ranking the outliers. [16] it provides privacy protection by add Laplacian noise on attribute value frequencies. The advantage of this method is high efficiency, but it only provides privacy protection from the perspective of information theory, which does not satisfy the security definition of cryptography. Furthermore, adding noise to data could damage the availability of data and reduce the accuracy of the final results.

In this paper, we focus on Local Distance-based Outlier Factor (LDOF) [19], which is sensitive to outliers in scattered datasets and more suitable for the real-world applications, and adopt the two-server model, commonly used by previous work on privacy protection via MPC [17,18]. Our scheme consists of two phases, in a setup phase, the data owners (participants) process, encrypt and/or secret-share their data among two non-colluding servers. In the computation phase, the two servers can detect outliers on the participants' joint data without learning any information beyond the outlier detection algorithm.

In our protocols, we perform arithmetic operations which takes place inside LDOF on arithmetic circuits instead of boolean circuits, and perform sorting operations on boolean circuits. It is well-known that boolean circuits are not suitable for performing arithmetic operations, but it performs comparison operations efficiently. Our protocols are naturally divided into a data-independent offline phase and a much faster online phase, both arithmetic and sorting operations are performed in an efficiently privacy manner. Efficient circuit combination ensures that our scheme can be executed more efficiently in arbitrarily partitioned data. Compared with previous schemes, our protocol is more competitive.

The paper is organised as follows: In Sect. 2, we introduce related notations and some primitive secure protocols used in our protocol. In Sect. 3, we provide the overview of the problem formulation and security definition. In Sect. 4, we give the detail of our privacy-preserving outlier detection protocol, and the analysis of its security discussion. The experimental results on real data are discussed in Sect. 5. Finally, we conclude the whole paper and discusses future work in Sect. 6.

2 Preliminaries

Before we present the details of our protocols, we give an overview of some primitives and definitions on which we rely for our construction.

2.1 Outlier Detection

In this section, we briefly review the outlier detection algorithms considered in this paper: *Local Distance-based Outlier Factor* (LDOF) [19], which is sensitive to outliers in scattered datasets and more suitable for the real-world applications. LDOF uses the relative location of an object to its neighbours to determine the degree to which the object deviates from its neighbourhood.

The local distance-based outlier factor of x_p is defined as:

$$LDOF_k(x_p) := \frac{\overline{d}_{x_p}}{\overline{D}_{x_p}} \tag{1}$$

Let N_p be the set of the k-nearest neighbours of object x_p (excluding x_p), $\overline{d}_{x_p}$ the k-nearest neighbours distance of x_p equals the average distance from x_p to all objects in N_p. Given the k-nearest neighbours set N_p of object x_p, the k-nearest neighbours inner distance $\overline{D}_{x_p}$ is defined as the average distance among objects in N_p. If we regard the k-nearest neighbours as a neighbourhood system, LDOF captures the degree to which object x_p deviates from its neighbourhood system. It has the clear intuitive meaning that LDOF is the distance ratio indicating how far the object x_p lies outside its neighbourhood system. When LDOF ≤ 1 it means that x_p is surrounded by a data cluster. On the contrary, when LDOF ≥ 1, x_p is outside the whole cluster. It is easy to see that the higher LDOF is, the farther x_p is away from its neighbourhood system.

2.2 Secure Computation

Secure multiparty computation (SMC) is a method for parties to jointly compute a function over their inputs while keeping those inputs private. Basically, SMC base protocols are employed to ensure that no information other than the specified output and auxiliary information as per protocol specification is reveled to the parties during execution of the protocol computing a function.

Garbled Circuit is a cryptographic protocol that enables two-party secure computation in which two mistrusting parties can jointly evaluate a function over their private inputs without the presence of a trusted third party. In the garbled circuit protocol, the function has to be described as a Boolean circuit. More detailed description and proof of security against a semi-honest adversary is in [20].

Oblivious transfer (OT) is a fundamental cryptographic primitive that is commonly used as building block in SMC. We use $1 - out - of - 2$ OT in our protocol. In a 1–2 oblivious transfer protocol, the sender has two messages m_0 and m_1, and the receiver has a bit b, and the receiver wishes to receive m_b, without the sender learning b, while the sender wants to ensure that the receiver receives only one of the two messages.

We uses OTs to compute Arithmetic multiplication triple in the offline phase and in the online phase for LODF functions in order to securely compute the Multiplication [21–23]. In this paper, we use the $OT(x_0, x_1; b)$ to denote a protocol realizing this functionality.

Secret Sharing and Multiplication Triplets. In our protocols, all intermediate values are secret-shared between the two servers.We employ three different sharing schemes: Arithmetic sharing(Shr^A), Boolean sharing(Shr^B) and Yao sharing(Shr^Y). We briefly review these schemes but refer the reader to [24, 25] for more details.

Every sharing circuit is a sequence of addition and multiplication gates. P_0 has shared values $\langle x \rangle$, and P_1's shared values is $\langle y \rangle$. Let ADD_i^A, MUL_i^A denote addition and multiplication operation by Arithmetic sharing, respectively. To reconstruct the shared value, we perform REC_i^A. Multiplication is performed using a pre-computed Arithmetic multiplication triple [26] of the form $\langle c \rangle^A = \langle a \rangle^A \cdot \langle b \rangle^A$. P_i locally sets $\langle e \rangle_i^A = \langle x \rangle_i^A - \langle a \rangle_i^A$ and $\langle f \rangle_i^A = \langle y \rangle_i^A - \langle b \rangle_i^A$, both parties perform $\text{Rec}_i^A(e)$ and $\text{Rec}_i^A(f)$, and P_i sets $\langle z \rangle_i^A = i \cdot e \cdot f + f \cdot \langle a \rangle_i^A + e \cdot \langle b \rangle_i^A + \langle c \rangle_i^A$.

In our protocol, we explicitly use Arithmetic sharing and Yao sharing. We need convert between different sharings. Converting an Arithmetic share $\langle x \rangle^A$ to a Yao share $\langle x \rangle^Y$ ($A2Y$) can be done by securely evaluating an addition circuit.

A conversion from a Yao share $\langle x \rangle^Y$ to an Arithmetic share $\langle x \rangle^A$ was described in [24]. However, in this framework, where the $(Y2B)$ conversion is for free (*The key insight is that the permutation bits of $\langle x \rangle_o^Y$, $\langle x \rangle_1^Y$ already form a valid Boolean sharing of x*), and converting a Boolean share $\langle x \rangle^B$ to an Arithmetic share $\langle x \rangle^A$ is cheaper in terms of computation and communication, we propose to compute $\langle x \rangle^A = Y2A\left(\langle x \rangle^Y\right) = B2A\left(Y2B\left(\langle x \rangle^Y\right)\right)$.

3   Defining Private Outlier Detection

3.1   Problem Formulation

With a database X is partitioned among multiple parties $P_1, P_2, ..., P_N$. we consider how they could collaborate to calculate the LDOF value of each object. Formally, let $X = \{x_1, x_2, ..., x_n\}$ be a dataset, and k be a parameter to be used later. Each object $x_i = \{x_{i,1}, x_{i,2}, ..., x_{i,m}\}$ is an m-dimensional point. They wish to detect their joint data using LDOF outlier detection algorithm. Both of the parties want to obtain the LDOF value of each object in dataset X without leaking private information. We do not make any assumptions on how the data is distributed among the parties. A natural solution is to perform a secure multiparty computation where each data owner plays the role of one party. While this approach satisfies the privacy properties we are aiming for, it has several drawbacks. First, it requires the parties to be involved throughout the protocol. Second, unlike the two-party case, techniques for more than two parties (and a dishonest majority) are significantly more expensive and not scalable to large input sizes or a large number of parties.

Hence, we consider a server-aided setting where the parties outsource the computation to two untrusted but non-colluding servers S_0 and S_1. Server-aided MPC has been formalized and used in various previous work (e.g. see [27]). This setting has two important advantages (1) parties can distribute (secret-share) their inputs among the two servers in a setup phase but not be involved in any future computation, and (2) we can benefit from a combination of efficient techniques for boolean computation such as garbled circuits and OT-extension, and arithmetic computation such as offline/online multiplication triplet shares.

The two servers can also be representatives of the different subsets of parties and assumes that the two servers are untrusted but do not collude. We discuss the security definition in detail next.

3.2   Security Definition

We assume the existence of secure communication channels among the parties and a semi-honest adversary A who can corrupt any subset of the clients and at most one of the two servers. He will follow the protocol, but try to obtain extra information (not allowed by the privacy definition). Servers S_0 and S_1 involved in the protocols are also assumed to be noncolluding before, meaning they will not share any information which they are not explicitly instructed to share with each other. We do not put any restrictions on collusion among the parties and between the parties and the servers.

The security definition should require that such an adversary only learns the data of the parties it has corrupted and the final output but nothing else about the remaining honest parties data.

We define security using the framework of Universal Composition (UC) [28]. The target ideal functionality F_{mf} for our protocols: accurate ciphertext results can be obtained by executing protocols between T participants and two servers.

An execution in the UC framework involves a collection of (non-uniform) interactive Turing machines. In this work we consider an admissible and semi-honest adversary A as discussed above. The participants exchange messages according to a protocol. Protocol inputs of uncorrupted participants are chosen by an environment machine. Uncorrupted participants also report their protocol outputs to the environment. At the end of the interaction, the environment outputs a single bit. The adversary can also interact arbitrarily with the environment — without loss of generality the adversary is a dummy adversary which simply forwards all received protocol messages to the environment and acts in the protocol as instructed by the environment.

Security is defined by comparing a real and ideal interaction. Let real $[Z, A, \pi, \lambda]$ denote the final (single-bit) output of the environment Z when interacting with adversary A and honest participants who execute protocol π on security parameter λ. This interaction is referred to as the real interaction involving protocol π.

In the ideal interaction, participants simply forward the inputs they receive to an uncorruptable functionality machine and forward the functionality's response to the environment. Hence, the trusted functionality performs the entire computation on behalf of the participants. Let ideal $[Z, S, F_{mf}, \lambda]$ denote the output of the environment Z when interacting with adversary S and honest parties who run the dummy protocol in presence of functionality F on security parameter λ.

We say that a protocol π securely realizes a functionality F_{mf} for every admissible adversary A attacking the real interaction (without loss of generality, we can take A to be the dummy adversary), there exists an adversary S (called a simulator) attacking the ideal interaction, such that for all environments Z, the following quantity is negligible (in λ):

$$|\Pr\left[real\left[Z, A, \pi, \lambda\right] = 1\right] - \Pr\left[ideal\left[Z, S, F_{mf}, \lambda\right] = 1\right]|$$

Intuitively, the simulator must achieve the same effect (on the environment) in the ideal interaction that the adversary achieves in the real interaction. Note that the environment's view includes (without loss of generality) all of the messages that honest parties sent to the adversary as well as the outputs of the honest parties.

4   Privacy Preserving Outlier Detection

In this section, we present our protocols for privacy preserving outlier detection using LDOF. We first describe a protocol for LDOF in Sect. 4.1, based solely on arithmetic secret sharing and multiplication triplets. Next, we discuss how to efficiently generate these multiplication triplets in the offline phase in Sect. 4.2.

4.1   Privacy-Preserving LDOF Outlier Detection Protocol

In this section, we present our privacy-preserving outlier detection protocol. At first, we consider how two servers can construct distance matrices just using their own data information. Then based on the distance matrices, we present our secure method to compute k-NN distance and KNN inner distance of x_p. Lastly, we securely calculate LDOF value for each object. We separate our protocol into two phases: online and offline. The online phase computes the each object's LDOF value, while the offline phase consists mainly of multiplication triplet generation. We focus on the online phase in this section, and discuss the offline phase in Sect. 4.2.

Constructing Distance Matrices. Recall that we assume the data to be detected is secret shared between two servers S_0 and S_1. We denote the shares by $\langle X \rangle_0$, $\langle X \rangle_1$, In practice, the parties can distribute the shares between the two servers, or encrypt the first share using the public key of S_0, upload both the first encrypted share and the second plaintext share to S_1. S_1 then passes the encrypted shares to S_0 to decrypt.

As described in Sect. 2.1, The objective function for constructing distance matrices is $dis^2(x_i, x_j) = \sum_{k=1}^{m}(x_{ik} - x_{jk})^2$. We also want to reduce the computational complexity of the Arithmetic circuit. To achieve this, we generalize the pre-calculated operations on values to be shared. The parties prepare two matrices Xhr and Xqr. each object Xhr_i is $\sum_{k=1}^{m}(x_{ik}^2)$ and $Xqr_i = \{x_{i,1}, x_{i,2}, ..., x_{i,m}\}$. Thus the objective function for constructing distance matrices can be expressed simply as

$$dis^2(x_i, x_j) = Xhr_i + Xhr_j - (Xqr_i \cdot 2Xqr_j) \tag{2}$$

Applying the method to objective function, our protocol of constructing distance matrices consist of additions, subtraction and multiplications. Servers obtains two n dimensional shared vector $\langle SXhr \rangle$, $\langle CXhr \rangle$, and two shared matrices $n \times m$ $\langle SXqr \rangle$, $m \times n$ $\langle CXqr \rangle$, each element in matrix $\langle CXqr \rangle$ is $2x_{n,m}$. Matrix addition can be computed non-interactively by letting $\langle SXhr \rangle + \langle CXhr \rangle$. To multiply two shared matrices $\langle SXqr \rangle$, $\langle CXqr \rangle$, instead of using independent multiplication triplets, we take shared matrices $\langle A \rangle$, $\langle B \rangle$, $\langle C \rangle$, where each element in A and B is uniformly random in $\mathbb{C}_{2^l}$, A has the same dimension as $\langle SXqr \rangle$, B has the same dimension as $\langle CXqr \rangle$ and $C = A \times B$ mod 2^l. S_t computes $\langle E \rangle_t = \langle SXqr \rangle_t - \langle A \rangle_t$, $\langle F \rangle_t = \langle CXqr \rangle_t - \langle B \rangle_t$ and sends it to each other. Both servers reconstruct E and F and set $\langle SXqr \times CXqr \rangle_t = t \cdot E \times F + \langle SXqr \rangle_t \times F + E \times \langle CXqr \rangle_t + \langle C \rangle_t$. The each element in matrix $SXqr$ is always masked by the same random element in U, while it is multiplied by different elements in $CXqr$ in the matrix multiplication. So it does not affect security of the protocol, but makes the protocol significantly more efficient. Therefore, we apply the corresponding addition, subtraction and multiplication algorithms for secret shared values to construct distance matrices. which is

$$\langle dis^2(x_i, x_j) \rangle = SUB^A \left[ADD^A \left(\langle SXhr \rangle_i, \langle CXhr \rangle_j \right), \right.$$
$$\left. MUL^A \left(\langle SXqr \rangle_i, \langle CXqr \rangle_j \right) \right] \tag{3}$$

we get a $n \times (n-1)$ distance matrix $\langle D \rangle = (\langle d_{i,j} \rangle)$, $\langle d_{i,j} \rangle = \langle dis^2(x_i, x_j) \rangle$. Obviously, the matrix $\langle D \rangle$ contains the distances information between any two

Algorithm 1. Secure LDOF value Calculating

1. S_t computes $\langle E \rangle_t = \langle SXqr \rangle_t - \langle U \rangle_t$ for $t \in \{0,1\}$. Then parties run $REC\left(\langle E \rangle_0, \langle E \rangle_1\right)$ to obtain E.

2. S_t computes $\langle F \rangle_t = \langle CXqr \rangle_t - \langle V \rangle_t$ for $t \in \{0,1\}$. Then parties run $REC\left(\langle F \rangle_0, \langle F \rangle_1\right)$ to recover F.

3. for $q = 1,...,n$ do

3.   for $p = 1,...,m$ do

4. S_t computes $\langle temp \rangle_t = t \cdot E_{q,p} \times F_{q,p} + \langle SXqr_{q,p} \rangle_t \times F_{q,p} + E_{q,p} \times \langle CXqr_{q,p} \rangle_t + \langle Z_{q,p} \rangle_t$

5. $\langle temptum \rangle_t += \langle temp \rangle_t$

6. $\langle d_{i,j} \rangle_t = \langle SXhr_{q,p} \rangle_t + \langle CXhr_{q,p} \rangle_t - \langle temptum \rangle_t$

7. S_t converts Arithmetic shares $\langle d_{i,j} \rangle_t^A$ to Yao shares $\langle d_{i,j} \rangle_t^Y$, and runs the k-NN algorithm to find k-first elements D_{knn}.

8. S_t executes $(Y2A)$ on each element of D_{knn} to obtain the N_p for each object.

9. for $p = 1,...,n$ do

10. S_t executes addition $\langle \overline{x} \rangle_t = \frac{1}{k} \sum_{x_i \in N_p} \langle x_i \rangle_t$.

11. S_t computes distance matrix $\langle AXi_p \rangle_t : \langle \|x_p - \overline{x}\|^2 \rangle_t$ (*The calculation process is the same as above*).

12.   for $q = 1,...,k$ do

13. S_t computes $\langle AXp \rangle_t : \langle \sum_{x_p \in N_p} \|x_p - \overline{x}\|^2 \rangle_t$.

14. S_t run $REC^A\left(\langle AXi \rangle_0, \langle AXi \rangle_1\right)$.

15. S_t run $REC^A\left(\langle AXp \rangle_0, \langle AXp \rangle_1\right)$.

objects in dataset X, and the *ith* row vector of $\langle D \rangle$ contains the shared distances information between object x_i and any other objects in dataset X.

Computing k-NN Distance and KNN Inner Distance. In this subsection, we present a secure method to compute k-NN distance and KNN inner distance. The input of secure k-NN protocol is arithmetic shares of matrix $\langle D \rangle$, the desired output $\langle D_{knn} \rangle$ is shares of k elements $d_1,...,d_k$ such that $d_1,...,d_k$ are the first k smallest elements in $\langle D \rangle$. According to this output $\langle D_{knn} \rangle$, we could compute k-NN distance of each object.

In our secure k-NN computing protocol, sorting algorithm is the important part. Therefore, we apply the corresponding comparisons algorithms for secret shared values to update the sequence. However, comparisons algorithms need a Boolean circuit, thus we convert an Arithmetic share $\langle d_{i,j} \rangle^A$ to a Yao share $\langle d_{i,j} \rangle^Y (A2Y)$. After converting $(A2Y)$, servers run the k-NN algorithm to find k-first elements D_{knn}.

Combining the information of two matrices D_{knn} and X, we could easily obtain $k \times m$ matrix $\langle N_p \rangle$ which is the set of the k-nearest neighbours of each object x_p (excluding x_p). The k-nearest neighbours distance of x_p equals the average distance from x_p to all objects in $\langle N_p \rangle$, the k-nearest neighbours inner distance of x_p is defined as the average distance among objects in $\langle N_p \rangle$. The method of calculating distance is the same as that described in the previous paragraph. Before calculating distance, we convert a Yao share $\langle d_{i,j} \rangle^Y$ to an Arithmetic share $\langle d_{i,j} \rangle^A (Y2A)$. After distance calculating, we get the $\langle \|x_p - \overline{x}\|^2 \rangle$ and $\langle \|x_i - \overline{x}\|^2 \rangle$ value of each object x_p.

Calculating LDOF Value. In this subsection, we present the further steps of LDOF values calculation. Based on the former steps, two servers can obtain the $\langle \|x_p - \overline{x}\|^2 \rangle$ and $\langle \|x_i - \overline{x}\|^2 \rangle$ value of each object x_p. To calculate LDOF value of each object x_p more directly, We can compare $\langle AXi \rangle$ and $\langle AXp \rangle$ instead of calculating $\langle \overline{d}_{xp} \rangle$ divided by $\langle \overline{D}_{xp} \rangle$.

$$\langle AXi \rangle = \langle \frac{k}{k(k-1)} \sum_{x_i \in N_p} \|x_p - \overline{x}\|^2 \rangle$$
$$\langle AXp \rangle = \langle \|x_p - \overline{x}\|^2 \rangle$$

Hence severs reconstruct $\langle AXi \rangle^A$ and $\langle AXp \rangle^A$. If the AXp is larger than AXi. That means x_p lies outside its neighbourhood system, it is an outlier. This process is given in Algorithm 1.

As is known to all, a major source of inefficiency in prior work on privacy preserving outlier detection stems from computing on shared/encrypted decimal numbers. In our protocol, we employ a simple but effective solution to support decimal arithmetics in an integer field. This truncation technique [29] also works when decimal number is secret shared. In particular, the two servers can truncate their individual shares independently. Given two decimal numbers x, y with at most l_D bits in the fractional part, we first transform the numbers to integers by letting $x' = 2^{l_D} x$ and $y' = 2^{l_D} y$ and then multiply them to obtain the product $z = x'y'$. z has at most $2l_D$ bits representing the fractional part of the product, so we simply truncate the last l_D bits of z such that it has at most l_D bits representing the fractional part. More concretely, if z is decomposed into two parts $z = z_1 \cdot 2^{l_D} + z_2$, where $0 \leq z_2 < 2^{l_D}$, then the truncation results is z_1.

4.2 The Offline Phase

We describe how to implement the offline phase as a two party protocol between S_0 and S_1 by generating the desired shared multiplication triplets. We present a protocol for doing so based on oblivious transfer (OT). Recall that given shared random matrices $\langle U \rangle$ and $\langle V \rangle$, the key step is to compute the shares of their product by $\langle U \rangle$ and a column from $\langle V \rangle$. This is repeated n times to generate $\langle Z \rangle$. For simplicity, we want to compute $C = A \times B$.

To generate an Arithmetic multiplication triple, we can write $\langle A \rangle^A \times \langle B \rangle^A = (\langle A \rangle_0^A + \langle A \rangle_1^A)(\langle B \rangle_0^A) + \langle B \rangle_1^A) = \langle A \rangle_0^A \langle B \rangle_0^A + \langle A \rangle_1^A \langle B \rangle_1^A + \langle A \rangle_0^A \langle B \rangle_1^A + \langle A \rangle_1^A \langle B \rangle_0^A$. It suffices to compute $\langle A \rangle_0^A \langle B \rangle_1^A$ and $\langle A \rangle_1^A \langle B \rangle_0^A$ as the other two terms can be computed locally.

We compute the product of two secret-shared values using OT. In the following we describe the protocol that uses more efficient correlated OT extension. We first compute the shares of the product $\langle a_{ij} \cdot b_{ji} \rangle$ $i = 1, ..., n$ and $j = 1, ..., m$. In this way, We have S_0 and S_1 engage in a C-OT, where S_0 is the sender and S_1 is the receiver. For $k = 1, ..., l$, S_1 inputs $\langle b \rangle_1^A [k]$ as choice bit and S_0 sets the correlation function of C-OT $f_{\Delta_k}(x) = \langle a \rangle_0^A \cdot 2^k - x \mod 2^\ell$. As output from the k-th C-OT, S_0 obtains $(s_{k,0}, s_{k,1})$, $s_{k,0} \in R^{\mathbb{Z}_{2^\ell}}$ and $s_{k,1} = f_{\Delta_k}(s_{k,0}) = \langle a \rangle_0^A \cdot 2^k - s_{k,0}$

mod 2^ℓ and and S_1 obtains $s_{k,\langle b\rangle_1^A[k]} = \langle b\rangle_1^A[k] \cdot \langle a\rangle_0^A \cdot 2^k - s_{k,0}$ mod 2^ℓ. Finally, S_0 sets $\langle a_{ij} \cdot b_{ji}\rangle_0 = \sum_{k=1}^l s_{k,0}$ mod 2^ℓ, and S_1 sets $\langle a_{ij} \cdot b_{ji}\rangle_1 = \sum_{k=1}^l s_{k,\langle b\rangle_1^A[k]}$ mod 2^ℓ.

4.3 Security Discussion

We sketch a proof for the following Theorem on security of our protocol.

Theorem 1. *Consider a protocol where participants distribute shares of their data among two servers who run the algorithm 1 and send the output to participants. This protocol realizes the ideal functionality F_{mf} for the outlier detection function, in presence of a semi-honest admissible adversary.*

Proof. Consider a protocol where t participants $P_1, P_2, ..., P_t$ distribute shares of their data among two servers S_0, S_1 who run the algorithm 1 and send the output to participants. An admissible adversary A in our model can corrupt one server and any subset of the participants. Given that the protocol is symmetric with respect to the two servers, we simply need to consider the scenario where the adversary corrupts one of servers S_0 and $t-1$ participants $P_1, P_2, ..., P_{t-1}$.

We describe a simulator S that simulates the above adversary in the ideal world. S submits the corrupted participants' inputs data to the functionality and receives the final output of the outlier detection algorithm, the LDOF value of the data. S then runs A. On behalf of the honest participants S sends a random share in $\mathbb{Z}_{2^\ell}$ to A for each value in the held by that participants. This is the only message where participants are involved. In the remainder of the protocol, generate random matrices and vectors corresponding to the honest server's shares of $\langle SXhr\rangle$, $\langle SXqr\rangle$, $\langle CXhr\rangle$, $\langle CXqr\rangle$ and $\langle A\rangle$, $\langle B\rangle$, $\langle C\rangle$. And play the role of the honest server in interactions with A using those randomly generated values. Because, S_0 does not collude with another server, they cannot get the original data of each shared value. This immediately follows from the security of the secret sharing and the fact that the matrices/vectors generated in the offline phase are indeed random. In particular, all value sent and received and reconstructed in the protocol are generated using uniformly random shares in both the real protocol and the simulation described above. Therefore, there is no leakage of data information.

5 Experimental Evaluation

5.1 Experimental Setup

We carried out extensive empirical analysis using four real datasets obtained from the UCI Machine Learning repository. The system is implemented in C++. In all our experiments, the field size is set to 2^{64}. Mohassel P observes that the modulo operations can be implemented using regular arithmetics on the unsigned long integer type in C++ with no extra cost. This is significantly faster than any number-theoretic library that is able to handle operations in arbitrary field, they have proved that an integer addition (multiplication) is 100× faster than a modular addition (multiplication) in the same field implemented in the GMP [30] or the NTL [31] library. The experiments were conducted on personal computers with an i5 3.2-GHz processor and 8 GB of RAM.

5.2   Results and Discussion

In this work, we measure effectiveness of the privacy-preserving approach by comparing how well it performs in terms of detecting outliers with respect to the original LDOF approach. The effect of truncation technique has been proofed [29], we use 6, 13 bits to represent the fractional part of LDOF value. We implemented our protocol on real datasets ,Wisconsin Breast Cancer, obtained from the UCI Machine Learning repository. This dataset has 699 records and nine attributes. Each record is labeled as either benign or malignant. we randomly picked a subset of records labeled as malignant such that they made up 8% of the dataset, and we considered them to be outliers. In Fig. 1, the x-axis is the number of neighbourhood size k and the y-axis is the precision of the outlier detection on the real dataset. Figure 1 shows the experimental result for different values of k with privacy preserving 6 and 13 bits. In the experiments, we progressively increase the value of k and calculate the detection precision for base LDOF approach and our privacy-preserving LDOF protocol. In each case, the precisions is computed. With the increase of k, the precisions increases, and when k = 30, the precisions reaches the highest level, and then decreases with the increase of k. As is to be expected, the precisions of the privacy-preserving 13 bits algorithm approaches that of the base algorithm. This is because we only introduce a small error on the 13th bit of the decimal part of LDOF value. This error is negligible.

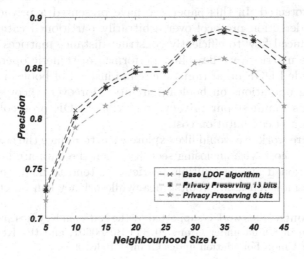

Fig. 1. Precisions in WBC dataset

As above, our protocol mainly consists of arithmetic operation and sorting operation. Then we analyzed the execution time and communication cost of sort circuits and arithmetic circuits. As shown in Tables 1 and 2. The execution time and communication cost increases linearly with the increase of number of tuples. Meanwhile, execution time of arithmetic circuits is much more than sort circuits (about nine times), and communication costs required by sort is about four times as large as arithmetic circuits. Thus, performing arithmetic operations which takes place inside LDOF on arithmetic circuits instead of boolean circuits is more efficient than previous schemes.

Table 1. Communication cost

Number of tuples	16	32	64	128	256	512
Arith	749 KB	1.49 MB	2.99 MB	5.99 MB	11.97 MB	21.86 MB
Sort	666 KB	2.01 MB	5.71 MB	15.45 MB	40.28 MB	102.01 MB

Table 2. Execution time

Number of tuples	16	32	64	128	256	512
Arith	1.226 s	2.352 s	5.525 s	12,47 s	22.89 s	43.13 s
Sort	16.139 ms	61.462 ms	130.21 ms	351.18 ms	933.6 ms	2.46 s

6   Conclusion and Future Work

Outlier detection is a critical analytics task that can be computationally quite intensive, especially when the data is split between multiple parties and privacy needs to be protected. In this paper, we have presented a privacy-preserving LDOF outlier detection protocol over arbitrarily partitioned categorical data. We have introduced how to efficiently construct distance matrices. Then based on the distance matrices, we flexibility performed arithmetic operations which takes place inside LDOF on arithmetic circuits instead of boolean circuits, and perform sorting operations on boolean circuits. Moreover, theoretical analysis and experiments manifest our privacy-preserving LDOF protocol has desired communication and computation cost.

For the future work, we would like explore ways to reduce the communication and computation cost without losing security when the data are horizontally or vertically partitioned among multiple parties. We tend to increase offline work to decrease the indispensable circuits, meanwhile privacy can be guaranteed.

Acknowledgments. This work is supported by the National Key Research and Development Program of China under Grant 2016YFB0800601, and the Key Program of NSFC-Tongyong Union Foundation under Grant U1636209.

References

1. Vaidya, J., Clifton, C., Kantarcioglu, M.: Tools for privacy preserving distributed data mining. ACM SIGKDD Explor. Newsl. **4**, 28–34 (2002)
2. Clifton, C., Kantarcioglu, M.: Privacy-preserving distributed mining of association rules on horizontally partitioned data. IEEE Trans. Knowl. Data Eng. **16**, 1026–1037 (2004)
3. Clifton, C., Vaidya, J.: Privacy preserving association rule mining in vertically partitioned data. In: 8th ACMSIGKDD International Conference on Knowledge Discovery and Data Mining (KDD02), pp. 639–644 (2002)
4. Wright, R., Jagannathan, G.: Privacy-preserving distributed k-means clustering over arbitrarily partitioned data. In: 11th ACM SIGKDD International Conference on Knowledge Discovery in Data Mining (KDD05), pp 593–599 (2005)
5. Ghosh, J., Merugu, S.: Privacy-preserving distributed clustering using generative models. In: 3rd IEEE International Conference on Data Mining (ICDM03), pp. 211–218 (2003)
6. Clifton, C., Vaidya, J.: Privacy-preserving k-means clustering over vertically partitioned data. In: 9th ACMSIGKDD International Conference on Knowledge Discovery and Data Mining (KDD 2003), pp 206–215 (2003)
7. Srikant, R., Agrawal, R.: Privacy-preserving data mining. In: ACMSIGMOD International Conference on Management of Data (SIGMOD 2000), pp. 439–450 (2000)
8. Pinkas, B., Lindell, Y.: Privacy preserving data mining. In: 20th Annual International Cryptology Conference (CRYPTO 2000), pp. 36–54 (2000)
9. Clifton, C., Vaidya, J.: Privacy preserving naive Bayes classifier for vertically partitioned data. In: SIAM International Conference on Data Mining (SDM 2004), pp. 522–526 (2004)
10. Wang, S., Zhao, W., Zhang, N.: A new scheme on privacy-preserving data classification. In: 11th ACM-SIGKDD International Conference on Knowledge Discovery and Data Mining (KDD 2005), pp. 374–383 (2005)
11. Aggarwal, C.C.: Outlier Analysis. Springer-Verlag, New York (2013). https://doi.org/10.1007/978-1-4614-6396-2
12. Rastogi, R., Shim, K., Ramaswame, S.: Efficient algorithms formining outliers from large data sets. In: ACMSIGMOD International Conference on Management of Data (SIGMOD 2000), pp. 427–438 (2000)
13. Atallah, M., Du, W.: Privacy-preserving cooperative statistical analysis. In: 17th Annual Computer Security Applications Conference (ACSAC 2001), pp. 102–110 (2001)
14. Syverson, P., Goldschlag, D., Reed, M.: Onion routing. Commun. ACM **42**, 39–41 (1999)
15. Vaidya, J., Clifton, C.: Privacy-preserving outlier detection. In: 4th IEEE International Conference on Data Mining, pp. 233–240 (2004)
16. Asif, H., Talukdar, T., Vaidya, J.: Differentially private outlier detection in a collaborative environment. Int. J. Coop. Inf. Syst. **27**(03), 1850005 (2018)
17. Nikolaenko, V., Ioannidis, S., Weinsberg, U., Joye, M., Taft, N., Boneh, D.: Privacy-preserving matrix factorization. In: ACM SIGSAC Conference on Computer Communications Security, pp. 801–812 (2013)
18. Nikolaenko, V., Weinsberg, U., Ioannidis, S., Joye, M., Boneh, D., Taft, N.: Privacy-preserving ridge regression on hundreds of millions of records. In: IEEE Symposium on Security and Privacy, pp. 334–348 (2013)

19. Zhang, K., Hutter, M., Jin, H.: A new local distance-based outlier detection app- roach for scattered real-world data. In: Theeramunkong, T., Kijsirikul, B., Cercone, N., Ho, T.-B. (eds.) PAKDD 2009. LNCS (LNAI), vol. 5476, pp. 813–822. Springer, Heidelberg (2009). https://doi.org/10.1007/978-3-642-01307-2_84

20. Lindell, Y., Pinkas, B.: A proof of security of Yaos protocol for two-party compu- tation. J. Cryptology **22**, 161–188 (2009)

21. Ishai, Y., Kilian, J., Nissim, K., Petrank, E.: Extending oblivious transfers effi- ciently. In: Boneh, D. (ed.) CRYPTO 2003. LNCS, vol. 2729, pp. 145–161. Springer, Heidelberg (2003). https://doi.org/10.1007/978-3-540-45146-4_9

22. Schneider, T., Asharov, G., Lindell, Y., Zohner, M.: More efficient oblivious transfer and extensions for faster secure computation. In: ACM CCS 2013, pp. 535–548 (2013)

23. Nielsen, J.B., Nordholt, P.S., Orlandi, C., Burra, S.S.: A new approach to practi- cal active-secure two-party computation. In: Safavi-Naini, R., Canetti, R. (eds.) CRYPTO 2012. LNCS, vol. 7417, pp. 681–700. Springer, Heidelberg (2012). https://doi.org/10.1007/978-3-642-32009-5_40

24. Demmler, D., Schneider, T., Zohner, M.: ABY-a framework for efficient mixed- protocol secure two-party computation. In: NDSS (2015)

25. Nisan, N., Pinkas, B., Sella, Y., Malkhi, D., et al. : Fairplay a secure two-party computation system. In: 13th Conference on USENIX Security Symposium, vol. 13, pp. 20–20 (2004)

26. Beaver, D.: Efficient multiparty protocols using circuit randomization. In: Feigen- baum, J. (ed.) CRYPTO 1991. LNCS, vol. 576, pp. 420–432. Springer, Heidelberg (1992). https://doi.org/10.1007/3-540-46766-1_34

27. Kamara, S., Mohassel, P., Raykova, M.: Outsourcing multiparty computation. IACR Cryptology ePrint Archive 272 (2011)

28. Canetti, R.: Universally composable security: a new paradigm for cryptographic protocols. In: 42nd IEEE Symposium on Foundations of Computer Science (FOCS 2001), pp. 136–145 (2001)

29. Zhang, Y., Mohassel, P.: SecureML: a system for scalable privacy-preserving machine learning. In: IEEE Symposium on Security and Privacy (SP), pp. 19– 38 (2017)

30. GMP library. https://gmplib.org

31. NTL library. http://www.shoup.net/ntl

An SVM Based Secural Image Steganography Algorithm for IoT

Weifeng Sun[1](✉), Minghan Jia[1], Shumiao Yu[1], Boxiang Dong[2], and Xinyi Li[3]

[1] School of Software, Dalian University of Technology, Dalian 116620, China
wfsun@dlut.edu.cn, 15665993071@163.com,
yusml1995@outlook.com
[2] Stevens Institute of Technology, Hoboken, NJ 07030, USA
dongb@montclair.edu
[3] AI/Algorithm Team, GuanData Co. Ltd., Hangzhou 310000, China
2583433490@qq.com

Abstract. With the fast development of IoT network, there are more and more images generated by sensors and other devices, which increases the transmission expenses. By adopting image steganography, the images can deliver more information than they could. Therefore, the transmission expenses could be significantly reduced. However, the safety and quality of steganographic algorithms is not promising nowadays. To improve this situation, we propose an SVM-based steganography algorithm. The algorithm takes advantage of four features, including the variance of the image, the overall difference, the shape context matching and the smoothness. The analysis and experimental results show that the information hiding algorithm can effectively optimize the information steganography and anti-steganography analysis, which could be used in IoT.

Keywords: IoT · Image steganography · LSB embedding · Anti-steganography analysis

1 Introduction

With the development of Internet technology, a new generation of network, the Internet of Things (IoT) is coming. The applications and sensors in IoT generate enormous data. The data security and transmission are play a key role in the era of Big Data. The information security and efficient transmission problems have become increasingly important. The information steganography, as a type of secure communication technology, has been studied and applied due to its unique concealment. The information steganography can protect the privacy, hide the information, and reduce the round trips for the combining data. At present, information steganography based on digital images has been studied, and steganography detection technology has also been developed. Thus, we can apply this technology on the pictures that we collect from sensors in the IoT. Some systems have certain requirements for information security, such as Medical Record Image Management System, Ticket Digital Image Management System, and Library Fingerprint Management System. Therefore, images obtained from image

J. Vaidya et al. (Eds.): CSS 2019, LNCS 11983, pp. 357–371, 2019.
https://doi.org/10.1007/978-3-030-37352-8_32

sensors can be steganographic. The image sensor with steganographic function is used to conceal information that needs to be encrypted, such as location (longitude, latitude, etc.), date, acquisition time of the image and the name of the person in the picture. It can make the information more confidential and secure in the transmission process on the network.

Though LSB-based steganography is easy to operate, it is difficult to perceive the existence of hidden messages by the naked eye. However, when the LSB (Least Significant Bit) plane is extracted separately, it is easy to find the anomalies in the steganography images. This image steganography method is unsafe because the LSB embedding method always implant the messages in the lowest bits. To solve this problem, we can introduce a pseudo-random number generator, and pick random bits to embed the information. The random selection of the location of the pixel embedded in the message can make the hidden information no longer at the lowest bits, which can make camouflage more covert. In the steganographic system, a pseudo-random number generator (PRNG) is introduced to select the location of the embedded message pixels according to the sequence generated by PRNG, which makes the distribution of the disguised message more random. However, it is noteworthy that the initial value of the PRNG must be exchanged by both parties before they can be used as the secret key of the system. In fact, the condition of the secure channel for exchanging secret keys is difficult to be satisfied, and it is impossible to guarantee that the hidden data can be randomly distributed in the image in an ideal way. Therefore, it is more effective to choose the method of random embedding under the condition of the unsafe channel. At the same time, LSB steganography is insecure because there are many LSB stegano-graphic analysis methods such as test, sample pair analysis, and RS steganalysis. The existence of these methods poses a great threat to the security of LSB-based steganography. To solve these problems, in this paper, we propose an information hiding algorithms based on SVM, which is more secure against steganographic analysis.

The main contributions of this paper are as follows: We employ information hiding algorithms based on SVM to generate a safer steganographic analysis method. This method can select the position of a picture randomly, which can improve security. We propose a method to select features, including variance, overall difference, SC matching, and smoothness, and these features are used as safety evaluation indexes. An SVM-based LSB steganography optimization scheme is proposed and analyzed.

The rest parts of the paper are organized as follows: Sect. 2 introduces the related work. Section 3 describes the LSB steganography based on the SVM. Section 4 proposes the selection of the feature value of the image block. Section 5 carries on the simulation and the result analysis. Section 6 summarizes the whole article and puts forward some ideas for future work.

2 Related Work

In order to improve the security of steganography, many existing works have proposed methods that need to examine the characteristics of the image and the secret message to select the embedding location [1] adaptively. These methods have been applied in classical LSB-based image hiding methods such as LSB substitution and LSB matching [2]. The method of finding a location that is suitable for hiding information is mainly based on the difference in pixel values. The LSB mechanism [3, 4] is replaced according to the difference of one pixel and its four adjacent pixels, which enables the steganographer to embed the most secret data on the sharp edges and makes the information more difficult to be detected by the human eye. However, this method is easy to be detected by RS steganalysis [5] and other analysis methods, so the security is weak.

Nagaraj et al. proposed an embedding method [6]. First, Laplacian detectors were deployed on each pixel size image block without overlap to find edges. Then, a sharper edge was selected according to a threshold, and next to the central pixels of the image blocks on these edges were hidden [7]. The mechanism based on pixel value difference (PVD) is another method to find image blocks suitable for hiding data. The number of embedded pixels is determined by the difference between a pixel and its adjacent pixels. The larger the difference, the more secret bits can be embedded [8]. In General, PVD-based methods can provide larger embedding capacity. But these PVD-based methods are not ideal in countering statistical steganographic analysis [9]. In an edge-adaptive LSB matching, re-access steganography method is proposed. This method adjusts the definition and selection of edge regions according to the embedding rate and considers the relationship between secret message size and image [10]. The method of finding edge regions is also based on the difference between pixels.

3   LSB Steganography Optimization Based on SVM

We assume the application scenario as follows: overhead information like secret keys is not allowed; the first bit is the embedded position of the hidden information length and the next bit length of the pixels is embedded in a coordinate.

The image consists of $m \times n$ pixels and the pixel value are 8 bits. The $l_1 + l_2$ bits of auxiliary information is embedded in the image, including the length of the secret message and the coordinates of the initial steganographic pixel. The embedding rate is close to 0 when $l_1 + l_2 \ll m \times n$ and the existing LSB steganographic analysis methods cannot detect the low embedding rate information. Therefore, the embedding of these auxiliary messages before $l_1 + l_2$ bits of the image is safe. The distribution of LSB for each pixel of an image is shown in Fig. 1. The image blocks for embedding messages represented by dotted lines are not necessarily continuous in space. The grey positions represent the pixels without embedding messages, and they are not operated on during steganography.

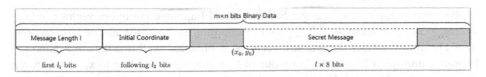

Fig. 1. Distribution scheme of each position in LSB plane of image.

Through the introduction of LSB steganography methods mentioned above, it is easy to find that the steganography based on LSB has some shortcomings in security and is vulnerable to the attack of steganalysis methods. To solve this problem, we introduce the concept of learning to find a location of the pixels which is suitable for hiding secret messages. As a new machine learning method, Support Vector Machine (SVM) has a good effect in data classification application. The combination of the two methods is helpful to improve the accuracy of steganalysis.

The training sample set with a given capacity of N, $D = \{(x_1, y_1), (x_2, y_2), \cdots \cdots (x_N, y_N)\}$ in which $yi \in \{-1, 1\}$, the relevant features of each image block i are marked as x_i. Then the classic steganographic analysis method and mark as y_i evaluate whether the camouflage image is safe. There may be several hyperplanes which can be linearly divided according to the value of Y. It is necessary to select the best hyperplane as the classification boundary. The criterion for selecting the best hyperplane by SVM method is to minimize the sum of the distances from the nearest vector to the hyperplane in two classes of sample vectors. The sum of the distances is also called interval. The vector closest to the hyperplane in the sample of each class is called support vector.

The output of SVM is normal vector **w** of hyperplane and intercept in sample space. These two coefficients can uniquely identify a hyperplane that can be used for sample classification.

For any vector **X** the classification result can be obtained by substituting the function $f(x) = sign (\mathbf{w}^T \mathbf{x} + b)$.

The sample image is divided into blocks, and the eigenvector x_i is calculated for each image block. The result of the steganalysis is recorded as y_i. The hyperplane that can segment samples of different types and maximize the interval can be found by training samples with SVM, and its expression is formula (1).

$$\max_{\mathbf{w},b} \frac{2}{\|\mathbf{w}\|}$$
$$s.t. \quad y_i(\mathbf{w}^T x_i + b) \geq 1, i = 1, 2 \ldots N \tag{1}$$

However, the process of solving directly from this formula is complicated. This problem can be converted into the corresponding dual formula (2) by using Lagrange multiplier method, the convex quadratic programming problem.

$$\max_{\alpha} \sum_{i=1}^{N} \alpha_i - \frac{1}{2} \sum_{i=1}^{N} \sum_{j=1}^{N} \alpha_i \alpha_j y_i y_j \mathbf{x}_i^T \mathbf{x}_j$$
$$s.t. \quad \sum_{i=1}^{N} \alpha_i y_i = 0$$
$$\alpha_i \ldots 0, i = 1, 2, \ldots N \tag{2}$$

By solving Eq. (2), we can get N-dimensional Lagrange multiplier vector $\boldsymbol{\alpha} = [\alpha_1, \alpha_2 \ldots \alpha_n]$, and coefficient $\mathbf{w} = \sum_{i=1}^{n} \alpha_i y_i x_i$. According to the constraint of $\alpha_1(y_i (\mathbf{w}^T \mathbf{x} + b) - 1) = 0$ in the KKT condition, a vector $\mathbf{x_i}$ is obtained such that the corresponding Lagrange multiplier α_i is zero. The value of b is obtained according to $\mathbf{x_i}$. In this way, the Sequential Minimal Optimization (SMO) algorithm is used to speed up the calculation.

As mentioned above, the original SVM method have some limitations, such as the inability to obtain closed solutions for linear indivisible training sets, and the pursuit of the maximum interval may lead to over-fitting. Therefore, the concept of core technique or soft interval can be introduced to improve the applicability of SVM.

In the case of linear inseparability, the dimension vector x is transformed into φ(x) in a new d-dimensional feature space. In General, the problems that cannot be solved in low-dimensional space often seek solutions in high-dimensional space. If we specify that the dot product of two vectors in the new feature space can be represented by the function k (·,·), k(x, x') = φ(x)T · φ(x'), this function is called a kernel function. The kernel function is used to replace the low-dimensional inner product operation of the objective function in the primal-dual problem, as shown in formula (3).

$$\sum_{i=1}^{N} \alpha_i - \frac{1}{2} \sum_{i=1}^{N} \sum_{j=1}^{N} \alpha_i \alpha_j y_i y_j k(x_i, x_j) \tag{3}$$

And the final training result is formula (4). The computational technique is known as the nuclear technique.

$$f(x) = sign(\mathbf{w}^\mathbf{T} \varphi(x) + b)$$
$$sign(\sum_{i=1}^{N} \alpha_i y_i k(\mathbf{x_i}, x_j) + b) \tag{4}$$

However, it is difficult to directly calculate the high-dimensional inner product. Thus, the inner product is directly calculated by using the kernel function, which is equivalent to the corresponding space transformation operation of the kernel function. In the process of setting the parameters of SVM, the kernel function is chosen, which is the specific form of space transformation.

When the kernel matrix $k_{i,j}$ = f(x_i, x_j) is a semi-definite matrix, it can be used as a kernel function of the SVM. Therefore, in addition to common kernel functions, practical kernel functions are designed by means of linear combination and direct product.

When dealing with linearly inseparable sample sets, the sample space is transformed, and the surface that can completely separate the heterogeneous samples is found by the kernel technique. However, it is difficult to determine the kernel function that can correctly classify the training set in the training process. Even if such a kernel function is found, it is the result of over-fitting to a large extent, and the prediction effect is not ideal. Therefore, when training the classifier, a more robust SVM classifier is obtained by sacrificing the correctness of sample classification. This is the idea of the soft interval SVM. In order to represent the "degree of deviation" of samples violating classification rules, linear hinge loss function formula (5) is used to quantify.

$$l_{hinge}\left(y_i\left(w^T x_i + b\right)\right) = max\left(0, 1 - y_i\left(w^T x_i + b\right)\right) \tag{5}$$

The new objective function is obtained by multiplying a coefficient C with the original minimization optimization objective function. A convex quadratic programming expression which is almost identical to the hard interval SVM is obtained by the similar solution method. The difference is that the constraints of α_i are reduced from the original $\alpha_i \geq 0$ to $0 \geq \alpha_i \geq c$. The function of parameter C is to adjust the ratio of interval size to the weight of classification accuracy of training set samples. In General, the bigger the C is, the higher the accuracy is. And the lower the tolerance for violation of classification is, and the smaller the final interval is. When C tends to infinity, the SVM degrades into a hard interval SVM, and the classification error is zero.

In order to obtain a high-performance SVM classifier, a soft space SVM with kernel function is selected to conduct classification training on image samples and steganographic effects, and then to predict the pixel location suitable for hiding secret information in a given image.

Table 1. The pseudocode of training SVM

Pseudocode: Training SVM
1. TrainSet1 = TrainSet(1001:1338)
2. TrainSet2 = TrainSet(1:1000)
3. SVM_parameters = Training (TrainSet2)
4. testing_rate = Testing (SVM_parameters,TrainSet1)
5. if testing_rate < 0.92
6.   SVM_parameters = Training (TrainSet2)
7. else
8.   return SVM_parameters
9. Improving SVM by Kernel Function and Soft Spacing SVM

The use of SVM can be divided into two stages. One is the training stage of (Table 1) building a model for using data sets, and the other is the prediction stage of classifying samples as models. The latter includes the testability prediction during the testing and adjustment of the training process, but the main usage scenario is the application stage after training.

In our optimization scheme, the trained SVM is used as the input of embedded message processing together with a secret message and carrier image. Therefore, for the whole steganographic system, a SVM with good performance needs to be trained in the pretreatment process, and the trained SVM can be used for the next steganography (Table 2).

Table 2. The use of SVM

Pseudocode: The Use Of SVM
1. Input:Image,SM 2. Output:Image with SM 3. n=$\lceil 2\sqrt{2l} \rceil$ 4. graphics = Random (Graphic) 5. strings = GraphicToString(graphics) 6. Use the results of SVM training 7. $x_i \leftarrow (x_{i1}, x_{i2}, x_{i3}, x_{i4})$ 8. if SVM (x_{i1}) == 1 9. Steganography(graphics)

4 Selection of Image Block Feature Value

The length of the secret message stored in 8 bits is l. The size of the carrier image is M × N, the edge length N must satisfy formula (6)

$$(n-1)^2 < 8l \tag{6}$$

It is easy to get n = $\lceil 2\sqrt{2l} \rceil$ where n < min (M, N).

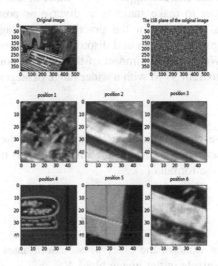

Fig. 2. Selects different locations on the carrier image

The edge length n of the image block is calculated according to the message length l. The size of the image block is determined. The information of l embedded in the first

l_1 bit of the image. After SVM training, several image blocks are obtained as the input of SVM, the appropriate image blocks for embedding messages are selected, and the initial coordinates (x_0, y_0) are inserted into l_2 bit of the image.

Figure 2 shows a carrier image of 384×512 size. Each position of the image expresses different things. If the length of the embedded message is 384B, we can choose a 40×40 image block to embed in its LSB plane. Figure 2 also shows six image blocks of different sizes, and the effect of hiding them is different. By extracting the features of the six image blocks for analysis, we can judge whether the six positions are suitable for hiding.

In the process of constructing a training set, in order to evaluate whether a given image block is suitable for hiding a given message, four features are selected to describe the image block. These four features are variance, global difference, SC matching, and smoothness. They reflect the diversity of image block pixel values, the similarity of the distribution of pixel values with the whole image, the matching degree between LSB plane and the secret message of the image block, and the continuity of image block itself. Through the above steganographic analysis methods to evaluate the single feature of the image, it can better evaluate whether the image block hides data.

For each small image, four corresponding features are extracted as the feature vectors $x_i = (x_{i1}, x_{i2}, x_{i3}, x_{i4})$ of the sample. After embedding the message in the small image block, the RS steganalysis algorithm based on the threshold is used to determine whether the whole camouflage image can be identified as a suspicious image hiding the message. The result of steganalysis is used as the label of the sample, where $y_i \in (-1, 1)$. In the pre-processing stage with enough resources, the sampling method can be used to construct a large enough sample set. The sample set is divided into training set, test set, and test set. We use the embedding rate as an index to test the sample group. It is worth noting that in order to make samples as diverse as possible, we use random arrays for each sample. However, in the practice of message steganography, the message cannot be completely random and disorderly, and there is some regularity in the binary expression. We ignore the impact of this rule on our training, because the purpose of this paper is to train SVM with a wider range of steganography applications.

4.1   Variance

Each pixel in the image block is taken as a sample, and the whole image blocks calculated as a sample set. The variance of the image block B of $m \times n$ pixels can be calculated according to the formula (7):

$$war(B) = \frac{\sum_{n=1}^{m} \sum^{n} j = 1 (x_{i,j} - \bar{x})}{(m \times n - 1)} \tag{7}$$

Here, $x_{i,j}$ denotes the value of the pixel whose coordinates are (i, j) and $\bar{x}$ is the average value of all the pixels in the image block.

In General, the smoother the image block variance is, the smaller the difference between the contained pixels is, the more unsuitable for hiding data.

4.2   The Overall Discrepancy

The overall discrepancy reflects the relationship between the image block and the original image. We use the frequency of the pixel value to describe some characteristics of the image and the image block, and use the sum of squares of the differences between them, to enlarge the difference between the image block and the original image. Frequency vectors **fre** are calculated by formulas (8) and (9) respectively for image blocks B and I with size m × n and size M × N.

$$fre(B)_i = \frac{\sum_{k=1}^{m} \sum_{j=1}^{n} p(x_{k,j} = i)}{m \times n} \quad 0 \leq i \leq 255, \ i \in Z$$

$$fre(I)_i = \frac{\sum_{k=1}^{M} \sum_{j=1}^{N} p(x_{i,j} = i)}{M \times N} \quad 0 \leq i \leq 255, \ i \in Z$$

(8)

The **p** (·) function is a logical judgment function whose range is 0,1. When the value of the independent variable expression is true, the value of P function is 1. Otherwise, it is 0. The value of **fre** (·) is a 256-dimensional vector. The formula above gives the calculation method of each value in the vector, where the index value counts from zero. Next, we calculate the sum of squares of the differences between the corresponding pixel values in the two vectors as the overall difference.

$$D_{B,I} = \sum_{i=0}^{255} [fre(B)_i - fre(I)_i]^2$$

(9)

4.3   SC Match

The secret message of length is converted into 8-bit binary data and expressed as M_{Binary} by 0/1 vector. At the same time, the LSB bits of the first 1×8 pixels in the image block are taken in the natural order and the 0/1 vector B_{LSB} is recorded as SC matching degree, which is calculated according to formula (10).

$$sc\_match = \frac{\sum_{i=1}^{8l} p(M_{Binary}(i) = B_{LSB}(i))}{8l}$$

(10)

Here, M_{Binary} and B_{LSB} are used to denote the i_{th} element of M_{Binary} and B_{LSB}, respectively. And the definition of the function p(.) is identical to the function p(.) in the overall degree of difference to determine the same bit in the two binary expressions.

4.4   Smoothness

For the non-edged pixel x_i, there are eight pixels around it. These eight pixels are located in eight different directions of the pixel. This extended difference calculation is also applied in some steganalysis algorithms, which can be expressed as a set of x_i according to the direction:

$$S_i = \{x_i{\leftarrow}, x_i \rightarrow, x_i{\uparrow}, x_i{\downarrow}, x_i{\searrow}, x_i{\nearrow}, x_i{\nwarrow}, x_i{\diagdown}\} \tag{11}$$

For the edge pixels, the corresponding S_i set lacks some direction data, only retain the surrounding pixels. Thus, we use the sum of formula (12) to calculate the smoothness of image block B with m×n size.

$$Smooth(B) = \frac{\sum_{i=1}^{m}\sum_{j=1}^{n}\sum_{x' \in s_{i,j}} |x_{i,j}x'|}{m \times n} \tag{12}$$

At this time, the smoothness function takes full account of the relationship between the pixels and the adjacent pixels in all directions. However, some differences are also calculated repeatedly. Because of the large amount of calculation directly using the above formula, the smoothness can be calculated by matrix offset method.

The B $((x_1, y_1), (x_2, y_2))$ denotes the pixel matrix with (x_1, y_1) as the starting coordinate (upper left corner), (x_2, y_2) as the terminating coordinate (lower right corner). Then the whole image block B is denoted as B $((1, 1), (m, n))$. The absolute difference matrix of pixels in each direction is calculated by formula (13).

$$\begin{aligned} AD_{\rightarrow} &= |B((1,1),(m,n-1)) - B((1,2),(m,n))| \\ AD_{\uparrow} &= |B((1,1),(m-1,n)) - B((2,1),(m,n))| \\ AD_{\nearrow} &= |B((1,1),(m-1,n-1)) - B((2,2),(m,n))| \\ AD_{\nwarrow} &= |B((2,1),(m,n-1)) - B((1,2),(m-1,n))| \end{aligned} \tag{13}$$

The sum operation of each element in the four matrices obtained from formula (13) can avoid repeated calculation. In addition, the calculation efficiency is greatly improved by directly calculating the matrix.

5 Simulation and Result Analysis

The UCID image data set of the V2 version is used as an image resource in this experiment. The UCID data set contains 1,338 uncompressed RGB color images, each of which is 384×512 or 512×384 pixels in size and in TIF format. The images are rich in themes, including landscapes, buildings, animals, plants and people. In order to simplify the operation and highlight the experimental results, we transform these images into gray images. The operating system used in the experiment is Windows 10.

Part of the data preprocessing and collection is accomplished by Python 3.5. Most of the operations are implemented in MATLAB 2015b. The training and prediction of the relevant parts of SVM are accomplished by LIBSVM3.21 toolbox.

We use 80 sets of different parameters to train SVM. These parameters include the type, number, coefficient of the kernel function, and the cost of the soft-spaced SVM.

Their error rate E_0 of the training set and the error rate E_1 of the test set are shown in the scatter plot. The size of the scatter points in Fig. 3 is determined by the parameters of the soft-spaced SVM, the cost C. And the color is determined by the number of polynomial kernels and the RBF kernels [7].

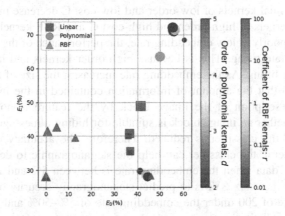

Fig. 3. Error rates of SVM classifiers trained with different parameters.

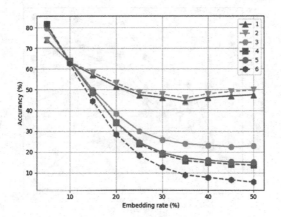

Fig. 4. Prediction accuracy of six SVMs for RS steganalysis under different embedding rates

The coefficients jointly determine the kernel of lower order polynomials. The effect of coefficient change on training effect is small, but it is sensitive to the change of cost. The sample feature space is mapped to the infinite multi-dimensional RBF kernels [11], which keeps a low error rate in the performance of the training set. However, the error rate of RBF kernels SVM with high cost and large test set coefficient increase obviously, which is an over-fitting phenomenon. We choose six sets of typical parameters with better properties to get SVM for subsequent experiments.

Next, we use six SVM classifiers to classify 10 groups of images with embedding rates of 5%–50%. Five blocks of images are randomly selected from 1,338 images to embed messages. The results are shown in Fig. 4.

In Fig. 4, the prediction accuracy of all classifiers for RS steganalysis shows a downward trend with the increase of embedding rate. But the difference is that the linear and polynomial kernels of low-order and low-cost C decrease more slowly than the polynomial kernels of high-order and high-cost C and RBF kernels. Although the former performs poorly at low embedding rate, the performance of the former is stable with embedding rate rising. This is because high-order kernels and high-cost probability lead to over-fitting. As the embedding rate increases, the size of the image block also increases, so that the amount of information contained in the image block also increases. The description of the image block by the feature is not accurate. The uncertainty of whether an image block is suitable for hiding a message increases. The decision level of the classifier is reduced. Therefore, the accuracy of the classifier decreases. In general, the classifier can help the steganographic to determine exactly where to hide the data when the embedding rate is between 5% and 25%.

Then, we use these six SVMs to predict steganography security on image blocks with a sample size of 200 under the embedding rate of 5%–50% and use SPA to test the accuracy of prediction.

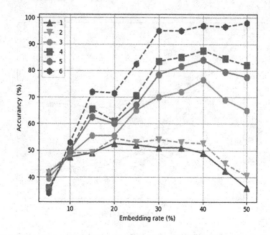

Fig. 5. Prediction accuracy of sample pair analysis (SPA) by six SVMs with different embedding rates.

In Fig. 5, with the increase of embedding rate between 5% and 25%, the accuracy of all SVM classifiers has an upward trend. When the embedding rate reaches 25%, the performance of low-order and low-cost kernels begins to decline, but high-order kernels shows a great improvement. This result is just contrary to the results of RS steganography prediction, and also shows high-order kernels is very effective against SPA attacks. The RS steganalysis mainly considers the simple change of feature itself, while SPA analysis considers many possible features, and the process of analysis is more complex. In this case, the use of high-order kernels can achieve better prediction results.

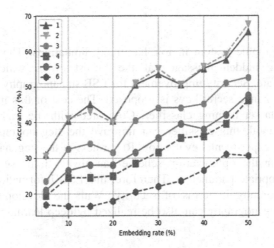

Fig. 6. Prediction accuracy of six SVMs for χ^2 test analysis under different embedding rates.

The 10 sets of camouflage image samples with embedding rate of 5%–50% and the corresponding sample size of 200 are randomly sampled. The χ^2 test is used to evaluate whether the images is steganographic. Then the six SVMs is used to predict the image. The prediction accuracy is shown in Fig. 6.

From Fig. 6, the changing trend of the accuracy of the χ^2 test is similar to RS steganalysis and SPA analysis. On the one hand, the results of the χ^2 test, like RS steganalysis, are best performed by low-order and low-cost kernels, while the high-order and high-cost kernels are always unsatisfactory.

On the other hand, the prediction accuracy of the χ^2 test also increases with the increase of embedding rate, which is similar to the prediction accuracy of the SPA method. The χ^2 test is a simple analysis method, so it is better to use low-order kernels to simulate the classification process. Compared with RS steganalysis, the χ^2 test is more sensitive to the embedding rate, so the classification of SVM is more advantageous in the case of high embedding rate. At this time, the SVM can quickly find unsuitable hiding location and improve the security. But the SVM may be difficult to find a suitable hiding location. It is necessary to find better features from larger image block samples. In the case of high embedding rate, although the accuracy of hiding data increases, the efficiency of hiding data decreases, which is also an unavoidable problem for all steganography methods. The evaluation results of the χ^2 test depend heavily on the nature of the carrier image. When the selection of the carrier image is limited in most practical application scenarios, the significance of the prediction results is not significant. The main reference for the optimization evaluation should be the accuracy of RS steganography and SPA steganography. Thus, selecting the appropriate SVM can make LSB steganography achieve at least 10% improvement in security.

6 Conclusion

The LSB steganographic system in IoT has many limitations. The LSB embedding method keeps the hidden messages at the lowest order, which makes image steganography unsafe. Security improvement for LSB steganography in the absence of secure channel exchange secret keys is proposed. The cost of this improvement is to find a suitable data set training classifier. Compared with the traditional sequential steganography method, this classifier can improve the steganography security to a certain extent after experimental evaluation. Regardless of the steganalysis method, the SVM introduced in the optimization scheme can always improve the accuracy by choosing the appropriate parameters. Therefore, this LSB information hiding method optimizes steganography in terms of security. With the development of in-depth learning, image steganography can also be realized by deep learning.

7 Acknowledgements

This research was supported by National Key R&D Program of China (2018YFB1700100), the Fundamental Scientific Research Project of Dalian University of Technology (DUT18JC28), the National Science Foundation of China (61772113, 61672131).

References

1. Menon, N., Vaithiyanathan: A survey on image steganography. In: 2017 International Conference on Technological Advancements in Power and Energy (TAP Energy), Kollam, pp. 1–5 (2017)
2. Jois, A., Tejaswini, L., et al.: Survey on LSB data hiding techniques. In: 2016 International Conference on Wireless Communications, Signal Processing and Networking (WiSPNET), Chennai, pp. 656–660 (2016)
3. Lin, Q., Liu, J., Guo, Z.: Local ternary pattern based on path integral for steganalysis. In: 2016 IEEE International Conference on Image Processing (ICIP), pp. 2737–2741 (2016)
4. Teng, D., Shi, R., Zhao, X.: DCT image watermarking technique based on the mix of time-domain. In: 2010 IEEE International Conference on Information Theory and Information Security (ICITIS), pp. 826–830 (2010)
5. Kaur, H., Kakkar, A.: Comparison of different image formats using LSB Steganography. In: 2017 4th International Conference on Signal Processing, Computing and Control (ISPCC), IEEE, pp. 97–101 (2017)
6. Nagaraj, V., Vijayalakshmi, V., Zayaraz, G.: RS steganalysis on block based octal pair pixel value differencing method. In: 2016 International Conference on Signal Processing, Communication, Power and Embedded System (SCOPES), IEEE (2016)
7. Chang, C.C., Chuang, J.C., Hu, Y.C.: Spatial domain image hiding scheme using pixel-values differencing. Fundamenta Informaticae 171–184 (2006). IOS Press
8. Singh, A., Rawat, M., Shukla, A.K., Kumar, A., Singh, B.: An overview of pixel value differencing based data hiding techniques. In: 2018 Eleventh International Conference on Contemporary Computing (IC3), Noida, pp. 1–3 (2018)

9. Tan, S., Li, B.: Targeted steganalysis of adaptive pixel-value differencing steganography. In: 2012 19th IEEE International Conference on Image Processing, Orlando, FL, pp. 1129–1132 (2012)
10. Tyagi, A., Roy, R., Changder, S.: High capacity image steganography based on pixel value differencing and pixel value sum. In: 2015 Second International Conference on Advances in Computing and Communication Engineering, Dehradun, pp. 488–493 (2015)
11. Talabani, H., Avci, E.: Impact of various kernels on support vector machine classification performance for treating wart disease. In: 2018 International Conference on Artificial Intelligence and Data Processing (IDAP), Malatya, Turkey, pp. 1–6 (2018)

A Blockchain-Based Mobile IOT Network Interconnection Security Trusted Protocol Model

Baochang Zhang[1] (ID), Juan Li[2(✉)], Xi Zheng[1], Jingjun Ge[3], and Juan Sun[1]

[1] Information Technology Center, Jining Medical University, Rizhao, China
zhangbc@mail.jnmc.edu.cn
[2] School of Medical Information Engineering,
Jining Medical University, Rizhao, China
94587807@qq.com
[3] Health Big Data Research Center, Jining Medical University, Rizhao, China

Abstract. With the continuous development of information technology and internet of things, technology of the mobile Internet of Things (mobile IOT) has been widely used in medical and health, smart home, transportation, logistics and other industries. At the same time, the network security issues of mobile IOT have become increasingly prominent. What's more serious is that the destructive power of these cyber threats has grown geometrically by taking the advantage of cloud computing and big data. This threat can be summarized as a non-trusted model threat under a "centralized" network architecture. By analyzing such security threats through real-world cases, this paper proposes a model to solve such security problems. Firstly, a variety of smart home and intelligent voice-controlled robots in the market are selected as research objects, and then the Man-in-the-Middle Attacks such as intelligence mining and data packet hijacking are used to detect the security vulnerabilities of such mobile IOT schemes. Through illustrating the huge network security threat faced by mobile IOT under the new situation, the example summarizes the current security risks in such mobile IOT solutions, and propose a secure and trusted mobile IOT network interconnection security model based on blockchain technology to remedy this problem.

Keywords: Blockchain · Mobile IOT · Trusted interconnection model · Man-in-the-Middle Attack · Security protocol

1 Introduction

The concept of the Internet of Things was first proposed by the Massachusetts Institute of Technology in 1999. It is a new type of information technology in the Internet Era. The development of mobile computing technology has plugged in the wings into the development of the Internet of Things. The convergence of the them gave birth to the mobile Internet of Things [1, 2], namely mobile IOT. In the past two years, with the rapid development of mobile IOT, various technologies and products such as drones,

© Springer Nature Switzerland AG 2019
J. Vaidya et al. (Eds.): CSS 2019, LNCS 11983, pp. 372–381, 2019.
https://doi.org/10.1007/978-3-030-37352-8_33

self-driving cars, robots, and smart homes have appeared in the market. The unveiling of the self-driving car of Baidu unveiled at the Spring Festival Gala in 2018 has made scientific and technological strength and development speed of China catch the eyes of the world. Nevertheless, behind the development of mobile IOT scenery, "Security" problem has become more prominent to us. The primary challenge for the development of the Internet of Things will be security [2]. Among many security factors, server-centric "centralized" control commands for secure transmission will be an important part of security issues. On the one hand, the server as the control center can easily become the "target" of internet attacks. On the other hand, the transmission of information such as control commands faces a variety of "man-in-the-middle attacks". This paper proposes a new secure and trusted mobile IOT interconnection model to achieve decentralized secure and trusted transmission of control instructions.

2 Security Case Study

2.1 Research Ideas

The commercial IOT brand products such as robots and smart home systems that are being sold on the market are selected as research objects. Try to find out the hidden dangers by data analysis, packet hijacking, password deciphering etc. This type of mobile IOT solution has some common features, such as the gateway control device on the local end, the device transmit signals "down" by the Bluetooth, ZigBee, WIFI and other protocols to connect the lower-end sensor device and control device. The device transmit signals "upwards" by WIFI or the wired network method converts the Internet of Things protocol into the traditional TCP/IP mode to connect to the Internet, and realizes basic setting and remote control through the mobile phone APP. Through consulting materials and e-commerce platforms, it is found that this type of solution has a high market share, covering the mainstream smart home, robot brand and development board market.

The specific research ideas for the above product safety issues are:

Firstly, technical parameters adopted by products are mined by product descriptions and web search engines, and the relevant information is summarized by using cloud computing and big data environment.

Secondly, trying out the product, obtain detailed information such as APP account and set process. During the process of using the product, carry out data packet hijacking and then analyze the packet to obtain vulnerability information of the cloud platform.

Thirdly, by analyzing the problems in this case, summarize the security risks in the overall solution of such products to find countermeasures.

2.2 Research Process

By reading product data, searching engine retrieval etc., the smart home system uses "smart home gateway" as the connection center of various smart devices. The gateway accesses the Internet by WIFI and further connects to the cloud server; The switch realizes remote control by transmitting control and execution signals by WIFI patch. Remote control of lights, curtains, background music and various home appliances can be realized by mobile phone APP or voice. Meanwhile, a series of application scenarios can be established, such as sleep mode, video and audio mode, with complete functions and simple operation. The robot connected to its server via WIFI and has the function of intelligent voice interaction, which can be used as the control entrance of intelligent furniture. The working principle of such devices is to set different variable parameters on the server and change the assignment of these parameters by the mobile APP. Different assignments of parameters represent different states of the terminal device, such as opening and closing. The controlled device detects these corresponding parameter changes in real time and changes its state.

Download their APP login respectively for trial and packet hijacking of the process. It is found that the user name of smart home APP is the ID of the gateway (9-digit Arabic number) or scan the QR code at the bottom of the gateway directly (24-digit hexadecimal number). Data packets hijacking is performed, and the results are shown in the figures as follows (Figs. 1, 2 and 3):

Fig. 1. Screenshot of the packet when logging in to the app

Fig. 2. Screenshot of the packet when the light is turned on

Fig. 3. Screenshot of the packet when the light is off

It can be seen that the URL is partially encrypted, when the URL information is complemented and decrypted, the final result is the complete URL as shown below (Fig. 4):

[image] :8080/asyncApi/hostop?
hostid=05DAFF383134424243216309&timeout=10&osType=1&lang=ch&appid=getui_1&channelid=f99e0c17dbbc467ba749efa1187
32da4&params=READ, BINDBASE, 2

Fig. 4. The URL of logging in

By analyzing the above URLs, can be got very important intelligence information. Obviously, the server with the above IP address provides the WEB service, and the access port is 8080. Further interpretation of URL and APP login information can be inferred as follows:

HostID is the unique identifier of the smart home gateway. The original login user name is the last 6 digits of the HostID.

"Timeout" is the timeout period, "osType" is the type of the operating system, and "lang" is the language type.

When using iphone and Android mobile phones to log in to the same smart home gateway respectively, the "HostID" is unchanged but the "ChannelID" is changed.

The control instruction statement is the statement following "params", the first group of parameters behind "Params" represents the command mode, and the "CONTROL" is the control mode, and the parameters behind it are to send control signals to the terminal (perhaps there are other modes such as detecting the state of the terminal, etc.), The second group digitally identifies the type of terminal device ("SPL" means switch, "PW" means curtain), the third group of numbers is the number of the terminal device (indicating which switch or curtain to send control commands to), and the fourth group of numbers is a specific remote control command.

Further testing, it is found that the control instruction of the smart home terminal can be directly realized by using the browser or use other tools to post the data to the server. Change the control command parameter "0" to "1" or "1" to "0", the remote light and curtain can be turned on or off. Repeating the above operation after changing the "ChannelID" arbitrarily, finding that control instructions can still be parsed and executed, Which means that the "ChannelID" should only be an identification code that records the identity of the intelligent terminal device, rather than verification information. Then in this way the most important security point is to focus on the "HostID". If you decrypt the specific meaning of the "HostID", you can control all the smart home terminals which using the smart solutions. It may be difficult to decipher the meaning of a hexadecimal bit array like "05DAFF383134424243216309". We can think about it from another perspective:

(1) Use the tool to send a correct control command, we can find that the smart home terminal can be controlled, and return a json file with the content "{"code": 0, "msg": "success", "data": "CONTROL, SPL, 76, OK"}". Modify the "hosted" arbitrarily and find that it also returns a json file with the content {"code": 4, "msg": "Cannot find 05DAFF383134abc243216589 host", "data": ""}, this shows that at least one program can be written to guess the "HostID" violently.

(2) Trying to make violent guesses from a large amount of data, up to 24 to the 16th power, theoretically feasible, and practically not operational. However, in the era of cloud computing and big data, a variety of intelligence can be detected from the Internet to shorten the guess time. The following existing HostID information can be obtained through various channels (Table 1).

Table 1. HostID information.

Number	HostID	User
1	0671FF565552837267121912	267121912
2	066DFF565552837267122136	267122136
3	066DFF565552837267122242	267122242
4	05DAFF383134424243216309	243216309
5	05DAFF383134424243185122	243185122
6	05DAFF383134424243185513	243185513

Analyzing these "HostID" reveals that these arrays are not ciphertext but regular plaintext. Multiple digits in front of the four "HostID" are duplicates. This should be the same batch of products, in this way, the probability of guessing the meaning of "HostID" is greatly increased. Try to change the "HostID" to the above list value and send it to the server, find that the returned json file prompts "success", indicating that the remote unknown smart home has been illegally operated without authorization. This is undoubtedly a very serious vulnerability, and it can be imagined how much harm will be caused once the vulnerability and related information are illegally exploited. Through the official website of the product solution manufacturer, the wireless control solution has been applied to many smart home brands, industrial intelligent control and other fields, and even various big data analysis charts of terminal data, which is very terrible.

The same research procedure was used to analyze the robot system. After the data packet hijacking, it was found that it used a Pass cloud computing open platform and Tencent cloud to provide voice and video services. All the software and hardware development materials can be easily obtained. When sending commands such as "dance" or "sing a song", it was found that it also adopted a control signal transmission mode similar to smart home, except that the identity verification was added to the URL. Further analysis of the data packet revealed that the transmission of the robot system control command was to add the post and check of "user" and "pwd" after the similar URL. We try to do the following operation: first send a control instruction, then intercept the instruction with the packet capture software, change some control instructions without moving the identity verification information, and then release the changed instructions. The result shows that the robot successfully executed and was changed. After the "pseudo-instructions", this shows that the robot also has similar illegal execution loopholes.

2.3   Statement of Problem

The above examples show clearly that the man-in-the-middle attack (MITM) method such as packet hijacking in the traditional network environment is still effective in the mobile IOT field [3]. In other words, the mobile IOT has a "trust" vulnerability in the process of network data transmission. For the time being, we named this vulnerability as "a non-trusted interconnect vulnerability of mobile IOT network based on TCP/IP in the cloud computing and big data environment." Mobile IOT control instructions are not trusted during transmission, which is very scary. So, how can we fundamentally solve this loophole and ensure the safe development of mobile IOT? Succeeding in solving this problem will directly affect the development prospects of mobile IOT.

3 Analysis of the Problem

Mobile IOT is actually a network that forms intelligent identification, positioning, tracking, monitoring and management, which connects items to the Internet via wired or wireless gateways through various means such as radio frequency, infrared, sensor, etc. Its main function is data transmission. The TCP/IP protocol has been widely used in the Internet. The protocol can also meet all the requirements of IoT data transmission. Together with the use of the gateway, the data of any type sensor can be identified, extracted and transmitted. Therefore, the solution of mobile IOT remote control using IoT gateway and TCP/IP protocol has become one of the most popular and popular mobile IOT solutions [4].

Mobile IOT is usually implemented through three levels—the first level is the perception layer, which senses the location, temperature, and light of the object; the second level is the network layer, which acts to transmit the perceived information to the outside world; The last level is the application layer, which can meet a variety of different application needs. Let's take the smart home as an example to analyze the network structure of mobile IOT, shown as in Fig. 5.

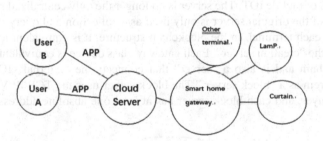

Fig. 5. Smart home network structure

The Internet of Things terminal uses Bluetooth, Zig-Bee, RFID and other technologies to sense information such as temperature and humidity, switch status of the luminaire, and switch status of the curtain, and then sends the perceived terminal information to the cloud server through the smart home gateway. The user obtains the relevant information of the terminal at any time through the APP and sends the control command to the cloud server, and the smart furniture gateway monitors the status of the relevant parameters of the server (control instruction) in real time, and sends the instruction to the corresponding terminal for execution [5].

There are two common used ways to transmit data: http and https. The transmission of data by http is more dangerous to attack by the middleman. The data is transmitted by https, because only part of the data is encrypted, such threats still exist [6].

The above vulnerabilities are threats to the data instructions during transmission. In fact, this type of solution stores and sends instruction data through a centralized server. If someone illegally controls the server or the administrator manually sends an illegal command, they are also "untrustworthy" factors [7], which can be attributed to the above categories of untrustworthy vulnerabilities.

4 Solution

To fundamentally solve the "untrusted interconnect vulnerability of mobile IOT network based on TCP/IP in cloud computing big data environment", the primary and core problem is to solve the problem of centralized server as the only control instruction storage and sending device, the second problem is to change the sending and receiving mechanism of control instructions [8]. This completely changes the framework of the traditional mobile IOT network protocol model. Here we propose a new mobile IOT network interconnection model based on blockchain technology. This model is named as "a blockchain-based Mobile IOT Network Interconnection Security Trusted Protocol Model".

4.1 Framework of the Proposed Model

The new model is designed based on the blockchain model, adopts the distributed block server setting up mode. On this basis, the model is upgraded and improved with the characteristics of mobile IOT. The server is no longer the only centralized server device. The function of the original server is only used as a collection and query device for the status data of each terminal. In the blockchain structure, it is equivalent to the creation block, called the "creation server". Each gateway class device is equivalent to a "block" in the blockchain and is also a "server" that connects the "internal" IOT terminals, referred to herein as a "block server." The block server uses the TCP/IP V6 protocol at the network layer, and each block server has at least one absolute address [9].

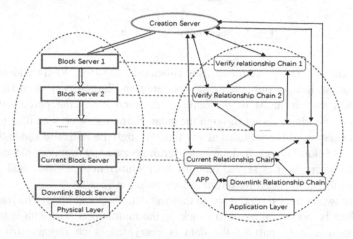

Fig. 6. Framework of new model

As shown in Fig. 6, which is a framework structure diagram of the new model, the model relates to physical layer and an application layer in network protocol. The orange oval represents the "creation server", the blue rectangle represents the physical existence of the "block server", and the red rounded rectangle represents the random check relationship chain generated by the current block server and any other physical "block server". It corresponds to the physical block server one by one, and is the virtual link of the verification relationship network of the physical block server. Each physical block server periodically sends an online command to the Creation Server and synchronizes the manipulation information in the block server to the Creation Server at any time. When the mobile phone APP logs into the original server for the first time, it needs to complete the identity check and binding of its own block, and accept the "chain" information of the blockchain sent by the creation server (That is, the chain formed by the sequential links of the left block server in Fig. 10). The "chain" includes information such as "Uplink ID", "HostID", IP address, MAC address, "Downlink ID" of all block servers. When the new block server is registered, the last block server in the chain is automatically set as the "upper block server", and after completion, the block server is updated to update the chain information. The APP randomly detects at least N (N can be customized, N must first include its own block) online block servers according to the chain information, and records the HostID, IP address and other information of these blocks to form its own check block server. Sub-chain. After the first login, operations such as editing and adding of the terminal device can be performed. Then, the APP generates a ciphertext set of the encryption operation command of the terminal device according to the information about the N sub-chains of the check block. The so-called operation instruction ciphertext set means that the data submitted to the server by each remote control in this model is no longer a combination of characters such as identification variables and state variables as shown in Fig. 5, but is combined in the APP. The information of the N check blocks is encrypted to form a set of hash arrays grouped by instruction type. As shown in Fig. 7.

Number	Instruction	Operating Object	Operational Instruction
1			c3f7feaa3dda17399eaacb7d84c911f8f7e49111
2	Turn On	Smart	e570445090ca1dc682c3f124c98b6d923caed209
3	The Light	Switch 1	1956bc43dc47d61fd01f493b1bfefc829a3ca052
4			bc58593762e6ff74a3cbbfeb7bf9aac0fa3ae7ee
......			......
6			dd387ff71ed4a4105e0676e81761886fe437b6ff
7	Turn Off	Smart	e2a7ede2015213f898c7342ce73b3f088375d846
8	The Light	Switch 1	949475ab9f37fa3e55c2fa11c25e918d5b212dab
9			......

Fig. 7. Operation instruction ciphertext set

After logging in for the first time, the system prompts you to log in again. During the re-login process, the APP sends verification information to the above-mentioned N check block servers to complete identity verification and log in to its own block server.

If it is not detected that its own block server is online, any one of the above N block servers can log in online. If it is not online, log in again to the creation block server and send a message indicating that the corresponding block server is offline. All the data is transmitted by HTPPS encryption [10].

The APP periodically sends these instruction sets to N blocks for storage, in preparation for later data verification, and updates the relevant instruction set or even the encryption algorithm according to the set conditions. When a remote command is initiated from the APP, such as the light-on command, the APP automatically randomly extracts an instruction code (such as c3f7feaa3dda17399eaacb7d84c911f8f7e49111) from the light-in commands ciphertext set to send to the logged-in block server. After receiving the instruction ciphertext, the server directly searches in the synchronized instruction set. When the instruction is retrieved in the light-on group, the light-on operation is directly performed. Then the APP and the block server will delete the instruction code from the corresponding instruction set, and broadcast the operation to the above N block servers. After receiving the broadcast information, the N block servers complete the deletion instruction, and record the relevant operation log, finally send the log back to the creation block server, thereby completing the entire process of remote lighting control. Since the instruction information of the light-on data has been synchronized in the block server, the related operation can be performed without decryption, so the reaction speed can be greatly improved. In addition, the instruction set received by the block server can be verified not only from its own instruction set database, but also from any other block server that is randomly selected in the N verify block servers, which greatly improves the security.

4.2   Analysis of Model Safety and Difficulty in Generalization

This model completely changed the function of the original mobile IOT system server, removing its original absolute centralization status [11], making it a "simple" function server for log storage and query. The server acts as the login main server of the APP. Refusing to remotely control the IOT terminal directly from the server background, and must perform the relevant operation after receiving the instruction sent by the APP, which prevents improper operation after the block server is illegally controlled. In addition, the APP and the server use the https protocol for transmission, so that even if only some data is encrypted by https, since the control command transmitted by itself is ciphertext, the security factor is very high [12].

5   Conclusion

Overall, the above model has solved the "untrusted" problem of mobile IOT and realized the trusted interconnection of mobile IOT. If the model is implemented and established, it is extremely feasible in both technical and theoretical aspects. However, it may take long time for large-scale commercial production. The reason is that the current TCP/IP internet protocol Version 4 and related devices still occupy the dominant position in the market from a global perspective [13]. To achieve the fast block server mode architecture based on IOT gateway devices and meet the requirements of industrial promotion, there is still a long way to go in many aspects [14]. Fortunately, the popularization speed of Chinese Internet Protocol Version 6. I believe that with the continuous development and popularization of IPV6 and 5G technologies, this model will contribute to the application of mobile IOT security development.

Acknowledgment. This work is partially supported by Ministry of Education Humanities and Social Sciences Project (11YJCZH021, 15YJCZH111). Shandong Social Science Planning Research Project (17CHLJ41, 16CTQJ02, 18CHLJ34). Teachers Research Support Foundation of Jining Medical University 2018 (JYFC2018KJ063, JYFC2018KJ025, JY2017KJ054). Education Research Project of Jining Medical University (18048).

References

1. Li, S., Zhao, S., Yang, P., Andriotis, P., Xu, L., Sun, Q.: Distributed consensus algorithm for events detection in cyber physical systems. IEEE Internet Things J. **6**(2), 2299–2308 (2019)
2. Li, S., Choo, K.-K. R., Sun, Q., Buchanan, W., Cao, J.: IoT forensics: Amazon Echo as a use case. IEEE Internet Things (2019). ISSN: 2327-4662
3. Algorithms; study findings on algorithms are outlined in reports from G. Oliva and Colleagues (Distributed calculation of edge-disjoint spanning trees for robustifying distributed algorithms against man-in-the-middle attacks). Comput. Networks Commun. (2019)
4. Information technology - Information forensics and security; new findings from Ben Gurion University of the Negev in the area of information forensics and security reported (Vesper: using echo analysis to detect man-in-the-middle attacks in LANs). Comput. Networks Commun. (2019)
5. Li, S., Zhao, S., Yuan, Y., Sun, Q., Zhang, K.: Dynamic security risk evaluation via hybrid Bayesian risk graph in cyber-physical social systems. IEEE Trans. Comput. Soc. Syst. **5**(4), 1133–1141 (2018)
6. Li, S., Tryfonas, T., Li, H.: The Internet of Things: a security point of view. Internet Res. **26**(2), 337–359 (2016)
7. Li, S., Tryfonas, T., Russell, G., Andriotis, P.: Risk assessment for mobile systems through a multilayered hierarchical Bayesian network. IEEE Trans. Cybern. **46**(8), 1749–1759 (2016)
8. Ahmad, F., Adnane, A., Franqueira, V., Kurugollu, F., Liu, L.: Man-in-the-middle attacks in vehicular ad-hoc networks: evaluating the impact of attackers' strategies. Sensors (Basel, Switzerland) **18**(11), 4040 (2018)
9. Elakrat, M.A., Jung, J.C.: Development of field programmable gate array–based encryption module to mitigate man-in-the-middle attack for nuclear power plant data communication network. Nucl. Eng. Technol. **50**(5), 780–787 (2018)
10. Fei, Y.Y., Meng, X.D., Gao, M., Wang, H., Ma, Z.: Quantum man-in-the-middle attack on the calibration process of quantum key distribution. Sci. Rep. **8**(1), 4283 (2018)
11. Qian, Y., et al.: Towards decentralized IoT security enhancement: a blockchain approach. Comput. Electr. Eng. **72**, 266–273 (2018)
12. Si, H., Sun, C., Li, Y., Qiao, H., Shi, L.: IoT information sharing security mechanism based on blockchain technology. Future Gener. Comput. Syst. **101**, 1028–1040 (2019)
13. Tariq, N., et al.: The security of big data in fog-enabled IoT applications including blockchain: a survey. Sensors (Basel, Switzerland) **19**(8), 1788 (2019)
14. Derhab, A., et al.: Blockchain and random subspace learning-based IDS for SDN-enabled industrial IoT security. Sensors (Basel, Switzerland) **19**(14), 3119 (2019)

Privacy-Preserving Attribute-Based Multi-keyword Search Encryption Scheme with User Tracing

Zhenhua Liu[1], Yan Liu[1]($^{(\boxtimes)}$), Jing Xu[1], and Baocang Wang[2]

[1] School of Mathematics and Statistics, Xidian University, Xi'an 710071, China
1742271353@qq.com
[2] State Key Laboratory of Integrated Services Networks, Xidian University, Xi'an 710071, China

Abstract. Attribute-based keyword search encryption (ABKSE) can provide fine-grained data sharing and keyword search over encrypted data. However, most of the existing ABKSE schemes need a large amount of computation cost in the encryption phase and only support single-keyword queries in the search phase, and the access policy embedded in the ciphertext cannot be hidden, which will leak some sensitive information to malicious user. Furthermore, some malicious authorized users could leak their secret keys to others for benefits, but it is difficult to identify the malicious users who disclosed the secret keys when the same attributes are shared by many users. To address the above problems, we propose a privacy-preserving attribute-based multi-keyword search encryption scheme with user tracing. In the proposed scheme, we adopt the AND gate on multi-value attribute technique to hide the access policy. Meanwhile, an aggregate technique is used to achieve fast multi-keyword search and Shamir's threshold scheme is utilized to trace the malicious users. The security analysis demonstrates that the proposed scheme is selectively secure and fully traceable. Performance analysis shows that the proposed scheme is efficient and practical.

Keywords: Attribute-based encryption · Privacy-preserving · Multi-keyword search · User tracing

1 Introduction

With the rapid development of cloud computing, more and more individuals and enterprises store their data in the cloud server, which can provide more convenience. To protect data confidentiality, sensitive data must always be encrypted before uploading to the cloud server. However, encryption operation may hinder data retrieval from encrypted data in the cloud. To solve this issue, searchable encryption (SE) is introduced. SE contains two types: symmetric searchable encryption (SSE) and asymmetric searchable encryption (ASE). Song et al. [1] first proposed the concept of symmetric searchable encryption. Boneh et al. [2]

© Springer Nature Switzerland AG 2019
J. Vaidya et al. (Eds.): CSS 2019, LNCS 11983, pp. 382–397, 2019.
https://doi.org/10.1007/978-3-030-37352-8_34

introduced the first public-key encryption with keyword search (PEKS) scheme. However, all above schemes can only provide single-keyword search, which are inefficient in practice since the search results may contain a very large number of data items and only a small proportion of them are relevant. Furthermore, multi-keyword search scheme [3] was introduced, which avoids the problem.

Traditional searchable encryption is "one-to-one" model, which can not support a more expressive data sharing. Fortunately, Sahai et al. [4] firstly proposed the concept of attribute-based encryption (ABE) in 2005, which can provide "one-to-many" service and be considered as one of the most appropriate encryption technologies for cloud storage. There are two kinds of attribute-based encryption: ciphertext-policy ABE (CP-ABE) [5,6], where the ciphertext is associated with access policy, and key-policy ABE (KP-ABE) [7], where the secret key is associated with access policy.

To achieve keyword queries and fine-grained access control, a lot of attribute-based keyword search encryption (ABKSE) schemes have been proposed. For example, Wang et al. [8] proposed a CP-ABE scheme supporting keyword search function. In their scheme, data owners encrypt the data with access policy, and generate indexes for the corresponding keyword, and then outsource them to cloud server. Only the users whose attribute set satisfies the access policy can search and decrypt the encrypted data. Furthermore, to verify the searching result, Zheng et al. [10] proposed a verifiable attribute-based keyword search encryption scheme using bloom filter and digital signature techniques. Although ABKSE schemes can support fine-grained access control over encrypted data in the cloud, there are still some problems to be resolved.

Firstly, most of the existing CP-ABKSE schemes can only provide single-keyword search, which is not practical. Single-keyword search wastes network bandwidth and computing resources, since it returns a large number of irrelevant results. Therefore, it is necessary to support multi-keyword search in the CP-ABKSE schemes. i.e. when a data user uses multi-keyword search, the cloud server will return relatively few number of files containing these keywords, thus the search result is much more accurate than single-keyword search. Furthermore, Miao et al. [11] presented an attribute-based multi-keyword search scheme in multi-owner settings. Wang et al. [12] presented a verifiable and multi-keyword searchable attribute-based encryption scheme.

Secondly, in the conventional CP-ABKSE, an access policy may leaks some sensitive information. For example, in an electronic health record system, if the access policy embedded in the ciphertext is public, one can infer some sensitive information from the patient's access policy. Hence, it is necessary to design a CP-ABKSE scheme with hidden access policy. Qiu et al. [13] presented a hidden policy ciphertext-policy attribute-based encryption with keyword search against keyword guessing attack. Chaudhari et al. [14] presented a privacy-preserving attribute-based keyword search scheme with hidden access policy, which is applicable in a scenario that there are multiple data owners and multiple data receivers.

Thirdly, most of the CP-ABKSE schemes do not consider the situation that a malicious user leaks its secret keys to some unauthorized users for profits. The secret key is associated with a set of attributes, but the same attributes may be shared by many users. Thus, it is essential to support user tracing in the existing CP-ABKSE schemes. Fortunately, Liu et al. [15] proposed the first white-box traceable CP-ABE scheme, which can trace a malicious user who leaks his secret key to others for benefits. Ning et al. [16] proposed a white-box traceable ciphertext-policy attribute-based encryption supporting flexible attributes.

To the best of our knowledge, there is few schemes supporting fast multi-keyword search, hidden-policy and user tracing, simultaneously. Inspired by Wang et al.'s scheme [17], we propose a privacy-preserving attribute-based multi-keyword search encryption scheme with user tracing (P2ABMKSE-UT).

Our Contributions are summarized as follows:

- We present an attribute-based encryption scheme, which can provide fast multi-keyword search, hidden-policy, and user tracing, simultaneously.
- We adopt the AND gate on multi-value attribute technique from Wang et al.'s scheme [17] to realize hidden-policy, and make use of an aggregate technique to achieve fast keyword search. In addition, the proposed scheme can also provide multi-keyword search, which enables the users to quickly search the most relevant records.
- Shamir's $(\hat{t}, \hat{n})$ threshold scheme [16] is utilized to trace a malicious user who leaks the secret key to others for benefits. The storage cost for traceability is constant and only depends on the threshold $\hat{t}$.
- Finally, we provide thorough analysis of security and performance, which shows that the proposed scheme is efficient and practical.

1.1   Organization

The rest of this paper is organized as follows. Some preliminaries and system architecture are described in Sect. 2. We describe a formal definition and security model in Sect. 3. The proposed P2ABMKSE-UT scheme is presented in Sect. 4. The security proof and performance analysis are given in Sect. 5. Finally, we make the conclusions in Sect. 6.

2   Preliminaries

2.1   Multilinear Maps

The definition of multilinear maps and multilinear map groups is described as follows. Given a security parameter λ and prime p, a 3-multilinear map consists of 3 cyclic groups $(\mathbb{G}_0, \mathbb{G}_1, \mathbb{G}_2)$ with order p, and 2 mappings $\hat{e}_i : \mathbb{G}_0 \times \mathbb{G}_i \to \mathbb{G}_{i+1}, i = 0, 1$. The 3-multilinear map should satisfy the following properties [17]:

1. Let $g_0 \in \mathbb{G}_0$ be a generator of $\mathbb{G}_0$, then $g_{i+1} = \hat{e}_i(g_0, g_i)$ is a generator of $\mathbb{G}_{i+1}$.
2. $\hat{e}_i(g_0^a, g_i^b) = \hat{e}_i(g_0, g_i)^{ab}$ for all $a, b \in \mathbb{Z}_p$.
3. There is an efficient polynomial-time algorithm to compute $\hat{e}_i$.

2.2   Access Structure

A series of AND gate on multi-value attribute [17] are defined as follows. Let n be the total number of attributes, and all attributes be indexed as $L = \{att_1, att_2, \cdots, att_n\}$. Each attribute $att_i \in L, i \in [1, n]$ has a set of possible value $V_i = \{v_{i,1}, v_{i,2}, \cdots, v_{i,n_i}\}$, where n_i is the number of the possible value for att_i. An attribute list S for a user is $S = (\lambda_1, \lambda_2, \cdots, \lambda_n)$, where $\lambda_i \in V_i$. The access policy in ciphertext is $\mathbb{P} = \{P_1, P_2, \cdots, P_n\}$, where $P_i \in V_i$. The attribute list S satisfies the access policy $\mathbb{P}$ if and only if $\lambda_i \in P_i, (i = 1, 2, \cdots, n)$.

2.3   Generic Group Model

Let $\Upsilon = (p, \mathbb{G}_0, \mathbb{G}_1, \mathbb{G}_2, \hat{e}_0, \hat{e}_1) \leftarrow \mathbf{PairGen}(1^\lambda)$. There are three random encodings $\psi_0, \psi_1, \psi_2 : \mathbb{Z}_p \rightarrow \{0, 1\}^\ell$, where $\ell > 3 \log(p)$. For $i = 0, 1, 2$, we have $\mathbb{G}_i = \{\psi_i(x) | x \in \mathbb{Z}_p\}$. We use the oracles to execute the respective actions on $\mathbb{G}_0, \mathbb{G}_1, \mathbb{G}_2$ and compute a non-degenerate bilinear map $\hat{e}_i : \mathbb{G}_0 \times \mathbb{G}_i \rightarrow \mathbb{G}_{i+1}$. A random oracle is used to represent the hash function [18].

2.4 φ-Strong Diffie-Hellman (φ-SDH) Assumption

Let $\mathbb{G}_0$ be a bilinear group of prime order p and g_0 be a generator of $\mathbb{G}_0$. The φ-Strong Diffie-Hellman (φ-SDH) problem [16] in $\mathbb{G}_0$ is defined as follows. Given a $(\varphi + 1)$-tuple $(g_0, g_0^x, g_0^{x^2}, \cdots, g_0^{x^\varphi})$, where the probability is over the random choice of x in $\mathbb{Z}_p^*$, the φ-Strong Diffie-Hellman (φ-SDH) problem is to output a pair $(c, g_0^{c+x}) \in \mathbb{Z}_p \times \mathbb{G}_0$. An algorithm $\mathcal{C}$ has advantage ϵ in solving φ-SDH problem in $\mathbb{G}_0$ if

$$\Pr[\mathcal{C}(g_0, g_0^x, g_0^{x^2}, \cdots, g_0^{x^\varphi}) = (c, g_0^{c+x})] \geq \epsilon.$$

φ-**Strong Diffie-Hellman (φ-SDH) Assumption.** We say that the φ-SDH assumption holds in $\mathbb{G}_0$ if no polynomial-time algorithm has advantage at least ϵ in solving the φ-SDH problem in $\mathbb{G}_0$.

2.5   Shamir's Threshold Scheme

In Shamir's threshold scheme $\Gamma_{(\hat{t}, \hat{n})}$ [16], a secret can be divided into $\hat{n}$ part, which are sent to each participant a unique part. All of them can be used to reconstruct the secret. Suppose that the secret is assumed to be an element in a finite field $\mathbb{F}_p^*$. Choose $\hat{t} - 1$ random coefficients $a_1, a_2, \cdots, a_{\hat{t}-1} \in \mathbb{F}_p$ and set the secret in the constant term a_0. Note that, we have such a polynomial:

$$f(x) = a_0 + a_1 \cdot x + a_2 \cdot x^2 + \cdots + a_{\hat{t}-1} \cdot x^{\hat{t}-1}.$$

Every participant is given a point (x, y) on the above curve, that is, the input to the polynomial x and its output $y = f(x)$. Given a subset with any $\hat{t}$ points, we can recover the constant term a_0 using the Lagrange interpolation.

2.6   System Framework

As shown in Fig. 1, there are four entities in our scheme: Trusted authority (TA), data owner (DO), data user (DU) and cloud server (CS).

Trusted authority: TA is in charge of generating the public parameter and secret keys for DO and DU. And TA can trace the malicious users if some secret keys are disclosed.

Data owner: DO encrypts the sensitive data, generates an encrypted keyword index, and then uploads them to the cloud server. To achieve fine-grained access control, an access policy is embedded in the ciphertext in the encryption phase, where the ciphertext will be shared with the data users whose attributes satisfy the access policy embedded in the ciphertext.

Data user: DU owns a set of attributes, and her or his secret key is associated with the attribute set. Given a keyword and a secret key, DU can generate a valid trapdoor and send it to the cloud server.

Cloud server: CS stores the encrypted data and searches the intended data. We assume that the cloud server is honest-but-curious. i.e., it will honestly execute the operations but try to acquire much more information about the sensitive data.

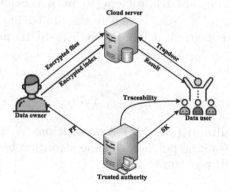

Fig. 1. The architecture of P2ABMKSE-UT scheme

3   Formal Definition and Security Model

3.1   Formal Definition

We describe the formal definition of P2ABMKSE-UT as follows:

- **Setup**(1^λ) → (PP, MSK): TA takes the security parameter λ as input, and outputs the public parameter PP and a master secret key MSK.

- **KeyGen**$(PP, MSK, S, id) \rightarrow SK_{S,id}$: TA takes the public parameter PP, the master secret key MSK, a set of attribute S and a data user's identifier id as input. This algorithm outputs a secret key $SK_{S,id}$.
- **Encrypt**$(PP, F, k, W, \mathbb{P}) \rightarrow (CT, I_W)$: DO takes the public parameter PP, a set of file F, a symmetric key k, a set of keywords W and the AND gate access policy $\mathbb{P}$ as input. This algorithm outputs a ciphertext CT and an encrypted index I_W.
- **Trapdoor**$(SK_{S,id}, W') \rightarrow T_{W'}$: DU takes the secret key $SK_{S,id}$, an intended keyword set W' as input, and outputs a trapdoor $T_{W'}$.
- **Test**$(I_W, T_{W'}) \rightarrow 0$ or 1: This algorithm takes the index I_W and the trapdoor $T_{W'}$ as input. CS returns 1 if the attribute set matches the access policy embedded in the ciphertext and $W = W'$. Otherwise returns 0.
- **Decrypt**$(SK_{S,id}, CT) \rightarrow k$: DU takes the secret key $SK_{S,id}$ and the ciphertext CT as input. This algorithm outputs the symmetric key k if the attribute set satisfies the access policy embedded in the ciphertext; otherwise outputs $\perp$.
- **Trace**$(PP, \Gamma_{(\hat{t},\hat{n})}, MSK, SK_{S,id}) \rightarrow id$ or $\perp$: This algorithm takes the public parameters PP, an instance of Shamir's threshold scheme $\Gamma_{(\hat{t},\hat{n})}$, the master secret key MSK and a secret key $SK_{S,id}$ as input. This algorithm outputs an identity id from $\Gamma_{(\hat{t},\hat{n})}$ implying that $SK_{S,id}$ is linked to id if $SK_{S,id}$ is well-formed. Otherwise, output $\perp$.

3.2 Security Model

IND-sCP-CKA Game. According to Wang et al.'s scheme [17], we describe the indistinguishability against selective ciphertext-policy and chosen-keyword attack (IND-sCP-CKA) game between an adversary $\mathcal{A}$ and a challenger $\mathcal{C}$ as follows:

- **Setup.** $\mathcal{A}$ selects a challenging access policy $\mathbb{P}^*$, and then sends it to $\mathcal{C}$. Then, $\mathcal{C}$ runs the *Setup* algorithm, sends the public parameter PP to $\mathcal{A}$, and keeps the master secret key MSK for himself.
- **Phase 1.** $\mathcal{A}$ issues polynomial-time secret key queries for (S_i, id_i) and trapdoor queries as follows:
  - $\mathcal{O}_{KeyGen(S_i, id_i)}$: If S_i satisfies the chosen access policy $\mathbb{P}^*$, $\mathcal{C}$ runs $KeyGen$ to output secret key SK_{S_i, id_i} and returns to $\mathcal{A}$.
  - $\mathcal{O}_{Trapdoor}(S_i, W')$: Given a set of keywords W', $\mathcal{C}$ executes $Trapdoor$ algorithm to generate a trapdoor $T_{W'}$ by leveraging SK_{S_i, id_i}, and then sends the trapdoor to $\mathcal{A}$.
- **Challenge.** $\mathcal{A}$ selects two keyword set W_0 and W_1 to $\mathcal{C}$. If $\mathcal{A}$ gets access to $T_{W'}$ on the condition that S_i meets the challenging access policy $\mathbb{P}^*$ in Phase 1, we define $W_0 = W_1$. Then, $\mathcal{C}$ selects a random element $b \in \{0, 1\}$ and generates an index $I_{W'_b}$ by utilizing $\mathbb{P}^*$. Finally, $\mathcal{C}$ sends $I_{W'_b}$ to $\mathcal{A}$.
- **Phase 2.** Same as Phase 1 with the restriction that if $W_0 \neq W_1$, then $\mathcal{A}$ cannot find S_i that satisfies $\mathbb{P}^*$.
- **Guess.** $\mathcal{A}$ outputs its guess b' of b and wins the game if $b' = b$.

The advantage of $\mathcal{A}$ is defined as follows:

$$Adv_{\mathcal{A}}^{IND\text{-}sCP\text{-}CKA} = \left| \Pr[b' - b] - \frac{1}{2} \right|.$$

Definition 1. *A privacy-preserving attribute-based multi-keyword search encryption scheme with user tracing is IND-sCP-CKA secure if all polynomial-time adversaries have at most a negligible advantage in the above game.*

Traceability. Based on Ning et al.'s scheme [16], we will present the traceability definition for our P2ABMKSE-UT scheme. Let q_t be the total number of key queries that the attacker makes. The game between an adversary $\mathcal{A}$ and a challenger $\mathcal{C}$ is as follows:

- **Setup**: $\mathcal{C}$ runs the *Setup* algorithm and sends the public parameters PP to $\mathcal{A}$.
- **Key Query**: $\mathcal{A}$ submits a set of attributes (S_i, id_i) to request the corresponding secret keys.
- **Key Forgery**: $\mathcal{A}$ will output a secret key $SK_{S,id}^*$. If

$$Trace(PP, \Gamma_{(\hat{t},\hat{n})}, MSK, SK_{S,id}^*) \neq \perp$$

and

$$Trace(PP, \Gamma_{(\hat{t},\hat{n})}, MSK, SK_{S,id}^*) \notin \{id_1, id_2, \cdots, id_{q_t}\},$$

then $\mathcal{A}$ will win the game.

The advantage of $\mathcal{A}$ in this game is defined as:

$$Adv_{\mathcal{A}}^{Traceability} = \Pr[Trace(PP, \Gamma_{(\hat{t},\hat{n})}, MSK, SK_{S,id}^*) \notin \{\perp, id_1, id_2, \cdots, id_{q_t}\}].$$

Definition 2. *A privacy-preserving attribute-based multi-keyword search encryption scheme with user tracing is fully traceable if there is no polynomial-time adversary that has non-negligible advantage in the above game.*

4   Our Concrete Construction

In this section, the construction of our scheme is described as follows:

- **Setup**(1^λ): We define a hash function $H_1 : \{0,1\}^* \to \mathbb{Z}_p$. TA runs this algorithm as follows:
  1. Run the group generator algorithm $PairGen(1^\lambda)$ and get the groups and the multilinear mapping description $\Upsilon = (p, \mathbb{G}_0, \mathbb{G}_1, \mathbb{G}_2, \hat{e}_0, \hat{e}_1)$, where g_0 is a generator of $\mathbb{G}_0$.
  2. Choose a probabilistic encryption scheme (Enc, Dec), which satisfies the map: $\{0,1\}^* \to \mathbb{Z}_p^*$ with different key k_1, k_2. Initialize an instance of Shamir's threshold scheme $\Gamma_{(\hat{t},\hat{n})}$, and keep a polynomial $f(x)$ and $\hat{t} - 1$ points $(x_1, y_1), (x_2, y_2), \cdots, (x_{\hat{t}-1}, y_{\hat{t}-1})$ on $f(x)$ secret.

3. Select $\alpha, a \in \mathbb{Z}_p$ randomly and compute $Y = \hat{e}_0(g_0, g_0)^{\alpha}, h = g_0^a$.
4. Publish the public parameter

$$PP = (Y, g_0, H_1, \Gamma_{(\hat{t}, \hat{n})}, Enc, Dec, Y, h)$$

and keep the master secret key $MSK = (\alpha, a, k_1, k_2)$ secret.

- **KeyGen**(PP, MSK, S, id): This algorithm takes the public parameter PP, the master secret key MSK, a data user with identifier id and a set of attribute $S = \{\lambda_1, \lambda_2, \cdots, \lambda_n\}$. TA runs this algorithm as follows:
  1. Compute $x = Enc_{k_1}(id), y = f(x), K' = c = Enc_{k_2}(x||y)$.
  2. Choose $r_i \in \mathbb{Z}_p, i = 1, 2, \cdots, n$, and compute $r = \sum_{i=1}^{n} r_i, K = g_0^{\frac{\alpha+r}{a+c}}$.
  3. Select $r' \in \mathbb{Z}_p$ and compute $L = g_0^{r'}, L' = g^{ar'}$, and $\{K_i = g_0^{r_i} \cdot H_1(\lambda_i)^{r'}, \tilde{K} = \prod_{i=1}^{n} H_1(\lambda_i)^a | \lambda_i \in S\}$.
  4. Send the secret key $SK_{S,id} = (K', K, L, L', \tilde{K}, \{K_i | \lambda_i \in S\})$ to DU.

- **Encrypt**$(PP, \mathcal{F}, k, W, \mathbb{P})$: DO takes the public parameter PP, a set of files $\mathcal{F} = \{f_1, f_2, \cdots, f_d\}$, a symmetric key $k \in \mathbb{G}_1$, a set of keyword W, and the AND gate access policy $\mathbb{P} = \{P_1, P_2, \cdots, P_n\}$ as input, where each file is encrypted as $c_l = Enc_k(f_l), l \in [1, d]$ by using of Enc defined in the *Setup* algorithm. This algorithm runs as follows:
  1. Select a random $s \in \mathbb{Z}_p$, and compute $C = k \cdot Y^s, C_{0,1} = h^s, C_{0,2} = g_0^s$. For each attribute in the AND gate $\mathbb{P}$, set $C_i = H_1(P_i)^s, i = 1, \cdots, n$.
  2. Extract a set of keywords $W = (w_1, w_2, \cdots, w_m)$ from the data files $\mathcal{F}$, select a random $s' \in \mathbb{Z}_p$ and compute $C_W = \hat{e}_0(h, g_0^{H_1(w_j)})^{s'}, j \in [1, m]$ and $C_{0,3} = (g_0^s)^{s'}$.
  3. Send the ciphertext $CT = (\{c_l\}_{l=1}^{d}, C, C_{0,1}, C_{0,2}, \{C_i\}_{i=1}^{n})$ and the index $I_W = (\{C_i\}_{i=1}^{n}, C_W, C_{0,3})$ to the cloud server.

- **Trapdoor**$(SK_{S,id}, W')$: Taking the secret key SK and an intended keyword set $W' = (w_1', w_2', \cdots, w_t')$ as input. This algorithm runs as follows:
  1. Compute a trapdoor $T_{W'} = \hat{e}_0(\tilde{K}, \prod_{j=1}^{t} g_0^{H_1(w_j')})$.
  2. Send the trapdoor $T_{W'}$ to the cloud server.

- **Test**$(I_W, T_{W'})$: This algorithm takes the index I_W and a trapdoor $T_{W'}$ as input. If the attribute list S satisfies the access policy $\mathbb{P}$, i.e. $\lambda_i \in P_i$, this algorithm runs as follows:
  1. Check whether the equation $\hat{e}_1(T_{W'}, C_{0,3}) = \hat{e}_1(\prod_{i=1}^{n} C_i, C_W)$ holds.
  2. Return 1 if the equation holds and send the corresponding ciphertext CT to the data user; otherwise return 0.

- **Decrypt**$(SK_{S,id}, CT)$: DU takes the ciphertext CT and the secret key $SK_{S,id}$ as input. If the attribute list S matches the access policy embedded in the ciphertext, i.e. $\lambda_i \in P_i$, this algorithm runs as follows:
  1. Compute the partial decryption ciphertext

$$Q_{CT} = \prod_{i=1}^{n} \frac{\hat{e}_0(K_i, C_{0,2})}{\hat{e}_0(L, C_i)} = \hat{e}_0(g_0, g_0)^{rs}.$$

2. Decrypt the symmetric key of data file $k = \dfrac{C}{\hat{e}_0(K, C_{0,1} \cdot C_{0,2}^{K'})/Q_{CT}}$.

- **Trace**$(PP, \Gamma_{(\hat{t},\hat{n})}, MSK, SK_{S,id}) \to id$ or $\bot$: This algorithm takes PP, the instance of Shamir's threshold scheme $\Gamma_{(\hat{t},\hat{n})}$, the master secret key MSK and $SK_{S,id}$ as inputs. TA runs this algorithm as follows:
  1. If $SK_{S,id}$ is not well-formed, output a symbol $\bot$.
  2. Otherwise, $SK_{S,id}$ is a well-formed, and execute the following steps:
     (a) **Step1**: Run the algorithm $Dec_{k_2}(K')$ to extract $(x^* = x', y^* = y')$.
     (b) **Step2**: Check whether $SK_{S,id}$ is issued by TA. If $(x^* = x', y^* = y') \in \{(x_1, y_1), (x_2, y_2), \cdots, (x_{\hat{t}-1}, y_{\hat{t}-1})\}$, compute $Dec_{k_1}(x^*)$ to get id to identify the malicious user directly; otherwise run the next step.
     (c) **Step3**: Compute the secret a_0^* of $\Gamma_{(\hat{t},\hat{n})}$ by interpolating with $\hat{t} - 1$ points $(x_1, y_1), (x_2, y_2), \cdots, (x_{\hat{t}-1}, y_{\hat{t}-1})$ and (x^*, y^*). If $a_0^* = f(0)$, compute $Dec_{k_1}(x^*)$ to get id to identify the malicious user; otherwise, output $\bot$.

5   Security and Performance

5.1   Correctness

Test: If $W = W'$, we have the following equation:

$$
\hat{e}_1(T_{W'}, C_{0,3}) = \hat{e}_1(\hat{e}_0(\tilde{K}, \prod_{j=1}^{t} g_0^{H_1(w_j')}), g_0^{ss'}) = \hat{e}_1(\hat{e}_0((\prod_{i=1}^{n} H_1(\lambda_i))^a, \prod_{j=1}^{t} g^{H_1(w_j')}), g_0^{ss'})
$$

$$
= \hat{e}_1(\prod_{i=1}^{n} H_1(\lambda_i)^s, \hat{e}_0(\prod_{j=1}^{t} g_0^{H_1(w_j')^{s'}}, g_0^a))
$$

$$
= \hat{e}_1(\prod_{i=1}^{n} H_1(\lambda_i)^s, \hat{e}_0(\prod_{j=1}^{t} g_0^{H_1(w_j')}, h)^{s'})
$$

$$
= \hat{e}_1(\prod_{i=1}^{n} C_i, C_W)
$$

Decryption: If the attribute list matches the access policy, i.e. $\lambda_i \in P_i$, the following equation holds:

$$
Q_{CT} = \prod_{i=1}^{n} \frac{\hat{e}_0(K_i, C_{0,2})}{\hat{e}_0(L, C_i)} = \prod_{i=1}^{n} \frac{\hat{e}_0(g_0^{r_i} H_1(\lambda_i)^{r'}, g_0^s)}{\hat{e}_0(g_0^{r'}, H_1(P_i)^s)}
$$

$$
= \frac{\hat{e}_0(g_0^{\sum_{i=1}^{n} r_i} \prod_{i=1}^{n} H_1(\lambda_i)^{r'}, g_0^s)}{\hat{e}_0(H_1(P_i)^s, g_0^{r'})}
$$

$$
= \frac{\hat{e}_0(g_0^r, g_0^s) \cdot \hat{e}_0(\prod_{i=1}^{n} H_1(\lambda_i), g_0)^{rs'}}{\hat{e}_0(H_1(P_i), g_0)^{r's}}
$$

$$
= \hat{e}_0(g_0, g_0)^{rs}
$$

$$
\frac{C}{\hat{e}_0(K, C_{0,1} \cdot C_{0,2}^{K'})/Q_{CT}} = \frac{k \cdot \hat{e}_0(g_0, g_0)^{as}}{\hat{e}_0(g_0^{\frac{\alpha+r}{a+c}}, g_0^{(a+c)s})/\hat{e}_0(g_0, g_0)^{rs}} = \frac{k \cdot \hat{e}_0(g_0, g_0)^{as}}{\hat{e}_0(g_0, g_0)^{as}} = k
$$

5.2   Security Analysis

Theorem 1. *Let* $\Upsilon = (p, \mathbb{G}_0, \mathbb{G}_1, \mathbb{G}_2, \hat{e}_0, \hat{e}_1)$ *be defined in Sect. 2.4. If any adversary* $\mathcal{A}$ *makes at most* q *oracle queries in order to compute the interaction with the IND-sCP-CKA security game, then the advantage of the adversary* $\mathcal{A}$ *in the IND-sCP-CKA security game is* $\mathcal{O}(q^2/p)$.

Proof. We initialize $g_0 = \psi_0(1), g_1 = \psi_1(1), g_2 = \psi_2(1)$. In the following queries, the adversary $\mathcal{A}$ will communicate with the simulator $\mathcal{C}$ using the ψ-representations of the group elements. $\mathcal{C}$ interacts with $\mathcal{A}$ in the security game as follows:

- **Setup:** $\mathcal{A}$ selects the challenging access policy $\mathbb{P}^*$, and then sends them to $\mathcal{C}$. $\mathcal{C}$ chooses $\alpha, a \in \mathbb{Z}_p$, computes $Y = \hat{e}_0(g_0, g_0)^\alpha, h = g_0^a$, and sends the public parameters $PP = (\Upsilon, g_0, H_1, \Gamma_{(\hat{t}, \hat{n})}, Enc, Dec, Y, h)$ to $\mathcal{A}$. Finally, $\mathcal{C}$ keeps the master secret key $MSK = (\alpha, a, k_1, k_2)$ for himself. When $\mathcal{A}$ calls for the evaluation of H_1 on any string λ_i, a new random value $t_i \in \mathbb{Z}_p$ is chosen, and the simulation provides $g_0^{t_i}$ as the response to $H_1(\lambda_i)$.
- **Phase 1:** $\mathcal{A}$ issues polynomial-time secret key queries for (S_i, id_i) and trapdoor queries as follows:
  - $\mathcal{O}_{KeyGen(S_i)}$: If S_i satisfies the chosen access policies $\mathbb{P}^*$, $\mathcal{C}$ sets $x = Enc_{k_1}(id), y = f(x), K' = c = Enc_{k_2}(x\|y)$. Then $\mathcal{C}$ selects new random values r^*, r_i^*, r'^* from $\mathbb{Z}_p$. For each attribute $\lambda_i \in S_i$, $\mathcal{C}$ computes $K_i = g_0^{r_i^* + t_i^* r'^*}, i \in [1, n], K = g_0^{\frac{\alpha + r^*}{a + c}}, L = g_0^{r'^*}, L' = g_0^{ar'^*}$ and $\tilde{K} = g_0^{a(\sum\limits_{i=1}^{n} t_i^*)}$. The secret key is well formulated as

$$SK^*_{S,id} = (K', K, L, L', \tilde{K}, \{K_i | \lambda_i \in S\}).$$

  - $\mathcal{O}_{Trapdoor}(S_i, W')$: On $\mathcal{A}$'s trapdoor query for set $S_i = \{\lambda_1, \lambda_2, \cdots, \lambda_n\}$ and a keyword set W', $\mathcal{C}$ generates a trapdoor of the chosen keyword w'_j as:

$$T_{W'} = \hat{e}_0(\tilde{K}, \prod_{j=1}^{t} g_0^{H_1(w'_j)}) = \hat{e}_0(g_0^{a(\sum\limits_{i=1}^{n} t_i^*)}, \prod_{j=1}^{t} g_0^{H_1(w'_j)}).$$

    And then sends the trapdoor to $\mathcal{A}$.
- **Challenge:** $\mathcal{A}$ issues a keyword set $W_0 = \{w_{j_0}\}_{j \in [1,m]}$ and $W_1 = \{w_{j_1}\}_{j \in [1,m]}$ that it wishes to be challenged on. $\mathcal{A}$ gives a challenging access policy $\mathbb{P}^*$. For each attribute in the AND gate $\mathbb{P}^*$, $\mathcal{C}$ selects random number $s, s' \in \mathbb{Z}_p$, computes $C_i = g_0^{t_i s}, i \in [1, n], C_W = \hat{e}_0(h, y_0^{H_1(w_{i_b}) s'}), C_{0,3} = g_0^{ss'}$. And sends the challenge index $I_W^* = (C_i, C_W, C_{0,3})$ to $\mathcal{A}$.
- **Phase 2:** The same as Phase 1 with the restriction $W_0 \neq W_1$ and the attribute set S_i satisfies the challenging access policy $\mathbb{P}^*$.
- **Guess:** $\mathcal{A}$ outputs guess b of b, where $b' \in \{0, 1\}$.

In the IND-sCP-CKA game, $\mathcal{A}$ can query at most q times and attempts to distinguish $\hat{e}_0(h, g_0^{H_1(w_{j_1})s'})$ from $\hat{e}_0(h, g_0^{H_1(w_{j_b})s'})$. We can instead consider a modified game in which the real challenging ciphertext via substituting $\hat{e}_0(h, g_0^{H_1(w_{j_b})s'})$ for $\hat{e}_0(g_0, g_0)^\theta$. The probability for distinguish $\hat{e}_0(h, g_0^{H_1(w_{j_1})s'})$ from $\hat{e}_0(g_0, g_0)^\theta$ is equal to half of the probability for distinguishing $\hat{e}_0(h, g_0^{H_1(w_{j_0})s'})$ from $\hat{e}_0(h, g_0^{H_1(w_{j_1})s'})$.

Next, we describe a detail analysis of $\mathcal{C}$'s simulation. We say that $\mathcal{C}$'s simulation is perfect as long as no "unexpected collision" happens. The probability that "unexpected collision" occurs at most $\mathcal{O}(q^2/p)$ before substitution by the Schwartz-Zipple lemma [19]. Now we show that the adversary's view would have been identically distributed even if $\mathcal{C}$ substitutes as' for variable θ. Since θ only occurs as $\hat{e}_0(g_0, g_0)^\theta$, we must have that $\nu - \nu' = \gamma as' - \gamma'\theta$. We show that the adversary can almost never construct a query for $\hat{e}_0(g_0, g_0)^{\gamma as'}$, and analysis the following two cases: (1) To construct as', $\mathcal{A}$ can pairing sa with ss' if and only if $s = 1$. The probability $\Pr[s = 1]$ is $\mathcal{O}(1/p)$; (2) $\mathcal{A}$ can query the trapdoor $T_{W'}$ of form $\hat{e}_0(g_0, g_0)^{a\left(\sum_{i=1}^{n} t_i^*\right)t^*}$, which can be used to construct the term as'. By the Schwartz-Zipple lemma, the probability $\Pr[(\sum_{i=1}^{n} t_i^*)t^* = s']$ is at most $\mathcal{O}(q^2/p)$.

Theorem 2. *If the φ-SDH assumption holds, then our privacy-preserving attribute-based multi-keyword search encryption scheme with user tracing scheme is fully traceable on condition that $q_t < \varphi$.*

Proof. Suppose that there exists a polynomial-time adversary $\mathcal{A}$ that has nonnegligible advantage in winning the traceability game after making q_t key queries ($\varphi = q_t + 1$), we construct a polynomial-time algorithm $\mathcal{C}$ that has non-negligible advantage in breaking the φ-SDH assumption.

$\mathcal{C}$ is given an instance $(g_0, g_0^x, g_0^{x^2}, \cdots, g_0^{x^\varphi})$. It aims at outputting a tuple $(c_i, v_i) \in \mathbb{Z}_p \times \mathbb{G}_0$ satisfying $v_i = g_0^{1/(a+c_i)}$ for solving φ-SDH problem. Before starting the traceability game with $\mathcal{A}$, $\mathcal{C}$ takes $(\mathbb{G}_0, \mathbb{G}_1, p, g_0, g_0^a, g_0^{a^2}, \cdots, g_0^{a^\varphi})$ as inputs and sets $B_i = g_0^{a^i}, i = 0, 1, \cdots, \varphi$, then interacts with $\mathcal{A}$ in the traceability game as follows:

- **Setup:** $\mathcal{C}$ initializes an instance of Shamir's threshold scheme $\Gamma_{(\hat{t},\hat{n})}$ and keeps $\hat{t} - 1$ points $(x_1, y_1), (x_2, y_2), \cdots, (x_{\hat{t}-1}, y_{\hat{t}-1})$ on $f(x)$ and a polynomial $f(x)$ secret. Then, $\mathcal{C}$ chooses random $\alpha, a \in \mathbb{Z}_p$, computes $Y = \hat{e}_0(g_0, g_0)^\alpha, h = g_0^a$, and gives $PP = (g_0, H_1, \Gamma_{(\hat{t},\hat{n})}, Enc, Dec, Y, h)$ to $\mathcal{A}$.
- **Key Query:** $\mathcal{A}$ submits (S_i, id_i) to $\mathcal{C}$ to query a secret key. When it comes to the i-th query, we assume $i \leq q_t$. Let $f_i(x) = f(x)/(x + c_i) = \prod_{j=1, j \neq i}^{q_t} (x + c_j)$. Expand $f_i(x)$ and write $f_i(x) = \sum_{j=0}^{q_t-1} \beta_j x^j$. $\mathcal{C}$ computes $\sigma_i = \prod_{j=0}^{q_t-1} (B_j)^{\beta_j} = g_0^{f_i(a)} = g_0^{f(a)/(a+c_i)} = g_0^{1/(a+c_i)}, x = Enc_{k_1}(id), y = f(x), K' = c =$

$Enc_{k_2}(x||y)$. $\mathcal{C}$ chooses $r_i, r' \in \mathbb{Z}_p$ randomly, computes $r = \sum_{i=1}^{n} r_i$, $K =$
$g_0^{\frac{\alpha+r}{a+c}}, L = g_0^{r'}, L' = g_0^{ar'}, \tilde{K} = \prod_{i=1}^{n} H_1(\lambda_i)^a, \{K_i = g_0^{r_i} \cdot H_1(\lambda_i)^{r'}|\lambda_i \in S\}$,
and gives $SK_{S,id}^* = (K, K', L, L', \tilde{K}, \{K_i|\lambda_i \in S\})$ to $\mathcal{A}$.

- **Key Forgery**: $\mathcal{A}$ submits a secret key $SK_{S,id}^*$ to $\mathcal{C}$. Let $\epsilon_\mathcal{A}$ denotes the event that $\mathcal{A}$ wins the game. If $\epsilon_\mathcal{A}$ does not happen, $\mathcal{C}$ chooses a random tuple $(c_s, v_s) \in \mathbb{Z}_p \times \mathbb{G}_0$ as the solution to φ-SDH problem. If $\epsilon_\mathcal{A}$ happens, using long division, $\mathcal{C}$ writes the polynomial f as $f(x) = \gamma(x)(x + K') + \gamma - 1$ for some polynomial $\gamma(x) = \sum_{i=0}^{q_t}(\gamma_i x_i)$ and some $\gamma - 1 \in \mathbb{Z}_p, (\gamma - 1 \neq 0)$. And $\mathcal{C}$ computes a tuple $(c_s, v_s) \in \mathbb{Z}_p \times \mathbb{G}_0$ as follows. If $\gcd(\gamma - 1, p) = 1$, assume $L = g_0^{r'}$, where $r' \in Z_p$ is unknown, we have $L' = g_0^{ar'}$. Then $\mathcal{C}$ computes $1/(\gamma - 1) \mod p$ and gets the following (c_s, v_s): $\sigma = K^{(\alpha+r)^{-1}} = g_0^{1/(a+K')} = g_0^{f(a)/(a+K')} = g_0^{\gamma(a)} g_0^{\frac{\gamma-1}{a+K'}}, v_s = (\sigma \cdot \prod_{i=0}^{q_t-1} B_i^{-\gamma_i})^{\frac{1}{\gamma-1}} = g_0^{\frac{1}{a+K'}}, c_s = K'$ $\mod p \in \mathbb{Z}_p$. Therefore (c_s, v_s) is a solution for the φ-SDH problem. Otherwise, $\mathcal{C}$ chooses a random tuple $(c_s, v_s) \in \mathbb{Z}_p \times \mathbb{G}_0$ as the solution to φ-SDH problem.

Next, we analysis the advantage of $\mathcal{C}$ in breaking φ-SDH assumption. Let $\epsilon_{SDH}(c_s, v_s)$ denote the event that (c_s, v_s) is a solution for the φ-SDH problem, which can be verified by checking whether $\hat{e}_0(g_0^a \cdot g_0^{c_s}, v_s) = \hat{e}_0(g_0, g_0)$ holds. Therefore, $\mathcal{C}$ solves the φ-SDH problem with the probability

$$\Pr[\epsilon_{SDH}(c_s, v_s)]$$
$$= \Pr[\epsilon_{SDH}(c_s, v_s)|\overline{\mathcal{A} \ win}] \cdot \Pr[\overline{\mathcal{A} \ win}]$$
$$+ \Pr[\epsilon_{SDH}(c_s, v_s)|\mathcal{A} \ win \wedge \gcd(\gamma - 1, p) \neq 1] \cdot \Pr[\mathcal{A} \ win \wedge \gcd(\gamma - 1, p) \neq 1]$$
$$+ \Pr[\epsilon_{SDH}(c_s, v_s)|\mathcal{A} \ win \wedge \gcd(\gamma - 1, p) = 1] \cdot \Pr[\mathcal{A} \ win \wedge \gcd(\gamma - 1, p) = 1]$$
$$= 0 + 0 + 1 \cdot \Pr[\mathcal{A} \ win \wedge \gcd(\gamma - 1, p) = 1]$$
$$= \Pr[\mathcal{A} \ win \wedge \gcd(\gamma - 1, p) = 1]$$
$$= \Pr[\mathcal{A} \ win] \cdot \Pr[\gcd(\gamma - 1, p) = 1]$$
$$= \epsilon_\mathcal{A}.$$

5.3 Performance Analysis

In this section, we will give the performance analysis from the perspective of functionalities, computational cost, and efficiency analysis. In Table 1, we define the symbols that will be used in this section.

Functionalities. We compare the proposed scheme with some existing ABKSE schemes in features of keyword search, constant-size ciphertext, hidden-policy, multi-keyword search and traceability. From Table 2, scheme [10] can only support keyword search. scheme [13] can achieve keyword search and hidden-policy, but not support fast multi-keyword search, traceability and the constant-size ciphertext. Compared with the above two schemes, the functionalities of the proposed scheme are better.

Computational Cost. We compare the computational costs with Zheng et al.'s scheme [10] and Qiu et al.'s scheme [13]. Since the operation cost over $\mathbb{Z}_p$ is much less than group and pairing operation, we ignore the computational time over $\mathbb{Z}_p$ and only focus on the computation cost of costly operations: bilinear pairing and exponentiation operation. From Table 3, the computational cost of our scheme is similar to that of scheme [10] and [13] in the *KeyGen* algorithm. During the *Encrypt* algorithm, since we add the pairing operation in encrypting the keyword index, the computational overhead is less efficient than scheme [10] and [13]. In the *Trapdoor* algorithm, the computational cost of our scheme needs one pairing operation and t exponentiation operation, which is a little efficient than the other two schemes. In the *Test* algorithm, the computational cost of our scheme is less than that of scheme [10] and [13].

Efficiency Analysis. We implement the proposed scheme on a Windows machine with Intel Core 2 processor running at 3.30 GHz and 4.00G memory. The running environment of our scheme is Java Runtime Environment 1.7, and the Java Virtual Machine (JVM) used to compile our programming is 64 bit which brings into correspondence with our operation system. We select the Type A curves in the pairing-based cryptography library [20].

Table 1. Notations used in performance analysis

Notations	Description
P	The pairing operation
E	The group exponentiation in $\mathbb{G}_0$
E_T	The group exponentiation in $\mathbb{G}_1$
n	The number of system attributes in the system
t	The number of keywords a data user wants to search for

Table 2. Comparisons of the functionalities

	Zheng et al.'s scheme [10]	Qiu et al.'s scheme [13]	Ours
Keyword search	$\checkmark$	$\checkmark$	$\checkmark$
Constant-size ciphertext	$\times$	$\times$	$\checkmark$
Fast multi-keyword search	$\times$	$\times$	$\checkmark$
Hidden-policy	$\times$	$\checkmark$	$\checkmark$
Traceability	$\times$	$\times$	$\checkmark$

Table 3. Computational cost comparisons

Operations	Zheng et al.'s scheme [10]	Qiu et al.'s scheme [13]	Ours
KeyGen	$(2n+2)E$	$(2n+1)E+E_T$	$(2n+2)E$
Encrypt	$(2n+4)E$	$(2n+1)E+2E_T$	$(n+4)E+2E_T+P$
Trapdoor	$(2n+4)E$	$(2n+1)E$	$P+tE$
Test	$(2n+3)P+nE_T$	$(2n+1)P+E_T$	$2P+nE$

In our experiments, the modulus of the elements in the group is chosen to be 512 bits. Assume that the number of attributes in the system is n, and n ranges from 10 to 50. From Fig. 2, the search time of scheme [10] and [13] is increasing linearly with respect to the number of included attributes. However, the search time of our scheme is less than the other two schemes. For example, we set the number of attributes in system $n = 30$, our scheme only needs 71 ms to search, while scheme [10] costs 1068 ms and scheme [13] needs 966 ms. Therefore, compared with the above two schemes, the proposed scheme is more suitable for practical application and efficient.

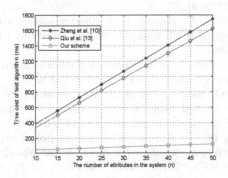

Fig. 2. Comparison of keyword search efficiency.

6 Conclusions

In this paper, we have proposed a privacy-preserving attribute-based multi-keyword encryption with user tracing. In the proposed scheme, the access policy embedded in the ciphertext can be hidden in the encryption phase, and the size of ciphertext is constant. Meanwhile, the proposed scheme can achieve the fast multi-keyword search. In addition, the trusted authority can trace the malicious users directly when the malicious users leak their secret keys to the unauthorized users. The security analysis has demonstrated that the proposed scheme is selectively security and fully traceable. Performance analysis shows that our scheme is efficient and practical.

Acknowledgments. This work is supported by the National Natural Science Foundation of China under Grants No. 61807026, the Natural Science Basic Research Plan in Shaanxi Province of China under Grant No. 2019JM-198, the Plan For Scientific Innovation Talent of Henan Province under Grant No. 184100510012, and in part by the Program for Science and Technology Innovation Talents in the Universities of Henan Province under Grant No. 18HASTIT022.

References

1. Song, D., Wagner, D., Perrig, A.: Practical techniques for searches on encrypted data. In: Proceedings of IEEE Symposium on Security and Privacy, pp. 44–55. IEEE, Berkeley (2000)
2. Boneh, D., Di Crescenzo, G., Ostrovsky, R., Persiano, G.: Public key encryption with keyword search. In: Cachin, C., Camenisch, J.L. (eds.) EUROCRYPT 2004. LNCS, vol. 3027, pp. 506–522. Springer, Heidelberg (2004). https://doi.org/10.1007/978-3-540-24676-3_30
3. Cao, N., Wang, C., Li, M., et al.: Privacy-preserving multi-keyword ranked search over encrypted cloud data. IEEE Trans. Parallel Distrib. Syst. **25**(1), 222–233 (2011)
4. Sahai, A., Waters, B.: Fuzzy identity-based encryption. In: Cramer, R. (ed.) EUROCRYPT 2005. LNCS, vol. 3494, pp. 457–473. Springer, Heidelberg (2005). https://doi.org/10.1007/11426639_27
5. Bethencourt, J., Sahai, A., Waters, B.: Ciphertext-policy attribute-based encryption. In: Proceedings of IEEE Symposium on Security and Privacy, pp. 321–334. ACM, Berkeley (2007)
6. Wang, H., Dong, X., Cao, Z., et al.: Secure and efficient attribute-based encryption with keyword search. Comput. J. **61**(8), 1133–1142 (2018)
7. Goyal, V., Pandey, O., Sahai, A., et al.: Attribute-based encryption for fine-grained access control of encrypted data. In: Proceedings of the 13th ACM Conference on Computer and Communications Security, pp. 89–98. ACM, Alexandria (2006)
8. Wang, C., Li, W., Li, Y., Xu, X.: A ciphertext-policy attribute-based encryption scheme supporting keyword search function. In: Wang, G., Ray, I., Feng, D., Rajarajan, M. (eds.) CSS 2013. LNCS, vol. 8300, pp. 377–386. Springer, Cham (2013). https://doi.org/10.1007/978-3-319-03584-0_28
9. Sun, W., Yu, S., Lou, W., et al.: Protecting your right: verifiable attribute-based keyword search with fine-grained owner-enforced search authorization in the cloud. IEEE Trans. Parallel Distrib. Syst. **27**(4), 1187–1198 (2016)
10. Zheng, Q., Xu, S., Ateniese, G.: VABKS: verifiable attribute-based keyword search over outsourced encrypted data. In: Proceedings of IEEE Conference on Computer Communications, pp. 522–530. IEEE, Toronto (2014)
11. Miao, Y., Ma, J., Liu, X., et al.: m2-ABKS: attribute-based multi-keyword search over encrypted personal health records in multi-owner setting. J. Med. Syst. **40**(11), 1–12 (2016)
12. Wang, S., Jia, S., Zhang, Y.: Verifiable and multi-keyword searchable attribute-based encryption scheme for cloud storage. IEEE Access **7**, 50136–50147 (2019)
13. Qiu, S., Liu, J., Shi, Y., et al.: Hidden policy ciphertext-policy attribute-based encryption with keyword search against keyword guessing attack. Sci. China Inf. Sci. **60**(5), 1 (2016)

14. Chaudhari, P., Das, M.: Privacy preserving searchable encryption with fine-grained access control. IEEE Trans. Cloud Comput. (2019). https://doi.org/10.1109/TCC.2019.2892116
15. Liu, Z., Cao, Z., Wong, D.: White-box traceable ciphertextpolicy attribute-based encryption supporting any monotone access structures. IEEE Trans. Inf. Forensics Secur. **8**(1), 76–88 (2013)
16. Ning, J., Dong, X., Cao, Z., et al.: White-box traceable ciphertext-policy attribute-based encryption supporting flexible attributes. IEEE Trans. Inf. Forensics Secur. **10**(6), 1274–1288 (2015)
17. Wang, H., Dong, X., Cao, Z.: Multi-value-independent ciphertext-policy attribute based encryption with fast keyword search. IEEE Trans. Serv. Comput. (2017). https://doi.org/10.1109/TSC.2017.2753231
18. Boneh, D., Boyen, X., Goh, E.-J.: Hierarchical identity based encryption with constant size ciphertext. In: Cramer, R. (ed.) EUROCRYPT 2005. LNCS, vol. 3494, pp. 440–456. Springer, Heidelberg (2005). https://doi.org/10.1007/11426639_26
19. Schwartz, J.: Fast probabilistic algorithms for verification of polynomial identities. J. ACM **27**(4), 701–717 (1980)
20. Caro, A., Iovino, V.: JPBC: Java pairing based cryptography. In: Proceedings of 2011 IEEE Symposium on Computers and Communications, pp. 850–855. IEEE, Kerkyra (2011)

Authentication

Facial Localization Based on Skin Color Modeling

Wei Li and Nan Li[✉]

Shenyang University of Technology, Shenyang, China
569666325@qq.com

Abstract. In recent years, due to the application value of facial localization in the fields of secure access control, visual monitoring and content-based retrieval, it has gradually received the attention of researchers. In this thesis, facial region localization is mainly carried out by modeling the skin color. This method obtains the missed detection rate (20.28%) and the false detection rate (14.80%) by performing repeated experiments on 100 facial color images in the FERET face database. Compared with the other two methods, the accuracy and real-time of the integrated facial localization, the facial localization based on skin color modeling has a better detection effect.

Keywords: Facial localization · Skin color detection · Skin color modeling · Euler number

1 Introduction

In recent years, facial localization technology has attracted widespread attention in many fields such as computer vision, pattern recognition, and human-computer interaction. The increasing demand for various applications based on facial processing makes facial localization technology of great significance in the field of computer vision and the like. The research on facial image processing is mainly divided into: facial localization, facial recognition and expression analysis. Among them, face detection and localization is the key to facial research. Only accurate localization can make face recognition and expression recognition better.

Facial localization refers to the use of a computer to analyze the input image to locate the entire area of the face. At present, the research on related algorithms of facial localization is mainly divided into two categories, methods based on explicit features and methods based on implicit features. Among them, the methods based on explicit features mainly include methods based on skin color modeling, methods based on template matching and methods based on knowledge. The method based on skin color modeling is to use skin color to detect human face. Because the color is the most obvious on the facial surface, the detection is more accurate. The method based on template matching is to predefine a standard facial template by calculating the image and template to locate the face area, but the size of the template is artificially set, so it can not be dynamically positioned, and the versatility is low. The knowledge-based approach uses a face mosaic that conforms to the facial physiology to create a knowledge base about the face and detect whether it meets the prior knowledge of the

J. Vaidya et al. (Eds.): CSS 2019, LNCS 11983, pp. 401–408, 2019.
https://doi.org/10.1007/978-3-030-37352-8_35

face in the knowledge base, but when the knowledge of the face is converted into a rule, the rule cannot be accurately defined, so the correct rate cannot be guaranteed. The methods based on implicit features mainly include feature face method, artificial neural network method, support vector machine method and integral image feature method. But due to system restrictions, the detection speed is low. At present, there is no unified standard to quantitatively evaluate the performance of various algorithms, and it depends on the development of related disciplines such as artificial intelligence to provide higher technical support.

This thesis mainly uses the method based on skin color modeling in the explicit feature method to realize the research of facial localization. Convert RGB color space to YCbCr color space. The skin color Gaussian model is established by collecting the skin color data, and all the skin color regions included in the input image are discriminated by the Gaussian model, and the number of holes existing in the connected region is further calculated by the Euler number to determine the face region.

2 Facial Localization Based on Skin Color Information

2.1 Color Space Conversion

In color images, color is one of the most prominent features of the face, so the application of skin color modeling to identify faces is becoming more and more widespread due to the important characteristics of skin color. Of course, the skin color model is related to the color space. In addition to the RGB color space, there are other color spaces such as HIS, Luv, GLHS, and YCbCr. Different color spaces are used to create the skin color model, and the clustering effects are also different. Therefore, selecting a color space with good clustering effect to establish the skin color model is very important for the subsequent skin color segmentation. The accuracy of skin color segmentation will affect the success of facial localization based on color information.

In this thesis, YCbCr color space is used. YCbCr color space can separate brightness and chromaticity and provide a compact skin color cluster. Therefore, the input color image is subjected to color space conversion, and is converted from the RGB space with high color component correlation to the YCbCr color space with small color component correlation. The conversion formula for RGB and YCbCr is:

$$
\begin{bmatrix} Y \\ C_b \\ C_r \\ 1 \end{bmatrix} = \begin{bmatrix} 0.2990 & 0.5870 & 0.1140 & 0 \\ -0.1687 & -0.3313 & 0.5000 & 128 \\ 0.5000 & -0.4187 & -0.0813 & 128 \\ 0 & 0 & 0 & 1 \end{bmatrix} \begin{bmatrix} R \\ G \\ B \\ 1 \end{bmatrix} \tag{1}
$$

2.2 Skin Color Gaussian Modeling

Skin color is a stable feature inherent in human face. It is not affected by the texture, scale, direction, posture and expression changes of the face. As long as there is a difference in color between the face and the background, the face region can be separated by constructing a suitable skin color model.

Depending on the skin color information, accurate and reliable detection of the face area involves four key issues. The color of the skin color varies depending on the individual, gender and ethnicity. Choosing the right color space can make different skin colors. The difference in description is small, and the description of non-skin and skin color is quite different, that is, the selection of color space. For some colors, if the Euclidean distance is used to measure the difference in color, it is likely to accept a lot of non-skinned colors, that is, the problem of skin color distance measurement. The skin color region is not yet a face region, but it is only a candidate region of the face region, that is, how to select the region in which the face exists in the candidate region with an indeterminate number of regions. In some cases, the obtained facial area is too large or incomplete, that is, the area optimization problem is obtained for the obtained facial area.

Because YCbCr color space is obtained by linear transformation of RGB, it is generally considered that the Y channel does not contain color information, and the skin color has good clustering characteristics on the CbCr plane, so using this feature is the key to skin color modeling and segmentation of faces. The histogram distribution of a typical skin color in the CbCr space is shown in Fig. 1. The distribution of skin color is basically a Gaussian shape, so a single Gaussian model is used to describe the skin color. An ideal Gaussian model corresponding to the above real skin color distribution is shown in Fig. 2.

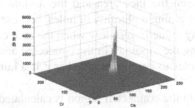 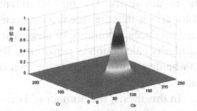

Fig. 1. Distribution of Skin Pixels in Cb-Cr Space   **Fig. 2.** Ideal skin color Gaussian model

2.3 Skin Color Area Discrimination

The Gaussian function is used to describe the probability that a pixel belongs to the skin color. In fact, the Gaussian function is used as a distance measurement function between the current pixel color value and the ideal skin color center color value. The characteristics of the Gaussian function make the distance metrics have higher tolerance for similar colors, and when the color difference is greater than a certain limit, the similarity probability decreases rapidly, so as to minimize the interference color introduction. The single Gaussian skin color modeling method is a simple and effective skin color detection method and is widely used. The specific steps of constructing skin color Gaussian modeling and calculating the probability that a pixel belongs to skin color are as follows:

1. Determine two unknown parameters of the two-dimensional Gaussian model N(M, C), that is, the mean vector and the covariance matrix, the formula of the mean vector and the covariance matrix are defined as follows:

$$M = (\overline{C_b}, \overline{C_r}) \tag{2}$$

$$C = cov(C_b, C_r) = \begin{pmatrix} \sigma_{C_b}^2 & \sigma_{C_b}\sigma_{C_r} \\ \sigma_{C_r}\sigma_{C_b} & \sigma_{C_r}^2 \end{pmatrix} \tag{3}$$

In the above formula, $\overline{C_b} = \frac{1}{N}\sum_{i=1}^{N} C_{bi}$, $\overline{C_r} = \frac{1}{N}\sum_{i=1}^{N} C_{ri}$, N is the number of pixels used for Gaussian modeling.

2. Based on the skin color Gaussian model, the probability that a single pixel belongs to the skin color is defined as follows

$$p(x|skin) = \frac{1}{(2\pi)^{\frac{n}{2}}|C|^{\frac{1}{2}}} \exp\left(-\frac{1}{2}(x-M)^T C^{-1}(x-M)\right) \tag{4}$$

In addition to the area exclusion, the center position, and the aspect ratio for area exclusion, the face area detection requires further determination of the area that satisfies the requirements. The biggest difference between the face area and the normal skin color area is that the face is a connected area containing a plurality of holes, because the face produces a plurality of areas where the gray value is very low when the skin color similarity calculation is performed. By analyzing the topology in the connected area, it can be determined whether the area contains holes to determine whether it is a human face.

In this thesis, the number of holes existing in the connected region is calculated by using the image Euler number, and the discrimination of the face area is realized in this way. The relationship between the Euler number and the number of image holes is defined as follows:

$$E = C - H \tag{5}$$

In the above formula, E is the Euler number, C is the number of connected components, and H is the number of holes in the area. Since only one area to be tested is examined at a time, the number of connected components is always 1, so the area in the area to be inspected The number of holes can be obtained by:

$$H = 1 - E \tag{6}$$

3   Implementation of Facial Localization

In this thesis, color skin samples are collected to determine the skin color Gaussian model. The skin color model is used to determine the probability of belonging to the skin area. First, the image is preprocessed to obtain the face candidate area. Then calculate the Euler number in the candidate area and determines the final face area, thereby achieving facial localization.

Using 100 facial color images in the FERET face database as the source of the face area, repeated experiments on them. The rate of missed detection and false detection rate were obtained, and compared with the other two methods, the detection effect of the facial localization were compared. A flowchart of facial localization in this thesis is shown in Fig. 3.

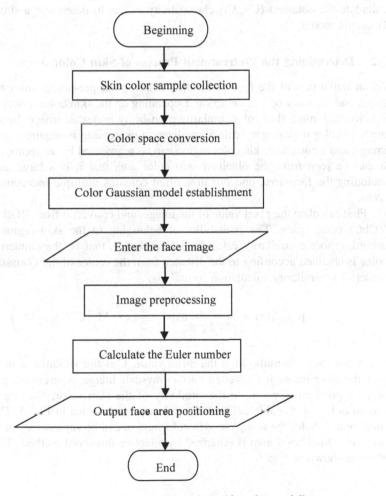

Fig. 3. Facial localization flowchart based on skin color modeling

3.1 Skin Color Sample Collection

Skin color sample selection directly affects the effect of face detection. In order to accurately count the skin color clustering features of the facial region, this paper uses the FERET face database for skin color sample collection. The FERET face database is created by the FERET project. This image set contains a large number of face images, and each image has only one human face, in the database, each person's image contains different expressions, lighting, posture and age changes. The FERET face database includes more than 10,000 face images and is one of the most widely used face databases in the field of face recognition.

Firstly, 100 color images are selected from the FERET face database as the source of the face region. After dividing the images, the skin color pixel values are obtained, and the RGB values of the segmented face regions are converted into the YCbCr color space to obtain each skin color pixel. The chromaticity values (Cb, Cr) are used to calculate the obtained (Cb, Cr) chromaticity values to determine a simple skin color Gaussian model.

3.2 Determining the Pretreatment Process of Skin Color Area

As an initial part of the face detection process, good pre-processing can improve the speed and accuracy of face detection. Depending on the skin color model, a color image is converted into a skin color similarity probability grayscale image. In order to extract the skin color region, grayscale normalization processing is required for the grayscale image, and a complete skin color region can be segmented by an appropriate threshold. It can be seen from the obtained skin color area that it is a large candidate range including the face area, and this area often contains multiple independent connected areas.

First calculate the pixel value of the image, and convert it from RGB color space to YCbCr color space. The probability of belonging to the skin region is calculated according to the similarity calculation formula (7), that is, the similarity of the skin color is obtained according to the distance from the center of the Gaussian distribution center. The similarity calculation formula is:

$$p(x|skin) = \frac{1}{(2\pi)^{\frac{n}{2}}|C|^{\frac{1}{2}}} \exp\left(-\frac{1}{2}(x - M)^{T} C^{-1} (x - M)\right) \qquad (7)$$

In the above formula, M is the mean value, C is the variance, x is $(C_b, C_r)^{T}$, and then the color image is converted into a grayscale image, wherein the grayscale value of each pixel corresponds to the similarity of the skin color, the original image As shown in Fig. 4, the skin color likelihood map is as shown in Fig. 5. Then, through a suitable threshold, the complete skin color region can be segmented. In this paper, the skin color likelihood map is binarized by adaptive threshold method. The binarization effect is shown in Fig. 6.

Fig. 4. The original image   **Fig. 5.** Skin color likelihood map   **Fig. 6.** Binarized image

3.3 Face Area Discrimination

After the original image is preprocessed to obtain a binarized image, a candidate region of the face is obtained, and the face region is further obtained by Euler number. Under normal circumstances, the face area will include holes in the non-skin area such as eyes, eyebrows, and mouth. The so-called Euler number is the number of holes in the image.

By calculating whether or not the hole is included in the connected region, a true face region is finally selected in the face candidate region, and the face candidate region is as shown in Fig. 7, and the result of the face region discrimination is as shown in Fig. 8.

Fig. 7. Face candidate area   **Fig. 8.** Face location result

3.4 Face Localization Result Analysis

In order to verify the superiority of face positioning based on skin color modeling, this thesis compares HBEL ellipse template matching method and GA-BP neural network method. The results are shown in Table 1. The method of HBEL ellipse template matching has high missed detection rate and false detection rate. This method has higher requirements on the orientation of the face. Therefore, misjudgment may occur in the case of a face or a non-positive face region in the image.

Although the method in this thesis is slightly higher than the missed detection rate and false detection rate of GA-BP neural network method, the positioning process of GA-BP neural network solves the computational complexity and affects the speed of facial localization. The real-time nature of face positioning is not guaranteed.

Table 1. Statistics of experimental results of the three methods

Method	Missed detection rate (%)	False detection rate (%)
HBEL ellipse template matching [2]	24.86	25.43
GA-BP neural network [4]	18.53	13.86
Method in this thesis	20.28	14.80

4   Conclusion

The content in this thesis is the basic work of facial research. It is proved by experiments that the skin color Gaussian model can distinguish the skin color region well and has fewer restrictions on the facial region in the image, and it has a good localization effect on facial images in different backgrounds.

There are still have problems in facial localization based on skin color modeling, the accuracy of special cases such as wearing glasses and hair occlusion is low, and this problem needs to be solved in the future.

References

1. Zou, G., Fu, G., et al.: Summary of multi-pose face recognition. Pattern Recogn. Artif. Intell. **28**(7), 613–624 (2015). Author, F., Author, S.: Title of a proceedings paper. In: Editor, F., Editor, S. (eds.) Conference 2016, LNCS, vol. 9999, pp. 1–13. Springer, Heidelberg (2016)
2. Liu, W., Zhu, J., et al.: Fast face localization based on integral projection. J. Comput. Aided Des. Motion **31**(4), 36–42 (2017). Author, F.: Contribution title. In: 9th International Proceedings on Proceedings, pp. 1–2. Publisher, Location (2010)
3. Mahmoodi, M.R., Sayedi, S.M.: Color_based skin segmentation in videos using a multi-step spatial method. Multimedia Tools Appl. **76**(7), 9785–9801 (2017)
4. Qingsong, Z.: Application of multi-core support vector domain description in face recognition based on image set matching. J. Image Graph. **21**(8), 1021–1027 (2016)
5. Liang, H., Yi, S., et al.: Real-time expression recognition based on pixel mode and feature point mode. J. Image Graph. **22**(12), 1737–1749 (2017)
6. Song, W., Wu, D., Xi, Y.: Motion-based skin region of interest detection with a real-time connected component labeling algorithm. Multimedia Tools Appl. **76**(9), 11199–11214 (2017)

A Textual Password Entry Method Resistant to Human Shoulder-Surfing Attack

Shudi Chen[1] and Youwen Zhu[1,2(✉)]

[1] College of Computer Science and Technology, Nanjing University of Aeronautics
and Astronautics, Nanjing 211106, China
zhuyw@nuaa.edu.cn
[2] Collaborative Innovation Center of Novel Software Technology
and Industrialization, Nanjing 210023, China

Abstract. Textual password is one of the most widely used authentication methods today. However, entering password in public is vulnerable to shoulder-surfing attacks. The attacker can observe or use the device to record the authentication session to obtain the password. Then the account is invaded and that will cause loss of data and property to the user. In this paper, we propose a new method MapPass for human shoulder-surfing resistant textual password entry by significantly increasing the limitation of cognitive ability of the attacker. Besides, we put forward the concept of attack alert, that is, the system can detect the failed shoulder-surfing attack and timely remind the user. We add this function to the method MapPass to improve the security of the method. Additionally, we analyze the security and usability of the proposed method.

Keywords: Shoulder-surfing attack · Password entry · Identity authentication · Information security

1 Introduction

Password is one of the well-known authentication methods used in many situations, such as accessing a personal account and unlocking a mobile device. Nowadays people attach great importance to privacy protection [1], and password is an important means of privacy protection [2]. In a regular authentication, the user inputs a textual password or a graphical password on the system interface [3]. However, the entry process is vulnerable to shoulder-surfing attacks which refer to attacks that obtain private information by observing others [4]. That is to say, when the user enters the password in unsafe environments such as public places, anyone around him/her can easily obtain the password by looking or recording the login procedure. Textual passwords are limited in length so that they are convenient for users to remember. But this advantage makes the attacker to memorize the user's password easily too. A simple and memorable textual password may be memorized by an attacker at one attack.

© Springer Nature Switzerland AG 2019
J. Vaidya et al. (Eds.): CSS 2019, LNCS 11983, pp. 409–420, 2019.
https://doi.org/10.1007/978-3-030-37352-8_36

Passwords are the security of many kinds of accounts, even bank accounts [5]. Once they are disclosed, users will suffer heavy losses of information and property [6]. In addition, many users use the same password or similar passwords on their other accounts, which makes the problem more serious [4]. Therefore, it is necessary to design an advanced password entry method to protect identity authentication security.

Some of the schemes focus on textual password [7–11], some focus on graphical password [12–14] and some focus on PIN [3,4,15–18]. There are also methods that change the form of password, such as combining PIN with color or gaze gesture [19,20]. Instead of directly entering the password, these schemes adopt their own secret transfer approaches to separate the visible password entry process from the secret itself.

The first kind of schemes utilize the limitation of the cognitive ability of the attacker to design the method. They significantly increases the amount of short term memory required in the attack. In the textual password scheme proposed by Matsumoto and Imai [9], the system and the user share a password and an ordered symbol set in secret. The user has memorized the additional symbol set in advance and does proper character substitutions in the authentication, which will fatigue the user. The PIN entry method proposed by Lee [15] and ColorPIN [19] cannot resist intersection attacks.

The second kind of schemes avoid full exposure of interaction information in an authentication session by using auxiliary channels. Vibrapass [10] uses the vibration signal to indicate the user to input correct or error character. This scheme cannot resist intersection attacks because the attacker is aware of all the correct characters. TimeLock [17] also uses the haptical channel, where the user counts the irregular vibration and enters the counted digit by stopping counting. The range of digit is 1 to 5, which reduces the password space greatly. Phone-Lock [16] uses the acoustic channel to inform the user of the keyboard numbers. That requires the user to wear the earphone, which brings inconvenience to the user.

Another kind of schemes physically protect some secret information in the visual channel. The work of De Luca [11] adds a number of moving fake cursors to the keyboard to cover the real input, but the actual effect is not ideal. In PassMatrix [14], the user obtains the secret information by using palm to shield the screen, which protects the security of information at the same time. This scheme needs to solve the hot-spot problem of the graphical password.

In this paper, we propose a new textual password entry method. Our new method can resist human shoulder-surfing attack effectively by significantly increasing the amount of short-term memory required in an attack. Besides, we introduce a new security notion of attack alert, which is embodied in our method to improve the security. This function enables the system to detect failed shoulder-surfing attacks and alert the legitimate user to prevent further attacks by the attacker.

The rest of this paper is organized as follows. In Sect. 2, we introduce the attack model and security notions for the password entry method. In Sect. 3, we present our new textual password entry method MapPass. In Sect. 4, we specifically analyze the security. Then we analyze the usability of the proposed method in Sect. 5. At last, we conclude this paper in Sect. 6.

2 Threat Model and Security Notions

2.1 Threat Model

In an authentication session, the password is used in conjunction with the account or the corresponding mobile device. Considering that attacker can try to know the account or steal mobile device of the user, which will be more easier if the attacker is an acquaintance of the user, we do not take into account other factors needed for an authentication expect the password. The password entry process can be seen as the interactions between the user and the system. The user completes the identity authentication by responding to the challenge from the system. For a regular password entry method, the challenge is to input the password directly. For a shoulder-surfing resistant method, the system challenges the user to enter the information converted from the password. Then the system judges whether the user is a legitimate user according the information.

The threat model is composed of three entities, user, system and attacker. The attacker observes or records all interactions between the user and the system in an authentication session and tries to obtain the password. Then the attacker impersonates the legitimate user with the password obtained from the attack.

2.2 Security Definition

We consider the security of the method against guessing attacks and shoulder-surfing attacks. Based on the means the attacker uses, we classify shoulder-surfing attacks into two types, human shoulder-surfing attack and recording attack.

Guessing Attack. In a guessing attack, the attacker guesses the password without knowing any information and tries to authenticate with the guessed password. To simplify analysis, we assume that the distribution of passwords is uniform. We define the security of a password entry method against the guessing attack as follows.

Definition 1. *The success probability of guessing attack, denoted by $P_G^n(n \geq 1)$, is the probability that the attacker authenticates successfully by guessing the correct password in n trials.*

Human Shoulder-Surfing Attack. In a human shoulder-surfing attack, the attacker observes the entire authentication session by naked eyes and tries to obtain the password. Then the attacker uses the password to authenticate. The security of a password entry method against the human shoulder-surfing attack is defined as follows.

Algorithm 1. Generation Algorithm

Input: figure sequences $figureSeq$s; position buttons pbs; shift buttons $shift$s
Output: the candidate set pwd; entry behavior $behavior$

1: **while** the user inputs $figureSeq$, pb and $shift$ **do**
2:    **for** $i = 0, \cdots, 11$ **do**
3:       $m \leftarrow figureSeq[i]$
4:       **if** $shift = false$ **then**
5:          $pwd_m \leftarrow pwd_m + L_i(pb)$
6:       **else**
7:          $pwd_m \leftarrow pwd_m + U_i(pb)$
8:       **end if**
9:       $behavior \leftarrow behavior + pb$
10:    **end for**
11:    **if** the user inputs OK **then**
12:       break
13:    **end if**
14: **end while**
15: **return** pwd and $behavior$

Definition 2. *The success probability of human shoulder-surfing attack, denoted by $P_H^n (n \geq 1)$, is the probability that the attacker authenticates successfully in only one trial using the password obtained during n human shoulder-surfing attacks on the same account.*

Recording Attack. In a recording attack, the attacker uses a smartphone or a camera to record the entire authentication session and tries to obtain the password. Then the attacker uses the password to authenticate. We give the definition for the security of a password entry method against the recording attack as follows.

Definition 3. *The success probability of recording attack, denoted by $P_R^n (n \geq 1)$, is the probability that the attacker authenticates successfully in only one trial using the password obtained during n recording attacks on the same account.*

2.3 Attack Alert

For shoulder-surfing attacks, the attacker can access the account with the correct password. If the attacker uses a wrong password, he/she will fail to authenticate and may continue to try. Attack alert means that the system can detect failed shoulder-surfing attack in an authentication and promptly remind the legitimate user to modify the password and step up his/her vigilance. If the authentication session is failed, the system will distinguish whether the user is a legitimate user or a shoulder-surfing attacker. If the system detects the shoulder-surfing attack, the system can notify the legitimate user to modify the password in time by sending a message and force the user to authenticate with the second factor, such as verification code. We add attack alert function to our method, and it will effectively prevent the attacker from continuing to authenticate.

3   MapPass

In this section, we propose a new textual password method against shoulder-surfing attacks called MapPass. The basic layout of our method comprises a horizontal array of squares which contain characters, juxtaposed with another array of twelve familiar figures such ■ and ★, as shown in Fig. 1(a). The figures can be replaced by other meaningful symbols, such as letters or zodiacs. The design of basic layout is inspired by a PIN-entry method LIN_4 [15]. Our method supports input of 96 characters, including digits from 0 to 9, lower case letters from a to z, upper case letters from A to Z and some common symbols. A square is composed of 4 characters, and a total of 48 characters can be displayed in a square array. The remaining 48 characters are displayed on the second interface, and the user can switch to the other interface by pressing the "Shift" button in the lower left corner of the interface as in Fig. 1(b).

Algorithm 2. Attack Detection Algorithm

Input: the candidate set pwd; entry behavior $behavior$
Output: true or false

1: **if** $behavior \neq userBehavior$ **then**
2:    **return** false
3: **end if**
4: **for** $i = 0, \cdots, 11$ **do**
5:    **if** NUMBEROFSC(pwd_i) $\geq$ LENGTH($userPwd$)/2 **then**
6:       **return** false
7:    **end if**
8: **end for**
9: **return** true

For a k-character password, the user needs k rounds of input. In the first round, the user recognizes the temporary session figure key and inputs the first character of the password. And the user inputs the remaining $k-1$ characters in the next $k-1$ rounds. In the first round, twelve randomly arranged figures are displayed on the interface, as shown in Fig. 1(a). The user recognizes the figure below the first character of the password as the session figure key. According to the position of the first character in the square (upper left, upper right, lower left or lower right), the user presses the button of the corresponding position in the 2×2 buttons (we call them the position buttons) below the array of figures to input the character. In the example shown in Fig. 1, where the password is 2ac73?, the user determines ▲ as the session figure key, which is below the square where the character 2 is located. Then the user presses the position button on the upper left to input the character because 2 is at the upper left of the square

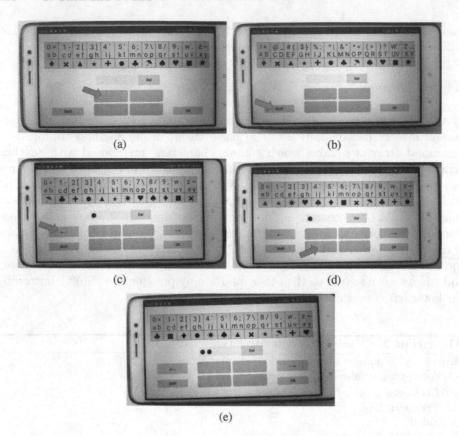

(a)   (b)

(c)   (d)

(e)

Fig. 1. Example of a password entry procedure for password 2ac73?, in which the session key is ▲. (a) Recognizing the session key is ▲ and pressing the position button on the upper left to input the character 2. (b) The user can switch to the other interface by pressing the "Shift" button. (c) The interface after inputting 2. (d) The session key ▲ is moved to the position below the square where a is located. Pressing the position button on the lower left to input the character a. (e) The interface after inputting a.

as in Fig. 1(a). In each of the remaining $k - 1$ rounds, the user inputs the next character in the password. In the beginning of these rounds, the array of figures will be rearranged randomly as in Fig. 1(c). The user rotates the figure array to place the session figure key directly below the square of the character which the user wants to input, then presses the position button corresponding to the position of the character in the square. Here the user can press two additional buttons ("←" and "→") to rotate the array to the left or right. In the example shown in Fig. 1(c), to input the second character a, the user presses the "←" button four times to move the session key ▲ to the position below the square where a is located, and presses the position button on the lower left to input the character a as in Fig. 1(d). After that, the figure array is rearranged randomly again as shown in Fig. 1(e), and the user enters the remaining characters in the same way. We name our method MapPass after the mapping relationship among the character, the figure and the position button.

In each entry round, the session figure key is collocated with the password character. Therefore, the key points out the square where the character is located. According to the position button, the system gets the character, and finally gets the password of the user. For other figures that are not used as the session figure key, the system can also get the corresponding passwords according to the figure and the position button. The system and the user do not negotiate the specified key before authentication, and the session key is randomly arranged in a session, which is below the first character of the correct password. Thus, the system has no idea the session key and gets 12 candidates corresponding to 12 figures. The pseudo-code of the candidate set generation algorithm is shown in Algorithm 1, where $figureSeq$ is the current order of figures; pwd_m is the password corresponding to the mth figure; $L_i(pb)$ is the character corresponding the position button pb in the ith square of the first interface; $U_i(pb)$ is the character corresponding the position button pb in the ith square of the second interface. The authentication rule is that if the correct password is included in the set of candidate passwords, the user is considered to be a legitimate user.

We add the function of attack alert into our method, which is that the system can detect the failed shoulder-surfing attack by the attacker and remind the user. In a human shoulder-surfing attack, the attacker needs to observe the corresponding relationship between the figures, character squares and the position button in each round. Because of the limited short term memory of human beings, the attacker cannot remember all the information. He/she can only try to memorize a password corresponding to one figure or memorize the sequence of position buttons which the user presses. For the recording attack, the attacker can get the set of 12 candidate passwords like the system by watching the video repeatedly. After observing or recording the authentication process, the attacker attempts to authenticate with the password obtained from the attack. The recording attacker chooses one password from the candidate set to try.

Authenticating with the wrong candidate password or simply imitating the user to press the position buttons can be regarded as the shoulder-surfing attack. For a human shoulder-surfing attack and a recording attack, the sequences of position buttons pressed by the attacker are the same as entering the correct password, because these attacks depend on the sequence of position buttons which the user inputs to obtain and enter the correct password. Therefore, we use the sequence of position buttons as the entry behavior of the user to detect the shoulder-surfing attack. The pseudo-code of the entry behavior generation algorithm is shown in Algorithm 1, where the system generates the entry behavior and the candidate set simultaneously. If the user fails the authentication, but the entry behavior is identical to that of the legitimate user, the user may be a shoulder-surfing attacker. Considering that the legitimate user may make mistakes, we cannot generalize the above situation. For the attacker, if the attacker authenticates with a wrong candidate password, each character in this password is different from the corresponding one in the correct password because a character can only be determined by a unique combination of figure and position button. Besides, if the attacker simply imitates the entry behavior of the user, attacker does not use the session figure key which is below the first character of the correct password to indicate the remaining characters of the password. Thus, the session figure key cannot point out the correct password. And other figures also cannot point out the correct password because only the session key is likely to do that. For the legitimate user, he/she may enter a few wrong characters in an authentication session, but most of the characters are right. Therefore, we base our judgement on the number of wrong characters in the password. A rough criterion is whether the number of wrong characters is more than half the length of the password. When the authentication fails and the corresponding entry behavior is correct, the system will check whether there is a candidate with wrong characters less than half in the candidate set obtained from the authentication. If such a candidate exists, the user is considered as a legitimate user, but if it does not exist, the authentication is regarded as a shoulder-surfing attack. The pseudo-code of the entry behavior generation algorithm is shown in Algorithm 2, where $userBehavior$ is the entry behavior of the legitimate user; NUMBEROFSC(x) counts the number of the same characters in x and the correct password; $userPwd$ is the correct password.

4   Security Analysis

In this section, we analyze the security of the proposed method in theory, considering the guessing attack, the shoulder-surfing attack and the attack alert.

4.1   Guessing Attack

The attacker tries to authenticate with a predicted password, and the system obtains the candidate set containing the password of the attacker through the input to verify whether there is a correct password. Thus, the attacker tests 12 passwords in a session. If the length of the password is $k(k > 0)$, the success probability of a guessing attack theoretically is $P_G^1 = 12/96^k$. The success rate of two attacks is roughly estimated as $P_G^2 = \frac{12 \times 2}{96^k}$. For n guessing attacks $(n \geq 1)$, the success rate is roughly estimated as $P_G^n = \frac{12n}{96^k}$.

4.2   Human Shoulder-Surfing Attack

Because of the limited human short term memory, the attacker cannot memorize all the information observed during the authentication process. The study of Miller [21] suggests that the average person can only remember 7 ± 2 symbols in a short time. Thus, the attacker can try to obtain one candidate password corresponding to a figure where the attacker only needs to memorize one figure and the corresponding password. If the length of the password is 8, it is possible for the attacker who can remember 9 symbols to memorize a password. While the figure array moves rapidly or the session key is near the correct position, the attacker may not have enough time to acquire the character of the password.

In this case, he/she can only memorize and imitate the entry behavior of the user. If the attacker obtains a candidate password smoothly, the success probability is $P_H^1 = 1/12$ because there are 11 wrong passwords in the candidate set which cannot be used to authenticate in the subsequent session.

For multiple human shoulder-surfing attacks, the attacker tries to authenticate after several times of observation. Assuming that the attacker can get a candidate password in each observation, the success probability of two attacks is $P_H^2 = 2 \times \frac{11}{12} \times \frac{1}{12} \times \frac{1}{2} + \frac{1}{12} \times \frac{1}{12} = \frac{1}{12}$, and the success rate of three attacks is $P_H^3 = 3 \times \frac{11}{12} \times \frac{11}{12} \times \frac{1}{12} \times \frac{1}{3} + 3 \times \frac{11}{12} \times \frac{1}{12} \times \frac{1}{12} + \frac{1}{12^3} = \frac{155}{1728}$. If the attacker observes n times $(n \geq 2)$, the success probability is

$$P_H^n = \frac{11^{n-1}}{12^n} + \sum_{i=2}^{n} C_n^i \frac{11^{n-i}}{12} \times \frac{1}{12}^i .$$

4.3   Recording Attack

The attacker can record all the information during the authentication session of the user. Thus, he/she can get all the candidate passwords by watching the video. For a single recording attack, the attacker chooses one candidate from the candidate set to log on, the success rate is $P_R^1 = 1/12$. For multiple recording attacks, because candidate sets from different authentication sessions all contain the correct password, the attacker can determine that the same password in different candidate sets is the correct password, and the success rate is $P_R^n = 1 (n > 1)$. Therefore, our method cannot resist multiple recording attacks. In this regard, we can improve the method with the auxiliary channel. In the input process, the system can inform the user to use a specific figure one or more times through the earphone. In this way, it is very likely that the candidate set does not contain the correct password. Therefore, it is difficult to get the correct password from multiple recording attacks.

4.4   Attack Alert

In shoulder-surfing attacks, the attacker obtains the corresponding character according to the combination of figure and position button. For the human shoulder-surfing attack, because of limited capacity of memory, the attacker may get one candidate password corresponding to one figure or not be able to get a complete password. The first case is the same as the attacker chooses one candidate password in the candidate set to authenticate in a recording attack. In the second case, even though the attacker cannot get all characters in a password, he/she can obtain the intermediate information, the sequence of position buttons. The attacker will try a string that the corresponding sequence of position buttons is the same as the sequence he/she observed from the previous shoulder-surfing attack to approach the correct password. If the attacker fails to authenticate, the system will determine whether it is a shoulder-surfing attack or not. It is hard for the attacker who imitates the entry behavior to choose a password similar to the correct one. Additionally, the wrong candidate password is totally inconsistent with the correct one. For the recording attack, as analyzed above, it is the same as the first case of human shoulder-surfing attack. Therefore, the system will detect these failed shoulder-surfing attacks and alert the user, that is to say, the attacker has no chance to try other passwords. For multiple shoulder-surfing attacks, if the authentication fails, the system will also detect the attacks.

5   Usability Analysis

In this section, we evaluate the usability of our method and compare it with the regular textual password entry method (REG) through the experiment. We implemented MapPass and REG on a Redmi Note3 smartphone running Android 5.0.2 and used the keyboard of the mobile phone system in REG. Then we conducted a usability study to evaluate the authentication time and the error rate.

We recruited 10 participants from the university. All participants had many years of experience using the mobile phone, and they were familiar with REG. The experiment procedure was designed as follows. First, we introduced our method MapPass and explained the use of MapPass and REG to participants. We gave a specific example to illustrate the operation of password input in each method and ensured that each participant understood the input procedure. Then, each participant submitted a 8-character password, which was used in the training and testing. The following procedure was then repeated for each method. At the training phase, each participant needed to log on successfully three times to be familiar with the entry process and showed us one successful session, i.e., four successful sessions in all. Each authentication session allowed a maximum of three attempts. At the testing phase, each participant was asked to perform one authentication session within a maximum of three trials. The entry time and authentication result were logged for the subsequent analysis. After the testing phase, the participant switched to the other authentication method. We counterbalanced the order of the authentication methods with the Latin square approach to reduce learning effects.

Figure 2 graphically illustrates the successful password entry times for the two password entry methods. A paired t-test shows that these two methods have significant difference on the entry time ($t(9) = 12.021, p < 0.01$). Compared with REG, MapPass takes much longer to input. This is because the user needs to change the position of session figure key before he/she inputs the character.

As for the error rates, we recorded whether the participant authenticates successfully and the number of trials had been used. For both entry methods, all participants authenticated themselves successfully at the first attempt. MapPass does not affect the error rate.

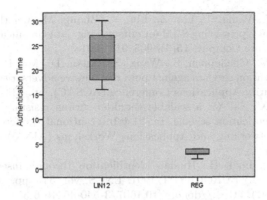

Fig. 2. Password entry time of a successful authentication session.

6 Conclusions

In this paper, we proposed a new textual password entry method. Our method can resist human shoulder-surfing attack effectively by taking advantage of the limitation of human short term memory. Besides, we presented the security notion of attack alert and added this function to our method so that the system can detect the failed shoulder-surfing attacks, whether it is a single attack or a intersection attack. This function prevents the shoulder-surfing attackers from trying repeatedly. Additionally, we analyzed the security and usability of the proposed method. The limit of our method is that it cannot resist multiple recording attacks, and we put forward the measure to improve it.

Acknowledgments. This work is partly supported by the National Key Research and Development Program of China (No. 2017YFB0802300), and the Natural Science Foundation of China (No. 61602240).

References

1. Li, X., Zhu, Y., Wang, J.: Highly efficient privacy preserving location-based services with enhanced one-round blind filter. IEEE Trans. Emerg. Top. Comput. (2019). https://doi.org/10.1109/TETC.2019.2926385
2. Zhu, Y., Zhang, Y., Li, X., Yan, H., Li, J.: Improved collusion-resisting secure nearest neighbor query over encrypted data in cloud. Concurrency Comput. Pract. Exp. (2018). https://doi.org/10.1002/cpe.4681
3. Kwon, T., Hong, J.: Analysis and improvement of a pin-entry method resilient to shoulder-surfing and recording attacks. IEEE Trans. Inf. Forensics Secur. 10(2), 278–292 (2017)
4. Roth, V., Richter, K., Freidinger, R.: A pin-entry method resilient against shoulder surfing. In: Proceedings of the 11th ACM Conference on Computer and Communications Security, CCS 2004, pp. 236–245. ACM, New York (2004)
5. Li, X., Zhu, Y., Wang, J., Zhang, J.: Efficient and secure multi-dimensional geometric range query over encrypted data in cloud. J. Parallel Distrib. Comput. 131, 44–54 (2019)

6. Li, X., Zhu, Y., Wang, J., Liu, Z., Liu, Y., Zhang, M.: On the soundness and security of privacy-preserving SVM for outsourcing data classification. IEEE Trans. Dependable Secure Comput. **15**(5), 906–912 (2018)

7. Bai, X., Gu, W., Chellappan, S., Wang, X., Xuan, D., Ma, B.: PAS: predicate-based authentication services against powerful passive adversaries. In: 2008 Annual Computer Security Applications Conference (ACSAC), pp. 433–442 (2008)

8. Zhao, H., Li, X.: S3PAS: a scalable shoulder-surfing resistant textual-graphical password authentication scheme. In: 21st International Conference on Advanced Information Networking and Applications Workshops (AINAW 2007), vol. 2, pp. 467–472 (2007)

9. Matsumoto, T., Imai, H.: Human identification through insecure channel. In: Davies, D.W. (ed.) EUROCRYPT 1991. LNCS, vol. 547, pp. 409–421. Springer, Heidelberg (1991). https://doi.org/10.1007/3-540-46416-6_35

10. De Luca, A., von Zezschwitz, E., Hussmann, H.: VibraPass: secure authentication based on shared lies. In: Proceedings of the SIGCHI Conference on Human Factors in Computing Systems, CHI 2009, pp. 913–916. ACM, New York (2009)

11. De Luca, A., von Zezschwitz, E., Pichler, L., Hussmann, H.: Using fake cursors to secure on-screen password entry. In: Proceedings of the SIGCHI Conference on Human Factors in Computing Systems, CHI 2013, pp. 2399–2402. ACM, New York (2013)

12. Weinshall, D.: Cognitive authentication schemes safe against spyware. In: 2006 IEEE Symposium on Security and Privacy (S&P 2006), pp. 295–300 (2006)

13. Wiedenbeck, S., Waters, J., Sobrado, L., Birget, J.-C.: Design and evaluation of a shoulder-surfing resistant graphical password scheme. In: Proceedings of the Working Conference on Advanced Visual Interfaces, AVI 2006, pp. 177–184. ACM, New York (2006)

14. Sun, H., Chen, S., Yeh, J., Cheng, C.: A shoulder surfing resistant graphical authentication system. IEEE Trans. Dependable Secure Comput. **15**(2), 180–193 (2018)

15. Lee, M.K.: Security notions and advanced method for human shoulder-surfing resistant pin-entry. IEEE Trans. Inf. Forensics Secur. **9**(4), 695–708 (2017)

16. Bianchi, A., Oakley, I., Kostakos, V., Kwon, D.-S.: The phone lock: audio and haptic shoulder-surfing resistant pin entry methods for mobile devices, pp. 197–200 (2011)

17. Bianchi, A., Oakley, I., Dong, S.K.: Counting clicks and beeps: exploring numerosity based haptic and audio pin entry. Interact. Comput. **24**(5), 409–422 (2012)

18. Perkovic, T., Cagalj, M., Rakic, N.: SSSL: shoulder surfing safe login. In: SoftCOM 2009–17th International Conference on Software, Telecommunications Computer Networks, pp. 270–275 (2009)

19. De Luca, A., Hertzschuch, K., Hussmann, H.: ColorPIN: securing pin entry through indirect input. In: Proceedings of the SIGCHI Conference on Human Factors in Computing Systems, CHI 2010, pp. 1103–1106. ACM, New York (2010)

20. Khamis, M., Alt, F., Hassib, M., von Zezschwitz, E., Hasholzner, R., Bulling, A.: GazeTouchPass: multimodal authentication using gaze and touch on mobile devices. In: Proceedings of the 2016 CHI Conference Extended Abstracts on Human Factors in Computing Systems, CHI EA 2016, pp. 2156–2164. ACM, New York (2016)

21. Miller, G.A.: The magical number seven, plus or minus two: some limits on our capacity for processing information. Psychol. Rev. **63**(2), 81–97 (1956)

Speaker Recognition Based on Lightweight Neural Network for Smart Home Solutions

Haojun Ai[1,2(✉)], Wuyang Xia[1(✉)], and Quanxin Zhang[3]

[1] School of Cyber Science and Engineering, Wuhan University, Wuhan,
People's Republic of China
aihj@whu.edu.cn, 904419717@qq.com
[2] Key Laboratory of Aerospace Information Security and Trusted Computing,
Ministry of Education, Wuhan, China
[3] School of Computer Science and Technology, Beijing Institute of Technology,
Beijing, People's Republic of China
zhangqx@bit.edu.cn

Abstract. With the technological advancement of smart home devices, the lifestyles of people have been gradually changed. Meanwhile, speaker recognition is available in almost all smart home devices. Currently, the mainstream speaker recognition service is provided by a very deep neural network which trained on the cloud server. However, these deep neural networks are not suitable for deployment and operation on smart home devices. Aiming at this problem, in this paper, we propose a packet bottleneck method to improve SqueezeNet which has been widely used in the speaker recognition task. In the meantime, a lightweight structure named TrimNet has been designed. Besides, a model updating strategy based on transfer learning has been adopted to avoid model deteriorates due to the cold speech. The experimental results demonstrate that the proposed lightweight structure TrimNet is superior to SqueezeNet in classification accuracy, structural parameter quantity, and calculation amount. Moreover, the model updating method can increase the recognition rate of cold speech without damaging the recognition rate of other speakers.

Keywords: Speaker recognition · Smart home · Transfer learning

1 Introduction

Voice-based smart home devices such as Amazon's Alexa and Google's Google Home have gradually become the center of interaction between home and the Internet [1]. Personalized services can be provided for users such as online shopping, song recommendations and news feeds. Therefore, it is very important to perform user authentication. Speaker recognition is a very effective way to verify users' identities. Existing solutions, such as Google Home, Siri, Cortana and other deep learning-based speaker recognition technologies, are deployed in the cloud [2]. These solutions have limitations in terms of user privacy protection and network reliability. In order to protect the privacy of users, it would be better to deploy the neural network on a user's personal device. Then, the speaker recognition service can be provided locally instead

© Springer Nature Switzerland AG 2019
J. Vaidya et al. (Eds.): CSS 2019, LNCS 11983, pp. 421–431, 2019.
https://doi.org/10.1007/978-3-030-37352-8_37

of transmitting the data to a cloud server. Moreover, systems deployed locally also do not have network bandwidth limitation and can reduce service response time. To meet these needs, we need design a neural network-based speaker recognition solution that can run on smart home devices.

Speaker recognition technology based on deep neural network has developed rapidly [3], such as Bhattacharya [4], and explored the speaker recognition method based on DNN and RNN. Directly using CNN to train spectrogram data is also a new research direction [5–8]. Although the above models are excellent in performance, they are getting deeper and deeper and cannot be applied to low hardware resource conditions in a smart home environment.

In order to deploy the neural network in an embedded device, other researchers have proposed a lightweight structure of the neural network. In 2016, Landola borrowed the design idea of the Inception module and proposed the Fire module to propose a lightweight neural network SqueezeNet [9, 10]. The Fire module uses only 1×1 and 3×3 convolution kernels to effectively reduce the amount of structural parameters. In order to reduce the computational load caused by the 1×1 convolution kernel, in 2017, Jian Sun et al. introduced group convolution in the 1×1 convolution kernel [11], but the group convolution resulted in no information between channels.

In this paper, we aimed to design a lightweight neural network model that can be deployed on smart home devices that provides fast response and high-precision speaker recognition results. Our contribution is to solve the problem of non-circulation of information between the channels of the grouped volume integral group by using the packet bottleneck strategy, so as to improve SqueezeNet, propose a lightweight neural network model TrimNet, and use transfer learning to update the model.

The rest of the paper is organized as follows. Section 2 introduces our own dataset, the PBSD, wherein all speakers use smartphones to record. In Sect. 3, we present the lightweight neural network TrimNet and describe results that include precision, recall, F1 scores, inference time, parameter quantity and calculation amount. In Sect. 4, we introduce the model updating strategy. Section 5 concludes the paper.

2 Database (PBSD) Construction

In order to evaluate the performance of proposed method, a new database named PBSD (Phone-based Speech Database) has been constructed. It contains 23 speakers, 13 male and 10 females, with a mean age in 25 years old. Several guidelines and requirements for recording have been set up in order to guarantee the quality of data. The prompt text is 0–9 numbers and sentences in Chinese. The time of one session varies from person to person. The length of reading materials is approximately 2.5–4 min. All sessions were recorded in lossless pcm-encoded WAV format via the Luyinbao app (from Iflytek CO., LTD.) with sampling rate of 16 kHz. Speakers were required to use the same phone throughout the entire recording time. Each session was recorded in a relatively quiet environment be it indoor or outdoor (i.e., their daily environment) with background noise below 45 dB. Each session was given three tags: date, phone model, and physiological status.

We removed any audible unwanted noises to limit variable factors (apart from aging) for the sake of consistency, since the recording conditions were varied. We examined the recorded spectral content and any with significant frequency artefacts (e.g., microphone interference, popping) were discarded. So far, each speaker produced 20–40 effective sessions spanning a range of 30–50 days. There were 14 sessions in total with common time nodes, so the current database contains 322 sessions, totally 13 h of speech data.

In our experiment, we convert the voice file in wav format into a spectrogram. A spectrogram is a visual representation of an audio signal that completely includes the voiceprint characteristics of the speaker. The picture below shows the display of "0901-Samsung S8-No Cold" (this is the naming of voice files in the self-built voice database, 0901 represents the recording date, and Samsung S8 stands for the recording device) (Fig. 1).

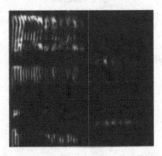

Fig. 1. Spectrogram of "0901-Samsung S8-No Cold"

3 Lightweight Neural Network

SqueezeNet is equal to AlexNet in classification accuracy and structural calculations, with a structural parameter of 5.3 megabytes and an AlexNet structural parameter of 61.10 megabytes [12, 13]. The compute volume of SqueezeNet is the same as AlexNet, which is not conducive to deployment on mobile devices. After deriving the calculation amount of the Fire module, it is found that the reason for the excessive calculation is that the number of input channels in the compression layer is large, and the 1 × 1 convolution operation for reducing the number of channels accounts for a large proportion of the output channel of the expansion layer. The 1 × 1 and 3 × 3 convolution operations for feature learning are more computationally intensive. Although group convolution can reduce the amount of calculation [14], it will cause the channel less information to affect the recognition accuracy. For this problem, we propose a packet bottleneck.

3.1 Packet Bottleneck

In order to solve the problem of channel information non-circulation caused by group convolution, we find that the bottleneck module in ResNet [15] may solve this problem.

The bottleneck module is shown in Fig. 2. The bottleneck module first uses 1×1 convolution to reduce the number of input channels. The number of channels changes from 256 to 64, then 3×3 convolutions on 64 channels to learn features, and finally use 1×1 convolution to recover the number of channels. Change to 256. The number of channels in the module has undergone a process of decreasing first and then increasing the last, similar to the bottleneck, so called the bottleneck module. The goal is to reduce the number of input and output channels for a 3×3 convolution to 64 to reduce the training time of the structure. The right line in Fig. 2 connects the inputs and outputs to an identity map, the purpose of which is to use residual learning.

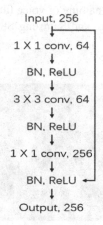

Fig. 2. Bottleneck module

Due to the large number of input or output channels of 1×1 convolution in the bottleneck module, the number of input and output channels of 3×3 convolution is small, so this paper proposes that 1×1 convolution uses group convolution to reduce the parameter amount of the structure. And the amount of computation, 3×3 convolution uses conventional convolution to re-circulate information between channels and is named the packet bottleneck.

3.2   TrimNet

We use the above strategy to improve SqueezeNet, and introduces Batch Normalization (BN) to improve SqueezeNet's Fire module. Improve the overall structure of SqueezeNet, cascade the Trim module, increase the number of pooling layers and Trim modules, add Softmax, and propose TrimNet.

The Fire module does not have a bottleneck design. To improve with the packet bottleneck, the Fire module is first improved into a bottleneck module, and the packet bottleneck is introduced. Specifically, reduce the number of output channels of the 3×3 convolution in the Fire module so that the number of input and output channels is the same, followed by a 1×1 convolution for amplifying the number of channels to form a bottleneck module. Using a packet bottleneck, a group convolution is applied to the 1×1 convolution in the module. At the same time, the nonlinear transformation of 1×1 convolution is discarded. In addition, it was found that there is no batch normalization in the Fire module. Batch normalization speeds up the training process and improves classification accuracy.

After adding batch normalization, this paper proposes the Trim module, as shown in Fig. 3. The Trim module consists of a compression layer, a convolution layer and an extension layer. It has four hyperparameters, which are the grouping number g of the compression layer and the expansion layer, the convolution layer convolution kernel s, and the convolution layer convolution kernel number c. And the expansion layer convolution kernel number e, where s = c, s < e, c < e.

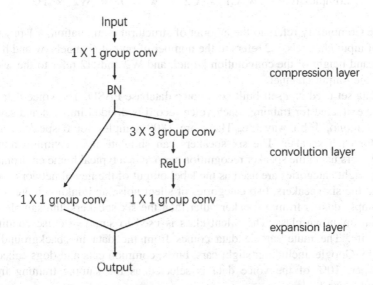

Fig. 3. Trim module

The Trim module is cascaded for feature learning, followed by a classifier for speaker. Since the input, output channels of the Trim module and the Fire module are the same in width, height and quantity, this article cascades the Trim module according to the SqueezeNet overall structure, and adds an additional pooling layer and two Slim modules to the structure. The last layer of SqueezeNet's convolutional layer uses a 1×1 convolution to change the number of output classifications, increasing the number of channels from 512 to 1 000. This operation takes up a lot of calculations, so the convolutional layer is removed and the fully connected layer is added to change the number of output classifications. Also, add the Softmax function at the end of the structure. The Softmax function is used in the multi-classification process to map the output values of the structure to a range of 0 to 1, and the sum of the outputs is 1, which can be regarded as a probability.

3.3 Experiment

This experiment uses classification accuracy, structural parameter quantities, and structural calculations as evaluation indicators. Compare the performance of SqueezeNet and TrimNet to demonstrate the effectiveness of the lightweight method proposed in this paper. The classification accuracy is the recognition rate of the speaker on the test set, and the parameter quantity is the capacity of the model. The structural calculation refers to the number of floating-point operations required to infer a spectrum by the structure GFLOPI (Giga Floating-Point Operations Per Image). The formula is as follows [16]:

$$Complexity = 2 \times C1 \times C2 \times w \times h \times W2 \times H2$$

Where Complexity refers to the amount of structural computation, C1 refers to the number of input channels, C2 refers to the number of output channels, w and h refer to the width and height of the convolution kernel, and W2 and H2 refer to the width and height of the output channel.

The data set used is a self-built cold voice database PBSD. The voice data of 6 of them were extracted for training. Each voice record is divided into 1 s and saved as a 16000 Hz, mono, 16bit wav file. There are 1800 samples for 6 speakers and 300 samples for each speaker. The six speakers can simulate the maximum number of registered users using the speaker recognition service in a typical home environment. In this paper, eight categories are used as the label output of the neural network model. In addition to the six speakers, two categories of silent noise and unknown are set. If the speech sample data is from a speaker other than the six speakers, the sample is identified as an unknown class. The Silent class is used to simulate noise conditions in everyday life. The mute sample data comes from the data in "background_noise" provided by Google, including: slight cars, birds, common cats and dogs called noise. In this paper, 10% of the voice data is selected as the sample training from the background noise folder.

The hyperparameters are set as follows: This paper classifies the dataset according to the training set, verification set, and test set. The classification ratio is 80:10:10, the dropout rate is 0.5, the learning rate is 0.00001, the training step is 30000, and the batch size is 10 (Table 1).

Table 1. Validation metrics

Model name	Average precision	Average recall	Average F1 score
TrimNet	0.91	0.92	0.91
SqueezeNet	0.89	0.89	0.88

Table 2. Comparison of parameter quantity and calculation amount

Model name	Parameter quantities	Calculations
TrimNet	4.2 M	4.5 GFLOPI
SqueezeNet	5.3 M	7.2 GFLOPI

At the same time, the experiment records parameters quantities and calculations, as shown in Table 2. The packet bottleneck effectively reduces the amounts of structural parameters and the amount of calculation. TrimNet reduces the parameter amount by 21% and the calculation amount by 37%.

Table 3. Average inference time during live experiment

Inference time	
TrimNet	SqueezeNet
57.7 ± 3.7 ms	360.45 ± 76.82 ms

As can be seen from the table, TrimNet has less parameter and calculation while maintaining a higher recognition rate.

To prove that the TrimNet are suitable to run on embedded devices we measured the inference time of processing 10 samples per speaker on Samsung S8 based on Snapdragon 835 processor. The results are shown in the table below (Table 3).

4 Pathology Situation

4.1 SR Rate Curve from Cold-Suffering to Health

We designed experiments based on TrimNet to determine the overall SR rate curve of 6 speakers over time. The model was registered using a session of about N (2/5/10) seconds on the first day for each speaker. After VAD operation, we took speech data about 1 s long for testing per person per day. There were three who caught a cold during the recording time (labeled "c-speaker1" "c-speaker3"). We observed changes in their SR rates over time as well as those of the three "h-speakers" (healthy speakers) for comparative analysis. The recording time was about 40 days and covered the whole process of physiological changes from healthy to cold-suffering to healthy again.

Figure 4 show that the three h-speakers' recognition curves remain stable over the observation period. By contrast, the recognition curves of each c-speaker during the cold-suffering period (Fig. 5) show various degrees of decline related to the severity of the cold. Indeed, suffering a cold can significantly reduce the accuracy of SR even as the training template time progresses.

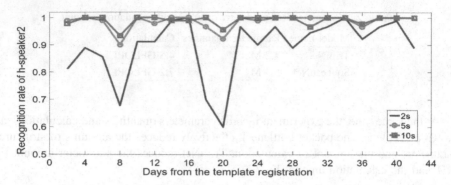

Fig. 4. SR rate curve over time of one healthy speaker (h-speaker2).

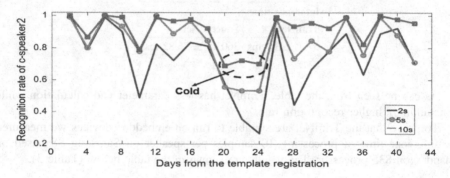

Fig. 5. SR rate curve over time of one cold-suffering speaker (c-speaker2).

4.2　Transfer Learning-Based Template Strategy

We tried transfer learning technique to update our model. The essence of transfer learning [17] is to improve the generalization of another distribution P2 by using the prior knowledge of learning a certain distribution P1. Specifically, we want to solve the problem of a specific domain A, but we have very little data in this field (in this case, there is not enough cold voice dataset). We can get enough in another similar domain B. So, knowledge transfer in different fields begins to take place. The data set A is improved using the knowledge learned from the data set obtained from the domain B, where the two data sets do not need to come from the same domain and the data set B is much larger than the data set A. The large data set in Domain B helps to learn the generalized representation in the small amount of data obtained from Domain A. That is to say, the idea of knowledge transfer makes transfer learning in deep learning model training possible, and transfer learning has been proved to be helpful for classification, regression and clustering [18–21].

We directly utilized the trained TrimNet structure, weights, and hyper parameters. We kept the original structure unchanged, replaced only the original output layer with a new single, fully connected layer and the activation function was softmax. The layer of the original structure was used to extract features and train only the newly added layers.

During training, the weights of the original layer were frozen and only the weights of the subsequent layers were updated. This prevented any damage to the aforetrained model while improving the recognition rate of cold-suffering users.

We adopted 10 s utterance data of the cold-suffering user to retrain the last layer and update the new template.

As shown in Figs. 6 and 7, whether based on the new template or old template, h-speaker3 consistently received a high recognition rate. By contrast, the SR rate of c-speaker2 under the new template significantly improved especially during points where the user had a cold, where the recognition rate increased to over 90%. In effect, the proposed updating strategy effectively ensures a high SR rate regardless of whether the user is suffering a cold.

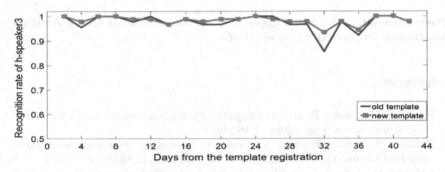

Fig. 6. SR rate curve over time based on new template and old template of one healthy speaker (h-speaker3).

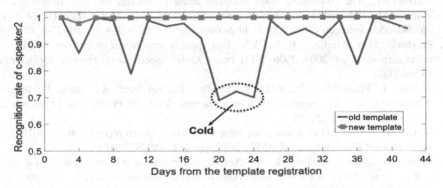

Fig. 7. SR rate curve over time based on new template and old template of one cold-suffering speaker (c-speaker2).

5   Conclusion

In this paper, we focused on lightweight neural network used for recognizing speakers using spectrograms generated from audio files on embedded devices for smart home solutions. With the preliminary results, it can be found that TrimNet has achieved decent accuracy (precision $\sim 91\%$) and it is suitable for an embedded device because of the small memory (4.2 MB) requirement and short inference time (60 ms).

On the other hand, an available dataset PBSD has been introduced for assessing SR accuracy in daily usage. The PBSD consists of data from 23 individuals and spans 40 days, where each session is recorded in lossless pcm-encoded WAV format. Based on PBSD, 6 speakers were selected as a set for our SR experiment. We used samples of training speech with a length between 2 to 10 s and the test voice of 1 s to analyze the recognition performance based on TrimNet. In PBSD, three complete voice samples of cold-suffering users were included. When the adaptation template was not actively updated, the recognition rate first decreased and then increased. The results of experiments have indicated that the transfer learning updating strategy can effectively ensure a high SR rate as the user recovering from cold-suffering to healthy.

Acknowledgement. This paper is supported by the National Natural Science Foundation of China (General Program). Grant No. 61971316.

References

1. Hansen, J.H.L., Hasan, T.: Speaker recognition by machines and humans: a tutorial review. IEEE Signal Process. Mag. **32**(6), 74–99 (2015)
2. Richards, H., Haynes, R., Kim, Y., Bridle, J.: Generalised discriminative transform via curriculum learning for speaker recognition. In: 2018 IEEE ICASSP, pp. 5324–5328 (2018)
3. Ghiurcau, M.V., Rusu, C., Astola, J.: A study of the effect of emotional state upon text-independent speaker identification. In: 2011 IEEE International Conference on ICASSP, 2011, pp. 4944–4947 (2011)
4. Matveev, Y.: The problem of voice template aging in speaker recognition systems. In: Železný, M., Habernal, I., Ronzhin, A. (eds.) SPECOM 2013. LNCS (LNAI), vol. 8113, pp. 345–353. Springer, Cham (2013). https://doi.org/10.1007/978-3-319-01931-4_46
5. Przybocki, M.A., Martin, A.F., Le, A.N.: Nist speaker recognition evaluations utilizing the mixer corporal 2004, 2005, 2006. IEEE Trans. Audio Speech Lang. Process. **15**(7), 1951–1959 (2007)
6. Wagner, J., Fraga-Silva, T., Josse, Y., Schiller, D., Sei-derer, A., Andre, E.: Infected phonemes: how a cold impairs speech on a phonetic level. In: Proceedings of Interspeech 2017, pp. 3457–3461 (2017)
7. Bengio, Y.: End-to-end attention-based large vocabulary speech recognition. In: 2016 IEEE Inter- national Conference on ICASSP, 2016, pp. 4945–4949 (2016)
8. Berry, D.A., Herzel, H., Titze, I.R., Krischer, K.: Interpretation of biomechanical simulations of normal and chaotic vocal fold oscillations with empirical eigenfunctions. J. Acoust. Soc. Am. **95**(6), 3595–3604 (1994)
9. Godino Llorente, J.I., Díazde María, F.: Characterization of healthy and pathological voice through measures based on nonlinear dynamics. IEEE Trans. Audio Speech Lang. Process. **17**(6), 1186–1195 (2009)
10. Hansen, J.H.L., Gavidia Ceballos, L., Kaiser, J.F.: A nonlinear operator-based speech feature analysis method with application to vocal fold pathology assessment. IEEE Trans. Biomed. Eng. **45**(3), 300–313 (1998)
11. Tull, R.G., Rutledge, J.C., Larson, C.R: Cepstral analysis of cold-speech for speaker recognition: a second look. Ph.D. thesis, ASA (1996)

12. Cole, R.A., Noel, M., Noel, V.: The CSLU speaker recognition corpus. In: Fifth International Conference on Spoken Language Processing (1998)
13. Beigi, H.: Effects of time lapse on speaker recognition results. In: 2009 16th Inter- national Conference on Digital Signal Processing, pp. 1–6 (2009)
14. Reynolds, D.A., Rose, R.C., et al.: Robust text-independent speaker identification using gaussian mixture speaker models. IEEE Trans. Speech Audio Process. 3(1), 72–83 (1995)
15. Ouellet, P.: Front-end factor analysis for speaker verification. IEEE Trans. Speech Audio Process. 19(4), 788–798 (2011)
16. Senior, I., Lopez-Moreno, A.: Improving DNN speaker independence with i-vector inputs. In: 2014 IEEE International Conference on ICASSP, 2014, pp. 225–229 (2014)
17. Kenny, P.: Bayesian speaker verification with heavy tailed priors. In: Odyssey 2010, p. 14 (2010)
18. Rohdin, J., Silnova, A., Diez, M., Plchot, O., Matějka, P., Burget, L.: End-to-end DNN based speaker recognition inspired by i-vector and PLDA. In: 2018 IEEE ICAS-SP, 2018, pp. 4874–4878 (2018)
19. Yamada, T., Wang, L., Kai, A.: Improvement of distant-talking speaker identification using bottleneck features of DNN. In: Interspeech 2013, pp. 3661–3664 (2013)
20. Lei, Y., Scheffer, N., Ferrer, L., McLaren, M.: A novel scheme for speaker recognition using a phonetically- aware deep neural network. In: 2014 IEEE International Conference on ICASSP, 2014, pp. 1695–1699 (2014)
21. Torfi, A., Dawson, J., Nasrabadi, N.M.: Text-independent speaker verification using 3d convolutional neural networks. In: 2018 IEEE ICME, 2018, pp. 1–6 (2018)

A Fine-Grained Authorized
Keyword Secure Search Scheme
in the Cloud Computing

Fan Wang[1]📷, Zheng Qin[1](✉)📷, and Hui Yin[2]📷

[1] College of Computer Science and Electronic Engineering,
Hunan University, Changsha, China
{shelywf,zqin}@hnu.edu.cn
[2] College of Computer Engineering and Applied Mathematics,
Changsha University, Changsha, China
3913115@qq.com

Abstract. The development of the Internet and the Internet of Things has led to a sharp increase in the amount of data. The great advantages of big data have promoted the research and usage of a series of related technologies in various fields. In the field of government, data from various departments is being aggregated to acquire more value which can help to improve the efficiency and quality of public service. Cloud computing, as an infrastructure of big data, is also applied in government big data. However, the sensitivity of government data determines that the data stored in the cloud must be well protected. Meanwhile, fine-grained data sharing is also important for the public services of government. Recently, several searchable attribute-based encryption schemes have been proposed to achieve fine-grained data access control and search on ciphertext simultaneously. Unfortunately, each of them has some imperfections in efficiency or access policy. In this paper, we propose a fine-grained authorized keyword secure search scheme by leveraging the attribute-based encryption primitive, whose access policy supports AND, OR, and threshold gates. We give the concrete construction, rigorous verification of correctness, detailed security analysis, and prove that our solution is efficiency through several experiments.

Keywords: CP-ABE · Access control · Searchable encryption

1 Introduction

Government data appeared in the 1980s when e-government was applied, and as time goes on, more and more data has been collected. Recently, with the rapid development of the Internet, technologies, such as the Internet of things, industry 4.0 and machine intelligence, are becoming more and more mature, which enables us to extract more value from data. Government departments have realized the importance of integrating government data, and hope that

© Springer Nature Switzerland AG 2019
J. Vaidya et al. (Eds.): CSS 2019, LNCS 11983, pp. 432–447, 2019.
https://doi.org/10.1007/978-3-030-37352-8_38

these integrated government data can create great value and promote the formation of a new management mode. The data that was originally divided by geography, functions, topics, etc. and the data which was stored in different departments due to the limitations in storage, communication and computing can be aggregated and further processed now. As a result, more valuable information can be obtained from the data. However, when the data stored locally is transferred to the cloud server after aggregation, new security issues will arise in data storage and access. The specific explanation is as follows. When the data of each department is stored in its own department, the amount of data and the scope of data content are relatively small. Meanwhile, the generation, exchange and use of data are all within the department. In this situation, the department that holds government data enables to ensure the safety of the data by standardizing the internal regulations and using traditional security means such as security assurance architecture of E-government mentioned in [17]. However, as for the aggregated data, it has some new characteristics, such as large volume, variety, great value and strong confidentiality requirements. Besides, government big data is closely related to national interests and people's livelihood. Therefore, it is necessary for us to ensure the security of the aggregated government data, otherwise it will cause very serious consequences once the data is obtained illegally or abused.

Data encryption is one of the effective means to ensure the security of government big data. However, data encryption causes that traditional keyword-based information retrieval technologies are no longer applicable in the cipher text environment. Further, the sharing and utilization of data will be seriously hindered, and it will be difficult for the government to use government big data to achieve value creation and pattern innovation. Fortunately, searchable encryption algorithm, as a cryptographic that ensures both confidentiality and searchability of the data, can effectively solve these problems. There exist many searchable encryption schemes [5,6,8,10,11,15,18]. However, unlike ordinary data stored in a cloud, government big data contains information from multiple domains and departments, and the users of government big data have different access rights (i.e., users with different attribute should have different data access rights). So a fine-grained data access control algorithm is also needed. An intuitive idea is to design an encryption algorithm based on user's attribute. Attribute-based encryption (ABE) [14] happens to be an algorithm that can realize fine-grained access control. To better share and apply government big data, it's necessary to design an algorithm that satisfies both fine-grained access control and efficient query. The combination of CP-ABE and searchable encryption, that is, CP-ABE searchable encryption protocol well be a good solution. In recent years, a few searchable encryption schemes with authorized keyword search are proposed. However each of them has some imperfection in efficiency [12] or access policies [7,13,16,19,20] (See Sect. 2 for details). So we design a fine-grained authorized keyword secure search scheme with practical time cost, to realize a data access structure which supports AND, OR, and threshold gates.

In the paper, our contributions are organized as follows:

(1) We design a searchable encryption scheme based on CP-ABE, which satisfies both fine-grained access control and keyword search on ciphertext.
(2) We verify the correctness of our scheme and give detailed security proof.
(3) We implement our scheme and evaluate it's performance by several experiments. The results show that our scheme is effective.

2   Related Works

Searchable encryption can be classified into symmetric searchable encryption (SSE) and asymmetric searchable encryption according to the encryption algorithm. Since the first practical searchable encryption scheme proposed by Song [15] in 2000, many people have done research in this field and got some achievements, such as advanced symmetrical searchable encryption schemes [10,11] and search functionality explored in the public-key cryptosystem [5,6,8,18]. Unfortunately, none of the scheme mentioned above can achieve fine-grained access control. But, attribute-based encryption (ABE) [14] can solve the problem. The origin of ABE can be traced back to identity-based encryption, where Sahai and Waters first proposed the concept [14]. The formal definition and classification of ABE (ciphertext policy attribute based encryption and key policy attribute based encryption, i.e., CP-ABE and KP-ABE) as well as the first construction of KP-ABE were proposed by Goyal [9], while the first CP-ABE was constructed in [4]. Recently, Some attribute-based searchable encryption have been proposed to achieve fine-grained access control and ciphertext search [7,12,13,16,19,20]. The first attribute-based keyword search scheme with efficient user revocation proposed by Sun [16] only support AND policies. The schemes proposed in [7,13] support more policies, but threshold gates aren't still supported by these schemes. It is noteworthy that the reason why [7,13] don't support threshold gates is the inherent flaw of the Linear Secret Sharing Scheme (LSSS) used by these schemes. In addition, the scheme proposed in [12] can't be applied to practice, due to the high computational cost. So it is necessary to design a fine-grained authorized keyword secure search scheme with practical time cost, to realize a data access structure which supports AND, OR, and threshold gates.

3   Preliminaries

This section will introduce some background knowledge, which will be used in our construction.

Definition 1. *Let $\mathbb{G}_1$, $\mathbb{G}_T$ be two cyclic multiplication groups with the uniform order p and g is a generator of $\mathbb{G}_1$. We define a mapping as $e : \mathbb{G}_1 \times \mathbb{G}_1 \to \mathbb{G}_T$. We say that e is a bilinear map, if and only if it satisfies the following conditions:*

(1) Bilinearity: for $\forall\, x, y, x_1, x_2 \in \mathbb{G}_1$, and $\forall\, a, b \in \mathbb{Z}_p^*$, the following equation are true: $e(x^a, y^b) = e(x, y)^{ab}$, $e(x_1 x_2, y) = e(x_1, y)e(x_2, y)$, $e(x, y) = e(y, x)$;

(2) *Non-degeneracy: there exists one pair of elements* $x, y \in \mathbb{G}_1$, *making the following equation is true:* $e(x, y) \neq 1_{\mathbb{G}_T}$, *where* $1_{\mathbb{G}_T}$ *is a generator of* $\mathbb{G}_T$;

(3) *Computability: for* $\forall x, y \in \mathbb{G}_1$, *we can calculate* $e(x, y) \in \mathbb{G}_T$ *within a polynomial time algorithm.*

Definition 2. *Access Control Tree. A access control tree is a tree structure that can be used to represent access policies. Currently, access control trees have been widely used in ABE. We use* T *to denote a access control tree and* x *to denote the node of the access control tree. Then we define several notations for a better description of a access control tree.* $parent(x)$ *is used to indicate the parent of a node* x. $index(x)$ *is used to indicate the order of a node* x *relative to its parent node* $parent(x)$. *For instance,* $index(x) = 1$ *indicates that* x *is the leftmost child (i.e., the first child) of the node* $parent(x)$, *and so on.* $attr(x)$ *is used to indicate the attribute associated with a leaf node* x *in an attribute-based encryption system. Further, we use* num_x *and* k_x *to denote the number of children and threshold value of* $x \in T$, *respectively. According to the value of* num_x *and* k_x, *a non-leaf node* x *can represent an AND gate, an OR gate or a threshold gate, the specific description is as follows: Node* x *is (1) an OR gate, if* $k_x = 1$; *(2) an AND gate, if* $k_x = num_x$; *(3) a threshold gate, if* $1 < k_x < num_x$. *Besides, we define* $k_x = 1$ *and* $num_x = 0$, *when* x *is a leaf node.*

Definition 3. *Decisional Bilinear Diffie-Hellman (DBDH) assumption. Let* $e :$ $\mathbb{G}_1 \times \mathbb{G}_1 \to \mathbb{G}_T$ *be a bilinear map, where* $\mathbb{G}_1$ *and* $\mathbb{G}_T$ *are two multiplicative groups with order* p, *and* $\mathbb{G}_1$ *has a generator denoted by* g. *We choose four elements* $a, b, c, z \in \mathbb{Z}_p^*$ *randomly and get* $g^a, g^b, g^c \in \mathbb{G}_1$, $e(g, g)^{abc}$, $Z = e(g, g)^z \in \mathbb{G}_T$. *The DBDH assumption is defined as follows: no probabilistic polynomial-time adversary* $\mathcal{A}$ *can distinguish* $e(g, g)^{abc}$ *from* Z *with a non-negligible advantage.*

Definition 4. *Discrete Logarithm (DL) assumption. Let* $\mathbb{G}$ *be a group with prime order* p, *which has a generator denoted by* g. *We choose* $a \in \mathbb{Z}_p^*$ *at random uniformly, the DL problem assumption is defined as follows: give* g *and* g^a, *no probabilistic polynomial-time adversary* $\mathcal{A}$ *can compute the number* a *with a non-negligible advantage.*

4 System Model and Security Model

4.1 System Model

The system model of our scheme can be described as the interaction of the data owner, the server as well as the data users, which is shown in Fig. 1. The concrete interaction is divided into three stages.

In the first stage, the data owner uploads data to the server. To ensure the searchability and confidentiality of data files, data owner first encrypts the data files and builds a secure searchable index embedded by an access control tree before uploads these encrypted data files and the corresponding keyword indexes.

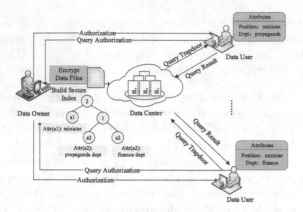

Fig. 1. A system model of search over encrypted data on a remote cloud center.

In the next stage, the users request the certificate from the data owner. When users request to join the system, they need to get the authorization from the data owner. Authorized users will own a group of keys according to their attributes.

In the final stage, the users search for data on the server. The users first use their key to generate a valid search trapdoor and submit the query request to the server. Then, a search on the secure searchable index is performed by the server without any leakage of the data file information and the search query. Finally, the result is returned.

4.2 Security Model

First of all, we assume that: (1) the server is "curious but honest"; (2) authorized data users can be trusted, which means they does don't leak the received security parameters to other illegal users; (3) the secure communication channels which is used to transfer keys from the data owner to the authorized data users is exit.

Informally, we say that a keyword index based searchable algorithm achieve a security goal means that any polynomial-size adversaries can't get the keyword information from the searchable index and query trapdoor. So, in this paper, we prove that our scheme is secure under the $ikus - cpa$ and $qtus - eav$ models mentioned in [20].

5   Fine-Grained Authorized Keyword Based Secure Search Scheme

In this section, We propose a Fine-Grained Authorized Keyword Based Secure Search Scheme and present the detailed of its constructions.

5.1   Setting Initialization

Let $\mathbb{G}_1$ and $\mathbb{G}_T$ be two cyclic multiplicative groups with a large prime order p, while g is a generator of group $\mathbb{G}_1$. Let $e : \mathbb{G}_1 \times \mathbb{G}_1 \to \mathbb{G}_T$ be a bilinear map with three properties mentioned in Sect. 3. We define two cryptography hash functions $H_1 : \{0, 1\}^* \to \mathbb{Z}_p^*$ hashing an arbitrary length string to an element in $\mathbb{Z}_p^*$ and $H_2 : \{0, 1\}^* \to \mathbb{G}_1$ hashing an arbitrary length string to a group element in $\mathbb{G}_1$. We also define Lagrange coefficients as follows: $\Delta_{i,S}(x) = \prod_{j \in S, j \neq i} \frac{x-j}{i-j}$, where S denotes a set of elements in $\mathbb{Z}_p^*$ and $i, j \in \mathbb{Z}_p^*$.

5.2   Key Generation

In this phase, the data owner takes advantage of the initialized setting to generate the public parameters and system keys under the protection of a security parameter. Specifically, the data owner chooses two random elements α, $\beta \in \mathbb{Z}_p^*$, and generates the public parameter PK and two key groups sk_1, sk_2 as follows:

$$\begin{aligned} \mathbb{KEY} = (PK &= (\mathbb{G}_1, \mathbb{G}_T, g, e, H_1, H_2), \\ sk_1 &= (\beta, \frac{1}{\beta}, g^\alpha), sk_2 = (e(g, g)^\alpha, h = g^\beta), \end{aligned} \tag{1}$$

where PK is the public parameter and can be accessed by all entities in the system, while sk_1 and sk_2 are holden only by the data owner. In our scheme, the data owner uses sk_1 to grant query privilege for newly joined data users and sk_2 is used to encrypted index keywords for constructing secure searchable indexes.

5.3   Secure Inverted Index Construction and Data Outsourcing

To prevent the cloud server from obtaining useful information of keywords and data files from the inverted index, before outsourcing data, the data owner has to encrypt each keyword and corresponding data files that contain the keyword in a posting list. Normally, the security of data files can be easily guaranteed by using any symmetric encryption scheme such as AES under a key k. For each keyword associating with each posting list (without loss of generality, we use w to denote a keyword), to achieve effective and efficient matching between the encrypted keyword in a posting list and a query trapdoor submitted by an authorized data user, in this paper, the data owner first takes three steps to encrypt the keyword w. First, w is mapped an element in $\mathbb{Z}_p^*$ by using the hash function H_1 as $H_1(w)$. Second, the data owner converts $H_1(w)$ to a group element in $\mathbb{G}_1$ by computing $g^{H_1(w)}$. Finally, he further uses the bilinear pairing map e to encode the group element $g^{H_1(w)}$ under the secret parameter $\gamma = \{r_1, r_2\}$ as follows:

$$\varepsilon_\gamma(w) = e(g^{H_1(w) \cdot r_1}, g)^{r_2} = e(g, g)^{H_1(w) r_1 r_2}, l = g^{r_2}. \tag{2}$$

We use $\varepsilon(w)_\gamma$ to denote the ciphertext of keyword w encrypted by the key γ.

On the other hand, to achieve fine-grained authorized keyword search and allow the data owner to determine the keyword w can be searched by which authorized data users in a fine-grained manner, the attribute-based access control is embedded into the keyword w under a access control tree structure T_w which is defined by the data owner. Only the user whose attribute set satisfies the tree structure T_w is able to use the keyword w to request data files. We describe the encryption process in detail as follows.

Given a keyword w, the data owner first defines an access control tree T_w and chooses a polynomial q_x for each node x in T_w. These polynomials are chosen in a top-down manner, starting from the root node R. For each polynomial q_x of x, the data owner sets the degree d_x of q_x to be one less than the threshold value k_x of the node x, i.e., $d_x = k_x - 1$. For the root node R, he sets d_R, chooses a random element $s \in \mathbb{Z}_p^*$, and then sets $q_R(0) = s$ and other points of q_R randomly to completely define it. For any other node x in T_w, he sets $q_x(0) = q_p(x)(index(x))$, then chooses d_x and other points to completely define q_x, where p is $parent(x)$. Let Y be the set of leaf nodes in T_w, based on the ciphertext $\varepsilon(w)_\gamma \in \mathbb{G}_1$ of the keyword w, the data owner computes:

$$CT_w = (T_w, C = \varepsilon(w)_\gamma \cdot e(g,g)^{\alpha s}, C' = h^s, l = g^{r_2}$$
$$\forall y \in Y : C_y = g^{q_y(0)}, C'_y = H_2(attr(y))^{q_y(0)}).$$
(3)

Finally, the data owner uses CT_w to associate with all encrypted data files that contain the keyword w to form the corresponding posting list and then outsources them to the cloud server.

5.4   Data User Grant

When a data user wishes to join the system to search data files of interest from the cloud server, he first needs to obtain the query privilege from the data owner. In this paper, the data owner achieves fine-grained authorized keyword query control for data users by defining different attribute sets for different data users according to keywords query privilege owned by a data user. Only when the attribute set assigned a data user satisfies the access control tree that encrypts a certain keyword w in the corresponding posting list, the data user can use the keyword w to search data from server. In order to grant the access permission to a new user, the data owner assigns a set of attributes S for the new data user and generates the secret key associated with these attributes in S as:

$$SK = (D = g^{(\alpha+r)/\beta}, \forall a \in S, D_a = g^r \cdot H_2(a)^{r_a}, D'_a = g^{r_a}),$$
(4)

where r is a random element in $\mathbb{Z}_p^*$ and r_a also denotes a random element in $\mathbb{Z}_p^*$ for each attribute a in S. Then, the data owner sends tuple (k, γ, S, SK) to the data user through secure communication channels, and the user stores the received tuple locally, where k, γ are data files encryption key and keywords encryption key respectively, which are securely stored by the data owner.

5.5   Trapdoor Generation

Assume the data user wants to search all data files that contain a certain keyword w, before submitting the keyword to the cloud server, the data user needs to encrypt the query keyword for protecting his query privacy and realizing encrypted keyword matching with encrypted inverted index stored at the cloud server. On the other hand, to achieve trapdoor unlinkability, the generated trapdoor should be different every time even for the same query keyword.

To meet the above conditions, the authorized data user takes the following two steps to generate the trapdoor for the query keyword w. First, he maps the keyword w into an element in $\mathbb{Z}_p^*$ as $H_1(w)$ and randomly chooses an element $\lambda \in \mathbb{Z}_p^*$ and gets two random group elements by computing $g^{H_1(w) \cdot \lambda}$ and g^λ. Second, to realize encrypted keyword matching with encrypted inverted index, he further encrypts $g^{H_1(w) \cdot \lambda}$ and g^λ using the keyword encryption key γ. Eventually, the data user gets the trapdoor of query keyword w as follows:

$$T_r(w) = (T_1 = g^{H_1(w)r_1} \cdot g^\lambda, T_2 = g^{\lambda \cdot r_2}, SK), \tag{5}$$

and submits the trapdoor to the cloud server. We can see that the T_1 is the encryption of the keyword w and the randomly chosen element γ guarantees unlinkability of the trapdoor. SK is a necessary factor of the trapdoor to determine whether the data user holds the query privilege of keyword w.

5.6   Secure Search over Encrypted Inverted Index

Cloud server is equipped with powerful storage capacity and computation power, besides storing all encrypted data files of the data owner, it is also responsible for performing search on behalf of data users and returning the qualified query results. In our scheme, upon receiving a query trapdoor $T_r(w)$ of the query keyword w submitted by a data user u, the cloud server begins to perform search over encrypted inverted index and then returns all encrypted data files that contain the keyword w if and only if the following two conditions are satisfied simultaneously: (1) the cloud server can find a posting list with a certain keyword w_0 that satisfies $w = w_0$ and (2) the data user u must hold the query privilege of the keyword w_0, i.e., u's attribute set assigned by the data owner must satisfy the access control tree that encrypts the keyword w_0 in the corresponding posting list. Otherwise, u cannot obtain any data files from the cloud server. Moreover, in the whole query process, a basic security requirement is that the cloud server cannot know any plaintext contents of data files and query keywords.

In what follows, we detailedly introduce the secure search process performed by the cloud server. Without loss of generality, we use $T_r(w)$ to denote a query trapdoor of a keyword w submitted by a data user u, an posting list of the keyword w_0 encrypted by an access control tree T_{w_0} as CT_{w_0}. Essentially, the search is the encrypted keyword matching process between $T_r(w)$ and CT_{w_0}, which includes the following two steps as a whole.

The first step is that the cloud server tries to decrypt the CT_{w_0} to obtain $\varepsilon(w_0)_\gamma$ only when $T_r(w)\_SK$, which is associated with the u's attribute set S, satisfies the access control tree T_{w_0}. The decryption process can be performed from down to top as follows.

For each leaf node x, let $a = attr(x)$ denotes the attribute associated with x, if $a \in S$, then computes:

$$
\begin{aligned}
F_x &= \frac{e(D_a, C_x)}{e(D'_a, C'_x)} = \frac{e(g^r \cdot H_2(a)^{r_a}, g^{q_x(0)})}{e(g^{r_a}, H_2(a)^{q_x(0)})} \\
&= \frac{e(g^r, g^{q_x(0)}) \cdot e(H_2(a), g)^{r_a \cdot q_x(0)}}{e(H_2(a), g)^{r_a \cdot q_x(0)}} \\
&= e(g, \cdot g)^{r q_x(0)}.
\end{aligned}
\tag{6}
$$

If $a \notin S$, we define $F_x = \perp$. For each non-leaf node x in T_{w_0}, let S_x denote an arbitrary k_x-sized set of child nodes z such that $F_z \neq \perp$, We arbitrarily choose k child nodes, for each node z that satisfy $F_z = 1$, to form a set which is represented as S_x. If the set S_x doesn't exist then the node is not satisfied by u's attribute set S and define $F_x = \perp$; otherwise, compute by using Lagrange interpolation:

$$
\begin{aligned}
F_x &= \prod_{z \in S_x} F_z^{\Delta_{i,S'_x}(0)} \\
&= \prod_{z \in S_x} (e(g,g)^{r \cdot q_z(0)})^{\Delta_{i,S'_x}(0)} \\
&= \prod_{z \in S_x} (e(g,g)^{r \cdot q_{parent(z)}(index(z))})^{\Delta_{i,S'_x}(0)} \\
&= \prod_{z \in S_x} e(g,g)^{r \cdot q_x(i) \cdot \Delta_{i,S'_x}(0)} \\
&= e(g,g)^{r \cdot q_x(0)}.
\end{aligned}
\tag{7}
$$

Where $i = index(z)$, $S'_x = (\forall z \in S_x : index(z))$, and Δ_{i,S'_x} is the Lagrange coefficient. For the root node R of the tree T_{w_0}, according to the above operation, if $F_R = \perp$ then T is not satisfied by the u's attribute set S, otherwise,

$$
F_R = e(g, g)^{r \cdot q_R(0)} = e(g, g)^{rs}.
\tag{8}
$$

After finishing the above operations, if $F_R = \perp$ then it means that the data owner does not authorize the privilege of searching the posting list of the keyword w_0 to the data user u. Otherwise, the cloud server continues to perform the second step of the search to judge whether the query keyword w satisfies $w = w_0$ without knowing the plaintext information of w and w_0 by verifying whether the following equation is true:

$$
\frac{C}{e(C', D)/F_R} \cdot e(T_2, g) = e(T_1, l).
\tag{9}
$$

If the equation is true, it means that $w = w_0$ holds, the data user u obtains all encrypted data files that contain keyword $w\,(w_0)$ according to the corresponding posting list from the cloud server. Finally, u uses the symmetric key k to decrypt them locally.

Now, we verify the correctness of the search by the following derivation:

$$\frac{C}{e(C', D)/F_R} \cdot e(T_2, g) = \frac{\varepsilon(w_0) \cdot e(g, g)^{\alpha s}}{e(h^s, g^{(\alpha+r)/\beta})/e(g, g)^{rs}} \cdot e(g^{\lambda \cdot r_2}, g)$$

$$= \frac{\varepsilon(w_0) \cdot e(g, g)^{\alpha s}}{e(g, g)^{\alpha s}} \cdot e(g^{\lambda \cdot r_2}, g)$$

$$= \varepsilon(w_0) \cdot e(g^{\lambda \cdot r_2}, g) \tag{10}$$

$$= e(g, g)^{H_1(w_0) r_1 r_2} \cdot e(g^{\lambda \cdot r_2}, g)$$

$$= e(g^{r_2 \cdot (H_1(w_0) r_1 + \lambda)}, g)$$

$$= e(g^{(H_1(w_0) r_1 + \lambda)}, g^{r_2}).$$

If the query keyword w is exactly the same as w_0 (i.e., $w = w_0$) then,

$$\frac{C}{e(C', D)/F_R} \cdot e(T_2, g) = e(g^{(H_1(w_0) r_1 + \lambda)}, g^{r_2})$$

$$= e(g^{(H_1(w) r_1 + \lambda)}, g^{r_2}) \tag{11}$$

$$= e(g^{H_1(w) r_1} \cdot g^{\lambda}, g^{r_2})$$

$$= e(T_1, l).$$

6   Analysis of Correctness and Security

In this section, we will analyze the correctness and security of the scheme we proposed. To prove the correctness of the scheme we proposed, we only need to prove that the trapdoor can match an encrypted index keyword. However, we have prove it in Subsect. 5.6, so we can affirm that the scheme we proposed is correct. Next, we will analyze the security of our algorithm in detail as follows.

Now we prove that our scheme is secure under the $ikus - cpa$ model and $qtus - eav$ model mentioned in Subsect. 4.2.

Theorem 1. *If DBDH assumption is true, then our proposed fine-grained authorized keyword based secure search scheme achieves $ikus - cpa$ model.*

Proof. If there exists a polynomial-time adversary $\mathcal{A}$ that can obtain the index keyword information from the corresponding encrypted index keyword with a non-negligible advantage ϵ, it means that we can build a simulator $\mathcal{B}$ that can solve the DBDH problem with advantage $\frac{\epsilon}{2}$.

The challenger $\mathcal{C}$ first sets up the system public parameters including $\mathbb{G}_1$, $\mathbb{G}_T$, a bilinear map e (constructed by $\mathbb{G}_1$ and $\mathbb{G}_T$), and a generator g of $\mathbb{G}_1$. Then $\mathcal{C}$ chooses a bit v from $\{0, 1\}$ at randomly. If $v = 0$, the tuple $(g, A = g^a, B = g^b, C = g^c, Z = e(g, g)^{abc})$, denoted by t_0, is sent to $\mathcal{B}$, otherwise the tuple sent to $\mathcal{B}$ is $(g, A = g^a, B = g^b, C = g^c, Z = e(g, g)^z)$, denoted by t_1, where a, b, c, z are chosen from $\mathbb{Z}_p^*$ randomly. Next, the simulator $\mathcal{B}$ plays the game based on $ikus - cpa$ with the adversary $\mathcal{A}$ as follows.

Setup. $\mathcal{B}$ sets the public parameter $Y = e(A, B) = e(g, g)^{ab}$ and transmits it to $\mathcal{A}$. At same time $\mathcal{A}$ specifies an access control tree $T^{\#}$ that he wishes to be challenged and sends it to $\mathcal{B}$.

Phase 1. $\mathcal{A}$ adaptively issues queries for the private keys corresponding to attribute sets $S_1, S_2, \cdots S_n$ (none of them satisfy the challenge access control tree $T^{\#}$) and the encrypted keywords $CT_{w_1}, CT_{w_2}, \cdots, CT_{w_m}$ of index keywords $w_1, w_2, \cdots, w_m$ from $\mathcal{B}$. $\mathcal{B}$ responses the private keys and encrypted keywords, which satisfy the conditions as follows.

(1) We can generate a valid query trapdoor by any private key.
(2) Given a private key and a query keyword we can generate a query trapdoor. There exists an encrypted index keyword, that we can get the data files containing the query keyword by the search algorithm.

Challenge. $\mathcal{A}$ chooses two keywords w_0' and w_1' and sends them to the $\mathcal{B}$. Then, $\mathcal{B}$ randomly chooses a bit b from $\{0, 1\}$, and generates the ciphertext as follows: $CT_{w_b'}^{\#} = (T^{\#}, C^{\#} = Z^{H_1(w_b')} \cdot e(g,g)^{\alpha s}, (C')^{\#} = h^s, l^{\#} = A \forall y \in Y^{\#} : C_y^{\#} = g^{q_y(0)}, (C_y')^{\#} = H_2(attr(y))^{q_y(0)})$, where $Y^{\#}$ denotes the leaf node set of $T^{\#}$. Finally, $CT_{w_b'}^{\#}$ is sent to $\mathcal{A}$ by $\mathcal{B}$.

Phase 2. $\mathcal{A}$ continues to adaptively issue queries for the private keys corresponding to attribute sets $S_{n+1}, S_{n+2}, \cdots$ (none of them satisfy the challenge access control tree $T^{\#}$) and the encrypted keywords $CT_{w_{m+1}}, CT_{w_{m+2}}, \cdots$, of index keywords $w_{m+1}, w_{m+2}, \cdots$ from $\mathcal{B}$.

Guess. $\mathcal{A}$ outputs the guess b' of b. We know that $\mathcal{A}$ can't guess a correct of b by executing a search operation with keyword (w_0' or w_1') to get the valid output, because all attribute sets held by $\mathcal{A}$ don't satisfy $T^{\#}$. So, the only way to judge the value of b is to recover the index keyword information from $CT_{w_b'}^{\#}$. This problem has two conditions as follows:

(1) If $v = 0$, $\mathcal{C}$ sends t_0 to $\mathcal{B}$, then $Z = e(g,g)^{abc}$, we get $CT_{w_b'}^{\#} = (T^{\#}, C^{\#} = e(g,g)^{abc \cdot H_1(w_b')} \cdot e(g,g)^{\alpha s}, (C')^{\#} = h^s, l^{\#} = g^a, \forall y \in Y^{\#} : C_y^{\#} = g^{q_y(0)}, (C_y')^{\#} = H_2(attr(y))^{q_y(0)})$. Due to r_1, r_2 are randomly chosen in the index keyword encryption, we set $a = r_2$ and $bc = r_1$, the encrypted index keyword can be written as $CT_{w_b'}^{\#} = (T^{\#}, C^{\#} = e(g,g)^{r_2 r_1 \cdot H_1(w_b')} \cdot e(g,g)^{\alpha s}, (C')^{\#} = h^s, l^{\#} = g^{r_2}, \forall y \in Y^{\#} : C_y^{\#} = g^{q_y(0)}, (C_y')^{\#} = H_2(attr(y))^{q_y(0)})$. It suggests that $(CT_{w_b'})^{\#}$ is the correct encrypted index keyword of w_b'.

(2) If $v = 1$, $\mathcal{C}$ sends t_1 to $\mathcal{B}$, then $Z = e(g,g)^z$, we get $CT_{w_b'}^{\#} = (T^{\#}, C^{\#} = e(g,g)^{z \cdot H_1(w_b')} \cdot e(g,g)^{\alpha s}, (C')^{\#} = h^s, l^{\#} = g^{r_2}, \forall y \in Y^{\#} : C_y^{\#} = g^{q_y(0)}, (C_y')^{\#} = H_2(attr(y))^{q_y(0)})$. From $\mathcal{A}$'s point of view, $CT_{w_b'}^{\#}$ is random without any information about w_b', due to z is random.

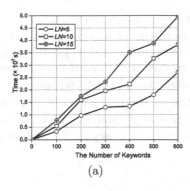
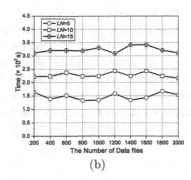

(a)   (b)

Fig. 2. The time cost of Secure Inverted Index Construct algorithm. (a) Time cost of encrypting index keywords for different number of index keywords with fixed number of data files $n = 2000$. (c) Time cost of encrypting index keywords for different number of data files with fixed number of index keyword $i = 400$.

$\mathcal{A}$ outputs the guess b' of b, then $\mathcal{B}$ output $v' = 0$, when $b' = b$, $\mathcal{C}$ transits the valid tuple t_0 to $\mathcal{B}$. Since the advantage of $\mathcal{A}$ to recover $H_{(w'_b)}$ from $CT^{\#}_{w'_b}$ is ϵ, the probability that $\mathcal{A}$ outputs $b' = b$ is $\frac{1}{2} + \epsilon$. If $b' \neq b$, then $\mathcal{B}$ output $v' = 1$, and $\mathcal{C}$ transits the valid tuple t_1 to $\mathcal{B}$. The probability that $\mathcal{A}$ outputs $b' = b$ is $\frac{1}{2}$. The overall advantage for $\mathcal{A}$ to solve the DBDH problem in the game mentioned above is as follows: $|\frac{1}{2}Pr[v = v'|v = 0] + \frac{1}{2}Pr[v = v'|v = 1] - \frac{1}{2}| = ||\frac{1}{2}(\frac{1}{2} + \epsilon) + \frac{1}{2} \cdot \frac{1}{2}] - \frac{1}{2}| = \frac{\epsilon}{2}$.

If ϵ is non-negligible, then $\frac{\epsilon}{2}$ is also non-negligible, which means that $\mathcal{B}$ can solve the DBDH problem with a non-negligible advantage. However it contradicts the DBDH assumption.

Theorem 2. *If DL assumption is true, then our proposed fine-grained authorized keyword based secure search scheme achieves qtus − eav model.*

Proof. We prove the above theorem by a game between the adversary $\mathcal{A}$ and the challenger $\mathcal{C}$ as follows.

Phase 1. $\mathcal{A}$ issues queries of trapdoor corresponding to keywords $w_1, w_2, \cdots, w_n$ from $\mathcal{B}$. For each k_i, $1 \leq i \leq n$, $\mathcal{C}$ responses the ciphertext as follows: $T_{r\mathcal{A}}(w_i) = (T_1 = g^{H_1(w_i)r_1} \cdot g^{\lambda}, T_2 = g^{\lambda \cdot r_2}, SK_{\mathcal{A}})$, where $SK_{\mathcal{A}}$ denotes the attribute set of $\mathcal{A}$.

Challenge. The adversary $\mathcal{A}$ chooses two keywords w'_0 and w'_1 and sends them to $\mathcal{C}$. Then, $\mathcal{C}$ randomly chooses a bit b from $\{0, 1\}$, and generates the ciphertext of w'_b as follows: $T^{\#}_{r\mathcal{A}}(w'_b) = (T^{\#}_1 = g^{H_1(w'_b)r_1} \cdot g^{\lambda}, T^{\#}_2 = g^{\lambda \cdot r_2}, SK_{\mathcal{A}}{}^{\#})$ Finally, $T^{\#}_{r\mathcal{A}}(w'_b)$ is sent to $\mathcal{A}$ by $\mathcal{C}$.

Phase 2. $\mathcal{A}$ continues to issue queries for the trapdoors corresponding to keywords $w_{m+1}, w_{m+2}, \cdots$ from $\mathcal{C}$.

Guess. $\mathcal{A}$ outputs the guess b' of b. We know that $\mathcal{A}$ can't guess a correct of b by executing a search operation with keyword (w'_0 or w'_1) to get the valid output, because the queries of the challenge keyword (w'_0 and w'_1) is forbidden. So, the only way to judge the value of b is to recover the keyword information from $T_{r\,\mathcal{A}}^{\#}(w'_b)$. However, according to the DL assumption, $\mathcal{A}$ can't compute $H_1(w'_b)r_1$ with a non-negligible advantage. Then $\mathcal{A}$ can't compute r_1 or $H_1(w'_b)$ in polynomial time, so $\mathcal{A}$ can't compute the trapdoor of w'_0 and w'_1 effectively. So, the probability that $\mathcal{A}$ outputs $b' = b$ is $\frac{1}{2} + \epsilon$ (where ϵ is negligible) as long as the DL assumption is true.

7   Experimental Evaluation

In this section, we present several tests to evaluate the performances of our scheme. We choose 2000 files from the Comments Database (RFC) [3] and get 600 index keywords by Hermetic Word Frequency Counter [2] tool to form the data set of our experiments. All the tests are processed by using JPBC library [1]

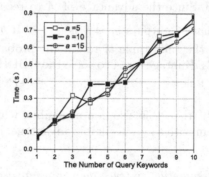

Fig. 3. The time cost of trapdoor generation

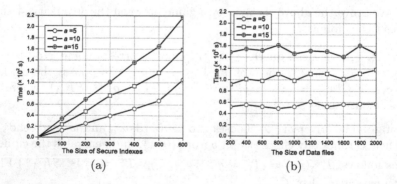

Fig. 4. Time cost of search over encrypted data. (a) Time cost of search for different number of index keywords with fixed size of data files $n = 2000$. (b) Time cost of search for different size of data files with fixed number of index keyword $i = 400$.

on server with an Ubuntu 16.04 system with 3.60-GHz Intel Core (TM) i7-7700 CPU and 8-GB RAM, and client with an Windows 7 desktop system 2.3-GHz Intel Core (TM) i5-6200U and 4-GB RAM.

7.1 Evaluation of Secure Index Construction

We evaluate the performs of the secure index construction by testing the time cost with experiments, whose dependent variable is the number of leaf nodes in the access control tree, the number of index keywords and the number of data files. These test results show that the more leaf nodes the access control tree have, the more time we spend. The results are similar when the number of the index keyword is the dependent variable. However, there is no obvious relationship between the number of data files and the time cost. The detailed results are shown in Fig. 2(a) and (b), where notation LN denotes the number of leaf nodes in the access control tree.

7.2 Evaluation of Trapdoor Generation

From the Fig. 3, we can see that the time cost of query keyword encryption is linear to the number of query keywords and is independent of the number of attributes, where notation a denotes the number of attributes.

7.3 Evaluation of Secure Search

In order to evaluate the efficiency of search over encrypted data, we organize keywords and encrypted documents to form an invert index structure. Besides, the trapdoor we used in our test satisfies all access control trees in our experiment, so that the efficiency of testing can be improved. The experimental results shows that the search time increases linearly with the increase of the number of keywords, while the number of files has little effect on the time overhead of the search algorithm. The detailed results are shown in Fig. 4(a) and (b), where notation a denotes the number of attributes.

8   Conclusion

In this paper, We designed a searchable encryption algorithm based on CP-ABE to satisfy both fine-grained access control and keyword search on ciphertext. We give the specific construction, rigorous verification of correctness, detailed analysis of safety, and prove that our solution is efficiency through several experiments. The experimental results show that our scheme has good performance.

Acknowledgement. This work is supported by the National Natural Science Foundation of China under Grant 61772191, 61472131, Science and Technology Key Projects of Hunan Province (2015TP1004, 2016JC2012), and Science and Technology Key Projects of Changsha (kq1801008, kq1804008).

References

1. JPBC: The Java Pairing Based Cryptography Library, December 2013. http://gas. dia.unisa.it/projects/jpbc/index.html
2. Hermetic Systems: Hermetic Word Frequency Counter (2015). http://www. hermetic.ch/wfc/wfc.htm
3. IETF: Request for Comments Database, August 2018. http://www.ietf.org/rfc. html
4. Bethencourt, J., Sahai, A., Waters, B.: Ciphertext-policy attribute-based encryption. In: 2007 IEEE Symposium on Security and Privacy, Berkeley, CA, USA, pp. 321–334. IEEE (2007)
5. Boneh, D., Di Crescenzo, G., Ostrovsky, R., Persiano, G.: Public key encryption with keyword search. In: Cachin, C., Camenisch, J.L. (eds.) EUROCRYPT 2004. LNCS, vol. 3027, pp. 506–522. Springer, Heidelberg (2004). https://doi.org/10. 1007/978-3-540-24676-3_30
6. Boneh, D., Waters, B.: Conjunctive, subset, and range queries on encrypted data. In: Vadhan, S.P. (ed.) TCC 2007. LNCS, vol. 4392, pp. 535–554. Springer, Heidelberg (2007). https://doi.org/10.1007/978-3-540-70936-7_29
7. Cui, H., Wan, Z., Deng, R.H., Wang, G., Li, Y.: Efficient and expressive keyword search over encrypted data in cloud. IEEE Trans. Dependable Secur. Comput. 15(3), 409–422 (2018)
8. Golle, P., Staddon, J., Waters, B.: Secure conjunctive keyword search over encrypted data. In: Jakobsson, M., Yung, M., Zhou, J. (eds.) ACNS 2004. LNCS, vol. 3089, pp. 31–45. Springer, Heidelberg (2004). https://doi.org/10.1007/978-3-540-24852-1_3
9. Goyal, V., Pandey, O., Sahai, A., Waters, B.: Attribute-based encryption for fine-grained access control of encrypted data. In: Proceedings of the 13th ACM Conference on Computer and Communications Security, pp. 89–98. ACM, New York (2006)
10. Kamara, S., Papamanthou, C., Roeder, T.: Dynamic searchable symmetric encryption. In: Proceedings of the 2012 ACM Conference on Computer and Communications Security, pp. 965–976. ACM, New York (2012)
11. Kim, K.S., Kim, M., Lee, D., Park, J.H., Kim, W.H.: Forward secure dynamic searchable symmetric encryption with efficient updates. In: Proceedings of the 2017 ACM SIGSAC Conference on Computer and Communications Security, pp. 1449–1463. ACM, New York (2017)
12. Lai, J., Zhou, X., Deng, R.H., Li, Y., Chen, K.: Expressive search on encrypted data. In: Proceedings of the 8th ACM SIGSAC Symposium on Information, Computer and Communications Security, Hangzhou, China, pp. 243–252. ACM (2013)
13. Peng, T., Liu, Q., Hu, B., Liu, J., Zhu, J.: Dynamic keyword search with hierarchical attributes in cloud computing. IEEE Access 6, 68948–68960 (2018)
14. Sahai, A., Waters, B.: Fuzzy identity-based encryption. In: Cramer, R. (ed.) EUROCRYPT 2005. LNCS, vol. 3494, pp. 457–473. Springer, Heidelberg (2005). https:// doi.org/10.1007/11426639_27
15. Song, D.X., Wagner, D., Perrig, A.: Practical techniques for searches on encrypted data. In: Proceeding 2000 IEEE Symposium on Security and Privacy, Berkeley, CA, USA, pp. 44–55. IEEE (2000)
16. Sun, W., Yu, S., Lou, W., Hou, Y.T., Li, H.: Protecting your right: attribute-based keyword search with fine-grained owner-enforced search authorization in the cloud. In: IEEE INFOCOM 2014 - IEEE Conference on Computer Communications, Toronto, ON, Canada, pp. 226–234. IEEE (2014)

17. Wang, Z., Han, W., Lin, Y., Li, J.: Research on security assurance architecture of e-government. Comput. Appl. **28**(s1), 55–58 (2008)
18. Yin, H., et al.: Secure conjunctive multi-keyword search for multiple data owners in cloud computing. In: ICPADS 2016, Wuhan, China, pp. 761–768. IEEE (2016)
19. Yin, H., Xiong, Y., Zhang, J., Ou, L., Liao, S., Qin, Z.: A key-policy searchable attribute-based encryption scheme for efficient keyword search and fine-grained access control over encrypted data. Electronics **8**(256), 1–20 (2019)
20. Yin, H., et al.: CP-ABSE: a ciphertext-policy attribute-based searchable encryption scheme. IEEE Access **7**, 5682–5694 (2019)

Implementing Fingerprint Recognition on One-Time Password Device to Enhance User Authentication

Xiaochun Cheng$^{(\boxtimes)}$ (iD), Andreas Pitziolis, and Aboubaker Lasebae

Faculty of Science and Technology, Middlesex University, London, UK
{x.cheng,A.Lasebae}@mdx.ac.uk, apl520@live.mdx.ac.uk

Abstract. The banking sector uses One-Time Passwords (OTPs) to provide extra user authentication in contrast to basic security methods used, such as the "Card and PIN" or "online username and password". There have been several known attacks against OTPs, this paper provides an addition to the authentication process by the use of biometric authentication, such as fingerprint recognition. Finally, the solution is implemented by designing a smart IoT device using Arduino Uno, Fingerprint Sensor, RFID Card Reader and SIM/GSM/GPRS Shield.

Keywords: Internet of Things (IoT) · One-Time Password (OTP) · Fingerprint · Arduino Uno

1 Introduction

The banks engage information technology. Mobile IoT technology provides flexible access for the customers, and reduces costs for banks as physical transactions in banks are less needed [1]. Although IT provides many benefits, the disadvantages, such as attacks, have been increasing. The mobile banking has led to authentication challenges. Without proper authentication in mobile banking system, valid users and attackers cannot be distinguished; thus, invalid users might access clients' banking details, such as credit card numbers and account names. This might lead to the fraudsters undertaking unauthorized transactions in their favor. Mobile user authentication in the banking sector is considered of high noteworthiness due to the importance of the assets that are managed in such organizations. To prevent the above stated case, the banks introduced OTPs to provide Multi-Factor Authentication. By the passing of time, though, attackers figured out ways to compromise OTPs. This paper aims to enhance the security of online transactions by the use of biometrics such as fingerprint recognition in addition to OTPs, which will provide an additional step of user authentication.

2 Review Online Banking Authentication Methods

The banking sector is considered high in risk due to the importance of the assets that it handles, thus, security is of high level of concern. The lack of strong authentication procedure is the reason behind all major attacks taking place in the banking sector.

J. Vaidya et al. (Eds.): CSS 2019, LNCS 11983, pp. 448–461, 2019.
https://doi.org/10.1007/978-3-030-37352-8_39

Mentioned below are some of the most important authentication procedures used by banks to authenticate users to their accounts.

2.1 Single-Factor Authentication (SFA)

SFA uses only one authentication factor. The factors that it may use are knowledge-based, such as: a PIN, a passphrase, or a password. Even though with SFA, attackers have an easy task to acquire the single factor rather that multiple factors required for a successful authentication entry to a system, SFA offers simplicity and convenience as only one factor is required for authentication [2].

2.2 Multi-factor Authentication (MFA)

MFA is considered a more secure authentication protocol in contrast to SFA, since two or more independent security factors are used to authenticate users [2]. MFA is more complex and slower than SFA, but provides additional security.

2.3 Biometric Authentication

Biometrics can be defined as a pattern recognition system that can use both physiological and behavioral attributes of any individual in order to prove his/her identity [3]. Some examples of physiological attributes include face, fingerprint, hand geometry, and iris recognition, whereas, some examples of behavioral attributes include written signature and voice [4].

This paper mainly focuses on fingerprint recognition, not only because it is the most popular biometric method but also because that it is the most successfully implemented technique [5]. Even though fingerprint recognition will be described in details mainly in this paper, most biometric methods can be implemented using similar process [6].

Biometrics are a very important asset to organizations that have security as a high priority. This is because biometrics offer uniqueness and permanence of a pattern, non-reputation, and most importantly, are almost impossible to forge [7]. Research has shown that it is expected that the use of biometrics will soon replace the current authentication methods such as passwords and PINs that are currently in use by organizations. This is because biometrics are directly linked to an individual and cannot be used by another person, unlike PINs and passwords [8].

2.4 One-Time Passwords

OTP devices are most commonly used as an additional authentication factor of MFA in the banking sector in pursuance of enhancing security. OTPs are requested in specific or random situations, and are basically dynamically changing passwords. They are generated by handheld devices owned by the user, or by organizations that deal with the system the user is trying to log in. As stated above, OTPs are generated when a user requests access to his/her account, can be only used for a specific account, and have a limited amount of lifetime. This means that after the first use of the OTP, it cannot be used for any future transactions, nor after a specific amount of time, which is generally set at 60 s [12].

3   Analyzing Biometrics

The emerging phenomenon of biometrics as a means of more accurately identifying people has seen a significant increase in the last couple of years. In contrast to other identification methods, such as PINs and passwords, biometrics have the major advantage of neither being forgotten, overheard, lost, or stolen, thus, increasing the difficulty of fraudsters gaining access to user's accounts. As it has already been stated in previous sections, fingerprint recognition is the most popularly used biometric method. Such biometric methods are used in many businesses and organizations nowadays such as law enforcement, corporate databases, airports security, granting access to buildings/cars, as well as used to unlock the most recent smartphones in contrast to using a password or a pattern method.

3.1   Accuracy of Biometrics

The authentication process in biometric systems involves the comparison of the sample template, which is acquired using the sensor and the reference template, which is acquired during the enrolment phase [5]. The sensitivity of the sensor correspondingly plays an important role in the pattern matching phase since that phase has a direct effect on the decision-making phase [9]. False Acceptance Rate (FAR) and False Rejection Rate (FRR) are measurements about the accuracy of the matching process [10].

3.2   Processes Involved in a Biometric System

There are four main processes [10] involved in a biometric system, which include "Enrollment" [5], "Verification" [9], "Feature Extraction" [9] [11], and "Matching".

3.3   Biometrics- Fingerprint Recognition: Advantages and Disadvantages

The following Table 1 illustrates the advantages and disadvantages of fingerprint recognition.

3.4   Henry Classes

Henry classes are used to perform the task of classification to determine, which category an acquired fingerprint belongs to. Henry classes come into act when a user's fingerprint is entered at the sensor and sent for processing. Usually, the acquired fingerprint will be compared to all the fingerprint templates in the database until the system finds a match and grants access to the user, or else, prevent an unregistered user from logging into the system. Going through all the fingerprint templates that are stored in the database will take time, and thus, decrease the performance of such usage.

Table 1. The advantages and disadvantages of fingerprint recognition

Advantages	Disadvantages
Low cost hardware implementation	Affected by fingers cuts, bruises or dirt
Widely accessible	Users may mask the finger to avoid/fake the match
Easily integrated with hardware with wireless communication capability	Ability to force a false match
Information need for recognition is available	Noise can be captured. May prevent access to legitimate users or accept spurious users
High performance due to the uniqueness of the fingerprint	Elastic distortion of the skin when pressing it against the fingerprint sensor might affect the access decision
Sensor captures the fingerprint and fast access can be granted to legitimate users	Most applications need improve the recognition performance

A given fingerprint is classified into one of five Henry classes [16]: Whorl, Left loop, Right loop, Arch, and Tented arch.

It is widely known that every finger of any user's hand has its unique fingerprint. The system separates the fingerprint templates once registered to above five classes. When a user requests access using his/her fingerprint, the sample fingerprint will be set to one of the five classes before being compared to each fingerprint at that specific class. This method decreases the amount of time for comparisons between fingerprint templates since the comparison will only be undertaken only on a specific class containing a smaller percentage of fingerprints rather than on all fingerprints.

4   Analyzing One-Time Passwords

One-Time Passwords (OTP) came into existence mostly to decrease the attack surface in online security by the means of providing an improved authentication procedure for users. OTPs are basically passwords that are generated at a specific time that the user wishes to make online payments or withdrawals, and are valid for only a limited amount of time and only for a single transaction [13]. The OTP is often sent via the "Short Message Service" (SMS) to the registered user's mobile phone, which is associated with the specific account, where the user is expected to input the code in the required field. There are also other ways that OTPs can be generated, such as by specific devices for that credit card and the PIN input are required.

4.1   Popular Attacks that One-Time Passwords Defend Against

- **Eavesdropping** is secretly listening to a conversation or intercepting communication without any legitimate authorization.
- **Replay attacks**: Valid data is maliciously repeatedly transmitted. It is carried out by a Man-In-The-Middle (MITM) who intercepts the data and retransmits it as part of a masquerade attack [14].

- **Phishing** is the fraudulent practice of sending emails that are claimed to be from a reputable source when in fact they are not, thus, misleading individuals into revealing personal information, such as: passwords and credit card numbers [15].

4.2   Generation Methods of One-Time Passwords

As it has previously been stated, OTP is an authentication service that creates a one-time password whenever it is requested by the host or application been used. Synchronization is required between the server and the terminal that creates the OTP in order for OTPs to be created. Compatibility between the two is achieved by using either event-based synchronization, time-based synchronization or a combination of the two called hybrid-type synchronization. Research has shown that "time-based synchronization" is the most universally used type [17]. OTPs retain attributes of two-factor authentication since when OTPs are created, they can be transmitted either through SMS, mobile-phone applications, and/or hardware-type tokens [12].

Additionally, there are several methods on how OTPs are generated. The generation methods are random and can be either undertaken through software or hardware. In this section, both SMS based and hardware device generated OTP methods will be discussed as seen below.

Method 1: This method uses software and goes as follows:

- "User A" wants to make an online purchase, therefore logs into the service provider's website, where an SSL session is established.
- The user enters username, password and OTP status in order for the server to be synchronized with the client.
- The user is then requested by the server to enter new indexes in his OTP generator in order to get a new corresponding OTP.
- The user can then enter the new OTP generated and the server will then compare the received (new) OTP from the user to the calculated one.
- Depending on the validity of the data entered, authorization access is granted or communication is terminated.

Method 2: This method uses hardware. One of the most famous hardware devices that will be used as a reference here is the PINSENTRY device used by BARCLEYS bank in the UK and goes as follows:

- "User A" wants to make an online purchase
- The correct card details are entered in the website including the 16-digit code on the card, Card Verification Value (CVV), expiry date, and the name associated with the card
- If the details are entered correctly, for "User A" to continue the payment, User A is prompted to enter the OTP that can be generated using the "PINSENTRY" device.
- "User A" is required to input his credit card into the "PINSENTRY" device, and enter his credit card's Personal Identification Number (PIN).
- If the PIN is valid, the "PINSENTRY" device generates an OTP, which "User A" in turn is required to input into the required field online.
- If "User A" inputs the valid OTP, the payment is successfully made; if not, continuation of the payment is halted.

4.3 How One-Time Password Devices Work

OTP devices contain data that is required for generation of a sequence of passwords. The same data is also stored in a database, which is controlled by the bank. As it has been previously stated, when users want to access their accounts, a new password is needed to be generated in pursuance of gaining access to their accounts. When the users enter the password into the required field, the interface associated with the field sends the password to the server of the bank where it is processed. The server in turn accesses the database of the bank to get the data of the given device and compares the password sent by the user to determine if it is a valid password.

4.4 Problems Associated with One-Time Passwords

Although OTPs provide security authentication service, attackers can still intercept the codes or compromise the OTPs solution, then perform unauthorized transactions or payments. Some known attacks to OTPs [18] are explained in the following.

- Regarding SMS based OTPs, the security lays mostly on the confidentiality of the SMS messages, which are relayed on the cellular networks. As it has been seen, there are several attacks regarding GSM and mobile networks and this is to explain that confidentiality cannot be fully provided with SMS messages [20]. For example, the telecommunications company controls the SMS communications, a malicious or compromised employer from the telecommunications company can access and leak the SMS messages.
- The smart phone or SIM can be cloned and OTPs through mobile phone SMS can be monitored.
- The so called "mobile phone Trojans" are a new trend adopted by cybercriminals in pursuance of intercepting OTP based transactions [21]. Trojans are computer programs that can be downloaded on computers or smartphones by clicking on certain links that can be most commonly found in electronic mails. They mislead users of their true identity and steal information without their permission [18].

4.5 Strengths and Weaknesses of One-Time Passwords

The strengths and weaknesses of OTPs are highlighted in the following.

Strengths: Instead of using the same password for various applications or transactions that could lead to more than one account theft, OTPs lower the risk by disposing the passwords generated right after their usage as well as do not create the same password again. Although OTPs can be intercepted by an attacker, experiments undertaken by security professionals conclude that OTPs are still safer than user name and password authentication method because the OTPs' lifetime is approximately 60 s and thus, requiring attackers to use powerful computers as well as forcing them to act swiftly in performing their attacks, which in most cases is impossible [19]. In addition, OTPs are cost effective, easy to use, and there are cases where no additional hardware is needed for delivery.

Weaknesses: Researches carried out by the banking sector concluded that there are frequent OTP input failures regarding the limited acceptable amount of time. This can be seen from older people that are unfamiliar with OTP technology and/or slow in typing speed, and thus, are unsuccessful in typing the OTP in the time boundary. For this reason, many banks such as the Citibank have increased the lifetime of OTPs to over 3 min thus, giving more time for attackers to intercept the OTP and use it for their financial gain [12]. In addition, the evolution of hacking methods such as the Man-in-the-Middle (MITM) [22] or Man-in-the-Browser (MITB) [23] can be used to intercept messages and seize information transferred.

5   Hardware Used for Implementation of the Final Device

5.1   Arduino Uno

The Arduino Uno is based on the ATmega328P chip, it can be powered via the USB connection or by an external power supply. It has a number of facilities for communicating either with a computer, another Arduino board, other microcontrollers such as the Raspberry Pi, external hardware components such as VCR and DVD players, and finally computers. The ATmega328P chip that this project uses provides 32 kB of flash memory for storing the uploaded code.

5.2   Fingerprint Sensor (TTL GT511C1R)

The fingerprint sensor used in this project is the "TTL GT51C1R Fingerprint Sensor". The specific fingerprint sensor module communicates over the TTL Serial port and is developed by ADH-Tech industries. The module has an embedded on-board optical sensor that is responsible of reading and identifying the fingerprints as well as a 32-bit CPU [24]. Getting started, the fingerprint module works by first registering fingerprints of given users, which is done by pressing a finger on the scanner when prompted from the serial monitor. The registering process works by creating templates of the fingerprints that are scanned, and then saving them in the fingerprint module database, which can store a maximum of 20 fingerprints. The second step is verifying the stored fingerprints, which need that the user presses the finger on the scanner.

5.3   RFID Card Reader (RFID RC522)

The RFID Card Reader used in this project is the "RFID RC522 Module". This module was selected for the benefits that it has such as simplicity and effectiveness for both the ability to interface with an Arduino as well as the accuracy of the scanned cards that it provides. "RFID" stands for "Radio Frequency Identification" and such modules work by using electromagnetic fields to transfer data between the card and the reader using the SPI (Serial Peripheral Interface) protocol. Each card has specific data and when placed in front of a reader, the reader can read that data and depending on the way the reader is programmed, it can have a variety of effects such as enabling or preventing access. In contrast to barcodes and barcode readers, RFID reader module do not have to be in the line of sight of the card to be detected and read.

5.4   GSM Shield (SIM900 GPRS/GSM Shield)

The GSM shield used in this project is the "SIM900 GPRS/GSM Shield". This module was selected because it is specially built for interfacing with Arduino microcontrollers, as well as other capabilities such as allowing users to connect to the internet, send SMS, receive SMS and make voice call; some of which are essential for this project (OTP generated will be sent to the user's smartphone through SMS).

Although this shield is designed for Arduino microcontrollers, it only works out of the box on the "Arduino Uno" microcontroller since it fits exactly on top of it. Since in this project the microcontroller used is the "Arduino Uno", no modifications need be undertaken in pursuance for it to successfully work (plug and play). On other Arduino microcontrollers such as the Arduino Mega, modifications must be made in order for it to successfully work since the default communication of the GMS shield to the attached Arduino requires the use of digital pins 2 and 3, where pin 2 is the GSM_TX pin, and sends information to the Arduino. The interrupt on pin 2 is what lets the Arduino know when information is available to read. Since the libraries of the GMS shield are already installed in the Arduino IDE, users do not need to make any changes to the code. The software program makes all the necessary changes automatically when the selection of the board used in the Arduino IDE (Tools/Board) is made by the client.

6   Final Device

The final device design with all peripheral hardware parts is in Fig. 1 below.

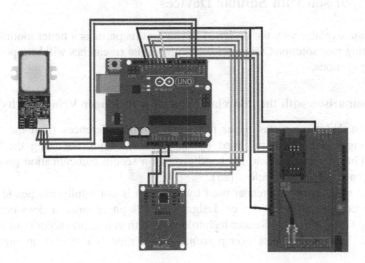

Fig. 1. The design of the IoT MFA device with connected. Arduino Uno, Fingerprint Sensor, RFID Card Reader, SIM/GSM/GPRS Shield.

Biometrics (fingerprint), used with card, pin, OTPs; provide an additional step of security to the Multi-Factor Authentication (MFA). Communications between the fingerprint sensor and Arduino Uno support following activities: register a fingerprint by storing it in the internal database; scan a fingerprint to compare it with the stored fingerprints in the database. Communications between RFID-RC522 sensor and the Arduino Uno support following activities: when a card is scanned on the reader, the card ID and user name will be recorded in the system. Communications between the GPRS/GSM Shield and the Arduino Uno support following activities: the code be uploaded to the Arduino IDE; SMS message containing the OTP be sent to the user's phone; the OTP is generated randomly.

The designed device provides the additional step of security using biometrics technology. Biometrics are almost impossible to forge, copy, or misinterpret. Run time fingerprint recognition can uniquely authenticate legitimate users. Hence, the designed device provides extra security against known attacks to bank card and pin and OTPs, such as: ATM shoulder surfing, brute force attacks, Card, SIM or Phone cloning or hacking as well as OPTs attacks mentioned in Sect. 4.4.

Previous banking security methods only required the user to input the bank card and PIN associated with the specific bank account, and use the OTP as MFA of bank transactions. The more complex solution in this paper provides improved authentication for bank authentication. The designed device of this paper can incorporate card and pin, OTP, and biometrics. Overall, the designed device not only provides improved security, it also is easy to use, for mobile banking.

7   Comparison with Similar Devices

This section explains why the designed device in this paper is a better mobile solution than existing past solutions. Comparisons with similar researches will be reported in the following sections.

7.1   Comparison with the "Barclays IPortal with Finger Vein Security"

The designed device in this paper has some minor differences from the "Barclays iPortal Finger Vein Security" used by the Barclays Bank regarding the biometric method. Finger vein scans on one hand provide a secure authentication procedure as can be seen from Table 2 below [25]:

On the other hand, the reader used by Barclays is not a fully independent mobile device in contrast with the device designed in this paper since it does not have an embedded GSM, and Card Reader technology, and therefore, the security of the user is decreased dramatically since user personal information is scattered amongst several places.

Table 2. Finger vein VS Fingerprint authentication

Finger-vein authentication	Fingerprint authentication
More accurate – has lower False Rejection Rate (FRR) and False Acceptance Rate (FAR) than fingerprint authentication	Less accurate – has higher False Rejection Rate (FRR) and False Acceptance Rate (FAR) than finger vein authentication
Less invasive & more hygienic – does not require the subject to place his finger in contact with the scanner. Does not leave any fingerprints behind on the scanning surface that can be intercepted by fraudsters. It also requires less maintenance since no cleaning of the scanner is required	More invasive & less hygienic – requires the subject to place his finger in contact with the scanner in order for the fingerprint to be acquired. May leave traces of fingerprints behind on the scanner. Finally, for the above stated reasons it also requires more maintenance since cleaning of the scanner from previous fingerprints are required
Not affected by age or scratch on the skin surface since it scans veins	Decision may be affected by minor scratches and bruises on the skin surface

7.2 Comparison with the "OTP System Using Elliptic Curve Cryptography with Palm-Vein Biometrics"

The designed device in this paper has some minor differences with the "OTP system using Elliptic Curve Cryptography with palm-vein biometrics" regarding the biometric method. Palm-vein scans on one hand provide a secure authentication procedure just like finger-vein scans that were mentioned in Sect. 7.1. This comparison is reported in Table 3 below [26]:

Table 3. Palm-vein VS Fingerprint authentication

Palm-vein authentication	Fingerprint authentication
More accurate – has lower False Rejection Rate (FRR) and False Acceptance Rate (FAR) than fingerprint authentication	Less accurate – has higher False Rejection Rate (FRR) and False Acceptance Rate (FAR) than palm vein authentication
Less invasive & more hygienic – does not require the subject to place his palm in contact with the scanner. Does not leave any fingerprints behind on the scanning surface that can be intercepted by fraudsters. Finally, it also requires less maintenance since no cleaning of the scanner is required	More invasive & less hygienic – requires the subject to place his finger in contact with the scanner in order for the fingerprint to be acquired. May leave traces of fingerprints behind on the scanner. It also requires more maintenance since cleaning of the scanner from previous fingerprints are required
Not affected by age or scratch related effects on the skin surface since it scans veins	Decision may be affected by minor scratches and bruises on the skin surface
Requires a larger scanner since users may have large hands and palms	Does not require a large scanner since only a single finger is scanned from a user

On the other hand, the "OTP system using Elliptic Curve Cryptography with palm-vein biometrics" is just a research with no actual implemented device whereas, the device designed in this paper is one that is implemented using an Arduino Micro-controller, and tested to be a fully functional mobile device.

7.3   Comparison with "Fingerprint and Iris Biometric Controlled Smart Banking Machine Embedded with GSM Technology for OTP"

The designed device in this paper has some minor differences from the "Fingerprint and iris biometric controlled smart banking machine embedded with GSM technology for OTP" regarding the biometric method as well as where it is used. Iris scans on one hand provide a secure authentication procedure just like finger-vein scans palm-vein scans as can be seen from Table 4 below:

Table 4. Iris VS Fingerprint authentication

Iris authentication	Fingerprint authentication
More accurate – has lower False Rejection Rate (FRR) and False Acceptance Rate (FAR) than fingerprint authentication	Less accurate – has higher False Rejection Rate (FRR) and False Acceptance Rate (FAR) than iris authentication
Less invasive & more hygienic – does not require the subject to place his finger in contact with the scanner. In addition, it has the advantage of not leaving any fingerprints behind on the scanning surface that can be copied by fraudsters and used against the users. Finally, for the above stated reasons it also requires less maintenance since no cleaning of the scanner is required	Less hygienic – requires the subject to place his finger in contact with the scanner in order for the fingerprint to be acquired. May leave traces of fingerprints behind on the scanner. Finally, for the above stated reasons it also requires more maintenance since cleaning of the scanner from previous fingerprints are required
Not affected by age or scratch related effects on the skin surface since it scans veins	Decision may be affected by minor scratches and bruises on the skin surface
The eyesight of the users might be affected from the long-term usage of the scanner. The scan might be affected by people with eye conditions such as cataracts, myopia, and astigmatism that are conditions that develop through time	A person's fingerprints do not change through time. The only problem that a fingerprint scan might be affected from are cuts, bruises and burns to the skin of the finger

On the other hand, the "Fingerprint and iris biometric controlled smart banking machine embedded with GSM technology for OTP" is used at ATM machine terminals for more of a physical security since it provides shutters that fall in front of the ATM terminal in contrast with the designed device that is implemented in this paper, which is used for online transactions at home or work. Lastly, there is the danger of the shutter falling on users and injuring them.

7.4   Comparison with the "Secure OTP and Biometric Verification Scheme for Mobile Banking"

The designed device in this paper has some minor differences with the "Secure OTP and biometric verification scheme for mobile banking" regarding the biometric methods used. There is no specific biometric method required by the "Secure OTP and biometric verification scheme for mobile banking" system since the biometric method that might be asked is linked to the specifications of the mobile phone used by the user. This is because the user might not have a fingerprint scanner on his phone like the latest smartphone models currently out in the market, and/or a front camera. There are also some limitations to this system. For example, the user's phone might be of an old model with an old or low-quality camera, which will affect the photo biometric reading. Additionally, users with old mobile phones that do not have fingerprint sensors or cameras, are not able to use this system. Finally, smartphones are a target to mobile phone Trojans or other viruses that can steal personal information as well as biometrics of the user, and thus, an attacker can use the specific information and data in his favor.

7.5   Function Comparison of Devices

This section compares the devices that can perform the following functions:

- **Biometrics:**

  - Designed Device
  - Barclays iPortal with finger vein security
  - OTP using ECC with palm vein biometrics
  - Fingerprint and iris banking machine with GSM technology for OTP
  - OTP and biometric verification for mobile banking

- **OTP:**

  - Designed Device
  - OTP using ECC with palm vein biometrics
  - Fingerprint and iris banking machine with GSM technology for OTP
  - OTP and biometric verification for mobile banking

- **GSM Technology:**

  - Designed Device
  - Fingerprint and iris banking machine with GSM technology for OTP
  - OTP and biometric verification for mobile banking

- **Card Reader:**

  - Designed Device
  - Fingerprint and iris banking machine with GSM technology for OTP

- **Portable:**

  - Designed Device
  - OTP and biometric verification for mobile banking
  - Barclays iPortal with finger vein security

- **Low cost:**

  - Designed Device

8   Conclusions

One Time Passwords (OTPs) method has been used by many banks. Due to the OTP attacks stated in Sect. 4.4, there is need to improve the banking authentication. Among increasing researches on IoT security [27–32], this paper presents the design of one IoT MFA device with connected Arduino Uno, Fingerprint Sensor, RFID Card Reader, SIM/GSM/GPRS Shield for banking authentication, detailed in Sect. 5 for components and in Sect. 6 for whole system, evaluated in Sect. 7.

The designed easy-to-use IoT device in this paper provides enhanced user authentication as an addition to the already set-in-place measures that are popular in the banking sector, based on ready to use mechanisms, such as Card, pin, OTP and fingerprint recognition. The designed device improves the security by integrating multiple authentication mechanisms. Run time fingerprint recognition can prevent access by attackers who can compromise OTPs as explained in Sect. 4.4, or who compromise online user name and password authentication by guessing attacks, relay attacks, brute force attacks, or who compromise card and pin authentication by ATM card jammer and ATM shoulder surfing.

The implementation of the IoT device designed in this paper provides addition advantage over OTP authentication procedure currently used by the banks, it is also designed with acceptable usability by banks.

References

1. First Data, (2015). Cards and Payments: Seeing Past the Hi-Tech Hype. First Data
2. Prabhakar, S., Pankanti, S., Jain, A.: Biometric recognition: security and privacy concerns. IEEE Secur. Priv. Mag. **1**(2), 33–42 (2003)
3. Valavan, T., Kalaivani, R.: Biometric authentication system using finger vein. Int. J. Comput. Sci. Mob. Appl. **2**, 50–55 (2014)
4. González-Agulla, E., Otero-Muras, E., García-Mateo, C., Alba-Castro, J.: A multiplatform Java wrapper for the BioAPI framework. Comput. Stand. Interfaces **31**(1), 186–191 (2009)
5. Vacca, J.: Biometric Technologies and Verification Systems. Butterworth-Heinemann/Elsevier, Amsterdam (2007)
6. Woodward, J., Orlans, N., Higgins, P.: Biometrics. McGraw-Hill/Osborne, New York (2003)
7. Barral, C.: Biometrics & Security: Combining Fingerprints, Smart Cards and Cryptography. Ph.D. École Polytechnique Fédérale de Lausanne (2010)
8. Jain, A., Nandakumar, K., Nagar, A.: Fingerprint template protection: from theory to practice. In: Campisi, P. (ed.) Security and Privacy in Biometrics, pp. 187–214. Springer, Heidelberg (2013). https://doi.org/10.1007/978-1-4471-5230-9_8
9. Nanavati, S., Thieme, M., Nanavati, R.: Biometrics. Wiley, New York (2002)

10. Bazen, A.: Fingerprint identification - feature extraction, matching, and database search. Ph.D. (2002)
11. Bolle, R.: Guide to Biometrics. Springer, New York (2011). https://doi.org/10.1007/978-1-4757-4036-3
12. Ku, W.C., Tasi, H.C., Tsaur, M.J.: Stolen-verifier attack on an efficient smartcard-based one-time password authentication scheme. IEICE Trans. Commun. E87-B(8), 2374–2376 (2005)
13. Karovaliya, M., Karedia, S., Oza, S., Kalbande, D.: Enhanced security for ATM machine with OTP and facial recognition features. Procedia Comput. Sci. 45, 390–396 (2015)
14. Smith, D., Wiliem, A., Lovell, B.: Face recognition on consumer devices: reflections on replay attacks. IEEE Trans. Inf. Forensics Secur. 10(4), 736–745 (2015)
15. Seo, S., Kang, W.: Technical status of otp & cases of introducing otp in domestic financial institutions. Korea Inst. Inf. Secur. Cryptol. 3(17), 18–25 (2007)
16. Savvides, M.: Introduction to Biometric Technologies and Applications. [ebook] ECE & CyLab, Carnegie Mellon University (n.d.). https://users.ece.cmu.edu/~jzhu/class/18200/F06/L10A_Savvides_Biometrics.pdf
17. Yoo, C., Kang, B., Kim, H.: Case study of the vulnerability of OTP implemented in internet banking systems of South Korea. Multimed. Tools Appl. 74(10), 3289–3303 (2014)
18. Qi, A., Shen, Y.: Design and research of a new secure authentication protocol in GSM networks. In: MATEC Web of Conferences, vol. 61, p. 03010 (2016)
19. Burkholder, P.: SSL Man-in-the-Middle Attacks. SANS Institute 2002 (2002)
20. Lawton, G.: Is it finally time to worry about mobile Malware? Computer 41(5), 12–14 (2008)
21. Villalba, J., Lleida, E.: Preventing replay attacks on speaker verification systems. In: 2011 Carnahan Conference on Security Technology (2011)
22. Cain, C.: Analyzing Man-in-the-Browser (MITB) Attacks. SANS Institute (2014)
23. O'Gorman, L.: Comparing passwords, tokens, and biometrics for user authentication. Proc. IEEE 91(12), 2021–2040 (2003)
24. Mavoungou, S., Kaddoum, G., Taha, M., Matar, G.: Survey on threats and attacks on mobile networks. IEEE Access, 4, pp. 4543–4572 (2016)
25. Bayometric: Fingerprint vs. Finger-Vein Biometric Authentication (2017). https://www.bayometric.com/fingerprint-vs-finger-vein-biometric-authentication/
26. Lin, C., Fan, K.: Biometric verification using thermal images of palm-dorsa vein patterns. IEEE Trans. Circuits Syst. Video Technol. 14(2), 199–213 (2004)
27. Gao, C., Lv, S., Wei, Y., Wang, Z., Liu, Z., Cheng, X.: An effective searchable symmetric encryption with enhanced security for mobile devices. IEEE Access 6, 38860–38869 (2018). ISSN 2169-3536
28. Wang, C., Zhao, Z., Gong, L., Zhu, L., Liu, Z., Cheng, X.: A distributed anomaly detection system for in-vehicle network using HTM. IEEE Access 6(1), 9091–9098 (2018)
29. Wang, C., et al.: Accurate Sybil attack detection based on fine-grained physical channel information'. Sensors 18(3), 878, 23 p. (2018). ISSN 1424-8220
30. Dinculeană, D., Cheng, X.: Vulnerabilities and limitations of MQTT protocol used between IoT devices, special issue "Access Control Schemes for Internet of Things" at Applied Sciences Journal published at MDPI 9(5), 848 (2019). https://doi.org/10.3390/app9050848
31. Shi, F., Chen, Z., Cheng, X.: Behaviour Modelling and Individual Recognition of Sonar Transmitter for Secure Communication in UASNs. IEEE Access (2019). Online early preprint, Print ISSN: 2169-3536, Online ISSN: 2169-3536. https://doi.org/10.1109/ACCESS.2019.2923059
32. Men, J., et al.: Finding sands in the eyes: vulnerabilities discovery in IoT with EUFuzzer on human machine interface. IEEE Access 7, 103751–103759 (2019)

A Secure Authentication Scheme Based on Chen's Chaotic System and Finger Vein's Auxiliary Data

Tingting Lan[1], Hui Wang[2], and Lin You[2](✉)

[1] School of Communication Engineering, Hangzhou Dianzi University, Hangzhou 310018, China
162080087@hdu.edu.cn
[2] School of Cybersecurity, Hangzhou Dianzi University, Hangzhou 310018, China
h.wang@hdu.edu.cn, mryoulin@gmail.com

Abstract. A secure authentication scheme based on Chen's chaotic system and finger vein's auxiliary data is proposed. In this scheme, the pixel positions of the finger vein feature template are shuffled by using Arnold cat transformation, and then the gray values of the shuffled pixels are encrypted by using Chen's chaotic system. The user's finger vein's auxiliary data are extracted to generate the encryption matrix by using the finger vein image centroid for this encryption process. Our scheme has a large key space and the experimental results show that it can resist statistical analysis attack, correlation coefficient analysis attack and the known-plaintext attack.

Keywords: Secure authentication · Finger vein · Auxiliary data · Arnold Cat transformation · Chaotic system · Feature template encryption

1 Introduction

Finger veins are the biometric features located beneath the surface of human finger skin, which are different and unique for each person. Finger vein patterns cannot be stolen and will not be changed by the influence of the external environment or skin. Since the non-contact feature extraction equipment inflicts no harm on human body, it is a better choice for users to accept this technology [1]. The above reasons make the finger vein technology develop rapidly, but how to improve the security of the finger vein related authentication system has become a hot issue in recent years. If the finger vein information is transmitted or saved in a public network without any encryption operation, the data on personal identity related to this finger vein information will be threatened by malicious

This research is partially supported by the key program of the Nature Science Foundation of Zhejiang province of China (No. LZ17F020002) and the National Science Foundation of China (No. 61772166).

attackers, and the identity authentication system will be broken by the forged user information of the finger vein. Therefore, an effective algorithm for finger vein security authentication is urgently needed.

In recent years, chaotic systems have been applied for image encryption. Compared with the traditional cryptographical methods, chaotic system has the following advanced properties [2].

- Chaotic systems are very sensitive to initial values. Even the initial values have a slightly change, the sequences generated by chaotic systems will be very different.
- Since chaotic systems have internal randomness, they have complex behavior which are very difficult to be predicted or analyzed.
- The signals produced by a chaotic system have the statistical characteristic of white noises, which can be regarded as random signals.

Since the evolution of chaotic systems is from simple to complex, people are more likely to use several chaotic systems in an encryption process [3]. For example, in some research works, both Arnold cat map and Henon map are used to encrypt an image, both Holmes Map and singular value decomposition are used to encrypt biometric data, and the combination of Arnold cat map and Chen's chaotic map are used to encrypt the iris data [4–6]. Especially in the literature [6], the Arnold cat map is used to shuffle the positions of pixels, while the Chen's chaotic map is used to change the pixels' values. The algorithm proposed in [6] has a large key space, which can resist statistical analysis and correlation coefficient analysis. As for auxiliary data, its function in a biometric template encryption is used to rebuild and generate secret keys [7,8]. Essentially, auxiliary data is a kind of information related to biometric features, but it will not reveal any significant information about the real biometric features. In this paper, we propose a secure finger vein authentication algorithm based on Chen's chaotic system and some auxiliary data. In our proposed algorithm, the following functional improvements are achieved:

(1) Our algorithm has a complete registration and authentication function.
(2) The generation of encryption matrices and secret keys are related to the finger vein auxiliary data.
(3) In the authentication phase, our algorithm uses the centroid information of finger vein images to reconstruct encryption matrices.
(4) Our algorithm has a large key space and it can resist statistical analysis and correlation coefficient analysis.
(5) With the combination of Chen's chaotic map and auxiliary data, our algorithm can resist the known-plaintext attack and the chosen-plaintext attack, respectively.

2   Feature Encryption Based on Chen's Chaotic System and Auxiliary Data

Our finger vein security authentication algorithm is composed of the five steps:

(1) Selection of parameters: the coefficient of the Niblack algorithm is set to 0.05, and the coefficients of Chen's chaotic mapping are set to 35, 3 and 28.
(2) Preprocessing of finger vein images: in this phase, we use the centroid information of the finger vein image to finish the rotation correction and save the information in the database [9]. Then, we obtain the region of interest (ROI) of the image by using the sub-window method [10,11].
(3) Extraction of finger vein global features: in this phase, we use the Niblack algorithm to extract finger vein global features. In the Niblack algorithm, the coefficient k is set to 0.05, and the window size is set to 4.
(4) Shuffling of the pixels position: Arnold Cat transformation is used to shuffle the pixel positions.
(5) Encryption of the pixels' value: the shuffled pixel values are transformed based on Chen's chaotic system and the auxiliary data.

Our algorithm's flow diagram is shown as the following Fig. 1. In this flow diagram, the password and the iteration numbers are entered by user, the Database 1 is used to save the encrypted finger vein templates, and the Database 2 is used to save the information related to encryption. The following sections will give a detailed description about how this algorithm is used to encrypt finger vein feature templates.

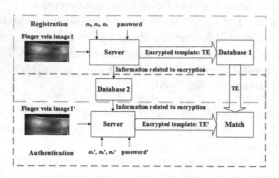

Fig. 1. The working principle flow diagram of our algorithm

2.1   Arnold Cat Transformation to Shuffle the Positions of Pixels

Arnold cat transformation is applied to stretch and fold the image many times in a finite field [4]. The original equation of Arnold cat map can be expressed as follows.

$$\begin{bmatrix} x_{n+1} \\ y_{n+1} \end{bmatrix} = \begin{bmatrix} 1 & 1 \\ 1 & 2 \end{bmatrix} \begin{bmatrix} x_n \\ y_n \end{bmatrix} \ mod \ 1 \tag{1}$$

The generally used Arnold cat map [5] can be expressed as follows.

$$\begin{bmatrix} x_{n+1} \\ y_{n+1} \end{bmatrix} = \begin{bmatrix} a & b \\ c & d \end{bmatrix} \begin{bmatrix} x_n \\ y_n \end{bmatrix} mod\ M \tag{2}$$

with the constant parameters a, b, c and d satisfying $ad - be = 1$. When the object of the transformation is an image matrix, M represents the size of the image, which means that the square image can, get better result. When the image matrix is not square, we need to cut the image matrix into a square and abandon the superfluous parts. Another choice to deal with the superfluous parts is to randomly select some elements and make the rest parts as a square. Before the Arnold cat transformation, the size of the global feature template is normalized to 64×96, and then the feature template is cut into three pieces. The size of each piece (which is called "sub-template" instead) are: 64×64, 32×32 and 32×32, respectively. The algorithm transforms these sub-templates independently, and the transformation matrices in each transformation step are different and independent. In both the registration and authentication processes, the three transformation matrices keep no change and are saved in Database 2. But in another registration and authentication process, the algorithm regenerates three new transformation matrices and replaces the old transformation templates in Database 2. The working principle of shuffling the positions of pixels by the Arnold cat transformation is shown in Fig. 2. The registration phase can be divided into the following steps:

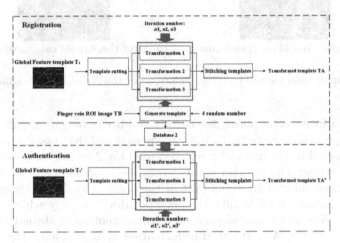

Fig. 2. The working principle flow diagram.

(1) Get the finger vein ROI image TR. Then we randomly select 4 pixels in the image and get their grayscale values.
(2) Multiply these 4 grayscale values by 4 different random numbers. Determine whether the result satisfies $ad - be = 1$. If not, try again until it satisfies $ad - be = 1$.

(3) Repeat the above steps three times and save the three transformation matrices in the Database 2.
(4) Cut the global feature template T_1 into three pieces, and set these three pieces as TS_1, TS_2 and TS_3.
(5) Prompt the user to enter three iteration numbers, set them as n_1, n_2, n_3. The accuracy of these numbers is within eight decimal numbers. The user saves these numbers by himself and regards them as a secret key: $K1(n_1, n_2, n_3)$.
(6) Iterate TS_1 for n_1 times, TS_2 for n_2 times and TS_3 for n_3 times, respectively. Later, joint them into a new template (matrix) and set it as TA.

Our algorithm's authentication phase can be are described as the following:

(1) Get three transformation matrices from the Database 2.
(2) Cut the global feature template T_1' into three pieces and set them as TS_1', TS_2' and TS_3'.
(3) Enter the iteration numbers by the algorithm prompts during the registration phase and set them as n_1', n_2' and n_3'.
(4) Transform three sub-templates and joint them together to get the result TA'.

The feature templates before and after the Arnold cat transformation are shown in Fig. 3.

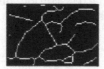 

(a) Before the Arnold cat transformation (b) After the Arnold cat transformation

Fig. 3. Finger vein feature template before/after the Arnold cat transformation

In the authentication phase, the correct result can be gotten only when the feature template is extracted from the same person and the iteration numbers are correctly entered by the users. But now our used Eq. 2 is likely to produce cycles, and it implies even if an attacker inputs wrong iteration numbers, the Arnold cat transformation can still get some part of the correct result. Furthermore, that the transformation simply shuffles the pixel positions can only achieve the visual disturbance. And so the transformation result cannot resist statistical analysis. This is because the Arnold cat transformation cannot change the statistical characteristics of the raw data. Therefore, we try to change the pixel values for higher security.

2.2 Transformation of the Pixel Values Based on Chen's Chaotic System

At present, some single chaotic systems and low-dimensional chaotic systems are still in use, e.g. one dimensional logistic chaotic system, one dimensional

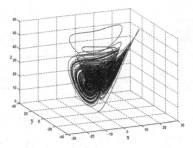

Fig. 4. Chen's chaotic attractor.

Chebyshev chaotic system and two dimensional Henon chaotic system [12–14]. Some attackers usually use the following methods to crack such kind of systems: space reconstruction, regression mappings and non-linear prediction. Take the one dimensional logistic system as an example. The initial values of the system are between 0 and 1, when the iteration time exceeds the specified precision, the sequences generated by the logistic system will be periodic [2]. Therefore, attackers can use non-linear prediction to crack this system to get some useful information. Relatively speaking, Chen's chaotic system not only has the basic properties of general chaotic systems, but also has a larger key space, which can achieve rapid diffusion. Chen's system can be described as the following equation expression:

$$\begin{cases} \dot{x} = a(y - x) \\ \dot{y} = (c - a)x - xz + cy \\ \dot{z} = xy - bz \end{cases} \tag{3}$$

When $(a, b, c) = (35, 3, 28)$, the above system becomes chaos state [6]. So the Chen's chaotic system is expressed as follows.

$$\begin{cases} \dot{x} = 35y - 35x \\ \dot{y} = -7x - xz + 28y \\ \dot{z} = xy - 3z \end{cases} \tag{4}$$

Although the Chen's chaotic equation is similar to Lorenz chaotic equation, it has totally different topology behavior [6,15]. Figure 4 shows the attractor of Chen's chaotic system. The attractor has three balance points, including a saddle point $S_0(0, 0, 0)$, two unstable focus points $S_+(7.937, 7.937, 21)$ and $S_-(-7.937, -7.937, 21)$. In order to make our algorithm resist the known-plaintext attack and the chosen-plaintext attack, we introduce the concept of auxiliary data. The auxiliary data in our algorithm is part of the information randomly selected form finger vein ROI. They are used to generate and reconstruct the encryption matrices, which will not reveal any significant information about the user' finger vein features.

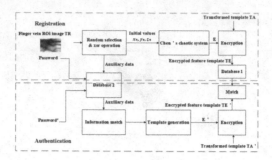

Fig. 5. The working principle of the transforming pixel values in the Chen's chaotic system

In addition, the registration and authentication process is slightly different. The working principle of the transforming pixel values in the Chen's chaotic system is shown in Fig. 5.

The registration phase can be divided into the following steps.

(1) We randomly generate 8 pairs of row and column numbers based on the size of the finger vein ROI image TR, and then get the 8 corresponding pixel grayscale values.

(2) Convert these pixel grayscale values into a 8-bit binary numbers. Later we will obtain four 16-bit binary numbers by combining the two 8-bit binary numbers into one binary number based on the pixel value sizes.

(3) Xor all the four 16-bit binary numbers to get the first initial value x_0. Then, we rotate it once to the left by one bit to get the second initial value y_0, and rotate y_0 once to the left by one bit to get the third initial value z_0. These three values are used as another key $K2(x_0, y_0, z_0)$.

(4) Put these three initial values into the Chen's chaotic system and iterate 192 times. In order to prevent the data from being too large to be generated by a computer, we take modular operation to the results of each iteration, and the modulus is set to be 2048.

(5) After we get three sequences, take the modular operation again, but this time the modulus is set to be 256. Set the finally acquired three sequences as L_1, L_2, and L_3, respectively.

(6) Xor L_1, L_2, and L_3 to get another sequences L_4, and these 4 sequences are arranged to form a matrix as a sub-encryption-matrix, and its size is 8×96.

(7) Repeat the above steps 8 times and generate 8 sub-encryption-matrices. Joint them together to become an encryption matrix E with the size 64×96.

(8) Prompt the user to enter a password used for securely saving the 64 pairs of rows and columns information and gray values in the generated Database 2.

(9) Make TA XOR with E to get the encrypted feature template set as TE. Save TE in the Database 1.

The following Fig. 6 shows the result when a finger vein feature template TA is encrypted by the Chen's chaotic system encryption.

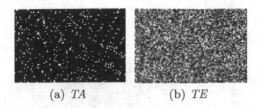

(a) TA (b) TE

Fig. 6. Encryption result of the Chen's chaotic system

If a user wants to authenticate his own identity, the first step in the algorithm is to get the correct encryption matrix. Because the Chen's chaotic system is sensitive to the initial values, it is an advantage of the algorithm security. But it also becomes an obstacle for the algorithm to generate encryption matrix accurately when the user is legitimate. Finger vein images will be affected by equipment, light and noises. Therefore, in the authentication phase, it is too difficult to get the same results as in the registration phase by only using row and column numbers saved in the Database 2. We use the intrinsic characteristic of the finger vein images, that is, the finger vain centroid, to solve the above problem. During the preprocessing of the registration phase, we have already saved the centroid information in the Database 2. The authentication steps are as follows.

(1) User enters the password to get the auxiliary data, and the password will be determined whether it is right. Otherwise, the algorithm will exit the current works, that is, the authentication fails.
(2) Compare the distance between the current centroid information with the centroid information stored in Database 2. If the distance is in $[0, \mu]$, the algorithm will extract grayscale values saved in Database 2 directly. If it is not, the algorithm will get the grayscale values from the current ROI image TR' according to the row and column numbers saved in Database 2.
(3) Generate the encryption matrix E'.
(4) Use E' to encrypt TA' and set the encrypted result as TE'.

Because the encryption of the finger vein features is operated bit by bit and so the results in the registration phase and the authentication phase can be compared in encryption domain. Hence, the user's finger vein information will not be exposed.

3   Experiments and Analysis

In our experiments, we used 1488 finger vein images from our lab database, which are collected from 186 users. The hardware for excusing the experiments is a computer with the third generation i5 processor, a 4G memory, and the 100G hard disk. The software environment is Windows10 64-bit operating system, and the simulation environment is Matlab R2014a.

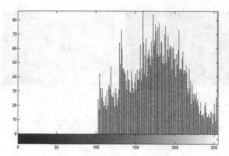

Fig. 7. Histogram of the original finger vein image.

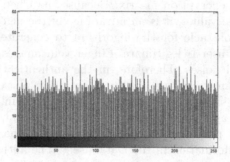

Fig. 8. Histogram of the encrypted finger vein image.

3.1 Histogram Analysis

In our experimental analysis, by comparing the histogram of finger vein features before and after the encryption, it can be found that there are great differences between them in the data distribution. In Fig. 7, it is obvious that the data is almost distributed between 100 and 255 before the encryption. But after the encryption, Fig. 8 shows that the data is relatively well-distributed between 0 and 255, except a few bulges. Hence, it is difficult for attackers to link the two feature templates by comparing the histograms before and after encryption. It shows that our algorithm can achieve the basic function of shuffling the positions of pixels. Our algorithm destroys the statistical characteristics of finger vein feature templates and achieves visual confusion.

3.2 Correlation Coefficient Analysis

The original finger vein image itself shows some inherent finger characteristics. When the finger vein features are extracted and preprocessed, a large part of the feature data will not be independent, and it means that there will have some more relationships in the feature data. Attackers usually try to analyze the correlation coefficients in original finger vein images and the encrypted finger vein images. In this way, attackers can get some useful information to crack the encrypted feature templates. To enhance the security of the algorithm, it is very important to destroy the correlation in the original data of finger vein images.

In this section, for both the original finger vein image and the encrypted finger vein image, we firstly randomly select 300 pairs of pixels in the horizontal direction and the vertical direction, respectively, then randomly select 64 pairs of pixels in the diagonal direction. Secondly, the pixel distribution of these three groups will be computed. Figs. 9, 10, 11, 12, 13 and 14 show the differences between the original image and the encrypted image. Thirdly, 50 groups of original finger vein images and encrypted images are selected and the first step is repeated for each image to get the data groups. Later, we calculate the correlation coefficients of each direction. Finally, we calculate the average values of each direction and get the results. Table 1 shows these results.

The following three figure sets (that is, Figs. 9, 10, 11, 12, 13 and 14) clearly show that the distribution of the original finger vein images tend to a straight line, but the distribution of the encrypted finger vein images is diffusive. In Table 1, where Or. and En. respectively denote original and encryption, the correlation coefficients of the original finger vein images are close to 1, and the correlation coefficients of the encrypted finger vein images are close to 0.06 to 0.03. It means that our encryption method obviously reduces the data correlation and so it enhances the ability of resisting attacks.

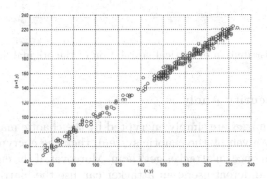

Fig. 9. Distribution of horizontal correlation of the original finger vein.

3.3 Key Space Analysis

In the Arnold cat transformation, the three iteration numbers' accuracy is set within 8 decimal numbers by the algorithm, therefore, in the Arnold cat transformation our key space is 10^{24}. In the Chen's chaotic encryption process, there are 8 encryption key sets with each having a 16-bit length, and so the size of the key space for this encryption process is 2128. Therefore, the key space of the entire system is $10^{24} \times 2^{128}$, which is close to 3.4×10^{62}.

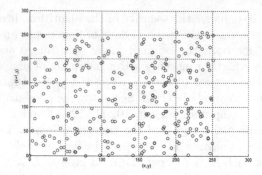

Fig. 10. Distribution of horizontal correlation of the encrypted finger vein.

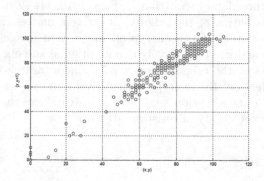

Fig. 11. Distribution of vertical correlation of the original finger vein.

3.4 System Security Analysis

If the finger vein images are simply encrypted by the chaotic map and the initial values are directly given by the chaotic system, then the encryption matrix will be easily generated once an attacker get them. Moreover, if the encryption matrix is reused by some different users, an attacker can use the matrix to get a lot of useful information from the different users, and the security of the algorithm can no longer be guaranteed. In our algorithm, the real initial values are generated by the auxiliary data without being directly exposed to the encryption process. This enables our method to resist known-plaintext attacks and chosen-plaintext attacks. Our proposed algorithm can resist the known-plaintext attack. It is because that the encryption matrix has the same size as the feature template and it has pseudo-random characteristic, an attacker cannot get the complete encryption matrix or feature template and he can only employ a part of feature template information and its ciphertext.

For resisting the chosen-plaintext attack in the registration process, the Arnold cat transformation matrices and the Chen's chaotic initial values are generated by the auxiliary data. The selection of the auxiliary data is random and unpredictable, which makes the generation of the matrices unpredictable

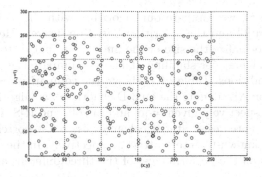

Fig. 12. Distribution of vertical correlation of the encrypted finger vein.

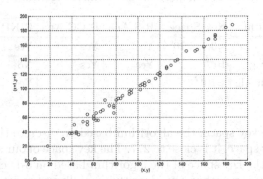

Fig. 13. Distribution of diagonal correlation of the original finger vein.

Table 1. Correlation coefficients' averages (CCA) of the finger vein images

Direction	Total num. of pixel pairs	CCA of Or. Image	CCA of En. Image
Horizontal	1500	0.9961	0.0554
Vertical	1500	0.9893	0.0442
Diagonal	300	0.8983	0.0363

and distinctive. An attacker who uses the existing plaintext can only get the encryption result of the current operation, while he cannot use these information to decrypt other ciphertext messages.

3.5 Comparison of Similar Algorithms

In this paper, we focus on the following four aspects:

(1) Key space.
(2) Whether the algorithm can resist statistical analysis.
(3) Whether the algorithm can resist correlation coefficient analysis.
(4) Whether the algorithm can resist known-plaintext attack.

For these aspects, we compare our algorithm with the algorithm based on 3-D chaotic system [6] and the algorithm based on discrete Henon system [14], respectively. We normalize the size of the finger vein images to 64×96 and use 8 bits in Arnold cat map for shuffling. Thus, we compare the algorithms under the same basic conditions. Table 2 has shown the comparison results, where the 3-D Alg. and Henon Alg. denote the on 3-D chaotic-based algorithm and Henon-based algorithm respectively given in [6] and in [14], and R-S Ana., R- CC Ana. and R-KP Att. denote resist statistical analysis, resist correlation coefficient analysis and resist known-plaintext attack, respectively. In the following, we will give some analysis on the performances of the three different algorithms.

Table 2. Comparisons of the three algorithms

Algorithm	Key Space	R-S Ana	R-CC Ana	R-KP Att
Ours	$\approx 3.4 \times 10^{62}$	Yes	Yes	Yes
3-D Alg	10^{50}	Yes	Yes	No
Henon Alg	$\approx 10^{77}$	No	Yes	Yes

In terms of the key space, the algorithm based on discrete Henon system [14] has the largest key space, it is close to 277. The key space of our algorithm is close to 3.4×1062 and the key space of the algorithm based on 3-D chaotic system [6] is 1050. In order to strengthen the algorithm's ability to resist known-plaintext attacks and known-plaintext attacks, we should make some little sacrifice on key space, but it will not greatly affect the security of the algorithm. For resisting the statistical analysis, our algorithm and the algorithm based on 3-D chaotic system can achieve the security purpose, but the Henon system cannot resist the statistical analysis. This is because that Henon system only shuffles the pixel positions and destroys the correlation between pixels, but it cannot destroy the statistical characteristics of the raw data. We know that in our algorithm, the encryption matrix is generated from the finger vein's auxiliary data randomly selected from the finger vein ROI image and the selection range of the auxiliary data run through the entire finger vein ROI image. The attacker cannot reconstruct all the current selected auxiliary data by employing only some part of the plaintext.

According to the reconstruction of the encryption matrix in the user authentication phase, it is necessary to match the centroid position of the finger vein feature template to obtain the auxiliary data. Since the centroid is the unique information of a complete finger vein image, it cannot be calculated by using only some parts of the finger vein image. Even if the attacker uses the ciphertext corresponding to the parts of the plaintext to retrieve some parts of the encryption matrix, but since the size of the encryption matrix is the same as that of the finger vein feature template, it will not pose a security threat to the encrypted finger vein feature template.

In conclusion, our algorithm has more comprehensive security performance.

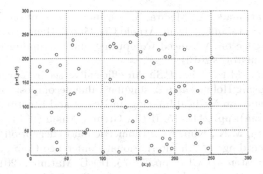

Fig. 14. Distribution of diagonal correlation of the encrypted finger vein.

4   Conclusion

In this paper, we propose a secure authentication algorithm based on Chen's chaotic system and finger vein's auxiliary data. First, Arnold Cat transform is used to scramble the feature pixel positions of user's finger vein through some inputted keys. Then, some auxiliary data generated from user's finger vein is applied in Chen's chaotic system to encrypt the finger vein feature pixel gray values for the protection of the user's original finger veins from illegal disclosure. In order to reduce the rejection rate during the authentication process, the centroid position matching is used for the reconstruction of the encryption matrix. Experiment results show that our scheme has a large key space and it can resist statistical analysis attacks and correlation coefficient analysis attacks, and it can achieve the ability to resist known-plaintext attacks.

Because of the sensitivity of the chaotic system to the initial values, many finger vein encryption algorithms based on chaotic theory are unable to reach a satisfactory recognition rate. This property of the chaotic system is just like a double-edged sword. In some algorithms, the encryption results have a great randomness to resist specific attack, but in some other algorithms, the encryption results cannot get the ideal state because of the fuzzy generation of the secret keys. Therefore, how to improve the recognition rate of the authentication algorithm on the basis of reaching relative safety is another research issue that need further research study.

References

1. Guo, G.-H., Qiao, B.: Research on the finger vein image capture and finger edge extraction. In: Proceedings of IEEE Conference on Mechatronics and Automation, pp. 275–279. IEEE, Takamatsu (2017)
2. Cai, J.: Chaotic encryption technology of digital image. Digit. Technol. Appl. **1**, 196–198 (2017)
3. Li, Y., Chen, G., Tang, W.K.S.: Controlling a unified chaotic system to hyperchaotic. IEEE Trans. Circuits Syst. II: Express Briefs **52**(4), 204–207 (2005)

4. Prusty, A.K., Pattanaik, A., Mishra, S.: An image encryption & decryption approach based on pixel shuffling using Arnold Cat Map & Henon Map. In: Proceedings of IEEE Conference on Advanced Computing and Communication Systems, pp. 1–6. IEEE, Coimbatore (2013)

5. Mehta, G., Dutta, M.K., Kim, P.S.: An efficient & secure encryption scheme for biometric data using Holmes map & singular value decomposition. In: Proceedings of IEEE Conference on Medical Imaging, m-Health and Emerging Communication Systems (MedCom), pp. 211–215. IEEE, Greater Noida (2014)

6. Mehta, G., Dutta, M.K., Kim, P.S.: Biometric data encryption using 3-D chaotic system. In: Proceedings of 2th International Conference Communication, Control and Intelligent Systems (CCIS), pp. 72–75. IEEE, Mathura (2016)

7. Boyen, X., Dodis, Y., Katz, J., Ostrovsky, R., Smith, A.: Secure remote authentication using biometric data. In: Cramer, R. (ed.) EUROCRYPT 2005. LNCS, vol. 3494, pp. 147–163. Springer, Heidelberg (2005). https://doi.org/10.1007/11426639_9

8. Gemeren, C.V., Poppe, R., Veltkamp, R.C.: Lend me a hand: auxiliary image data helps interaction detection. In: Proceedings of 12th International Conference Automatic Face and Gesture Recognition (FG 2017), pp. 538–543. IEEE, Washington, DC (2017)

9. Ma, H., Wang, K.: A region of interest extraction method using rotation rectified finger vein images. Chin. Assoc. Artif. Intell. (CAAI) Trans. Intell. Syst. **7**(3), 230–234 (2012)

10. Liu, C., Kim, Y.H.: An efficient finger-vein extraction algorithm based on random forest regression with efficient local binary patterns. In: Proceedings of IEEE Conference on Image Processing (ICIP), pp. 3141–3145. IEEE, Phoenix (2016)

11. Yang, J., Shi, Y.: Finger-vein ROI localization and vein ridge enhancement. Pattern Recognit. Lett. **33**(12), 1569–1579 (2012)

12. Mehta, G., Dutta, M.K., Kim, P.S.: A secure encryption method for biometric templates based on chaotic theory. In: Gavrilova, M.L., Tan, C.J.K. (eds.) Transactions on Computational Science XXVII. LNCS, vol. 9570, pp. 120–140. Springer, Heidelberg (2016). https://doi.org/10.1007/978-3-662-50412-3_8

13. Cai, Z., Feng, Y., Zhang, J., Gan, Y., Zhang, Q.: A Chebyshev-map based one-way authentication and key agreement scheme for multi-server environment. Int. J. Secur. Its Appl. **9**(6), 147–156 (2015)

14. Ping, P., Mao, Y., Lv, X., Xu, F., Xu, G.: An image scrambling algorithm using discrete Henon map. In: Proceedings of IEEE Conference on Information and Automation, pp. 429–432. IEEE, Lijiang (2015)

15. He, C., Bao, S.: An encryption algorithm based on chaotic system for 3G security authentication. In: Proceedings of IEEE Conference on Information, Computing and Telecommunications, pp. 351–354. IEEE, Beijing (2010)

Machine Learning and Security

Image Denoising Based on Sparse Representation over Learned Dictionaries

Juan Wang, Guanghui Li, Fei Du, Meng Wang, Yong Hu, Meng Yu,
Aiyun Zhan, and Yuejin Zhang[✉]

School of Information Engineering, East China Jiaotong University,
Nanchang 330013, China
zyjecjtu@foxmail.com

Abstract. Image is an important carrier of information, but the existence of noise will affect the quality and efficiency of information interaction. Image denoising is a classical problem in image processing, in order to improve the denoising effect, we proposed a method based on improved K-SVD algorithm. First, the high frequency and low frequency of the original noisy image are separated. Besides, the improved K-SVD algorithm is used for sparse reconstruction of the high frequency part of the image. Finally, the denoised high frequency part and the low frequency part are superimposed to make the final clean image. The experiments show that this method can achieve better denoising effect compared with DCT based denoising algorithm, K-SVD algorithm and LC-KSVD model.

Keywords: Sparse representation · Denoising · Dictionary

1 Introduction

In the past few decades, digital image processing has been widely studied and applied to many fields. As a basic issue of image processing, image denoising lays good foundation for the subsequent image processing [1]. Image denoising based on sparse representation is to separate signal and noise, making use of the feature that random noise cannot be sparsely represented, and to finally reconstruct the image reasonably [2]. Sparse representation aims at describing the original signal with as few coefficients as possible [3, 4], which has attracted a lot attention due to its efficiency.

In 2006, Aharon et al. [5] proposed a K-SVD algorithm based on sparse representation, it is a method of training an overcomplete dictionary by updating the dictionary atoms and the sparse representation. In [6], Eland and Aharon applied K-SVD algorithm to image denoising. However, the denoising result of traditional K-SVD algorithm is not good in the case of low Signal to Noise Ratio (SNR) [7], besides, the noise atom and the noiseless atom in the learned dictionary have a high similarity,

This work was supported in part by the National Natural Science Foundation of China under Grant 11862006, Grant 61862025, in part by the Jiangxi Provincial Natural Science Foundation under Grant 2018ACB21032, 20181BAB211016, in part by the Scientific and Technological Research Project of Education Department in Jiangxi Province under Grant GJJ170381, Grant GJJ170383.

J. Vaidya et al. (Eds.): CSS 2019, LNCS 11983, pp. 479–486, 2019.
https://doi.org/10.1007/978-3-030-37352-8_41

which may make the image too smooth [8, 9]. A new incoherent dictionary learning model was proposed in [10], this model adds a penalty term for dictionary coherence under the K-SVD algorithm minimization objective function. The learned dictionary is used for image denoising. In [11, 12], denoising algorithms based on image block classification and sparse representation are proposed, which can well preserve the image details when denoising, but training dictionary will be very time consuming.

In this paper, we aim to improve the denoising effect. The original noisy image is separated into high frequency and low frequency parts, and the improved K-SVD algorithm is applied to sparse reconstruction of the high frequency part. Finally, the denoised high frequency part and the low frequency part are superimposed to make the final clean image.

2 Image Denoising Based on K-SVD

Sparse representation is a technique of representing high-dimensional signal in a low-dimensional way, which can be described as recovering an unknown signal X from an observed signal Y:

$$Y = X + N \tag{1}$$

where $X = \sum_{i=0}^{n-1} <R_i$, $N = \sum_{i=n}^{\infty} <R_i$ is additive noise. K-SVD algorithm is capable of build an overcomplete dictionary, assume that X can be represented by $X = D\alpha$, the objective equation of K-SVD algorithm is:

$$\alpha' = \arg \min_{\alpha} ||\alpha||_0 \text{ subject to } ||D\alpha - Y||_2^2 \le T \tag{2}$$

where α is the sparse representation coefficient, T denotes the maximum number of sparse coefficients, further, the sparse representation model of the image is modified by using Lagrange multiplier as follows:

$$\alpha' = \arg \min_{\alpha} ||D\alpha - Y||_2^2 + \mu ||\alpha||_0 \tag{3}$$

where μ is regularization parameter which needs to be selected appropriately. Therefore, the constraint is transformed into a penalty term [13].

For an input noisy image Y whose size is $\sqrt{N} \times \sqrt{N}$, $(\sqrt{N} - \sqrt{n} + 1)^2$ smaller image patched sized $\sqrt{n} \times \sqrt{n}$ can be extracted from it. Then the following denoising objective function can be established:

$$\left\{ \alpha'_{ij}, D', X' \right\} = \arg \min_{\alpha_{ij}, D, X} \lambda ||X - Y||_2^2 + \sum_{ij} \mu_{ij} ||\alpha_{ij}||_0 + \sum_{ij} || D\alpha_{ij} - R_{ij}X ||_2^2 \tag{4}$$

where the first term is used to measure the overall similarity between images before and after denoising, which is called the fidelity term [14]. The second term is the sparsity constraint, and the third term is used to ensure that the image patches of the denoised image can be sparsely represented.

When dictionary D is assumed known, initialize X = Y, using OMP algorithm to compute the sparse representation coefficient α_{ij}:

$$\alpha_{ij}' = \arg\min_{\alpha} \mu_{ij}||\alpha||_0 + ||D\alpha - x_{ij}||_2^2 \tag{5}$$

the iteration stops when residual reaches a certain threshold. When the sparse representation of all image patches is solved, fix coefficient α_{ij} and X, then the solution of (4) is shown as following:

$$D' = \arg\min_{D} \sum_{ij} \mu_{ij} \| \alpha_{ij} \|_0 + \sum_{ij} \| D\alpha_{ij} - R_{ij}X \|_2^2 \tag{6}$$

using K-SVD algorithm to update one column each time until all the update of the dictionary is completed, then fix D and α_{ij}, the image X can be restored by solving the following formula:

$$X' = \arg\min_{X} \lambda||X - Y||_2^2 + \sum_{ij} ||D\alpha_{ij}' - R_{ij}X||_2^2 \tag{7}$$

which leads to:

$$X' = (\lambda I + \sum_{ij} R_{ij}^T R_{ij})^{-1}(\lambda Y + \sum_{ij} R_{ij}^T D\alpha_{ij}') \tag{8}$$

where I is unit matrix, and X' is the expected denoised image.

3   Denoising Strategy Optimization Design

As the high-frequency part of an image contains a lot of boundary detail information [15], as well as almost all the noise, it will be effective to process separately the high-frequency and low-frequency parts of an image, denoising the high- frequency part by sparse representation and leaving the low-frequency part unchanged. However, this will make the coherence of the overcomplete dictionary greater, which may cause overfitting of the training sample and affect signal reconstruction performance.

We settled that problem by adopting an improved Low Coherence K-SVD (LC-KSVD) algorithm, which adds a penalty term to describe the coherence of the dictionary to reduce the dictionary coherence as follows:

$$\arg\min_{D,\{c_i\}} \sum_{i=1}^{\sqrt{N}} \frac{1}{2} \| y - Dc_i \|_2^2 + \mu \| c_i \|_0 + \gamma \| D^T D - I \|_2^2 \tag{9}$$

where $D \in R^{n \times k}$, c_i is the sparse representation coefficient of y, μ and γ are Lagrange multiplier, which are used to control reconstruction error and minimize the tradeoff between coherence and sparsity of the dictionary.

Randomly select K samples to construct dictionary D, as D is known, model (9) can be rewritten as

$$\min_{\{c_i\}} \frac{1}{2} \| y - Dc_i \|_2^2 + \mu \| c \|_0 \tag{10}$$

Using OMP algorithm to compute the sparse representation coefficient $\{c_i\}$, whose matrix can be noted as C. When the sparse representation is solved, fix coefficient C, then the dictionary updating objective function is given by

$$\min_D \sum_{i=1}^{\sqrt{N}} \frac{1}{2} \| y - Dc_i \|_2^2 + \gamma \| D^T D - I \|_2^2 \tag{11}$$

whose matrix form is

$$\min_D \sum_{i=1}^{\sqrt{N}} \frac{1}{2} \| Y - DC \|_2^2 + \gamma \| D^T D - I \|_2^2 \tag{12}$$

K-SVD is applied to update the dictionary D and sparse representation coefficient, with u_i and v_i of singular value decomposition $D = U \sum V^T$ that minimize the following formula:

$$\min_D \frac{1}{2} \| Y - DC \|_2^2 + \gamma \| V \sum^2 V^T - I \|_2^2 \tag{13}$$

once $\| Y - D_{(k)} C_{(k)} \|_2^2$ gets small enough, the iteration, and dictionary D is acquired.

To achieve better performance in denoising, we separate an image into high-frequency and low-frequency parts, denoising the high-frequency part with the improved LC-KSVD algorithm and leaving another part unchanged. Then superimpose the denoised high frequency part and the low frequency part to make the final clean image. The flow chart of the detailed process of our model is shown in Fig. 1.

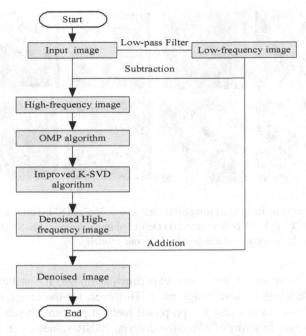

Fig. 1. Flow chart of proposed method

4 Experimental Results

In order to prove the validity of the above model, the traditional DCT based denoising algorithm, K-SVD algorithm, LC-KSVD model and our proposed method are used to compare and draw relevant conclusions.

The following Figs. 2 and 3 show the denoising effects of the Lena image with Gaussian noise "$\delta = 10$" and "$\delta = 25$", respectively. The comparison of PSNR values is shown in the following table.

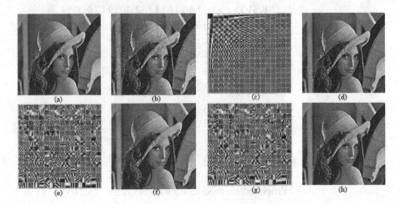

Fig. 2. (a) Original Lena image; (b) Image with noise $\delta = 10$; (c) DCT dictionary; (d) Denoised image based on DCT; (e) K-SVD dictionary; (f) Denoised image based on K-SVD; (g) Dictionary based on our model; (h) Denoised image based on our model.

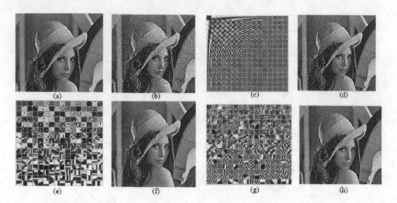

Fig. 3. (a) Original Lena image; (b) Image with noise δ = 25; (c) DCT dictionary; (d) Denoised image based on DCT; (e) K-SVD dictionary; (f) Denoised image based on K-SVD; (g) Dictionary based on our model; (h) Denoised image based on our model.

From the comparison of the above experimental image, it can be seen that all methods can effectively remove image noise. However, for the image with the same noise, the denoising result using the proposed method performs better in preserving details of the image. In terms of objective criteria, PSNR values of each image with different algorithms are shown in Table 1 below:

Table 1. The peak signal-to-noise ratio (PSNR) of images after denoising using different methods with different noise levels.

Test image	Method	PSNR/dB		
		$\sigma = 10$	$\sigma = 25$	$\sigma = 50$
Lena	Noising image	28.1369	27.1680	14.1633
	DCT	35.2938	30.1618	27.7231
	K-SVD	35.4036	31.3086	27.7324
	LC-KSVD	36.1613	32.4059	28.0254
	Proposed method	36.3601	32.8091	28.7420
Barbara	Noising image	28.1409	20.1727	14.1625
	DCT	33.9722	28.5415	24.7620
	K-SVD	34.2809	29.0632	25.4626
	LC-KSVD	34.3043	29.4267	26.0509
	Proposed method	34.3514	29.7505	26.5813
Peppers	Noising image	28.1019	20.1811	14.1227
	DCT	33.9564	29.0197	25.5733
	K-SVD	34.1808	29.7890	26.0554
	LC-KSVD	34.2142	29.5051	26.1189
	Proposed method	34.3905	30.1259	26.2103

From the comparison of the corresponding peak signal-to-noise ratios, it can be seen that all those methods can improve the PSNR value of the image, but the proposed method has the greatest improvement. Comparing above experiments, the experimental results can reflect the superiority of the method introduced in this paper, which shows better characteristics in both image effects and objective mathematical standards. Since the atoms of the dictionary has a lower coherence, the structure of the original image can be expressed more effectively, thus further optimizing the image denoising effect.

5   Conclusions

The existence of noise brings great inconvenience to the transmission and reading of information, therefore, researches in this area are also deepening. Focusing on image denoising, this paper introduces an image denoising method based on sparse representation, and studies the idea of sparse representation in detail. The section of denoising strategy optimization design mainly introduces a new method that can get a better denoising performance. The experiments proved that the proposed method based on the improved K-SVD algorithm can reduce the coherence of the dictionary effectively, as well as speed up the sparse coding, avoid the over-fitting of the training sample. The details of the image are preserved, making the denoising effect superior.

References

1. Liu, Y., Wang, Z.: Simultaneous image fusion and denoising with adaptive sparse representation. Image Process. IET 9(5), 347–357 (2014)
2. Guo, D.Q., Yang, H.Y., Liu, D.Q., et al.: Overview on sparse image denoising. Appl. Res. Comput. 29, 406–413 (2012)
3. Zhang, L., Zhou, W., Chang, P.: Kernel sparse representation-based classifier. IEEE Trans. Signal Process. 60(4), 1684–1695 (2012)
4. Wang, J., Cai, J.F., Shi, Y., et al.: Incoherent dictionary learning for sparse representation based image denoising. In: IEEE International Conference on Image Processing. IEEE (2015)
5. Aharon, M., Elad, M., Bruckstein, A.: K-SVD: An Algorithm for Designing Overcomplete Dictionaries for Sparse Representation. IEEE Press, Piscataway (2006)
6. Elad, M., Aharon, M.: Image denoising via sparse and redundant representations over learned dictionaries. IEEE Trans. Image Process. 15(12), 3736–3745 (2006)
7. Kong, Y.H., Hu, Q.Y.: An image denoising algorithm via sparse and redundant representations over improved K-singular value decomposition algorithm. Sci. Technol. Eng. 18(1), 287–292 (2018)
8. Romano, Y., Elad, M.: Improving K-SVD denoising by post-processing its method noise. In: IEEE International Conference on Image Processing. IEEE (2014)
9. Shi, J., Wang, X.H.: Image super-resolution reconstruction based on improved K-SVD dictionary-learning. Acta Electron. Sin. 41(5), 997–1000 (2013)
10. Niu, B., Li, H.Y.: Research on low dictionary coherence K-SVD algorithm. Comput. Digit. Eng. 47(01), 97–103 (2019)

486   J. Wang et al.

11. Tan, C., Wei, Z.H., Wu, Z.B., et al.: Parallel optimization of K-SVD algorithm for image denoising based on Spark. In: 2016 IEEE 13th International Conference on Signal Processing (ICSP). IEEE (2017)
12. Wang, X.Y.: The Research of Sparse Decomposition in the Field of Image Denoising. Anhui University (2014)
13. Huang, H F. Research on Methods and Applications of Digital Image Sparse Representation. South China University of Technology (2016)
14. Wu, D., Du, X., Wang, K.Y.: An effective approach for underwater sonar image denoising based on sparse representation, pp. 389–393. https://doi.org/10.1109/icivc.2018.8492877
15. Jing, C.M., Xiao, L.: An improved image enhancement algorithm. Wuhan Univ. J. Nat. Sci. 22(1), 85–92 (2017)

Cyclic DenseNet for Tumor Detection and Identification

Di Jiang[1,2], Hui Liu[1,2(✉)], Qiang Guo[1,2], and Caiming Zhang[2,3]

[1] School of Computer Science and Technology,
Shandong University of Finance and Economics, Jinan 250014, China
liuh_lh@sdufe.edu.cn
[2] Digital Media Technology Key Laboratory of Shandong Province,
Jinan 250014, China
[3] Software College, Shandong University, Jinan 250101, China

Abstract. How to correctly and efficiently detect and identify tumors has always been a core issue in the medical field. In order to improve the accuracy and efficiency of tumor detection, we proposed a DenseNet-based tumor recognition and classification model Cyclic DenseNet. First, Cyclic DenseNet inherits the fully-connected architecture of DenseNet and fully exploits the image features. Secondly, Cyclic DenseNet introduces the group concept and uses Group Normalization instead of Batch Normalization, in order to improve the stability of the parameters. At the same time, we extract the features deep after each Dense Block, which reinforces the features reuse and strengthens the advantages of DenseNet. Finally, in order to reduce the high time overhead caused by the reuse of multiple features, we adopt the optimal block extraction method, which greatly improves the training efficiency. The experimental results show that this method can effectively improve the accuracy and efficiency of tumor detection and recognition. Compared with the existing algorithms, it has achieved better results in the area under the receiver operating curve (ROC) and other criteria.

Keywords: Densenet · Group Normalization · Tumor detection · Tumor identification

1 Introduction

In recent years, with the rapid development of convolutional neural network (CNN) [7], their applications have also appeared in many aspects [9]. In 2014, in the ImageNet Large Scale Visual Recognition Competition (ILSVRC) [1], the VGGNet [12] won the second place, reducing the Top-5 error rate to 7.3%. In the same year, GoogLeNet [13] won the first place in the competition. And the following year, ResNet [2] won the championship in ILSVRC2015, with an error rate of 3.57% on top5 and a lower parameter than VGGNet.

In 2017, as the Best Paper of CVPR 2017, DenseNet [4], a structure that borrowed from GoogleNet and ResNet, appeared. It is dedicated to improving

© Springer Nature Switzerland AG 2019
J. Vaidya et al. (Eds.): CSS 2019, LNCS 11983, pp. 487–493, 2019.
https://doi.org/10.1007/978-3-030-37352-8_42

network performance from the perspective of feature reuse, effectively solving the problem of gradient disappearance [10], enhancing feature propagation, and supporting feature reuse [8]. In response to the long-standing problem of tumor identification and detection [15] in the medical field, we have adopted a rapidly developing deep learning method. The specific measure is to improve densenet so that it can be used more effectively in the detection and identification of tumors.

At the same time, we also combine the latest papers.

FC-DenseNets [6] released in 2017 improved and used densenet for task segmentation, with no post-processing model and fewer parameters. Memory-efficient DenseNets [11] reduces the model video memory by means of sharing storage space for intermediate feature, which makes it possible to train DenseNet deeper under the limit of GPU video memory and improves the problem that DenseNet occupies a large amount of video memory. Residual Dense Network [16] (RDN) improves the problem of relatively low performance in DenseNet due to the insufficient use of original low resolution (LR) image stratification features. ConDenseNet [3] mainly lies in the optimization of DenseNet network to make its calculation efficiency higher and parameter storage less.

We integrated the advantages of the above network and finally completed our Cyclic DenseNet.

2   Cyclic DenseNet for Tumor Detection and Identification

We constructed a DenseNet-based tumor recognition and classification model Cyclic DenseNet. The network structure is shown in Fig. 1, which includes Convolution, Dense Block, and Transition. Transition includes convolution, pooling, and Group Normalization (GN) [14]. In addition, there is an optimal block extraction structure after each Dense Block.

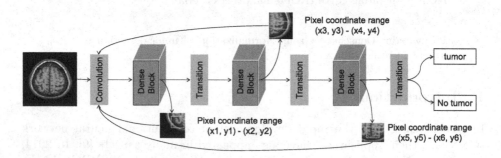

Fig. 1. Cyclic DenseNet

We have three innovations for the overall network architecture:

First, we used the Dense block structure in DenseNet, which greatly reduces the number of iterations of Cyclic DenseNet by taking advantage of its feature reuse. Densenet enhances functional reuse and has fewer parameters than resnet, which has a certain regularity effect and alleviates the problems of gradient disappearance and model degradation.

$$X_l = H_l([X_0, X_1, ..., X_{l-1}]) \tag{1}$$

Second, we use GN instead of BN. Group Normalization is a new deep learning normalization method that can replace Batch normalization (BN) [5]. The batch dimension of BN problem is not fixed, which may lead to the inconsistency of training, verification and testing. The standardization of GN avoids the impact of batch size on the model, thus solving this problem and achieving better results.

The formula for BN is:

$$\mu_i = \frac{1}{m} \sum_{k \in S_i} x_k, \quad \sigma_i = \sqrt{\frac{1}{m} \sum_{k \in S_i} (x_k - \mu_i)^2 + \theta}$$
$$y_i = \gamma \hat{x}_i + \beta \tag{2}$$

The difference between BN and GN is:

BN: batch direction, calculate the mean value of N*H*W.

GN: divide the channel direction into groups, and then normalize each group to calculate the mean value of (C//G)*H*W.

Thirdly, we use the optimal block structure to judge in the whole process of feature extraction of the model. Optimal block extraction greatly reduces the feature redundancy problem generated by DenseNet, and reduces the training time of the model and improves the accuracy.

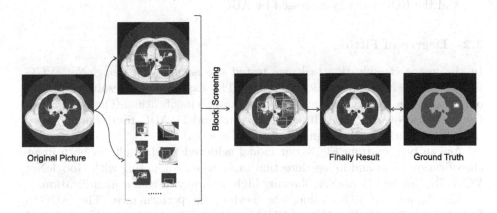

Fig. 2. Classification judgment

Our Cyclic DenseNet has two main functions, one is the classification function to identify whether the image contains tumors as shown in Fig. 1, and the other is the recognition function to identify where the tumor is located as shown in Fig. 2.

3 Experiment

We selected medical images of lungs, brain tumors or nodules from Shandong Qianfo Hospital and labeled the images. A total of 2,600 annotation data were used, including 2,200 training sets, 200 test sets, and 200 verification sets. The experiment was implemented using the TensorFlow framework. The experimental hardware facilities are Intel(R)Xeon(R)E5-2643 v4@3.40 GHz CPU, Nvidia Geforce GTX 1080M GPU, 256 GB RAM, and the operating system is Ubuntu 14.04.

3.1 Evaluation Index

In the experiment, we compared our network with GoogleNet, VGG, ResNet and DenseNet in terms of accuracy, misclassification rate, precision, recall, F1 score, Receiver Operating Characteristic (ROC) curve, Area Under the Curve (AUC), PR curve, AP, MAP, etc. Finally, accuracy, ROC curve and AUC were selected as the accuracy of predicting the final tumor location of the model, as shown in Fig. 3. The formula for accuracy is:

$$Accuracy = \text{Calculated} - \text{groundtruth} \leq 0.05 \tag{3}$$

The formula for Receiver Operating Characteristic is

$$AUC = \frac{\sum \text{ins}_i \in positiveclass \text{rank}_{\text{ins}_i} - \frac{M \times M + 1}{2}}{M \times N} \tag{4}$$

And the ROC curve is expressed by AUC.

3.2 Degree of Fitting

In the image classification task, we tested the accuracy of GoogleNet, VGG, ResNet, DenseNet and Cyclic DenseNet. The experimental results show that our model has the highest accuracy for image classification. The accuracy of Cyclic DenseNet is 98.75%. In addition, our model's AUC results are the best in image detection and recognition tasks (Table 1).

As can be seen from Fig. 3, our model achieved good results in both image classification tasks and image detection tasks when competing with GoogleNet, VGG, ResNet and DenseNet, showing high accuracy in tumor identification.

The larger the ROC value, the better the performance. The AUC of GoogleNet is 0.8681, The AUC of VGG is 0.8244, The AUC of ResNet is 0.8943, The AUC of DenseNet is 0.9117, and The AUC of Cyclic DenseNet is 0.9216.

Not only did we compare the AUC, ROC and accuracy for GoogleNet, VGG, ResNet, DenseNet and Cyclic DenseNet, we also compared efficiency with the latest DenseNet network, such as FC-DenseNets, Memory-efficient, and Con-DenseNet. As can be seen from the table, when the number of images is increasing, Cyclic DenseNet takes less time to process the images than FC-DenseNets,

Table 1. Comparison of AUC and accuracy of GoogleNet, VGG, ResNet, DenseNet and Cyclic DenseNet.

Model	AUC	Accuracy
GoogleNet	0.8681	97.16%
VGG	0.8244	96.59%
ResNet	0.8943	97.74%
DenseNet	0.9117	98.30%
Cyclic DenseNet	**0.9216**	**98.75%**

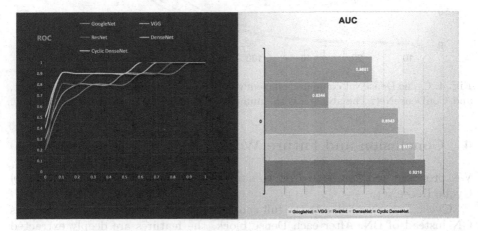

Fig. 3. Our Cyclic DenseNet works best compared to several other advanced models. And our model has an AUC of 0.9216 and works best.

Table 2. The time efficiency of FC-DenseNets, Memory-efficient, ConDenseNet and Cyclic DenseNet. T is time, and the number followed by T is the number of images, with a size of 512×512.

Model	T(10)/s	T(100)/s	T(1000)/s
FC-DenseNets	2.47	19.77	191.35
Memory-efficient	3.02	26.49	255.98
ConDenseNet	**2.10**	17.82	177.82
Cyclic DenseNet	2.11	**17.35**	**168.44**

Memory-efficient and ConDenseNet. The experimental results show that Cyclic DenseNet has a higher processing efficiency under the experimental data (Fig. 4 and Table 2).

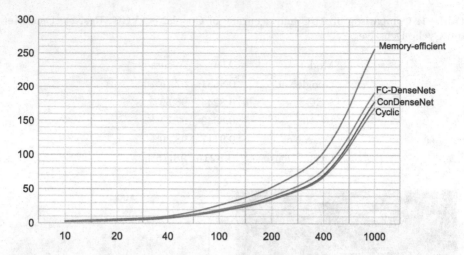

Fig. 4. Cyclic DenseNet compared efficiency with the FC-DenseNets, Memory-efficient, and ConDenseNet. The abscissa is the number of images and the ordinate is the time.

4   Conclusion and Future Work

We proposed a DenseNet-based tumor recognition and classification model Cyclic DenseNet.

Cyclic DenseNet inherits the full connection structure of DenseNet and uses GN instead of BN. After each Dense block, the features are deeply extracted and the optimal block extraction is used to improve the training efficiency. The experimental results show that the method effectively improves the accuracy and efficiency of detecting and identifying tumors.

On the other hand, Cyclic DenseNet does not optimize the storage structure too much, and still needs a lot of space for use. How to reduce the space utilization rate while ensuring the efficiency of Cyclic DenseNet is the research direction of the next problem.

References

1. Deng, J., Berg, A., Satheesh, S., Su, H., Khosla, A., Fei-Fei, L.: ImageNet large scale visual recognition competition. ILSVRC2012 (2012)
2. He, K., Zhang, X., Ren, S., Sun, J.: Deep residual learning for image recognition. In: Proceedings of the IEEE Conference on Computer Vision and Pattern Recognition, pp. 770–778 (2016)
3. Huang, G., Liu, S., Van der Maaten, L., Weinberger, K.Q.: CondenseNet: an efficient DenseNet using learned group convolutions. In: Proceedings of the IEEE Conference on Computer Vision and Pattern Recognition, pp. 2752–2761 (2018)
4. Huang, G., Liu, Z., Van Der Maaten, L., Weinberger, K.Q.: Densely connected convolutional networks. In: Proceedings of the IEEE Conference on Computer Vision and Pattern Recognition, pp. 4700–4708 (2017)

5. Ioffe, S., Szegedy, C.: Batch normalization: accelerating deep network training by reducing internal covariate shift. arXiv preprint arXiv:1502.03167 (2015)
6. Jégou, S., Drozdzal, M., Vazquez, D., Romero, A., Bengio, Y.: The one hundred layers tiramisu: fully convolutional densenets for semantic segmentation. In: Proceedings of the IEEE Conference on Computer Vision and Pattern Recognition Workshops, pp. 11–19 (2017)
7. Kalchbrenner, N., Grefenstette, E., Blunsom, P.: A convolutional neural network for modelling sentences. arXiv preprint arXiv:1404.2188 (2014)
8. LeCun, Y., Bengio, Y., Hinton, G.: Deep learning. Nature **521**(7553), 436 (2015)
9. Michie, D., Spiegelhalter, D.J., Taylor, C., et al.: Machine learning. Neural Stat. Classif. **13** (1994)
10. Pickup, G., Chewings, V.: A grazing gradient approach to land degradation assessment in arid areas from remotely-sensed data. Remote Sens. **15**(3), 597–617 (1994)
11. Pleiss, G., Chen, D., Huang, G., Li, T., van der Maaten, L., Weinberger, K.Q.: Memory-efficient implementation of densenets. arXiv preprint arXiv:1707.06990 (2017)
12. Simonyan, K., Zisserman, A.: Very deep convolutional networks for large-scale image recognition. arXiv preprint arXiv:1409.1556 (2014)
13. Szegedy, C., et al.: Going deeper with convolutions. In: Proceedings of the IEEE Conference on Computer Vision and Pattern Recognition, pp. 1–9 (2015)
14. Wu, Y., He, K.: Group normalization. In: Proceedings of the European Conference on Computer Vision (ECCV), pp. 3–19 (2018)
15. Zeindl-Eberhart, E., et al.: Detection and identification of tumor-associated protein variants in human hepatocellular carcinomas. Hepatology **39**(2), 540–549 (2004)
16. Zhang, Y., Tian, Y., Kong, Y., Zhong, B., Fu, Y.: Residual dense network for image super-resolution. In: Proceedings of the IEEE Conference on Computer Vision and Pattern Recognition, pp. 2472–2481 (2018)

Stock Prediction Model Based on Wavelet Packet Transform and Improved Neural Network

Xin Liu[1,3], Hui Liu[1,3]($\boxtimes$), Qiang Guo[1,3], and Caiming Zhang[2,3]

[1] School of Computer Science and Technology,
Shandong University of Finance and Economics, Jinan 250014, China
liuh_lh@sdufe.edu.cn
[2] School of Software, Shandong University, Jinan 250100, China
[3] Digital Media Technology Key Laboratory of Shandong Province,
Jinan 250014, China

Abstract. With the advent of the era of big data, the network's intervention in the stock market has deepened and the security of the stock market has been seriously threatened. In order to maintain the security of the stock market, this paper proposes a long short term memory prediction model based on wavelet packet decomposition and attention mechanism (Wav-att-LSTM). First, Wav-att-LSTM uses the XGBoost algorithm to select important feature variables from the stock data, and then uses wavelet packet decomposition to extract stock frequency features, which are used as the next input. Finally, the LSTM with the attention mechanism is used as the prediction model to predict the frequency component. This paper uses the stock dataset of the $S\delta P500$ for performance verification. The experimental results show that Wav-att-LSTM has higher prediction accuracy and less hysteresis than some advanced methods.

Keywords: Stock price prediction · Wavelet packet transform · Attention mechanism · Long short term memory

1 Introduction

Financial time series forecasting, especially stock price forecasting, has always been one of the most difficult issues for researchers and investors. Stock forecasting plays a key role in financial markets [1]. Effective stock forecasting can make better use of existing information for analysis and decision making, and maintain the security of the stock market. Therefore, stock models with outstanding performance are very popular [2]. The most common predictive model is LSTM. LSTM is an efficient nonlinear recurrent neural network that takes into account the time series and nonlinear characteristics of the data. Moreover, LSTM is gradually applied to the field of stock forecasting [3].

© Springer Nature Switzerland AG 2019
J. Vaidya et al. (Eds.): CSS 2019, LNCS 11983, pp. 494–500, 2019.
https://doi.org/10.1007/978-3-030-37352-8_43

Although the LSTM network model can fully reflect long-term historical processes in the input time series data, it ignores the frequency information of the data. Wavelet packet transform can extract the frequency information of stocks by wavelet packet decomposition, and explore the trading mode inside stock data [4]. Therefore, this paper adds wavelet packet decomposition before LSTM. This connection can not only extract the frequency mode of the data but also achieve the denoising effect.

The combination of wavelet packet transform and neural network can capture the multi-frequency trading mode of the market. However, the prediction performance is not ideal. Because the neural network does not highlight key features, and the historical information of the stock context is not fully utilized. However, attention can help the neural network assign different probability weights to hidden layer units, and can focus on more critical features [5]. The most important point is that attention does not increase the computational complexity and storage overhead of the model, which means that the efficiency of the model has not changed. At present, attention has been widely used in many fields, such as image annotation [6], image segmentation [7], machine translation [8] and time series prediction [9], etc.

In order to mine the frequency information of stocks and improve the model prediction ability, this paper proposes an improved neural network based on wavelet packet decomposition and attention mechanism. The experimental results proved the excellent performance of the model.

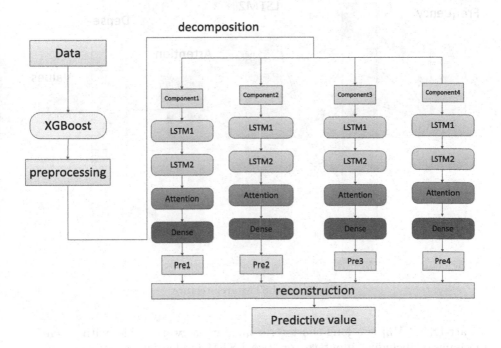

Fig. 1. Wav-att-LSTM architecture

2   Wav-att-LSTM Model

The model architecture diagram for this article is shown in Fig. 1. XGBoost [10] is an improved algorithm based on gradient decision tree [11], which can construct the enhanced tree and parallel operation effectively. The core of XGBoost algorithm is to construct the gradient enhancement tree to obtain the feature importance score. In this paper, xgboost is used to measure the feature importance of the data at t time of the stock sequence, and the important features are selected as the input of the model. Wavelet packet decomposition [12] is an improvement of wavelet decomposition. Wavelet decomposition only decomposes the low-frequency part, and the wavelet packet analysis not only decomposes the low-frequency part, but also decomposes the high-frequency part, refines the stock sequence in multiple scales and multi-faceted, and extracts more frequency information. The wavelet packet is essentially a function cluster, and its decomposition formula is as follows (Fig. 2):

$$X_{2n,j}(k) = \sum h_0(m - 2k)X_{n,j-1}(m) \tag{1}$$

$$X_{2n+1,j}(k) = \sum h_1(m - 2k)X_{n,j-1}(m) \tag{2}$$

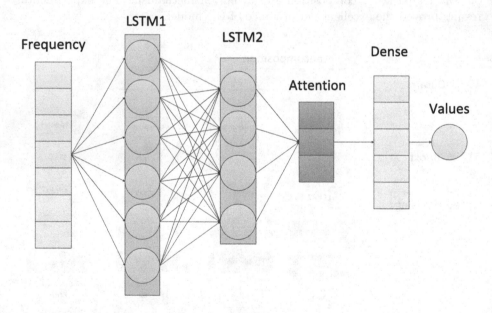

Fig. 2. att-LSTM architecture

att-LSTM [13] is a long short term memory network model with attention mechanism, including input vector, two LSTM hidden layers, attention layer, fully connected layer and output layer. In the attention, the weight vector is first calculated from the hidden layer state vector of the LSTM, and then the weight vector is merged with the input vector of the current layer to obtain a new vector, which is the input of the fully connected layer. The resulting predicted frequency is obtained in the fully connected layer Because the training requires a lot of time, it is generally better to choose a solution with less effect and less time. This paper sets up two layers of LSTM. It can get good results in less time. The attention layer is used to assign the feature weights learned by the model to the input vector in the next time step, highlighting the influence of key features on the predicted stock price.

The final step in the model is to reconstruct the frequency components from the predicted values using the inverse transform of the wavelet packet decomposition.

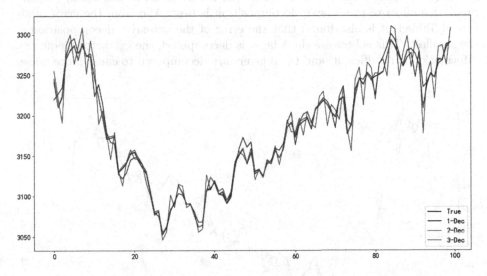

Fig. 3. Parameter comparison chart

3   Experiment

In this section, we conducted experiments to test the proposed Wav-att-LSTM. This article uses the stock data of the $S\delta P500$ as a data set and uses the mean absolute percentage error ($MAPE$) and the root mean square error ($RMSE$) as the evaluation indicators.

$$MAPE = \frac{1}{T} \sum^{T} \frac{\left| \hat{Y}_t - Y_t \right|}{Y_t} \tag{3}$$

$$RMSE = \sqrt{\frac{1}{T} \sum^{T} (\hat{Y}_t - Y_t)^2} \tag{4}$$

Where Y_t represents the actual value of the tth sample in the stock sequence, and $\hat{Y}_t$ represents the experimentally derived prediction.

3.1 Parameter Analysis

The complexity of the model is mainly measured by the number of decomposition layers of the wavelet packet. In theory, the error in the training process can be reduced by a sufficiently complex model. However, the low error on the training set does not mean a lower test set error, and the complex model also increases the risk of overfitting.

Figure 3 shows the prediction curve of the number of wavelet packet decomposition layers. It can be seen from Figure that the 1, 2, and 3 layer decomposition of wavelet packet decomposition can fit the future trend of the stock, but the prediction effect of the 2 layer decomposition is best. And from the error analysis of Table 1, it is also found that the error of the two-layer decomposition is the smallest. This is because the 1 layer is decomposed, the extracted frequency information is insufficient, and the 3 layers are decomposed to cause more noise.

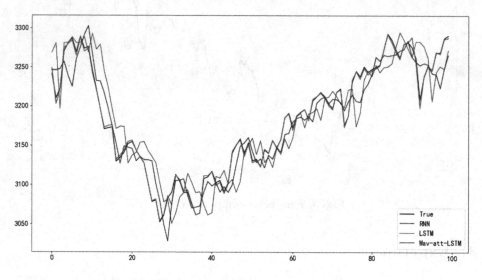

Fig. 4. Baseline comparison chart

3.2 Baseline Model Comparison

To test our model, we compare Wav-att-LSTM with other advanced methods, such as: ARMA [14], RNN [15] and LSTM [3]. Figure 4 is a fitting curve of the Wav-att-LSTM model and the baseline model. It can be seen from the figure that all four models can predict the future trend of stock prices, but the prediction accuracy is quite different. The prediction curve of Wav-att-LSTM has the highest accuracy compared to other algorithms The most important point is that the fitting curve of the model in the fluctuations such as peaks and troughs is the highest precision and the lag is smaller than the other models. This highlights he excellent performance of the Wav-att-LSTM model for predicting non-stationary sequences.

Table 1. Wav-att-LSTM wavelet decomposition layer error analysis

	MAPE	RMSE
ARMA	2.7526	1.3269
RNN	2.5074	1.2182
LSTM	2.0071	0.9821
1 dec Wav-att-LSTM	2.1201	0.8438
2 dec Wav-att-LSTM	**1.9306**	**0.7614**
3 dec Wav-att-LSTM	2.4671	1.0182

4   Conclusion and Future Work

This paper proposes a novel stock forecasting model (Wav-att-LSTM). Wav-att-LSTM takes into account the advantages of XGBoost, wavelet packet transform, LSTM, attention mechanism in time series decomposition and price prediction of stock sequences. The experiment found that compared with other advanced models, Wav-att-LSTM has stronger predictability and less lag. However, there are some defects in this paper. Our next step is to adaptive the model parameters and dynamically adjust them with time series to reduce the complexity of the model.

References

1. Li, Y., Zhang, L.: Short selling pressure, stock price behavior, and management forecast precision: evidence from a natural experiment. J. Account. Res. **53**(1), 79–117 (2015)
2. Spanos, G., Angelis, L.: The impact of information security events to the stock market: A systematic literature review. Comput. Secur. **58**, 216–229 (2016)
3. Petersen, N.C., Rodrigues, F., Pereira, F.C.: Multi-output bus travel time prediction with convolutional LSTM neural network. Expert Syst. Appl. **120**, 426–435 (2019)
4. Meng, A., Ge, J., Yin, H., et al.: Wind speed forecasting based on wavelet packet decomposition and artificial neural networks trained by crisscross optimization algorithm. Energy Convers. Manag. **114**, 75–88 (2016)
5. Vaswani, A., Shazeer, N., Parmar, N., et al.: Attention is all you need. In: Advances in Neural Information Processing Systems, pp. 5998–6008 (2017)
6. Liu, W., Tao, D.: Multiview Hessian regularization for image annotation. IEEE Trans. Image Process. **22**(7), 2676–2687 (2013)

7. Wang, Y., Zhou, Y., Shen, W., et al.: Abdominal multi-organ segmentation with organ-attention networks and statistical fusion. Med. Image Anal. **55**, 88–102 (2019)

8. Johnson, M., Schuster, M., Le, Q.V., et al.: Googles multilingual neural machine translation system: enabling zero-shot translation. Trans. Assoc. Comput. Linguist. **5**, 339–351 (2017)

9. Li, L., Wu, Y., Zhang, Y., et al.: Time+ user dual attention based sentiment prediction for multiple social network texts with time series. IEEE Access **7**, 17644–17653 (2019)

10. Zheng, H., Yuan, J., Chen, L.: Short-term load forecasting using EMD-LSTM neural networks with a Xgboost algorithm for feature importance evaluation. Energies **10**(8), 1168 (2017)

11. Rao, H., Shi, X., Rodrigue, A.K., et al.: Feature selection based on artificial bee colony and gradient boosting decision tree. Appl. Soft Comput. **74**, 634–642 (2019)

12. Acharya, U.R., Sudarshan, V.K., Rong, S.Q., et al.: Automated detection of premature delivery using empirical mode and wavelet packet decomposition techniques with uterine electromyogram signals. Comput. Biol. Med. **85**, 33–42 (2017)

13. Gao, L., Guo, Z., Zhang, H., et al.: Video captioning with attention-based LSTM and semantic consistency. IEEE Trans. Multimedia **19**(9), 2045–2055 (2017)

14. Rounaghi, M.M., Zadeh, F.N.: Investigation of market efficiency and financial stability between $S\delta P500$ and London stock exchange: monthly and yearly forecasting of time series stock returns using ARMA model. Phys. A: Stat. Mech. Its Appl. **456**, 10–21 (2016)

15. Rather, A.M., Agarwal, A., Sastry, V.N.: Recurrent neural network and a hybrid model for prediction of stock returns. Expert Syst. Appl. **42**(6), 3234–3241 (2015)

An Image Denoising Algorithm Based on Singular Value Decomposition and Non-local Self-similarity

Guoyu Yang[1,2], Yilei Wang[1], Banghai Xu[2], and Xiaofeng Zhang[3(✉)]

[1] School of Information Science and Engineering,
Qufu Normal University, Rizhao 276826, China
[2] School of Information and Electrical Engineering,
Ludong University, Yantai 264025, China
[3] School of Computer Science and Technology,
Shandong Technology and Business University, Yantai 264005, China
iamzxf@126.com

Abstract. Image denoising is a basic but important step in image pre-processing, computer vision, and related areas. Based on singular value decomposition (SVD) and non-local self-similarity, This paper proposed an image denoising algorithm which is simple in computation. The proposed algorithm is divided into three steps: firstly, the block matching technique is used to find similar patches to construct one matrix, which is of low rank; secondly, SVD is performed on this matrix, and the singular value matrix is processed by principal component analysis (PCA); finally, all similar patches are aggregated to retrieve the denoised image. Since the noise in the image will affect the computation of similar patches, this procedure is iterated many times to enhance the performance. Simulated experiments on different images show that the proposed algorithm performs well in denoising images. Compared with most denoising algorithms, the proposed algorithm is of high efficiency.

Keywords: Singular value decomposition · Non-local self-similarity · Principal component analysis

1 Introduction

In the process of image retrieval and transmission, image will be contaminated inevitably by noise. Generally speaking, noise is redundant or disturbed information, which will reduce image quality and affect corresponding applications greatly. To improve the visual effect of image, many researchers and scholars have conducted deep and extensive research in image denoising algorithms [1]. In the past several decades, many denoising algorithms were proposed, such as non-local mean filtering, block matching 3D(BM3D), and etc.

In digital images, each pixel doesn't exist in isolation, and it is relevant to some pixels, which is illustrated by similar intensities or geometric similarity.

© Springer Nature Switzerland AG 2019
J. Vaidya et al. (Eds.): CSS 2019, LNCS 11983, pp. 501–510, 2019.
https://doi.org/10.1007/978-3-030-37352-8_44

For example, pixels in the edge of one object often have similar intensity values. Based on this phenomenon, some scholars proposed a denoising algorithm based on mean filtering. In this algorithm, a searching window is designed, the intensity value of a pixel in the denoised image is the mean value of all pixels falling in the searching window [2]. Commonly, when the noise level is low, the size of the searching window is small, and when the image is contaminated by noise greatly, the size is big to retrieve good performance. However, when the noise level is high, any big searching window cannot perform well. Further research find that pixel similarity is not limited to local searching window, but the whole image. For example, pixels in the long edge may have similar intensity values and similar textures, which don't belong to the local searching window of a given pixel. Hence, a denoising algorithm based on non-local self-similarity is proposed [3]. In the algorithm, the redundant information of the given image is mined, and all image patches with similar structure features will be retrieved. The contaminated image will be denoised by considering the information in these similar image patches simultaneously. The principle of non-local algorithms is similar as that of mean filtering algorithms, and the intensity value of a pixel is based on the intensities of related pixels. However, in non-local denoising algorithms, pixel relevance is considered, and the intensity value of a pixel is the weighted value of all pixels in the while image. Experimental results show that non-local desnoising algorithms have good performance, but perform poor in images contaminated by noise of high level.

From the viewpoint of image representation, the similarity of pixel features can be expressed by the sparsity or low rank of coefficients in frequency domain. Due to the sparse representation, the noise is propagated in the transform domain uniformly, resulting in the fact that the main information of the image is concentrated on a small number of large eigenvalues. Based on the sparse representation, the most fractions of a signal can be retrieved by only a small number of atoms in a given super-complete dictionary. Based on non-local denoising algorithms and the sparse representation of image, Dabov et al. proposed a collaborative filtering denoising algorithm using block matching and sparse 3D transformation(BM3D) [4]. In BM3D, block matching algorithm is adopted to retrieve the similar image patches, and then one 3D array is constructed. After that, sparse 3D transform will be performed on the array, and Wiener filtering is utilized to remove image noise in transform domain. To our knowledge, BM3D can almost retrieve the best performance, yet with high computation.

2   Preliminaries

Suppose X is a grayscale image, and based on the theory of signal representation, the image can be denoted as the weighted sum of some basis functions, formalized as follows,

$$X = \sum_{i=1}^{N} \phi_i a_i \tag{1}$$

where ϕ_i is the basis function, and a_i is the corresponding coefficient related to $\phi_i(i = 1, 2, \ldots, n)$.

Considering the diversity of image noise, this manuscript will analyze and design the denoising algorithms of Gaussian white noise. Suppose the noisy image is denoted as Y, and based on the property of Gaussian white noise, Y can be represented as

$$Y = X + E \tag{2}$$

where E is the Gaussian white noise, and X is the reference image without noise. In this manuscript, a vectorized version of this model is adopted, i.e.

$$y = x + e \tag{3}$$

Block matching is a common method in image denoising and motion estimation. For a image patch, all neighboring image patches will be matched, and the most nearest L patches will be retrieved. Block matching algorithms can be classified into two categories: local searching and global searching. In local searching, similar patches is retrieved in a local searching window, while global searching will find similar patches in the whole image.

Singular value decomposition, abbreviated as SVD, is an important matrix decomposition method, and is the extension of feature decomposition on any matrix. The singular value is mainly applied into the dimensionality reduction and low rank approximation of high dimensional matrices. SVD can be formalized as [5]

$$P = U\Sigma V^T \tag{4}$$

where U and V are unitary matrices, and Σ is a diagonal matrix, in which the diagonal elements are the singular values. In SVD, the singular values in Σ are deceasing, and the first r singular values are often adopted to represent all information approximately.

Commonly, principal component analysis (PCA) [6] and SVD are similar, which are adopted to perform matrix approximation by dimension reduction. However, more computation is required in PCA. While for low-rank matrix, SVD can estimate it by low-rank approximation. Therefore, SVD will be adopted instead of PCA in this manuscript, and a simple but effective denoising algorithm will be proposed.

3   Proposed Algorithm for Image Denoising

The proposed denoising algorithm can be divided into two steps: basic estimation and final estimation. In the proposed algorithm, each step contains 3 phases: image patches grouping, denoising and aggregation. In the first step, N image patches are extracted from the noisy image y, denoted as $\{y_i\}_{i=1}^N$, in which y_i is the vector model of the i-th image patch. For each image patch y_i, the L nearest image patches from $\{y_i\}_{i=1}^N$ will be retrieved to form the low rank matrix. Then, SVD will be adopted to perform low rank approximation. Finally all approximated image patches are aggregated to construct the denoised image.

The second step is the improvement of the first step, which will use residual image to perform back projection, which will enhance the result further (Fig. 1).

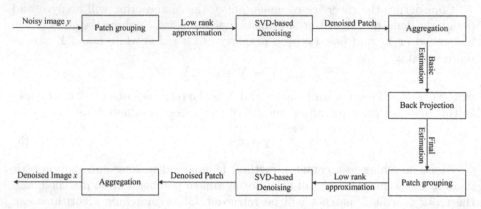

Fig. 1. The work flow of the proposed algorithm.

3.1 Similar Patches Grouping

Patch grouping is a problem which is extensively applied in such areas as image processing, computer vision, and etc. Many algorithms were proposed after several decades of deep and extensive research, such as block matching, K-means, and etc [7]. In these algorithms, block matching is a method with less computation, and has good performance. Hence, this manuscript will adopt block matching for similar patch grouping.

Considering there are two matching techniques, this manuscript will adopted global searching to retrieve similar patches based of the property of non-local self-similarity in images. For a reference image patch with size of $\sqrt{m} \times \sqrt{m}$, block matching will retrieve similar patches from $\{y_i\}_{i=1}^N$ based on similarity measurement. Since there are many measurements to evaluate the similarity between image patches, this manuscript adopts Euclidean distance, which is simple but effective. For two image patches y_i and y_j, the Euclidean distance between the two patches is defined as follows.

$$D(y_i, y_j) = \|y_i - y_j\|_2^2 \tag{5}$$

where $\| \cdot \|_2$ denotes the Euclidean distance, and y_j is the candidate patch. The smaller $D(y_i, y_j)$ is, the more similar y_i and y_j are. In this manuscript, the most L similar patches with y_i are selected to construct the matrix P_i. Since image noise exists, P_i can be expressed as

$$P_i = Q_i + E_i \tag{6}$$

where Q_i is the noise-free matrix, and E_i is the noise one.

Generally speaking, the number of similar patches should not be too small or too big. If L is too small, less similar patches will be selected, which will make the algorithm with low robustness. If the L is too big, the dissimilar patches will be considered into the matrix P_i, resulting in incorrect estimation of P_i, and the final image will still contains image noise.

3.2 Image Denoising Based on SVD

For more simple description, we will replace P_i with P, and Q_i with Q by a slight abuse of notation. The target is to estimate the noise-free image Q from the noisy image P. As is well known, different image patches are relevant due to the similarity of their features, meaning that Q is also of low rank, and can be approximated.

In SVD, the noisy image P can be expressed as

$$P = U \Sigma V^T \tag{7}$$

When low rank approximation is performed, the following equation will be retrieved

$$P_r = U \Sigma_r V^T \tag{8}$$

where Σ_r is the diagonal matrix with the first r singular values of Σ, formalized as,

$$\Sigma_r = diag(\sigma_1, \sigma_2, \ldots, \sigma_r, 0, \ldots, 0) \tag{9}$$

In the proposed algorithm, the key problem is to decide the value of r. Considering that 10% or even 1% of all singular values can represent 99% of the given image. From the analysis and comparison in different noisy images, we found that the ideal value of r can be decided by $\sum_{i=r}^{n} \sigma_i^2 = \beta \sum_{i=1}^{n} \sigma_i^2$, in which β is the scale factor of image noise. Therefore, the value r can be retrieved by the following inequality,

$$\sum_{i=r}^{n} \sigma^2 > \beta \sum_{i=1}^{n} \sigma_i^2. \tag{10}$$

3.3 Image Patch Aggregation

After the two steps above, each image patch is estimated by low rank approximation. We can compute the denoised image by aggregating the L nearest patches. First, mean processing will be performed on L nearest patches, and the image patch x_i will be computed as

$$x_i = \frac{1}{L} \sum_{i=1}^{L} x_{i,j} \tag{11}$$

where $x_{i,j}$ is the j-th estimation of x_i. Then the image patches are aggregated to retrieve the denoised image. To our knowledge, weighted averaging is the common method to aggregate image patches. Also, weighted averaging can resist image noise farther to retrieve more accurate image. In weighted averaging, there are two methods of weight assignment: fixed weight and adaptive one. It is the simplest to assign the similar blocks with the same weights, but this will result in over-smoothing and some detailed information will be lost. According to SVD and principal component analysis (PCA), this manuscript proposes an adaptive weight assignment schema which is based on bias and unbiased estimation. The bigger the singular value is, the bigger weight is assigned. Subsequent analysis shows the proposed weight assignment schema can highlight the important structures and features of the given image, and good performance can be retrieved. For the j-th patch, the adaptive weight is defined as,

$$w_j = \frac{\sum_{i=1}^{r} \sigma_i}{n \times m} \tag{12}$$

where n and m is the row and column of the matrix Σ, and r is the rank of Σ.

With the help of the adaptive weights, the estimation of the i-th image patch can be computed as

$$x_i = \frac{1}{W} \sum_{j=1}^{n} w_j x_{i,j} \tag{13}$$

where $W = \sum_{j=1}^{n} w_j$ is the normalization factor.

3.4 Back Projection

Though most image noise can be removed by the steps mentioned above, there is still some noise in the image. The reason is that the noise in the initial image affect the patch grouping. Some dissimilar patches may be classified into the same group, resulting in an inaccurate patch grouping. Therefore, different from other iterative schemas, this manuscript adopts a two-stage strategy: basic estimation and final one. Based on back projection, the residual image will be adopted to enhance the result of basic estimation in the final estimation. In back projection, the filtered noise will be added to the denoised image to retrieve a novel noisy image, formalized as,

$$y_i = x_i + \delta(y - x_i) \tag{14}$$

where $\delta \in (0, 1)$ is the parameter of back projection. Since the noise in y_i changes, the standard deviation should be re-computed as,

$$\tau' = \gamma \sqrt{\tau^2 - \|y - x_0\|_F^2} \tag{15}$$

where γ is the scale factor, τ is the standard deviation of the original image, and $\| \cdot \|_F$ is the F-norm.

4   Simulated Experiments

In this section, the proposed algorithm will be compared with other denoising algorithms, including mean filtering, median filtering, non-local mean filtering and BM3D. In the experiments, Gaussian noise of different levels are added.

To compare the results quantitatively, two measurements are adopted, peak signal to noise ratio (PSNR) and structural similarity index (SSIM), which are applied extensively. The two measurements are defined as follows.

$$PSNR = 10 \times \log_{10} \left(\frac{(2^n - 1)^2}{MSR} \right) \tag{16}$$

where n is the number of intensity values, and MSE is the mean square error, denoting the average square error between the noisy image and denoised one. Formally, MSE can be computed as

$$MSE = \frac{1}{N} \sum_{i=1}^{N} (\tilde{x}_i - x_i)^2 \tag{17}$$

$\tilde{x}_i$ and x_i is the intensity value of the i-th pixel in the denoised image and original one, and N is the number of pixels in the given image.

Another measurement $SSIM$ is the similarity of structure. The bigger $SSIM$, the closer the structure of the denoised image and the original one is. Formally,

$$SSIM(x, \tilde{x}) = \frac{(2\mu_x\mu_{\tilde{x}} + c_1)(2\sigma_{x\tilde{x}} + c_2)}{(\mu_x^2 + \mu_{\tilde{x}}^2 + c_1)(\sigma_x^2 + \sigma_{\tilde{x}}^2 + c_2)} \tag{18}$$

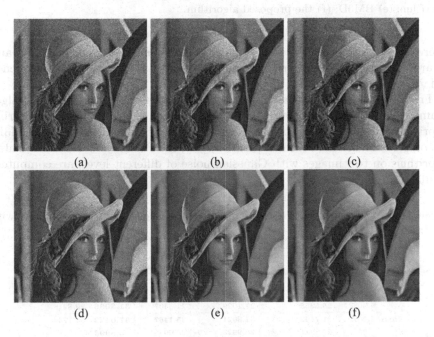

Fig. 2. Denoised images of *Lenna* with Gaussian noise of 30% level; (a) noisy image; (b) median filtering algorithm; (c) mean filtering algorithm; (d) non-local denoising algorithm; (e) BM3D; (f) the proposed algorithm.

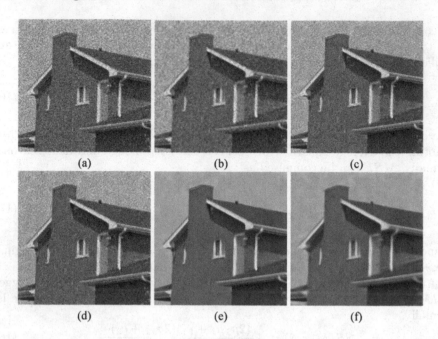

(a)   (b)   (c)

(d)   (e)   (f)

Fig. 3. Denoised images of *House* with Gaussian noise of 30% level; (a) noisy image; (b) median filtering algorithm; (c) mean filtering algorithm; (d) non-local denoising algorithm; (e) BM3D; (f) the proposed algorithm.

where μ_x and $\mu_{\tilde{x}}$ are the mean values of the noisy and denoised image, σ_x^2 and $\sigma_{\tilde{x}}^2$ are the standard variation of x and $\tilde{x}$, and $\sigma_{x\tilde{x}}^2$ is the covariance between x and $\tilde{x}$.

From Figs. 2 and 3, we can see that the visual effects of the proposed algorithm on these images are better than mean filtering algorithm, median filtering algorithm and non-local denoising one, and are comparable with that of BM3D. To compare the denoised results quantitatively, the PSNRs and SSIMs of related algorithms on test images with Gaussian noise of different levels are computed, tabulated in Tables 1 and 2.

Table 1. Comparison of PSNR of different denoising algorithms on test images with different noise levels

	Noise level	Median filtering	Mean filtering	Non-local denoising	BM3D	Proposed algorithm
Lenna	10%	32.1601	32.3003	34.9843	**36.0726**	34.4228
	20%	28.3748	29.5924	26.6964	**33.2015**	31.3240
	30%	25.5258	27.1029	21.3407	**31.3996**	29.8218
House	10%	31.7192	31.3021	35.1467	**37.0122**	34.1744
	20%	27.9947	28.9923	26.6995	**33.8993**	31.3485
	30%	25.1818	26.7241	21.3493	**32.1251**	30.0193

Table 2. Comparison of SSIM of different denoising algorithms on test images with different noise levels

	Noise level	Median filtering	Mean filtering	Non-local denoising	BM3D	Proposed algorithm
Lenna	10%	0.9913	0.9915	0.9955	**0.9965**	0.9949
	20%	0.9795	0.9843	0.9705	**0.9932**	0.9894
	30%	0.9611	0.9725	0.9055	**0.9897**	0.9849
House	10%	0.9895	0.9883	0.9953	**0.9969**	0.9940
	20%	0.9755	0.9803	0.9679	**0.9937**	0.9885
	30%	0.9541	0.9672	0.8979	**0.9905**	0.9843

Table 3. Comparison of running time of different denoising algorithms on test images with different noise levels

	Noise level	Median filtering	Mean filtering	Non-local denoising	BM3D	Proposed algorithm
Lenna	10%	3.3762	**0.6884**	175.0388	1160.6442	35.7824
	20%	3.0573	**0.6572**	178.0489	1159.9875	35.1343
	30%	2.9736	**0.6408**	175.8655	1159.6549	25.7978
House	10%	0.8788	**0.4413**	46.5749	1038.0303	8.1956
	20%	0.8329	**0.4439**	44.5558	1039.4123	9.8960
	30%	0.8186	**0.4646**	42.9115	1038.9542	7.2719

From Tables 1 and 2, we can see that the PSNR and SSIM of the proposed algorithm are better than those of median filtering, mean filtering and non-local denoising algorithms, and is comparable with those of BM3D. In addition, the running time of related are recorded, shown in Table 3. As is shown from Table 3, the running time of mean filtering is the best, then median filtering, the proposed algorithm, non-local denoising algorithm and BM3D. Comparing these algorithms synthetically, the visual effect and two quantitative measurements of the proposed algorithm are not better than BM3D, but the running time of the proposed algorithm is more acceptable than BM3D. Therefore, the proposed algorithm is a good algorithm synthetically.

5   Conclusions

In this paper, a simple but effective denosing algorithm is proposed based on non-local self-similarity and singular value decomposition. Based on non-local self-similarity, all information coving the whole image can be utilized to resist the image noise. By singular value decomposition, low rank is adopted to resist the effect of image noise. Experiments on different images show that the proposed algorithm can retrieve satisfying performance, especially when the noise level is high.

Acknowledgements. The research is supported by the NSF of China under granted nos. 61873117, 61873145, 61602229. Shandong educational science planning "special research subject for educational admission examination", No.: ZK1337123A002. Key Research and Development Program of Shandong Province (No. 2019GGX101025).

References

1. Guo, Q., Zhang, C., Zhang, Y., Liu, H.: An efficien SVD-based method for image denoising. IEEE Trans. Circuits Syst. Video Technol. **26**(5), 868–880 (2016)
2. Shao, L., Yan, R., Li, X., Liu, Y.: From heuristic optimization to dictionary learning: a review and comprehensive comparison of image denoising algorithms. IEEE Trans. Cybern. **44**(7), 1001–1013 (2014)
3. Buades, A., Coll, B., Morel, J.M.: A non-local algorithm for image denoising. In: Proceeding of IEEE Computer Society Conference on Computer Vision and Pattern Recognition, pp. 60–65 (2015)
4. Dabov, K., Foi, A., Katkovnik, V., Egiazarian, K.: Image denoising by sparse 3-D transform-domain collaborative filtering. IEEE Trans. Image Process. **16**(8), 2080–2095 (2007)
5. Liu, W., Lin, W.: Additive white Gaussian noise level estimation in SVD domain for images. IEEE Trans. Image Process. **22**(3), 872–883 (2013)
6. Mauldin Jr., F.W., Lin, D., Hossack, J.A.: The singular value filter: a general filter design strategy for PCA-based signal separation in medical ultrasound imaging. IEEE Trans. Med. Imag. **30**(11), 1951–1964 (2011)
7. Chatterjee, P., Milanfar, P.: Patch-based near optimal image denoising. IEEE Trans. Image Process. **21**(4), 1635–1649 (2012)

Dummy Trajectory Generation Scheme Based on Deep Learning

Jiaji Pan[1,2], Jingkang Yang[1], and Yining Liu[1(✉)]

[1] School of Computer and Information Security, Guilin University of Electronic Technology, Guilin, China
ynliu@guet.edu.cn
[2] College of Computer Science and Technology, HenyangNormal University, Henyang 421002, China

Abstract. Nowadays, the traditional dummy trajectory generation algorithm used to protect users' trajectory privacy usually uses statistical methods to build trajectory model. Because the human mobility model is a complex equation, it is difficult to use mathematical methods to model, so the established trajectory model can not consider the human mobility model which restricts the formation of trajectory. Therefore, traditional dummy trajectory generation algorithms can not defend against data mining attacks based on in-depth learning. In this paper, LSTM (Long Short-Term Memory) is used to design the real and dummy trajectory discriminator. Experiments show that data mining based on deep learning can eliminate more than 95% of the algorithm generated trajectories, and the error rate of real trajectory is less than 10%. We restrict the traditional dummy trajectory generation algorithm to human mobility model, and design a dummy trajectory generation strategy so that the generated trajectory can defend against multiple recognition attacks.

Keywords: Dummy trajectory · Human mobility model · LSTM

1 Introduction

In today's society, LBS (Location based services) [1–7] has developed rapidly and is widely used in smart mobile terminals. The LBS service provider and the customer use the trajectory data as the information entity and the Internet as the information carrier for information interaction. A large amount of trajectory data is generated during the interaction process. These trajectory data have rich time and space information, and information about the user's personal interests and social status can be obtained through data mining. However, the trajectory information contains too much data on personal privacy and therefore cannot be published directly. Therefore, how to protect the privacy of users in data distribution and LBS can make the trajectory data play a role and is concerned by researchers. In recent years, researchers have also applied the proposed new technology to data privacy and trajectory privacy protection in LBS. However, the algorithms proposed by current researchers can only resist traditional data mining attacks, and can not resist data mining attacks based on deep learning.

© Springer Nature Switzerland AG 2019
J. Vaidya et al. (Eds.): CSS 2019, LNCS 11983, pp. 511–523, 2019.
https://doi.org/10.1007/978-3-030-37352-8_45

Aiming at the problem of trajectory privacy protection of intelligent mobile terminals, a large number of solutions have emerged in the academic world, which can be roughly divided into two categories: a trusted third-party server-based method and a mobile terminal-based distributed method. These schemes are mainly implemented by means of spatial cloaking, mix-zone, path confusion, and dummy trajectory.

Among them, the dummy trajectory method is most practical because it does not need a trusted third party, can defend against channel-side attacks, and its operation is simple and does not need to cooperate with other users.

However, current researchers have been unable to evade the problems of what trajectory conforms to the real trajectory when designing the dummy trajectory generation algorithm. Most researchers use mathematical modeling methods to try to explain whether the trajectory conforms to the real trajectory characteristics from the perspective of probability theory and statistics and has achieved a series of results. However, it is always impossible to explain the constraints of the formation of the trajectory.

In order to verify that there are some constraints in the process of trajectory formation that can not be explained in the current paper, we design and train a LSTM-based trajectory discriminator in the third part of this paper. We put the dummy trajectory generated by the algorithm ADTGA [10], MLN [8] and MN [8] into the trained LSTM trajectory discriminator, respectively, to prove that the dummy trajectory generated by the classical algorithm can not resist trajectory identification attack based on LSTM. The trajectory discrimination attack proves that the dummy trajectory generated by the classical algorithm and the real trajectory are not distributed in the same space-time, and proves that the dummy trajectory generated by the classical algorithm does not conform to the real human mobility model. In the next part, a complete scheme of dummy trajectory generation is designed.

Contributions. In this paper, we:

- Define trajectory points with four-dimensional vectors and describe the space-time distribution of trajectory sections composed of n points with n × 4 matrix.
- Design a trajectory detector based on LSTM, which can detect most of the generated trajectories of the algorithm, but the error rate of the real trajectory is very low.
- Combine background information, human movement mode and classical dummy trajectory generation algorithm to design a complete real-time continuous trajectory privacy protection scheme.

The rest of the paper is organized as follows. Section 2 introduces Related Works, LSTM-based trajectory discriminator. The LSTM-based trajectory discriminator described in Sect. 3. We propose dummy trajectory generation strategy in Sect. 4. Section 5 concludes the paper.

2 Related Works

Kido et al. [8, 9] proposed that users could use dummy locations generated by two requests to form dummy trajectories, which pioneered the use of dummy trajectories to protect trajectory privacy. Wu et al. [10] proposed that virtual trajectories could be generated by adding disturbance, taking into account the distance between real trajectories and dummy trajectories and the distance between dummy trajectories, so that the final generated trajectory set could meet the needs of user privacy protection. Ray et al. In order to protect user's trajectory privacy, a method of adding intersection points to the trajectory after rotation is proposed. Kato R et al. [11] assumes that user movement is known beforehand, and proposes a dummy anonymity method based on user movement, in which dummy objects move naturally when multiple locations stop. Niu et al. [12] fully considered the probability information of users sending requests at each location, and formalized the background information using information entropy. A dummy location generation algorithm based on background information was proposed to ensure that the generated dummy location could effectively confuse opponents.

In our paper, in order to verify that the dummy trajectories generated by the traditional dummy trajectory generation scheme do not conform to the human mobility model, we select three algorithms of MN, MLN and ADTGA in the traditional dummy trajectory generation algorithm to generate dummy trajectories, and use our LSTM-based dummy trajectory discriminator to identify these generated dummy trajectories.

3 Dummy Trajectory Recognition Scheme Based on LSTM

Traditional dummy trajectory generation schemes are implemented by mathematical modeling. These algorithms attempt to generate dummy trajectories with the same distribution as real trajectories. In order to prove that the trajectory model established by traditional mathematical modeling methods can not describe the spatial and temporal distribution of real trajectories, we have done the following work to verify our conclusions.

3.1 Dummy Trajectory Identification Scheme

We define a series of trajectory points to form a trajectory section, and two adjacent points form a trajectory segment.

Suppose our detector can detect the trajectory section from m to n points. When a trajectory is detected, it is firstly divided into sections of equal trajectory points (points from m to n). If the number of points in the last part is less than m, it is discarded. Otherwise, use detector to detect.

The dummy trajectory identification scheme is shown in Fig. 1. We divide a trajectory into n trajectory sections. Each trajectory section is detected by a trajectory detector, and n results are obtained. It is assumed that k of the n results are dummy. If k/n is greater than the set threshold, the trajectory is judged to be dummy or real.

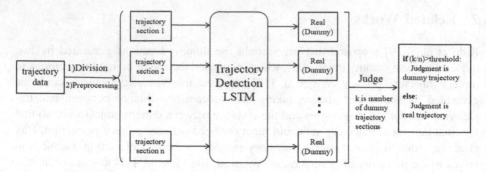

Fig. 1. Dummy trajectory detection model framework based on LSTM

3.2   LSTM Trajectory Discriminator Framework

The LSTM-based trajectory discriminator framework is shown in Fig. 2.

- **Input Layer:** First, we transform the trajectory from longitude and latitude to plane rectangular coordinate system, then divide the trajectory into equal trajectory sections, and finally preprocess the trajectory points into time series matrix. The trajectory set includes real trajectory and algorithm generated trajectory.
- **Network Layer:** The first position state of the trajectory section is input into the LSTM network in time sequence, and the final result is transmitted to the output layer through the fully connected layer.
- **Output Layer:** Softmax operation is performed on the output of the fully connected layer to get the classification results.
- **Network Training Layer:** In the network training stage, the label of the trajectory section (true or dummy) and the output of the output layer are combined to calculate the loss value. The weight matrix and bias of the network layer are updated by gradient descent method to reduce the loss value, so that the prediction results are closer to the real results.

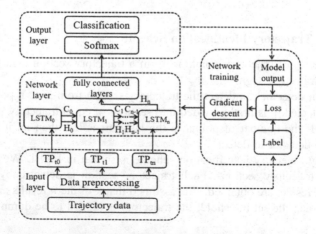

Fig. 2. LSTM-based trajectory discriminator framework

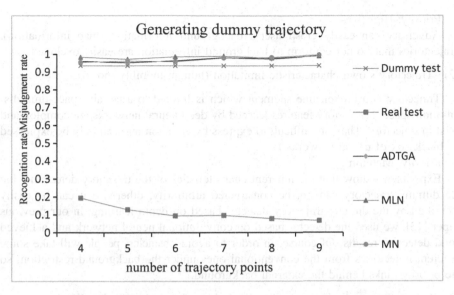

Fig. 3. Detection performance of LSTM-based dummy trajectory detector

Figure 3 shows the detection performance of LSTM-based dummy trajectory detector. On the whole, the average detection rate of this detector is over 95% for the dummy trajectory generated by the classical algorithm, and about 10% for the real trajectory. With the increase of the number of trajectory points in each trajectory section, the detection rate of the generated trajectory increases slightly, and the error rate of the real trajectory decreases greatly.

Experiments show that the dummy trajectories based on LSTM designed by us can detect most of the generated trajectories which do not conform to the real trajectories' spatial and temporal distribution, while for the real trajectories, the error rate is low. With the increase of trajectory points, the recognition rate of the generated trajectory is slightly improved, while for the real trajectory, the error rate is significantly reduced, that is, the more the trajectory points are sampled, the better the detection effect is. When the number of trajectory points reaches 9, the error rate of real trajectory is only 6.6%.

4   Improved Dummy Trajectory Generation Scheme

4.1   Consider Three Constraints of Dummy Trajectory Generation (Priority from High to Low)

(1) External background constraints, such as inaccessible areas such as waters, green areas, etc.

Priority: High

Adversary can easily grasp user's background information (map information). Trajectories that do not conform to background information are easily excluded.

(2) Trajectory's own characteristic limitation (human mobility model):

Trajectory is a broken line segment which is limited to a certain space-time distribution space. (Trajectory features learned by deep neural networks are complex and exist in trajectory. They are difficult to express by equation and can only be expressed by black box of neural networks.)

Priority: Medium

Experiments show that the inherent characteristics of the trajectory determine that the dummy trajectory can not be constructed arbitrarily, otherwise it can be easily identified by the dummy trajectory detector based on depth learning. in our previous paper [13], we used the detector based on convolutional neural network and achieved good detection results. Of course, in order to avoid obstacles, people will take some different trajectories from the conventional ones under the background restriction, so the priority ranks behind the external background.

(3) Inter-trajectory limitation, space limitation of trajectory point distribution and some other limitations. (Trajectory features modeled by mathematical methods such as probability and statistics are simple and easy to be expressed by equation. Researchers construct trajectory features based on experience, and the description of features is not necessarily accurate or irrelevant to trajectory.)

Priority: Low

Background information must be given priority, and the inherent attributes of the trajectory parsed by the deep learning classifier are more reliable than the trajectory characteristics based on empirical mathematical modeling, because the ability of deep learning to obtain deep information is stronger than that of mathematical modeling.

Of course, so far, researchers have designed many excellent pseudo-trajectory generation algorithms. Our dummy trajectory generation strategy combines these excellent dummy trajectory generation algorithms to construct dummy trajectories on the basis of considering background information and inherent attributes of the trajectory itself, so that the generated dummy trajectories can mix the spurious with the genuine.

4.2 Precondition for Constructing Reasonable Dummy Trajectories

The constraints of generating trajectory explain the internal and external causes of forming trajectory.

Internal Causes: Human movement model

External Cause: Background information, as long as there are obstacles on the map, the trajectory must be avoided.

Also, when generating multiple dummy trajectories, the dispersion of positions between trajectories should be considered to reduce the leakage probability.

In confronting an adversary, we assume that the adversary has all the information, namely:

(1) The adversary has the background information of the location when user requests the LBS service.
(2) Adversary trained classifier with deep learning tool to recognize real trajectory and arithmetic generated trajectory.
(3) The opponent has some other methods to distinguish dummy trajectories, and some other methods proposed in related papers.

Therefore, in order to confront the adversary who knows all the information, the generated dummy trajectory is restricted by these three conditions. Considering these constraints, the dummy trajectory scheme needs the following preconditions.

Background Information
Our scheme uses simplified background information design. We divide the background into three levels as shown in Fig. 4:

(1) Hot region: Pedestrian flow $> \alpha$
    Hot region is represented by green grid, which represent densely populated areas. When trajectory generation, trajectory points are selected first.
(2) Ordinary region: $\alpha \geq$ Pedestrian flow $> \beta$
    Ordinary region is represented by yellow grid, which represents the relatively sparse region of pedestrian flow, and is the secondary area of trajectory points when trajectory generation.
(3) Forbidden region: Pedestrian flow $\leq \beta$
    Forbidden region is represented by red grid, which represent areas with little pedestrian flow. Trajectory points should avoid these areas when generating trajectories.

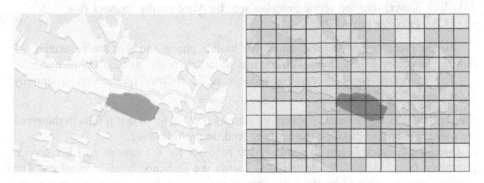

Fig. 4. Map background information (Color figure online)

Appropriate Trajectory Discriminator

In order to make the generated dummy trajectories conform to the human mobility model, it is necessary to design a reasonable trajectory discriminator to distinguish the real trajectory from the generated trajectory which is not in the same distribution space as the real trajectory, so as to screen the generated trajectory which is the same distribution as the real trajectory.

Experiments show that our LSTM-based trajectory discriminator can recognize more than 95% of dummy trajectories, and the error rate for real trajectories is less than 10%. It proves that our designed trajectory discriminator has the ability to distinguish whether a trajectory is in the same distribution as the real trajectory.

Dummy Trajectory Generation Strategies for Some Other Attack Methods

In the work done by previous researchers, various dummy trajectory generation strategies for enemy attacks have been proposed, and remarkable results have been achieved. These mature strategies against opponent's dummy trajectory prediction can be combined with the former two to design a set of perfect dummy trajectory generation strategies.

4.3   Dummy Trajectory Generation Scheme

Our scheme is to establish the generation of each dummy trajectory point under three restrictions. Under our scheme, we can ensure that user Alice is free from trajectory privacy theft.

Alice travels to a tourist village. Starting from place A of the tourist village, she wants to know some interest points (restaurants, scenic spots, accommodation points, etc.). So she opens an APP to inquire about nearby interest points, but she does not want to reveal her trajectory privacy. At this time, she faces two potential trajectory privacy thieves (assuming that the stealer has the ability to analyze the trajectory and master the background information of the trajectory):

(1) Bob intercepting the service request sent by Alice on the channel side
(2) LBS Provider (an APP)

So she preprocessed the request on her mobile phone and sent the generated k-1 dummy trajectory points along with the real trajectory points to the LBS provider.

The trajectory point processing process is as follows (generating a dummy trajectory):

Step1: Initialize $k - 1$ dummy trajectory starting point at t_0, so that it falls in the green area within a certain distance from Alice. And do the following.

Operation1: Alice began to send service requests for k locations to LBS service providers. Only Alice's mobile terminal knows the authenticity of k locations. The service requests returned by the LBS service provider to Alice's mobile terminal are returned to k locations. Alice's mobile terminal filters out $k - 1$ dummy requests and returns the results returned by the LBS server to Alice (Fig. 5).

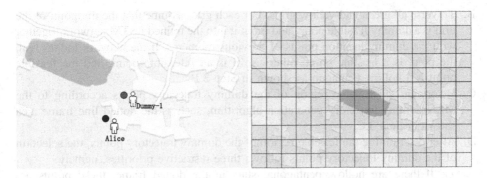

Fig. 5. Step 1 of Dummy trajectory generation strategy (Color figure online)

Step2: At t_1 and t_2, since the designed LSTM needs at least three locations to determine whether the trajectory conforms to the real trajectory distribution, the traditional dummy generation algorithm is used to generate dummy points (here we use the classical dummy trajectory generation algorithm MLN). The restriction is that the generated dummy trajectory points must fall in the green or yellow region.

If the feasible region of the dummy trajectory points generated by MLN algorithm does not intersect with the feasible region of the background, the dummy trajectory points that meet the background constraints are selected first, and the trajectory points are as close as possible to the feasible region of the dummy trajectory points generated by MLN algorithm.

Do Operation1.

Step3: From time t_3 to the end of the request service, Alice's mobile terminal does the following:

A. According to the points of the previous moment, the range of the dummy position points at the current moment is determined and divided into grids. The priority of each grid's landing point is identified by different colors, the red area represents the non-landing point, and the green area represents the priority selection area (Fig. 6).

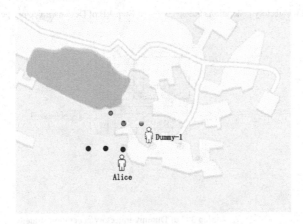

Fig. 6. Step 2 of Dummy trajectory generation strategy

B. Traverse all green and yellow grids. For each grid, assume that the midpoint of the grid is a dummy feasible point, and input it into the trained LSTM network together with the dummy location points of previous moments. If the network judges real, the point is a feasible point, otherwise it is an infeasible point, and the feasible point is a hollow Pentagon as shown in Step 3.B.

C. Determine the feasible region of the dummy trajectory points according to the MLN dummy trajectory generation algorithm, such as the dotted line frame area shown in Step 3.C.

D. After determining the feasible region of the dummy trajectory points, the selection of the dummy trajectory points follows three restrictive priorities, namely:

   (1) If there are hollow pentagonal stars in the dotted frame, these points are selected as the set of points to be selected for dummy trajectory, and one point in the set of points is selected randomly as the set of dummy trajectory points. The set of points to be selected is shown by the solid Pentagon in the figure.

   (2) If there is no pentagonal star in the dotted frame, look for the pentagonal star outside the dotted frame near the dotted frame as the dummy trajectory point.

   (3) If there is no pentagonal star in the background feasible region, the random points in the dashed frame are selected, such as the intersection of the dashed frame and the background feasible region, and the points in the background feasible region are selected as the dummy trajectory points (Fig. 7).

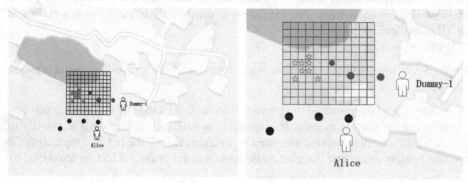

Step 3.A of Dummy trajectory generation strategy   Step 3.B of Dummy trajectory generation strategy

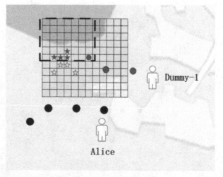

Step 3.C of Dummy trajectory generation strategy.

Fig. 7. Step 3 of Dummy trajectory generation strategy (Color figure online)

Algorithm 1: Group t Dummy locations Generation Algorithm

1 **For** i in range (k-1):

2 Determining feasible grids based on background information

3 Generated = 0

4 **If (t <= 3)**:

5   Generating candidate dummy trajectory point set Using Classical Algorithms

6   **If** (feasible grid and candidate dummy trajectory point set intersect):

7   Random selection of intersection points

8   Generated = 1

9 **Else**:

10   Determining feasible points HMMPs (Points conforming to Human Mobility Model) using LSTM

11   **If** (feasible grid and HMMPs intersect):

12   Generating candidate dummy trajectory point set Using Classical Algorithms

13   **If** feasible grids and HMMPs and candidate dummy trajectory point set intersect:

14   Random selection of intersection point (feasible grids and HMMPs and

15   candidate dummy trajectory point set)

16   Generated = 1

17   **Else**:

18   Random selection of intersection point (feasible grids and HMMPs)

19   Generated = 1

20 **If not** Generated:

21   Random selection of point in feasible grids

22   Adding the point to the dummy location dataset

23 Outputting **k − 1** dummy locations

24 Fusing 1 real-time location data with **k − 1** dummy locations

4.4 Experience and Analysis

Figure 8 shows the performance of each scheme against LSTM-based discriminator. Among them, MLN, MN and ADTGA do not consider the human mobility model, but all consider the background information. The experimental results show that the probability of our scheme being recognized is very low, that is, the generated dummy trajectory basically conforms to the human movement pattern.

4.5 Security Analysis

- *Resistance to collusion attacks:* Collusion attacks occur when a group of users connect and share information. Our scheme does not need to cooperate with other parties, so it can resist collusion attacks.

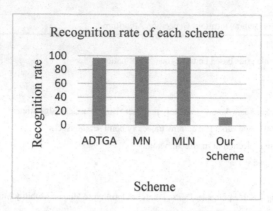

Fig. 8. Performance of each scheme against LSTM-based discriminator

- *Resist to inference attacks:* Inference Attack is an attack launched by an opponent based on prior knowledge such as map information and query probability. Our scheme takes full account of the map background information, and the selected trajectory points at each moment conform to the real trajectory's temporal and spatial distribution, so the scheme can resist inference attacks.
- *Resist to channel attacks:* Because the generation and publication of dummy trajectory points are in mobile intelligent terminals and do not pass through communication channels before the fusion of k trajectory point, the attacker can not obtain the real trajectory points from the channel end.

5 Summary

In this paper, we designed a LSTM-based dummy trajectory detection scheme and tested some trajectories generated by the classical dummy trajectory generation algorithm. The experimental results show that for the dummy trajectories generated by these algorithms, the average detection rate can reach more than 95%, and for real trajectories, the dummy positive rate is only about 10%. The experimental results show that the dummy trajectory generated by the classical algorithm does not conform to the human mobility model, that is, the spatio-temporal distribution that does not conform to the real trajectory. After that, we design a complete set of dummy trajectory generation schemes for the shortcomings of existing dummy trajectory generation algorithms. This scheme restricts the generated trajectory points to three major constraints. Because our design scheme can resist collusion attacks, inference attacks and channel attacks, it can effectively protect the user's trajectory privacy.

Acknowledgment. This work was partly supported by National Natural Science Foundation of China (61662016), Key projects of Guangxi Natural Science Foundation (2018JJD170004), and Fundamental Research Funds for the Central Universities (Program No. 201-510318070).

References

1. Krumm, J.: A survey of computational location privacy. Pers. Ubiquitous Comput. **13**, 391–399 (2009). https://doi.org/10.1007/s00779-008-0212-5
2. Wernke, M., Skvortsov, P., Dürr, F., Rothermel, K.: A classification of location privacy attacks and approaches. Pers. Ubiquitous Comput. **18**(1), 163–175 (2014). https://doi.org/10.1007/s00779-012-0633-z
3. Tang, M., Wu, Q., Zhang, G., He, L., Zhang, H.: A new scheme of LBS privacy protection. In: 2009 5th International Conference on Wireless Communications, Networking and Mobile Computing, Beijing, pp. 1–6 (2009)
4. He, W.: Research on LBS privacy protection technology in mobile social networks. In: 2017 IEEE 2nd Advanced Information Technology, Electronic and Automation Control Conference (IAEAC), Chongqing, pp. 73–76 (2017)
5. Xu, T., Cai, Y.: Feeling-based location privacy protection for location-based services. In: Proceedings of the ACM Conference on Computer and Communications Security, pp. 348–357 (2009). https://doi.org/10.1145/1653662.1653704
6. Xu, T., Cai, Y.: Exploring historical location data for anonymity preservation in location-based services. In: IEEE INFOCOM 2008 - The 27th Conference on Computer Communications, Phoenix, AZ, pp. 547–555 (2008)
7. Wang, Y., Xu, D., He, X., et al.: L2P2: location-aware location privacy protection for location-based services. In: 2012 Proceedings IEEE INFOCOM, Orlando, FL, pp. 1996–2004 (2012)
8. Kido, H., Yanagisawa, Y., Satoh, T.: An anonymous communication technique using dummies for location-based services. In: ICPS 2005. Proceedings. International Conference on Pervasive Services, 2005, Santorini, Greece, pp. 88–97 (2005)
9. Kido, H., Yanagisawa, Y., Satoh, T.: Protection of location privacy using dummies for location-based services. In: 21st International Conference on Data Engineering Workshops (ICDEW 2005), Tokyo, Japan, pp. 1248–1248 (2005)
10. Wu, X., Sun, G.: A novel dummy-based mechanism to protect privacy on trajectories. In: 2014 IEEE International Conference on Data Mining Workshop, Shenzhen, pp. 1120–1125 (2014)
11. Kato, R., Iwata, M., Hara, T., et al.: A dummy-based anonymization method based on user trajectory with pauses. In: Proceedings of the 20th International Conference on Advances in Geographic Information Systems (SIGSPATIAL 2012), pp. 249–258. ACM, New York (2012)
12. Niu, B., Li, Q., Zhu, X., et al.: Achieving k-anonymity in privacy-aware location-based services. In: IEEE INFOCOM 2014 - IEEE Conference on Computer Communications, Toronto, ON, pp. 754–762 (2014)
13. Pan, J., Liu, Y., Zhang, W.: Detection of dummy trajectories using convolutional neural networks. Secur. Commun. Netw. **2019**, 12 (2019)

Explaining Concept Drift of Deep Learning Models

Xiaolu Wang[1], Zhi Wang[1,2]($\boxtimes$), Wei Shao[1], Chunfu Jia[1,2]($\boxtimes$), and Xiang Li[3]

[1] College of Cyber Science, Nankai University, Tianjin 300350, China
{zwang,cfjia}@nankai.edu.cn
[2] Tianjin Key Laboratory of Network and Data Security Technology,
Tianjin 300350, China
[3] National Key Laboratory of Science and Technology
on Information System Security, Beijing, China

Abstract. Deep learning has been widely used in many fields and has achieved excellent performance, especially in the field of malware detection. Since attackers constantly change malware to avoid being detected by machine learning algorithms, the concept drift phenomenon often occurs when deep neural networks are used for malware classification, degrading the effect of the detection model over time. In this paper, we analyze the characteristics of neural nodes from the internal structure of neural network models. A threshold method is used to prove that different classes of samples activate different neurons whileas samples of the same class activate the same neurons. We explore the reason for concept drift of deep learning models and further improve the interpretability of neural networks by analyzing the distribution of samples before and after the concept drift.

Keywords: Deep learning · Concept drift · Explaining

1 Introduction

In recent years, deep learning [1] has shown great potential in security applications. Researchers have successfully applied deep learning models to many areas such as malware detection [2–4], security event prediction [5] and network intrusion detection [6–8]. Although deep learning models have shown good performance, sometimes they are not trusted in security field given the lack of transparency.

Many researchers have began to study the results of deep learning models and their internal structure in order to improve the transparency of deep neural networks (DNNs). Kexin et al. [9] studied the correlation structure and classification results of neural networks through the overlapping ratios of their internal nodes activated by samples of the same or different categories; Guo et al. [10] proposed the LEMNA method to interpret the classification results of deep learning models for security applications; Bastani et al. [11] interpreted the black box

© Springer Nature Switzerland AG 2019
J. Vaidya et al. (Eds.): CSS 2019, LNCS 11983, pp. 524–534, 2019.
https://doi.org/10.1007/978-3-030-37352-8_46

model by simulating deep learning classification results using a decision tree. While exploring the nature of RNN, Radford et al. [12] found that each node in a neural network independently extracted specific features from the input rather than extracting features together with other nodes. Inspired by previous work, in this paper we analyze the classification results of DNNs that classify malware and observe its intermediate layer output to explore the interpretability of neural networks. We observe the nodes activated by malicious and benign samples to see if they are non-overlapping and stable. We also study reasons for concept drift [13] of DNN models from their internal structure. The experimental results show that the nodes inside a neural network activated by different types of samples have two important properties: stability and distinguishability. Stability refers to the fact that the actived neurons by the same category sample are the same. Distinguishability refers to the fact that the actived neurons by different category are different. As the decrease of the detection effect of the model, the distinguishability of node activation gradually decreases. The output distribution of correct and misclassified samples at the intermediate nodes shows that the concept drift of a neural network occurs because many samples have values that exceed the threshold at internal network nodes. Structurally analyzing the characteristics of neural networks can further improve the interpretability of deep neural networks and to improve the transparency of neural networks.

2   Malware Concept Drift

With the rapid evolution of malware, traditional malware detection technology has become less capable in detecting variant. Machine learning, specialized in extracting information from large amount of data is widely applied to malware analysis and detection system. Machine learning has a good predictive performance on the premise that the underlying distribution of training data and test data has certain stability. However, malware usually change constantly to avoid machine learning detection, resulting in changes in the underlying data distribution and the degradation of machine learning models [14].

Machine learning faces the problem of concept drift [15]. Figure 1 shows the model aging phenomenon of DNN model. This model is trained by Andriod malicious and benign samples in 2014 and is tested by the monthly samples from 2015 to 2017 to evaluate the accuracy of the DNN model in each month. The result shows that the detection effect of the DNN model on malware is gradually decreases over time, from which we can draw the conclusion that model degradation is real and inevitable.

As far as we know, the reason for the degradation phenomenon have not been fully explained due to the unexplainable nature of deep neuron networks. Figures 2 and 3 show the tsne dimensionality reduction results of the hidden layer output values of all samples. According to the results in these figures, it can be found that the two types of samples before the model degradation have obvious decision boundaries on the output of the hidden layers but the output of hidden layers after the model is degraded does not effectively distinguish between the

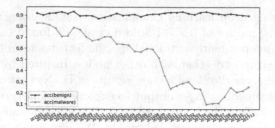

Fig. 1. DNN model aging

two types of samples. So we assume that the degradation of the model is directly related to the performance anomaly of the hidden layers. In order to explore our assumption is correct or not, we attempt to explain the effect of concept drift on the classification result of DNN models from the internal structure of neural networks and study the causes of misclassification in this paper.

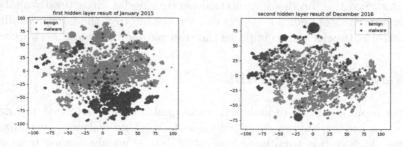

Fig. 2. Tsne result of first hidden layer

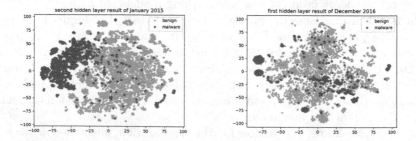

Fig. 3. Tsne result of second hidden layer

3   Explaining Concept Drift of DNN

3.1   DNN Architecture

DNN refers to a deep neural network whose structure is shown in Fig. 4. A DNN usually has at least three layers: an input layer, an output layer, and one or more hidden layers. Each layer has multiple neurons, and each neuron is directly connected to the neurons in the next layer. A neuron is an independent computational unit inside the DNN. Each neuron of DNN applies a linear and an activation function on its input and passes the result to the neurons of the next layer. The linear function is defined as $z = \sum w_i x_i + b$, where x_i represents the output value of the i-th neuron in the upper layer and w_i represents its weight connecting to the node. The weight is obtained through the training process. The activation function usually is sigmoid, hyperbolic tangent or ReLU.

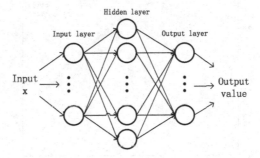

Fig. 4. DNN architecture

3.2   The Activation of Neurons and Our Threshold Method

We use the method of threshold analysis to determine the state of activity of neurons in this paper. Let the set $N = n_1, n_2, \ldots$ represents all neurons in a DNN, and the set $T = x_1, x_2, \ldots$ represents all test samples. The function $out(n, x)$ calculates the output of neuron n in the DNN under the condition that the input sample is x. Let t be the threshold for judging the state of the neurons. If $out(n, x) > t$, we consider that the neuron is active when the input sample is x, otherwise it is inactive. In this paper, we consider the sensitivity and specificity of test samples to determine the threshold of each neuron. Sensitivity is the predictive accuracy of benign samples in the test set and specificity is the predictive accuracy of malicious samples. They are defined as: $sensitity = \frac{TP}{TP+FN}$, $specificity = \frac{TN}{FP+TN}$. Where TP, FN, FP, TN means true positive, false negative, false positive and true negtive. False and true refer to the predicted result is correct or not. Positive indicates that the predict result is benign and negtive indicates that the predict result is malware. The point where the sensitivity curve and the specificity curve intersect is taken as the optimal threshold point.

We adopt a dynamic threshold method to determine the threshold of each neuron due to the fact that the weight of each neuron is different, and a uniform threshold cannot determine its state. Figure 5 shows the threshold of the sixth neuron of the second layer. We first analyze the output of this node and draw the sensitivity curve and the specificity curve of the sample set afterward. The abscissa of the intersection point is 0.11, indicating the threshold of this neuron. It means that for this node, the classification accuracy of malwares and benign samples can all reach more than 90% with 0.11 as the threshold.

Note that the different intermediate layer output values of DNNs in different range, so we scale the output to be within $[0, 1]$ by computing $(out - min(out))/(max(out) - min(out))$ where out is the vector denoting the output of all neurons of a given layer.

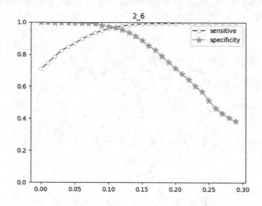

Fig. 5. The threshold of the sixth neuron of the second layer

4   Experiments

4.1   The Dataset and Model

we choose Android application samples from 2014 to 2017 as the original dataset and use the drebin algorithm [16] to extract the static feature of all samples. The extracted features can be divided into 8 categories as shown in Table 1. We use a binary notation to indicate whether a feature appears in an application. After feature extraction and transformation, the feature of each Android application is represented as a binary feature vector $x \in \{0, 1\}^M$, where M = 2342987 in this paper.

We use 314440 samples from 2014 as training sets (including 52749 malwares and 261601 benign samples). The detection accuracy of the model on the training set is 95.44%. We use 16471 correctly classified samples (including 2622 malwares and 13848 benign samples) to test the stability of neurons. In addition to the

Table 1. Features of Android applications

Feature ID	Feature name	Manifest file	Disassembly file
S_1	Hardware components	✓	
S_2	Requested permissions	✓	
S_3	App components	✓	
S_4	Filtered intents	✓	
S_5	Restricted API calls		✓
S_6	Used permissions		✓
S_7	Suspicious API calls		✓
S_8	Network addresses		✓

above samples, we add 1060 misclassified samples for studying the state change of active neurons.

We use a fully connected deep neuron network [17], which contains two hidden layers, each layer consists of 200 neurons, using RELU activation function, and the output layer uses sigmoid activation function.

4.2 Experimental Results and Analysis

By analyzing each neuron of the model and statistically observing its activation state, we learn that the activation of neurons in the model is mainly as follows:

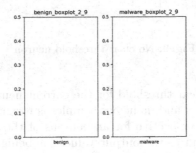

Fig. 6. Inactive neuron for both benign and malicious

(1) When the current neuron is inactive for both benign and malicious samples, the output values for both at this neuron are zero (see Fig. 6);

(2) When the current neuron is activated by benign samples (see Fig. 7);

(3) When the current neuron is activated by malwares (see Fig. 8);

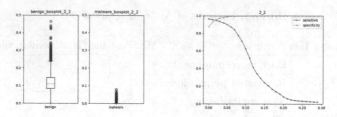

Fig. 7. Benign active neuron

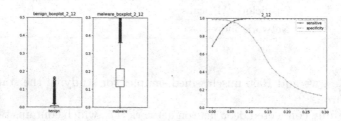

Fig. 8. Malware active neuron

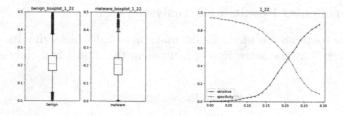

Fig. 9. No clear threshold neuron

(4) When there is no clear threshold for the current neuron, the distinction of the output for benign and malicious samples is irregular (see Fig. 9).

From a statistical perspective for all neurons of the hidden layers such as those in Tables 2 and 3, the output values for benign and malicious samples at most neurons have obvious discrimination, which indicate that the neurons activated by both classes in the neural network are stable and distinguishable.

Table 2. Activation of the first layer neurons

Neuron state	Neuron number
Inactive on both benign sample and malware	19
Benign active	83
Malware active	69
No clear threshold	29

Table 3. Activation of the second layer neurons

Neuron state	Neuron number
Inactive on both benign sample and malware	34
Benign active	86
Malware active	69
No clear threshold	11

Figure 10 compares the output distribution of the sample at the 23-th neuron of the second layer in January 2015 and December 2016. Left sub graph is the situation of January 2015 and right is December 2016. According to the result, there is a significant difference in the output distribution of the sample at the intermediate layer before and after the concept drift occurs. Other neurons have similar tendency.

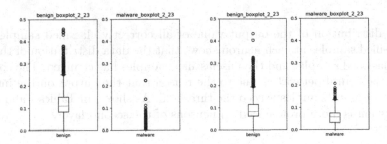

Fig. 10. Intermediate layer output distribution comparison

Table 4. The distribution of malicious samples in each neuron

Layer	Node	Threshold	gt rate of error	lt rate of error	gt rate of correct	lt rate of correct
1	1	0.009	0.908115	0.091885	0.111323	0.888677
1	3	0.06	0.020286	0.979714	0.896683	0.103317
1	4	0.085	0.612172	0.387828	0.023637	0.976363
1	6	0.261	0.386635	0.613365	0.709493	0.290507
1	8	0.009	0.288783	0.711217	0.137629	0.862371
1	9	0	0.159905	0.840095	0.690812	0.309188
1	10	0.103	0.235084	0.764916	0.702631	0.297369
1	11	0	0.315036	0.684964	0.842928	0.157072
1	13	0.03	0.862768	0.137232	0.129623	0.870377
1	14	0	0.698091	0.301909	0.045368	0.954632
2	1	0.063	0.198091	0.801909	0.895539	0.104461
2	2	0.02	0.750597	0.249403	0.048037	0.951963
2	3	0.033	0.772076	0.227924	0.04003	0.95997
2	4	0	0.109785	0.890215	0.81586	0.18414
2	5	0.04	0.385442	0.614558	0.120091	0.879909
2	6	0.11	0.105012	0.894988	0.967594	0.032406
2	7	0.08	0.542959	0.457041	0.05223	0.94777
2	10	0.015	0.834129	0.165871	0.050324	0.949676
2	12	0.055	0.151551	0.848449	0.959207	0.040793
2	24	0.04	0.120525	0.879475	0.905071	0.094929

The distribution of the output value of all correctly classified samples and misclassified samples at each neuron shows that the data distribution of the correctly classified samples and the misclassified samples has changed. The concept drift of the neural network is due to the reason that the output on the internal neurons for many samples exceed the threshold. As shown in Tables 4 and 5, the phenomenon is more pronounced on neurons of the second layer.

Table 5. The distribution of benign samples in each neuron

Layer	Node	Threshold	gt rate of error	lt rate of error	gt rate of correct	lt rate of correct
1	1	0.009	0.454954955	0.545045	0.879333	0.120667
1	3	0.06	0.315315315	0.684685	0.120378	0.879622
1	4	0.085	0.653153153	0.346847	0.029463	0.970537
1	6	0.261	0.779279279	0.220721	0.305676	0.694324
1	8	0.009	0.157657658	0.842342	0.846982	0.153018
1	9	0	0.689189189	0.310811	0.29961	0.70039
1	10	0.103	0.536036036	0.463964	0.308059	0.691941
1	11	0	0.914414414	0.085586	0.155907	0.844093
1	13	0.03	0.310810811	0.689189	0.886049	0.113951
1	14	0	0.072072072	0.927928	0.68277	0.31723
2	1	0.063	0.896396396	0.103604	0.117562	0.882438
2	2	0.02	0.027027027	0.972973	0.946996	0.053004
2	3	0.033	0.058558559	0.941441	0.96411	0.03589
2	4	0	0.707207207	0.292793	0.164789	0.835211
2	5	0.04	0.09009009	0.90991	0.886843	0.113157
2	6	0.11	0.914414414	0.085586	0.03004	0.96996
2	7	0.08	0.094594595	0.905405	0.955878	0.044122
2	10	0.015	0.09009009	0.90991	0.948512	0.051488
2	12	0.055	0.981981982	0.018018	0.036612	0.963388
2	24	0.04	0.801801802	0.198198	0.090555	0.909445

5 Conclusion

This paper analyzes the characteristics of internal neurons of deep learning models to reveal the reasons for concept drift of malware classification models. The threshold method is used to determine the different types of samples that affect different neurons. We preliminarily explored the causes of concept drift of deep learning models and improved the interpretability for them by analyzing the distribution of output values of the samples at each neuron before and after the concept drift. In future work, we will modify some characteristics of samples to explore the influence of different features on neurons to further enhance the transparency of deep learning models and improve the interpretability of neuron networks.

Acknowledgment. This work is partially supported by the National Natural Science Foundation (61872202), the CERNET Innovation Project (NGII20180401).

References

1. Bengio, Y.: Learning deep architectures for AI. Found. Trends Mach. Learn. **2**(1), 1–127 (2009)
2. Yuan, Z., Lu, Y., Xue, Y.: Droiddetector: android malware characterization and detection using deep learning. Tsinghua Sci. Technol. **21**(1), 114–123 (2016)
3. Ye, Y., Chen, L., Hou, S., Hardy, W., Li, X.: Deepam: a heterogeneous deep learning framework for intelligent malware detection. Knowl. Inf. Syst. **54**(2), 265–285 (2018)
4. Yuan, X.Y.: Ph.D. forum: deep learning-based real-time malware detection with multi-stage analysis, pp. 1–2, May 2017
5. Shen, Y., Mariconti, E., Vervier, P.A., Stringhini, G.: Tiresias: predicting security events through deep learning. In: Proceedings of the 2018 ACM SIGSAC Conference on Computer and Communications Security, CCS 2018, New York, NY, USA, pp. 592–605. ACM (2018)
6. Shone, N., Ngoc, T.N., Phai, V.D., Shi, Q.: A deep learning approach to network intrusion detection. IEEE Trans. Emerging Topics Comput. Intell. **2**(1), 41–50 (2018)
7. Roy, S.S., Mallik, A., Gulati, R., Obaidat, M.S., Krishna, P.V.: A deep learning based artificial neural network approach for intrusion detection. In: Giri, D., Mohapatra, R.N., Begehr, H., Obaidat, M.S. (eds.) ICMC 2017. CCIS, vol. 655, pp. 44–53. Springer, Singapore (2017). https://doi.org/10.1007/978-981-10-4642-1_5
8. Kang, M., Kang, J.: A novel intrusion detection method using deep neural network for in-vehicle network security. In: 2016 IEEE 83rd Vehicular Technology Conference (VTC Spring), pp. 1–5, May 2016
9. Pei, K., Cao, Y., Yang, J., Jana, S.: Deepxplore: automated whitebox testing of deep learning systems, pp. 1–18, October 2017
10. Guo, W., Mu, D., Xu, J., Su, P., Wang, G., Xing, X.: Lemna: explaining deep learning based security applications. In: Proceedings of the 2018 ACM SIGSAC Conference on Computer and Communications Security, CCS 2018, New York, NY, USA, pp. 364–379. ACM (2018)
11. Bastani, O., Kim, C., Bastani, H.: Interpreting blackbox models via model extraction. CoRR, abs/1705.08504 (2017)
12. Radford, A., Józefowicz, R., Sutskever, I.: Learning to generate reviews and discovering sentiment. CoRR, abs/1704.01444 (2017)
13. Jordaney, R., et al.: Transcend: detecting concept drift in malware classification models. In: 26th USENIX Security Symposium (USENIX Security 17), pp. 625–642. USENIX Association, Vancouver, BC (2017)
14. Wang, Z., Qin, M., Chen, M., Jia, C., Ma, Y.: A learning evasive email-based P2P-like botnet. China Commun. **15**(2), 15–24 (2018)
15. Wang, Z., et al.: A hybrid learning system to mitigate botnet concept drift attacks. J. Internet Technol. **18**(6), 1419–1428 (2017)
16. Arp, D., Spreitzenbarth, M., Hubner, M., Gascon, H., Rieck, K.: Drebin: effective and explainable detection of android malware in your pocket, February 2014
17. Grosse, K., Papernot, N., Manoharan, P., Backes, M., McDaniel, P.: Adversarial perturbations against deep neural networks for malware classification, June 2016

Attention Bilinear Pooling for Fine-Grained Facial Expression Recognition

Liyuan Liu, Lifeng Zhang$^{(\boxtimes)}$, and Shixiang Jia

School of Information and Electrical Engineering, Ludong University,
Yantai, China
lifengzhang@ldu.edu.cn

Abstract. Subtle differences in human facial expressions may convey quite distinct sentiment, which makes expression recognition a challenging task. The previous studies has achieved good results on the regular expression datasets, but it shows poor recognition accuracy and robustness for facial images with small discrimination. The high dimensional space representation of bilinear model can perceive small distinctions among images, which is crucial to the fine-grained facial expression categorization. Hence, we propose to utilize the bilinear pooling to enhance the discriminate capabilities of the deep convolution networks. Meanwhile, with the aid of attention mechanism, the roles of the important spatial positions in the feature map are highlighted. Finally, With extensive experiments, we demonstrate that our model can obtain competitive performance and robustness against state-of-the-art baselines on Fer2013 and CK+ datasets.

Keywords: Bilinear pooling · Attention model · Fine-grained facial expression recogintion

1 Introduction

Facial expressions are important approaches to reflect the emotional signals and psychological activities. Facial expression recognition techniques empower a wide range of applications, e.g., intelligent guidance, learning state detection and sentiment analysis [1]. Therefore, it has attracted much research enthusiasm in human-computer interaction and sentiment computing. However, the existing studies focus on the facial categorization scenarios with given salient features and pre-labeled images under specific controlled environments. In contrast, the practical facial expression classification tasks tend to have subtle differences. To improve the recognition accuracy and efficiency for fine-grained facial expressions, we introduce bilinear method to obtain the second-order local statistical information of latent space, which contributes to boost the fine-grained discriminating capabilities significantly.

© Springer Nature Switzerland AG 2019
J. Vaidya et al. (Eds.): CSS 2019, LNCS 11983, pp. 535–542, 2019.
https://doi.org/10.1007/978-3-030-37352-8_47

The bilinear method exploits sum pooling to aggregate the bilinear feature with same weights for all positions, which ignores the various importance of feature representations in different regions. In this paper, the contribution degree of the spatial location is automatically learned, the position weights are used to enhance the useful location information and suppress the useless one. For the sake of improving the robustness, the dropout policy is introduced to stop activating certain neurons with a given probability p, which can help to eliminate the joint adaptability of the unity neuron nodes.

The experiments prove that our model has small network scale while maintain a high recognition accuracy and robustness. It can achieve 73.18% and 98.73% classification accuracy on the data sets Fer2013 and CK+ respectively, which outperforms most of rivals.

2 Related Work

Generally, facial expression recognition is divided into three steps: image pre-processing, feature extraction and classification model. Feature extraction is a key step in expression recognition. The integrity and robustness of the extracted features directly affect the accuracy of recognition. There are two common ways to realize feature extraction in prior research: geometry feature and textural feature extraction.

Geometry feature extraction focuses on locating the key points and building the geometrical relations of the key points in salient features. [3] proposed to extract geometry features from points, lines, and triangles and use the AdaBoost algorithm to select the most discriminative geometric features, but the accuracy of facial feature point is prune to be affected by the illumination and posture, etc.

Textural feature extraction is based on the gray distribution of the spatial neighborhood. Gabor wavelet transform and LBP (local binary pattern) are classical approaches, however, texture feature extraction is mainly used for local regions, lacking global information lead to it difficult to obtain the genetic or dependence of pixels at texture scales.

In recent years, convolution neural networks show remarkable advantages in feature extraction in that it can maintain the invariance of the geometric position (or relative position). Meanwhile, with the increasing of network depth, the model can extract the high-level semantic information of the image, effectively narrowing the gap between the underlying features and the high-level semantics.

[10] used the embedded attention model and used local features extracted by 10 layers convolution network to automatically determine the region of interest and local features of these regions are blended to infer emotional tags. [6] attempts to select features that have influences on facial appearance/shape changes by a learning network, then [6] enhances strong classifier to improve the discriminating ability.

Combining the traditional feature extraction methods with neural networks to fuse multiple features from different angles have become a hot topic [9]. [5] combines deep learning with LBP/VAR features to impair the effect of the illumination and rotation. [2] fuses the central symmetric local binary mode (CS-LBP) with the DBN to make use of local and global feature extraction capability.

However, that's not the whole story. Multi-feature fusion tends to cause high dimensionality curse. less researchers concern on the fusion of shallow and deep features. Some subtle, small-resolution facial expressions require deep features to strengthen the ability of recognition.

The main contributions of this paper are summarized as follows:

- We propose to exploit the bilinear pooling to model the fine-grained facial expression recognition in that the high order statistics of latent space can benefit to capture the subtle differences among features.
- Considering that the information provided by different spatial positions have distinct significance to final decision, we introduce attention module to learning the weight metrics of locations, which can identify and reinforce the salient neuron units autonomously.
- In order to prevent over-fitting of CNN, this paper adopts crop10 method for pre-processing and a dropout layer to decrease computation overhead. Experiments show that on the Fer2013, CK+ datasets, our method identification accuracy rate reached 73.18% and 98.73%.

3   Facial Expression Recognition Model

Facial expression recognition is a branch field of fine-grained classification, so we can draw some enlightenment from it. As is known, high-order statistics of latent space is benefit to identify the subtle variation of the face expressions. Therefore, after feature extraction through CNN network, our model try to capture the pairwise correlation and interdependencies between the feature channels by multiplying the elements from different channel using the outer product at each location. Then, to identify and address the important contributions from some specific locations, we exploit attention mechanism to adaptively recalibrate location-wise feature responses by explicitly modelling location weights, so that the network is able to increase its sensitivity to informative region features which can be exploited to subtle discriminate.

Overall, our model is implemented as follows (as is shown in Fig. 1):

(1) We first extend the data set by crop10 method and input them to resnet18 to generate the latent space representation.
(2) The bilinear layer is used to model the high order statistics of latent space.
(3) To make use of the information aggregated in step 2, we follow it with an attention operation that aims to fully capture position-wise significance.

3.1   Attention Enhanced Bilinear Model

Bilinear is proposed as a feature coding layer that can be used after the convolution layer to improve performance in multiple visual tasks. The bilinear is

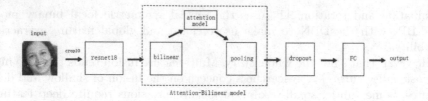

Fig. 1. The network pipeline structure

suitable for modeling the effects of pair factors, such as the influence of style and content, or the posture and light flow on the faces. The bilinear model consists of a feature extractor that performs an outer product on the different channels at each position of the feature space and pools it to obtain a descriptor for the images. Bilinear pooling can model local pairwise feature interactions in transform invariance mode, which has be proven to a powerful tool to tackle the fine-grained recognition tasks. The full pipeline of attention enhanced bilinear model is illustrated in Fig. 2.

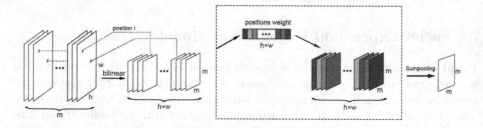

Fig. 2. The attention-bilinear model

Bilinear Features. To calculate the bilinear features of facial expressions, we extract feature maps of the final layer of resnet18. Let $\chi \in R^{h \times w \times m}$ represents the feature maps, where h, w, m represent the height, width and number of feature channels, respectively. The description vector $x_i \in R^m$ represents the feature vector of the feature map spatial position i, where the spatial coordinate index is [1, hw]. Description matrix $X \in R^{m \times hw}$ can be defined as

$$X = [x_1 x_2 \cdots x_{hw}]$$

For each point, we calculate the outer product $x_i x_i^T$, and the feature matrix of the position i is denoted as Eq. 1.

$$Z_i = x_i x_i^T \tag{1}$$

The bilinear pooling operation is acquired with the pairwise correlation between the feature channels, which can be calculate by the Gram matrix $\mathbf{G} \in R^{m \times m}$:

$$\mathbf{G} = \frac{1}{hw} \sum_{i=1}^{hw} \mathbf{x}_i \mathbf{x}_i^T = \frac{1}{hw} \mathbf{X}\mathbf{X}^T \tag{2}$$

$\mathbf{G}$ is the overall representation of the feature space, it captures the second-order statistical information of feature activations, which is also closely related to the covariance matrix.

Bilinear Attention Model. Attention can be interpreted as a means of biasing the allocation of available credits towards the most informative components of a signal. Intuitively, some specific locations (i.e., canthus and mouth corners, etc.) express extremely important signals for distinguishing the emotions. Hence, these locations should be paid more attentions than others to strengthen the representational power of the feature matrix $\mathbf{G}$. The attention module explicitly models the position significance, and automatically acquires weight layer through network learning. Our attention module is illustrate as Fig. 3.

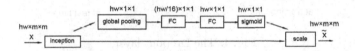

Fig. 3. The attention model

The position weight vector obtained by the attention module is denoted as

$$\boldsymbol{\omega} = [\omega_1 \omega_2 \cdots \omega_{hw}], \omega_i \in R$$

Then Gram matrix $\mathbf{G}$ is rewrited as

$$\tilde{\mathbf{G}} = \frac{1}{hw} \sum_{i=1}^{hw} \omega_i \mathbf{x}_i \mathbf{x}_i^T = \frac{1}{hw} \tilde{\mathbf{X}}\tilde{\mathbf{X}}^T \tag{3}$$

For the seek of compressing the computing overhead, we normalize $\tilde{\mathbf{G}}$ by mean square root operation.

$$\tilde{\mathbf{G}} \to \sqrt[2]{\tilde{\mathbf{G}}}$$

Finally, we obtain the bilinear feature by expanding the Gram matrix into vectors

$$\mathbf{s} = vec\tilde{\mathbf{G}} \in R^{m^2}$$

As a consequence, the benefits of the location recalibration performed by attention blocks can be accumulated through the network. We further demonstrate that attention blocks bring significant improvements in performance for existing state-of-the-art CNNs at slight additional computational cost.

3.2   Linear Classifier

We employ a fully connected layers as classifiers, the categorization result is decided by Eq. 4.

$$y = (vec\mathbf{W})^T(vec\tilde{\mathbf{G}}) + b = \frac{1}{hw}(vec\mathbf{W})^T(vec\tilde{\mathbf{X}}\tilde{\mathbf{X}}^T) + b \qquad (4)$$

Where $\mathbf{W}$ is weight vector and b is bias. To decrease computational overhead, dropout layer before the a fully connected layer is added. It forces a neural unit to work with other randomly selected neural units, alleviating the weakening of the joint adaptability between the neuron nodes (Fig. 4).

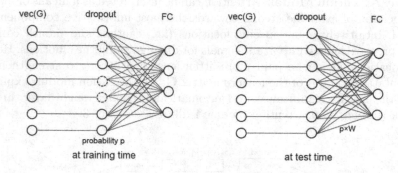

Fig. 4. The Dropout layer

4   Experiments and Results

4.1   Experiments Setup

Our model is implemented with a resnet18 network to generate the latent space, we augment the data sets with crop10 operation, the drop probability of the dropout layer is set to 0.6. We choose Fer2013 and CK+ as training and testing data sets. Among them, the Fer2013 data set has a low image resolution, and the difference between some different categories of expressions is very subtle, resulting in the accuracy of recognition has not been high. This experiment focuses on verifying the fine-grained recognition of this data set. The size of input images are crop to 44×44 before.

4.2   Experimental Results

We choose several typical research work to verify the network scale and recognition accuracy on Fer2013. Table 1 summarizes the proposed methods as well as the baseline under different experiment settings. Compared to other methods, we can achieve a higher accuracy rate on smaller models.

Results including Average Precision are shown in Table 2, in which the accuracy of CK+ experiments are presented. The results imply that our model has distinct advantages over the counterparts [7,8,12] at a similar network.

Table 1. Network size and accuracy on Fer2013

Models	Network size	Accuracy
Tang et al. [11]	12.0 m	71.20%
Zhang et al. [13]	21.3 m	75.10%
Guo et al. [4]	2.6 m	71.33%
Attention-Bilinear model	11.2 m	73.18%

Table 2. Accuracy on CK+

Models	Accuracy
Meng et al. [8]	95.37%
Liu et al. [7]	97.10%
Yang et al. [12]	97.30%
Attention-Bilinear model	98.73%

4.3   Validation of Attention Module

In this section, we focus on validating the actual role of the attention mechanism for the face expression fine-grained recognition task. Hence, we only compared our results with those obtained by the baseline algorithms, as Table 3 shows. Since the attention module employed had a significant impact on the final performance, we showed performance results separately based on the same network pipeline. Table 3 indicates that the performance of the original bilinear model is better than that of the resent18, and on the Fer2013 dataset, attention module helps to boost about 10% accuracy that its rivals.

Table 3. Accuracy on Fer2013 and CK+

Models	Fer2013 Accuracy	CK+ Accuracy
Original bilinear model	61.10%	94.24%
Original bilinear model + attention model	70.97%	96.68%
Resnet18	58.57%	87.17%
Resnet18 + attention model	60.20%	90.20%

5   Conclusion

In this paper, we propose to exploit bilinear pooling that incorporates the idea of attention to improve accuracy of fine-grained facial expression recognition. To make full use of the important detail information from some specific locations, we design an attention module to learn the weight matrix that can coordinate with bilinear pooling. Finally, we design multiple experiments to verify accuracy and validation of our model on several facial expression data-sets, and the results show that strong discriminate features captured by our attention module can improve the accuracy significantly comparing to its counterparts. We hope this insight may be useful for other facial expression tasks.

Acknowledgements. This work was supported by the Natural Science ShanDong Province of China under Grant No. ZR2016FM23, and Shandong Key Research and Development Program under Grant No. 2017GHY215009.

References

1. Chen, J., Luo, N., Liu, Y., Liu, L., Zhang, K., Kolodziej, J.: A hybrid intelligence-aided approach to affect-sensitive e-learning. Computing **98**(1), 215–233 (2016)
2. Li, C., Wei, W., Wang, J., Tang, W., Zhao, S.: Face recognition based on deep belief network combined with center-symmetric local binary pattern. In: Park, J., Jin, H., Jeong, Y.S., Khan, M. (eds.) Advanced Multimedia and Ubiquitous Engineering. Lecture Notes in Electrical Engineering, vol. 393, pp. 277–283. Springer, Singapore (2016). https://doi.org/10.1007/978-981-10-1536-6_37
3. Ghimire, D., Lee, J., Li, Z., Jeong, S.: Recognition of facial expressions based on salient geometric features and support vector machines. Multimedia Tools Appl. **76**(6), 7921–7946 (2017)
4. Guo, Y., Tao, D., Yu, J., Hao, X., Li, Y., Tao, D.: Deep neural networks with relativity learning for facial expression recognition. In: IEEE International Conference on Multimedia & Expo Workshops, pp. 1–6 (2016)
5. He, J., Cai, J., Fang, L., He, Z., Amp, D.E.: Facial expression recognition based on LBP/VAR and DBN model. Appl. Res. Comput. **33**, 453–461 (2016)
6. Kuang, L., Zhang, M., Pan, Z.: Facial expression recognition with CNN ensemble. In: International Conference on Cyberworlds, pp. 163–166 (2016)
7. Liu, X., Kumar, B.V.K.V., You, J., Ping, J.: Adaptive deep metric learning for identity-aware facial expression recognition. In: IEEE Conference on Computer Vision & Pattern Recognition Workshops, pp. 522–531 (2017)
8. Meng, Z., Ping, L., Jie, C., Han, S., Yan, T.: Identity-aware convolutional neural network for facial expression recognition. In: IEEE International Conference on Automatic Face & Gesture Recognition, pp. 558–565 (2017)
9. Shihui, Z., Huan, H., Lingfu, K.: Fusing multi-feature for video occlusion region detection based on graph cut. Acta Optica Sin. **35**(4), 0415001 (2015)
10. Sun, W., Zhao, H., Jin, Z.: A visual attention based ROI detection method for facial expression recognition. Neurocomputing **296**, 12–22 (2018)
11. Tang, Y.: Deep learning using linear support vector machines. arXiv preprint arXiv: 1306.0239 (2013)
12. Yang, H., Ciftci, U., Yin, L.: Facial expression recognition by de-expression residue learning. Int. J. Comput. Sci. Eng. 2168–2177 (2018)
13. Zhang, Z., Luo, P., Loy, C.C., Tang, X.: Learning social relation traits from face images. In: IEEE International Conference on Computer Vision, pp. 3631–3639 (2015)

Cyberspace Safety

A Secure Collision Avoidance Warning Algorithm Based on Environmental Characteristics and Driver Characteristics

Yuejin Zhang[✉], Fei Du, Meng Wang, Juan Wang, Yong Hu,
Meng Yu, Guanghui Li, and Aiyun Zhan

School of Information Engineering, East China Jiaotong University,
Nanchang 330013, China
zyjecjtu@foxmail.com

Abstract. Aiming at the requirements of vehicle safety collision avoidance system, a safe collision avoidance warning algorithm based on environmental characteristics and driver characteristics is proposed. By analyzing the relationship between collision avoidance time and the environment, a safe time model is established. In the established safety time model, parameters based on driver characteristics are added, which increases the flexibility of the algorithm. The algorithm can adapt to more different driving conditions and give appropriate warning thresholds. Through simulation modeling, the safety collision distance between the algorithm and MAZDA algorithm, Berkeley algorithm and Honda algorithm is compared in four cases. The effectiveness and feasibility of the algorithm are verified, and the safety of vehicle driving can be improved.

Keywords: Vehicle network · Traffic safety · Safe collision avoidance warning · Collision avoidance time · Environmental characteristics · Driver characteristics

1 Introduction

Since entering the 21st century, the number of cars has increased exponentially. As one of the important means to reduce traffic accidents, vehicle anti-collision warning system has received more and more attention. The existing collision warning algorithms are mainly divided into two categories, namely the safety time algorithm and the safety distance algorithm [1]. The safety time logic algorithm compares the collision time between the two workshops with the safety time threshold to determine the safety status [2]. The safety distance model refers to the minimum distance between the vehicle and the obstacle that the vehicle needs to maintain to avoid the collision with the obstacle under the current conditions of the vehicle [3]. However, neither the TTC model nor the safety distance model is flexible enough to adapt to various situations during driving. Based on the alarm-avoidance algorithm of collision avoidance time TTC, this paper proposes a secure collision avoidance warning algorithm that adapts to environmental characteristics and driver characteristics. The algorithm is simulated by MATLAB, and the effectiveness of the algorithm is verified.

© Springer Nature Switzerland AG 2019
J. Vaidya et al. (Eds.): CSS 2019, LNCS 11983, pp. 545–552, 2019.
https://doi.org/10.1007/978-3-030-37352-8_48

2 Model Establishment

2.1 Scene Analysis

For a frontal collision, since the two cars that are relatively driven are generally not in a straight line, when the center line of the two cars is larger than the average of the two car widths, even if the distance between the two cars is already very small, but driving in different lanes, there is no possibility of collision. Therefore, only when the distance between the two vehicles perpendicular to the traveling direction is less than the average value k of the two vehicle widths (the A vehicle width is W_A and the B vehicle width is W_B), $k \leq |d \times \sin \theta_1|$. The general vehicle width is about 1.5 meters to 1.8 meters, so here k takes 2 m [4]. The distance between the two vehicles $d = \sqrt{(x_2 - x_1)^2 + (y_2 - y_1)^2}$ can be derived from the vehicle coordinates received by the DSRC module in meters [5]. The self-vehicle speed is V_A, the adjacent car speed is V_B, and the unit is km/h. For the frontal collision shown in Fig. 1, the time required is $t = 4.3 \times (d \times |\cos \theta_1| - 5)/(v_A + v_B)$ [6]. When $|\theta_1| < 90°$ and $|\theta_2| > 90°$, the calculation of the collision time is performed; if it is $|\theta_1| \geq 90°$ and $|\theta_2| \geq 90°$, the processing is not performed.

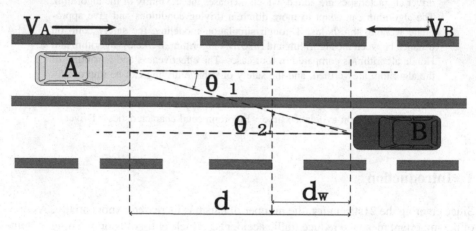

Fig. 1. Frontal collision algorithm model

For the rear-end model, most of the rear-end collisions occur in the same lane. Therefore, we no longer consider the heading angle factor and only consider the relative motion of the vehicle [7]. For the rear-end collision model shown in Fig. 2, when the vehicle is actively rear-end, if $V_A > V_B$, the time required for the collision-finding collision is $t = d/(V_A - V_B)$; if $V_A < V_B$, the collision-proof algorithm is not processed [8]. When the car is passive rear-end collision, if $V_A > V_B$, the time required for the collision-finding collision is $t = d/(V_A - V_B)$; if $V_A < V_B$, the anti-collision algorithm is not processed [9].

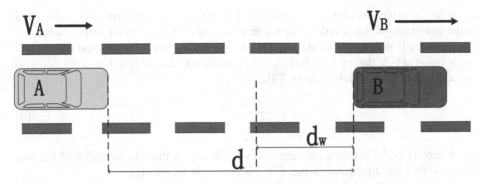

Fig. 2. Rear-end collision algorithm model

2.2 Design of Secure Collision Avoidance Warning Algorithm

According to research by Yu et al., the early warning algorithm considering the driver's driving style can adapt to the driving needs of different drivers to a certain extent, and during the driving process, the driver can perform according to his own physical condition and driving environment [1, 10].

With the change of driving mode, this algorithm can better reflect the driving characteristics of the driver. However, it is not enough to consider only one characteristic of the driver. The driver's age, driving age, vision, physical condition and mental condition are all factors to be considered [10]. We assign different weights to the above factors to determine the impact of the driver's personal factors on the safety warning time. We set the driver's age X_1 (weight $\omega_1 = 0.3$), driving age X_2 (weight $\omega_2 = 0.3$), physical health status X_3 ($X_3 = 1, 2, 3, 4, 5$) (weight $\omega_3 = 0.2$), mental state X_4 ($X_4 = 1, 2, 3, 4, 5$) (weight $\omega_4 = 0.4$), visual acuity X_5 (weight $\omega_5 = 0.1$), using the formula:

$$Y_i = \sum_{i,j=1}^{5} X_i \omega_j \tag{1}$$

$$\tau_{dr} = 1.2\sqrt{\frac{75}{Y_i}} \tag{2}$$

correct the reaction time [3].

Braking system response time includes the reaction time of the brake system, the time of brake coordination and the time of continuous braking [11]. Here, the reaction time of the brake system is t_1, the brake action time is t_2, and the continuous braking time is set to t_3. In the continuous braking time, we assume that the deceleration is constant, and the calculation formula is as follows:

$$t_3 = \frac{v}{3.6 \times g \times a\mu} - \frac{t_2}{2} \tag{3}$$

Where v is the vehicle speed, unit km/h, which is the driving speed of the vehicle; g is the gravitational acceleration, the value is 9.8 m/s^2; μ is the road surface adhesion coefficient; a is the environmental coefficient. According to Pei's study, the rainy day a has a value of 0.5, the icy road surface is 0.1, the snow surface is 0.3, and the dry road surface is 1 [12]. The definition of TTC is:

$$TTC = \frac{D}{v_\tau} \tag{4}$$

Where D is the distance between two vehicles, v_τ is the relative speed of the two vehicles, and the dimension of the TTC parameter is seconds(s).

According to the above analysis, the risk warning from the safety collision warning system to the minimum time that the driver takes the reaction to stop the vehicle or avoid the danger, the safety collision warning time threshold TTC is calculated as:

$$TTC = t_1 + \frac{t_2}{2} + \frac{v}{3.6 + g + a\mu} + 1.2 \sqrt{\frac{75}{\sum\limits_{i,j=1}^{5} X_i \omega_i}} \tag{5}$$

The value of X_i is input according to the actual situation of the driver.

The collision avoidance time is converted into the corresponding vehicle distance using Eq. (5) and the variables are normalized. The corresponding safety warning/brake algorithm is as follows:

$$\begin{cases} D_w = v_\tau \left(t_1 + \frac{t_2}{2} + \frac{v}{3.6 \times g \times a\mu} + 1.2 \sqrt{\frac{75}{\sum\limits_{i,j=1}^{5} X_i \omega_i}} \right) \\ D_b = v_\tau \left(\frac{t_2}{2} + \frac{v}{3.6 \times g \times a\mu} \right) \end{cases} \tag{6}$$

Where: D_w is the warning distance; D_b is the brake distance; v_τ is the relative speed; t_1 is the brake reaction time; t_2 is the brake action time; t_3 is the continuous braking time; g is the gravity acceleration; a is the environmental coefficient; μ is the road surface adhesion coefficient; X_i and ω_i are the driver characteristics and their weights, respectively.

The algorithm flow chart of the collision early warning algorithm is (Fig. 3):

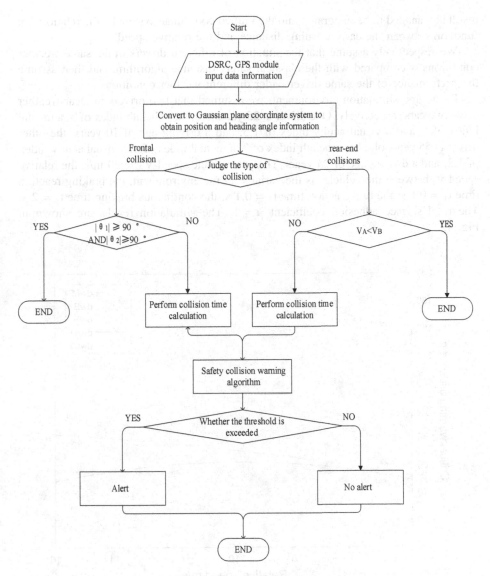

Fig. 3. Algorithm Flowchart

3   Simulation Experiment

After understanding the working principle and construction idea of the algorithm, we use Matlab software to simulate the proposed algorithm and the classical safety distance algorithm MAZDA algorithm, Berkeley algorithm, Honda algorithm based on the real-world simulation environment setting, in the simulation In the process, the variable is set to the unique variable of the relative speed of the two vehicles, and the simulation result is managed to be integrated into the unified coordinate system by the relationship function between the early warning distance and the relative speed.

We respectively assume that the situation of different drivers in the same weather conditions is compared with the classical safety distance algorithm, and then assume the performance of the same driver under different weather conditions.

In the first simulation environment, we assumed that two drivers in clear weather drive two cars respectively. One driver is 35 years old, has a health index of 5, a mental index of 5, and a visual acuity index of 1.5. and a driving age of 10 years; the other driver is 55 years old, has a health index of 3, a mental index of 4, a visual acuity index of 1.2, and a driving age of 25 years. The rear vehicle speed $V_A = 20$ m/s, the relative speed v_τ between the vehicles is the variable in the environment, the braking reaction time $t_1 = 0.1$ s; the brake action time $t_2 = 0.1$ s; the continuous braking time $t_3 = 2$ s; The road surface adhesion coefficient $\mu = 1$. The simulation results are shown in Fig. 4:

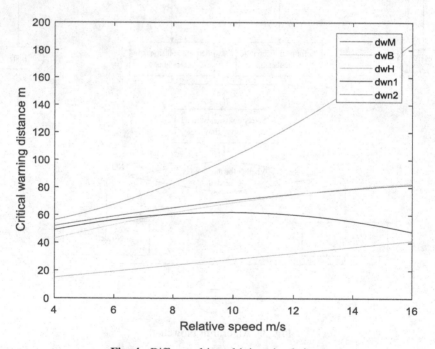

Fig. 4. Different driver driving simulations

As can be seen from Fig. 4, because the second driver is older and has a poorer health, the second driver has the longest collision warning distance and the first collision warning. For the first driver, the speed of the collision is less than 10 m/s. The collision distance of the algorithm is close to the MAZDA algorithm and the Berkeley algorithm. When the speed is greater than 10 m/s, the collision distance of the algorithm is smaller, avoiding frequent reminders. And interfere with the driver.

In the second simulation environment, we assume that a driver is 35 years old, has a health index of 5, a mental index of 5, a visual acuity index of 1.5, and a driving age of 10 years. The driver drove in snowy weather and rainy weather. The rear vehicle speed $V_A = 20$ m/s, the relative speed v_τ between the vehicles is the variable in the environment, the braking reaction time $t_1 = 0.1$ s; the brake action time $t_2 = 0.1$ s; the continuous braking time t_3 is 4 s the snow weather and the rainy weather is 2.5 s; the road adhesion coefficient $\mu = 1$. The simulation results are shown in Fig. 5:

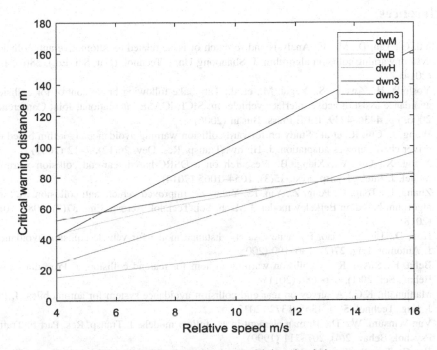

Fig. 5. Different environment driving simulation

According to Fig. 5, it can be seen that in the snowy weather, the algorithm sets the safety collision distance very conservatively. The snowy weather roadside is very slippery, the longer the safety warning distance, the earlier the warning time, the more favorable to driving safety. In the rainy weather, due to the decrease of visibility, the road is also weakened by the accumulated water friction. When the vehicle speed reaches about 12 m/s, the safety warning distance of the algorithm is longer and safer than the MAZDA algorithm and the Berkeley algorithm.

4   Conclusion

This paper establishes a corresponding early warning algorithm by analyzing the relationship between collision avoidance time and weather environment characteristics and driver characteristics. The algorithm not only considers the relative positional relationship between vehicles, but also considers the influence of different weather conditions on safe driving, and adds weather factors to the collision warning algorithm. Because different drivers have different driving habits and reaction time characteristics, driver characteristics are also an important factor affecting safe driving. This factor is also reflected in this algorithm. Through the simulation of the algorithm, the effectiveness is verified and the driving safety efficiency is improved.

References

1. Yu, G., Tan, D., Ma, F.: Analysis and research of issue related to automotive anti-collision system warning/collision algorithm. J. Shandong Univ. Technol. (Nat. Sci. Ed.). **28**(6), 1–5 (2014)
2. Yoshida, H., Awano, S., Nagai, M., et al.: Targetake following brake control for collision avoidance assist of active interface vehicle. In: SICE-ICASE International Joint Conference 2006, pp. 4436–4439. IEEE Press, Busan (2006)
3. Wang, J., Chi, R., et al.: Study on forward collision warning-avoidance algorithm based on driver characteristics adaptation. J. Highw. Transp. Res. Dev. **26**(12), 7–12 (2009)
4. Xiang, X., Qin, W., Xiang, B.: Research on a DSRC-based rear-end collision warning model. J. Intell. Transp. Syst. **15**(3), 1054–1065 (2014)
5. Zhang, L., Teng, F., Peng, Z., Yin, R., Yuan, X.: Improved vehicle anti-collosion warning algorithm based on Berkeley model. J Mech. Sci. Technol. Aerosp. Eng. **37**(7), 1082–1088 (2018)
6. Hou, D., Liu, G., Gao, F.: A new safety distance model for vehicle collision avoidance. J. Automot. Eng. **27**(2), 186–190 (2005)
7. Bella, F., Russo, R.: A collision warning system for rearend collision. J. Procedia - Soc. Behav. Sci. **20**(1), 676–686 (2011)
8. Manjunath, K.G.: A survey on rear end collision avoidance system for automobiles. J. Int. J. Eng. Technol. **5**(2), 1368–1372 (2013)
9. Van Winsum, W.: The Human element in car follow models. J. Transp. Res. Part F: Traffic Psychol. Behav. **2**(4), 207–211 (1999)
10. Yu, G., Tan, D., Tian, H.: Warning/barke algorithm based on time of longitudinal collision avoidance. J. Henan Univ. Sci. Technol. (Nat. Sci. Ed.) **36**(2), 30–35 (2015)
11. Tang, A., Yip, A.: Collision avoidance timing analysis of DSRC-based vehicles. J. Accid. Anal. Prev. **42**(1), 182–195 (2010)
12. Pei, X., et al.: Safe distance model and obstacle detection algorithms for a collision warning and collision avoidance system. J. Automot. Saf. Energy **3**(1), 26–33 (2012)

Research on Safety Early Warning Transmission Control Algorithm Based on Driving Stability

Aiyun Zhan, Meng Wang, Juan Wang, Fei Du, Yong Hu, Meng Yu, Guanghui Li, and Yuejin Zhang(✉)

School of Information Engineering, East China Jiaotong University,
330013 Nanchang, China
zyjecjtu@foxmail.com

Abstract. As the number of cars continues to grow and traffic accidents occur frequently, it is of great significance to study the safety warning problem based on the Internet of Vehicles. Because the broadcast frequency of fixed parameters can not adapt to the characteristics of fast Internet access, high topology and high quality of service requirements, and the vehicle risk factors of different driving conditions are also very different. Therefore, this paper proposes a security early warning information transmission control algorithm based on vehicle speed and acceleration fusion, and adaptively controls the broadcast frequency according to the vehicle driving stability. Based on SUMO and NS2 simulation software, the modeling and simulation experiments are carried out. The simulation results show that the algorithm of this paper improves the data transmission delay and throughput.

Keywords: Internet of Vehicles · Driving stability · Adaptive transmission control · SUMO · NS2

1 Introduction

In the vehicle self-organizing network, the vehicle keeps moving, and the network topology and the number of nodes are always changing [1–3]. Vehicles ensure that other vehicles receive data in real time by increasing their broadcast frequency [4, 5]. However, in practice, when the communication channel capacity is limited, and the number of vehicles is too large or the road conditions are complicated, the nodes send a large amount of data at the same time, causing channel blockage. Causes retransmission and packet loss [6–8], further aggravating congestion and making early warning information lose its effect.

This work was supported in part by the National Natural Science Foundation of China under Grant 11862006, Grant 61862025, in part by the Jiangxi Provincial Natural Science Foundation under Grant 2018ACB21032, 20181BAB211016, in part by the Scientific and Technological Research Project of Education Department in Jiangxi Province under Grant GJJ170381, Grant GJJ170383.

J. Vaidya et al. (Eds.): CSS 2019, LNCS 11983, pp. 553–561, 2019.
https://doi.org/10.1007/978-3-030-37352-8_49

In order to study the information transmission problem of the Internet of Vehicles [9], a road traffic awareness model is proposed, which can identify a high-speed car in a certain range and reduce the occurrence of safety accidents; the literature [10] proposes a DPLD model, which can effectively Predict the expected link delay of 2 cars; the literature [11] designed the highway safety warning system by wireless communication and networking technology; the literature [12] proposed an adaptive power control strategy based on fuzzy logic. The strategy can predict traffic flow density and predict the transmission range of the packet delivery rate to avoid channel congestion. However, the performance requirements of the Internet of Vehicles cannot be well satisfied. Therefore, an algorithm that can adaptively adjust the broadcast frequency of the vehicle according to the real-time communication situation is of great value.

2 Broadcast Frequency Adaptive Adjustment Algorithm Based on Driving Stability

2.1 Position Prediction Error Analysis

In the Internet of Vehicles application, the vehicle broadcasts its own latitude, longitude, speed, acceleration and other driving status information to other vehicles, and other vehicles receive data and perform position prediction [13]. In addition to the error of the positioning system itself, the data transmission delay and packet loss rate are factors that affect the position prediction error [14, 15]. Vehicles generally reduce the error of other vehicles' perception of their position by increasing the broadcast frequency of the data, but due to limited channel resources, it is impossible to achieve that all vehicles broadcast at a large frequency [16, 17]. Therefore, this paper proposes a broadcast frequency adaptive adjustment algorithm based on driving stability, which gives higher priority broadcast frequencies to higher priority vehicles and lowers the broadcast frequency of vehicles with lower priority. This paper uses the position prediction error to determine the priority of the vehicle.

During the driving process, the vehicle accelerates, decelerates, changes lanes and turns, etc., which are prone to collision and rear-end collision. If the vehicle can accurately sense other vehicle positions, it can be early warning to avoid accidents [18–20]. The larger the position prediction error, the more likely it is to cause a safety accident. Therefore, the vehicle with a large position prediction error should be given a higher priority so that other vehicles can better perceive their position. The linear tracking algorithm [19] is now used for error analysis during position prediction.

Assume that the vehicle is located at the origin of the plane rectangular coordinate system. After Δt time, its position is located at:

$$x = \int_t^{t'} v(t) \cos \theta(t) dt \tag{1}$$

$$y = \int_t^{t'} v(t) \sin \theta(t) dt \tag{2}$$

The predicted position of the linear tracking algorithm is:

$$x_1 = v_0 \Delta t \cos \theta_0 \tag{3}$$

$$y_1 = v_0 \Delta t \sin \theta_0 \tag{4}$$

And because t is very short, the acceleration and angular velocity can be considered unchanged, so there is

$$x = \int_t^{t'} v(t) \cos \theta(t) dt = \int_t^{t'} (v_0 + a\Delta t) \cos(w\Delta t + \theta_0) dt \tag{5}$$

$$y = \int_t^{t'} v(t) \sin \theta(t) dt = \int_t^{t'} (v_0 + a\Delta t) \sin(w\Delta t + \theta_0) dt \tag{6}$$

Then the position prediction error k is:

$$k = \sqrt{(x_1 - x)^2 + (y_1 - y)^2} \tag{7}$$

2.2   Broadcast Frequency Adaptive Adjustment Algorithm

It can be observed from Eq. 7 that the position prediction error of the vehicle is positively correlated with the acceleration, speed and Δt of the vehicle. The acceleration, angular velocity and speed of the vehicle are controlled by the vehicle and the driver. At the transmission control level, the communication delay can be reduced by reducing the Δt as much as possible, that is, increasing the data broadcast frequency, and the accuracy of the position prediction is improved. The acceleration and speed are defined as the stability of the vehicle's travel. Therefore, the idea of the transmission control algorithm is to reduce the broadcast frequency of a stable traveling vehicle while increasing the broadcasting frequency of an unstable traveling vehicle.

Now defined:

$$S = 2 - H_1 * a - H_2 * v \tag{8}$$

H is a weight parameter to characterize the stability of the vehicle's travel.

Message broadcast frequency adaptive adjustment algorithm based on vehicle driving stability:

$$M = [R^* e^{\ s}] + c \tag{9}$$

"[]" is the rounding function and R is the calibration message generation rate, which is 10 Hz. Selection of parameters H and c: the speed of the vehicle on the ordinary road is generally 60 km/h, about 17 m/s, and the acceleration value range is 0–6. Take $H_1 = 0.15 \approx \frac{1}{6}$, $H_2 = 0.06 \approx \frac{1}{17}$. The frequency is observed by Matlab drawing, and the offset C = 5 is selected. The relationship between broadcast frequency and speed and acceleration is shown in Fig. 1(a) and (b):

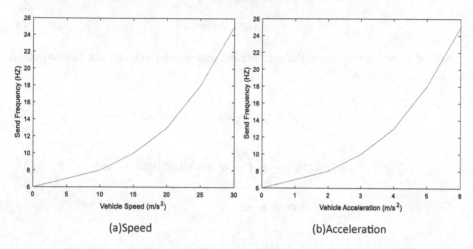

(a)Speed   (b)Acceleration

Fig. 1. Relationship between broadcast frequency with speed and acceleration

The message broadcast frequency adaptive adjustment algorithm based on driving stability can realize the data broadcasting frequency when the position prediction error is large, reduce the broadcasting frequency when the error is small, and provide a higher quality early warning information transmission service when the channel capacity is constant. And the exponential adaptive adjustment algorithm compares the threshold-type adaptive adjustment algorithm, and the change is more real-time and accurate.

3 Urban Environment Implementation

In order to obtain the vehicle node movement model of the real city map, the map.osm map file exported by OpenStreetMap [21] is configured by SUMO [22] software into a script file that can be used in NS2 [23], thereby importing the real urban environment into Network simulation in NS2, the basic implementation process is as follows:

(1) Use OpenStreetMap to get the map.osm map file;
(2) Use the SUMO command to configure the node motion path, node motion model, etc.
(3) Use the SUMO command to output the fcd (Floating Car Data) file;
(4) Use traceExproter.py to convert the fcd file generated in the previous step into the config.tcl, mobility.tcl and activity.tcl files required by NS2;
(5) Embed the three files generated in the previous step into the NS2 code, configure the relevant simulation conditions, and perform network simulation through NS2.

Figures 2 and 3 show the real map of a street in Nanchang and its topology, which are generated by SUMO.

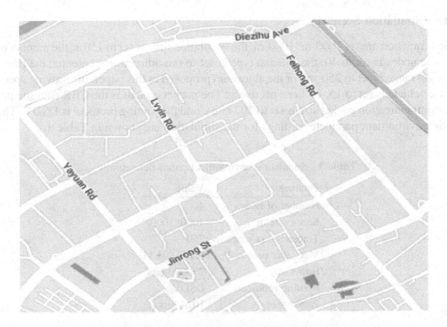

Fig. 2. Nanchang partial map data

Fig. 3. Nanchang local map topology

4   Comparison of Performance Simulations of Different Broadcast Frequencies

4.1   Simulation Scenario

The simulation area is 1000 m*1000 m, the simulation time is set to 150 s, the number of vehicle nodes is set to 40; the antenna type is set to omnidirectional antenna; the transmission range is set to 250 m; for the algorithm proposed in this paper, the moving speed of the vehicle is set to 15, 19 m respectively; The packet type uses the CBR data stream, the communication packet size is set to 1024 bits, and the routing protocol is DSDV. The basic environment parameter settings for the simulation are shown in Table 1.

Table 1. Simulation environment parameter settings

Parameter	Value
Number of nodes	40
Scene size/m	1000*1000
Transmission range/m	250
Mac layer protocol/p	IEEE 802.11
Buffer size	256000 bits
Routing protocol	DSDV
Packet size	1024 bits

4.2   Simulation Analysis

The moving speed of the vehicle node will affect the topology of the node, and the severity of the topology change will have a certain impact on the communication between vehicles. Therefore, the moving speed of the vehicle is the key factor of the algorithm. In order to better explore the performance of the proposed algorithm, based on the urban vehicle scene built in the previous chapter, the NS2 simulation platform is used to simulate the calibration frequency and the performance of the adaptive transmission frequency algorithm. The simulation results are shown in the figure below.

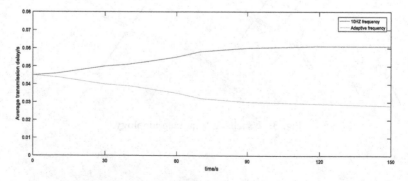

Fig. 4. Comparison of average transmission delay between two scenes

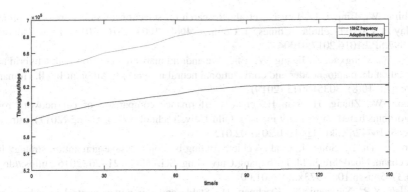

Fig. 5. Comparison of two scene throughputs

As can be seen from Fig. 4, the change in speed has an impact on the end-to-end delay performance. The calibrated message generation rate cannot meet the communication speed between vehicles when the vehicle speed is too fast, resulting in a long delay; while the adaptive transmission frequency of this paper can adjust the transmission frequency according to the speed, the delay caused by the calibration is more obvious than the calibration frequency improve. As can be seen from Fig. 5, the speed change also has a certain impact on throughput. The adaptive algorithm has a significantly increased throughput compared to the calibrated frequency.

In general, the algorithm in this paper can better adapt to the communication between vehicles with faster speed.

5 Summary

The urban road file obtained by SUMO software is converted into a script file that can be used by NS2, and the node motion model under NS2 is extended. Based on this, the routing performance of the calibration transmission frequency and the adaptive transmission frequency at different node moving speeds is analyzed. It can be seen from the simulation results that the adaptive transmission frequency of this paper is better than the calibration transmission frequency. However, the results of this paper are not applied to real maps, and the number of vehicle motion models is not large. Therefore, the transmission control algorithm combined with urban scenes is our main research direction.

References

1. Fadilah, S.I., Shariff, A.R.M., Hilmi, M.N.M.: Crash avoidance based periodic safety message dissemination protocol for vehicular ad hoc network. In: 2019 IEEE 89th Vehicular Technology Conference (VTC2019-Spring), pp. 1–7. IEEE (2019)
2. Wang, W., Luo, T., Kang, H.: A local information sensing-based broadcast scheme for disseminating emergency safety messages in IoV. Mobile Inf. Syst. (2019)

3. Libing, W., Bingyi, L., Lei, N., et al.: Research on selection of safety message broadcast relay in VANET-cellular. Chinese J. Comput. **40**(4), 1004–1016 (2017). https://doi.org/10.11897/SP.J.1016.2017.01004

4. Wei, W., Mengxue, Z., Jigang, W.: Effective android malware detection with a hybrid model based on deep autoencoder and convolutional neural network. J. Ambient Intell. Humanized Comput. **10**(8), 3035–3043 (2019)

5. Dong, W., Zhang, H., Lin, H., et al.: Performance comparison of car network routing algorithms based on real city maps. J. Qilu Univ. Technol. **31**(2), 56–62 (2017). https://doi.org/10.16442/j.cnki.qlgydxxb.2017.02.012

6. Mo, Y., Yu, D., Song, J., et al.: Vehicle routing beacon message generation strategy based on channel load threshold. J. Zhejiang Univ. (Eng. Sci.) **50**(1), 21–26 (2016). https://doi.org/10.3785/j.issn.1008-973x.2016.01.004

7. Fallah, Y.P., Nasiriani, N., Krishnan, H.: Stable and fair power control in vehicle safety networks. IEEE Trans. Veh. Technol. **65**(3), 1662–1675 (2016)

8. Xu, J., Ao, X.: Comparative research on routing algorithms of wireless ad-hoc network based on location information. Ship Electron. Eng. **39**(2), 110–114 (2019). https://doi.org/10.3969/j.issn.1672-9730.2019.02.027

9. Hu, Q., Xu, L.: Real-time road traffic awareness model based on optimal multi-channel self-organized time division multiple access algorithm. Comput. Electr. Eng. **58**, 299–309 (2017)

10. Wang, X., Cui, G., Wang, C.: Dynamic prediction of time delay of V2 V link in urban vehicle network. Comput. Res. Dev. **54**(12), 2721–2730 (2017). https://doi.org/10.7514/issn1000-1239.2017.20158391

11. Zeng, Yu.: Design of Highway Safety Early Warning System Based on Vehicle Network. Chang'an University, Shaanxi (2017)

12. Li, S., Tan, G., Zhang, F., et al.: An adaptive power control strategy for vehicle networking. Small Comput. Syst. **38**(1), 72–76 (2017)

13. Huang, J., Li, J., Li, Y.: An adaptive routing algorithm based on social relationships in mobile social networks. Comput. Digit. Eng. **47**(4), 748–755 (2019). https://doi.org/10.3969/j.issn.1672-9722.2019.04.003

14. Xu, C.: Research on mutual authentication scheme for Internet of Vehicle. Beijing University of Posts and Telecommunications (2019)

15. Fallah, Y.P., Nasiriani, N., Krishnan, H.: Stable and fair power control in vehicle safety networks. IEEE Trans. Veh. Technol. **65**(3), 1 (2015)

16. Hao, L., Li, J., Rong, T., et al.: Trajectory tracking of unmanned vehicles based on MPC. Automot. Pract. Technol. **20**, 53–55 (2017). https://doi.org/10.16638/j.cnki.1671-7988.2017.20.018

17. Nan, J., Li, B., Wan, T., Liu, L.: C-POEM: comprehensive performance optimization evaluation model for wireless sensor networks. Soft. Comput. **21**(12), 3377–3385 (2017). (SCI: EV8QE)

18. Ye, M., Guanm, L., Quddus, M.: MPBRP-mobility prediction based routing protocol in VANETs. In: 2019 International Conference on Advanced Communication Technologies and Networking (CommNet), pp. 1–7. IEEE (2019)

19. Yang, L., Zhe, W., Zhang, C., et al.: Trajectory prediction algorithm for vehicle self-organizing network routing. Comput. Res. Dev. **54**(11), 2419–2433 (2017). https://doi.org/10.7544/issn1000-1239.2017.20170359

20. Na, Y., Shi, W., Zhao, X.: Intersection speed guidance information management system in IoV. Meas. Control Technol. **38**(4), 142–147 (2019). https://doi.org/10.19708/j.ckjs.2019.04.029

21. OpenStreetMap Community. OpenStreetMap world map [EB/OL]. http://www.openstreet map.org. Accessed 23 May 2015
22. Behrisch, M., Bieker, L., Erdmann, J., et al.: SUMO-simulation of urban mobility: an overview. In: Simulation DLR, pp. 63–68 (2011)
23. Zhang, J.: Installation of network simulation software NS2 based on VMware environment. Electron. World, (16), 444–445 (2014). https://doi.org/10.3969/j.issn.1003-0522.2014.16. 436

Body-Weight Estimation of Plateau Yak with Simple Dimensional Measurement

Yu-an Zhang[1]($\boxtimes$), Xiaofeng Qin[1]🆔, Minghao Zhao[2], Meiyun Du[1], and Rende Song[3]

[1] Department of Computer Technology and Applications,
Qinghai University, Xining, China
2011990029@qhu.edu.cn
[2] Tsinghua University, Beijing, China
zhaominghao.thu@gmail.com
[3] Yushu Prefecture Animal Husbandry and Veterinary, Yushu, Qinghai, China

Abstract. Animal husbandry is the economic backbone in large areas around the world, especially in rural and under-developing countries. In the Sanjiangyuan region of China, the cultivation and depasturing of yak is one of the most representative industries and the main source of revenue for the shepherds. In yak-breeding, body weight is an essential index for evaluating the body (health) status of the livestock. However, as a pasture-raised large-body-size animal, it is not easy for the herdsmen to weigh them. In this paper, we attempt to investigate the feasibility to acquire yaks' body-wight with easy effort, i.e., via just measuring some dimensional features with ordinary rulers. To achieve this, we collect large-scale data about body dimensional features and the body weight of the yaks, and use machine learning methods to get the model to estimate the body weight. Through in-depth evaluation and analysis, we find that the estimation method by utilizing Random Forest achieves the best performance, i.e., with the test precision of 0.95 (The test precision of *LR* and *SVMs* is 0.92, 0.7 respectively). Finally, we develop the PC software and Android App based on our method and freely issue to the herdsmen to use. Our research greatly facilitates herdsmen's livestock production.

Keywords: Yushu yak · Yak weight estimation · Linear regression · Support vector machines · Random forest

1 Introduction

The livestock sector is an important industry around the world. It is reported that the livestock systems cover nearly 30% of the planet's ice-free terrestrial surface area [1] and there are about 1.3 billion people engaged in animal husbandry related works globally [2]. The importance of the livestock sector is not only confined in under developing countries, in which 600 million poor smallholder farmers rely on livestock for living [3], but also in developed countries.

© Springer Nature Switzerland AG 2019
J. Vaidya et al. (Eds.): CSS 2019, LNCS 11983, pp. 562–571, 2019.
https://doi.org/10.1007/978-3-030-37352-8_50

For example, in The U.S.A., the animal agriculture contributes to 1.85 million in jobs, $346 billion in total economic, $60 billion in household income and $15 billion in tax revenue [4].

In the Sanjiangyuan region[1] of China, the animal husbandry and farming take over other industries (such as manufacturing, construction, service and financial industry) and became the backbone of the local economy. With total acreage of nearly 3.63 million square kilometers, this area is mainly covered with alpine meadow. An overwhelming majority of the people (90%) in this area are Tibetan and more than 50% of the total population is engaged in animal-raising-related works. The detailed natural scenery and anthropological spectacle can be found in [5].

Among this region, the yak (with biological nomenclature of Poëphagus Grunniens) is the main and representative livestock raised here. This is mainly because of the fact that, with special physiologic characteristics (as demonstrated in [6,7]), the yak is perhaps the only (large sized) domestic animal that adapts to the extreme natural environments (extremely cold and low oxygen concentration). Up to now, the raising of yak has been the source of income, as well as the resource of human life and production for the local residents, especially for the Tibetans. In Qinghai province, the scale of yak cultivation is expanding year by year, and yak-raising has become a distinguishing feature of the local graziery. Recently, the yak has become the emblem for the culture of this area.

In terms of animal raising, the body weight is one of the most important index figures that indicate the growth status of the animal. It serves as a basic indicator or gauge for hybridization, forage feeding, physical condition monitoring, and dosage calculation. However, it is not easy for the herdsmen to weigh the yaks. This is mainly because the yaks are normally raised in a free-range farming manner and they are overwhelmingly weighty (roughly weighing several hundred kilograms for a grown yak).

Traditionally, when it is required to get the body weight of a yak, the herdsmen has to capture the yak in the pasture, tie it up and then drag them on the top of a mechanical steelyard. Obviously, this leads to taxing and onerous workload to the breeder. Even now, almost all the individual herdsmen and (state-owned) livestock farm use the arduous method to measure the yak's body weight. Expect for the laboriousness, the precision deficiency of the mechanical steelyard makes the measurement inaccurate to some extent.

In this work, we attempt to provide an easy way for the shepherds to estimate the yak body weight with high precision. Specifically, we adopt the machine learning method, such that enables the shepherds just provide some dimensional data (can simply be metered with a tape measure) and get the estimated body weight with our scheme. In order to achieve this goal, we firstly collect large scale the body features and body weight data of yaks. Latterly, we used the collected data to train the machine learning model; and through in-depth performance

---

[1] Also known as "the Source of Three Rivers, which derives his name as this area is the source of three crucial rivers – the Yangtze River, the Yellow River, and the Mekong.

evaluation, we find that the random forest outweighs other method and achieves better precision (over 95%). Finally, based on the aforementioned method, we develop a PC software as well as an Android App, and freely release them to the herdsmen.

Related Works. At present, the analysis of body weight and body size of Qinghai yak indicates that there is a clear linear relationship between yak body weight and body size, the correlation between yak body size and body weight has been quantitatively analyzed and explained, and a multivariate linear regression equation of yak body weight and body size was established to describe the growth performance of yak [8–11]. Pei [12] used the path analysis method to calculate the direct and indirect effects of body weight traits on the body weight of yak, indicating that the direct effect of yak chest circumference on body weight is greater than the effect of other traits on body weight, and the indirect effect of chest circumference is on body height and Body length has made a major contribution to the effects of body weight. Fan [13] studied the effects of different feeding patterns on the growth and development of juvenile calves. By studying the changes in body size and body weight data of yak found that the patterns conducive to growth and development, the use of cowshed management and feeding methods can accelerate the growth and development of young yaks. Zhao [14] studied the performance of Changtai Yak in the germplasm resources of different genders and age groups, which provided a data basis for the improved breeding of yak. Wu [15] pointed out that chest circumference, body length, breast height and depth have important effects on the milk yield of yak when studying Maiwa yak (Maiwa yak is a rare animal breeding resource on the Qinghai-Tibet plateau, which has black hair on its while body, developed forechest, long body, short limbs and solid hooves so that people call it "god cow") and suggested that the above factors should be considered in yak breeding. Han [16] analyzed the body size and body weight of hybrid calves of different ages and genders found that the growth performance of hybrid improved yak was significantly improved, and the evaluation of the growth performance of hybrid yak was achieved.

Based on the above research, it can be found that although it has a big contribution to the research and breeding of traditional yak, while the mining methods and results are too simple, and the data set is very small (only a few dozen yaks were typically measured) and the algorithm they used is relatively onefold (machine learning algorithms are rarely used but only analysed by correlation analysis, Linear regression, etc.). Therefore, the key point of our current research is to mining yak body size and weight data with better performance algorithm and obtain more accurate weight prediction model.

1.1 Our Contribution

- *A large-scale dataset on yak body feature.* Our professionals measured the characteristics of 600 male and female yaks at different ages in Yushu prefecture, the data set includes abundant features such as the body size (height, body length, chest girth, cannon bone girth), weight, age, gender, appearance grade, genital condition, limb hoof condition, comprehensive level, etc. of yaks and their parents. In this paper, body size, weight, age, gender and other data were selected for mining with different methods.

- *A machine learning method for yak body-weight estimation.* The Linear regression, Support vector machines and Random forest algorithm of machine learning methods were used to conduct data mining and prediction, and established a yak weight prediction model, the test accuracy of the methods $(LR, SVMs, RF)$ is 0.92, 0.7, 0.95 respectively.
- *Freely released PC software and Android application.* We developed a PC software (decision support system of yak breeding for Sanjiangyuan region) that embedded in a variety of machine learning algorithm to detect yak growth, at the same time, the system shows the pastoral area ecological environment, changes in the meadows, herders family situation, the information of government policy, etc., which provides a platform for rational breeding. Similarity, the application based on android can predict changes in yak weight or body size by machine learning algorithms to monitor the yak growth real-time.

2 The Dataset

2.1 Dataset Overview

In this paper, 600 healthy yaks (male and female yaks) in Yushu Prefecture of Qinghai Province was collected as the research object, the age of yak range is from 0 (the newborn yaks) to 5 years old. The researchers from Yushu Animal Husbandry and Veterinary Station measured the body weight of yak by weighbridge, and the yak was on an empty stomach after 12 h. The body length, body height, chest girth and cannon bone girth were measured by stick (Biltmore stick) and tape rulers. The yak picture in Yushu Prefecture is shown in Fig. 1, and the schematic diagram of measurement is shown in Fig. 2.

2.2 The Metrics

The body length (BL): The body length, also known as the lean body length, refers to the distance from the shoulder blade to the ischium. It can be measured by measuring stick (Biltmore stick) or tape rulers.

Height (H): The body height, also known as the withers height, refers to the vertical height measured from the withers (the highest embossment on the dorsum) to the ground. It is normally measured with a measuring stick (Biltmore stick).

Chest girth (CG): The chest girth refers to the perimeter measured at the posterior margin of the scapula. This figure is captured with a type-ruler to encircle the beast "chest" for one round, and the preferable tightness is to slightly cover the yak's hair and two fingers can freely slither in the type-ruler circle.

Circumference of cannon bone (CCB): The circumference of cannon bone indicates the circumference of the thinnest part of the ankle bone, which usually

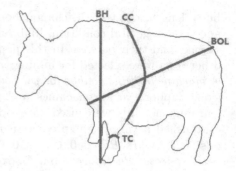

Fig. 1. The picture of Yushu prefecture yak

Fig. 2. The measurement of yak body size figure

refers to the horizontal circumferential diameter of the upper third (thinnest part) of the canal bone if the left forelimb and measured by the flexible ruler.

Weight (W): The body weight of yak value was measured at early morning by weighbridge after the yak has been fasted 12 h, recording the data with kilogram (kg) unit.

2.3   Data Pre-processing and Cleaning

There are some eigenvalues missing in the data set, especially the CCB data missing. The CCB missing data were filled through regression prediction method, the other data were filled according to the data of similar body size in each same age group. Skewness-Kurtosis detection method was used to detect the outliers and remove them for smoothing noise data. (Skewness detection method is suitable for the situation where the outliers appear on the one side, the Eq. 1 shows the processing method of Skewness detection. Kurtosis detection method is suitable for bilateral cases, which processing method is shown in Eq. 2).

$$b_s = \frac{\sqrt{n}\sum_{i=1}^{n}(x_i - \overline{x})^3}{\left[\sum_{i=1}^{n}(x_i - \overline{x})^2\right]^{3/2}} = \frac{\sqrt{n}\left[\sum_{i=1}^{n}x_i^3 - 3\overline{x}\sum_{i=1}^{n}x_i^2 + 2n(\overline{x})^3\right]}{\left[\sum_{i=1}^{n}x_i^2 - n\overline{x}^2\right]^{3/2}} \tag{1}$$

In the formula, the ith data arranged from the smallest sample to the largest sample is called x_i. Determine the detected level α, check the critical value table whether the $b_s \geq bP(n)$, if greater than then judged as an abnormal value, otherwise no abnormal value is found. When there are more than one outlier, the innermost outlier is selected to test. For example, when there are two upper outliers x_n and x_{n-1}, temporarily remove x_n and subtract 1 from the measurement times to check whether x_{n-1} is an outlier. If it is not an outlier, the measurement times are n, and then check whether x_n is an outlier, if x_{n-1} is an outlier, then x_n is naturally discarded.

$$b_k = \frac{n \sum_{i=1}^{n}(x_i - \overline{x})^4}{\left[\sum_{i=1}^{n}(x_i - \overline{x}^2)\right]^2} = \frac{n\left[\sum_{i=1}^{n} x_i^4 - 4\overline{x}\sum_{i=1}^{n} x_i^3 + 6\overline{x}^2 \sum i = 1^n x_i^2 - 3n\overline{x}^4\right]}{\left[\sum_{i=1}^{n} x_i^2 - n\overline{x}^2\right]^2}$$

(2)

Determine the detected level α, check the threshold values for kurtosis test table value $bP(n)$, when the $bk > bP(n)$ determines that the furthest value from mean $\overline{x}$ is an abnormal value. After removing the abnormal value, the repeated kurtosis detection tests wether there is still an abnormal value, otherwise no abnormal value is found.

2.4 Machine Learning Tools

Support Vector Machines (*SVMs*). The support vector machines (*SVMs*) is a new supervised machine learning algorithm that firstly proposed by Vapnik and et al. at 1964, which based theoretically on statistical learning theory to solve the practical problems such as small samples, nonlinearity, over learning, high dimension and local minima that has very high generalization [17].

The Support vector machines is a kind of generalized linear classifier for binary classification of data which were originally designed for binary classification. It is an ongoing research issue to effectively extend SVMs for multiclass classification, and there are two methods for multiclass *SVMs*, One is by constructing and combining multiple binary classifiers, and other is to directly consider all data in an optimization formulation [18]. Nowadays, *SVMs* has been used for isolated handwritten digit recognition [19], object recognition [20], speaker identification [21], face detection in images [22], and text categorization [23].

Linear Regression. The Linear regression (*LR*) is a data mining tool based on regression analysis in statistics and the quantitative function of regression analysis is one of the common methods in statistical analysis, the purpose is to find a line or a high-dimensional hyperplane that minimizes the error between the predicted value and the true value [24]. The problem of learning regression is equivalent to function fitting, that is using a function curve to make it well fit known functions and predict unknown data. The procedure is divided into model learning and prediction, firstly build a model based on the given training data set and secondly predict the corresponding output according to the new input data. Linear regression is widely used in social, economic, technological and many natural science research that studies how to effectively organize and analyze randomly affected data and make inferences and predictions on the issues examined [25].

Random Forests. The Random forest (*RF*, also known as *random decision forest*), firstly proposed by Ho [26] and formalized by Breiman [27] is a supervised learning technique. As the name suggests, it forms forest-like structures with decision trees that are generated using the random sampling with replacement.

Actually, the organized decision trees can either be the classification trees or the regression trees; as a result, the random forest can be used to solve both classification problems and regression problems.

The random forest adopts the parallelization technique to provide multiple trained decision tree classifiers for the testing phase to improve the learning performance, and uses the Bootstrapping (applied at the training phase) and Bagging (applied at the testing phase) technique to optimize the classification objectives. As a result, the decision tree method achieves high prediction precision, performs well tolerated for outliers and noise values, and is not prone to overfitting Until to now, it has been widely used in many practical areas, such as image processing, bio-medical data analyses, ecosystem modeling, commercial behavior prediction and information security ensurance.

3   Experiments and Findings

3.1   Experiments and Results

The training set selected by random function (The data was divided into train set and test set in a ratio of 4:1). Yak body weight was taken as the dependent variable and the body size characteristics (BL, H, CG, CCB) with strong correlation with body weight were selected as the independent variables. The comparison between the predicted results and the real values of three algorithms are shown in figures (Figs. 3, 4 and 5), training set accuracy, test set accuracy, MSE (Mean Square Error, which is the value of squared difference between the estimated value of the parameter and the true value of the parameter that can evaluate the degree of data change, the smaller the value of MSE is, the more accurate the prediction model is to describe experimental data.) and $RMSE$ (Root Mean Square Error, which is arithmetic square root of the MSE.) were used to compare the performance of algorithms shown as Table 1. The LR algorithm predicted values is shown in Fig. 3 that has a good result. The $SVMs$ algorithm predicted results are relatively poor than LR algorithm which shown in Fig. 4. The RF algorithm predicted result is shown in Fig. 5 that is the most accurate model for the yak weight prediction.

Table 1. Performance comparison of LR, $SVMs$ and RF algorithm

Algorithm	Training set accuracy	Test set accuracy	MSE	$RSME$
LR	0.91	0.92	300.21	17.33
$SVMs$	0.7	0.7	1449.67	38.07
RF	0.99	0.95	202.93	14.25

The predicted results by these three machine learning algorithms are not significantly different from the actual values that can be seen from Figs. 3, 4 and 5, which confirm that estimate yak weight by these three machine learning

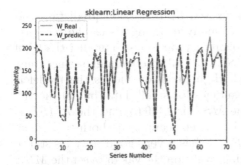

Fig. 3. The predicted results and real data comparison figure. The black line indicates the real values of yak weight, and the red line indicates the predicted value of yak weight by Linear regression algorithm. The horizontal coordinate is the serial number of data, and the vertical coordinate is the weight of yak in kilograms(kg). (Color figure online)

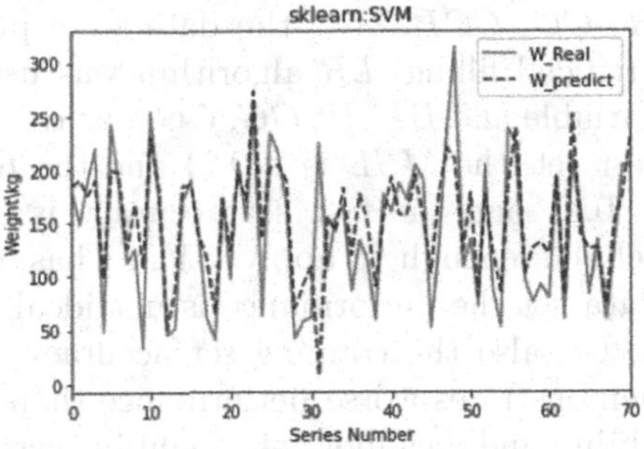

Fig. 4. The predicted results and real data comparison figure. The black line indicates the real values of yak weight, and the red line indicates the predicted value of yak weight by Support vector machines algorithm. The horizontal coordinate is the serial number of data, and the vertical coordinate is the weight of yak in kilograms(kg). (Color figure online)

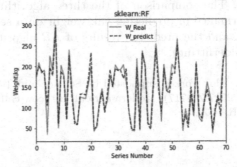

Fig. 5. The predicted results and real data comparison figure. The black line indicates the real values of yak weight, and the red line indicates the predicted value of yak weight by Random forest algorithm. The horizontal coordinate is the serial number of data, and the vertical coordinate is the weight of yak in kilograms(kg). (Color figure online)

algorithms is feasible. Among them, the fitting degree of RF algorithm is better than $SVMs$, and the LR is better than $SVMs$. And Table 1 shows the performance indicators of LR, $SVMs$, RF like accuracy of training set and test set, MSE, $RMSE$.

3.2 The Findings and Conclusion

In this paper, we selected 600 healthy yaks form Yushu prefecture as the research objects, with the help of professionals we measured the yak data such as W, BL,

H, CG, CCB, etc., the data were preprocessed by regression prediction and artificial filling. LR algorithm was used to analyze taking W as the response variable and BL, H, CG, CCB as the explanatory variables to predict the W of test set, the MSE is 300.21 and the $RMSE$ is 17.33, the training set accuracy is 0.91 and the test set accuracy is 0.92. High precision means the model is reliable enough to apply. $SVMs$ has advantages for small data, but in the yak data set the performance is not ideal, the MSE is 1449.67 and the $RMSE$ is 38.07, also the training set accuracy and test set accuracy is both 0.7, which demonstrates worse performance than LR. RF has a very good nosy resistance ability and it cannot get caught in overfitting easily, on the yak data set the MSE is 202.93 and the $RMSE$ is 14.25, the training set accuracy is 0.99 and the test set accuracy is 0.95. As we can see from the Table 1, the overall performance of each algorithm is good but there are still differences. The training set accuracy and test set accuracy is the same indicates the $SVMs$ algorithm is under fitting, and the large value of MSE and $RMSE$ means the error of regression prediction results is quite large. The training set accuracy of RF algorithm is 0.99 and the test set accuracy is 0.95, indicating that there is overfitting condition of RF algorithm. The R^2 of LR algorithm is 0.92, the accuracy of training set and test set is 0.91, 0.92 respectively, which indicates the model fits well and has a great performance. The comparison of the three algorithms shows that the RF has a best performance in predicting yak weight data set although it exits overfitting condition, and the predicted results of LR algorithm is better than $SVMs$ algorithm (underfitting).

Acknowledgements. This work is supported by Science and Technology Project in Qinghai Province (No. 2017-ZJ-717); Modern agriculture (cow calf) industrial technology system project (CRA-37).

References

1. Steinfeld, H., et al.: Livestocks Long Shadow: Environmental Issues and Options. Food and Agriculture Organization, Rome (2006)
2. Thornton, P.K.: Livestock production: recent trends, future prospects. Philos. Trans. R. Soc. Lond. B Biol. Sci. **365**(1554), 2853–2867 (2010)
3. Thornton, P., Jones, P., Owiyo, T., Kruska, R., Herrero, M., Kristjanson, P.: Mapping climate vulnerability and poverty in Africa, report to the department for international development (2006)
4. Economic Benefits of the Livestock Industry. http://igrow.org/livestock/profit-tips/economic-benefits-of-the-livestock-industry
5. Foggin, M.: Pastoralists and wildlife conservation in western China: collaborative management within protected areas on the Tibetan plateau. Pastoralism Res. Policy Pract. **2**(1), 17 (2012)
6. Harris, R.B.: Rangeland degradation on the Qinghai-Tibetan plateau: a review of the evidence of its magnitude and causes. J. Arid Environ. **74**(1), 1–12 (2010)
7. Wu, X., et al.: Association of novel single-nucleotide polymorphisms of the vascular endothelial growth factor-a gene with high-altitude adaptation in yak (Bos grunniens). Genet. Mol. Res. GMR **12**(4), 5506–5515 (2013)

8. Hongkang, L., Shoubao, Z.: Correlation analysis of body weight, body measurements in Datong yak. Chin. Qinghai J. Anim. Vet. Sci. **46**(4), 37–39 (2016)
9. Minqiang, W., Huiling, Z., Pingli, L.: Body weight growth model of Datong yak in Qinghai, China Herbivores (2005)(z2)
10. Da, Q., Quzong, L.: Correlation and regression analysis of the body weight and body size of adult female yak in Naqu. J. Anhui Agri. Sci. **39**(16), 9715–9716 (2011)
11. Guoqiang, S., Jiuhua, L., Lizhuang, H.: The model of the relationship between body weight and body size index of growing yak in Qinghai. Heilongjiang Anim. Sci. Vet. Med. **2018**(03), 225–229 (2018)
12. Jie, P., Ping, Y., Xian, G.: Multiple linear regression and path analysis between body measurement and weight on Datong yak. Chin. Herbivore Sci. **37**(6), 9–13 (2017)
13. Fengxia, F., Zhengjie, L.: Effects of different feeding patterns on growth and development of young yaks. Todays Anim. Husbandry Vet. **07**, 44–45 (2018)
14. Hongwen, Z., Xiaolin, L., Jinbin, M.: Study on the growth and development performance of Changtai yaks. Heilongjiang Anim. Sci. Vet. Med. **12**, 190–192 (2016)
15. Wu, J., He, S., Ai, Y.: Correlation between body size and breast traits and milk yield of Maiwa yak and principal component analysis. Heilongjiang Anim. Sci. Vet. Med. 149–152 (2019)
16. Xueyan, H., Zhongxin, Y., Yichao, J.: Effect of yak hybridization on its growth performance. Heilongjiang Anim. Sci. Vet. Med. **22**, 222–223 (2018)
17. Ma, L., Ha, M.: Support vector machine based on sectional set fuzzy k-means clustering In: Fuzzy Information and Engineering, ASC, vol. 54, pp. 420–425 (2009). https://doi.org/10.1007/978-3-540-88914-4_52
18. Hsu, C.W., Lin, C.J.: A comparison of methods for multiclass support vector machines. IEEE Trans. Neural Netw. **13**(2), 415–425 (2002)
19. Cortes, C., Vapnik, V.: Support-vector networks. Mach. Learn. **20**, 273–297 (1995)
20. Burges, C.J.C.: A tutorial on support vector machine for pattern recognition. Data Min. Knowl. Discov. **2**, 121–167 (1998). Bell Laboratories, Lucent Technologies
21. Schmidt, M.: Identifying speaker with support vector networks. In: Interface 96 Proceedings, Sydney (1996)
22. Osuna, E., Freund, R., Girosi, F.: An improved training algorithm for support vector machines. In: Proceedings of the 1997 IEEE Workshop on Neural Networks for Signal Processing, pp. 276–285 (1997)
23. Joachims, T.: Text categorization with support vector machines, Technical report, LS VII no. 23 (1997)
24. McNeil, K.A.: Meeting the goals on research with multiple linear regression. Multivar. Behav. Res. **5**(3), 375–386 (1970)
25. Bin, L.: Multiple linear regression analysis and its application. China Sci. Technol. Inf. **3**(6), 60–61 (2010)
26. Ho, T.K.: Random decision forests. In: Proceedings of the Third International Conference on Document Analysis and Recognition, vol. 1, pp. 278–282. IEEE (1995)
27. Breiman, L.: Random forests. Mach. Learn. **45**(1), 5–32 (2001)

Bank Card Number Identification Based on Template Matching Method

Wei Li and Zhilin Song[✉]

Shenyang University of Technology, Shenyang, China
715547476@qq.com

Abstract. In order to solve the identification problem of bank card number, an effective identification algorithm for bank card number based on template matching is proposed. The binary image is obtained by preprocessing the bank card image. According to the binary matrix feature of bank card number and based on template matching. The matrix of character image to be recognized is superimposed on the template matrix. In addition, the unmatched pixel statistics of the superimposed image are performed to obtain the matching factor. The minimum matching factor is regarded as the optimum matching. The results show that the proposed method is simple and effective, and with strong anti-interference performance and high identification rate. Moreover, the identification accuracy of bank card number is about 96%.

Keywords: Template matching · Bank card number · Binarization image

1 Introduction

In recent years, mobile payments have become more and more deep into everyone's lives. Mobile payment software is constantly emerging, and each mobile payment software requires users to bind bank cards. Therefore, input the bank card number becomes a necessary step. Because of the large number of bank card numbers, it is difficult for users to input bank card numbers correctly at one time, which leads to inefficiency. It is very positive for improving work efficiency and convenient people's live to design a fast and accurate identification of bank card numbers algorithm

Bank card number belongs to the print number. At present, there are mainly the following methods for printed digital recognition: Left and Right Contour Feature Method, Digital Structural Feature Method, Template matching method, Machine learning, etc. Based on the digital structure feature bank card recognition algorithm, the digital structure feature is used to extract the digital feature vector, and the Euclidean distance is used to compare the similarity between the feature vectors. However, the algorithm has a high probability of misjudgment, resulting in low recognition rate. Based on left and right contours is divided into six parts. By assigning different weights to six parts, the Euclidean distance of the eigenvector is calculated and the number with the smallest distance is selected. The recognition rate of this algorithm is very high. However, implementation is complex and therefore not widely used. Template matching is performed by making a digital template for superposition and selecting the best match with the template as the final result of recognition. Machine learning

© Springer Nature Switzerland AG 2019
J. Vaidya et al. (Eds.): CSS 2019, LNCS 11983, pp. 572–578, 2019.
https://doi.org/10.1007/978-3-030-37352-8_51

method has a high recognition rate, but it requires a large number of training datasets and a long design process.

In this paper, based on the binarization characteristics of the image of bank card number, an accurate and efficient recognition algorithm of bank card number based on template matching is proposed on the platform of OpenCV under Python. Then a large number of recognition experiments of bank card number image are carried out by template matching algorithm. Finally, the efficiency of the algorithm is compared with other algorithms by the comparison experiment.

2 Digital Image Preprocessing

2.1 Digital Image Acquisition

The image obtained is used a mobile phone camera to take bank card photo in this paper, as shown in Fig. 1. In theory, the higher the resolution of the image with the larger the amount of digital information contained in the image. So higher resolution with the accuracy of digital recognition. However, the amount of calculation required for the increase in resolution increases, resulting in recognition time slowing down Because of the structure of the printed digital is relatively simple, the amount of information required for recognition is relatively small, and the digital image obtained by the camera can fully satisfy the requirements of digital recognition.

Fig. 1. Bank card picture

2.2   Image Denoising

The image noisy is the sensor affected by its own factors and external environmental factors during the process of image acquisition and transmission, such as the quality of the camera's own components, the external light intensity during acquisition and other factors. Image denoising is to remove these interference factors to make the image clearer and get a more realistic image.

Because noise is concentrated on high frequency signals, it is easily recognized as a false edge. A Gaussian filter is applied to remove noise and reduce the identification of false edges. However, since the image edge information is also a high frequency signal, the radius selection of Gaussian blur is very important, and an excessive radius is easy to detect some weak edges. In this paper, the results of the experiments of Gaussian filtering and non-Gaussian filtering show that the pretreatment effect of surface Gaussian filtering is better.

2.3   Image Binarization

Binarization is the process of converting a digital gray image into a binary image with a gray value of 0 and 255. The function of binarization is to divide the image into two parts: target and background, eliminating unnecessary gray information in the process of processing. In the actual environment, there is no ensure that the brightness of each photo will be consistent when shooting. It is not possible to simply set a global threshold to achieve the purpose of binarization. Therefore, this paper use a local adaptive threshold segmentation method. The algorithm principle is to determine the binarization threshold at the pixel position according to the pixel value distribution of the neighborhood block of each pixel, which has the advantage that the binarization threshold at each pixel position is not fixed, It is determined by the distribution of pixels in its neighborhood. The binarization threshold of the image area with higher brightness is usually higher, and the binarization threshold of the image area with lower brightness is correspondingly smaller. Local image regions of different brightness will have corresponding local binarization thresholds. The local adaptive threshold segmentation of the target image can be achieved by the cv.Adaptive.Threshold() function provided by OpenCV.

2.4   Bank Card Tilt Correction

In the actual identification process, because of the arbitrariness of bank card placement, the obtained bank card character image usually has a certain angle of inclination. This state's recognition rate of the bank card in the tilt state is greatly reduced. In order to obtain a higher recognition rate, it is necessary to perform tilt correction on the bank card. Canny proposed three criteria for edge detection:

(1) Optimal Detection: the probability of missing the true edge and the probability of false detection of the non-edge are as small as possible.
(2) Optimal positioning criterion: the position of the detected edge point is closest to the position of the actual edge point, or the extent to which the detected edge deviates from the true edge of the object due to noise.

(3) The detection point corresponds to the edge point one to one correspondence: the edge point detected by the operator should correspond to the actual edge point one-to-one.

The basic idea of the Canny edge detection operator is to first select a certain Gauss filter to smooth the image, then use the non-maxima Suppression technique to process the smoothed image to obtain the final edge image. The main code for bank card edge detection using opencv's canny in Python is as follows: cv2.Canny (opened, 50, 150, apertureSize = 3).

Then this paper use morphological opening operation to erodes the unrelated area of the bank card frame and only retains the bank card border. The angle of the top line or the bottom line of the bank card after the canny detection is returned by the opencv Hough test. Get a level bank card by spinning. The Hough detection function lines = cv2.HoughLines(). The Hough test returns the distance between a straight line and the origin, and the vertical and horizontal angles. Calculate the two points on the line and return an angle through the math.atan() function, which is the angle at which the bank card rotates clockwise. The result is shown in Fig. 2.

Fig. 2. Rotating bank card

2.5 Bank Card Number Extraction and Segmentation

The outermost border of the bank card can be found through the findContours function of opencv. This will extract the bank card portion. According to prior knowledge, the bank card number is known to be in the upper 1/3 of the bank card, and the last one is about 2/5 of the bank card. This will extract the bank card number portion. The effect is shown in Fig. 3.

621669 0400000434475

Fig. 3. Bank card number part

By extracting the bank card each number portion, continue to use opencv's findContours to find the outermost border and extract the number.

3 Template Making

This paper's template is intercepted by entering 0–9 in the word software. The normalization of the number size refers to a unified geometric transformation of numeric characters of different sizes, making it a numeric character of uniform size. Adjust the numbers to a 16×16 picture. By writing a program, the transformation to a binary matrix is represented by 1 and the background is represented by 0. The effect of the number 7 is shown in Fig. 4.

```
1111111111111110
1111111111111110
0000000011111100
0000000011110000
0000000111100000
0000001111000000
0000011111000000
0000111111000000
0001111110000000
0011111100000000
0011111000000000
0011111000000000
0111111000000000
0111110000000000
0011110000000000
0011110000000000
```

Fig. 4. Number 7 template

4 Recongnition

The background of the number to be identified is expressed in 1 and the number part in 0. The number to be identified is superimposed on each template of 0–9. The matching coefficient is obtained by counting the mismatched pixels of the superimposed matrix, and the minimum value of the matching coefficient is the best matching.

5 Analysis of Results

Evaluate the quality of the pattern recognition system, focusing on accuracy and running time. Select bank card pictures from 10 different bank cards of Bank of China, 5 bank cards with different numbers from CCB, 5 bank cards with different numbers from ICBC, and 5 bank cards with different numbers from Shanghai Pudong Development Bank. And put the bank card in different rotation angles of different backgrounds. The sample picture is a total of 1000 pictures, and the picture is in jpg format. At the same time, with the bank card number identification method based on the left and right contour features and the method based on the digital structure feature, the comparison experiment is carried out under the condition that the experimental equipment, the running software version and the sample picture are consistent. And conduct an objective and fair evaluation of the experiment. The experimental results are calculated by the recognition rate calculation formula and the average response time calculation formula, and the statistics are shown in Table 1.

Table 1. Comparative test data sheet

Recognition algorithm	Recognition rate	Average response time(s)
Template matching algorithm	96.0%	1.3326523
Digital structure feature algorithm	80.2%	1.3554986
Left and right contour feature algorithm	88.5%	1.5646824

6 Conclusion

The paper design is based on the template matching method of the bank card number identification algorithm. The bank card image is preprocessed by the opencv module in Python language, and finally the bank card number is identified by template matching. The algorithm is simple and practical, and with good robustness. This algorithm recognition rate is 96.0%. It is can continue to develop applications in depth.

References

1. Han, J., Xu, F., Chen, Z., Liu, H.: An interactive phone number recognition method based on deep learning. J. Beijing Univ. Aeronaut. Astronaut. **44**(05), 1074–1080 (2018)
2. Wang, Y., Bai, B.: Research and implementation of digital recognition of printed body. J. Changchun Univ. Sci. Technol. (Nat. Sci. Ed.) **39**(01), 101–103 (2016)

3. Wei, H.: Research on Identification Method of Digital Reading of Water Meter Head. Nanjing University of Science and Technology, Nanjing (2007)
4. Rivera, A.R., Chae, O.: Spatiotemporal directional number transitional graph for dynamic texture recognition. IEEE Trans. Pattern Anal. Mach. Intell. **37**, 2146–2152 (2015)
5. Liu, Y., Pan, Q.: A digital recognition method based on BP neural network. Microcomput. Appl. **31**(7), 36–39 (2012)
6. Fareh, M., Boussaid, O., Chalal, R.: Semantic metadata mediation: XML, RDF and RuleML. In: ACS International Conference on Computer Systems and Applications (AICCSA), vol. 1, pp. 1–8 (2013)
7. He, K., Zhang, X., Ren, S., Sun, J.: Deep residual learning for image recognition. In: Proceedings of the IEEE Conference on Computer Vision and Pattern recognition, pp. 770–778. IEEE Press, Piscataway (2016)
8. Zhu, R.: Research and design of electronic homework correction system based on machine vision. Nanjing Normal University (2017)
9. Wang, J., Ma, X., Duan, G., Xue, H.: Handwritten numeral recognition in the context of edge intelligence. Comput. Appl., 1–11 (2019). http://kns.cnki.net/kcms/detail/51.1307.TP.20190723.1256.004.html
10. Ren, X., Ding, X., Tao, Z., Keys, H.X.: A multi-classifier based non-segmented handwritten numeric string recognition algorithm. Comput. Appl., Res. 1–6 (2019). https://doi.org/10.19734/j.issn.1001-3695.2019.03.0097

A Security Situation Assessment Method Based on Neural Network

Xiangyan Tang[2], Meizhu Chen[2(✉)], Jieren Cheng[1,2], Jinying Xu[2], and Hui Li[2]

[1] State Key Laboratory of Marine Resource Utilization in South China Sea, Hainan University, Haikou 570228, China
[2] School of Computer and Cyberspace Security, Hainan University, Haikou 570228, China
1073646111@qq.com

Abstract. In the big data environment, the scale of attacks of Distributed Denial of Service (DDoS) continues to expand rapidly. The traditional network situation assessment method cannot effectively evaluate the security situation of DDoS. A security situation assessment method based on deep learning and a security situation assessment model based on neural network are proposed. The model uses convolutional neural network (CNN), back propagation algorithm (BP) and Long Short-Term memory neural network (LSTM) to learn various network security indicators to achieve a comprehensive assessment of the network. The experimental results show that the model can more easily and accurately evaluate the network security status, which is more accurate and flexible than the existing evaluation methods.

Keywords: Distributed Denial of Service · Security situation assessment · Deep learning · Neural network

1 Introduction

Network security issues are increasingly becoming a major threat in the application, management and development of computer networks. The frequent occurrence of network intrusion has suffered huge losses to people's lives and social production. Among these network security threats, Distributed Denial of Service (DDoS) is gradually becoming one of the most devastating threats due to its serious potential impact and unpredictability. DDoS attacks seriously threaten the security of the network and become a major problem in the Internet environment [1, 2].

Under the new network environment, the traditional network situation assessment method cannot effectively evaluate the security situation of DDoS. This paper studies the deep learning methods, and establishes a security situation assessment evaluation model. The model uses Convolution Neural Network (CNN), Back Propagation Algorithm (BP) and Long Short-Term Memory (LSTM) to perform various network security indicators and to achieve a comprehensive assessment of the network security situation. The experimental results show that the proposed model can evaluate the network security situation more intuitively and effectively.

J. Vaidya et al. (Eds.): CSS 2019, LNCS 11983, pp. 579–587, 2019.
https://doi.org/10.1007/978-3-030-37352-8_52

2   Related Work

With the increasing complexity of the network environment and the continuous advancement of technology, the network attack behavior has gradually become distributed, remote and virtualized. Arbor Networks' report shows that DDos accounted for as much as 48% of all cyber threats in recent years [3], and it is clear that DDoS attacks have become the main cybercrime in today's society. Endsley first proposed the concept of Situation Assessment (SA). Then, Tim Bass introduced SA into the field of network security and propose the concept of network security situational awareness. Jian Xu et al. improved the Merkle Tree (DFHMT) algorithm based on dynamic complete homomorphic encryption, analyzed the security of DFHMT, and calculated the storage, communication and computational overhead of DFHMT. The results show that DFHMT achieves a performance balance between the client and the server, and has certain performance advantages for lightweight devices [4]. Li et al. proposed L-EncDB, a new lightweight encryption mechanism for databases that preserves the database structure and supports efficient SQL-based queries. Li built a new format-preserving Encryption (FPE) scheme that can be used to encrypt all types of strings stored in the database [5]. Wen et al. proposed the first lattice-based linearly homomorphic signatures in the standard model, which settle the open problem that there are still no lattice-based linearly homomorphic signature in the standard model [6]. Ma et al. present the generic secure outsourcing schemes enabling users to securely outsource the computations of exponentiations to the untrusted cloud servers. With the techniques, a batch of exponentiations can be efficiently computed by the user with only $O\,(n + t)$ multiplications, where n is the number of bits of the exponent [7].

However, the above methods also have some limitations. First, traditional methods are not easy to build a preventive reference model for various attacks, and it is difficult to identify logical relationships between alerts from multiple attack sources. Furthermore, the above method requires a large amount of engineering and professional domain knowledge in designing the feature extractor. The key advantage of deep learning is that it can perform feature learning through a common learning process, which greatly improves engineering efficiency. When constructing a model of non-linear complex relationships, the neural network can find the optimal value in the constant adjustment of weights, so that the model is continuously optimized. This is very important because in a networked environment, many of the relationships between inputs and outputs are non-linear and complex. This paper proposes and establishes a security situation assessment method based on deep learning and a security situation assessment model based on neural network. Firstly, data preprocessing is performed on the network traffic data, followed by further feature fusion after dimension reduction of the high dimensional feature data, and the pre-processed network traffic data is trained and class predicted using several different deep learning methods, and then reserved. The test data is taken into the trained these neural network models for testing experiments. Finally, the confusion output matrix is used to evaluate the model output results, and the output values are compared with the individual characteristic indicators.

3 Security Situation Assessment Model Based on Neural Network

3.1 DDoS Attack Data Preprocessing

Given a normal network flow U with n sample IP packets and a network flow V with m IP packets which need to be detected, we define each IP packet as (Ti, Si, Di), where Ti is the arrival time of the packet i, Si and Di denotes its source IP and the destination IP respectively, and we will take a same Δt as a parameter for both training and detection algorithm [2]. With the above definitions, in the training course, we collect a subgroup of samples IP packets G_k from normal network flow U within the k-th Δt. Once we've reached the end of every Δt, a filter is then applied to G_k to drop out all samples inside without a valid public IPv4 address of its S. Thus, the filtered sample group is defined as:

$$\forall G_{k_i} \in G_k \tag{1}$$

$G_{k_j} \in F_k$ if $S_{G_{k_j}}$ is valid public IPv4 address. While obtaining each Fk, we incrementally build an IP address set O which denotes our old users. O_{max} represents the maximum number of old user appeared in some certain Δt. We store all the source IP S in the dictionary W_k with S as the key and the times it occurs as the value, $W_k = [S_k, i, O_k, i]$. Then we let set G_k equals to all the keys in W_k, and we define the $W_k [S_k, i]$ as the times of the corresponding source IP S_k, i occurred in the k-th time interval. At the end of each Δt, we calculate four features of the k-th time interval. We define four features below.

Definition 1: The percentage of old user appeared in current k-th Δt over the maximum of our old user of some certain time intervals. We define this percentage as P_k:

$$P_k = \frac{|G_k \cap O| - O_{max}}{O_{max}} \tag{2}$$

Definition 2: The amount of changes of our new users in amount compared with the amount of the average new user N, We define this amount as C_k:

$$C_k = ||G_k \backslash O|| - N \tag{3}$$

Definition 3: The ratio of current new users to our maximum old users.

$$Z_k = \frac{||G_k \backslash O||}{O_{max}} \tag{4}$$

Definition 4: Current access rate of new users. To be specific, it denotes that there are average accessing requests per second per new user. We define this average accessing rate per new user per second as E_k:

$$E_k = \frac{\sum \left\{ W_k[S_{k,j}] | \forall_{S_{k,j}} \in (G_k \backslash O) \right\}}{||G_k \backslash O|| \Delta t} \tag{5}$$

3.2   Feature Classification Based on Neural Network

3.2.1   The Input Layer of Neural Network

Based on the results of the above feature extraction, this paper begins to assess the impact of DDoS attacks. We define the risk R, which represents the degree of risk of the system under the DDoS attack.

The mode of network feature classification algorithm based on neural network includes three steps, namely BP neural network construction, training and classification. The algorithm flow is shown in the following Fig. 1:

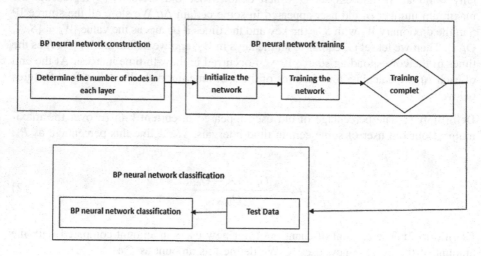

Fig. 1. BP neural network algorithm flow chart

Taking the extracted feature value α, P, C, Z and E as the input of the neural network. Since the input features are five-dimensional, the input layer of the BP neural network is set to five nodes. In the process of constructing a neural network, it is necessary to set a series of indicators [11, 12], which correspond to the neuron nodes of the input layer, respectively.

In order to make the neural network converge quickly, this paper normalizes these eigenvalues. The calculation process for normalizing [14] the feature value P is as shown in the formula (8), and similarly, the same normalization process is performed for C, Z, and E to obtain a new feature value group.

$$P_i = \frac{P_i - P_{\min}}{P_{\max} - P_{\min}} \tag{6}$$

3.2.2   The Hidden Layer of Neural Network

The hidden layer of the neural network completes the mapping of the neural network from M dimension to N dimension. In the process of constructing the hidden layer, because the number of neuron nodes in the input layer is relatively small, in order to prevent over-fitting phenomenon, the neural network security situation assessment mode uses a single-level structure [8–10]. In addition, determining the number of hidden layer nodes in the neural network hidden layer construction process is also related to the performance of the model. If the number of nodes is too large, the time of the neural network learning process will increase greatly. Excessive training will easily lead to over-fitting, resulting in poor learning results. To make the neural network get a better fitting effect, it is necessary to use an activation function, which acts on each neuron network node and increases the non-linear properties of the neural network. In this paper, the sigmoid function is used. The sigmoid function is a sigmoid curve, its formula is as follows.

$$y = sigmoid(x) = \frac{1}{1 + e^{-x}} \tag{7}$$

In the neural network structure, the logistic regression function is often used as a threshold function, and its output data is in the open interval of (0, 1), as shown in Fig. 2.

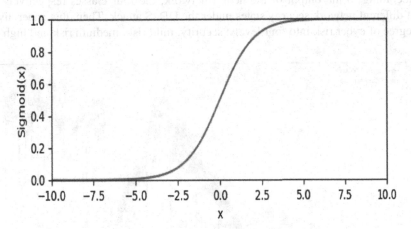

Fig. 2. The graph of Logistic function

Under normal circumstances, the number of new IPs accessing the website is small, the users accessing a website are basically fixed users, and the number of new IPs is relatively stable and maintained at a relatively small value. When a DDoS attack occurs, a large number of new IPs are accompanied for a certain period of time. Therefore, it is very meaningful to study the number of new IPs in the attack and the maximum number of new IPs in normal time. However, in order to avoid misinterpreting network congestion or hot events as DDoSe attacks, we pay extra attention to the number of IP addresses accessed in a short period of time. Under normal circumstances, when users visit the website, they find that the network is congested. After several attempts, they will give up or temporarily not access, but the zombies will continue to send requests continuously, so the IP address in a fixed period of time. We are introducing information entropy [15],

$$\text{Ent(D)} = -\sum_{k=1}^{|y|} P_k \log_2 P_k \tag{8}$$

The greater the information gain, the higher the accuracy of the network risk classification.

$$\text{Gain(D, a)} = \text{Ent(D)} - \sum_{V=1}^{V} \frac{|D^v|}{D} Ent(D^v) \tag{9}$$

Where D represents Sample collection, y represents the number of samples in the network collection, a is discrete attributes, V indicates feature number.

3.2.3   The Output Layer of Neural Network

Finally, based on the previous experiments, this paper constructs the output layer of the neural network in the security situation assessment model, and divides the network security state into four different risk levels, and establishes the output layer of the neural network with four nodes.

According to the output of the neural network, the four classes respectively represent different network security states under the DDoS attack. Then, this paper divides the degree of cyber risk into four levels: security, mild risk, medium risk and high risk.

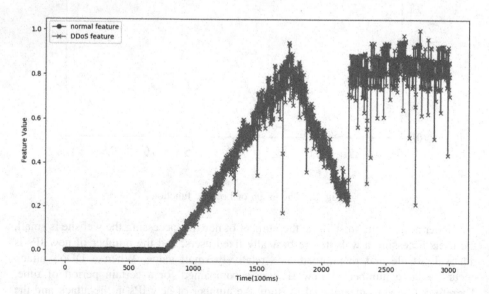

Fig. 3. PCZE value of the network flow at 100 ms

4 Experiment

This article uses the CAIDA DDoS Attack 2007 data as sample data to train CNN, BP, and LSTM, respectively. The total size of the dataset is 21 GB, and the attack started around 21:13, caused the network load to grow rapidly (in minutes) from about 200 kilobits per second to 80 megabits per second. We trained our model with different seconds, and the proposed algorithm successfully distinguished normal flow and DDoS flow as shown in Fig. 3.

The DDoS attack started around the 79th second. It is worth noting that the PCZE value dropped sharply around 219 s.

The CNN training adopts the feature fusion method, extracts the shallow and the deep features, and further tests and optimizes the obtained vector information. In the BP training process, the weight of ownership is randomly assigned. The BP algorithm adjusts the weights by repeating the two processes of forward propagation and error propagation to achieve to minimize the actual output value and the expected output. The first phase of LSTM is the Forgotten Gate. The Forgotten Layer determines which information needs to be forgotten from the state. The next phase is the input gate. The input gate determines which new information can be stored in the state. The last phase is the output gate, and the output gate determine output value.

The reserved test data is brought into the trained three neural network models for test experiments. The expected output values are compared with the various characteristic indicators to verify the scientific validity of the training model.

Table 1. Network security status

Risk level	Security level	Network status
R1	Security	Normal
R2	Mild risk	Minor impact
R3	Moderate risk	Large impact
R4	High risk	Serious damage

A portion of the output results of network situation assessment model based on CNN, BP, and LSTM are listed in Tables 1, 2, and 3, respectively.

Table 2. Output result of assessment model based on convolutional neural network

Input data	P	C	Z	E	β	Output	Risk level
T1	0.81	0.78	0.80	0.79	1	0.38	R1
T2	0.67	0.37	0.64	0.65	1	0.45	R2
T3	0.15	0.12	0.14	0.12	0	0.36	R1
T4	0.91	0.90	0.88	0.88	1	0.92	R4
T5	0.83	0.76	0.76	0.80	1	0.68	R3

Table 3. Output result of assessment model based on BP neural network

Input data	P	C	Z	E	β	Output	Risk level
T1	0.81	0.78	0.80	0.79	1	0.3	R1
T2	0.67	0.67	0.64	0.65	1	0.43	R2
T3	0.15	0.12	0.14	0.12	0	0.9	R1
T4	0.91	0.90	0.88	0.88	1	0.92	R4
T5	0.83	0.76	0.76	0.80	1	0.72	R3

Table 4. Output result of assessment model based on LSTM network

Input data	P	C	Z	E	β	Output	Risk level
T1	0.81	0.78	0.80	0.89	1	0.59	R1
T2	0.67	0.67	0.64	0.65	1	0.56	R2
T3	0.15	0.12	0.14	0.12	0	0.13	R1
T4	0.91	0.90	0.88	0.88	1	0.90	R4
T5	0.83	0.76	0.76	0.80	1	0.75	R3

It can be seen from Tables 2, 3 and 4 that the relationship between the five evaluation indicators P, C, Z, E and β is non-linear, and these indicators can reflect the security of the network. We use three neural network methods to extract and fuse the features in T1 = 50 ms, T2 = 100 ms, T3 = 500 ms, T4 = 1000, and T5 = 2000 ms. According to the evaluation results, the three methods are consistent in determining the risk level to which the network belongs, so we can make basic judgments on the network security situation.

5   Conclusion

For the new network environment, the traditional network situation assessment method cannot effectively evaluate the security situation of DDoS. This paper proposes a security situation assessment model based on neural network to quantitatively evaluate the security status of DDoS attacks across the network. In order to analyze and evaluate network security risks more reasonably, the model analyzes the application of deep learning network security situational awareness, and combines common deep learning methods and random gradient descent methods to quantitatively evaluate the security status of DDoS attacks on the entire network. Firstly, the security situation data is input, and the preliminary model is obtained by feature learning and parameter estimation. Then the model is optimized to obtain the security situation of the whole network. This method plays an important role on the research of network situational awareness model based on statistical pattern recognition. Experiments show that compared with related methods, the proposed model can more intuitively and effectively evaluate the security situation of DDoS attacks in the new network environment, and provides a powerful reference for taking appropriate preventive measures.

Acknowledgements. This work was supported by the Hainan Provincial Natural Science Foundation of China [2018CXTD333, 617048]; National Natural Science Foundation of China [61762033, 61702539]; Hainan University Doctor Start Fund Project [kyqd1328]; Hainan University Youth Fund Project [qnjj1444]; Social Development Project of Public Welfare Technology Application of Zhejiang Province [LGF18F020019]; Ministry of Education Humanities and Social Sciences Research Planning Fund Project (19YJA710010).

References

1. Cheng, J., Zhang, C., Tang, X., Sheng, V.S., Dong, Z., Li, J.: Adaptive DDoS attack: detection method based on multiple-kernel learning. Secur. Commun. Netw. **2018** (2018)
2. Cheng, J., Xu, R., Tang, X., Sheng, V.S., Cai, C.: An abnormal network flow feature sequence prediction approach for DDoS attacks detection in big data environment. Comput. Mater. Continua **55**(1), 095 (2018)
3. Arbor Networks: 2012 Infrastructure Security Report. http://tinyurl.com/ag6tht4. Accessed 22 May 2019
4. Xu, J., Wei, L., Zhang, Y., Wang, A., Gao, C.: Dynamic fully homomorphic encryption-based Merkle tree for lightweight streaming authenticated data structures. J. Netw. Comput. Appl. **107**, 113–124 (2018)
5. Li, J., Liu, Z., Chen, X., Xhafa, F., Tan, X., Wong, D.S.: L-EncDB: a lightweight framework for privacy-preserving data queries in cloud computing. Knowl.-Based Syst. **79**, 18–26 (2015)
6. Chen, W., Lei, H., Qi, K.: Lattice-based linearly homomorphic signatures in the standard model. Theor. Comput. Sci. **634**, 47–54 (2016). S0304397516300378
7. Ma, X., Li, J., Zhang, F.: Outsourcing computation of modular exponentiations in cloud computing. Cluster Comput. **16**(4), 787–796 (2013)
8. Guang, K., Guangming, T., Xia, D., Shuo, W., Kun, W: A network security situation assessment method based on attack intention perception. In: 2016 2nd IEEE International Conference on Computer and Communications (ICCC). IEEE (2016)
9. Xiang, S., Lv, Y., Xia, C., Li, Y., Wang, Z.: A method of network security situation assessment based on hidden Markov model (2015)
10. Luo, J.H., Wu, J., Lin, W.: [IEEE 2017 IEEE International Conference on Computer Vision (ICCV) - Venice, Italy, 22–29 October 2017] 2017 IEEE International Conference on Computer Vision (ICCV) - ThiNet: A Filter Level Pruning Method for Deep Neural Network Compression, pp. 5068–5076 (2017)
11. Wang, G., Lin, L., Ding, S., Li, Y., Wang, Q., Dari: distance metric and representation integration for person verification (2016)
12. Jian, S., Gui, Z., Ji, S., Shen, J., Tan, H., Yi, T.: Cloud-aided lightweight certificateless authentication protocol with anonymity for wireless body area networks. J. Netw. Comput. Appl. **106**, 117–123 (2018). S1084804518300031
13. Cheng, J., Yin, J., Liu, Y., Cai, Z., Li, M.: DDoS attack detection algorithm using IP address features. In: Deng, X., Hopcroft, J.E., Xue, J. (eds.) FAW 2009. LNCS, vol. 5598, pp. 207–215. Springer, Heidelberg (2009). https://doi.org/10.1007/978-3-642-02270-8_22
14. Gajera, V., Shubham, Gupta, R., Jana, P.K.: An effective multi-objective task scheduling algorithm using min-max normalization in cloud computing. In: International Conference on Applied & Theoretical Computing & Communication Technology. IEEE (2017)
15. Liang, J., Shi, Z.: The information entropy, rough entropy and knowledge granulation in rough set theory. Int. J. Uncertainty Fuzziness Knowl. Based Syst. **12**(01), 37–46 (2008)

Main Enabling Technologies in Industry 4.0 and Cybersecurity Threats

Lei Shi[1(✉)], Xiao Chen[1], Sheng Wen[1], and Yang Xiang[1,2]

[1] School of Software and Electrical Engineering, Swinburne University of Technology, Hawthorn, Australia
{lshi,xiaochen,swen,yxiang}@swin.edu.au
[2] State Key Laboratory of Integrated Service Networks, Xidian University, Xi'an, China

Abstract. Since 2012, at the Hanover Messe Fair, Germany introduced the concept of Industry 4.0 as using transformative technologies to connect the physical world to the cyber world. The past three industrial revolutions all had their own enabling technologies, but this is the first time that so many enabling technologies are impacting manufacturing industries at the same time. In the industrial areas, these enabling technologies open a lot of possibilities, for instance, predictive maintenance, virtual commission, re-configurable factory, remote data visualization and monitoring, data analytics, etc. which leads to Industry 4.0 revolution. This article provides an overview of the main enabling technologies in Industry 4.0 and possible cybersecurity threats to them.

Keywords: Industry 4.0 · Cybersecurity

1 Introduction

In the current industry, Industry 4.0 is the hottest topic. In Defining and Sizing the Industrial Internet [1] David Floyer estimated that, in respect to the global GDP, the value of Industry 4.0 will reach $15 trillion by 2020. Every major economy has invested tremendously to evolute their industries.

In each of the prior industrial revolutions, there are some key enabling technologies. Within the context of Industry 4.0, it is the first time that there is such a variety of enabling technologies, which creates new possibilities in manufacturing and other industrial areas. The main enabling technologies in the Industry 4.0 are as below [24]:

– 3D printing
– Cloud and edge computing
– Machine learning and data analytics
– Digital Twin
– Cobot
– AR (Augmented reality)

J. Vaidya et al. (Eds.): CSS 2019, LNCS 11983, pp. 588–597, 2019.
https://doi.org/10.1007/978-3-030-37352-8_53

These enabling technologies are the backbones of the Industry 4.0. Without them, it would not be possible to realize the blue print of the fourth industrial revolution. If we can understand the possible cybersecurity risks of each enabling technology, then analysis of cybersecurity of a complicated system within the context of Industry 4.0 can be simplified into two steps: step one, understand what enabling technologies that are used in the system; step two, based on the list generated in step one we can easily identify the possible threats.

In the current literature, there is a lack of research which looks at the cybersecurity of Industry 4.0 from the perspective of these enabling technologies. This article provides an overview of the main enabling technologies in Industry 4.0 and possible cybersecurity threats to them.

The structure of this article is that in Sect. 2, there is a brief review of the main enabling technologies in Industry 4.0. In Sect. 3, the cyber threats to each of main enabling technologies are explored. In Sect. 4, we brief introduce topics around the future work. In the end, we conclude the paper.

2   Main Enabling Technologies in Industry 4.0

2.1   3D Printing

With thirty years of development, 3D printing or additive manufacture has been widely used in the manufacturing industries and areas of Biomaterials, Aerospace, Buildings, Protective structures [20].

One main prospect of a smart factory in Industry 4.0 is reconfigurable manufacturing systems. Within this system, based on the order of customers, MES (manufacture execution system) can reconfigure the production process or functions to archive the manufacture of personalized product without needing the intervention of staff in the factory. Dongkyun Kim and Joon-Min Gil have introduced a Remote 3D Printing manufacturing process with 3D printing and software-defined networking (SDN) technologies [14]. Other related research work has presented the possibility of cloud-based manufacturing using remote 3D printing technology and new concepts based on remote 3D printing such as Cloud-Based Design and Manufacturing (CBDM) [26].

Within the examples above, 3D designed files can be shared among manufacturer sites which makes it possible to realize distributed manufacturing or collaborative design. Customized product can easily be built without much additional cost.

2.2   Machine Learning and Data Analytics

Machine learning and data analytics are both under the umbrella of data science which includes a lot of disciplines. Machine learning is also a subset of artificial intelligence. From the raw data that has been gathered, artificial intelligence needs to have the ability to gain their own knowledge by extracting the patterns them- selves, where machine learning is defined from this ability [13]. Data analytics is to acquire useful insights from gathered data but does not necessarily need to find the pattern. Overall, with machine learning and data analytics, people use the data gathered to either predict the future or create a new view to visualize the data.

2.3 Cloud and Edge Computing

NIST (National Institute of Standards and Technology) has defined cloud computing as a model for enabling ubiquitous, convenient, on-demand network access to a shared pool of configurable computing resources (e.g., networks, servers, storage, applications and services) that can be rapidly provisioned and released with minimal management effort or service provider interaction [18]. Edge or fog computing means the computing happens at the edge of a network, which is a complement to cloud computing. The existence of an edge device is generally due to the latency of cloud or pre-processing requirements before uploading data to the cloud. Siemens has come up with a cloud mainly for the Industrial 4.0 area which is called MindSphere. One of the main features of MindSphere is that it is designed to secure the Cyber-Physical infrastructure [25].

2.4 Digital Twin

Dr. Michael Grieves at the University of Michigan defined the term Digital Twin in around 2001 to 2002. The concept of this initial introduction is a virtual representation of what has been manufactured. Digital Twin is reported as the number 5 strategic trend for 2017 according to Gartners report titled Top 10 strategic Trends for 2017 [2]. The research has been focusing on different values of Digital Twin such as Visibility, Predictive or What if analysis.

Depending on the level of complexity and application, Digital Twin can be utilized in different fields. The simplest one is just a virtual representation of a physical asset. The second level is with Predictive or What if analysis ability. This is a more promising area but includes a lot more complexity. In this level, Digital Twin should be able to achieve one or more functions such as Collision analyses, Virtual commissioning and planning and optimization, etc.

2.5 Collaborative Robot

There is a shortage of labour around the world, and for a long time factories have been turning to automation to solve this problem. Traditionally, the industrial robots are big and very powerful. Usually, they are enclosed in a cage as their power and speed can injure or even cause death to employees. If the cage is opened, then the robot shuts itself down. The idea of collaborative robots comes from a mission in 1995 which aimed to come up with a way in which robots could safely work side by side with humans in their respective environments. In the current industry, collaborative robots, referred to as cobots, can be used in a wide range of production tasks to perform flexible and safe services teamed with humans.

2.6   AR

Augmented reality devices display virtual elements on top of the real physical environment. In real time, it can provide us with virtual data and information together with the real world. The main applications of Augmented reality in Industry 4.0 are: 1. Support production process and increase the productivity [17]. 2. Maintenance equipment in a factory or remote service [7].

3   Cybersecurity Threats to Enabling Technologies

Within the contexts of Industry 4.0, the enabling technologies which are introduced in Sect. 2 are the puzzle pieces and they are integrated to form a complicated system. If we can understand the cybersecurity threats to each enabling technology, then we can intuitively understand the threats to the whole system. For this very purpose, a taxonomy of such threats is presented. The tax- onomy in this section has been created according to the ISO/IEC 27000:2009 [12] which defines the information security model as availability, integrity, confidentiality. On top of these three, the fourth element is added which is safety. It is unique as cyber physical systems not only deal with the virtual world but also does control and gets feedback from the physical world.

Lezzi et al. in [16] has summarized the main threats within the scope of Industry 4.0. In Sect. 3, Table 4 of [16] is used as a reference to point out the possible threats to each main enabling technology in Industry 4.0.

3.1   3D Printing

3D printing or additive manufacturing is the key to reconfigurable manufacturing and distributed manufacturing. In such a system, 3D design files need to be sent from one machine to another during this process. Due to this process, data Integrity or more specifically, 3D design file integrity is the main problem. The attacker may tamper into the communication channels using Data tampering, spoofing or man-in-the-middle attacks. In traditional manufacturing, the design files are stored locally. However, confidentiality problems arise when the design files are shared among smart factories. Eavesdropping and Escalation of privilege are the possible threats which can cause the loss of confidentiality. As for availability, Denial of Service (DoS) attack using massive traffic can cause the unavailability of the 3D printer. Malware, worms and virus infections can be used to crush MES so that 3D printers are not able to receive customer orders. Safety problems arise when a design is hacked and modified through the process of communication as in Integrity threats. For instance, in the building area, if the 3D design file is modified by hackers which causes a defective printed pillar, it may lead to the crash of the building. In another scenario, it is possible to introduce a hidden structural defect to a drone propeller by attacking the 3D printing process [10].

3.2 Cloud and Edge Computing / Machine Learning and Data Analytics

Since the data is sent out to the cloud service provider, control over the data has been relinquished from the cloud user. Within the context of Industry 4.0, there are mainly 2 layers of threats to the cloud related service. One layer of threats is from network and communication channels when industrial field devices are linked to cloud. The other layer of threats is from the cloud service provider itself. Although cloud service providers are more specialised in remote storage and service, they are still facing a variety of threats from both internal and external sources which will affect data integrity, Confidentiality and availability.

We have included Machine learning and data analytics in this section as these services generally provide a cloud-based environment. Threats to these technologies are similar. It is worth pointing out that Machine learning and data analytics can be used as threat defence technology which can detect the threats to the CPS in Industry 4.0. To protect both physical and cyber parts of the system and detect anomalous activities, Nour Moustafa in [19] has proposed a threat intelligence technique based on beta mixture-hidden Markov models (MHMMs).

We use a real system, MindSphere as mentioned in Sect. 2, to explain the possible threats. As shown in Fig. 1, a digital factory which utilises the cloud service, there are 3 levels which are cloud level, factory level and field level. Edge devices are used at the edge of the network before data is uploaded to the cloud. Between MindSphere and the factory, a connection device called MindConnect is used to communicate directly from PLCs to MindSphere. The attacks can be launched against MindSphere or MindConnect. Regarding MindSphere, data stored in the cloud needs to be authenticated in case it has been modified in the process of communication. Solutions are proposed to try to keep the integrity of the data in the Cloud by audit [22]. Other threats can be from attacks to gain the access to the cloud storage using Malware, worms and viruses infection or Zero-day attacks methods. In term of confidentiality, BMI (Federal Office for Informa- tion Security) identifies the threat could be Cloud resources are not sufficiently isolated [3].

As a specialised industrial device, MindConnect has measures to defend itself. For example, it encrypts all the messages send out. Also, MindConnect uses one direction communication which means data can only flow from field level to cloud level, not vice versa. By using these measures, it is hard for the attacker to threaten the system with data manipulation attacks. At the same time, the attacker will not be able to cause safety threats by attacking the field due to one-way traffic setting of MindConnect, but availability of the Cloud may be attacked by DoS.

3.3 Digital Twin

Digital Twin has a very broad range of functions and applications. We can categorise the digital twin based on its real time ability. The main threats to

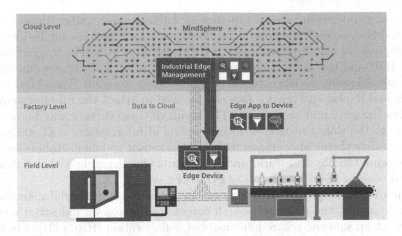

Fig. 1. MindSphere cloud in digital factory [4]

digital twins without real time ability are mainly from Malware, worms and virus infections (in an accidental or intentional way), Phishing and Insider attacks and unwitting behaviours.

Another type of Digital Twins can reflect the real time operation of a complicated system. To monitor the real time operation of an instance of a complicated system e.g. space vehicle, wind turbine, the Digital Twin in this level needs to have the real time analysis ability. It necessitates complete real-time management of complex materials, structures and systems.

As to this type of digital twin, confidentiality and integrity of data are under threat as the data is transferred from the field to a remote sever or another site. The threats can be from Data tampering, spoofing or man-in-the-middle attacks, Eavesdropping or data interface and Insider attacks, and unwitting behaviours. As for the availability, then threats like Jamming, Collision and False Routing Information can stop or modify the data being transferred. This can also cause Availability problems such as Dos threats. When it comes to the safety, the wrong information caused by an attack can make the machine or technical staff make wrong judgements of working conditions. Then it causes actual damage to the device and create threats to the safety.

Similar to machine learning and data analytics, digital twin itself can be used as a tool to analyse the CPS. It will be a very promising research field in the future [9].

3.4   Collaborative Robot

Safety is the main threat to a CPS or smart factory which uses Cobots, especially if these robots are designed to work side by side with humans. One difference between IT (information technology) and CPS in Industry 4.0 is that traditional security techniques individually focus on addressing security for system components rather than the interactions among these components. Hence, the main goal is addressing safety (absence of failure) issues rather than security (unauthorised access) [8]. One example of an attack is from an Insider such as a disgruntled employee who may use Escalation of privilege to grab control of the HMI and use the robot to create some damage. The threats can also be from external resources like external communication channels. Then Man-in-the-Middle and Replay (playback), Dos can be used to attack the robot system and threaten Integrity and availability. The result of these threats may be physical damage to the Robot instead of losing control of information in IT areas. The other possible threat also unique to Robots is sensor spoofing. Robots use sensors to sense the physical world and then react. One example is that a drone is crashed because of an attack to the gyroscope sensor [23].

Due to the complexity of threats to the robot in an industrial manufacturing environment, the present research targets to develop an industrial security framework for safe and secure human-robot collaboration (HRC) [21]. The other promising research is to develop framework to deriving and monitoring the Control Invariant of the robots. As this method extracts information from robots' physical properties, control algorithm and physics, any abnormality which causes safety threats will be detected, no matter if it is internal or external [11].

3.5   AR

To display the virtual information in the Augmented reality, AR devices generally need to exchange information with a remote server. During this process, as for integrity, there is a threat to the synchronisation between virtual representation and legitimate data. At the same time, when information is maliciously modified, the wrong information may cause fatal injury which is a serious safety issue. For instance, a service staff may touch a high voltage area which is indicated as a low voltage area by attacker. Regarding availability, again, Zero-day attacks may crash the AR device like a helmet or smart phone. Production staff or technicians then need to wait for the device to come back to normal before they can continue with production or servicing. In terms to the confidentiality, any VR device needs a camera to identify the physical world so that correct virtual information can be displayed. If the camera is compromised by Phishing or Insider attacks, then the attacker can see the site directly with the camera.

4   Future Work

For future work, one main obstacle is the lack of Industry 4.0 testbeds. Testbeds for similar purposes were built before [15], but none of them have been able to set up a full-scale factory which incorporates most of the main enabling technologies and capacities in Industry 4.0. Europe has started to build such a testbed which is aimed at designing, developing, integrating and demonstrating a set of main enabling capabilities to foster optimisation and resilience of the Digital Factory and Factories of the Future (FoF) [9]. In Australia, FoF in the Swinburne University of Technology is also building capacity in this area [6].

New technologies bring more opportunities, but they also at the same time bring cybersecurity threats. Cybersecurity threats analysis on other new Industry 4.0 technologies like smart sensors, blockchain and 5G are also necessary in future work.

5 Conclusion

Industry 4.0 system is generally a very complicated system with heterogeneous components and technologies and there is a great signage of cyber and physical elements in Industry 4.0 systems. For companies which plan to commit to evolute their factory and use enabling technologies in Industry 4.0, it is a challenge for them to understand the technology and possible cybersecurity threats. It would not be enough to use the security measures for traditional IT systems - further measures which can be applied to the Industry 4.0 environment need be researched and developed. But there is a lack of understanding and research from cybersecurity experts on the main enabling technologies in Industry 4.0.

Based on the characteristics and cyberthreats of the main enabling technologies in Industry 4.0, this paper briefly reviewed each of the main enabling technologies and the potential cybersecurity threats to them. Table 1 is a summary of threats to them. For each technology, threats are put into 4 types which are Integrity, Confidentiality, availability and Safety where safety is a unique aspect to an Industry 4.0 system.

Table 1. Possible cyber-security threats in the enabling technologies of Industry 4.0

	Integrity	Confidentiality	Availability	Safety
3D printing	3D design file may be tampered or modified during the process of communication	Eavesdropping and Escalation of privilege	1. Dos attack make 3D printer unavailable 2. Malware, worms and virus infection Compromise the MES	3D design file is hacked and modified by attacker during the process of communication
Cloud and edge computing/Machine learning	Attack against communication channels and access to the cloud	Resources in cloud are not sufficiently isolated	Exhausting of resources attacks	IoT connector device is compromised
Digital Twin	Attacks to the data transferring like Data tampering, spoofing	Attacks to the data transferring like Data tampering, spoofing	Jamming, Collision, and False Routing Information	False Data is used
Cobots	Insider attack	Threats not yet found	Exhausting of resources attacks	Sensor spoofing, disgruntled employee
AR	Data synchronization	Camera is compromised	Zero-day attacks cause devices crash	Virtual information is modified to give wrong information which cause fatal result

From Table 1 and Sect. 3, we can conclude that:

- The cybersecurity threats to the system are commonly interrelated.
- Some cybersecurity threats are more critical in certain technology e.g. Sensor Spoofing attack to cobot.
- Due to the complexity of the Industry 4.0 system, threats can be from various sources. A proactive approach must be used. Engineering technical staff like automation engineers need to understand the cybersecurity and take possible threats into consideration in the design phase of the industry 4.0 system.

Although Industry 4.0 is referred to as the fourth industrial revolution, due to cybercriminals and budgetary constraints, it is destined to be an evolution instead of revolution [5]. This means instead of changing all equipment at the same time, industries gradually introduce the Industry 4.0 technology and upgrade the equipment. Hopefully, this paper can help people understand the main enabling technologies in Industry 4.0 and possible cybersecurity threats to them.

References

1. Defining and sizing the industrial internet. http://wikibon.org/wiki/v/Defining_and_Sizing_the_Industrial_Internet. Accessed 01 July 2019
2. Gartner identifies the top 10 strategic technology trends for 2017. https://www.gartner.com/en/newsroom/press-releases/2016-10-18-gartner-identifies-the-top-10-strategic-technology-trends-for-2017. Accessed 01 July 2019
3. Industrial control system security top 10 threats and countermeasures 2019. https://www.allianz-fuer-cybersicherheit.de/ACS/DE/_/downloads/BSI-CS_005E.pdf?__blob=publicationFile&v=3. Accessed 01 July 2019
4. Industrial edge from siemens adds benefits from the cloud at the field level. https://www.siemens.com/press/en/pressrelease/?press=/en/pressrelease/2018/digitalfactory/pr2018040239dfen.htm. Accessed 01 July 2019
5. Industry 4.0 is an evolution, not a revolution. https://www.industryweek.com/technology-and-iiot/industry-40-evolution-not-revolution. Accessed 01 July 2019
6. World first industry 4.0 testlab for swinburne. https://www.swinburne.edu.au/news/latest-news/2018/03/swinburne-to-establish-world-first-industry-40-testlab.php. Accessed 01 July 2019
7. Aleksy, M., Vartiainen, E., Domova, V., Naedele, M.: Augmented reality for improved service delivery. In: 2014 IEEE 28th International Conference on Advanced Information Networking and Applications, pp. 382–389. IEEE (2014)
8. Ashibani, Y., Mahmoud, Q.H.: Cyber physical systems security: analysis, challenges and solutions. Comput. Secur. **68**, 81–97 (2017)
9. Bécue, A., et al.: Cyberfactory# 1-securing the industry 4.0 with cyber-ranges and digital twins. In: 2018 14th IEEE International Workshop on Factory Communication Systems (WFCS), pp. 1–4. IEEE (2018)
10. Belikovetsky, S., Yampolskiy, M., Toh, J., Gatlin, J., Elovici, Y.: dr0wned-cyber-physical attack with additive manufacturing. In: 11th USENIX Workshop on Offensive Technologies (WOOT 2017) (2017)

11. Choi, H., et al.: Detecting attacks against robotic vehicles: a control invariant approach. In: Proceedings of the 2018 ACM SIGSAC Conference on Computer and Communications Security, pp. 801–816. ACM (2018)
12. Disterer, G.: ISO/IEC 27000, 27001 and 27002 for information security management (2013)
13. Goodfellow, I., Bengio, Y., Courville, A.: Deep Learning. MIT Press, Cambridge (2016)
14. Kim, D., Gil, J.M.: Reliable and fault-tolerant software-defined network operations scheme for remote 3D printing. J. Electron. Mater. 44(3), 804–814 (2015)
15. Lee, S., Lee, S., Yoo, H., Kwon, S., Shon, T.: Design and implementation of cybersecurity testbed for industrial IoT systems. J. Supercomput. 74(9), 4506–4520 (2018)
16. Lezzi, M., Lazoi, M., Corallo, A.: Cybersecurity for industry 4.0 in the current literature: a reference framework. Comput. Ind. 103, 97–110 (2018)
17. Loch, F., Quint, F., Brishtel, I.: Comparing video and augmented reality assistance in manual assembly. In: 2016 12th International Conference on Intelligent Environments (IE), pp. 147–150. IEEE (2016)
18. Mell, P., Grance, T., et al.: The NIST definition of cloud computing (2011)
19. Moustafa, N., Adi, E., Turnbull, B., Hu, J.: A new threat intelligence scheme for safeguarding industry 4.0 systems. IEEE Access 6, 32910–32924 (2018)
20. Ngo, T.D., Kashani, A., Imbalzano, G., Nguyen, K.T., Hui, D.: Additive manufacturing (3D printing): a review of materials, methods, applications and challenges. Compos. Part B Eng. 143, 172–196 (2018)
21. Pichler, A., et al.: Towards shared autonomy for robotic tasks in manufacturing. Proc. Manuf. 11, 72–82 (2017)
22. Pratiba, D., Shobha, D.G.: Privacy-preserving public auditing for data storage security in cloud computing. Int. J. Comput. Eng. Technol. (IJCET) 4(3), 441–448 (2013)
23. Son, Y., et al.: Rocking drones with intentional sound noise on gyroscopic sensors. In: 24th USENIX Security Symposium (USENIX Security 2015), pp. 881–896 (2015)
24. Wan, J., Cai, H., Zhou, K.: Industrie 4.0: enabling technologies. In: Proceedings of 2015 International Conference on Intelligent Computing and Internet of Things, pp. 135–140. IEEE (2015)
25. Waurzyniak, P.: Securing manufacturing data in the cloud. Advanced Manufacturing (2016)
26. Wu, D., Rosen, D.W., Schaefer, D.: Cloud-based design and manufacturing: status and promise. In: Schaefer, D. (ed.) Cloud-Based Design and Manufacturing (CBDM), pp. 1–24. Springer, Cham (2014). https://doi.org/10.1007/978-3-319-07398-9_1

Author Index